Flight Stability and Automatic Control

SECOND EDITION

Dr. Robert C. Nelson

Department of Aerospace and Mechanical Engineering
University of Notre Dame

Boston, Massachusetts   Burr Ridge, Illinois   Dubuque, Iowa
Madison, Wisconsin   New York, New York   San Francisco, California
St. Louis, Missouri

WCB/McGraw-Hill

A Division of The McGraw·Hill Companies

FLIGHT STABILITY AND AUTOMATIC CONTROL

Copyright © 1998 by The McGraw-Hill Companies, Inc. All rights reserved. Previous editions ©
1989. Printed in the United States of America. Except as permitted under the United States
Copyright Act of 1976, no part of this publication may be reproduced or distributed in any form
or by any means, or stored in a data base or retrieval system, without the prior written permission
of the publisher.

This book is printed on acid-free paper.

1 2 3 4 5 7 8 9 0 DOC/DOC 9 0 9 8 7

ISBN 0-07-046273-9

Publisher: *Tom Casson*
Senior sponsoring editor: *Debra Riegert*
Marketing manager: *John Wannemacher*
Project manager: *Alisa Watson*
Production supervisor: *Heather Burbridge*
Senior designer: *Laurie J. Entringer*
Compositor: *Interactive Composition Corporation*
Typeface: *10/12 Times Roman*
Printer: *R. R. Donnelley & Sons Company*

Library of Congress Cataloging-in-Publication Data

Nelson, Robert C., 1942–
    Flight stability and automatic control / Robert C. Nelson.—2nd
ed.
        p.   cm.
    Includes bibliographical references and index.
    ISBN 0-07-046273-9
    1. Stability of airplanes.   2. Airplanes—Control systems.
3. Airplanes—Automatic control.   I. Title.
TL574.S7N45   1998
629.132'36—dc21   97-26109
                                                                          CIP

http://www.mhcollege.com

ABOUT THE AUTHOR

ROBERT C. NELSON received his B. S. and M. S. degrees in Aerospace Engineering from the University of Notre Dame and his Ph.D. in Aerospace Engineering from the Pennsylvania State University. Prior to joining Notre Dame, Dr. Nelson was an instructor of Aerospace Engineering at the Pennsylvania State University and an engineer for the Air Force Flight Dynamics Laboratory at Wright-Patterson Air Force Base, Fairborn, Ohio. While employed at AFFDL, he worked on an advanced development program to develop the technology for an air to air short range bomber defense missile. For his contribution to this effort he received a Technical Achievement award from the Air Force Systems Command.

In 1975, Dr. Nelson joined the faculty at Notre Dame and has been active in research dealing with the aerodynamics and flight dynamics of both aircraft and missiles. His present research interests include the aerodynamics of slender bodies at large angles of attack, flow visualization techniques, delta wing aerodynamics, and aircraft stability and control. He has written over 100 articles and papers on his research. Dr. Nelson is the chairman of the Department of Aerospace and Mechanical Engineering at Notre Dame. He has also been active as a consultant to government and industrial organizations. He is a Registered Professional Engineer and a Fellow of the American Institute of Aeronautics and Astronautics (AIAA). He served as the general chairman of the AIAA Atmospheric Flight Mechanics Conference in 1982 and was the chairman of the AIAA Atmospheric Flight Mechanics Technical Committee from May 1983–1985. Dr. Nelson also served as a member of the AIAA Applied Aerodynamics Technical Committee from 1986 to 1989. Other professional activities include participation as a lecturer and course coordinator of four short courses and one home study course sponsored by the AIAA (1982, 1984, 1989, 1995). He also has been an AGARD lecturer (1991, 1993, 1995, 1997). In 1991, Dr. Nelson received the John Leland Atwood Award from the AIAA and ASEE. This award is given annually for contributions to Aerospace Engineering Education.

PREFACE

An understanding of flight stability and control played an important role in the ultimate success of the earliest aircraft designs. In later years the design of automatic controls ushered in the rapid development of commercial and military aircraft. Today, both military and civilian aircraft rely heavily on automatic control systems to provide artificial stabilization and autopilots to aid pilots in navigating and landing their aircraft in adverse weather conditions. The goal of this book is to present an integrated treatment of the basic elements of aircraft stability, flight control, and autopilot design.

NEW TO THIS EDITION

In the second edition, I have attempted to improve the first six chapters from the first edition. These chapters cover the topics of static stability, flight control, aircraft dynamics and flying qualities. This is accomplished by including **more worked-out example problems, additional problems** at the end of each chapter, and new material to provide additional insight on the subject. The major change in the text is the addition of an **expanded section on automatic control theory** and its application to flight control system design.

CONTENTS

This book is intended as a textbook for a course in aircraft flight dynamics for senior undergraduate or first year graduate students. The material presented includes static stability, aircraft equations of motion, dynamic stability, flying or handling qualities, automatic control theory, and application of control theory to the synthesis of automatic flight control systems. Chapter 1 reviews some basic concepts of aerodynamics, properties of the atmosphere, several of the primary flight instruments, and nomenclature. In Chapter 2 the concepts of airplane static stability and control are presented. The design features that can be incorporated into an aircraft design to provide static stability and sufficient control power are discussed. The rigid body aircraft equations of motion are developed along with techniques to model the aerodynamic forces and moments acting on the airplane in Chapter 3. The aerodynamic forces and moments are modeled using the concept of aerodynamic stability derivatives. Methods for estimating the derivatives are presented in Chapter 3 along with a detailed example calculation of the longitudinal derivatives of a STOL transport. The dynamic characteristics of an airplane for free and forced response are presented in Chapters 4 and 5. Chapter 4 discusses the longitudinal dynamics while Chapter 5 presents the lateral dynamics. In both chapters the relationship between the rigid body motions and the pilot's opinion of the ease or difficulty of flying the airplane is explained. Handling or flying qualities are those control and dynamic characteristics that govern how well a pilot can fly a particular control task. Chapter 6 discusses the solution of the equations of motion for either arbitrary control input or atmospheric disturbances. Chapters 7–10 include the major changes incorporated into the second edition of this book. Chapter 7 provides a review of classical control concepts and discusses control system synthesis and design. The root locus method is used to design control systems to meet given time and frequency domain performance specifications. Classical control techniques are used to design automatic control systems for various flight applications in Chapter 8. Automatic control systems are presented that can be used to maintain an airplane's bank angle, pitch orientation, altitude, and speed. In addition a qualitative description of a fully automated landing system is presented. In Chapter 9, the concepts of modern control theory and design techniques are reviewed. By using state feedback design, it is theoretically possible for the designer to locate the roots of the closed loop system so that any desired performance can be achieved. The practical constraints of arbitrary root placement are discussed along with the necessary requirements to successfully implement state feedback control. Finally in Chapter 10 modern control design methods are applied to the design of aircraft automatic flight control systems.

LEARNING TOOLS

To help in understanding the concepts presented in the text I have included a number of worked-out example problems throughout the book, and at the end of each chapter one will find a problem set. Some of the example problems and selected problems at the end of later chapters require computer solutions. Commercially available computer aided design software is used for selected example problems and assigned problems. Problems that require the use of a computer are clearly identified in the problem sets. A major feature of the textbook is that the material is introduced by way of simple exercises. For example, dynamic stability is presented first by restricted single degree of freedom motions. This approach permits the reader to gain some experience in the mathematical representation and physical understanding of aircraft response before the more complicated multiple degree of freedom motions are analyzed. A similar approach is used in developing the control system designs. For example, a roll autopilot to maintain a wings level attitude is modeled using the simplest mathematical formulation to represent the aircraft and control system elements. Following this approach the students can be introduced to the design process without undue mathematical complexity. Several appendices have also been included to provide additional data on airplane aerodynamic, mass, and geometric characteristics as well as review material of some of the mathematical and analysis techniques used in the text.

ACKNOWLEDGEMENTS

I am indebted to all the students who used the early drafts of this book. Their many suggestions and patience as the book evolved is greatly appreciated. I would like to express my thanks for the many useful comments and suggestions provided by colleagues who reviewed this text during the course of its development, especially to:

Donald T. Ward	Texas A & M University
Andrew S. Arena, Jr.	Oklahoma State University
C. H. Chuang	Georgia Institute of Technology
Frederick H. Lutze	Virginia Polytechnic Institute and State University
Roberto Celi	University of Maryland

Finally, I would like to express my appreciation to Marilyn Walker for her patience in typing the many versions of this manuscript.

Robert C. Nelson

CONTENTS

CHAPTER 1

Introduction

"For some years I have been afflicted with the belief that flight is possible to man."

Wilbur Wright, May 13, 1900

1.1
ATMOSPHERIC FLIGHT MECHANICS

Atmospheric flight mechanics is a broad heading that encompasses three major disciplines; namely, performance, flight dynamics, and aeroelasticity. In the past each of these subjects was treated independently of the others. However, because of the structural flexibility of modern airplanes, the interplay among the disciplines no longer can be ignored. For example, if the flight loads cause significant structural deformation of the aircraft, one can expect changes in the airplane's aerodynamic and stability characteristics that will influence its performance and dynamic behavior.

Airplane performance deals with the determination of performance character-istics such as range, endurance, rate of climb, and takeoff and landing distance as well as flight path optimization. To evaluate these performance characteristics, one normally treats the airplane as a point mass acted on by gravity, lift, drag, and thrust. The accuracy of the performance calculations depends on how accurately the lift, drag, and thrust can be determined.

Flight dynamics is concerned with the motion of an airplane due to internally or externally generated disturbances. We particularly are interested in the vehicle's stability and control capabilities. To describe adequately the rigid-body motion of an airplane one needs to consider the complete equations of motion with six degrees of freedom. Again, this will require accurate estimates of the aerodynamic forces and moments acting on the airplane.

The final subject included under the heading of atmospheric flight mechanics is aeroelasticity. Aeroelasticity deals with both static and dynamic aeroelastic phenomena. Basically, aeroelasticity is concerned with phenomena associated with interactions between inertial, elastic, and aerodynamic forces. Problems that arise for a flexible aircraft include control reversal, wing divergence, and control surface flutter, to name just a few.

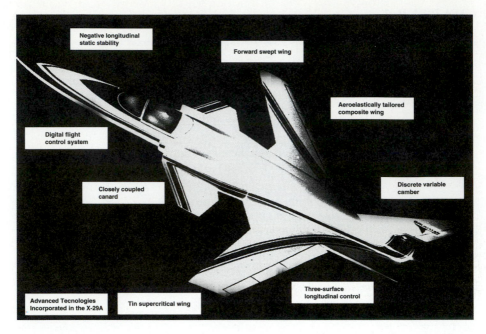

FIGURE 1.1
Advanced technologies incorporated in the X-29A aircraft.

This book is divided into three parts: The first part deals with the properties of the atmosphere, static stability and control concepts, development of aircraft equations of motion, and aerodynamic modeling of the airplane; the second part examines aircraft motions due to control inputs or atmospheric disturbances; the third part is devoted to aircraft autopilots. Although no specific chapters are devoted entirely to performance or aeroelasticity, an effort is made to show the reader, at least in a qualitative way, how performance specifications and aeroelastic phenomena influence aircraft stability and control characteristics.

The interplay among the three disciplines that make up atmospheric flight mechanics is best illustrated by the experimental high-performance airplane shown in Figure 1.1. The X-29A aircraft incorporates the latest advanced technologies in controls, structures, and aerodynamics. These technologies will provide substantial performance improvements over more conventional fighter designs. Such a design could not be developed without paying close attention to the interplay among performance, aeroelasticity, stability, and control. In fact, the evolution of this radical design was developed using trade-off studies between the various disciplines to justify the expected performance improvements.

The forces and moments acting on an airplane depend on the properties of the atmosphere through which it is flying. In the following sections we will review some basic concepts of fluid mechanics that will help us appreciate the atmospheric properties essential to our understanding of airplane flight mechanics. In addition we will discuss some of the important aircraft instruments that provide flight information to the pilot.

1.2
BASIC DEFINITIONS

The aerodynamic forces and moments generated on an airplane are due to its geometric shape, attitude to the flow, airspeed, and the properties of the ambient air mass through which it is flying. Air is a fluid and as such possesses certain fluid properties. The properties we are interested in are the pressure, temperature, density, viscosity, and speed of sound of air at the flight altitude.

1.2.1 Fluid

A fluid can be thought of as any substance that flows. To have such a property, the fluid must deform continuously when acted on by a shearing force. A shear force is a force tangent to the surface of the fluid element. No shear stresses are present in the fluid when it is at rest. A fluid can transmit forces normal to any chosen direction. The normal force and the normal stress are the pressure force and pressure, respectively.

Both liquids and gases can be considered fluids. Liquids under most conditions do not change their weight per unit of volume appreciably and can be considered incompressible for most engineering applications. Gases, on the other hand, change their weight or mass per unit of volume appreciably under the influences of pressure or temperature and therefore must be considered compressible.

1.2.2 Pressure

Pressure is the normal force per unit area acting on the fluid. The average pressure is calculated by dividing the normal force to the surface by the surface area:

$$P = \frac{F}{A} \qquad (1.1)$$

The static pressure in the atmosphere is nothing more than the weight per unit of area of the air above the elevation being considered. The ratio of the pressure P at altitude to sea-level standard pressure P_0 is given the symbol δ:

$$\delta = \frac{P}{P_0} \qquad (1.2)$$

The relationship between pressure, density ρ, and temperature T is given by the equation of state

$$P = \rho R T \qquad (1.3)$$

where R is a constant, the magnitude depending on the gas being considered. For air, R has a value 287 J/(kg°K) or 1718 ft²/(s²°R). Atmospheric air follows the equation of state provided that the temperature is not too high and that air can be treated as a continuum.

1.2.3 Temperature

In aeronautics the temperature of air is an extremely important parameter in that it affects the properties of air such as density and viscosity. Temperature is an abstract concept but can be thought of as a measure of the motion of molecular particles within a substance. The concept of temperature also serves as a means of determining the direction in which heat energy will flow when two objects of different temperatures come into contact. Heat energy will flow from the higher temperature object to that at lower temperature.

As we will show later the temperature of the atmosphere varies significantly with altitude. The ratio of the ambient temperature at altitude, T, to a sea-level standard value, T_0 is denoted by the symbol θ:

$$\theta = \frac{T}{T_0} \tag{1.4}$$

where the temperatures are measured using the absolute Kelvin or Rankine scales.

1.2.4 Density

The density of a substance is defined as the mass per unit of volume:

$$\rho = \frac{\text{Mass}}{\text{Unit of volume}} \tag{1.5}$$

From the equation of state, it can be seen that the density of a gas is directly proportional to the pressure and inversely proportional to the absolute temperature. The ratio of ambient air density ρ to standard sea-level air density ρ_0 occurs in many aeronautical formulas and is given the designation σ:

$$\sigma = \rho/\rho_0 \tag{1.6}$$

1.2.5 Viscosity

Viscosity can be thought of as the internal friction of a fluid. Both liquids and gases possess viscosity, with liquids being much more viscous than gases. As an aid in visualizing the concept of viscosity, consider the following simple experiment. Consider the motion of the fluid between two parallel plates separated by the distance h. If one plate is held fixed while the other plate is being pulled with a constant velocity u, then the velocity distribution of the fluid between the plates will be linear as shown in Figure 1.2.

To produce the constant velocity motion of the upper plate, a tangential force must be applied to the plate. The magnitude of the force must be equal to the

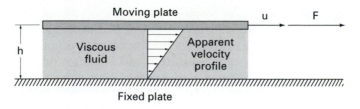

FIGURE 1.2
Shear stress between two plates.

friction forces in the fluid. It has been established from experiments that the force per unit of area of the plate is proportional to the velocity of the moving plate and inversely proportional to the distance between the plates. Expressed mathematically we have

$$\tau \propto \frac{u}{h} \tag{1.7}$$

where τ is the force per unit area, which is called the shear stress.

A more general form of Equation (1.7) can be written by replacing u/h with the derivative du/dy. The proportionality factor is denoted by μ, the coefficient of absolute viscosity, which is obtained experimentally.

$$\tau = \mu \frac{du}{dy} \tag{1.8}$$

Equation (1.8) is known as Newton's law of friction.

For gases, the absolute viscosity depends only on the temperature, with increasing temperature causing an increase in viscosity. To estimate the change in viscosity with the temperature, several empirical formulations commonly are used. The simplest formula is Rayleigh's, which is

$$\frac{\mu_1}{\mu_0} = \left(\frac{T_1}{T_0}\right)^{3/4} \tag{1.9}$$

where the temperatures are on the absolute scale and the subscript 0 denotes the reference condition.

An alternate expression for calculating the variation of absolute viscosity with temperature was developed by Sutherland. The empirical formula developed by Sutherland is valid provided the pressure is greater than 0.1 atmosphere and is

$$\frac{\mu_1}{\mu_0} = \left(\frac{T_1}{T_0}\right)^{3/2} \frac{T_0 + S_1}{T_1 + S_1} \tag{1.10}$$

where S_1 is a constant. When the temperatures are expressed in the Rankine scale, $S_1 = 198°R$; when the temperatures are expressed in the Kelvin scale, $S_1 = 110°K$.

The ratio of the absolute viscosity to the density of the fluid is a parameter that appears frequently and has been identified with the symbol ν; it is called the kinematic viscosity:

$$\nu = \frac{\mu}{\rho} \tag{1.11}$$

An important dimensionless quantity, known as the Reynolds number, is defined as

$$R_e = \frac{\rho V l}{\mu} = \frac{V l}{\nu} \tag{1.12}$$

where l is a characteristic length and V is the fluid velocity.

The Reynolds number can be thought of as the ratio of the inertial to viscous forces of the fluid.

1.2.6 The Mach Number and the Speed of Sound

The ratio of an airplane's speed V to the local speed of sound a is an extremely important parameter, called the Mach number after the Austrian physicist Ernst Mach. The mathematical definition of Mach number is

$$M = \frac{V}{a} \tag{1.13}$$

As an airplane moves through the air, it creates pressure disturbances that propagate away from the airplane in all directions with the speed of sound. If the airplane is flying at a Mach number less than 1, the pressure disturbances travel faster than the airplane and influence the air ahead of the airplane. An example of this phenomenon is the upwash field created in front of a wing. However, for flight at Mach numbers greater than 1 the pressure disturbances move more slowly than the airplane and, therefore, the flow ahead of the airplane has no warning of the oncoming aircraft.

The aerodynamic characteristics of an airplane depend on the flow regime around the airplane. As the flight Mach number is increased, the flow around the airplane can be completely subsonic, a mixture of subsonic and supersonic flow, or completely supersonic. The flight Mach number is used to classify the various flow regimes. An approximate classification of the flow regimes follows:

Incompressible subsonic flow	$0 < M < 0.5$
Compressible subsonic flow	$0.5 < M < 0.8$
Transonic flow	$0.8 < M < 1.2$
Supersonic flow	$1.2 < M < 5$
Hypersonic flow	$5 < M$

To have accurate aerodynamic predictions at $M > 0.5$ compressibility effects must be included.

The local speed of sound must be known to determine the Mach number. The speed of sound can be shown to be related to the absolute ambient temperature by the following expression:

$$a = (\gamma RT)^{1/2} \tag{1.14}$$

where γ is the ratio of specific heats and R is the gas constant. The ambient temperature will be shown in a later section to be a function of altitude.

1.3 AEROSTATICS

Aerostatics deals with the state of a gas at rest. It follows from the definition given for a fluid that all forces acting on the fluid must be normal to any cross-section within the fluid. Unlike a solid, a fluid at rest cannot support a shearing force. A consequence of this is that the pressure in a fluid at rest is independent of direction. That is to say that at any point the pressure is the same in all directions. This fundamental concept owes its origin to Pascal, a French scientist (1623–1662).

1.3.1 Variation of Pressure in a Static Fluid

Consider the small vertical column of fluid shown in Figure 1.3. Because the fluid is at rest, the forces in both the vertical and horizontal directions must sum to 0. The forces in the vertical direction are due to the pressure forces and the weight of the fluid column. The force balance in the vertical direction is given by

$$PA = (P + dP)A + \rho gA \, dh \tag{1.15}$$

or

$$dP = -\rho g \, dh \tag{1.16}$$

FIGURE 1.3
Element of fluid at rest.

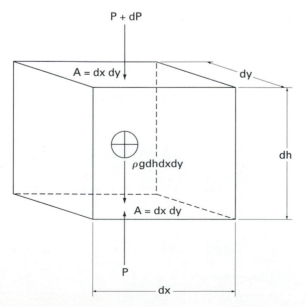

P + dP

A = dx dy

dy

ρgdhdxdy

dh

A = dx dy

P

dx

Equation (1.16) tells us how the pressure varies with elevation above some reference level in a fluid. As the elevation is increased, the pressure will decrease. Therefore, the pressure in a static fluid is equal to the weight of the column of fluid above the point of interest.

One of the simplest means of measuring pressure is by a fluid manometer. Figure 1.4 shows two types of manometers. The first manometer consists of a U-shaped tube containing a liquid. When pressures of different magnitudes are applied across the manometer the fluid will rise on the side of the lower pressure and fall on the side of the higher pressure. By writing a force balance for each side, one can show that

$$P_1 A + \rho g x A = P_2 A + \rho g (x + h) A \tag{1.17}$$

which yields a relationship for the pressure difference in terms of the change in height of the liquid column:

$$P_1 - P_2 = \rho g h \tag{1.18}$$

The second sketch shows a simple mercury barometer. The barometer can be thought of as a modified U-tube manometer. One leg of the tube is closed off and evacuated. The pressure at the top of this leg is 0 and atmospheric pressure acts on the open leg. The atmospheric pressure therefore is equal to the height of the mercury column; that is,

$$P_{atm} = \rho g h \tag{1.19}$$

In practice the atmospheric pressure is commonly expressed as so many inches or millimeters of mercury. Remember, however, that neither inches nor millimeters of mercury are units of pressure.

FIGURE 1.4
Sketch of U-tube manometer and barometer.

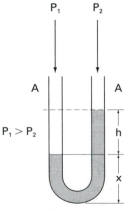

U-tube manometer

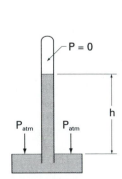

Barometer

1.4
DEVELOPMENT OF BERNOULLI'S EQUATION

Bernoulli's equation establishes the relationship between pressure, elevation, and velocity of the flow along a stream tube. For this analysis, the fluid is assumed to be a perfect fluid; that is, we will ignore viscous effects. Consider the element of fluid in the stream tube shown in Figure 1.5. The forces acting on the differential element of fluid are due to pressure and gravitational forces. The pressure force acting in the direction of the motion is given by

$$F_{\text{pressure}} = P \, dA - \left(P + \frac{\partial P}{\partial s} \, ds \right) dA \qquad (1.20)$$

or
$$= -dP \, dA \qquad (1.21)$$

The gravitational force can be expressed as

$$F_{\text{gravitational}} = -g \, dm \sin \alpha \qquad (1.22)$$

$$= -g \, dm \, \frac{dz}{ds} \qquad (1.23)$$

Applying Newton's second law yields

$$-dP \, dA - g \, dm \, \frac{dz}{ds} = dm \, \frac{dV}{dt} \qquad (1.24)$$

The differential mass dm can be expressed in terms of the mass density of the fluid element times its respective volume; that is,

$$dm = \rho \, dA \, ds \qquad (1.25)$$

Inserting the expression for the differential mass, the acceleration of the fluid can

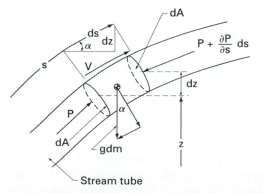

FIGURE 1.5
Forces acting on an element of flow in a stream tube.

be expressed as

$$\frac{dV}{dt} = -\frac{1}{\rho}\frac{dP}{ds} - g\frac{dz}{ds} \qquad (1.26)$$

The acceleration can be expressed as

$$\frac{dV}{dt} = \frac{\partial V}{\partial t} + \frac{\partial V}{\partial s}\frac{ds}{dt} \qquad (1.27)$$

The first term on the right-hand side, $\partial V/\partial t$, denotes the change in velocity as a function of time for the entire flow field. The second term denotes the acceleration due to a change in location. If the flow field is steady, the term $\partial V/\partial t = 0$ and Equation (1.27) reduce to

$$\frac{\partial V}{\partial s}\frac{ds}{dt} = -\frac{1}{\rho}\frac{dP}{ds} - g\frac{dz}{ds} \qquad (1.28)$$

The changes of pressure as a function of time cannot accelerate a fluid particle. This is because the same pressure would be acting at every instant on all sides of the fluid particles. Therefore, the partial differential can be replaced by the total derivative in Equation (1.28):

$$V\frac{dV}{ds} = -\frac{1}{\rho}\frac{dP}{ds} - g\frac{dz}{ds} \qquad (1.29)$$

Integrating Equation (1.29) along a streamline yields

$$\int_1^2 V\,dV = -\int_1^2 \frac{dP}{\rho} - g\int_1^2 dz \qquad (1.30)$$

which is known as Bernoulli's equation. Bernoulli's equation establishes the relationship between pressure, elevation, and velocity along a stream tube.

1.4.1 Incompressible Bernoulli Equation

If the fluid is considered to be incompressible, Equation (1.29) readily can be integrated to yield the incompressible Bernoulli equation:

$$P_1 + \frac{1}{2}\rho V_1^2 + \rho g z_1 = P_2 + \frac{1}{2}\rho V_2^2 + \rho g z_2 \qquad (1.31)$$

The differences in elevation usually can be ignored when dealing with the flow of gases such as air. An important application of Bernoulli's equation is the determination of the so-called stagnation pressure of a moving body or a body exposed to a flow. The stagnation point is defined as that point on the body at which the flow comes to rest. At that point the pressure is

$$P_0 = P_\infty + \frac{1}{2}\rho V_\infty^2 \tag{1.32}$$

where P_∞ and V_∞ are the static pressure and velocity far away from the body; that is, the pressures and velocities that would exist if the body were not present. In the case of a moving body, V_∞ is equal to the velocity of the body itself and P_∞ is the static pressure of the medium through which the body is moving.

1.4.2 Bernoulli's Equation for a Compressible Fluid

At higher speeds (on the order of 100 m/s), the assumption that the fluid density of gases is constant becomes invalid. As speed is increased, the air undergoes a compression and, therefore, the density cannot be treated as a constant. If the flow can be assumed to be isentropic, the relationship between pressure and density can be expressed as

$$P = c\rho^\gamma \tag{1.33}$$

where γ is the ratio of specific heats for the gas. For air, γ is approximately 1.4.

Substituting Equation (1.33) into Equation (1.30) and performing the indicated integrations yields the compressible form of Bernoulli's equation:

$$\frac{\gamma}{\gamma - 1}\frac{P}{\rho} + \frac{1}{2}V^2 + gz = \text{constant} \tag{1.34}$$

As noted earlier, the elevation term usually is quite small for most aeronautical applications and therefore can be ignored. The stagnation pressure can be found by letting $V = 0$, in Equation (1.34):

$$\frac{\gamma}{\gamma - 1}\frac{P}{\rho} + \frac{1}{2}V^2 = \frac{\gamma}{\gamma - 1}\frac{P_0}{\rho_0} \tag{1.35}$$

If we rearrange Equation (1.35), we obtain

$$1 + \frac{\gamma - 1}{2}\frac{1}{\gamma P/\rho}V^2 = \frac{P_0/P}{\rho_0\rho} \tag{1.36}$$

Equation (1.36) can be solved for the velocity by substituting the following expressions,

$$a^2 = \gamma RT = \gamma P/\rho \tag{1.37}$$

and

$$\frac{P_0}{P} = \left(\frac{\rho_0}{\rho}\right)^\gamma \tag{1.38}$$

into Equation (1.36) and rearranging to yield a relationship for the velocity and the Mach number as follows.

$$V = \left[\frac{2a^2}{\gamma - 1}\left[\left(\frac{P_0}{P}\right)^{(\gamma-1)/\gamma} - 1\right]\right]^{1/2} \tag{1.39}$$

$$M = \left[\frac{2}{\gamma - 1}\left[\left(\frac{P_0}{P}\right)^{(\gamma-1)/\gamma} - 1\right]\right]^{1/2} \tag{1.40}$$

Equations (1.39) and (1.40) can be used to find the velocity and Mach number provided the flow regime is below $M = 1$.

1.5
THE ATMOSPHERE

The performance characteristics of an airplane depend on the properties of the atmosphere through which it flies. Because the atmosphere is continuously changing with time, it is impossible to determine airplane performance parameters precisely without first defining the state of the atmosphere.

The earth's atmosphere is a gaseous envelope surrounding the planet. The gas that we call air actually is a composition of numerous gases. The composition of dry air at sea level is shown in Table 1.1. The relative percentages of the constituents remains essentially the same up to an altitude of 90 km or 300,000 ft owing primarily to atmospheric mixing caused by winds and turbulence. At altitudes above 90 km the gases begin to settle or separate. The variability of water vapor in the atmosphere must be taken into account by the performance analyst. Water vapor can constitute up to 4 percent by volume of atmospheric air. When the relative humidity is high, the air density is lower than that for dry air for the same conditions of pressure and temperature. Under these conditions the density may be reduced by as much as 3 percent. A change in air density will cause a change in the aerodynamic forces acting on the airplane and therefore influence its performance capabilities. Furthermore, changes in air density created by water vapor will affect engine performance, which again influences the performance of the airplane.

TABLE 1.1
Composition of atmospheric air

	Density		Percentage by volume	Percentage by weight
	kg/m³	slugs/ft³		
Air	1.2250	2.3769×10^{-3}	100	100
Nitrogen			78.03	75.48
Oxygen			20.99	23.18
Argon			0.94	1.29

The remaining small portion of the composition of air is made up of neon, helium, krypton, xenon, CO_2 and water vapor.

The atmosphere can be thought of as composed of various layers, with each layer of the atmosphere having its own distinct characteristics. For this discussion we will divide the atmosphere into four regions. In ascending order the layers are the troposphere, stratosphere, ionosphere, and exosphere. The four layers are illustrated in Figure 1.6. The troposphere and stratosphere are extremely important to aerospace engineers since most aircraft fly in these regions. The troposphere extends from the Earth's surface to an altitude of approximately 6–13 miles or 10–20 km. The air masses in the troposphere are in constant motion and the region is characterized by unsteady or gusting winds and turbulence. The influence of turbulence and wind shear on aircraft structural integrity and flight behavior continues to be an important area of research for the aeronautical community. The structural loads imposed on an aircraft during an encounter with turbulent air can reduce the structural life of the airframe or in an encounter with severe turbulence can cause structural damage to the airframe.

Wind shear is an important atmospheric phenomenon that can be hazardous to aircraft during takeoff or landing. Wind shear is the variation of the wind vector in both magnitude and direction. In vertical wind shear, the wind speed and direction

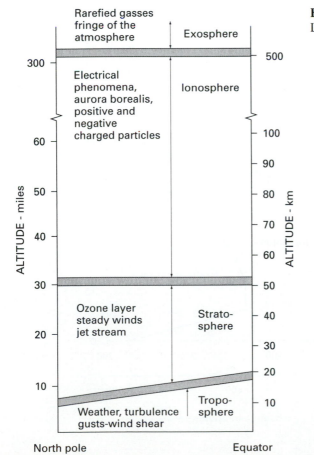

FIGURE 1.6
Layers of earth's atmosphere.

change with altitude. An airplane landing in such a wind shear may be difficult to control; this can cause deviations from the intended touchdown point. Wind shears are created by the movement of air masses relative to one another or to the earth's surface. Thunderstorms, frontal systems, and the earth's boundary layer all produce wind shear profiles that at times are severe enough to be hazardous to aircraft flying at a low altitude.

The next layer above the troposhere is called the stratosphere. The stratosphere extends up to over 30 miles, or 50 km, above the Earth's surface. Unlike the troposphere, the stratosphere is a relatively tranquil region, free of gusts and turbulence, but it is characterized by high, steady winds. Wind speeds of the order of 37 m/s or 120 ft/s have been measured in the stratosphere.

The ionosphere extends from the upper edge of the stratosphere to an altitude of up to 300 miles or 500 km. (The name is derived from the word *ion,* which describes a particle that has either a positive or negative electric charge.) This is the region where the air molecules undergo dissociation and many electrical phenomena occur. The aurora borealis is a visible electrical display that occurs in the ionosphere.

The last layer of the atmsophere is called the exosphere. The exosphere is the outermost region of the atmosphere and is made up of rarefied gas. In effect this is

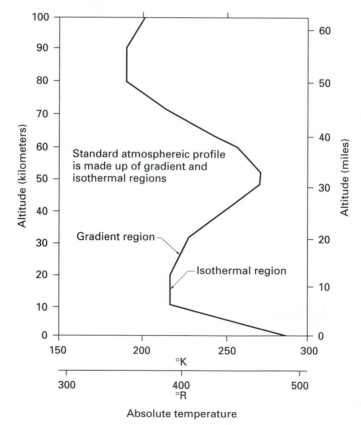

FIGURE 1.7
Temperature profile in the standard atmosphere.

TABLE 1.2
Properties of air at sea level in the standard atmosphere

	English units	SI units
Gas constant, R	1718 ft.lb/(slug · °R)	287 m²/(°K· s²)
Pressure, P	2116.2 lb/ft²	1.012×10^5 N/m²
	29.92 in Hg	760 mm Hg
Density, ρ	2.377×10^{-3} slug/ft³	1.225 kg/m³
Temperature	518.69°R	288.16°K
Absolute viscosity, μ	3.737×10^{-7} lb · s/ft²	1.789×10^{-3} N · s/m²
Kinematic viscosity, ν	1.572×10^{-4} ft²/s	1.460×10^{-5} m²/s
Speed of sound, a	1116.4 ft/s	340.3 m/s

a transition zone between the earth's atmosphere and interplanetary space. For many applications we can consider air resistance to cease in the exosphere.

As stated previously, the properties of the atmosphere change with time and location on the Earth. To compare the flight performance characteristics of airplanes and flight instruments, a standard atmosphere was needed. The modern standard atmosphere was first developed in the 1920s, independently in the United States and Europe. The National Advisory Committee for Aeronautics (NACA) generated the American Standard Atmosphere. The European standard was developed by the International Commission for Aerial Navigation (ICAN). The two standard atmospheres were essentially the same except for some slight differences. These differences were resolved by an international committee and an international standard atmosphere was adopted by the International Civil Aviation Organization (ICAO) in 1952.

The standard atmosphere assumes a unique temperature profile that was determined by an extensive observation program. The temperature profile consists of regions of linear variations of temperature with altitude and regions of constant temperature (isothermal regions). Figure 1.7 shows the temperature profile through the standard atmosphere. The standard sea-level properties of air are listed in Table 1.2.

The properties of the atmosphere can be expressed analytically as a function of altitude. However, before proceeding with the development of the analytical model of the atmosphere, we must define what we mean by altitude. For the present we will be concerned with three different definitions of altitude: absolute, geometric, and geopotential. Figure 1.8 shows the relationship between absolute and geometric altitude. Absolute altitude is the distance from the center of the Earth to

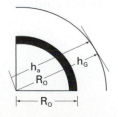

R_0 – Radius of the earth

h_G – Geometric altitude above earth's surface

h_a – Absolute altitude distance from the center of the earth to the point in question

FIGURE 1.8
Definition of geometric and absolute altitudes.

the point in question, whereas the geometric altitude is the height of the point above sea level. The absolute and geometric altitudes are related to each other in the following manner:

$$h_a = h_G + R_0 \qquad (1.41)$$

where h_a, h_G, and R_0 are the absolute altitude, geometric altitude, and radius of the earth, respectively.

Historically, measurements of atmospheric properties have been based on the assumption that the acceleration due to gravity is constant. This assumption leads to a fictitious altitude called the geopotential altitude. The relationship between the geometric and geopotential altitudes can be determined from an examination of the hydrostatic equation (Equation (1.16)). Rewriting the hydrostatic equation,

$$dP = -\rho g\, dh \qquad (1.42)$$

we see that the change in pressure is a function of the fluid density, and if we employ the acceleration due to gravity at sea level, then h is the geopotential altitude. Therefore, we have

$$dP = -\rho g_0\, dh \qquad (1.43)$$

when h is the geopotential height and

$$dP = -\rho g\, dh_G \qquad (1.44)$$

when h_G is the geometric height.

Equations (1.43) and (1.44) can be used to establish the relationship between the geometric and geopotential altitude. On comparing these equations we see that

$$dh = \frac{g}{g_0}\, dh_G \qquad (1.45)$$

Further it can be shown that

$$g = g_0 \left(\frac{R_0}{R_0 + h_G} \right)^2 \qquad (1.46)$$

which when substituted into Equation (1.45) yields

$$dh = \frac{R_0^2\, dh_G}{(R_0 + h_G)^2} \qquad (1.47)$$

Equation (1.47) can be integrated to give an expression relating the two altitudes:

$$h = \frac{R_0}{R_0 + h_G} h_G \qquad (1.48)$$

or

$$h_G = \frac{R_0}{R_0 - h} h \qquad (1.49)$$

In practice, the difference between the geometric and geopotential altitudes is quite small for altitudes below 15.2 km or 50,000 ft. However, for the higher altitudes the difference must be taken into account for accurate performance calculations.

Starting with the relationship for the change in pressure with altitude and the equations of state

$$dP = -\rho g_0 \, dh \tag{1.50}$$

and

$$P = \rho RT \tag{1.51}$$

we can obtain the following expression by dividing (1.50) by (1.51):

$$\frac{dP}{P} = -\frac{g_0}{R}\frac{dh}{T} \tag{1.52}$$

If the temperature varies with altitude in a linear manner, Equation (1.52) yields

$$\int_{P_1}^{P}\frac{dP}{P} = -\frac{g_0}{R}\int_{h_1}^{h}\frac{dh}{T_1 + \lambda(h - h_1)} \tag{1.53}$$

which on integration gives

$$\ln\frac{P}{P_1} = -\frac{g_0}{R\lambda}\ln\frac{T_1 + \lambda(h - h_1)}{T_1} \tag{1.54}$$

where P_1, T_1, and h_1 are the pressure, temperature, and altitude at the start of the linear region and λ is the rate of temperature change with altitude, which is called the lapse rate. Equation (1.54) can be rewritten in a more convenient form as

$$\frac{P}{P_1} = \left(\frac{T}{T_1}\right)^{-g_0/(R\lambda)} \tag{1.55}$$

Equation (1.55) can be used to calculate the pressure at various altitudes in any one of the linear temperature profile regions, provided the appropriate constants P_1, T_1, h_1, and λ are used.

The density variation can be easily determined as follows:

$$\frac{P}{P_1} = \frac{\rho T}{\rho_1 T_1} \tag{1.56}$$

and therefore

$$\frac{\rho}{\rho_1} = \left(\frac{T}{T_1}\right)^{-[1 + g_0/(R\lambda)]} \tag{1.57}$$

In the isothermal regions the temperature remains constant as the altitude varies. Starting again with Equation (1.52) we obtain

$$\ln\frac{P}{P_1} = -\frac{g_0}{RT_1}(h - h_1) \tag{1.58}$$

or

$$\frac{P}{P_1} = e^{-g_0(h-h_1)/(RT_1)} \tag{1.59}$$

TABLE 1.3
Properties of the atmosphere at the isothermal gradient boundaries

Geopotential altitude, H, km	Geometric altitude, Z, km	T, °K	P, N/m²	ρ, kg/m³	dT/dH, °K/km
0	0	288.15	1.01325×10^5	1.225	−6.5
11	11.019	216.65	2.2636×10^4	3.639×10^{-1}	0
20	20.063	216.65	5.474×10^3	8.803×10^{-2}	1
32	32.162	228.65	8.6805×10^2	1.332×10^{-2}	−2.8
47	47.350	270.65	1.1095×10^2	1.427×10^{-3}	0
52	52.429	270.65	5.9002×10^1	7.594×10^{-4}	−2
61	61.591	252.65	1.8208×10^1	2.511×10^{-4}	−4
79	79.994	180.65	1.03757	2.001×10^{-5}	0
88.74	90.0	180.65	0.16435	3.170×10^{-5}	

where P_1, T_1, and h_1 are the values of pressure, temperature, and altitude at the start of the isothermal region. The density variation in the isothermal regions can be obtained as

$$\frac{\rho}{\rho_1} = e^{-g_0(h-h_1)/(RT_1)} \tag{1.60}$$

Equations (1.55), (1.57), (1.59), and (1.60) can be used to predict accurately the pressure and density variation in the standard atmosphere up to approximately 57 miles, or 91 km. Table 1.3 gives the values of temperature, pressure, and density at the boundaries between the various temperature segments. The properties of the standard atmosphere as a function of altitude are presented in tabular form in Appendix A.

EXAMPLE PROBLEM 1.1. The temperature from sea level to 30,000 ft is found to decrease in a linear manner. The temperature and pressure at sea level are measured to be 40°F and 2050 lb/ft², respectively. If the temperature at 30,000 ft is −60°F, find the pressure and density at 20,000 ft.

Solution. The temperature can be represented by the linear equation

$$T = T_1 + \lambda h$$

where

$$T_1 = 499.6°\text{R}$$

and

$$\lambda = \frac{T - T_1}{h} = -0.00333° \text{ R/ft}$$

The temperature at 20,000 ft can be obtained as

$$T = 499.6 - (0.00333° \text{ R/ft})h$$

When $h = 20,000$ ft, $T = 432.9°\text{R}$. The pressure can be calculated from Equation (1.54); that is,

$$\frac{P}{P_1} = \left(\frac{T}{T_1}\right)^{-g_0/R\lambda} \qquad P = P_1\left(\frac{T}{T_1}\right)^{-g_0/R\lambda} = (2050 \text{ lb/ft}^2)\left(\frac{432.9°\text{R}}{499.6°\text{R}}\right)^{5.63} = 915 \text{ lb/ft}^2$$

The density can be found from either Equation (1.3) or (1.56). Using the equation of state,

$$P = \rho RT \qquad \rho = \frac{P}{RT}$$

$$\rho = \frac{915 \text{ lb/ft}^2}{(1718 \text{ ft}^2/(\text{s}^2 \cdot {}^{\circ}\text{R}))(432.9{}^{\circ}\text{R})} = 0.00123 \text{ slug/ft}^3$$

1.6
AERODYNAMIC NOMENCLATURE

To describe the motion of an airplane it is necessary to define a suitable coordinate system for the formulation of the equations of motion. For most problems dealing with aircraft motion, two coordinate systems are used. One coordinate system is fixed to the Earth and may be considered for the purpose of aircraft motion analysis to be an inertial coordinate system. The other coordinate system is fixed to the airplane and is referred to as a body coordinate system. Figure 1.9 shows the two right-handed coordinate systems.

The forces acting on an airplane in flight consist of aerodynamic, thrust, and gravitational forces. These forces can be resolved along an axis system fixed to the airplane's center of gravity, as illustrated in Figure 1.10. The force components are denoted X, Y, and Z; T_x, T_y, and T_z; and W_x, W_y, and W_z for the aerodynamic, thrust, and gravitational force components along the x, y, and z axes, respectively. The

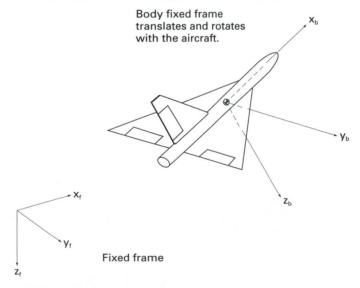

FIGURE 1.9
Body axis coordinate system.

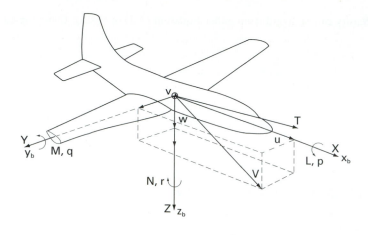

	Roll Axis x_b	Pitch Axis y_b	Yaw Axis z_b
Angular rates	p	q	r
Velocity components	u	v	w
Aerodynamic force components	X	Y	Z
Aerodynamic moment components	L	M	N
Moment of inertia about each axis	I_x	I_y	I_z
Products of inertia	I_{yz}	I_{xz}	I_{xy}

FIGURE 1.10
Definition of forces, moments, and velocity components in a body fixed coordinate

aerodynamic forces are defined in terms of dimensionless coefficients, the flight dynamic pressure Q, and a reference area S as follows:

$$X = C_x QS \qquad \text{Axial force} \tag{1.61}$$

$$Y = C_y QS \qquad \text{Side force} \tag{1.62}$$

$$Z = C_z QS \qquad \text{Normal force} \tag{1.63}$$

In a similar manner, the moments on the airplane can be divided into moments created by the aerodynamic load distribution and the thrust force not acting through the center of gravity. The components of the aerodynamic moment also are expressed in terms of dimensionless coefficients, flight dynamic pressure, reference area, and a characteristic length as follows:

$$L = C_l QSl \qquad \text{Rolling moment} \tag{1.64}$$

$$M = C_m QSl \qquad \text{Pitching moment} \tag{1.65}$$

$$N = C_n QSl \qquad \text{Yawing moment} \tag{1.66}$$

For airplanes, the reference area S is taken as the wing platform area and the characteristic length l is taken as the wing span for the rolling and yawing moment and the mean chord for the pitching moment. For rockets and missiles, the reference area is usually taken as the maximum cross-sectional area, and the characteristic length is taken as the maximum diameter.

The aerodynamic coefficients C_x, C_y, C_z, C_l, C_m, and C_n primarily are a function of the Mach number, Reynolds number, angle of attack, and sideslip angle; they are secondary functions of the time rate of change of angle of attack and sideslip, and the angular velocity of the airplane.

The aerodynamic force and moment acting on the airplane and its angular and translational velocity are illustrated in Figure 1.10. The x and z axes are in the plane of symmetry, with the x axis pointing along the fuselage and the positive y axis along the right wing. The resultant force and moment, as well as the airplane's velocity, can be resolved along these axes.

The angle of attack and sideslip can be defined in terms of the velocity components as illustrated in Figure 1.11. The equations for α and β follow:

$$\alpha = \tan^{-1} \frac{w}{u} \tag{1.67}$$

and
$$\beta = \sin^{-1} \frac{v}{V} \tag{1.68}$$

where
$$V = (u^2 + v^2 + w^2)^{1/2} \tag{1.69}$$

If the angle of attack and sideslip are small, that is, $< 15°$, then Equations (1.67)

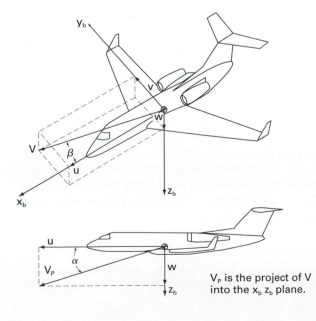

FIGURE 1.11
Definition of angle of attack and sideslip.

V_P is the project of V into the $x_b z_b$ plane.

and (1.68) can be approximated by

$$\alpha = \frac{w}{u} \tag{1.70}$$

and

$$\beta = \frac{v}{u} \tag{1.71}$$

where α and β are in radians.

1.7
AIRCRAFT INSTRUMENTS

The earliest successful airplanes were generally flown without the aid of aircraft instruments.* The pilots of these early vehicles were preoccupied primarily with maneuvering and controlling their sometimes temperamental aircraft. However, as new designs were developed, the performance, stability, and control steadily improved to the point where the pilot needed more information about the airplane's flight conditions to fly the airplane safely. One major change in aircraft design that led to improved performance was the evolution of the open-air cockpit. Prior to this development, pilots flew their airplanes in either a crouched or inclined position, exposed to the oncoming airstream. In addition to providing the pilot shelter from the airstream, the cockpit also provided a convenient place to locate aircraft instruments. The early open-cockpit pilots were hesitant to fly from a closed cockpit because this eliminated their ability to judge sideslip (or skid) by the wind blowing on one side of their face. They also used the sound of the slipstream to provide an indication of the airspeed.

A chronological development of aircraft instruments is not readily available; however, one can safely guess that some of the earliest instruments to appear on the cockpit instrument panel were a magnetic compass for navigation, airspeed and altitude indicators for flight information, and engine instruments such as rpm and fuel gauges. The flight decks of modern airplanes are equipped with a multitude of instruments that provide the flight crew with information they need to fly their aircraft. The instruments can be categorized according to their primary use as flight, navigation, power plant, environmental, and electrical systems instruments.

Several of the instruments that compose the flight instrument group will be discussed in the following sections. The instruments include the airspeed indicator, altimeter, rate of climb indicator, and the Mach meter. These four instruments, along with angle of attack and sideslip indicators, are extremely important for flight test measurement of performance and stability data.

---

*The Wright brothers used several instruments on their historic flight. They had a tachometer to measure engine rpm, an anemometer to measure airspeed, and a stopwatch.

1.7.1 Air Data Systems

The Pitot static system of an airplane is used to measure the total pressure created by the forward motion of the airplane and the static pressure of the ambient atmosphere. The difference between total and static pressures is used to measure airspeed and the Mach number, and the static pressure is used to measure altitude and rate of climb. The Pilot static system is illustrated in Figure 1.12. The Pilot static probe normally consists of two concentric tubes. The inner tube is used to determine the total pressure, and the outer tube is used to determine the static pressure of the surrounding air.

1.7.2 Airspeed Indicator

The pressures measured by the Pitot static probe can be used to determine the airspeed of the airplane. For low flight speeds, when compressibility effects can be safely ignored, we can use the incompressible form of Bernoulli's equation to show that the difference between the total and the static pressure is

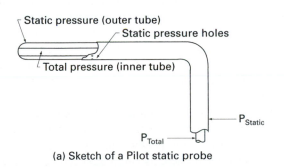

FIGURE 1.12
Pitot static system.

(a) Sketch of a Pilot static probe

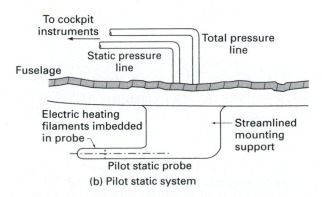

(b) Pilot static system

the dynamic pressure:

$$P_0 = P + \frac{1}{2}\rho V_\infty^2 \tag{1.72}$$

$$\frac{1}{2}\rho V_\infty^2 = P_0 - P \tag{1.73}$$

or
$$V_\infty = \left(\frac{2(P_0 - P)}{\rho}\right)^{1/2} \tag{1.74}$$

The airspeed indicator in the cockpit consists of a differential pressure gauge that measures the dynamic pressure and deflects an indicator hand proportionally to the pressure difference. As indicated by Equation (1.74), the airspeed is a function of both the measured pressure difference and the air density ρ. As was shown earlier, the air density is a function of altitude and atmospheric conditions. To obtain the true airspeed, the airspeed indicator would be required to measure the change in both pressure and air density. This is not feasible for a simple instrument and therefore the scale on the airspeed indicator is calibrated using standard sea-level air. The speed measured by the indicator is called the indicated airspeed (IAS).

The speed measured by an airspeed indicator can be used to determine the true flight speed, provided that the indicated airspeed is corrected for instrument error, position error, compressibility effects, and density corrections for altitude variations. Instrument error includes those errors inherent to the instrument itself; for example, pressure losses or mechanical inaccuracies in the system. Position error has to do with the location of the Pitot static probe on the airplane. Ideally, the probe should be located so that it is in the undisturbed freestream; in general this is not possible and so the probe is affected by flow distortion due to the fuselage or wing. The total pressure measured by a Pitot static probe is relatively insensitive to flow inclination. Unfortunately, this is not the case for the static measurement and care must be used to position the probe to minimize the error in the static measurement. If one knows the instrument and position errors, one can correct the indicated airspeed to give what is referred to as the calibrated airspeed (CAS).

At high speeds, the Pitot static probe must be corrected for compressibility effects. This can be demonstrated by examining the compressible form of the Bernoulli equation:

$$\frac{V^2}{2} + \frac{\gamma}{\gamma - 1}\frac{P}{\rho} = \frac{\gamma}{\gamma - 1}\frac{P_0}{\rho_0} \tag{1.75}$$

Equation (1.75) can be expressed in terms of the Mach number as follows:

$$P_0 = P\left(1 + \frac{\gamma - 1}{2}M^2\right)^{\gamma/(\gamma-1)} \tag{1.76}$$

Recall that the airspeed indicator measures the difference between the total and static pressure. Equation (1.76) can be rewritten as

$$Q_c = P_0 - P = P\left[\left(1 + \frac{\gamma - 1}{2}M^2\right)^{\gamma/(\gamma-1)} - 1\right] \tag{1.77}$$

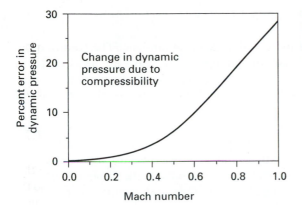

FIGURE 1.13
Percent of error in dynamic
pressure if compressibility is
neglected.

where Q_c is the compressible equivalent to the dynamic pressure. Figure 1.13 shows the percentage error in dynamic pressure if compressibility is ignored.

The equivalent airspeed (EAS) can be thought of as the flight speed in the standard sea-level air mass that produces the same dynamic pressure as the actual flight speed. To obtain the actual, or true, airspeed (TAS), the equivalent airspeed must be corrected for density variations. Using the fact that the dynamic pressures are the same, one can develop a relationship between the true and equivalent airspeeds as follows:

$$\frac{1}{2}\rho_0 V_{EAS}^2 = \frac{1}{2}\rho V_{TAS}^2 \tag{1.78}$$

$$V_{TAS} = \frac{V_{EAS}}{\sqrt{\sigma}} \tag{1.79}$$

where $\sigma = \rho/\rho_0$.

The definitions for the various airspeed designations are summarized in Table 1.4.

TABLE 1.4
Airspeed designations

Airspeed*	Definition
V_{IAS} Indicated airspeed	Airspeed indicated by the airspeed instrument. The indicated airspeed is affected by altitude, compressibility, instrument, and position error.
V_{CAS} Calibrated airspeed	Indicated airspeed corrected for instrument and position errors.
V_{EAS} Equivalent airspeed	Calibrated airspeed corrected for compressibility.
V_{TAS} True airspeed	Equivalent airspeed corrected for density altitude.

*When the prefix K is used in the subscript, the airspeed is in knots.

1.7.3 Altimeter

An altimeter is a device to measure the altitude of an airplane. The control of an airplane's altitude is very important for safe operation. Pilots use an altimeter to maintain adequate vertical spacing between their aircraft and other airplanes operating in the same area and to establish sufficient distance between the airplane and the ground.

Earlier in this chapter we briefly discussed the mercury barometer. A barometer can be used to measure the atmospheric pressure. As we have shown, the static pressure in the atmosphere varies with altitude, so that if we use a device similar to a barometer we can measure the static pressure outside the airplane, and then relate that pressure to a corresponding altitude in the standard atmosphere. This is the basic idea behind a pressure altimeter.

The mercury barometer of course would be impractical for application in aircraft, because it is both fragile and sensitive to the airplane's motion. To avoid this difficulty, the pressure altimeter uses the same principle as an aneroid* barometer. This type of barometer measures the pressure by magnifying small deflections of an elastic element that deforms as pressure acts on it.

The altimeter is a sensitive pressure transducer that measures the ambient static pressure and displays an altitude value on the instrument dial. The altimeter is calibrated using the standard atmosphere and the altitude indicated by the instrument is referred to as the pressure altitude. The *pressure altitude* is the altitude in the standard atmosphere corresponding to the measured pressure. The pressure altitude and actual or geometric altitude will be the same only when the atmosphere through which the airplane is flying is identical to the standard atmosphere.

In addition to pressure altitude two other altitudes are important for performance analysis: the density and temperature altitudes. The *density altitude* is the altitude in the standard atmosphere corresponding to the ambient density. In general, the ambient density is not measured but rather calculated from the pressure altitude given by the altimeter and the ambient temperature measured by a temperature probe. The *temperature altitude,* as you might guess, is the altitude in the standard atmosphere corresponding to the measured ambient temperature.

As noted earlier the atmosphere is continuously changing; therefore, to compare performance data for an airplane from one test to another or to compare different airplanes the data must be referred to a common atmospheric reference. The density altitude is used for airplane performance data comparisons.

An altimeter is an extremely sophisticated instrument, as illustrated by the drawing in Figure 1.14. This particular altimeter uses two aneroid capsules to increase the sensitivity of the instrument. The deflections of the capsules are magnified and represented by the movement of the pointer with respect to a scale on the surface plate of the meter and a counter. This altimeter is equipped with a

---

*Aneroid is derived from the Greek word *aneros,* which means "not wet."

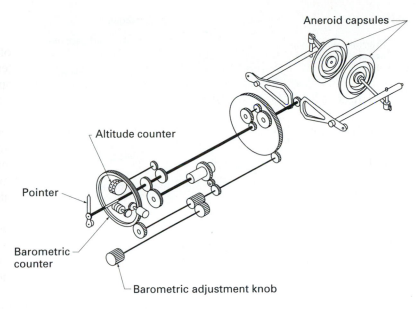

Aneroid capsules

Altitude counter

Pointer

Barometric counter

Barometric adjustment knob

FIGURE 1.14
Cutaway drawing of an altimeter.

barometric pressure-setting mechanism. The adjusting mechanism allows the pilot manually to correct the altimeter for variations in sea-level barometric pressure. With such adjustments, the altimeter will indicate an altitude that closely approaches the true altitude above sea level.

1.7.4 Rate of Climb Indicator

One of the earliest instruments used to measure rate of climb was called a statoscope. This instrument was used by balloonists to detect variation from a desired altitude. The instrument consisted of a closed atmospheric chamber connected by a tube containing a small quantity of liquid to an outer chamber vented to the atmosphere. As the altitude changed, air would flow from one chamber to the other to equalize the pressure. Air passing through the liquid would create bubbles and the direction of the flow of bubbles indicated whether the balloon was ascending or descending. A crude indication of the rate of climb was obtained by observing the frequency of the bubbles passing through the liquid.

Although the statoscope provided the balloonist a means of detecting departure from a constant altitude, it was difficult to use as a rate of climb indicator. A new instrument, called the balloon variometer, was developed for rate of climb measurements. The variometer was similar to the statoscope; however, the flow into the chamber took place through a capillary leak. The pressure difference across the leak was measured with a sensitive liquid manometer that was calibrated to indicate the rate of climb.

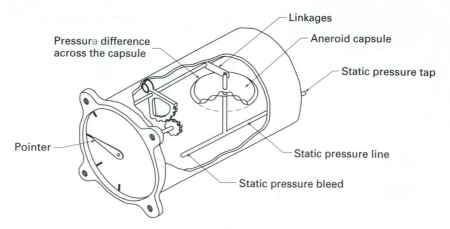

FIGURE 1.15
Sketch of the basic components of a rate of climb indicator.

Present-day rate of climb indicators are similar to the variometer. An example of a leak type rate of climb indicator is shown in Figure 1.15. This instrument consists of an insulated chamber, a diaphragm, a calibrated leak, and an appropriate mechanical linkage to measure the deflection of the diaphragm. The static pressure is applied to the interior of the diaphragm and also allowed to leak into the chamber by way of a capillary or orifice opening. The diaphragm measures the differential pressure across the leak and the deflection of the diaphragm is transmitted to the indicator dial by a mechanical linkage, as illustrated in the sketch in Figure 1.15.

1.7.5 Machmeter

The Pitot static tube can be used to determine the Mach number of an airplane from the measured stagnation and static pressure. If the Mach number is less than 1, Equation (1.40) can be used to find the Mach number of the airplane:

$$\frac{P_0}{P} = \left(1 + \frac{\gamma - 1}{2}M^2\right)^{\gamma/(\gamma-1)} \tag{1.80}$$

However, when the Mach number is greater than unity, a bow wave forms ahead of the Pitot probe, as illustrated in Figure 1.16. The bow wave is a curved detached shock wave. In the immediate vicinity of the Pitot orifice, the shock wave can be approximated as a normal shock wave. Using the normal shock relationships, the

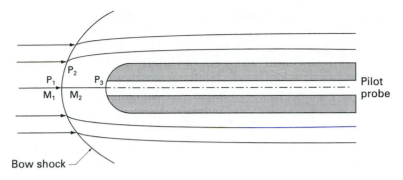

FIGURE 1.16
Detached shock wave ahead of a Pitot static probe.

pressure ratio across the shock can be written as

$$\frac{P_2}{P_1} = \left(\frac{2\gamma}{\gamma - 1}\right)M_1^2 - \left(\frac{\gamma - 1}{\gamma + 1}\right) \tag{1.81}$$

where M_1 is the Mach number ahead of the shock wave. The relationship between the Mach number M_1 ahead of the normal shock and the Mach number M_2 behind the shock is given by Equation (1.82):

$$M_2^2 = \frac{\frac{1}{2}(\gamma - 1)M_1^2 + 1}{\gamma M_1^2 - \frac{1}{2}(\gamma - 1)} \tag{1.82}$$

After passing through the shock wave, the air is slowed adiabatically to zero velocity at the total pressure orifice of the Pitot probe. The pressure ratio behind the shock can be expressed as

$$\frac{P_3}{P_2} = \left(1 + \frac{\gamma - 1}{2}M_2^2\right)^{\gamma/(\gamma - 1)} \tag{1.83}$$

On combining the previous equations, the ratio of stagnation pressure to static pressure in terms of the flight Mach number can be written:

$$\frac{P_3}{P_1} = \left[\left(\frac{2\gamma}{\gamma + 1}\right)M_1^2 - \left(\frac{\gamma - 1}{\gamma + 1}\right)\right]$$
$$\times \left[1 + \frac{\gamma - 1}{2}\left[\left(\frac{\frac{1}{2}(\gamma - 1)M_1^2 + 1}{\gamma M_1^2 - \frac{1}{2}(\gamma - 1)}\right)\right]\right]^{\gamma/(\gamma - 1)} \tag{1.84}$$

This expression is known as the Rayleigh Pitot tube formula, named after Lord Rayleigh, who first developed this equation in 1910. If we assume that the ratio γ

of specific heats for air is 1.4, the expression can be rewritten as

$$\frac{P_3}{P_1} = \frac{7M_1^2 - 1}{6}\left[1 + 0.2\left(\frac{M_1^2 + 5}{7M_1^2 - 1}\right)\right]^{3.5} \tag{1.85}$$

The preceding equations can be used to design a Mach meter.

The use of Rayleigh's formula is invalid for every high Mach numbers or altitudes. When the Mach number is high, appreciable heat will be exchanged, which violates the assumption of adiabatic flow used in the development of the equation. At very high altitude, air cannot be considered as a continuous medium and again the analysis breaks down.

1.7.6 Angle of Attack Indicators

The measurement of angle of attack is important for cruise control and stall warning. Several devices can be used to measure the angle of attack of an airplane, two of which are the vane and pressure-sensor type indicator. The pivot vane sensor is a mass-balanced wind vane that is free to align itself with the oncoming flow. The vane type angle of attack sensor has been used extensively in airplane flight test programs. For flight test applications the sensor usually is mounted on a nose boom or a boom mounted to the wing tips along with a Pitot static probe, as illustrated in Figure 1.17. Note that a second vane system is mounted on the boom to measure the sideslip angle.

The angle measured by the vane is influenced by the distortion of the flow field created by the airplane. Actually, the sensor measures only the local angle of attack. The difference between the measured and actual angles of attack is called the position error. Position error can be minimized by mounting the sensor on the fuselage, where the flow distortion is small. The deflection of the vane is recorded by means of a potentiometer.

A null-seeking pressure sensor also can be used to measure the angle of attack. Figure 1.18 is a schematic of a null-seeking pressure sensor. The sensor consists of the following components: a rotatable tube containing two orifices spaced at equal angles to the tube axis, a pressure transducer to detect the difference in pressure between the two orifices, a mechanism for rotating the probe until the pressure differential is 0, and a device for measuring the rotation or angle of attack. The device shown in Figure 1.18 consists of a rotable probe that protrudes through the

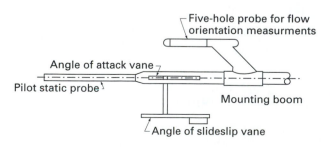

Five-hole probe for flow orientation measurments

Angle of attack vane

Pilot static probe

Mounting boom

Angle of slideslip vane

FIGURE 1.17
Flight test instrumentation, Pitot static probe, angle of attack and sideslip vanes, five-hole probe mounted on a nose or wing boom.

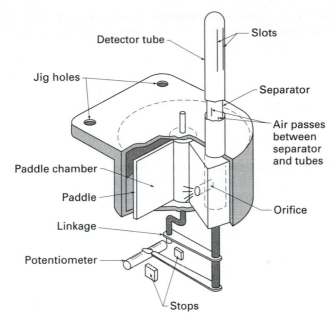

FIGURE 1.18
Null-sensing pressure probe for measuring angle of attack.

fuselage and an air chamber mounted inside the fuselage. The pressures from the two slits are vented to air chambers by a swivel paddle. If a pressure difference exists at the two slots, the swivel paddle will rotate. The paddle is connected by way of linkages so that, as the paddle moves, the pressure tube is rotated until the pressures are equalized. The angular position of the probe is recorded by a potentiometer.

EXAMPLE PROBLEM 1.2. An aircraft altimeter calibrated to the standard atmosphere reads 10,000 ft. The airspeed indicator has been calibrated for both instrument and position errors and reads a velocity of 120 knots. If the outside air temperature is 20°F, determine the true airspeed.

Solution. The altimeter is a pressure gauge calibrated to the standard atmosphere. If the altimeter reads 10,000 ft, the static pressure it senses must correspond to the static pressure at 10,000 ft in the standard atmosphere. Using the standard atmospheric table in the Appendix, the static pressure at 10,000 ft is given as

$$P = 1455.6 \text{ lb/ft}^2$$

The ambient density can be calculated using the equation of state:

$$\rho = \frac{P}{RT}$$

$$\rho = \frac{1455.6 \text{ lb/ft}^2}{(1716 \text{ ft}^2/(s^2 \cdot °R))(479.7°R)}$$

$$\rho = 0.001768 \text{ slug/ft}^3$$

A low-speed airspeed indicator corrected for instrument and position error reads the equivalent airspeed. The true speed and equivalent airspeed are related by

$$V_{TAS} = \frac{V_{EAS}}{\sqrt{\sigma}}$$

where σ is the ratio of the density at altitude to the standard sea-level value of density:

$$\sigma = \rho/\rho_0 = (0.001768/0.002739) = 0.7432$$

Now, solving for the true airspeed,

$$V_{KTAS} = \frac{V_{KEAS}}{\sqrt{\sigma}} = \frac{120 \text{ knots}}{\sqrt{0.7432}}$$
$$= 139 \text{ knots}$$

1.8
SUMMARY

In this chapter we examined the properties of air and how those properties vary with altitude. For the comparison of flight test data and calibrating aircraft instruments, a standard atmosphere is a necessity: The 1962 U.S. Standard Atmosphere provides the needed reference for the aerospace community. The standard atmosphere was shown to be made up of gradient and isothermal regions.

Finally, we discussed the basic concepts behind several basic flight instruments that play an important role in flight test measurements of aircraft performance, stability and control. In principle these instruments seem to be quite simple; they in fact, are, extremely complicated mechanical devices. Although we have discussed several mechanical instruments, most of the information presented to the flight crew on the newest aircraft designs comes from multifunctional electronic displays. Color cathode ray tubes are used to display air data such as attitude, speed, and altitude. Additional displays include navigation, weather, and engine performance information, to name just a few items. The improvements offered by this new technology can be used to reduce the workload of the flight crew and improve the flight safety of the next generation of airplane designs.

PROBLEMS

1.1. An altimeter set for sea-level standard pressure indicates an altitude of 20,000 ft. If the outside ambient temperature is $-5°F$, find the air density and the density altitude.

1.2. An airplane is flying at an altitude of 5000 m as indicated by the altimeter and the outside air temperature is $-20°C$. If the airplane is flying at a true airspeed of 300 m/s, determine the indicated airspeed.

1.3. A high-altitude, remotely piloted communications platform is flying at a pressure altitude of 60,000 ft and an indicated airspeed of 160 ft/s. The outside ambient temperature is −75°F. Estimate the Reynolds number of the wing based on a mean chord of 3.5 ft.

1.4. An airplane is flying at a pressure altitude of 10,000 ft and the airspeed indicator reads 100 knots. If there is no instrument error and the position error is given by Figure P1.4, find the true airspeed of the airplane.

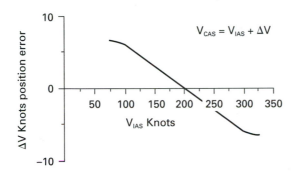

$V_{CAS} = V_{IAS} + \Delta V$

FIGURE P1.4
Position error versus indicated airspeed.

1.5. Under what conditions are following relationships valid?

$$V_{CAS} = V_{EAS} = V_{TAS}$$

$$V_{CAS} = V_{EAS} \neq V_{TAS}$$

$$V_{CAS} \neq V_{EAS} = V_{TAS}$$

1.6. A small right circular cylinder is used to measure the angle of attack of an airplane by measuring the difference in pressure at two port locations that are located at $\theta = \pm 20°$. Assuming that the flow on the forward face of the cylinder can be accurately modeled as an inviscid flow, the velocity along the cylinder surface can be expressed as

$$V_\theta = 2V_\infty \sin \theta$$

If, while flying at 200 ft/s under sea-level standard conditions, the pressure difference is 32.5 lb/ft², what is the angle of the airplane?

REFERENCES

1.1. Anderson, J. D. *Introduction to Flight*. New York: McGraw-Hill, 1978.
1.2. Domnasch, D. O.; S. S. Sherby; and T. F. Connolly. *Airplane Aerodynamics*. New York: Pitman, 1967.

1.3. Pallett, E. H. J. *Aircraft Instruments.* London: Pitman, 1982.
1.4. *U.S. Standard Atmosphere, 1962,* prepared under sponsorship of the National Aeronautics and Space Administration, United States Air Force, and United States Weather Bureau, Washington, DC, December 1962.
1.5. Putnam, T. W. "The X-29 Flight-Research Program." *AIAA Student Journal,* Fall 1984.

CHAPTER 2

Static Stability and Control

"Isn't it astonishing that all these secrets have been preserved for so many years just so that we could discover them!"

Orville Wright, June 7, 1903

2.1
HISTORICAL PERSPECTIVE

By the start of the 20th century, the aeronautical community had solved many of the technical problems necessary for achieving powered flight of a heavier-than-air aircraft. One problem still beyond the grasp of these early investigators was a lack of understanding of the relationship between stability and control as well as the influence of the pilot on the pilot-machine system. Most of the ideas regarding stability and control came from experiments with uncontrolled hand-launched gliders. Through such experiments, it was quickly discovered that for a successful flight the glider had to be inherently stable. Earlier aviation pioneers such as Albert Zahm in the United States, Alphonse Penaud in France, and Frederick Lanchester in England contributed to the notion of stability. Zahm, however, was the first to correctly outline the requirements for static stability in a paper he presented in 1893. In his paper, he analyzed the conditions necessary for obtaining a stable equilibrium for an airplane descending at a constant speed. Figure 2.1 shows a sketch of a glider from Zahm's paper. Zahm concluded that the center of gravity had to be in front of the aerodynamic force and the vehicle would require what he referred to as "longitudinal dihedral" to have a stable equilibrium point. In the terminology of today, he showed that, if the center of gravity was ahead of the wing aerodynamic center, then one would need a reflexed airfoil to be stable at a positive angle of attack.

In the 20 years prior to the Wright brothers' successful flight, many individuals in the United States and Europe were working with gliders and unpiloted powered models. These investigators were constantly trying to improve their vehicles, with the ultimate goal of achieving powered flight of a airplane under human control. Three men who would leave lasting impressions on the Wright brothers were Otto Lilienthal of Germany and Octave Chanute and Samuel Pierpont Langley of the United States.

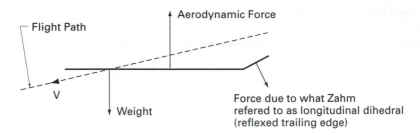

FIGURE 2.1
Zahm's description of longitudinal stability.

Lilienthal made a significant contribution to aeronautics by his work with model and human-carrying gliders. His experiments included the determination of the properties of curved or cambered wings. He carefully recorded the details of over 2000 glider flights. The information in his journal includes data on materials, construction techniques, handling characteristics of his gliders, and aerodynamics. His successful flights and recorded data inspired and aided many other aviation pioneers. Lilienthal's glider designs were statically stable but had very little control capability. For control, Lilienthal would shift his weight to maintain equilibrium flight, much as hang-glider pilots do today. The lack of suitable control proved to be a fatal flaw for Lilienthal. In 1896, he lost control of his glider; the glider stalled and plunged to earth from an altitude of 50 ft. Lilienthal died a day later from the injuries incurred in the accident.

In the United States, Octave Chanute became interested in gliding flight in the mid 1890s. Initially, he built gliders patterned after Lilienthal's designs. After experimenting with modified versions of Lilienthal's gliders, he developed his own designs. His gliders incorporated biplane and multiplane wings, controls to adjust the wings to maintain equilibrium, and a vertical tail for steering. These design changes represented substantial improvements over Lilienthal's monoplane gliders. Many of Chanute's innovations would be incorporated in the Wright brothers' designs. In addition to corresponding with the Wright brothers, Chanute visited their camp at Kitty Hawk to lend his experience and advice to their efforts.

Another individual who helped the Wright brothers was Samuel Pierpont Langley, secretary of the Smithsonian Institution. The Wright brothers knew of Langley's work and wrote to the Smithsonian asking for the available aeronautical literature. The Smithsonian informed the Wright brothers of the activities of many of the leading aviation pioneers and this information, no doubt, was very helpful to them.

Around 1890 Langley became interested in problems of flight. Initially his work consisted of collecting and examining all the available aerodynamic data. From the study of these data and his own experiments he concluded that heavier-than-air powered flight was possible. Langley then turned his attention to designing and perfecting unpiloted powered models. On May 6, 1896, his powered model flew for $1\frac{1}{2}$ minutes and covered a distance of three-quarters of a mile. Langley's success with powered models pioneered the practicality of mechanical flight.

After his successful model flights, Langley was engaged by the War Department to develop a human-carrying airplane. Congress appropriated $50,000 for the project. Langley and his engineering assistant, Charles Manley, started work on their own design in 1899. For the next four years, they were busy designing, fabricating, and testing the full-size airplane that was to be launched by a catapult fixed to the top of a houseboat. The first trial was conducted on September 7, 1903, in the middle of the Potomac River near Tidewater, Virginia. The first attempt ended in failure as the airplane pitched down into the river at the end of the launch rails. A second attempt was made on December 8, 1903; this time, the airplane pitched up and fell back into the river. In both trials, the launching system prevented the possibility of a successful flight. For Langley, it was a bitter disappointment and the criticism he received from the press deeply troubled him. He was one of the pioneering geniuses of early aviation, however, and it is a shame that he went to his grave still smarting from the ridicule. Some 20 years later his airplane was modified, a new engine was installed, and the airplane flew successfully.

The time had come for someone to design a powered airplane capable of carrying someone aloft. As we all know, the Wright brothers made their historic first flight on a powered airplane at Kitty Hawk, North Carolina, on December 17, 1903. Orville Wright made the initial flight, which lasted only 12 seconds and covered approximately 125 feet. Taking turns operating the aircraft, Orville and Wilbur made three more flights that day. The final flight lasted 59 seconds and covered a distance of 852 feet while flying into a 20 mph headwind. The airplane tended to fly in a porpoising fashion, with each flight ending abruptly as the vehicle's landing skids struck the ground. The Wright brothers found their powered airplane to be much more responsive than their earlier gliders and, as a result, had difficulty controlling their airplane.

Figure 2.2 shows two photographs of the Kitty Hawk Flyer. The first photograph shows Orville Wright making the historical initial flight and the second shows the airplane after the fourth and last flight of the day. Notice the damaged horizontal rudder (the term used by the Wright brothers). Today we use the term canard to describe a forward control surface. The world canard comes to us from the French word that means "duck." The French used the term canard to describe an early French airplane that had its horizontal tail located far forward of the wing. They thought this airplane looked like a duck with its neck stretched out in flight.

From this very primitive beginning, we have witnessed a remarkable revolution in aircraft development. In less than a century, airplanes have evolved into an essential part of our national defense and commercial transportation system. The success of the Wright brothers can be attributed to their step-by-step experimental approach. After reviewing the experimental data of their contemporaries, the Wright brothers were convinced that additional information was necessary before a successful airplane could be designed. They embarked on an experimental program that included wind-tunnel and flight-test experiments. The Wright brothers designed and constructed a small wind tunnel and made thousands of model tests to determine the aerodynamic characteristics of curved airfoils. They also conducted thousands of glider experiments in developing their airplane. Through their study of the works of others and their own experimental investigations, the Wright

FIGURE 2.2
Photographs of the Wright brothers' airplane, December 17, 1903, Kitty Hawk, North Carolina.

brothers were convinced that the major obstacle to achieving powered flight was the lack of sufficient control. Therefore, much of their work was directed toward improving the control capabilities of their gliders. They felt strongly that powerful controls were essential for the pilot to maintain equilibrium and prevent accidents such as the ones that caused the deaths of Lilienthal and other glider enthusiasts.

This approach represented a radical break with the design philosophy of the day. The gliders and airplanes designed by Lilenthal, Chanute, Langley, and other aviation pioneers were designed to be inherently stable. In these designs, the pilot's only function was to steer the vehicle. Although such vehicles were statically stable, they lacked maneuverability and were susceptible to upset by atmospheric disturbances. The Wright brothers' airplane was statically unstable but quite maneuverable. The lack of stability made their work as pilots very difficult. However, through their glider experiments they were able to teach themselves to fly their unstable airplane.

The Wright brothers succeeded where others failed because of their dedicated scientific and engineering efforts. Their accomplishments were the foundation on which others could build. Some of the major accomplishments follow:

1. They designed and built a wind-tunnel and balance system to conduct aerodynamic tests. With their tunnel they developed a systematic airfoil aerodynamic database.
2. They developed a complete flight control system with adequate control capability.
3. They designed a lightweight engine and an efficient propeller.
4. Finally, they designed an airplane with a sufficient strength-to-weight ratio, capable of sustaining powered flight.

These early pioneers provided much of the understanding we have today regarding static stability, maneuverability, and control. However, it is not clear whether any of these men truly comprehended the relationship among these topics.

2.2
INTRODUCTION

How well an airplane flies and how easily it can be controlled are subjects studied in aircraft stability and control. By stability we mean the tendency of the airplane to return to its equilibrium position after it has been disturbed. The disturbance may be generated by the pilot's actions or atmospheric phenomena. The atmospheric disturbances can be wind gusts, wind gradients, or turbulent air. An airplane must have sufficient stability that the pilot does not become fatigued by constantly having to control the airplane owing to external disturbances. Although airplanes with little or no inherent aerodynamic stability can be flown, they are unsafe to fly unless they are provided artificial stability by an electromechanical device called a stability augmentation system.

Two conditions are necessary for an airplane to fly its mission successfully. The airplane must be able to achieve equilibrium flight and it must have the capability to maneuver for a wide range of flight velocities and altitudes. To achieve equilibrium or perform maneuvers, the airplane must be equipped with aerodynamic and propulsive controls. The design and performance of control systems is an integral part of airplane stability and control.

The stability and control characteristics of an airplane are referred to as the vehicle's handling or flying qualities. It is important to the pilot that the airplane possesses satisfactory handling qualities. Airplanes with poor handling qualities will be difficult to fly and could be dangerous. Pilots form their opinions of an airplane on the basis of its handling characteristics. An airplane will be considered of poor design if it is difficult to handle regardless of how outstanding the airplane's performance might be. In the study of airplane stability and control, we are interested in what makes an airplane stable, how to design the control systems, and what conditions are necessary for good handling. In the following sections we will discuss each of these topics from the point of view of how they influence the design of the airplane.

2.2.1 Static Stability

Stability is a property of an equilibrium state. To discuss stability we must first define what is meant by equilibrium. If an airplane is to remain in steady uniform flight, the resultant force as well as the resultant moment about the center of gravity must both be equal to 0. An airplane satisfying this requirement is said to be in a state of equilibrium or flying at a trim condition. On the other hand, if the forces

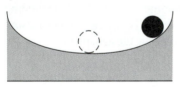

(a) Statically stable

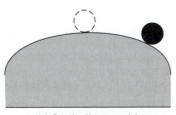

(b) Statically unstable

(c) Neutral stability

FIGURE 2.3
Sketches illustrating various conditions of static stability.

and moments do not sum to 0, the airplane will be subjected to translational and rotational accelerations.

The subject of airplane stability is generally divided into static and dynamic stability. Static stability is the initial tendency of the vehicle to return to its equilibrium state after a disturbance. An example of the various types of static stability is illustrated in Figure 2.3. If the ball were to be displaced from the bottom of the curved surface (Figure 2.3(*a*)), by virtue of the gravitational attraction, the ball would roll back to the bottom (i.e., the force and moment would tend to restore the ball to its equilibrium point). Such a situation would be referred to as a stable equilibrium point. On the other hand, if we were able to balance a ball on the curved surface shown in Figure 2.3(*b*), then any displacement from the equilibrium point would cause the ball to roll off the surface. In this case, the equilibrium point would be classified as unstable. In the last example, shown in Figure 2.3(*c*), the ball is placed on a flat surface. Now, if the wall were to be displaced from its initial equilibrium point to another position, the ball would remain at the new position. This would be classified as a neutrally stable equilibrium point and represents the limiting (or boundary) between static stability and static instability. The important point in this simple example is that, if we are to have a stable equilibrium point, the vehicle must develop a restoring force or moment to bring it back to the equilibrium condition.

2.2.2 Dynamic Stability

In the study of dynamic stability we are concerned with the time history of the motion of the vehicle after it is disturbed from its equilibrium point. Figure 2.4 shows several airplane motions that could occur if the airplane were disturbed from

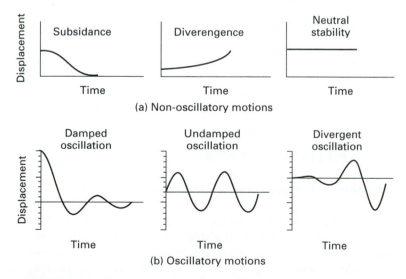

(a) Non-oscillatory motions

(b) Oscillatory motions

FIGURE 2.4
Examples of stable and unstable dynamic motions.

its equilibrium conditions. Note that the vehicle can be statically stable but dynamically unstable. Static stability, therefore, does not guarantee dynamic stability. However, for the vehicle to be dynamically stable it must be statically stable.

The reduction of the disturbance with time indicates that there is resistance to the motion and, therefore, energy is being dissipated. The dissipation of energy is called positive damping. If energy is being added to the system, then we have a negative damping. Positive damping for an airplane is provided by forces and moments that arise owing to the airplane's motion. In positive damping, these forces and moments will oppose the motion of the airplane and cause the disturbance to damp out with time. An airplane that has negative aerodynamic damping will be dynamically unstable. To fly such an airplane, artificial damping must be designed into the vehicle. The artificial damping is provided by a stability augmentation system (SAS). Basically, a stability augmentation system is an electromechanical device that senses the undesirable motion and moves the appropriate controls to damp out the motion. This usually is accomplished with small control movements and, therefore, the pilot's control actions are not influenced by the system.

Of particular interest to the pilot and designer is the degree of dynamic stability. Dynamic stability usually is specified by the time it takes a disturbance to be damped to half of its initial amplitude or, in the case of an unstable motion, the time it takes for the initial amplitude of the disturbance to double. In the case of an oscillatory motion, the frequency and period of the motion are extremely important.

So far, we have been discussing the response of an airplane to external disturbances while the controls are held fixed. When we add the pilot to the system, additional complications can arise. For example, an airplane that is dynamically stable to external disturbances with the controls fixed can become unstable by the pilot's control actions. If the pilot attempts to correct for a disturbance and that control input is out of phase with the oscillatory motion of the airplane, the control actions would increase the motion rather than correct it. This type of pilot-vehicle response is called pilot-induced oscillation (PIO). Many factors contribute to the PIO tendency of an airplane. A few of the major contributions are insufficient aerodynamic damping, insufficient control system damping, and pilot reaction time.

2.3
STATIC STABILITY AND CONTROL

2.3.1 Definition of Longitudinal Static Stability

In the first example we showed that to have static stability we need to develop a restoring moment on the ball when it is displaced from its equilibrium point. The same requirement exists for an airplane. Let us consider the two airplanes and their respective pitching moment curves shown in Figure 2.5. The pitching moment curves have been assumed to be linear until the wing is close to stalling.

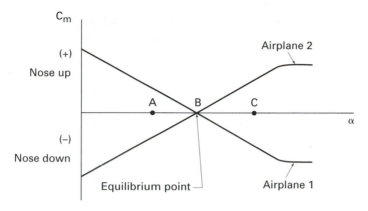

FIGURE 2.5
Pitching moment coefficient versus angle of attack.

In Figure 2.5, both airplanes are flying at the trim point denoted by B; that is, $C_{m_{cg}} = 0$. Suppose the airplanes suddenly encounter an upward gust such that the angle of attack is increased to point C. At the angle of attack denoted by C, airplane 1 would develop a negative (nose-down) pitching moment that would tend to rotate the airplane back toward its equilibrium point. However, for the same disturbance, airplane 2 would develop a positive (nose-up) pitching moment that would tend to rotate the aircraft away from the equilibrium point. If we were to encounter a disturbance that reduced the angle of attack, say, to point A, we would find that airplane 1 would develop a nose-up moment that would rotate the aircraft back toward the equilibrium point. On the other hand, airplane 2 would develop a nose-down moment that would rotate the aircraft away from the equilibrium point. On the basis of this simple analysis, we can conclude that to have static longitudinal stability the aircraft pitching moment curve must have a negative slope. That is,

$$\frac{dC_m}{d\alpha} < 0 \tag{2.1}$$

through the equilibrium point.

Another point that we must make is illustrated in Figure 2.6. Here we see two pitching moment curves, both of which satisfy the condition for static stability. However, only curve 1 can be trimmed at a positive angle of attack. Therefore, in addition to having static stability, we also must have a positive intercept, that is, $C_{m_0} > 0$ to trim at positive angles of attack. Although we developed the criterion for static stability from the C_m versus α curve, we just as easily could have accomplished the result by working with a C_m versus C_L curve. In this case, the requirement for static stability would be as follows:

$$\frac{dC_m}{dC_L} < 0 \tag{2.2}$$

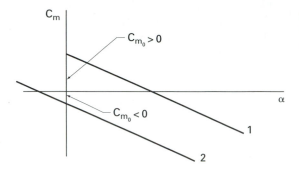

FIGURE 2.6
Flow field around an airplane
created by the wing.

The two conditions are related by the following expression:

$$C_{m_\alpha} = \frac{dC_m}{d\alpha} = \frac{dC_m}{dC_L}\frac{dC_L}{d\alpha} \tag{2.3}$$

which shows that the derivatives differ only by the slope of the lift curve.

2.3.2 Contribution of Aircraft Components

In discussing the requirements for static stability, we so far have considered only the total airplane pitching moment curve. However, it is of interest (particularly to airplane designers) to know the contribution of the wing, fuselage, tail, propulsion system, and the like, to the pitching moment and static stability characteristics of the airplane. In the following sections, each of the components will be considered separately. We will start by breaking down the airplane into its basic components, such as the wing, fuselage, horizontal tail, and propulsion unit. Detailed methods for estimating the aerodynamic stability coefficients can be found in the *United States Air Force Stability and Control Datcom* [2.7]. The *Datcom,* short for data compendium, is a collection of methods for estimating the basic stability and control coefficients for flight regimes of subsonic, transonic, supersonic, and hypersonic speeds. Methods are presented in a systematic body build-up fashion, for example, wing alone, body alone, wing/body and wing/body/tail techniques. The methods range from techniques based on simple expressions developed from theory to correlations obtained from experimental data. In the following sections, as well as in later chapters, we shall develop simple methods for computing the aerodynamic stability and control coefficients. Our emphasis will be for the most part on methods that can be derived from simple theoretical considerations. These methods in general are accurate for preliminary design purposes and show the relationship between the stability coefficients and the geometric and aerodynamic characteristics of the airplane. Furthermore, the methods generally are valid only for the subsonic flight regime. A complete discussion of how to extend these methods to higher-speed flight regimes is beyond the scope of this book and the reader is referred to [2.7] for the high-speed methods.

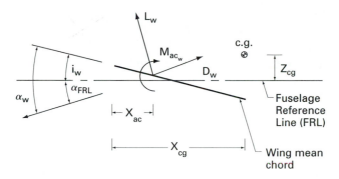

FIGURE 2.7
Wing contribution to the pitching moment.

2.3.3 Wing Contribution

The contribution of the wing to an airplane's static stability can be examined with the aid of Figure 2.7. In this sketch we have replaced the wing by its mean aerodynamic chord $\bar{c}$. The distances from the wing leading edge to the aerodynamic center and the center of gravity are denoted x_{ac} and x_{cg}, respectively. The vertical displacement of the center of gravity is denoted by z_{cg}. The angle the wing chord line makes with the fuselage reference line is denoted as i_w. This is the angle at which the wing is mounted onto the fuselage.

If we sum the moments about the center of gravity, the following equation is obtained:

$$\sum \text{Moments} = M_{cg_w}$$

$$
\begin{aligned}
M_{cg_w} = & L_w \cos(\alpha_w - i_w)[x_{cg} - x_{ac}] + D_w \sin(\alpha_w - i_w)[x_{cg} - x_{ac}] \\
& + L_w \sin(\alpha_w - i_w)[z_{cg}] - D_w \cos(\alpha_w - i_w)[z_{cg}] + M_{ac_w}
\end{aligned}
\tag{2.4}
$$

Dividing by $\frac{1}{2}\rho V^2 S\bar{c}$ yields

$$
\begin{aligned}
C_{m_{cg_w}} = & C_{L_w}\left(\frac{x_{cg}}{\bar{c}} - \frac{x_{ac}}{\bar{c}}\right)\cos(\alpha_w - i_w) + C_{D_w}\left(\frac{x_{cg}}{\bar{c}} - \frac{x_{ac}}{\bar{c}}\right)\sin(\alpha_w - i_w) \\
& + C_{L_w}\frac{(z_{cg})}{\bar{c}}\sin(\alpha_w - i_w) - C_{D_w}\frac{(z_{cg})}{\bar{c}}\cos(\alpha_w - i_w) + C_{m_{ac_w}}
\end{aligned}
\tag{2.5}
$$

Equation (2.5) can be simplified by assuming that the angle of attack is small. With this assumption the following approximations can be made:

$$\cos(\alpha_w - i_w) = 1, \qquad \sin(\alpha_w - i_w) = \alpha_w - i_w, \qquad C_L \gg C_D$$

If we further assume that the vertical contribution is negligible, then Equation (2.5) reduces to

$$C_{m_{cg_w}} = C_{m_{ac_w}} + C_{L_w}\left(\frac{x_{cg}}{\bar{c}} - \frac{x_{ac}}{\bar{c}}\right) \tag{2.6}$$

$$\left(\frac{x_{cg}}{\bar{c}} - \frac{x_{ac}}{\bar{c}}\right)$$

or

$$C_{m_{cg_w}} = C_{m_{ac_w}} + (C_{L_{0_w}} + C_{L_{\alpha_w}} \alpha_w)\left(\frac{x_{cg}}{\bar{c}} - \frac{x_{ac}}{\bar{c}}\right) \tag{2.7}$$

where $C_{L_w} = C_{L_{0_w}} + C_{L_{\alpha_w}} \alpha_w$. Applying the condition for static stability yields

$$C_{m_{0_w}} = C_{m_{ac_w}} + C_{L_{0_w}}\left(\frac{x_{cg}}{\bar{c}} - \frac{x_{ac}}{\bar{c}}\right) \tag{2.8}$$

$$C_{m_{\alpha_w}} = C_{L_{\alpha_w}}\left(\frac{x_{cg}}{\bar{c}} - \frac{x_{ac}}{\bar{c}}\right) \tag{2.9}$$

For a wing-alone design to be statically stable, Equation (2.9) tells us that the aerodynamic center must lie aft of the center of gravity to make $C_{m_\alpha} < 0$. Since we also want to be able to trim the aircraft at a positive angle of attack, the pitching moment coefficient at zero angle of attack, C_{m_0}, must be greater than 0. A positive pitching moment about the aerodynamic center can be achieved by using a negative-cambered airfoil section or an airfoil section that has a reflexed trailing edge. For many airplanes, the center of gravity position is located slightly aft of the aerodynamic center (see data in Appendix B). Also, the wing is normally constructed of airfoil profiles having a positive camber. Therefore, the wing contribution to static longitudinal stability is destabilizing for most conventional airplanes.

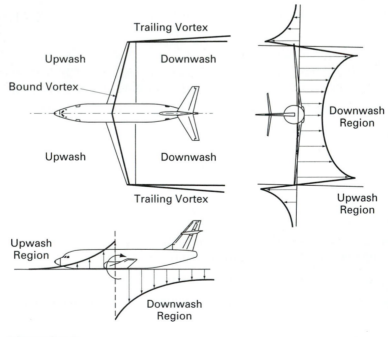

FIGURE 2.8
Flow field around an airplane created by the wing.

2.3.4 Tail Contribution—Aft Tail

The horizontal tail surface can be located either forward or aft of the wing. When the surface is located forward of the wing, the surface is called a canard. Both surfaces are influenced by the flow field created by the wing. The canard surface is affected by the upwash flow from the wing, whereas the aft tail is subjected to the downwash flow. Figure 2.8 is a sketch of the flow field surrounding a lifting wing. The wing flow field is due primarily to the bound and trailing vortices. The magnitude of the upwash or downwash depends on the location of the tail surface with respect to the wing.

The contribution that a tail surface located aft of the wing makes to the airplane's lift and pitching moment can be developed with the aid of Figure 2.9. In this sketch, the tail surface has been replaced by its mean aerodynamic chord. The angle of attack at the tail can be expressed as

$$\alpha_t = \alpha_w - i_w - \varepsilon + i_t \tag{2.10}$$

where ε and i_t are the downwash and tail incidence angles, respectively. If we assume small angles and neglect the drag contribution of the tail, the total lift of the wing and tail can be expressed as

$$L = L_w + L_t \tag{2.11}$$

or

$$C_L = C_{L_w} + \eta \frac{S_t}{S} C_{L_t} \tag{2.12}$$

where

$$\eta = \frac{\frac{1}{2}\rho V_t^2}{\frac{1}{2}\rho V_w^2} = \frac{Q_t}{Q_w} \tag{2.13}$$

The ratio of the dynamic pressures, called the tail efficiency, can have values in the range 0.8–1.2. The magnitude of η depends on the location of the tail surface. If

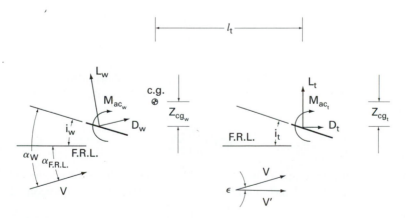

FIGURE 2.9
Aft tail contribution to the pitching moment.

the tail is located in the wake region of the wing or fuselage, η will be less than unity because $Q_t < Q_w$ due to the momentum loss in the wake. On the other hand, if the tail is located in a region where $Q_t > Q_w$, then η will be greater than unity. Such a situation could exist if the tail were located in either the slip stream of the propeller or in the exhaust wake of a jet engine.

The pitching moment due to the tail can be obtained by summing the moments about the center of gravity:

$$M_t = -l_t[L_t \cos(\alpha_{FRL} - \varepsilon) + D_t \sin(\alpha_{FRL} - \varepsilon)] \\ -z_{cg_t}[D_t \cos(\alpha_{FRL} - \varepsilon) - L_t \sin(\alpha_{FRL} - \varepsilon)] + M_{ac_t} \tag{2.14}$$

Usually only the first term of this equation is retained; the other terms generally are small in comparison to the first term. If we again use the small-angle assumption and that $C_{L_t} \gg C_{D_t}$, then Equation (2.14) reduces to

$$M_t = -l_t L_t = -l_t C_{L_t} \frac{1}{2} \rho V_t^2 S_t \tag{2.15}$$

$$C_{m_t} = \frac{M_t}{\frac{1}{2}\rho V^2 S\bar{c}} = -\frac{l_t S_t}{S\bar{c}} \eta C_{L_t} \tag{2.16}$$

or

$$C_{m_t} = -V_H \eta C_{L_t} \tag{2.17}$$

where $V_H = l_t S_t / (S\bar{c})$ is called the horizontal tail volume ratio.

From Figure 2.9, the angle of attack of the tail is seen to be

$$\alpha_t = \alpha_w - i_w - \varepsilon + i_t \tag{2.18}$$

The coefficient C_{L_t} can be written as

$$C_{L_t} = C_{L_{\alpha_t}} \alpha_t = C_{L_{\alpha_t}}(\alpha_w - i_w - \varepsilon + i_t) \tag{2.19}$$

where $C_{L_{\alpha_t}}$ is the slope of the tail lift curve. The downwash angle ε can be expressed as

$$\varepsilon = \varepsilon_0 + \frac{d\varepsilon}{d\alpha} \alpha_w \tag{2.20}$$

where ε_0 is the downwash at zero angle of attack.

The downwash behind a wing with an elliptic lift distribution can be derived from finite-wing theory and shown to be related to the wing lift coefficient and aspect ratio:

$$\varepsilon = \frac{2C_{L_w}}{\pi AR_w} \tag{2.21}$$

where the downwash angle is in radians. The rate of change of downwash angle with angle of attack is determined by taking the derivative of Equation (2.21):

$$\frac{d\varepsilon}{d\alpha} = \frac{2C_{L_{\alpha_w}}}{\pi AR_w} \tag{2.22}$$

where $C_{L_{\alpha_w}}$ is per radian. The preceding expressions do not take into account the position of the tailplane relative to the wing; that is, its vertical and longitudinal spacing. More accurate methods for estimating the downwash at the tailplane can be found in [2.7]. An experimental technique for determining the downwash using wind-tunnel force and moment measurements will be presented by way of a problem assignment at the end of this chapter.

Rewriting the tail contribution to the pitching moment yields

$$C_{m_{cg_t}} = -V_H \eta C_{L_t} \tag{2.23}$$

$$C_{m_{cg_t}} = \eta V_H C_{L_{\alpha_t}}(\varepsilon_0 + i_w - i_t) - \eta V_H C_{L_{\alpha_t}} \alpha \left(1 - \frac{d\varepsilon}{d\alpha}\right) \tag{2.24}$$

Comparing Equation (2.24) with the linear expression for the pitching moment given as

$$C_{m_{cg_t}} = C_{m_0} + C_{m_\alpha} \alpha \tag{2.25}$$

yields expressions for the intercept and slope:

$$C_{m_{0_t}} = \eta V_H C_{L_{\alpha_t}}(\varepsilon_0 + i_w - i_t) \tag{2.26}$$

$$C_{m_{\alpha_t}} = -\eta V_H C_{L_{\alpha_t}} \left(1 - \frac{d\varepsilon}{d\alpha}\right) \tag{2.27}$$

Recall that earlier we showed that the wing contribution to C_{m_0} was negative for an airfoil having positive camber. The tail contribution to C_{m_0} can be used to ensure that C_{m_0} for the complete airplane is positive. This can be accomplished by adjusting the tail incidence angle i_t. Note that we would want to mount the tail plane at a negative angle of incidence to the fuselage reference line to increase C_{m_0} due to the tail.

The tail contribution to the static stability of the airplane ($C_{m_{\alpha_t}} < 0$) can be controlled by proper selection of V_H and $C_{L_{\alpha_t}}$. The contribution of $C_{m_{\alpha_t}}$ will become more negative by increasing the tail moment arm l_t or tail surface area S_t and by increasing $C_{L_{\alpha_t}}$. The tail lift curve slope $C_{L_{\alpha_t}}$ can be increased most easily by increasing the aspect ratio of the tail planform. The designer can adjust any one of these parameters to achieve the desired slope. As noted here, a tail surface located aft of the wing can be used to ensure that the airplane has a positive C_{m_0} and a negative C_{m_α}.

EXAMPLE PROBLEM 2.1. The wing-fuselage pitching moment characteristics of a high-wing, single-engine, general aviation airplane follow, along with pertinent geometric data:

$$C_{m_{cg_{wf}}} = -0.05 - 0.0035\alpha$$

where α is the fuselage reference line angle of attack in degrees and wf means wing-fuselage

$S_w = 178$ ft^2	$x_{cg}/c = 0.1$
$b_w = 35.9$ ft	$AR_w = 7.3$
$\bar{c}_w = 5.0$ ft	$C_{L_{\alpha wf}} = 0.07$/deg $i_w = 2.0°$ $C_{L_{\alpha=0}} = 0.26$

Estimate the horizontal tail area and tail incidence angle, i_t, so that the complete airplane has the following pitching moment characteristics (illustrated in Figure 2.10):

$$C_{m\,cg_{wft}} = 0.15 - 0.025\alpha$$

where α is in degrees and wft is the wing-fuselage-horizontal tail contribution. Assume the following with regard to the horizontal tail:

$l_t = 14.75$ ft $\eta = 1$

$AR_t = 4.85$ $C_{L_{\alpha_t}} = 0.073/\deg$

Solution. The contribution of the horizontal tail to C_{m_0} and C_{m_α} can be calculated by subtracting the wing-fuselage contribution from the wing-fuselage-horizontal tail contribution, respectively:

$$C_{m_{0_t}} = C_{m_{0_{wft}}} - C_{m_{0_{wft}}}$$

$$= 0.15 - (-0.05) = 0.20$$

$$C_{m_{\alpha_t}} = C_{m_{\alpha_{wft}}} - C_{m_{\alpha_{wf}}}$$

$$= -0.025 - (-0.0035) = -0.0215/\deg$$

The horizontal tail area is found by determining the horizontal tail volume ratio required to satisfy the required static stability that needs to be created by the tail. Recall the $C_{m_{\alpha_t}}$ was developed earlier and is rewritten here:

$$C_{m_{\alpha_t}} = -\eta V_H C_{L_{\alpha_t}}\left(1 - \frac{d\varepsilon}{d\alpha}\right)$$

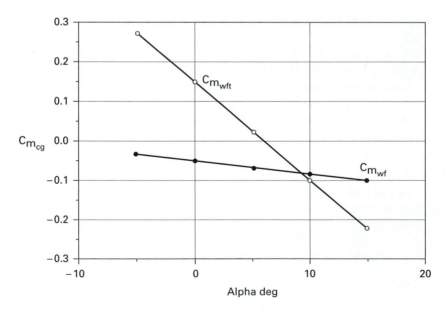

FIGURE 2.10
Pitching moment characteristic for airplane in Example Problem 2.1.

Solving this equation for the volume ratio yields

$$V_H = -\frac{C_{m\alpha_t}}{\eta C_{L_{\alpha_t}}\left(1 - \dfrac{d\varepsilon}{d\alpha}\right)}$$

The only quantity we do not know in this equation is the rate of change of the downwash angle with respect to the angle of attack, $d\varepsilon/d\alpha$. However, this can be estimated from the wing characteristics as follows:

$$\frac{d\varepsilon}{d\alpha} = \frac{2C_{L_{\alpha w}}}{\pi AR_w}$$

Using the wing-fuselage $C_{L_{\alpha wf}}$ as an approximation to $C_{L_{\alpha w}}$ we can obtain an estimate of $d\varepsilon/d\alpha$:

$$\frac{d\varepsilon}{d\alpha} = \frac{2(0.07/\text{deg})(57.3 \text{ deg/rad})}{\pi(7.3)}$$

$$\frac{d\varepsilon}{d\alpha} = 0.35$$

Substituting $d\varepsilon/d\alpha$ and the other quantities into the expression for V_H yields

$$V_H = -\frac{(-0.0215/\text{deg})}{(1.0)(0.073/\text{deg})(1 - 0.35)}$$

$$= 0.453$$

The horizontal tail volume ratio is expressed as

$$V_H = \frac{l_t S_t}{S\bar{c}}$$

and solving for the horizontal tail area yields

$$S_t = \frac{(0.453)(178 \text{ ft}^2)(5 \text{ ft})}{(14.75 \text{ ft})}$$

$$= 27.3 \text{ ft}^2$$

This is the tail area needed to provide the required tail contribution to $C_{m\alpha}$. Next we can determine the tail incidence angle, i_t, from the requirement for C_{mo_t}. The equation for C_{mo} due to the horizontal tail was shown to be

$$C_{mo_t} = V_H \eta C_{L_{\alpha_t}}(i_w + \varepsilon_0 - i_t)$$

The tail incidence angle, i_t, can be obtained by rearranging the preceding equation:

$$i_t = -\left(\frac{C_{mo_t}}{V_H \eta C_{L_{\alpha_t}}} - i_w - \varepsilon_0\right)$$

The only quantity that we do not know in this equation is ε_0; that is, the downwash angle at the tail when the wing is at zero angle of attack. This can be estimated using the following expression:

$$\varepsilon_0 = \frac{2C_{L_0}}{\pi AR_w}$$

$$= \frac{2[0.26]}{\pi[7.3]} = 0.0226 \text{ rad}$$

or
$$\varepsilon_0 = 1.3°$$

Substituting ε_0 and the other quantities into the expression for i_t yields

$$i_t = -\left[\frac{0.20}{(0.453)(1.0)(0.073/\text{deg})} - 2.0 - 1.3\right]$$

$$= -2.7 \text{ deg}.$$

The horizontal tail is mounted to the fuselage at a negative 2.7°.

In summary we have shown that the level of static stability can be controlled by the designer by proper selection of the horizontal tail volume ratio. In practice the only parameter making up the volume ratio that can be varied by the stability and control designer is the horizontal tail surface area. The other parameters, such as the tail moment arm, wing area, and mean wing chord, are determined by the fuselage and wing requirements, which are related to the internal volume and performance specifications of the airplane, respectively.

The horizontal tail incidence angle, i_t, is determined by trim angle of attack or lift coefficient. For a given level of static stability, that is, slope of the pitching moment curve, the trim angle depends on the moment coefficient at zero angle of attack, C_{m_0}. The tail incidence angle, i_t, can be adjusted to yield whatever C_{m_0} is needed to achieve the desired trim condition.

2.3.5 Canard—Forward Tail Surface

A canard is a tail surface located ahead of the wing. The canard surface has several attractive features. The canard, if properly positioned, can be relatively free from wing or propulsive flow interference. Canard control is more attractive for trimming the large nose-down moment produced by high-lift devices. To counteract the nose-down pitching moment, the canard must produce lift that will add to the lift being produced by the wing. An aft tail must produce a down load to counteract the pitching moment and thus reduce the airplane's overall lift force. The major disadvantage of the canard is that it produces a destabilizing contribution to the aircraft's static stability. However, this is not a severe limitation. By proper location of the center of gravity, one can ensure the airplane is statically stable.

2.3.6 Fuselage Contribution

The primary function of the fuselage is to provide room for the flight crew and payload such as passengers and cargo. The optimum shape for the internal volume at minimum drag is a body for which the length is larger than the width or height.

For most fuselage shapes used in airplane designs, the width and height are on the same order of magnitude and for many designs a circular cross-section is used.

The aerodynamic characteristics of long, slender bodies were studied by Max Munk [2.8] in the earlier 1920s. Munk was interested in the pitching moment characteristics of airship hulls. In his analysis, he neglected viscosity and treated the flow around the body as an ideal fluid. Using momentum and energy relationships, he showed that the rate of change of the pitching moment with angle of attack (per radian) for a body of revolution is proportional to the body volume and dynamic pressure:

$$\frac{dM}{d\alpha} = \text{fn}\left(\text{volume}, \frac{1}{2}\rho V^2\right) \tag{2.28}$$

Multhopp [2.9] extended this analysis to account for the induced flow along the fuselage due to the wings for bodies of arbitrary cross-section. A summary of Multhopp's method for C_{m_0} and C_{m_α} due to the fuselage is presented as follows:

$$C_{m_{0_f}} = \frac{k_2 - k_1}{36.5 S \bar{c}} \int_0^{l_f} w_f^2(\alpha_{0_w} + i_f) \, dx \tag{2.29}$$

which can be approximated as

$$C_{m_{0_f}} = \frac{k_2 - k_1}{36.5 S \bar{c}} \sum_{x=0}^{x=l_f} w_f^2(\alpha_{0_w} + i_f) \, \Delta x \tag{2.30}$$

where $k_2 - k_1$ = the correction factor for the body fineness ratio
$\quad\quad S$ = the wing reference area
$\quad\quad \bar{c}$ = the wing mean aerodynamic chord
$\quad\quad w_f$ = the average width of the fuselage sections
$\quad\quad \alpha_{0_w}$ = the wing zero-lift angle relative to the fuselage reference line
$\quad\quad i_f$ = the incidence of the fuselage camber line relative to the fuselage reference line at the center of each fuselage increment. The incidence angle is defined as negative for nose droop and aft upsweep.
$\quad\quad \Delta x$ = the length of the fuselage increments

Figure 2.11 illustrates how the fuselage can be divided into segments for the calculation of C_{m_0} and also defines the body width w_f for various body cross-sectional shapes. The correction factor $(k_2 - k_1)$ is given in Figure 2.12.

The local angle of attack along the fuselage is greatly affected by the flow field created by the wing, as was illustrated in Figure 2.8. The portion of the fuselage ahead of the wing is in the wing upwash; the aft portion is in the wing downwash flow. The change in pitching moment with angle of attack is given by

$$C_{m_{\alpha_f}} = \frac{1}{36.5 S \bar{c}} \int_0^{l_f} w_f^2 \frac{\partial \varepsilon_u}{\partial \alpha} \, dx \quad (\deg^{-1}) \tag{2.31}$$

which can be approximated by

$$C_{m_{\alpha_f}} = \frac{1}{36.5 S \bar{c}} \sum_{x=0}^{x=l_f} w_f^2 \frac{\partial \varepsilon_u}{\partial \alpha} \, \Delta x \tag{2.32}$$

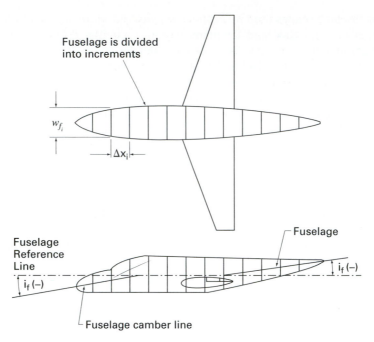

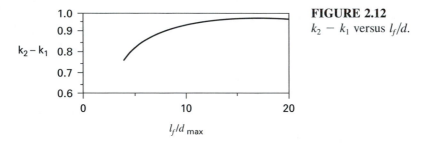

FIGURE 2.11
Procedure for calculating C_{m_0} due to the fuselage.

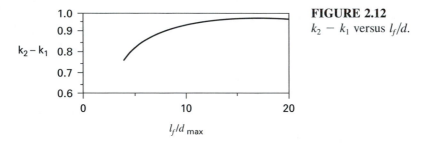

FIGURE 2.12
$k_2 - k_1$ versus l_f/d.

where S = the wing reference area and $\bar{c}$ = the wing mean aerodynamic chord.

The fuselage again can be divided into segments and the local angle of attack of each section, which is composed of the geometric angle of attack of the section plus the local induced angle due to the wing upwash or downwash for each segment, can be estimated. The change in local flow angle with angle of attack, $\partial \varepsilon_u/\partial \alpha$, varies along the fuselage and can be estimated from Figure 2.13. For locations ahead of the wing, the upwash field creates large local angles of attack; therefore, $\partial \varepsilon_u/\partial \alpha > 1$. On the other hand, a station behind the wing is in the downwash region of the wing vortex system and the local angle of attack is reduced. For the region behind the wing, $\partial \varepsilon_u/\partial \alpha$ is assumed to vary linearly from 0 to $(1 - \partial \varepsilon/\partial \alpha)$ at the tail. The region between the wing's leading edge and trailing edge is assumed

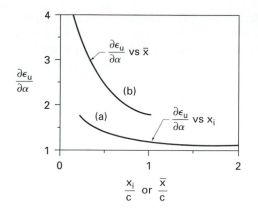

FIGURE 2.13
Variation of local flow angle along the fuselage.

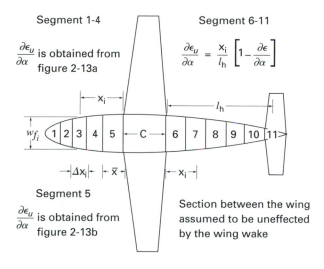

FIGURE 2.14
Procedure for calculating C_{m_α} due to the fuselage.

Segment 1-4

$\dfrac{\partial \epsilon_u}{\partial \alpha}$ is obtained from figure 2-13a

Segment 6-11

$$\frac{\partial \epsilon_u}{\partial \alpha} = \frac{x_i}{l_h}\left[1 - \frac{\partial \epsilon}{\partial \alpha}\right]$$

Segment 5

$\dfrac{\partial \epsilon_u}{\partial \alpha}$ is obtained from figure 2-13b

Section between the wing assumed to be uneffected by the wing wake

to be unaffected by the wing's flow field, $\partial \varepsilon_u / \partial \alpha = 0$. Figure 2.14 is a sketch showing the application of Equation (2.32).

2.3.7 Power Effects

The propulsion unit can have a significant effect on both the longitudinal trim and static stability of the airplane. If the thrust line is offset from the center of gravity, the propulsive force will create a pitching moment that must be counteracted by the aerodynamic control surface.

The static stability of the airplane also is influenced by the propulsion system. For a propeller driven airplane the propeller will develop a normal force in its plane of rotation when the propeller is at an angle of attack. The propeller's normal force will create a pitching moment about the center of gravity, producing a propulsion contribution to C_{m_α}. Although one can derive a simple expression for C_{m_α} due to the propeller, the actual contribution of the propulsion system to the static stability is much more difficult to estimate. This is due to the indirect effects that the propulsion system has on the airplanes characteristics. For example, the propeller slipstream can have an effect on the tail efficiency η and the downwash field. Because of these complicated interactions the propulsive effects on airplane stability are commonly estimated from powered wind-tunnel models.

A normal force will be created on the inlet of a jet engine when it is at an angle of attack. As in the case of the propeller powered airplane, the normal force will produce a contribution to C_{m_α}.

2.3.8 Stick Fixed Neutral Point

The total pitching moment for the airplane can now be obtained by summing the wing, fuselage, and tail contributions:

$$C_{m_{cg}} = C_{m_0} + C_{m_\alpha}\alpha \tag{2.33}$$

where

$$C_{m_0} = C_{m_{0_w}} + C_{m_{0_f}} + \eta V_H C_{L_{\alpha_t}}(\varepsilon_0 + i_w - i_t) \tag{2.34}$$

$$C_{m_\alpha} = C_{L_{\alpha_w}}\left(\frac{x_{cg}}{\bar{c}} - \frac{x_{ac}}{\bar{c}}\right) + C_{m_{\alpha_f}} - \eta V_H C_{L_{\alpha_t}}\left(1 - \frac{d\varepsilon}{d\alpha}\right) \tag{2.35}$$

Notice that the expression for C_{m_α} depends upon the center of gravity position as well as the aerodynamic characteristics of the airplane. The center of gravity of an airplane varies during the course of its operation; therefore, it is important to know if there are any limits to the center of gravity travel. To ensure that the airplane possesses static longitudinal stability, we would like to know at what point $C_{m_\alpha} = 0$. Setting C_{m_α} equal to 0 and solving for the center of gravity position yields

$$\frac{x_{NP}}{\bar{c}} = \frac{x_{ac}}{\bar{c}} - \frac{C_{m_{\alpha_f}}}{C_{L_{\alpha_w}}} + \eta V_H \frac{C_{L_{\alpha_t}}}{C_{L_{\alpha_w}}}\left(1 - \frac{d\varepsilon}{d\alpha}\right) \tag{2.36}$$

In obtaining equation 2.36, we have ignored the influence of center of gravity movement on V_H. We call this location the stick fixed neutral point. If the airplane's

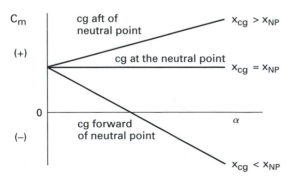

FIGURE 2.15
The influence of center of gravity position on longitudinal static stability.

center of gravity ever reaches this point, the airplane will be neutrally stable. Movement of the center of gravity beyond the neutral point causes the airplane to be statically unstable. The influence of center of gravity position on static stability is shown in Figure 2.15.

EXAMPLE PROBLEM 2.2. Given the general aviation airplane shown in Figure 2.16, determine the contribution of the wing, tail, and fuselage to the C_m versus α curve. Also determine the stick fixed neutral point. For this problem, assume standard sea-level atmospheric conditions.

Solution. The lift curve slopes for the two-dimensional sections making up the wing and tail must be corrected for a finite aspect ratio. This is accomplished using the formula

$$C_{L_\alpha} = \frac{C_{l_\alpha}}{1 + C_{l_\alpha}/(\pi AR)}$$

where C_{l_α} is given as per radian.

Substituting the two-dimensional lift curve slope and the appropriate aspect ratio yields

$$C_{L_{\alpha w}} = \frac{C_{l_{\alpha w}}}{1 + C_{l_{\alpha w}}/(\pi AR_w)}$$

$$= \frac{(0.097/\text{deg})(57.3 \text{ deg/rad})}{1 + (0.097/\text{deg})(57.3 \text{ deg/rad})/(\pi(6.06))}$$

$$= 4.3 \text{ rad}^{-1}$$

Flight condition

$W = 2750$ lb
$V = 176$ ft/sec
$X_{cg} = 0.295\bar{c}$

Wing airfoil characteristics

$C_{m_{ac}} = -0.116$
$C_{l_\alpha} = 0.097/\text{deg}$
$\alpha_{0_L} = -5°$
$X_{ac} = 0.25\bar{c}$
No Twist
$i_w = 1.0°$

Tail airfoil section

$C_{l_\alpha} = 0.01/\text{deg}$
$C_{m_{ac}} = 0.0$
$i_t = -1.0°$

Reference geometry

$S = 184$ ft^2 $S_H = 43$ ft^2
$b = 33.4$ ft $l_t = 16$ ft
$\bar{c} = 5.7$ ft

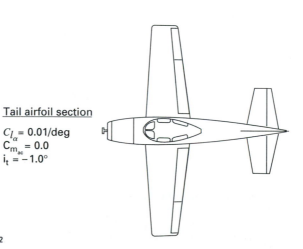

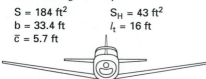

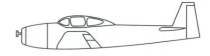

FIGURE 2.16
General aviation airplane.

In a similar manner the lift curve slope for the tail can be found:

$$C_{L_{\alpha_t}} = 3.91 \text{ rad}^{-1}$$

The wing contribution to C_{m_0} and C_{m_α} is found from Equations (2.8) and (2.9):

$$C_{m_{0_w}} = C_{m_{ac_w}} + C_{L_{0_w}}\left(\frac{x_{cg}}{\bar{c}} - \frac{x_{ac}}{\bar{c}}\right)$$

and

$$C_{m_{\alpha_w}} = C_{L_{\alpha_w}}\left(\frac{x_{cg}}{\bar{c}} - \frac{x_{ac}}{\bar{c}}\right)$$

The lift coefficient at zero angle of attack is obtained by multiplying the absolute value of the zero lift angle of attack by the lift curve slope:

$$C_{L_{0_w}} = C_{L_{\alpha_w}}|\alpha_0|$$
$$= (4.3 \text{ rad}^{-1})(5 \text{ deg})/(57.3 \text{ deg/rad})$$
$$= 0.375$$

Substituting the approximate information into the equations for $C_{m_{0_w}}$ and $C_{m_{\alpha_w}}$ yields

$$C_{m_{0_w}} = C_{m_{ac_w}} + C_{L_{0_w}}\left(\frac{x_{cg}}{\bar{c}} - \frac{x_{ac}}{\bar{c}}\right)$$
$$= -0.116 + (0.375)(0.295 - 0.250)$$
$$= -0.099$$

$$C_{m_{\alpha_w}} = C_{L_{\alpha_w}}\left(\frac{x_{cg}}{\bar{c}} - \frac{x_{ac}}{\bar{c}}\right)$$
$$= (4.3 \text{ rad}^{-1})(0.295 - 0.250)$$
$$= 0.1935 \text{ rad}^{-1}$$

For this particular airplane, the wing contribution to C_{m_α} is destabilizing.

The tail contribution to the intercept and slope can be estimated from Equations (2.26) and (2.27):

$$C_{m_{0_t}} = \eta V_H C_{L_{\alpha_t}}(\varepsilon_0 + i_w - i_t)$$
$$C_{m_{\alpha_t}} = -\eta V_H C_{L_{\alpha_t}}\left(1 - \frac{d\varepsilon}{d\alpha}\right)$$

The tail volume ratio V_H is given by

$$V_H = \frac{l_t S_t}{S\bar{c}}$$

or

$$V_H = \frac{(16 \text{ ft})(43 \text{ ft}^2)}{(184 \text{ ft}^2)(5.7 \text{ ft})} = 0.66$$

The downwash term is estimated using the expression

$$\varepsilon = \frac{2C_{L_w}}{\pi AR}$$

where ε is the downwash angle in radians,

$$\varepsilon_0 = \frac{2C_{L_{w_0}}}{\pi AR}$$

$$= \frac{2(0.375)}{\pi(6.06)} = 0.04 \text{ rad} = 2.3°$$

and

$$\frac{d\varepsilon}{d\alpha} = \frac{2C_{L_{\alpha w}}}{AR}$$

where $C_{L_{\alpha w}}$ is in radians,

$$\frac{d\varepsilon}{d\alpha} = \frac{2(4.3)}{\pi(6.06)} = 0.45$$

Substituting the preceding information into the formulas for the intercept and slope yields

$$C_{m_{0_t}} = \eta V_H C_{L_{\alpha_t}}(\varepsilon_0 + i_w - i_t)$$

$$= (0.66)(3.91 \text{ rad}^{-1})[2.3° + 1.0° - (-1.0°)]/57.3 \text{ deg/rad}$$

$$= 0.194$$

and

$$C_{m_{\alpha_t}} = -\eta V_H C_{L_{\alpha_t}}\left(1 - \frac{d\varepsilon}{d\alpha}\right)$$

$$= -(0.66)(3.91 \text{ rad}^{-1})(1 - 0.45)$$

$$= -1.42 \text{ rad}^{-1}$$

In this example, the ratio η of tail to wing dynamic pressure was assumed to be unity.

The fuselage contribution to C_{m_0} and C_{m_α} can be estimated from Equations (2.30) and (2.32), respectively. To use these equations, we must divide the fuselage into segments, as indicated in Figure 2.17. The summation in Equation (2.30) easily can be estimated from the geometry and is found by summing the individual contributions as illustrated by the table in Figure 2.17.

$$\sum_{x=0}^{l_B} w_f^2(\alpha_{0_w} + i_f)\,\Delta x = -1665$$

The body fineness ratio is estimated from the geometrical data given in Figure 2.16:

$$\frac{l_f}{d_{\max}} = 6.2$$

and the correction factor $k_2 - k_1$ is found from Figure 2.12, $k_2 - k_1 = 0.86$. Substituting these values into Equation (2.30) yields

$$C_{m_{0_f}} = -0.037$$

Station	Δx ft	w_f ft	$\alpha_{0_w} + i_f$	$w_f^2 \left[\alpha_{0_w} + i_t \right] \Delta x$
1	3.0	3.6	-5.0	-194
2	3.0	4.6	-5.0	-317
3	3.0	4.6	-5.0	-317
4	3.0	4.6	-5.0	-317
5	3.0	4.1	-5.0	-252
6	3.0	3.1	-5.0	-144
7	3.0	2.3	-5.0	-79
8	3.0	1.5	-5.0	-34
9	3.0	0.8	-5.0	-10

$i_f = 0$ at every station   Sum = -1664

FIGURE 2.17
Sketch of segmented fuselage for calculating C_{m_α} for the example problem.

In a similar manner C_{m_α} can be estimated. A table is included in Figure 2.17 that shows the estimate of the summation. $C_{m_{\alpha f}}$ was estimated to be

$$C_{m_{\alpha f}} = 0.12 \text{ rad}^{-1}$$

The individual contributions and the total pitching moment curve are shown in Figure 2.18.

The stick fixed neutral point can be estimated from Equation (2.36):

$$\frac{x_{NP}}{\bar{c}} = \frac{x_{ac}}{\bar{c}} - \frac{C_{m_{\alpha f}}}{C_{L_{\alpha w}}} + \eta V_H \frac{C_{L_{\alpha t}}}{C_{L_{\alpha w}}} \left(1 - \frac{d\varepsilon}{d\alpha} \right)$$

$$\frac{x_{NP}}{\bar{c}} = 0.25 - (0.12/4.3) + 0.66(3.91/4.3)(1 - 0.45)$$

$$\frac{x_{NP}}{\bar{c}} = 0.55$$

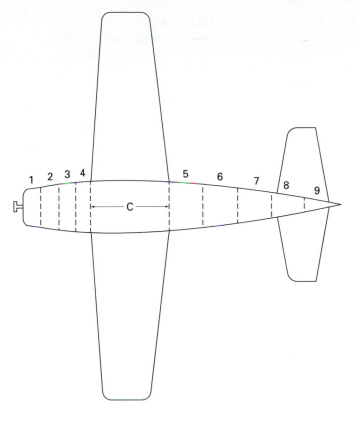

Station	Δx ft	w_f ft	x	$\dfrac{\partial \epsilon_\mu}{\partial \alpha}$	$w_f^2 \dfrac{\partial \epsilon_\mu}{\partial \alpha} \Delta x$
1	1.5	3.0	5.25	1.2	16.2
2	1.5	3.4	4.5	1.3	22.5
3	1.5	3.8	3.75	1.4	30.3
4	1.5	4.2	1.5	3.2	84.7
5	2.9	3.8	1.45	0.06	2.5
6	2.9	3.1	4.35	0.18	5.0
7	2.9	2.3	7.25	0.31	4.8
8	2.9	1.5	10.15	0.43	2.8
9	2.9	0.8	13.05	0.55	1.0

c = 6.5 ft l_h = 13 ft   Sum = 85.1

FIGURE 2.17
Continued.

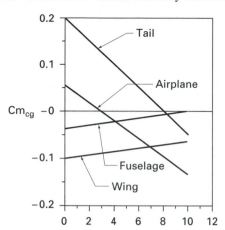

FIGURE 2.18
Component contributions to pitching moment for example problem.

2.4
LONGITUDINAL CONTROL

Control of an airplane can be achieved by providing an incremental lift force on one or more of the airplane's lifting surfaces. The incremental lift force can be produced by deflecting the entire lifting surface or by deflecting a flap incorporated in the lifting surface. Because the control flaps or movable lifting surfaces are located at some distance from the center of gravity, the incremental lift force creates a moment about the airplane's center of gravity. Figure 2.19 shows the three primary aerodynamic controls. Pitch control can be achieved by changing the lift on either a forward or aft control surface. If a flap is used, the flapped portion of the tail surface is called an elevator. Yaw control is achieved by deflecting a flap on the vertical tail called the rudder, and roll control can be achieved by deflecting small flaps located outboard toward the wing tips in a differential manner. These flaps are called ailerons. A roll moment can also be produced by deflecting a wing spoiler. As the name implies a spoiler disrupts the lift. This is accomplished by deflecting a section of the upper wing surface so that the flow separates behind the

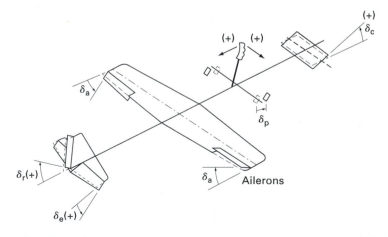

FIGURE 2.19
Primary aerodynamic controls.

spoiler, which causes a reduction in the lifting force. To achieve a roll moment, only one spoiler need be deflected.

In this section we shall be concerned with longitudinal control. Control of the pitch attitude of an airplane can be achieved by deflecting all or a portion of either a forward or aft tail surface. Factors affecting the design of a control surface are control effectiveness, hinge moments, and aerodynamic and mass balancing. Control effectiveness is a measure of how effective the control deflection is in producing the desired control moment. As we shall show shortly, control effectiveness is a function of the size of the flap and tail volume ratio. Hinge moments also are important because they are the aerodynamic moments that must be overcome to rotate the control surface. The hinge moment governs the magnitude of force required of the pilot to move the control surface. Therefore, great care must be used in designing a control surface so that the control forces are within acceptable limits for the pilots. Finally, aerodynamic and mass balancing deal with techniques to vary the hinge moments so that the control stick forces stay within an acceptable range.

2.4.1 Elevator Effectiveness

We need some form of longitudinal control to fly at various trim conditions. As shown earlier, the pitch attitude can be controlled by either an aft tail or forward tail (canard). We shall examine how an elevator on an aft tail provides the required control moments. Although we restrict our discussion to an elevator on an aft tail, the same arguments could be made with regard to a canard surface. Figure 2.20 shows the influence of the elevator on the pitching moment curve. Notice that the elevator does not change the slope of the pitching moment curves but only shifts them so that different trim angles can be achieved.

When the elevator is deflected, it changes the lift and pitching moment of the airplane. The change in lift for the airplane can be expressed as follows:

$$\Delta C_L = C_{L_{\delta_e}} \delta_e \qquad \text{where} \qquad C_{L_{\delta_e}} = \frac{dC_L}{d\delta_e} \qquad (2.37)$$

$$C_L = C_{L_\alpha} \alpha + C_{L_{\delta_e}} \delta_e \qquad (2.38)$$

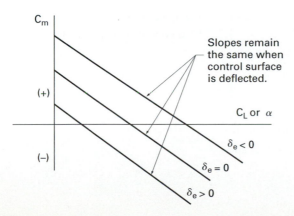

FIGURE 2.20
The influence of the elevator on the C_m versus α curve.

On the other hand, the change in pitching moment acting on the airplane can be written as

$$\Delta C_m = C_{m_{\delta_e}} \delta_e \qquad \text{where} \qquad C_{m_{\delta_e}} = \frac{dC_m}{d\delta_e} \qquad (2.39)$$

The stability derivative $C_{m_{\delta_e}}$ is called the elevator control power. The larger the value of $C_{m_{\delta_e}}$, the more effective the control is in creating the control moment.

Adding ΔC_m to the pitching moment equation yields

$$C_m = C_{m_0} + C_{m_\alpha} \alpha + C_{m_{\delta_e}} \delta_e \qquad (2.40)$$

The derivatives $C_{L_{\delta_e}}$ and $C_{m_{\delta_e}}$ can be related to the aerodynamic and geometric characteristics of the horizontal tail in the following manner. The change in lift of the airplane due to deflecting the elevator is equal to the change in lift force acting on the tail:

$$\Delta L = \Delta L_t \qquad (2.41)$$

$$\Delta C_L = \frac{S_t}{S} \eta \, \Delta C_{L_t} = \frac{S_t}{S} \eta \, \frac{dC_{L_t}}{d\delta_e} \delta_e \qquad (2.42)$$

where $dC_{L_t}/d\delta_e$ is the elevator effectiveness. The elevator effectiveness is proportional to the size of the flap being used as an elevator and can be estimated from the equation

$$\frac{dC_{L_t}}{d\delta_e} = \frac{dC_{L_t}}{d\alpha_t} \frac{d\alpha_t}{d\delta_e} = C_{L_{\alpha_t}} \tau \qquad (2.43)$$

The parameter τ can be determined from Figure 2.21.

$$C_{L_{\delta_e}} = \frac{S_t}{S} \eta \, \frac{dC_{L_t}}{d\delta_e} \qquad (2.44)$$

The increment in airplane pitching moment is

$$\Delta C_m = -V_H \eta \, \Delta C_{L_t} = -V_H \eta \, \frac{dC_{L_t}}{d\delta_e} \delta_e \qquad (2.45)$$

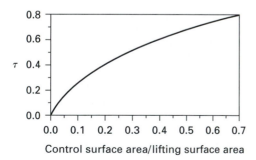

FIGURE 2.21
Flap effectiveness parameter.

or
$$C_{m_{\delta_e}} = -V_H \eta \frac{dC_{L_t}}{d\delta_e} = -V_H \eta C_{L_{\alpha_t}} \tau \tag{2.46}$$

The designer can control the magnitude of the elevator control effectiveness by proper selection of the volume ratio and flap size.

2.4.2 Elevator Angle to Trim

Now let us consider the trim requirements. An airplane is said to be trimmed if the forces and moments acting on the airplane are in equilibrium. Setting the pitching moment equation equal to 0 (the definition of trim) we can solve for the elevator angle required to trim the airplane:

$$C_m = 0 = C_{m_0} + C_{m_\alpha}\alpha + C_{m_{\delta_e}}\delta_e \tag{2.47}$$

or
$$\delta_{trim} = -\frac{C_{m_0} + C_{m_\alpha}\alpha_{trim}}{C_{m_{\delta_e}}} \tag{2.48}$$

The lift coefficient to trim is

$$C_{L_{trim}} = C_{L_\alpha}\alpha_{trim} + C_{L_{\delta_e}}\delta_{trim} \tag{2.49}$$

We can use this equation to obtain the trim angle of attack:

$$\alpha_{trim} = \frac{C_{L_{trim}} - C_{L_{\delta_e}}\delta_{trim}}{C_{L_\alpha}} \tag{2.50}$$

If we substitute this equation back into Equation (2.48) we get the following equation for the elevator angle to trim:

$$\delta_{trim} = -\frac{C_{m_0}C_{L_\alpha} + C_{m_\alpha}C_{L_{trim}}}{C_{m_{\delta_e}}C_{L_\alpha} - C_{m_\alpha}C_{L_{\delta_e}}} \tag{2.51}$$

The elevator angle to trim can also be obtained directly from the pitching moment curves shown in Figure 2.20.

EXAMPLE PROBLEM 2.3. The longitudinal control surface provides a moment that can be used to balance or trim the airplane at different operating angles of attack or lift coefficient. The size of the control surface depends on the magnitude of the pitching moment that needs to be balanced by the control. In general, the largest trim moments occur when an airplane is in the landing configuration (wing flaps and landing gear deployed) and the center of gravity is at its forwardmost location. This can be explained in the following manner. In the landing configuration we fly the airplane at a high angle of attack or lift coefficient so that the airplane's approach speed can be kept as low as possible. Therefore the airplane must be trimmed at a high lift coefficient. Deployment of the wing flaps and landing gear create a nose-down pitching moment increment that must be added to the clean configuration pitching moment curve. The additional nose-down or negative pitching moment increment due to the flaps and landing gear shifts the pitching moment curve. As the center of gravity moves forward the slope of the pitching moment curve becomes more negative (the airplane is more stable). This results in a large trim moment at high lift coefficients. The largest pitching moment that must be balanced by the elevator therefore occurs when the flaps and gear are deployed and the center of gravity is at its most forward position.

Assume that the pitching moment curve for the landing configuration for the airplane analyzed in Example Problem 2.2 at its forwardmost center of gravity position is as follows:

$$C_{m_{cg}} = -0.20 - 0.035\alpha$$

where α is in degrees. Estimate the size of the elevator to trim the airplane at the landing angle of attack of 10°. Assume that the elevator angle is constrained to +20° and −25°.

Solution. The increment in moment created by the control surface, $\Delta C_{m_{cg}}$, is both a function of the elevator control power, $C_{m_{\delta_e}}$, and the elevator deflection angle δ_e.

$$\Delta C_{m_{cg}} = C_{m_{\delta_e}} \delta_e$$

For a 10° approach angle of attack, the pitching moment acting on the airplane can be estimated as follows:

$$\Delta C_{m_{cg}} = -0.20 - 0.035 \, (10°) = -0.55$$

This moment must be balanced by an equal and opposite moment created by deflecting the elevator. The change in moment coefficient created by the elevator was shown to be

$$\Delta C_{m_{cg}} = C_{m_{\delta_e}} \delta_e$$

where $C_{m_{\delta_e}}$ is referred to as the elevator control power. The elevator control power is a function of the horizontal tail volume ratio, V_H, and the flap effectiveness factor, τ:

$$C_{m_{\delta_e}} = -V_H \eta \tau C_{L_{\alpha_t}}$$

The horizontal tail volume ratio, V_H, is set by the static longitudinal stability requirements; therefore, the designer can change only the flap effectiveness parameter, τ, to achieve the appropriate control effectiveness $C_{m_{\delta_e}}$. The flap effectiveness factor is a function of the area of the control flap to the total area of the lift surface on which it is attached. By proper selection of the elevator area the necessary control power can be achieved.

For a positive moment, the control deflection angle must be negative; that is, trailing edge of the elevator is up:

$$\Delta C_{m_{trim}}^{(+)} = C_{m_{\delta_e}}^{(-)} \delta_e^{(-)}$$

or

$$C_{m_{\delta_e}} = \frac{\Delta C_{m_{trim}}}{\delta_e} = \frac{0.55}{-25°} = -0.022/\text{deg}$$

Solving for the flap effectiveness parameter, τ,

$$\tau = -\frac{C_{m_{\delta_e}}}{V_H \eta C_{L_{\alpha_t}}}$$

Using the values of V_H, η, and $C_{L_{\alpha_t}}$ from Example Problem 2.2 we can estimate τ:

$$\tau = \frac{(-0.022/\text{deg})(57.3 \text{ deg/rad})}{(0.66)(1.0)(3.9/\text{rad})}$$

$$= 0.49$$

Knowing τ we can use Figure 2.21 to estimate the area of the elevator to the area of the horizontal tail:

$$S_e/S_t = 0.30$$

The elevator area required to balance the largest trim moment is

$$S_e = 0.30S_t$$
$$= (0.3)(43 \text{ ft}^2)$$
$$S_e = 13 \text{ ft}^2$$

This represents the minimum elevator area needed to balance the airplane. In practice the designer probably would increase this area to provide a margin of safety.

This example also points out the importance of proper weight and balance for an airplane. If the airplane is improperly loaded, so that the center of gravity moves forward of the manufacturers specification, the pilot may be unable to trim the airplane at the desired approach C_L. The pilot would be forced to trim the airplane at a lower lift coefficient, which means a higher landing speed.

2.4.3 Flight Measurement of X_{NP}

The equation developed for estimating the elevator angle to trim the airplane can be used to determine the stick fixed neutral point from flight test data. Suppose we conducted a flight test experiment in which we measured the elevator angle of trim at various air speeds for different positions of the center of gravity. If we did this, we could develop curves as shown in Figure 2.22.

Now, differentiating Equation (2.51) with respect to $C_{L_{trim}}$ yields

$$\frac{d\delta_{trim}}{dC_{L_{trim}}} = -\frac{C_{m_\alpha}}{C_{m_{\delta_e}} C_{L_\alpha} - C_{m_\alpha} C_{L_{\delta_e}}} \tag{2.52}$$

Note that when $C_{m_\alpha} = 0$ (i.e., the center of gravity is at the neutral point) Equation (2.53) equals 0. Therefore, if we measure the slopes of the curves in

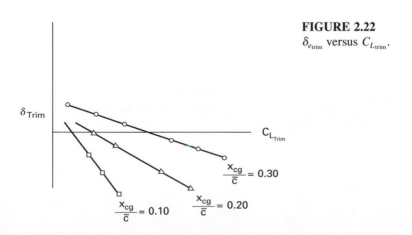

FIGURE 2.22
$\delta_{e_{trim}}$ versus $C_{L_{trim}}$.

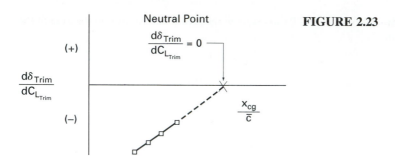

FIGURE 2.23

Figure 2.22 and plot them as a function of center of gravity location, we can estimate the stick fixed neutral point as illustrated in Figure 2.23 by extrapolating to find the center of gravity position that makes $d\delta_{trim}/dC_{L_{trim}}$ equal to 0.

2.4.4 Elevator Hinge Moment

It is important to know the moment acting at the hinge line of the elevator (or other type of control surface). The hinge moment, of course, is the moment the pilot must overcome by exerting a force on the control stick. Therefore to design the control system properly we must know the hinge moment characteristics. The hinge moment is defined as shown in Figure 2.24. If we assume that the hinge moment can be expressed as the addition of the effects of angle of attck, elevator deflection angle, and tab angle taken separately, then we can express the hinge moment coefficient in the following manner:

$$C_{h_e} = C_{h_0} + C_{h_{\alpha_t}} \alpha_t + C_{h_{\delta_e}} \delta_e + C_{h_{\delta_t}} \delta_t \tag{2.53}$$

where C_{h_0} is the residual moment and

$$C_{h_{\alpha_t}} = \frac{dC_h}{d\alpha_t} \qquad C_{h_{\delta_e}} = \frac{dC_h}{d\delta_e} \qquad C_{h_{\delta_t}} = \frac{dC_h}{d\delta_t} \tag{2.54}$$

The hinge moment parameters just defined are very difficult to predict analytically with great precision. Wind-tunnel tests usually are required to provide the control system designer with the information needed to design the control system properly.

$H_e = C_{h_e} \frac{1}{2}\rho V^2 S_e C_e$
S_e = Area aft of the hinge line
C_e = Chord measured from hinge
line to trailing edge of the flap

FIGURE 2.24
Definition of hinge moments.

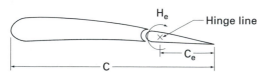

When the elevator is set free, that is, the control stick is released, the stability and control characteristics of the airplane are affected. For simplicity, we shall assume that both δ_t and C_{h_0} are equal to 0. Then, for the case when the elevator is allowed to be free,

$$C_{h_e} = 0 = C_{h_{\alpha_t}} \alpha_t + C_{h_{\delta_e}} \delta_e \qquad (2.55)$$

Solving for δ_e yields

$$(\delta_e)_{\text{free}} = -\frac{C_{h_{\alpha_t}}}{C_{h_{\delta_e}}} \alpha_t \qquad (2.56)$$

Usually, the coefficients $C_{h_{\alpha_t}}$ and $C_{h_{\delta_e}}$ are negative. If this indeed is the case, then Equation (2.56) tells us that the elevator will float upwards as the angle of attack is increased. The lift coefficient for a tail with a free elevator is given by

$$C_{L_t} = C_{L_{\alpha_t}} \alpha_t + C_{L_{\delta_e}} \delta_{e_{\text{free}}} \qquad (2.57)$$

$$C_{L_t} = C_{L_{\alpha_t}} \alpha_t - C_{L_{\delta_e}} \frac{C_{h_{\alpha_t}}}{C_{h_{\delta_e}}} \alpha_t \qquad (2.58)$$

which simplifies to

$$C_{L_t} = C_{L_{\alpha_t}} \alpha_t \left(1 - \frac{C_{L_{\delta_e}}}{C_{L_{\alpha_t}}} \frac{C_{h_{\alpha_t}}}{C_{h_{\delta_e}}} \right) = C'_{L_{\alpha_t}} \alpha_t \qquad (2.59)$$

where

$$C'_{L_{\alpha_t}} = C_{L_{\alpha_t}} \left(1 - \frac{C_{L_{\delta_e}}}{C_{L_{\alpha_t}}} \frac{C_{h_{\alpha_t}}}{C_{h_{\delta_e}}} \right) = C_{L_{\alpha_t}} f \qquad (2.60)$$

The slope of the tail lift curve is modified by the term in the parentheses. The factor f can be greater or less than unity, depending on the sign of the hinge parameters $C_{h_{\alpha_t}}$ and $C_{h_{\delta_e}}$. Now, if we were to develop the equations for the total pitching moment for the free elevator case, we would obtain an equation similar to Equations (2.34) and (2.35). The only difference would be that the term $C_{L_{\alpha_t}}$ would be replaced by $C'_{L_{\alpha_t}}$. Substituting $C'_{L_{\alpha_t}}$ into Equations (2.34) and (2.35) yields

$$C'_{m_0} = C_{m_{0w}} + C_{m_{0_f}} + C'_{L_{\alpha_t}} \eta V_H (\varepsilon_0 + i_w - i_t) \qquad (2.61)$$

$$C'_{m_\alpha} = C_{L_{\alpha_w}} \left(\frac{x_{\text{cg}}}{\bar{c}} - \frac{x_{\text{ac}}}{\bar{c}} \right) + C_{m_{\alpha_f}} - C'_{L_{\alpha_t}} \eta V_H \left(1 - \frac{\partial \varepsilon}{\partial \alpha} \right) \qquad (2.62)$$

where the prime indicates elevator-free values. To determine the influence of a free elevator on the static longitudinal stability, we again examine the condition in which $C_{m_\alpha} = 0$. Setting C'_{m_α} equal to 0 in Equation (2.62) and solving for $x/\bar{c}$ yields the stick-free neutral point:

$$\frac{x'_{\text{NP}}}{\bar{c}} = \frac{x_{\text{ac}}}{\bar{c}} + V_H \eta \frac{C'_{L_{\alpha_t}}}{C_{L_{\alpha_w}}} \left(1 - \frac{d\varepsilon}{d\alpha} \right) - \frac{C_{m_{\alpha_f}}}{C_{L_{\alpha_w}}} \qquad (2.63)$$

The difference between the stick fixed neutral point and the stick-free neutral point can be expressed as follows:

$$\frac{x_{NP}}{\overline{c}} - \frac{x'_{NP}}{\overline{c}} = (1 - f)V_H \eta \frac{C_{L_{\alpha_t}}}{C_{L_{\alpha_w}}} \left(1 - \frac{d\varepsilon}{d\alpha}\right) \tag{2.64}$$

The factor f determines whether the stick-free neutral point lies forward or aft of the stick fixed neutral point.

Static margin is a term that appears frequently in the literature. The static margin is simply the distance between the neutral point and the actual center of gravity position

$$\text{Stick fixed static margin} = \frac{x_{NP}}{\overline{c}} - \frac{x_{cg}}{\overline{c}} \tag{2.65}$$

$$\text{Stick-free static margin} = \frac{x'_{NP}}{\overline{c}} - \frac{x_{cg}}{\overline{c}} \tag{2.66}$$

For most aircraft designs, it is desirable to have a stick fixed static margin of approximately 5 percent of the mean chord. The stick fixed or stick-free static neutral points represent an aft limit on the center of gravity travel for the airplane.

2.5
STICK FORCES

To deflect a control surface the pilot must move the control stick or rudder pedals. The forces exerted by the pilot to move the control surface is called the stick force or pedal force, depending which control is being used. The stick force is proportional to the hinge moment acting on the control surface:

$$F = \text{fn}(H_e) \tag{2.67}$$

Figure 2.25 is a sketch of a simple mechanical system used for deflecting the elevator. The work of displacing the control stick is equal to the work in moving the control surface to the desired deflection angle. From Figure 2.25 we can write the expression for the work performed at the stick and elevator:

$$Fl_s \, \delta_s = H_e \, \delta_e \tag{2.68}$$

or

$$F = \frac{\delta_e}{l_s \, \delta_s} H_e \tag{2.69}$$

or

$$F = GH_e \tag{2.70}$$

where $G = \delta_e/(l_s \, \delta_s)$ called the gearing ratio, is a measure of the mechanical advantage provided by the control system.

Substituting the expression for the hinge moment defined earlier into the stick force equation yields

$$F = GC_{h_e} \frac{1}{2}\rho V^2 S_e \overline{c}_e \tag{2.71}$$

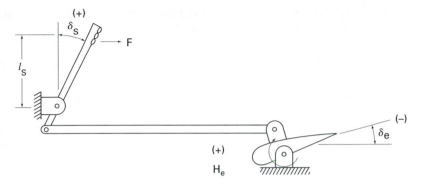

FIGURE 2.25
Relationship between stick force and hinge moment.

From this expression we see that the magnitude of the stick force increases with the size of the airplane and the square of the airplane's speed. Similar expressions can be obtained for the rudder pedal force and aileron stick force.

The control system is designed to convert the stick and pedal movements into control surface deflections. Although this may seem to be a relativey easy task, it in fact is quite complicated. The control system must be designed so that the control forces are within acceptable limits. On the other hand, the control forces required in normal maneuvers must not be too small; otherwise, it might be possible to overstress the airplane. Proper control system design will provide stick force magnitudes that give the pilot a feel for the commanded maneuver. The magnitude of the stick force provides the pilot with an indication of the severity of the motion that will result from the stick movement.

The convention for longitudinal control is that a pull force should always rotate the nose upward, which causes the airplane to slow down. A push force will have the opposite effect; that is, the nose will rotate downward and the airplane will speed up. The control system designer must also be sure that the airplane does not experience control reversals due to aerodynamic or aeroelastic phenomena.

2.5.1 Trim Tabs

In addition to making sure that the stick and rudder pedal forces required to maneuver or trim the airplane are within acceptabe limits, it is important that some means be provided to zero out the stick force at the trimmed flight speed. If such a provision is not made, the pilot will become fatigued by trying to maintain the necessary stick force. The stick force at trim can be made zero by incorporating a tab on either the elevator or the rudder. The tab is a small flap located at the trailing edge of the control surface. The trim tab can be used to zero out the hinge moment and thereby eliminate the stick or pedal forces. Figure 2.26 illustrates the concept of a trim tab. Although the trim tab has a great influence over the hinge moment, it has only a slight effect on the lift produced by the control surface.

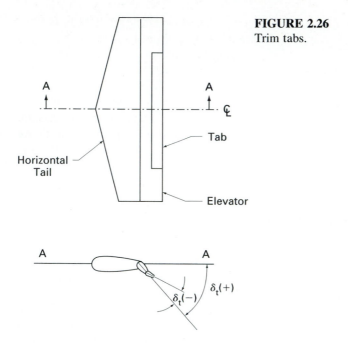

FIGURE 2.26
Trim tabs.

2.5.2 Stick Force Gradients

Another important parameter in the design of a control system is the stick force gradient. Figure 2.27 shows the variation of the stick force with speed. The stick force gradient is a measure of the change in stick force needed to change the speed of the airplane. To provide the airplane with speed stability, the stick force gradient must be negative; that is,

$$\frac{dF}{dV} < 0 \qquad (2.72)$$

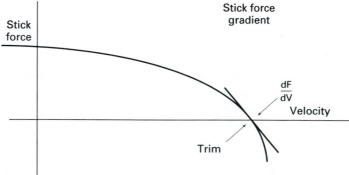

FIGURE 2.27
Stick force versus velocity.

The need for a negative stick-force gradient can be appreciated by examining the trim point in Figure 2.27. If the airplane slows down, a positive stick force occurs that rotates the nose of the airplane downward, which causes the airplane to increase its speed back toward the trim velocity. If the airplane exceeds the trim velocity, a negative (pull) stick force causes the airplane's nose to pitch up, which causes the airplane to slow down. The negative stick force gradient provides the pilot and airplane with speed stability. The larger the gradient, the more resistant the airplane will be to disturbances in the flight speed. If an airplane did not have speed stability the pilot would have to continuously monitor and control the airplane's speed. This would be highly undesirable from the pilot's point of view.

2.6
DEFINITION OF DIRECTIONAL STABILITY

Directional, or weathercock, stability is concerned with the static stability of the airplane about the z axis. Just as in the case of longitudinal static stability, it is desirable that the airplane should tend to return to an equilibrium condition when subjected to some form of yawing disturbance. Figure 2.28 shows the yawing

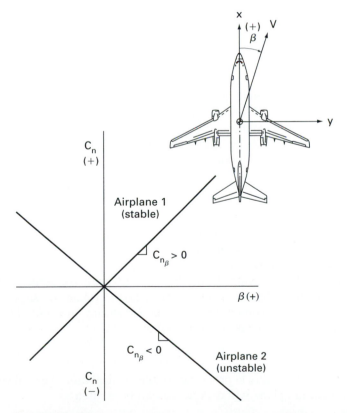

FIGURE 2.28
Static directional stability.

moment coefficient versus sideslip angle β for two airplane configurations. To have static directional stability, the airplane must develop a yawing moment that will restore the airplane to its equilibrium state. Assume that both airplanes are disturbed from their equilibrium condition, so that the airplanes are flying with a positive sideslip angle β. Airplane 1 will develop a restoring moment that will tend to rotate the airplane back to its equilibrium condition; that is, a zero sideslip angle. Airplane 2 will develop a yawing moment that will tend to increase the sideslip angle. Examining these curves, we see that to have static directional stability the slope of the yawing moment curve must be positive ($C_{n_\beta} > 0$). Note that an airplane possessing static directional stability will always point into the relative wind, hence the name weathercock stability.

2.6.1 Contribution of Aircraft Components

The contribution of the wing to directional stability usually is quite small in comparison to the fuselage, provided the angle of attack is not large. The fuselage and engine nacelles, in general, create a destabilizing contribution to directional stability. The wing fuselage contribution can be calculated from the following empirical expression taken from [2.7]:

$$C_{n_{\beta_{wf}}} = -k_n k_{Rl} \frac{S_{fs} l_f}{S_w b} \qquad \text{(per deg)} \qquad (2.73)$$

where k_n = an empirical wing-body interference factor that is a function of the fuselage geometry

k_{Rl} = an empirical correction factor that is a function of the fuselage Reynolds number

S_{fs} = the projected side area of the fuselage

l_f = the length of the fuselage

The empirical factors k_n and k_{Rl} are determined from Figures 2.29 and 2.30 respectively.

Since the wing-fuselage contribution to directional stability is destabilizing, the vertical tail must be properly sized to ensure that the airplane has directional stability. The mechanism by which the vertical tail produces directional stability is shown in Figure 2.31. If we consider the vertical tail surface in Figure 2.31, we see that when the airplane is flying at a positive sideslip angle the vertical tail produces a side force (lift force in the xy plane) that tends to rotate the airplane about its center of gravity. The moment produced is a restoring moment. The side force acting on the vertical tail can be expressed as

$$Y_v = -C_{L_{\alpha_v}} \alpha_v Q_v S_v \qquad (2.74)$$

where the subscript v refers to properties of the vertical tail. The angle of attack α_v that the vertical tail plane will experience can be written as

$$\alpha_v = \beta + \sigma \qquad (2.75)$$

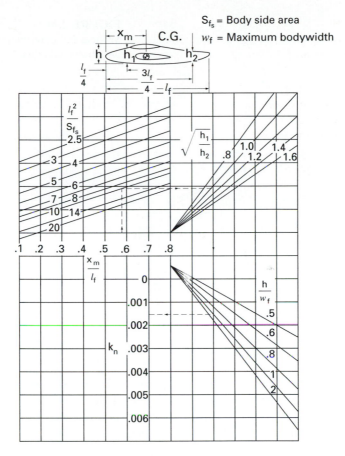

FIGURE 2.29
Wing body interference factor.

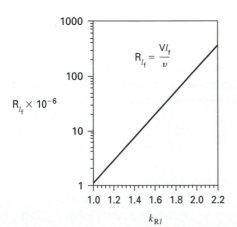

FIGURE 2.30
Reynolds number correction factor.

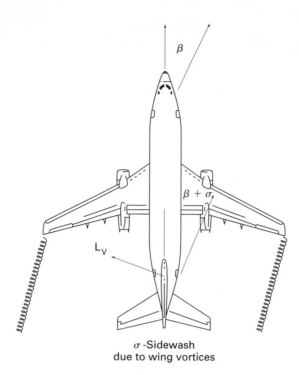

FIGURE 2.31
Vertical tail contribution to
directional stability.

σ -Sidewash
due to wing vortices

where σ is the sidewash angle. The sidewash angle is analogous to the downwash angle ε for the horizontal tail plane. The sidewash is caused by the flow field distortion due to the wings and fuselage. The moment produced by the vertical tail can be written as a function of the side force acting on it:

$$N_v = l_v Y_v = l_v C_{L_{\alpha_v}}(\beta + \sigma)Q_v S_v \tag{2.76}$$

or in coefficient form

$$C_n = \frac{N_v}{Q_w Sb} = \frac{l_v S_v}{Sb} \frac{Q_v}{Q_w} C_{L_{\alpha_v}}(\beta + \sigma) \tag{2.77}$$

$$= V_v \eta_v C_{L_{\alpha_v}}(\beta + \sigma) \tag{2.78}$$

where $V_v = l_v S_v/(Sb)$ is the vertical tail volume ratio and $\eta_v = Q_v/Q_w$ is the ratio of the dynamic pressure at the vertical tail to the dynamic pressure at the wing.

The contribution of the vertical tail to directional stability now can be obtained by taking the derivative of Equation (2.78) with respect to β:

$$C_{n_{\beta_v}} = V_v \eta_v C_{L_{\alpha_v}}\left(1 + \frac{d\sigma}{d\beta}\right) \tag{2.79}$$

A simple algebraic equation for estimating the combined sidewash and tail efficiency factor η_v is presented in [2.7] and reproduced here:

$$\eta_v\left(1 + \frac{d\sigma}{d\beta}\right) = 0.724 + 3.06 \frac{S_v/S}{1 + \cos \Lambda_{c/4w}} + 0.4 \frac{z_w}{d} + 0.009 AR_w \tag{2.80}$$

where S = the wing area

S_v = the vertical tail area, including the submerged area to the fuselage centerline

z_w = the distance, parallel to the z axis, from wing root quarter chord point to fuselage centerline

d = the maximum fuselage depth

AR_w = the aspect ratio of the wing

$\Lambda_{c/4w}$ = sweep of wing quarter chord.

2.7
DIRECTIONAL CONTROL

Directional control is achieved by a control surface, called a rudder, located on the vertical tail, as shown in Figure 2.32. The rudder is a hinged flap that forms the aft portion of the vertical tail. By rotating the flap, the lift force (side force) on the fixed vertical surface can be varied to create a yawing moment about the center of gravity. The size of the rudder is determined by the directional control requirements. The rudder control power must be sufficient to accomplish the requirements listed in Table 2.1.

The yawing moment produced by the rudder depends on the change in lift on the vertical tail due to the deflection of the rudder times its distance from the center of gravity. For a positive rudder deflection, a positive side force is created on the vertical tail. A positive side force will produce a negative yawing moment:

$$N = -l_v Y_v \tag{2.81}$$

where the side force is given by

$$Y_v = C_{L_v} Q_v S_v$$

Rewriting this equation in terms of a yawing moment coefficient yields

$$C_n = \frac{N}{Q_w Sb} = -\frac{Q_v}{Q_w} \frac{l_v S_v}{Sb} \frac{dC_{L_v}}{d\delta_r} \delta_r \tag{2.82}$$

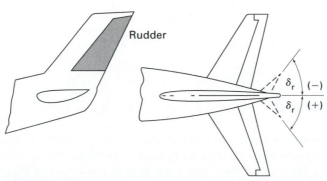

FIGURE 2.32
Directional control by means of the rudder.

TABLE 2.1
Requirements for directional control

Rudder requirements	Implication for rudder design
Adverse yaw	When an airplane is banked to execute a turning maneuver the ailerons may create a yawing moment that opposes the turn (i.e., adverse yaw). The rudder must be able to overcome the adverse yaw so that a coordinated turn can be achieved. The critical condition for adverse yaw occurs when the airplane is flying slow (i.e., high C_L.)
Crosswind landings	To maintain alignment with the runway during a crosswind landing requires the pilot to fly the airplane at a sideslip angle. The rudder must be powerful enough to permit the pilot to trim the airplane for the specified crosswinds. For transport airplanes, landing may be carried out for crosswinds up to 15.5 m/s or 51 ft/s.
Asymmetric power condition	The critical asymmetric power condition occurs for a multiengine airplane when one engine fails at low flight speeds. The rudder must be able to overcome the yawing moment produced by the asymmetric thrust arrangement.
Spin recovery	The primary control for spin recovery in many airplanes is a powerful rudder. The rudder must be powerful enough to oppose the spin rotation.

or

$$C_n = -\eta_v V_v \frac{dC_{L_v}}{d\delta_r} \delta_r \qquad (2.83)$$

The rudder control effectiveness is the rate of change of yawing moment with rudder deflection angle:

$$C_n = C_{n_{\delta_r}} \delta_r = -\eta_v V_v \frac{dC_{L_v}}{d\delta_r} \delta_r \qquad (2.84)$$

or

$$C_{n_{\delta_r}} = -\eta_v V_v \frac{dC_{L_v}}{d\delta_r} \qquad (2.85)$$

where

$$\frac{dC_{L_v}}{d\delta_r} = \frac{dC_{L_v}}{d\alpha_v} \frac{d\alpha_v}{d\delta_r} = C_{L_{\alpha_v}} \tau \qquad (2.86)$$

and the factor τ can be estimated from Figure 2.21.

2.8
ROLL STABILITY

An airplane possesses static roll stability if a restoring moment is developed when it is disturbed from a wings-level attitude. The restoring rolling moment can be shown to be a function of the sideslip angle β as illustrated in Figure 2.33. The requirement for stability is that $C_{l_\beta} < 0$. The roll moment created on an airplane

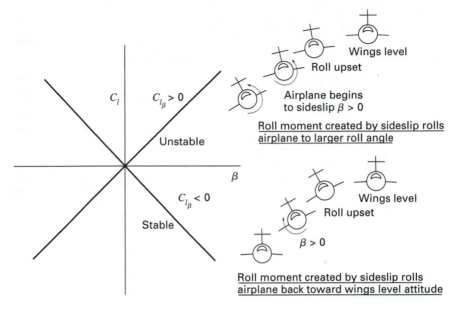

FIGURE 2.33
Static roll stability.

when it starts to sideslip depends on the wing dihedral, wing sweep, position of the wing on the fuselage, and the vertical tail. Each of these contributions will be discussed qualitatively in the following paragraphs.

The major contributor to C_{l_β} is the wing dihedral angle Γ. The dihedral angle is defined as the spanwise inclination of the wing with respect to the horizontal. If the wing tip is higher than the root section, then the dihedral angle is positive; if the wing tip is lower than the root section, then the dihedral angle is negative. A negative dihedral angle is commonly called anhedral.

When an airplane is disturbed from a wings-level attitude, it will begin to sideslip as shown in Figure 2.34. Once the airplane starts to sideslip a component of the relative wind is directed toward the side of the airplane. The leading wing experiences an increased angle of attack and consequently an increase in lift. The trailing wing experiences the opposite effect. The net result is a rolling moment that tries to bring the wing back to a wings-level attitude. This restoring moment is often referred to as the dihedral effect.

The additional lift created on the downward-moving wing is created by the change in angle of attack produced by the sideslipping motion. If we resolve the sideward velocity component into components along and normal to the wing span the local change in angle of attack can be estimated as

$$\Delta\alpha = \frac{v_n}{u} \tag{2.87}$$

where

$$v_n = V \sin \Gamma \tag{2.88}$$

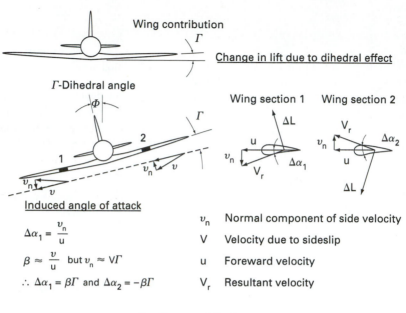

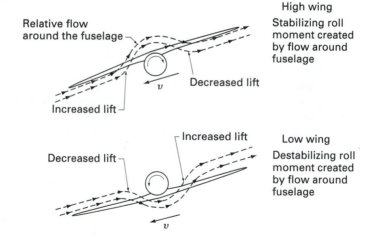

FIGURE 2.34
Wing and fuselage contribution to the dihedral

By approximating the sideslip angle as

$$\beta = \frac{v}{u} \qquad (2.89)$$

and assuming that Γ is a small angle, the change of attack can be written as

$$\Delta\alpha \cong \beta\Gamma \qquad (2.90)$$

The angle of attack on the upward-moving wing will be decreased by the same amount. Methods for estimating the wing contribution to C_{l_β} can again be found in [2.7].

Wing sweep also contributes to the dihedral effect. In a sweptback wing, the windward wing has an effective decrease in sweep angle and the trailing wing experiences an effective increase in sweep angle. For a given angle of attack, a decrease in sweepback angle will result in a higher lift coefficient. Therefore, the windward wing (with a less effective sweep) will experience more lift than the trailing wing. It can be concluded that sweepback adds to the dihedral effect. On the other hand, sweep forward will decrease the effective dihedral effect.

The fuselage contribution to dihedral effect is illustrated in Figure 2.34. The sideward flow turns in the vicinity of the fuselage and creates a local change in wing angle of attack at the inboard wing stations. For a low wing position, the fuselage contributes a negative dihedral effect; the high wing produces a positive dihedral effect. To maintain the same C_{l_β}, a low-wing aircraft will require a considerably greater wing dihedral angle than a high-wing configuration.

The horizontal tail also can contribute to the dihedral effect in a manner similar to the wing. However, owing to the size of the horizontal tail with respect to the wing, its contribution is usually small. The contribution to dihedral effect from the vertical tail is produced by the side force on the tail due to sideslip. The side force on the vertical tail produces both a yawing moment and a rolling moment. The rolling moment occurs because the center of pressure for the vertical tail is located above the aircraft's center of gravity. The rolling moment produced by the vertical tail tends to bring the aircraft back to a wings-level attitude.

2.9
ROLL CONTROL

Roll control is achieved by the differential deflection of small flaps called ailerons which are located outboard on the wings, or by the use of spoilers. Figure 2.35 is a sketch showing both types of roll control devices. The basic principle behind these devices is to modify the spanwise lift distribution so that a moment is created about the x axis. An estimate of the roll control power for an aileron can be obtained by a simple strip integration method as illustrated in Figure 2.36 and the equations that follow. The incremental change in roll moment due to a change in aileron angle can be expressed as

$$\Delta L = (\Delta \text{ Lift})y \tag{2.91}$$

which can be written in coefficient form as

$$\Delta C_l = \frac{\Delta L}{QSb} = \frac{C_l Qcy \, dy}{QSb} \tag{2.92}$$

$$= \frac{C_l cy \, dy}{Sb} \tag{2.93}$$

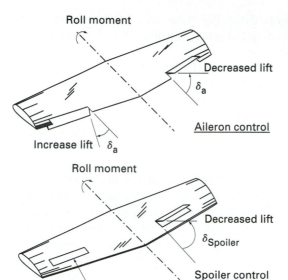

FIGURE 2.35
Aileron and spoilers for roll control.

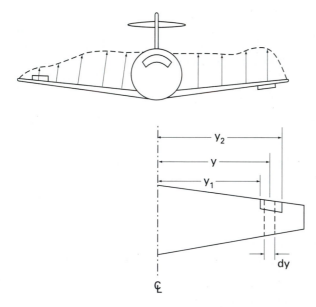

FIGURE 2.36
Strip theory approximation of roll control effectiveness.

The section lift coefficient C_l on the stations containing the aileron can be written as

$$C_l = C_{l_\alpha} \frac{d\alpha}{d\delta_a} \delta_a = C_{l_\alpha} \tau \delta_a \tag{2.94}$$

which is similar to the technique used to estimate the control effectiveness of an elevator and rudder. Substituting Equation (2.93) into Equation (2.94) and integrating over the region containing the aileron yields

$$C_l = \frac{2C_{L_{\alpha_w}} \tau \delta_a}{Sb} \int_{y_1}^{y_2} cy \, dy \qquad (2.95)$$

where $C_{L_{\alpha_w}}$ and τ have been corrected for three-dimensional flow and the factor of 2 has been introduced to account for the other aileron. The control power $C_{l_{\delta_a}}$ can be obtained by taking the derivative with respect to δ_a:

$$C_{l_{\delta_a}} = \frac{2C_{L_{\alpha_w}} \tau}{Sb} \int_{y_1}^{y_2} cy \, dy \qquad (2.96)$$

EXAMPLE PROBLEM 2.4. For the NAVION airplane described in Appendix B, estimate the roll control power, $C_{l_{\delta_a}}$. Assume that the wing and aileron geometry are as shown in Figure 2.37.

Solution. Equation (2.96) can be used to estimate the roll control power, $C_{l_{\delta_a}}$.

$$C_{l_{\delta_a}} = \frac{2C_{L_{\alpha_w}} \tau}{Sb} \int_{y_1}^{y_2} cy \, dy$$

b/2 = 16.7 ft.	λ = 0.54	c_r = 7.2 ft.
c_t = 3.9 ft.	y_1 = 11.1 ft.	y_2 = 16 ft.
S = 184 ft.^{2}	$C_{L_{\alpha_w}}$ = 4.44/rad.	c_a/c = 0.18 ft.

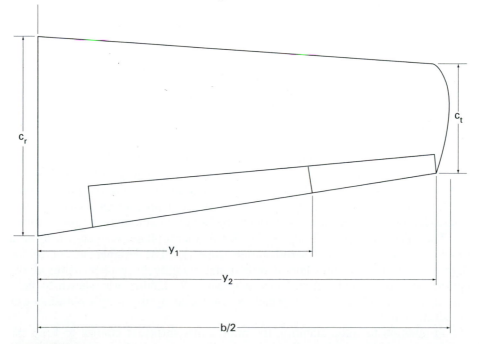

FIGURE 2.37
Approximate wing geometry of the NAVION airplane.

For a tapered wing the chord can be expressed as a function of y by the following relationship:

$$c = c_r\left[1 + \left(\frac{\lambda - 1}{b/2}\right)y\right]$$

Substituting the relationship for the chord back into the expression for $C_{l_{\delta a}}$ yields

$$C_{l_{\delta a}} = \frac{2C_{L_{\alpha w}}\tau C_r}{Sb}\int_{y_1}^{y_2}\left[1 + \left(\frac{\lambda - 1}{b/2}\right)y\right]y \, dy$$

or

$$C_{l_{\delta a}} = \frac{2C_{L_{\alpha w}}\tau C_r}{Sb}\left[\frac{y^2}{2} + \left(\frac{\lambda - 1}{b/2}\right)\frac{y^3}{3}\right]\Bigg|_{y_1}^{y_2}$$

This equation can be used to estimate $C_{l_{\delta a}}$ using the data in Figure 2.37 and estimating τ from Figure 2.21. Because the chord ratio is the same as the area ratio used in Figure 2.21, we can use $c_a/c = 0.18$ to estimate the flap effectiveness parameter, τ.

$$C_{l_{\delta a}} = \frac{2(4.3/\text{rad})(0.36)(7.2 \text{ ft})}{(184 \text{ ft}^2)(33.4 \text{ ft})}(90.4 \text{ ft}^2 - 49 \text{ ft}^2)$$

$$= 0.155/\text{rad}$$

The control derivative $C_{l_{\delta a}}$ is a measure of the power of the aileron control; it represents the change in moment per unit of aileron deflection. The larger $C_{l_{\delta a}}$, the more effective the control is at producing a roll moment.

2.10
SUMMARY

The requirements for static stability were developed for longitudinal, lateral directional, and rolling motions. It is easy to see why a pilot would require the airplane that he or she is flying to possess some degree of static stability. Without static stability the pilot would have to continuously control the airplane to maintain a desired flight path, which would be quite fatiguing. The degree of static stability desired by the pilot has been determined through flying quality studies and will be discussed in a later chapter. The important point at this time is to recognize that the airplane must be made statically stable, either through inherent aerodynamic characteristics or by artificial means through the use of an automatic control system.

The inherent static stability tendencies of the airplane were shown to be a function of its geometric and aerodynamic properties. The designer can control the degree of longitudinal and lateral directional stability by proper sizing of the horizontal and vertical tail surfaces, whereas roll stability was shown to be a consequence of dihedral effect, which is controlled by the wing's placement or dihedral angle.

In addition to static stability, the pilot wants sufficient control to keep the airplane in equilibrium (i.e., trim) and to maneuver. Aircraft response to control input and control force requirements are important flying quality characteristics determined by the control surface size. The stick force and stick force gradient are important parameters that influence how the pilot feels about the flying characteristics of the airplane. Stick forces must provide the pilot a feel for the maneuver initiated. In addition, we show that the stick force gradient provides the airplane with speed stability. If the longitudinal stick force gradient is negative at the trim flight speed, then the airplane will resist disturbances in speed and fly at a constant speed.

Finally, the relationship between static stability and control was examined. An airplane that is very stable statically will not be very maneuverable; if the airplane has very little static stability, it will be very maneuverable. The degree of maneuverability or static stability is determined by the designer on the basis of the airplane's mission requirements.

PROBLEMS

2.1. If the slope of the C_m versus C_L curve is -0.15 and the pitching moment at zero lift is equal to 0.08, determine the trim lift coefficient. If the center of gravity of the airplane is located at $X_{cg}/\bar{c} = 0.3$, determine the stick fixed neutral point.

2.2. For the data shown in Figure P2.2, determine the following:
(a) The stick fixed neutral point.
(b) If we wish to fly the airplane at a velocity of 125 ft/s at sea level, what would be the trim lift coefficient and what would be the elevator angle for trim?

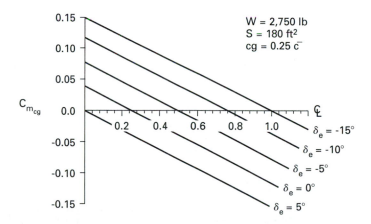

FIGURE P2.2

2.3. Analyze the canard-wing combination shown in Figure P2.3. The canard and wing are geometrically similar and are made from the same airfoil section.

$$AR_c = AR_w \qquad S_c = 0.2S_w \qquad \bar{c}_c = 0.45\bar{c}_w$$

(a) Develop an expression for the moment coefficient about the center of gravity. You may simplify the problem by neglecting the upwash (downwash) effects between the lifting surfaces and the drag contribution to the moment. Also assume small angle approximations.

(b) Find the neutral point for this airplane.

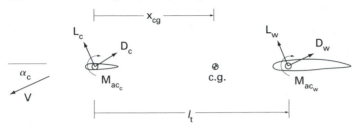

FIGURE P2.3

2.4. The C_m versus, α curve for a large jet transport can be seen in Figure P2.4. Use the figure and the following information to answer questions (a) to (c).

$$C_L = 0.03 + 0.08\alpha \text{ (deg.)}$$

$$-15° \le \delta_e \le 20°$$

(a) Estimate the stick fixed neutral point.
(b) Estimate the control power $C_{m_{\delta_e}}$.
(c) Find the forward center of gravity limit. Hint:

$$\frac{dC_{m_{cg}}}{dC_L} = \frac{X_{cg}}{\bar{c}} - \frac{X_{NP}}{\bar{c}}$$

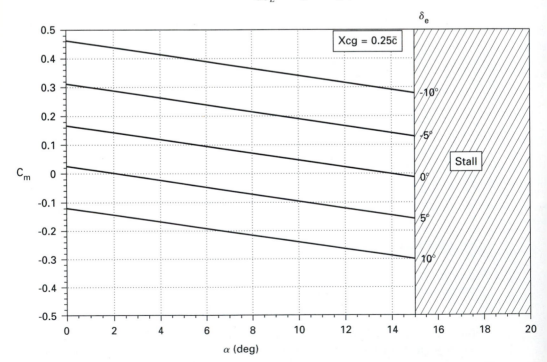

FIGURE P2.4

2.5. Using the data for the business jet aircraft included in Appendix B, determine the following longitudinal stability information at subsonic speeds:
(a) Wing contribution to the pitching moment
(b) Tail contribution to the pitching moment
(c) Fuselage contribution to the pitching moment
(d) Total pitching moment
(e) Plot the various contributions
(f) Estimate the stick fixed neutral point

2.6. An airplane has the following pitching moment characteristics at the center of gravity position:

$$x_{cg}/\overline{c} = 0.3.$$

$$C_{m_{cg}} = C_{m_0} + \frac{dC_{m_{cg}}}{dC_L} C_L + C_{m_{\delta_e}} \delta_e$$

where
$$C_{m_0} = 0.05 \qquad \frac{dC_{m_{cg}}}{dC_L} = -0.1 \qquad C_{m_{\delta_e}} = -0.01/\text{deg}$$

$$\frac{dC_{m_{cg}}}{dC_L} = \left[\frac{X_{cg}}{\overline{c}}\right] - \left[\frac{X_{NP}}{\overline{c}}\right]$$

If the airplane is loaded so that the center of gravity position moves to $x_{cg}/\overline{c} = 0.10$, can the airplane be trimmed during landing, $C_L = 1.0$? Assume that C_{m_0} and $C_{m_{\delta_e}}$ are unaffected by the center of gravity travel and that $\delta_{e_{max}} = \pm 20°$.

2.7. The pitching moment characteristics of a general aviation airplane with the landing gear and flaps in their retracted position are given in Figure P2.7.

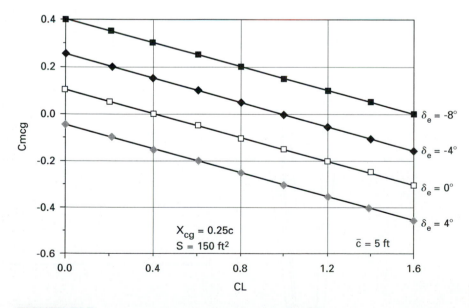

FIGURE P2.7
Pitching moment characteristics of a general aviation airplane.

(a) Where is the stick fixed neutral point located?

(b) If the airplane weighs 2500 lbs and is flying at 150 ft/s at sea level, $\rho = 0.002378$ slug/ft^3, what is the elevator angle required for trim?

(c) Discuss what happens to the pitching moment curve when the landing gear is deployed? How does the deflection of the high lift flaps affect the stability of the airplane?

2.8. Estimate the fuselage and engine nacelle contribution to C_{m_α} using the method discussed in section 2.3 for the STOL transport shown in Figure P2.8. The airplane has

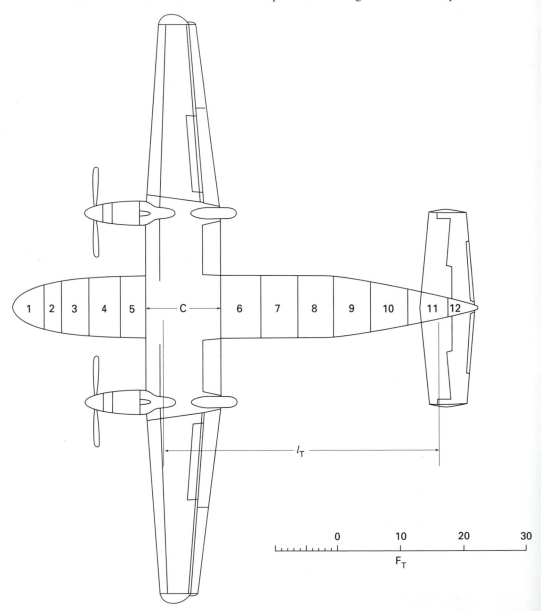

FIGURE P2.8

been divided into 12 sections as indicated in Figure P2.8. The section length, width, and distance from the wing leading or trailing edge to the midpoint of each section is given in the table below. The engine nacelles have been approximated by one section as indicated on the figure.

| Station | Fuselage | | |
	Δx ft	w_f ft	x_i ft
1	4.4	4.4	20.2
2	2.5	6.9	17.0
3	5.0	8.8	13.9
4	5.0	9.5	7.6
5	5.0	10.1	2.5
6	6.3	10.1	2.5
7	6.3	10.1	8.8
8	6.3	10.1	15.1
9	6.3	8.2	21.4
10	6.3	7.6	27.7
11	5.0	5.1	33.4
12	5.0	2.5	39.7

Assume that $c = 12.6$ ft (the fuselage region between the wing leading and trailing edge), $l_h = 34$ ft (the distance from the wing trailing edge to the quarter chord of the horizontal tail), and $d\varepsilon/d\alpha$ at the tail is 0.34.

2.9. The downwash angle at zero angle of attack and the rate of change of downwash with angle of attack can be determined experimentally by several techniques. The downwash angle can be measured directly by using a five- or seven-hole pressure probe to determine the flow direction at the position of the tail surface or indirectly from pitching moment data measured from wind-tunnel models. This latter technique will be demonstrated by way of this problem. Suppose that a wind-tunnel test were conducted to measure the pitching moment as a function of the angle of attack for various tail incidence settings as well as for the case when the tail surface is removed. Figure P2.9 plots such information. Notice that the tail-off data intersect the

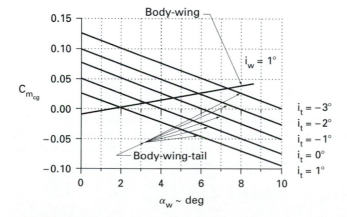

FIGURE P2.9

complete configuration data at several points. At the points of intersection, the contribution of the tail surface to the pitching moment curve must be 0. For this to be the case, the lift on the tail surface is 0, which implies that the tail angle of attack is 0 at these points. From the definition of the tail angle of attack,

$$\alpha_t = \alpha_w - i_w - \varepsilon + i_t$$

we obtain

$$\varepsilon = \alpha_w - i_w + i_t$$

at the interception points. Using the data of Figure P2.9 determine the downwash angle versus the angle of attack of the wing. From this information estimate ε_0 and $d\varepsilon/d\alpha$.

2.10. The airplane in Example Problem 2.2 has the following hinge moment characteristics:

$$C_{L_{\alpha w}} = 0.09/\text{deg} \qquad C_{h_\alpha} = -0.003/\text{deg} \qquad C_{h_\delta} = -0.005/\text{deg} \qquad V_H = 0.4$$

$$C_{L_{\alpha t}} = 0.08/\text{deg} \qquad C_{h_0} = 0.0 \qquad S_e/S_t = 0.35 \qquad d\varepsilon/d\alpha = 0.4$$

What would be the stick-free neutral point location?

2.11. As an airplane nears the ground its aerodynamic characteristics are changed by the presence of the ground plane. This change is called ground effect. A simple model for determining the influence of the ground on the lift drag and pitching moment can be obtained by representing the airplane by a horseshoe vortex system with an image as shown in Figure P2.11. Using this sketch, shown qualitatively, explain the changes that one might expect; that is, whether the forces and moment increase or decrease.

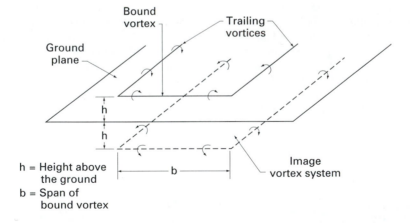

FIGURE P2.11

2.12. If the control characteristics of the elevator used in Example Problem 2.2 are as follows, determine the forwardmost limit on the center of gravity travel so that the airplane can be controlled during landing; that is, at $C_{L_{\max}}$. Neglect ground effects on the airplane's aerodynamic characteristics:

$$C_{m_{\delta e}} = -1.03/\text{rad} \qquad \delta_{e_{\max}} = \begin{cases} +10° \\ -20° \end{cases} \qquad C_{L_{\max}} = 1.4$$

2.13. Size the vertical tail for the airplane configuration shown in Figure P2.13 so that its weathercock stability has a value of $C_{n_\beta} = +0.1$ rad^{-1}. Clearly state your assumptions. Assume $V = 150$ m/s at sea level.

$S = 21.3$ m^2 $b = 10.4$ m $z_w = 0.4$ m $d = 1.6$ m

$l_f = 13.7$ m $x_m = 8.0$ m $w_f = 1.6$ m $S_{f_s} = 15.4$ m^2

$h = 1.6$ m $h_1 = 1.6$ m $h_2 = 1.07$ m

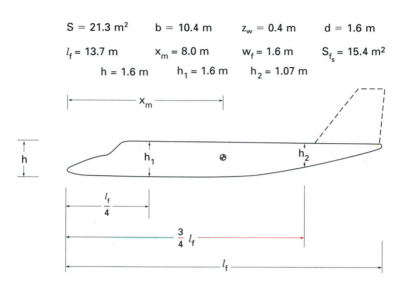

FIGURE P2.13

2.14. Figure P2.14 is a sketch of a wing planform for a business aviation airplane.
(*a*) Use strip theory to determine the roll control power.
(*b*) Comment on the accuracy of the strip theory integration technique.

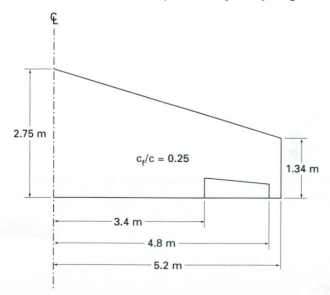

FIGURE P2.14

2.15. Suppose the wing planform in Problem 2.14 is incorporated into a low-wing aircraft design. Find the wing dihedral angle necessary to produce a dihedral effect of $C_{l_\beta} = -0.1$ rad^{-1}. Neglect the fuselage interference on the wing dihedral contribution.

2.16. For the twin engine airplane shown in Figure P2.16, determine the rudder size to control the airplane if one engine needs to be shut down. Use the flight information shown in the figure and

     Wing: $S = 980$ ft^2 $b = 93$ ft

     Vertical tail: $S_v = 330$ ft^2 $AR_v = 4.3$ $l_v = 37$ ft $\eta_v = 1.0$

     Rudder: $\delta_r = \pm 15°$

     Propulsion: $T = 14,000$ lb each $y_T = 16$ ft

     Flight condition: $V = 250$ ft/s $\rho = 0.002378$ slug/ft^3

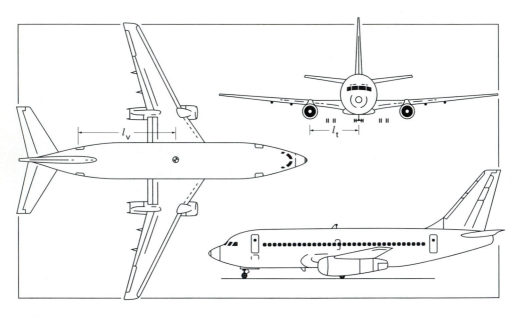

FIGURE P2.16

2.17. The elevator for a business jet aircraft is shown in Figure P2.17. Estimate the elevator's control power $C_{m_{\delta_e}}$ using the geometric information that follows:

$$S = 232 \text{ ft}^2 \qquad AR_t = 4.0$$
$$\bar{c} = 7.0 \text{ ft} \qquad l_t = 21.6 \text{ ft}$$
$$b_t = 14.7 \text{ ft} \qquad C_{l_{\alpha_t}} = 0.1/\text{deg(2D)}$$
$$S_t = 54 \text{ ft}^2$$

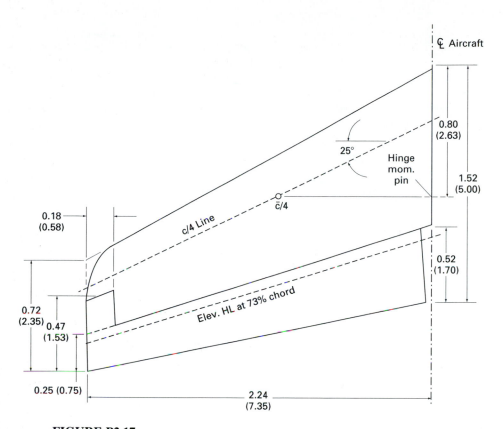

FIGURE P2.17

2.18. Develop an expression for the wing dihedral effect C_{l_β} for a wing planform that uses dihedral only for the outboard portion of the wing (see Figure P2.18). Clearly state all of your assumptions.

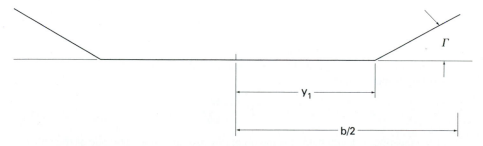

FIGURE P2.18

2.19. The trailing vortex wake left behind by an airplane can be a safety hazard to following aircraft as illustrated in Figure P2.19. The most likely place to encounter the wake of another aircraft is in the vicinity of the airport during takeoff or landing. To minimize

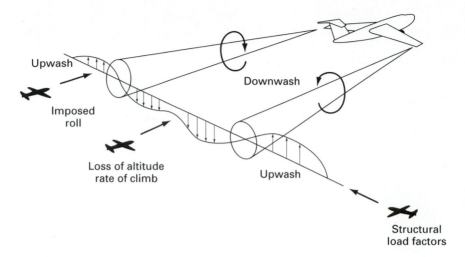

FIGURE P2.19

the possibility of a wake encounter the FAA has developed a separation criteria between aircraft of different sizes. If an elliptic wing loading is assumed, the strength of the trailing wake can be shown to be related to the size and speed of the generating aircraft.

$$L = W = \rho V \Gamma b'$$

where L = lift
W = weight
ρ = air density
V = velocity of the airplane
Γ = vortex strength
b' = effective span of vortices.

The effective span of the wing tip vortices for an elliptic load distribution can be shown to be

$$b' = \frac{\pi}{4}b$$

where b is the wingspan of the generating aircraft. Solving for the circulation (i.e., vortex strength) yields

$$\Gamma = \frac{W}{\rho V b'}$$

The tangential velocity field at some point downstream created by one of the vortices is given by

$$v_\theta = \left(\frac{\Gamma}{2\pi a_c}\right) r \qquad r \le a_c$$

$$v_\theta = \frac{\Gamma}{2\pi r} \qquad r \le a_c$$

From the simple analysis presented here it is clear that the vortex strength is proportional to the weight of the generating aircraft and inversely proportional to its speed. Therefore large heavy transports flying at approach or takeoff speeds will create the strongest wakes and the greatest hazard to following aircraft.

Wake vortices decay slowly in calm atmospheric conditions. Because the wake vortices decay very slowly in a calm atmosphere we will neglect vortex decay in this problem. Develop an expression for estimating the roll moment induced on an airplane wing when the wing is centered in the vortex core of another aircraft's trailing vortex wake.

2.20. Using the expression developed in Problem 2.19, estimate the roll moment induced by the wake of a large jet transport on several smaller aircraft. Use the data in Appendix B. Use the information for the 747 for the generating aircraft and evaluate the roll moment induced on the Convair 880, STOL transport, business jet, and the NAVION. Compare the induced roll moment to the maximum roll moment that could be developed by full aileron deflection. Assume the aileron maximum deflection is $\pm 25°$ for each aircraft.

REFERENCES

2.1. Dickman, E. W. *This Aviation Business.* New York: Brentano's, 1926.
2.2. Gibbs-Smith, C. H.; and T. D. Crouch. "Wilbur and Orville Wright—A 75th Anniversary Commemoration." *Astronautics and Aeronautics,* December 1978, pp. 8–15.
2.3. Perkins, C. D. "Development of Airplane Stability and Control Technology." *AIAA Journal of Aircraft* 7, no. 4 (1970).
2.4. Etkin, B. *Dynamics of Flight.* New York: Wiley, 1959.
2.5. Perkins, C. D.; and R. E. Hage. *Airplane Performance Stability and Control.* New York: Wiley, 1949.
2.6. McRuer, D.; I. Ashkenas; and D. Graham. *Aircraft Dynamics and Automatic Control.* Princeton, NJ: Princeton University Press, 1973.
2.7. *USAF Stability and Control Datcom,* Flight Control Division, Air Force Flight Dynamics Laboratory, Wright Patterson Air Force Base, Fairborn, OH.
2.8. Munk, M. M. *The Aerodynamic Forces on Airship Hulls,* NACA TR 184, 1924.
2.9. Multhopp, H. *Aerodynamics of Fuselage,* NACA TM-1036, 1942.

CHAPTER 3

Aircraft Equations of Motion

Success four flights Thursday morning all against 21 mile wind—started from
level with engine power alone average speed through air 30 miles—longest
57 seconds inform press home Christmas

Telegram message sent by Orville Wright, December 17, 1903

3.1
INTRODUCTION

In Chapter 2, the requirements for static stability were examined. It was shown that
static stability is a tendency of the aircraft to return to its equilibrium position. In
addition to static stability, the aircraft also must be dynamically stable. An airplane
can be considered to be dynamically stable if after being disturbed from its equilibrium flight condition the ensuing motion diminishes with time. Of particular
interest to the pilot and designer is the degree of dynamic stability. The required
degree of dynamic stability usually is specified by the time it takes the motion to
damp to half of its initial amplitude or in the case of an unstable motion the time
it takes for the initial amplitude or disturbance to double. Also of interest is the
frequency or period of the oscillation.

An understanding of the dynamic characteristics of an airplane is important in
assessing its handling or flying qualities as well as for designing autopilots. The
flying qualities of an airplane are dependent on pilot opinion; that is, the pilot's
likes or dislikes with regard to the various vechile motions. It is possible to design
an airplane that has excellent performance but is considered unsatisfactory by the
pilot. Since the early 1960s, considerable research has been directed toward quan-
tifying pilot opinion in terms of aircraft motion characteristics, such as frequency
and damping ratio of the aircraft's various modes of motion. Therefore, it is
important to understand the dynamic characteristics of an airplane and the relationship of the motion to the vehicle's aerodynamic characteristics and pilot
opinion.

Before developing the equations of motion, it is important to review the axis
system specified earlier. Figure 3.1 shows the body axis system fixed to the aircraft
and the inertial axis system that is fixed to the Earth.

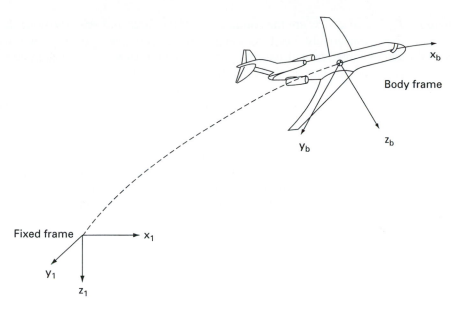

FIGURE 3.1
Body and inertial axis systems.

3.2
DERIVATION OF RIGID BODY EQUATIONS OF MOTION

The rigid body equations of motion are obtained from Newton's second law, which states that the summation of all external forces acting on a body is equal to the time rate of change of the momentum of the body; and the summation of the external moments acting on the body is equal to the time rate of change of the moment of momentum (angular momentum). The time rates of change of linear and angular momentum are referred to an absolute or inertial reference frame. For many problems in airplane dynamics, an axis system fixed to the Earth can be used as an inertial reference frame. Newton's second law can be expressed in the following vector equations:

$$\sum \mathbf{F} = \frac{d}{dt}(m\mathbf{v}) \tag{3.1}$$

$$\sum \mathbf{M} = \frac{d}{dt}\mathbf{H} \tag{3.2}$$

The vector equations can be rewritten in scalar form and then consist of three force equations and three moment equations. The force equations can be expressed as follows:

$$F_x = \frac{d}{dt}(mu) \qquad F_y = \frac{d}{dt}(mv) \qquad F_z = \frac{d}{dt}(mw) \tag{3.3}$$

where F_x, F_y, F_z and u, v, w are the components of the force and velocity along the x, y, and z axes, respectively. The force components are composed of contributions due to the aerodynamic, propulsive, and gravitational forces acting on the airplane. The moment equations can be expressed in a similar manner:

$$L = \frac{d}{dt} H_x \qquad M = \frac{d}{dt} H_y \qquad N = \frac{d}{dt} H_z \qquad (3.4)$$

where L, M, N and H_x, H_y, H_z are the components of the moment and moment of momentum along the x, y, and z axes, respectively.

Consider the airplane shown in Figure 3.2. If we let δm be an element of mass of the airplane, $\mathbf{v}$ be the velocity of the elemental mass relative to an absolute or inertial frame, and $\delta \mathbf{F}$ be the resulting force acting on the elemental mass, then Newton's second law yields

$$\delta \mathbf{F} = \delta m \frac{d\mathbf{v}}{dt} \qquad (3.5)$$

and the total external force acting on the airplane is found by summing all the elements of the airplane:

$$\sum \delta \mathbf{F} = \mathbf{F} \qquad (3.6)$$

The velocity of the differential mass δm is

$$\mathbf{v} = \mathbf{v}_c + \frac{d\mathbf{r}}{dt} \qquad (3.7)$$

where $\mathbf{v}_c$ is the velocity of the center of mass of the airplane and $d\mathbf{r}/dt$ is the velocity of the element relative to the center of mass. Substituting this expression for the

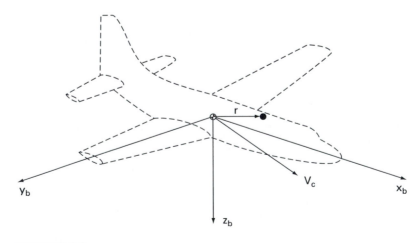

FIGURE 3.2
An element of mass on an airplane.

velocity into Newton's second law yields

$$\Sigma \, \delta\mathbf{F} = \mathbf{F} = \frac{d}{dt} \Sigma \left(\mathbf{v}_c + \frac{d\mathbf{r}}{dt} \right) \delta m \tag{3.8}$$

If we assume that the mass of the vehicle is constant, Equation (3.8) can be rewritten as

$$\mathbf{F} = m \frac{d\mathbf{v}_c}{dt} + \frac{d}{dt} \Sigma \frac{d\mathbf{r}}{dt} \delta m \tag{3.9}$$

or

$$\mathbf{F} = m \frac{d\mathbf{v}_c}{dt} + \frac{d^2}{dt^2} \Sigma \mathbf{r} \, \delta m \tag{3.10}$$

Because $\mathbf{r}$ is measured from the center of mass, the summation $\Sigma \, \mathbf{r} \, \delta m$ is equal to 0. The force equation then becomes

$$\mathbf{F} = m \frac{d\mathbf{v}_c}{dt} \tag{3.11}$$

which relates the external force on the airplane to the motion of the vehicle's center of mass.

In a similar manner, we can develop the moment equation referred to a moving center of mass. For the differential element of mass, δm, the moment equation can be written as

$$\delta\mathbf{M} = \frac{d}{dt} \delta\mathbf{H} = \frac{d}{dt} (\mathbf{r} \times \mathbf{v}) \, \delta m \tag{3.12}$$

The velocity of the mass element can be expressed in terms of the velocity of the center of mass and the relative velocity of the mass element to the center of mass:

$$\mathbf{v} = \mathbf{v}_c + \frac{d\mathbf{r}}{dt} = \mathbf{v}_c + \boldsymbol{\omega} \times \mathbf{r} \tag{3.13}$$

where $\boldsymbol{\omega}$ is the angular velocity of the vehicle and $\mathbf{r}$ is the position of the mass element measured from the center of mass. The total moment of momentum can be written as

$$\mathbf{H} = \Sigma \, \delta\mathbf{H} = \Sigma \, (\mathbf{r} \times \mathbf{v}_c) \, \delta m + \Sigma \, [\mathbf{r} \times (\boldsymbol{\omega} \times \mathbf{r})] \, \delta m \tag{3.14}$$

The velocity $\mathbf{v}_c$ is a constant with respect to the summation and can be taken outside the summation sign:

$$\mathbf{H} = \Sigma \, \mathbf{r} \, \delta m \times \mathbf{v}_c + \Sigma \, [\mathbf{r} \times (\boldsymbol{\omega} \times \mathbf{r})] \, \delta m \tag{3.15}$$

The first term in Equation (3.15) is 0 because the term $\Sigma \, \mathbf{r} \, \delta m = 0$, as explained previously. If we express the angular velocity and position vector as

$$\boldsymbol{\omega} = p\mathbf{i} + q\mathbf{j} + r\mathbf{k} \tag{3.16}$$

and

$$\mathbf{r} = x\mathbf{i} + y\mathbf{j} + z\mathbf{k} \tag{3.17}$$

then after expanding Equation (3.15), $\mathbf{H}$ can be written as

$$\mathbf{H} = (p\mathbf{i} + q\mathbf{i} + r\mathbf{k}) \sum (x^2 + y^2 + z^2)\, \delta m$$
$$- \sum (x\mathbf{i} + y\mathbf{i} + z\mathbf{k})(px + qy + rz)\, \delta m \qquad (3.18)$$

The scalar components of $\mathbf{H}$ are

$$H_x = p \sum (y^2 + z^2)\, \delta m - q \sum xy\, \delta m - r \sum xz\, \delta m$$
$$H_y = -p \sum xy\, \delta m + q \sum (x^2 + z^2)\, \delta m - r \sum yz\, \delta m \qquad (3.19)$$
$$H_z = -p \sum xz\, \delta m - q \sum yz\, \delta m + r \sum (x^2 + y^2)\, \delta m$$

The summations in these equations are the mass moment and products of inertia of the airplane and are defined as follows:

$$I_x = \iiint (y^2 + z^2)\, \delta m \qquad I_{xy} = \iiint xy\, \delta m$$

$$I_y = \iiint (x^2 + z^2)\, \delta m \qquad I_{xz} = \iiint xz\, \delta m \qquad (3.20)$$

$$I_z = \iiint (x^2 + y^2)\, \delta m \qquad I_{yz} = \iiint yz\, \delta m$$

The terms I_x, I_y, and I_z are the mass moments of inertia of the body about the x, y, and z axes, respectively. The terms with the mixed indexes are called the products of inertia. Both the moments and products of inertia depend on the shape of the body and the manner in which its mass is distributed. The larger the moments of inertia, the greater will be the resistance to rotation. The scaler equations for the moment of momentum follow:

$$H_x = pI_x - qI_{xy} - rI_{xz}$$
$$H_y = -pI_{xy} + qI_y - rI_{yz} \qquad (3.21)$$
$$H_z = -pI_{xz} - qI_{yz} + rI_z$$

If the reference frame is not rotating, then as the airplane rotates the moments and products of inertia will vary with time. To avoid this difficulty we will fix the axis system to the aircraft (body axis system). Now we must determine the derivatives of the vectors $\mathbf{v}$ and $\mathbf{H}$ referred to the rotating body frame of reference.

It can be shown that the derivative of an arbitrary vector $\mathbf{A}$ referred to a rotating body frame having an angular velocity $\boldsymbol{\omega}$ can be represented by the following vector identity:

$$\left. \frac{d\mathbf{A}}{dt} \right|_I = \left. \frac{d\mathbf{A}}{dt} \right|_B + \boldsymbol{\omega} \times \mathbf{A} \qquad (3.22)$$

where the subscripts I and B refer to the inertial and body fixed frames of reference.

Applying this identity to the equations derived earlier yields

$$F = m \frac{dv_c}{dt}\bigg|_B + m(\omega \times v_c) \tag{3.23}$$

$$M = \frac{dH}{dt}\bigg|_B + \omega \times H \tag{3.24}$$

The scalar equations are

$$F_x = m(\dot{u} + qw - rv) \qquad F_y = m(\dot{v} + ru - pw) \qquad F_z = m(\dot{w} + pv - qu)$$
$$L = \dot{H}_x + qH_z - rH_y \qquad M = \dot{H}_y + rH_x - pH_z \qquad N = \dot{H}_z + pH_y - qH_x \tag{3.25}$$

The components of the force and moment acting on the airplane are composed of aerodynamic, gravitational, and propulsive contributions.

By proper positioning of the body axis system, one can make the products of inertia $I_{yz} = I_{xy} = 0$. To do this we are assuming that the xz plane is a plane of symmetry of the airplane. With this assumption, the moment equations can be written as

$$L = I_x \dot{p} - I_{xz}\dot{r} + qr(I_z - I_y) - I_{xz}pq$$
$$M = I_y \dot{q} + rp(I_x - I_z) + I_{xz}(p^2 - r^2) \tag{3.26}$$
$$N = -I_{xz}\dot{p} + I_z \dot{r} + pq(I_y - I_x) + I_{xz}qr$$

3.3
ORIENTATION AND POSITION OF THE AIRPLANE

The equations of motion have been derived for an axis system fixed to the airplane. Unfortunately, the position and orientation of the airplane cannot be described relative to the moving body axis frame. The orientation and position of the airplane can be defined in terms of a fixed frame of reference as shown in Figure 3.3. At time $t = 0$, the two reference frames coincide.

The orientation of the airplane can be described by three consecutive rotations, whose order is important. The angular rotations are called the Euler angles. The orientation of the body frame with respect to the fixed frame can be determined in the following manner. Imagine the airplane to be positioned so that the body axis system is parallel to the fixed frame and then apply the following rotations:

1. Rotate the x_f, y_f, z_f frame about $0z_f$ through the yaw angle ψ to the frame to x_1, y_1, z_1.
2. Rotate the x_1, y_1, z_1 frame about $0y_1$ through the pitch angle θ bringing the frame to x_2, y_2, z_2.
3. Rotate the x_2, y_2, z_2 frame about $0x_2$ through the roll angle Φ to bring the frame to x_3, y_3, z_3, the actual orientation of the body frame relative to the fixed frame.

Remember that the order of rotation is extremely important.

Having defined the Euler angles, one can determine the flight velocities components relative to the fixed reference frame. To accomplish this, let the velocity components along the x_f, y_f, z_f frame be dx/dt, dy/dt, dz/dt and similarly let the

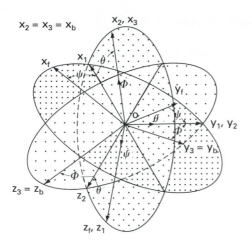

FIGURE 3.3
Relationship between body and inertial axes systems.

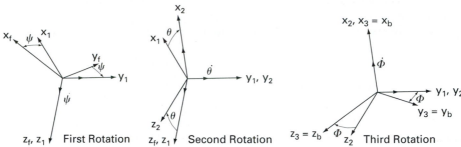

subscripts 1 and 2 denote the components along x_1, y_1, z_1 and x_2, y_2, z_2, respectively. Examining Figure 3.3, we can show that

$$\frac{dx}{dt} = u_1 \cos \psi - v_1 \sin \psi \qquad \frac{dy}{dt} = u_1 \sin \psi + v_1 \cos \psi \qquad \frac{dz}{dt} = w_1 \quad (3.27)$$

Before proceeding further, let us use the shorthand notation $S_\psi \equiv \sin \psi$, $C_\psi \equiv \cos \psi$, $S_\theta \equiv \sin \theta$, and so forth. In a manner similar to Equation (3.27), $u_1, v_1,$ and w_1 can be expressed in terms of $u_2, v_2,$ and w_2:

$$u_1 = u_2 C_\theta + w_2 S_\theta \qquad v_1 = v_2 \qquad w_1 = -u_2 S_\theta + w_2 C_\theta \quad (3.28)$$

and $\qquad u_2 = u \qquad v_2 = v C_\Phi - w S_\Phi \qquad w_2 = v S_\Phi + w C_\Phi \quad (3.29)$

where u, v, and w are the velocity components along the body axes x_b, y_b, z_b.

If we back-substitute the preceding equations, we can determine the absolute velocity in terms of the Euler angles and velocity components in the body frame:

$$\begin{bmatrix} \dfrac{dx}{dt} \\[2mm] \dfrac{dy}{dt} \\[2mm] \dfrac{dz}{dt} \end{bmatrix} = \begin{bmatrix} C_\theta C_\psi & S_\Phi S_\theta C_\psi - C_\Phi S_\psi & C_\Phi S_\theta C_\psi + S_\Phi S_\psi \\ C_\theta S_\psi & S_\Phi S_\theta S_\psi + C_\Phi C_\psi & C_\Phi S_\theta S_\psi - S_\Phi C_\psi \\ -S_\theta & S_\theta C_\theta & C_\Phi C_\theta \end{bmatrix} \begin{bmatrix} u \\ v \\ w \end{bmatrix} \quad (3.30)$$

Integration of these equations yields the airplane's position relative to the fixed frame of reference.

The relationship between the angular velocities in the body frame (p, q, and r) and the Euler rates ($\dot{\psi}$, $\dot{\theta}$, and $\dot{\Phi}$) also can be determined from Figure 3.3:

$$
\begin{bmatrix} p \\ q \\ r \end{bmatrix} = \begin{bmatrix} 1 & 0 & -S_\theta \\ 0 & C_\Phi & C_\theta S_\Phi \\ 0 & -S_\Phi & C_\theta C_\Phi \end{bmatrix} \begin{bmatrix} \dot{\Phi} \\ \dot{\theta} \\ \dot{\psi} \end{bmatrix}
\tag{3.31}
$$

Equation (3.31) can be solved for the Euler rates in terms of the body angular velocities:

$$
\begin{bmatrix} \dot{\Phi} \\ \dot{\theta} \\ \dot{\psi} \end{bmatrix} = \begin{bmatrix} 1 & S_\Phi \tan\theta & C_\Phi \tan\theta \\ 0 & C_\Phi & -S_\Phi \\ 0 & S_\Phi \sec\theta & C_\Phi \sec\theta \end{bmatrix} \begin{bmatrix} p \\ q \\ r \end{bmatrix}
\tag{3.32}
$$

By integrating these equations, one can determine the Euler angles ψ, θ, and Φ.

3.4
GRAVITATIONAL AND THRUST FORCES

The gravitational force acting on the airplane acts through the center of gravity of the airplane. Because the body axis system is fixed to the center of gravity, the gravitational force will not produce any moments. It will contribute to the external force acting on the airplane, however, and have components along the respective body axes. Figure 3.4 shows that the gravitational force components acting along the body axis are a function of the airplane's orientation in space. The gravitational

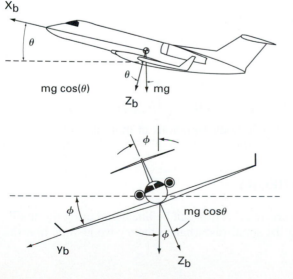

FIGURE 3.4
Components of gravitational force acting along the body axis.

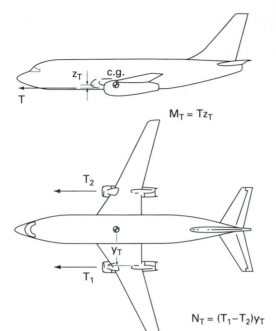

FIGURE 3.5
Force and moments due to propulsion system.

$M_T = Tz_T$

$N_T = (T_1 - T_2)y_T$

force components along the x, y, and z axes can be easily shown to be

$$(F_x)_{\text{gravity}} = -mg \sin \theta$$
$$(F_y)_{\text{gravity}} = mg \cos\theta \sin \Phi \qquad (3.33)$$
$$(F_z)_{\text{gravity}} = mg \cos \theta \cos \Phi$$

The thrust force due to the propulsion system can have components that act along each of the body axis directions. In addition, the propulsive forces also can create moments if the thrust does not act through the center of gravity. Figure 3.5 shows some examples of moments created by the propulsive system.

The propulsive forces and moments acting along the body axis system are denoted as follows:

$$(F_x)_{\text{propulsive}} = X_T \qquad (F_y)_{\text{propulsive}} = Y_T \qquad (F_z)_{\text{propulsive}} = Z_T \qquad (3.34)$$

and $\qquad (L)_{\text{propulsive}} = L_T \qquad (M)_{\text{propulsive}} = M_T \qquad (N)_{\text{propulsive}} = N_T \qquad (3.35)$

Table 3.1 gives a summary of the rigid body equations of motion.

3.5
SMALL-DISTURBANCE THEORY

The equations developed in the previous section can be linearized using the small-disturbance theory. In applying the small-disturbance theory we assume that the

TABLE 3.1
Summary of kinematic and dynamic equations

$$X - mgS_\theta = m(\dot{u} + qw - rv)$$
$$Y + mgC_\theta S_\Phi = m(\dot{v} + ru - pw) \qquad \text{Force equations}$$
$$Z + mgC_\theta C_\Phi = m(\dot{w} + pv - qu)$$

$$L = I_x\dot{p} - I_{xz}\dot{r} + qr(I_z - I_y) - I_{xz}pq$$
$$M = I_y\dot{q} + rq(I_x - I_z) + I_{xz}(p^2 - r^2) \qquad \text{Moment equations}$$
$$N = -I_{xz}\dot{p} + I_z\dot{r} + pq(I_y - I_x) + I_{xz}qr$$

$$p = \dot{\Phi} - \dot{\psi}S_\theta \qquad\qquad\qquad \text{Body angular velocities}$$
$$q = \dot{\theta}C_\Phi + \dot{\psi}C_\theta S_\Phi \qquad\qquad \text{in terms of Euler angles}$$
$$r = \dot{\psi}C_\theta C_\Phi - \dot{\theta}S_\Phi \qquad\qquad \text{and Euler rates}$$

$$\dot{\theta} = qC_\Phi - rS_\Phi \qquad\qquad\qquad \text{Euler rates in terms of}$$
$$\dot{\Phi} = p + qS_\Phi T_\theta + rC_\Phi T_\theta \qquad \text{Euler angles and body}$$
$$\dot{\psi} = (qS_\Phi + rC_\Phi)\sec\theta \qquad\qquad \text{angular velocities}$$

Velocity of aircraft in the fixed frame in terms of Euler angles and
body velocity components

$$
\begin{bmatrix} \dfrac{dx}{dt} \\[2ex] \dfrac{dx}{dt} \\[2ex] \dfrac{dz}{dt} \end{bmatrix}
=
\begin{bmatrix}
C_\theta C_\psi & S_\Phi S_\theta C_\psi - C_\Phi S_\psi & C_\psi S_\theta C_\psi + S_\Phi S_\psi \\
C_\theta S_\psi & S_\Phi S_\theta S_\psi + C_\Phi C_\psi & C_\Phi S_\theta S_\psi - S_\Phi C_\psi \\
-S_\theta & S_\Phi C_\theta & C_\Phi C_\theta
\end{bmatrix}
\begin{bmatrix} u \\[2ex] v \\[2ex] w \end{bmatrix}
$$

motion of the airplane consists of small deviations about a steady flight condition. Obviously, this theory cannot be applied to problems in which large-amplitude motions are to be expected (e.g., spinning or stalled flight). However, in many cases the small-disturbance theory yields sufficient accuracy for practical engineering purposes.

All the variables in the equations of motion are replaced by a reference value plus a perturbation or disturbance:

$$u = u_0 + \Delta u \qquad v = v_0 + \Delta v \qquad w = w_0 + \Delta w$$
$$p = p_0 + \Delta p \qquad q = q_0 + \Delta q \qquad r = r_0 + \Delta r$$
$$X = X_0 + \Delta X \qquad Y = Y_0 + \Delta Y \qquad Z = Z_0 + \Delta Z \qquad (3.36)$$
$$M = M_0 + \Delta M \qquad N = N_0 + \Delta N \qquad L = L_0 + \Delta L$$
$$\delta = \delta_0 + \Delta\delta$$

For convenience, the reference flight condition is assumed to be symmetric and the propulsive forces are assumed to remain constant. This implies that

$$v_0 = p_0 = q_0 = r_0 = \Phi_0 = \psi_0 = 0 \qquad (3.37)$$

Furthermore, if we initially align the x axis so that it is along the direction of the airplane's velocity vector, then $w_0 = 0$.

Now, if we introduce the small-disturbance notation into the equations of motion, we can simplify these equations. As an example, consider the X force equation:

$$X - mg \sin \theta = m(\dot{u} + qw - rv) \tag{3.38}$$

Substituting the small-disturbance variables into this equation yields

$$X_0 + \Delta X - mg \sin(\theta_0 + \Delta\theta)$$
$$= m \left[\frac{d}{dt}(u_0 + \Delta u) + (q_0 + \Delta q)(w_0 + \Delta w) - (r_0 + \Delta r)(v_0 + \Delta v) \right] \tag{3.39}$$

If we neglect products of the disturbance and assume that

$$w_0 = v_0 = p_0 = q_0 = r_0 = \Phi_0 = \psi_0 = 0 \tag{3.40}$$

then the X equation becomes

$$X_0 + \Delta X - mg \sin(\theta_0 + \Delta\theta) = m \, \Delta\dot{u} \tag{3.41}$$

This equation can be reduced further by applying the following trigonometric identity:

$$\sin(\theta_0 + \Delta\theta) = \sin \theta_0 \cos \Delta\theta + \cos \theta_0 \sin \Delta\theta = \sin \theta_0 + \Delta\theta \cos \theta_0$$

Therefore, $$X_0 + \Delta X - mg(\sin \theta_0 + \Delta\theta \cos \theta_0) = m \, \Delta\dot{u} \tag{3.42}$$

If all the disturbance quantities are set equal to 0 in these equation, we have the reference flight condition

$$X_0 - mg \sin \theta_0 = 0 \tag{3.43}$$

This reduces the X-force equation to

$$\Delta X - mg \, \Delta\theta \cos \theta_0 = m \, \Delta\dot{u} \tag{3.44}$$

The force ΔX is the change in aerodynamic and propulsive force in the x direction and can be expressed by means of a Taylor series in terms of the perturbation variables. If we assume that ΔX is a function only of u, w, δ_e, and δ_T, then ΔX can be expressed as

$$\Delta X = \frac{\partial X}{\partial u} \Delta u + \frac{\partial X}{\partial w} \Delta w + \frac{\partial X}{\partial \delta_e} \Delta\delta_e + \frac{\partial X}{\partial \delta_T} \Delta\delta_T \tag{3.45}$$

where $\partial X/\partial u$, $\partial X/\partial w$, $\partial X/\partial \delta_e$, and $\partial X/\partial \delta_T$, called stability derivatives, that are evaluated at the reference flight condition. The variables δ_e and δ_T are the change in elevator angle and throttle setting, respectively. If a canard or all-moveable stabilator is used for longitudinal control, then the control term would be replaced by

$$\frac{\partial X}{\partial \delta_H} \Delta\delta_H \quad \text{or} \quad \frac{\partial X}{\partial \delta_c} \Delta\delta_c$$

Substituting the expression for ΔX into the force equation yields:

$$\frac{\partial X}{\partial u} \Delta u + \frac{\partial X}{\partial w} \Delta w + \frac{\partial X}{\partial \delta_e} \Delta \delta_e + \frac{\partial X}{\partial \delta_T} \Delta \delta_T - mg \, \Delta\theta \cos \theta_0 = m \, \Delta \dot{u} \qquad (3.46)$$

or on rearranging

$$\left(m \frac{d}{dt} - \frac{\partial X}{\partial u} \right) \Delta u - \left(\frac{\partial X}{\partial w} \right) \Delta w + (mg \cos \theta_0) \, \Delta\theta = \frac{\partial X}{\partial \delta_e} \Delta \delta_e + \frac{\partial X}{\partial \delta_T} \Delta \delta_T$$

The equation can be rewritten in a more convenient form by dividing through by the mass m:

$$\left(\frac{d}{dt} - X_u \right) \Delta u - X_w \, \Delta w + (g \cos \theta_0) \, \Delta\theta = X_{\delta_e} \Delta \delta_e + X_{\delta_T} \Delta \delta_T \qquad (3.47)$$

where $X_u = \partial X / \partial u / m$, $X_w = \partial X / \partial w / m$, and so on are aerodynamic derivatives divided by the airplane's mass.

The change in aerodynamic forces and moments are functions of the motion variables Δu, Δw, and so forth. The aerodynamic derivatives usually the most important for conventional airplane motion analysis follow:

$$\left.\begin{aligned}
\Delta X &= \frac{\partial X}{\partial u} \Delta u + \frac{\partial X}{\partial w} \Delta w + \frac{\partial X}{\partial \delta_e} \Delta \delta_e + \frac{\partial X}{\partial \delta_T} \Delta \delta_T \\[2mm]
\Delta Y &= \frac{\partial Y}{\partial v} \Delta v + \frac{\partial Y}{\partial p} \Delta p + \frac{\partial Y}{\partial r} \Delta r + \frac{\partial Y}{\partial \delta_r} \Delta \delta_r \\[2mm]
\Delta Z &= \frac{\partial Z}{\partial u} \Delta u + \frac{\partial Z}{\partial w} \Delta w + \frac{\partial Z}{\partial \dot{w}} \Delta \dot{w} + \frac{\partial Z}{\partial q} \Delta q \\[2mm]
&\quad + \frac{\partial Z}{\partial \delta_e} \Delta \delta_e + \frac{\partial Z}{\partial \delta_T} \Delta \delta_T
\end{aligned}\right\} \qquad (3.48)$$

$$\left.\begin{aligned}
\Delta L &= \frac{\partial L}{\partial v} \Delta v + \frac{\partial L}{\partial p} \Delta p + \frac{\partial L}{\partial r} \Delta r + \frac{\partial L}{\partial \delta_r} \Delta \delta_r + \frac{\partial L}{\partial \delta_a} \Delta \delta_a \\[2mm]
\Delta M &= \frac{\partial M}{\partial u} \Delta u + \frac{\partial M}{\partial w} \Delta w + \frac{\partial M}{\partial \dot{w}} \Delta \dot{w} + \frac{\partial M}{\partial q} \Delta q \\[2mm]
&\quad + \frac{\partial M}{\partial \delta_e} \Delta \delta_e + \frac{\partial M}{\partial \delta_T} \Delta \delta_T \\[2mm]
\Delta N &= \frac{\partial N}{\partial v} \Delta v + \frac{\partial N}{\partial p} \Delta p + \frac{\partial N}{\partial r} \Delta r + \frac{\partial N}{\partial \delta_r} \Delta \delta_r + \frac{\partial N}{\partial \delta_a} \Delta \delta_a
\end{aligned}\right\} \qquad (3.49)$$

The aerodynamic forces and moments can be expressed as a function of all the motion variables; however, in these equations only the terms that are usually significant have been retained. Note also that the longitudinal aerodynamic control surface was assumed to be an elevator. For aircraft that use either a canard or combination of longitudinal controls, the elevator terms in the preceding equations can be replaced by the appropriate control derivatives and angular deflections.

The complete set of linearized equations of motion is presented in Table 3.2.

TABLE 3.2
The linearized small-disturbance longitudinal and lateral rigid body equation of motion

---

Longitudinal equations

$$\left(\frac{d}{dt} - X_u\right) \Delta u - X_w \, \Delta w + (g \cos \theta_0) \, \Delta\theta = X_{\delta_e} \, \Delta\delta_e + X_{\delta_T} \, \Delta\delta_T$$

$$-Z_u \, \Delta u + \left[(1 - Z_{\dot{w}})\frac{d}{dt} - Z_w\right] \Delta w - \left[(u_0 + Z_q)\frac{d}{dt} - g \sin\theta_0\right] \Delta\theta = Z_{\delta_e} \, \Delta\delta_e + Z_{\delta_T} \, \Delta\delta_T$$

$$-M_u \, \Delta u - \left(M_{\dot{w}}\frac{d}{dt} + M_w\right) \Delta w + \left(\frac{d^2}{dt^2} - M_q\frac{d}{dt}\right) \Delta\theta = M_{\delta_e} \, \Delta\delta_e + M_{\delta_T} \, \Delta\delta_T$$

Lateral equations

$$\left(\frac{d}{dt} - Y_v\right) \Delta v - Y_p \, \Delta p + (u_0 - Y_r) \, \Delta r - (g \cos\theta_0) \, \Delta\phi = Y_{\delta_r} \, \Delta\delta_r$$

$$-L_v \, \Delta v + \left(\frac{d}{dt} - L_p\right) \Delta p - \left(\frac{I_{yz}}{I_x}\frac{d}{dt} + L_r\right) \Delta r = L_{\delta_a} \, \Delta\delta_a + L_{\delta_r} \, \Delta\delta_r$$

$$-N_v \, \Delta v - \left(\frac{I_{xz}}{I_z}\frac{d}{dt} + N_p\right) \Delta p + \left(\frac{d}{dt} - N_r\right) \Delta r = N_{\delta_a} \, \Delta\delta_a + N_{\delta_r} \, \Delta\delta_r$$

3.6
AERODYNAMIC FORCE AND MOMENT REPRESENTATION

In previous sections we represented the aerodynamic force and moment contributions by means of the aerodynamic stability coefficients. We did this without explaining the rationale behind the approach.

The method of representing the aerodynamic forces and moments by stability coefficients was first introduced by Bryan over three-quarters of a century ago [3.1, 3.3]. The technique proposed by Bryan assumes that the aerodynamic forces and moments can be expressed as a function of the instantaneous values of the perturbation variables. The perturbation variables are the instantaneous changes from the reference conditions of the translational velocities, angular velocities, control deflection, and their derivatives. With this assumption, we can express the aerodynamic forces and moments by means of a Taylor series expansion of the perturbation variables about the reference equilibrium condition. For example, the change in the force in the x direction can be expressed as follows:

$$\Delta X(u, \dot{u}, w, \dot{w}, \ldots, \delta_e, \dot{\delta}_e)$$

$$= \frac{\partial X}{\partial u} \Delta u + \frac{\partial X}{\partial \dot{u}} \Delta\dot{u} + \cdots + \frac{\partial X}{\partial \delta_e} \Delta\delta_e + \text{H.O.T. (higher order terms)} \tag{3.50}$$

The term $\partial X/\partial u$, called the stability derivative, is evaluated at the reference flight condition.

The contribution of the change in the velocity u to the change ΔX in the X force is just $[\partial X/\partial u] \, \Delta u$. We can also express $\partial X/\partial u$ in terms of the stability coefficient C_{x_u} as follows:

$$\frac{\partial X}{\partial u} = C_{x_u} \frac{1}{u_0} QS \tag{3.51}$$

where
$$C_{x_u} = \frac{\partial C_x}{\partial(u/u_0)} \tag{3.52}$$

Note that the stability derivative has dimensions, whereas the stability coefficient is defined so that it is nondimensional.

The preceding discussion may seem as though we are making the aerodynamic force and moment representation extremely complicated. However, by assuming that the perturbations are small we need to retain only the linear terms in Equation (3.50). Even though we have retained only the linear terms, the expressions still may include numerous first-order terms. Fortunately, many of these terms also can be neglected because their contribution to a particular force or moment is negligible. For example, we have examined the pitching moment in detail in Chapter 2. If we express the pitching moment in terms of the perturbation variables, as indicated next,

$$M(u, v, w, \dot{u}, \dot{v}, \dot{w}, p, q, r, \delta_a, \delta_e, \delta_r)$$

$$= \frac{\partial M}{\partial u} \Delta u + \frac{\partial M}{\partial u} \Delta v + \frac{\partial M}{\partial w} \delta w + \cdots + \frac{\partial M}{\partial p} \Delta p + \cdots \tag{3.53}$$

it should be quite obvious that terms such as $(\partial M/\partial v) \Delta v$ and $(\partial M/\partial p) \Delta p$ are not going to be significant for an airplane. Therefore, we can neglect these terms in our analysis.

In the following sections, we shall use the stability derivative approach to represent the aerodynamic forces and moments acting on the airplane. The expressions developed for each of the forces and moments will include only the terms usually important in studying the airplane's motion. The remaining portion of this chapter is devoted to presentation of methods for predicting the longitudinal and lateral stability coefficients. We will confine our discussion to methods that are applicable to subsonic flight speeds. Note that many of the stability coefficients vary significantly with the Mach number. This can be seen by examining the data on the A-4D airplane in Appendix B or by examining Figure 3.6.

We have developed a number of relationships for estimating the various stability coefficients; for example, expressions for some of the static stability coefficients such as C_{m_α}, C_{n_β} and C_{l_β} were formulated in Chapter 2. Developing prediction methods for all of the stability derivatives necessary for performing vehicle motion analysis would be beyond the scope of this book. Therefore, we shall confine our attention to the development of several important dynamic derivatives and simply refer the reader to the *US Air Force Stability and Control DATCOM* [3.4]. This report is a comprehensive collection of aerodynamic stability and control prediction techniques, which is widely used through the aviation industry.

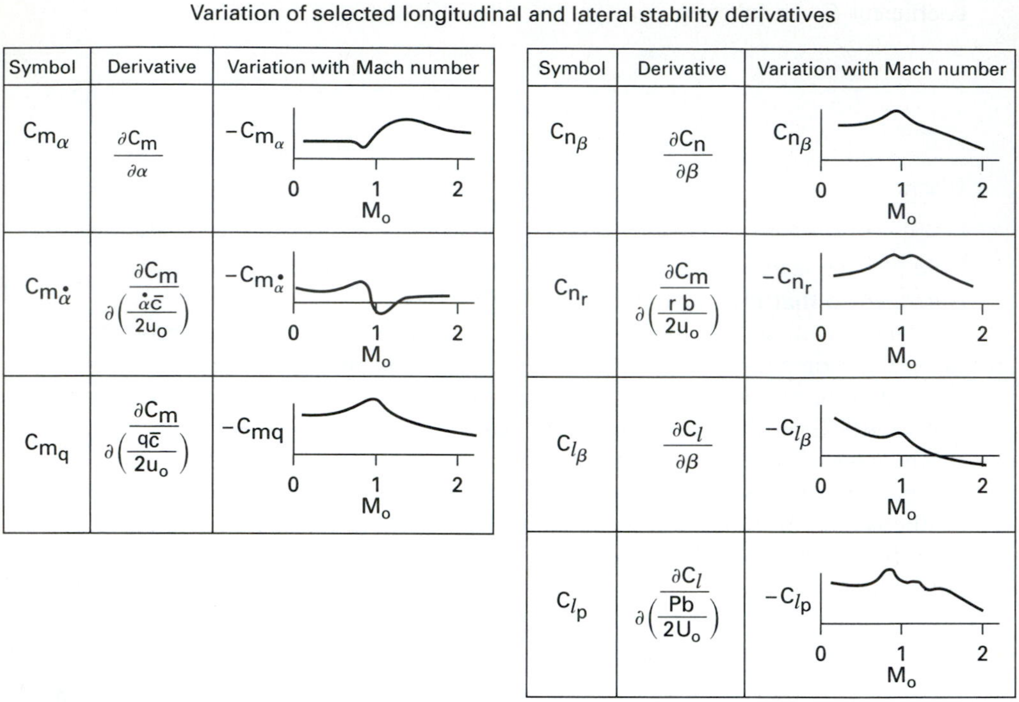

Variation of selected longitudinal and lateral stability derivatives

Symbol	Derivative	Variation with Mach number	Symbol	Derivative	Variation with Mach number
C_{m_α}	$\dfrac{\partial C_m}{\partial \alpha}$	$-C_{m_\alpha}$ 0 1 2 M_o	C_{n_β}	$\dfrac{\partial C_n}{\partial \beta}$	C_{n_β} 0 1 2 M_o
$C_{m_{\dot\alpha}}$	$\dfrac{\partial C_m}{\partial\left(\dfrac{\dot\alpha \bar c}{2u_0}\right)}$	$-C_{m_{\dot\alpha}}$ 0 1 2 M_o	C_{n_r}	$\dfrac{\partial C_m}{\partial\left(\dfrac{r\,b}{2u_0}\right)}$	$-C_{n_r}$ 0 1 2 M_o
C_{m_q}	$\dfrac{\partial C_m}{\partial\left(\dfrac{q\bar c}{2u_0}\right)}$	$-C_{mq}$ 0 1 2 M_o	C_{l_β}	$\dfrac{\partial C_l}{\partial \beta}$	$-C_{l_\beta}$ 0 1 2 M_o
			C_{l_p}	$\dfrac{\partial C_l}{\partial\left(\dfrac{P\,b}{2U_0}\right)}$	$-C_{l_p}$ 0 1 2 M_o

FIGURE 3.6
Variation of selected longitudinal and lateral derivatives with the Mach number.

3.6.1 Derivatives Due to the Change in Forward Speed

The drag, lift, and pitching moments vary with changes in the airplane's forward speed. In addition the thrust of the airplane is also a function of the forward speed. The aerodynamic and propulsive forces acting on the airplane along the X body axes are the drag force and the thrust. The change in the X force, that is, ΔX due to a change in forward speed, can be expressed as

$$\Delta X = \frac{\partial X}{\partial u}\Delta u = -\frac{\partial D}{\partial u}\Delta u + \frac{\partial T}{\partial u}\Delta u \qquad (3.54)$$

or
$$\frac{\partial X}{\partial u} = -\frac{\partial D}{\partial u} + \frac{\partial T}{\partial u} \qquad (3.55)$$

The derivative $\partial X/\partial u$ is called the speed damping derivative. Equation (3.55) can be rewritten as

$$\frac{\partial X}{\partial u} = -\frac{\rho S}{2}\left(u_0^2\,\frac{\partial C_D}{\partial u} + 2u_0\,C_{D_0}\right) + \frac{\partial T}{\partial u} \qquad (3.56)$$

where the subscript 0 indicates the reference condition. Expressing $\partial X/\partial u$ in coefficient form yields

$$C_{X_u} = -(C_{D_u} + 2C_{D_0}) + C_{T_u} \tag{3.57}$$

where $\quad\quad C_{D_u} = \dfrac{\partial C_D}{\partial(u/u_0)} \quad$ and $\quad C_{T_u} = \dfrac{\partial C_T}{\partial(u/u_0)} \tag{3.58}$

are the changes in the drag and thrust coefficients with forward speed. These coefficients have been made nondimensional by differentiating with respect to (u/u_0). The coefficient C_{D_u} can be estimated from a plot of the drag coefficient versus the Mach number:

$$C_{D_u} = \mathbf{M}\,\frac{\partial C_D}{\partial \mathbf{M}} \tag{3.59}$$

where $\mathbf{M}$ is the Mach number of interest. The thrust term C_{T_u} is 0 for gliding flight; it also is a good approximation for jet powered aircraft. For a variable pitch propeller and piston engine power plant, C_{T_u} can be approximated by assuming it to be equal to the negative of the reference drag coefficient (i.e., $C_{T_u} = -C_{D_0}$).

The change in the Z force with respect to forward speed can be shown to be

$$\frac{\partial Z}{\partial u} = -\frac{1}{2}\,\rho S u_0[C_{L_u} + 2C_{L_0}] \tag{3.60}$$

or in coefficient form as

$$C_{Z_u} = -[C_{L_u} + 2C_{L_0}] \tag{3.61}$$

The coefficient C_{L_u} arises form the change in lift coefficient with the Mach number. C_{L_u} can be estimated from the Prandtl-Glauent formula, which corrects the incompressible lift coefficient for the Mach number effects:

$$C_L = \frac{C_L|_{M=0}}{\sqrt{1 - \mathbf{M}^2}} \tag{3.62}$$

Differentiating the list coefficient with respect to the Mach number yields

$$\frac{\partial C_L}{\partial \mathbf{M}} = \frac{\mathbf{M}}{1 - \mathbf{M}^2}\,C_L \tag{3.63}$$

but $\quad\quad C_{L_u} = \dfrac{\partial C_L}{\partial(u/u_0)} = \dfrac{u_o}{a}\,\dfrac{\partial C_L}{\partial\left(\dfrac{u}{a}\right)} \tag{3.64}$

$$= \mathbf{M}\,\frac{\partial C_L}{\partial \mathbf{M}} \tag{3.65}$$

where a is the speed of sound.

C_{L_u} therefore can be expressed as

$$C_{L_u} = \frac{\mathbf{M}^2}{1 - \mathbf{M}^2}\,C_{L_0} \tag{3.66}$$

This coefficient can be neglected at low flight speeds but can become quite large near the critical Mach number for the airplane.

The change in the pitching moment due to variations in the forward speed can be expressed as

$$\Delta M = \frac{\partial M}{\partial u} \Delta u \tag{3.67}$$

or

$$\frac{\partial M}{\partial u} = C_{m_u} \rho \, S \bar{c} u_0 \tag{3.68}$$

The coefficient C_{m_u} can be estimated as follows:

$$C_{m_u} = \frac{\partial C_m}{\partial \mathbf{M}} \mathbf{M} \tag{3.69}$$

The coefficient C_{m_u} depends on the Mach number but also is affected by the elastic properties of the airframe. At high speeds aeroelastic bending of the airplane can cause large changes in the magnitude of C_{m_u}.

3.6.2 Derivatives Due to the Pitching Velocity, q

The stability coefficients C_{z_q} and C_{m_q} represent the change in the Z force and pitching moment coefficients with respect to the pitching velocity q. The aerodynamic characteristics of both the wing and the horizontal tail are affected by the pitching motion of the airplane. The wing contribution usually is quite small in comparison to that produced by the tail. A common practice is to compute the tail contribution and then increase it by 10 percent to account for the wing. Figure 3.7 shows an airplane undergoing a pitching motion.

As illustrated in Figure 3.7, the pitching rate q causes a change in the angle of attack at the tail, which results in a change in the lift force acting on the tail:

$$\Delta L_t = C_{L_{\alpha_t}} \Delta \alpha_t Q_t S_t \tag{3.70}$$

or

$$\Delta Z = -\Delta L_t = -C_{L_{\alpha_t}} \frac{q l_t}{u_0} Q_t S_t \tag{3.71}$$

$$C_Z = \frac{Z}{QS} \tag{3.72}$$

$$\Delta C_Z = -C_{L_{\alpha_t}} \frac{q l_t}{u_0} \eta \frac{S_t}{S} \tag{3.73}$$

$$C_{Z_q} \equiv \frac{\partial C_z}{\partial (q\bar{c}/2u_0)} = \frac{2u_0}{\bar{c}} \frac{\partial C_z}{\partial q} \tag{3.74}$$

$$C_{z_q} = -2C_{L_{\alpha_t}} \eta V_H \tag{3.75}$$

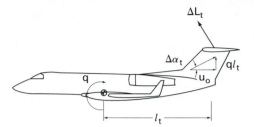

FIGURE 3.7
Mechanism for aerodynamic force due to pitch rate.

The pitching moment due to the change in lift on the tail can be calculated as follows:

$$\Delta M_{cg} = -l_t \, \Delta L_t \tag{3.76}$$

$$\Delta C_{m_{cg}} = -V_H \, \eta C_{L_{\alpha_t}} \frac{q l_t}{u_0} \tag{3.77}$$

$$C_{m_q} \equiv \frac{\partial C_m}{\partial (q\bar{c}/2u_0)} = \frac{2u_0}{\bar{c}} \frac{\partial C_m}{\partial q} \tag{3.78}$$

$$C_{m_q} = -2C_{L_{\alpha_t}} \eta V_H \frac{l_t}{\bar{c}} \tag{3.79}$$

Equations (3.75) and (3.79) represent the tail contribution to C_{z_q} and C_{m_q}, respectively. The coefficients for the complete airplane are obtained by increasing the tail values by 10 percent to account for the wing and fuselage contributions.

3.6.3 Derivatives Due to the Time Rate of Change of the Angle of Attack

The stability coefficients $C_{z_{\dot{\alpha}}}$ and $C_{m_{\dot{\alpha}}}$ arise because of the lag in the wing downwash getting to the tail. As the wing angle of attack changes, the circulation around the wing will be altered. The change in circulation alters the downwash at the tail; however, it takes a finite time for the alteration to occur. Figure 3.8 illustrates the lag in flow field development. If the airplane is traveling with a forward velocity u_0, then a change in circulation imparted to the trailing vortex wake will take the increment in time $\Delta t = l_t/u_0$ to reach the tail surface.

The lag in angle of attack at the tail can be expressed as

$$\Delta \alpha_t = \frac{d\varepsilon}{dt} \Delta t \tag{3.80}$$

where

$$\Delta t = l_t/u_0 \tag{3.81}$$

or

$$\Delta \alpha_t = \frac{d\varepsilon}{dt} \frac{l_t}{u_0} = \frac{d\varepsilon}{d\alpha} \frac{d\alpha}{dt} \frac{l_t}{u_0} \tag{3.82}$$

$$= \frac{d\varepsilon}{d\alpha} \dot{\alpha} \frac{l_t}{u_0} \tag{3.83}$$

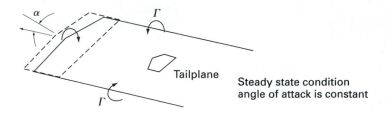

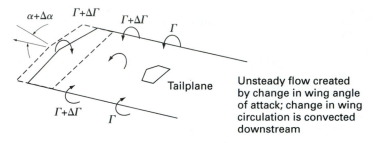

FIGURE 3.8
Mechanism for aerodynamic force due to the lag in flow field
development.

The change in the lift force can be expressed as

$$\Delta L_t = C_{L_{\alpha_t}} \, \Delta\alpha_t \, Q_t S_t \tag{3.84}$$

or in terms of the z force coefficient

$$\Delta C_z = -\frac{\Delta L_t}{QS} = -C_{L_{\alpha_t}} \, \Delta\alpha_t \, \eta \, \frac{S_t}{S} \tag{3.85}$$

$$= -C_{L_{\alpha_t}} \frac{d\varepsilon}{d\alpha} \, \dot\alpha \, \frac{l_t}{u_0} \, \eta \, \frac{S_t}{S} \tag{3.86}$$

$$C_{Z_{\dot\alpha}} \equiv \frac{\partial C_z}{\partial(\dot\alpha\bar c/2u_0)} = \frac{2u_0}{\bar c} \frac{\partial C_z}{\partial\dot\alpha} \tag{3.87}$$

$$= -2V_H \eta C_{L_{\alpha_t}} \frac{d\varepsilon}{d\alpha} \tag{3.88}$$

The pitching moment due to the lag in the downwash field can be calculated as
follows:

$$\Delta M_{cg} = -l_t \, \Delta L_t = -l_t C_{L_{\alpha_t}} \, \Delta\alpha_t \, Q_t S_t \tag{3.89}$$

$$\Delta C_{m_{cg}} = -V_H \eta C_{L_{\alpha_t}} \frac{d\varepsilon}{d\alpha} \, \dot\alpha \, \frac{l_t}{u_0} \tag{3.90}$$

$$C_{m_{\dot{\alpha}}} = \frac{\partial C_m}{\partial(\dot{\alpha}\overline{c}/2u_0)} = \frac{2u_0}{\overline{c}}\frac{\partial C_m}{\partial\dot{\alpha}} \tag{3.91}$$

$$= -2C_{L_{\alpha_t}}\eta V_H \frac{l_t}{\overline{c}}\frac{d\varepsilon}{d\alpha} \tag{3.92}$$

Equations (3.89) and (3.92) yield only the tail contribution to these stability coefficients. To obtain an estimate for the complete airplane these coefficients are increased by 10 percent. A summary of the equations for estimating the longitudinal stability coefficients is included in Table 3.3.

3.6.4 Derivative Due to the Rolling Rate, *p*

The stability coefficients C_{y_p}, C_{n_p}, and C_{l_p} arise due to the rolling angular velocity, p. When an airplane rolls about its longitudinal axis, the roll rate creates a linear velocity distribution over the vertical, horizontal, and wing surfaces. The velocity distribution causes a local change in angle of attack over each of these surfaces that results in a change in the lift distribution and, consequently, the moment about the center of gravity. In this section we will examine how the roll rate creates a rolling moment. Figure 3.9 shows a wing planform rolling with a positive rolling velocity. On the portion of the wing rolling down, an increase in angle of attack is created by the rolling motion. This results in an increase in the lift distribution over the downward-moving wing. If we examine the upward-moving part of the wing we observe that the rolling velocity causes a decrease in the local angle of attack and

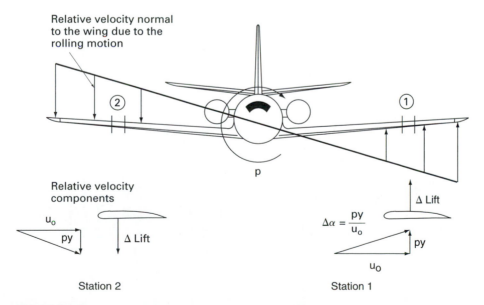

FIGURE 3.9
Wing planform undergoing a rolling motion.

TABLE 3.3
Equations for estimating the longitudinal stability coefficients

	X-force derivatives	Z-force derivatives	Pitching moment derivatives
u	$C_{X_u} = -[C_{D_u} + 2C_{D_0}] + C_{T_u}$	$C_{Z_u} = -\dfrac{M^2}{1 - M^2} C_{L_0} - 2C_{L_0}$	$C_{m_u} = \dfrac{\partial C_m}{\partial M} M_0$
α	$C_{X_\alpha} = C_{L_0} - \dfrac{2C_{L_0}\,C_{L\alpha}}{\pi e\; AR}$	$C_{Z_\alpha} = -(C_{L\alpha} + C_{D0})$	$C_{m\alpha} = C_{L_{0w}}\left(\dfrac{x_{cg}}{c} - \dfrac{X_{ac}}{c}\right) + C_{m_{a\,\text{fus}}} - \eta V_H C_{L\alpha t}\left(1 - \dfrac{d\varepsilon}{d\alpha}\right)$
$\dot\alpha$	0	$C_{Z\dot\alpha} = -2\eta C_{L\alpha t}\,V_H\,\dfrac{d\varepsilon}{d\alpha}$	$C_{m\dot\alpha} = -2\eta C_{L\alpha t}\,V_H\,\dfrac{l_t}{c}\dfrac{d\varepsilon}{d\alpha}$
q	0	$C_{Z_q} = -2\eta C_{L\alpha t}\,V_H$	$C_{m_q} = -2\eta C_{L\alpha t}\,V_H\,\dfrac{l_t}{c}$
α_e	0	$C_{Z\delta_e} = -C_{L\delta_e} = -\dfrac{S_t}{S}\,\eta\,\dfrac{dC_{L_t}}{d\delta_e}$	$C_{m\delta_e} = -\eta V_H\,\dfrac{dC_{L_t}}{d\delta_e}$

Subscript 0 indicates reference values and M is the Mach number.

AR	Aspect ratio
C_{D0}	Reference drag coefficient
$C_{L\alpha}$	Reference lift coefficient
$C_{L\alpha}$	Airplane lift curve slope
$C_{L_{0w}}$	Wing lift curve slope
$C_{L\alpha t}$	Tail lift curve slope
$\dfrac{}{c}$	Mean aerodynamic chord
e	Oswald's span efficiency factor
l_t	Distance from center of gravity to tail quarter chord
V_H	Horizontal tail volume ratio
M	Flight mach number
S	Wing area
S_t	Horizontal tail area
$\dfrac{d\varepsilon}{d\alpha}$	Change in downwash due to a change in angle of attack
η	Efficiency factor of the horizontal tail

116

the lift distribution decreases. The change in the lift distribution across the wing produces a rolling moment that opposes the rolling motion and is proportional to the roll rate, p. In Figure 3.9 the negative rolling velocity induces a positive rolling moment.

An estimate of the rolling damping derivative, C_{l_p}, due to the wing surface can be developed in the following manner. The incremental lift force created by rolling motion can be expressed as

$$d(\text{Lift}) = C_{l_\alpha} \Delta\alpha Qc \, dy \qquad (3.93)$$

where $\Delta\alpha = py/u_0$.

The incremental roll moment can be estimated by multiplying the incremental lift by the moment arm y:

$$dL = -C_{l_\alpha}\left(\frac{py}{u_0}\right)Qcy \, dy \qquad (3.94)$$

The total roll moment now can be calculated by integrating the moment contribution across the wing:

$$L = -2 \int_0^{b/2} C_{l_\alpha}\left(\frac{py}{u_0}\right) Qcy \, dy \qquad (3.95)$$

or in coefficient form

$$C_l = -\frac{2p}{Sbu_0} \int_0^{b/2} C_{l_\alpha} cy^2 \, dy \qquad (3.96)$$

To simplify this integral, the sectional lift curve slope is approximated by the wing lift curve slope as follows:

$$C_l = -\frac{2C_{L_{\alpha_w}}}{Sb}\left(\frac{p}{u_0}\right) \int_0^{b/2} cy^2 \, dy \qquad (3.97)$$

The roll damping coefficient C_{l_p} is defined in terms of a nondimensional roll rate:

$$C_{l_p} \equiv \frac{\partial C_l}{\partial\left(\dfrac{pb}{2u_0}\right)} \qquad (3.98)$$

Differentiating Equation (3.98) yields

$$C_{l_p} = -\frac{4C_{L_{\alpha_w}}}{Sb^2} \int_0^{b/2} cy^2 \, dy \qquad (3.99)$$

which provides an estimate to C_{l_p}, the roll damping coefficient due to wing surface. From this simple analysis we readily can see that C_{l_p} depends on the wing span. Wings of large span or high aspect ratio will have larger roll damping than low aspect ratio wings of small wing span.

The roll damping of the airplane is made up of contributions from the wing, horizontal, and vertical tail surfaces. The wing, typically being the largest aerodynamic surface, provides most of the roll damping. This is not necessarily the case for aircraft having low aspect ratio wings or missile configurations; for these configurations, the other components may contribute as much to the roll damping coefficients as the wing.

3.6.5 Derivative Due to the Yawing Rate, r

The stability coefficient C_{y_r}, C_{n_r}, and C_{l_r} are caused by the yawing angular velocity, r. A yawing rate causes a change in the side force acting on the vertical tail surface as illustrated in Figure 3.10. As in the case of the other angular rate coefficients the angular motion creates a local change in the angle of attack or in this case a change in sideslip angle of the vertical tail.

A positive yaw rate produces a negative sideslip angle on the vertical tail. The side force created by the negative sideslip angle is in the positive direction:

$$Y = -C_{L_{\alpha_v}} \Delta\beta \, Q_v \, S_v \tag{3.100}$$

where $\Delta\beta = -rl_v/u_0$ for a positive yawing rate. Rewritting Equation (3.100) in coefficient form yields

$$C_y = \frac{C_{L_{\alpha_v}}\left(\dfrac{rl_v}{u_0}\right)Q_v \, S_v}{QS} \tag{3.101}$$

$$= C_{L_{\alpha_v}}\left(\frac{rl_v}{u_0}\right)\eta_v \frac{S_v}{S} \tag{3.102}$$

The stability coefficient C_{y_r} is defined in terms of the nondimensional yaw rate as follows:

$$C_{y_r} \equiv \frac{\partial C_y}{\partial\left(\dfrac{rb}{2u_0}\right)} \tag{3.103}$$

Taking the derivative of C_y with respect to $rb/2u_0$ yields

$$C_{y_r} = 2C_{L_{\alpha_v}} \eta_v \frac{S_v}{S} \frac{l_v}{b} \tag{3.104}$$

The term $C_{L_{\alpha_v}} \eta_v \dfrac{S_v}{S}$ is approximately $-C_{y\beta_{\text{tail}}}$; therefore,

$$C_{y_r} = -2C_{y_{\beta_{\text{tail}}}} \frac{l_v}{b} \tag{3.105}$$

The stability coefficients, C_{n_r}, which is the change in yaw moment coefficient with respect to a nondimensional yaw rate $rb/(2u_0)$, is made up of contributions from the wing and the vertical tail. The vertical tail contribution is derived next. The yaw moment produced by the yawing rate is a result of the sideslip angle induced on the vertical tail. A positive yaw rate produces a negative sideslip at the

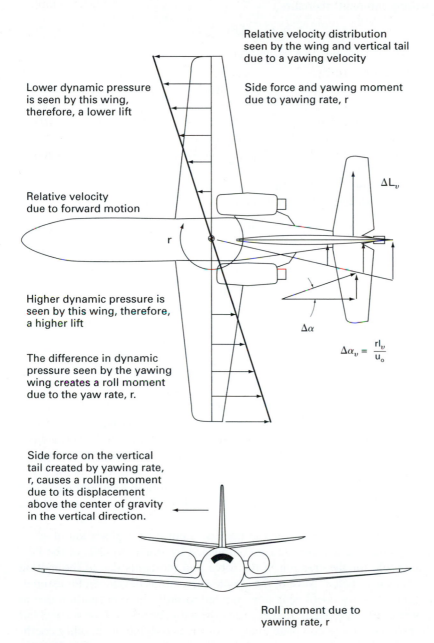

FIGURE 3.10
Influence of the yawing rate on the wing and vertical tail.

vertical tail or a positive side force on the tail. A positive side force causes a negative yawing moment; therefore,

$$N = C_{L_{\alpha_v}} \Delta\beta Q_v S_v l_v \tag{3.106}$$

But $\Delta\beta = -rl_v/u_0$ for a positive yawing rate:

$$N = -C_{L_{\alpha_v}} \left(\frac{rl_v}{u_0}\right) Q_v S_v l_v \tag{3.107}$$

Or in coefficient form

$$C_n = -C_{L_{\alpha_v}} \left(\frac{rl_v}{u_0}\right) \eta_v V_v \tag{3.108}$$

where $\eta_v = Q_v/Q$ and $V_v = S_v l_v/Sb$,
    The stability coefficient C_{n_r} is defined as

$$C_{n_r} \equiv \frac{\partial C_n}{\partial\left(\dfrac{rb}{2u_0}\right)} \tag{3.109}$$

$$= -2C_{L_{\alpha_v}} \eta_v V_v \frac{l_v}{b} \tag{3.110}$$

The vertical tail contribution to C_{n_r} also can expressed in terms of the side force coefficient with respect to sideslip:

$$C_{n_r} \simeq 2C_{y_{\beta_{\text{tail}}}} \left(\frac{l_v}{b}\right)^2 \tag{3.111}$$

The yaw rate, r, also produces a roll moment. The stability coefficient C_{l_r} is due to both the wing and the vertical tail. An expression for estimating C_{l_r} is given in Table 3.4. As shown earlier the yawing rate creates a side force on the vertical tail that is proportional to the yaw rate, r. Because this force acts above the center of gravity a rolling moment is created. The contribution of the wing to C_{l_r} is due to the change in velocity across the wing in the plane of the motion. Development of an expression for C_{l_r} due to the wing and the vertical tail is left as an exercise problem at the end of this chapter.
    In this section we have attempted to provide a physical explanation of some of the stability coefficients. This was accomplished by simple models of the flow physics responsible for the creation of the force and moments due to the motion variables such as p, q, and r . Most of the simple expressions developed for estimating a particular stability coefficient were limited to only the contribution due to the primary aircraft component; that is, either the wing, horizontal, or vertical tail surface. To provide a more complete analysis of the aerodynamic stability coefficients a more detailed analysis is required than has been presented in this chapter. References [3.4] and [3.5] provide a more complete set of stability and control prediction methods.
    The stability coefficients C_{l_p}, C_{n_r}, C_{z_q}, C_{m_q}, C_{z_α}, and C_{m_α} all oppose the motion of the vehicle and thus can be considered as damping terms. This will become more apparent as we analyze the motion of an airplane in Chapters 4 and 5.

TABLE 3.4
Equations for estimating the lateral stability coefficients

	Y-force derivatives	Yawing moment derivatives	Rolling moment derivatives
β	$C_{y_\beta} = -\eta\dfrac{S_v}{S}C_{L\alpha_v}\left(1 + \dfrac{d\sigma}{d\beta}\right)$	$C_{n_\beta} = C_{n_{\beta wf}} + \eta_v V_v C_{L\alpha_v}\left(1 + \dfrac{d\sigma}{d\beta}\right)$	$C_{l_\beta} = \left(\dfrac{C_{l_\beta}}{\Gamma}\right)\Gamma + \Delta C_{l_\beta}$ (see Figure 3.11)
p	$C_{y_p} = C_L\dfrac{AR + \cos\Lambda}{AR + 4\cos\Lambda}\tan\Lambda$	$C_{n_p} = -\dfrac{C_L}{8}$	$C_{l_p} = -\dfrac{C_{L\alpha}}{12}\dfrac{1 + 3\lambda}{1 + \lambda}$
r	$C_{y_r} = -2\left(\dfrac{l_v}{b}\right)(C_{y_\beta})_{\text{tail}}$	$C_{n_r} = -2\eta_v V_v\left(\dfrac{l_v}{b}\right)C_{L\alpha_v}$	$C_{l_r} = \dfrac{C_L}{4} - 2\dfrac{l_v}{b}\dfrac{z_v}{b}C_{y_{\beta\text{tail}}}$
δ_a	0	$C_{n_{\delta_a}} = 2KC_{L0}C_{l_{\delta_a}}$ (see Figure 3.12)	$C_{l_{\delta_a}} = \dfrac{2C_{L\alpha}\tau}{Sb}\displaystyle\int_{y_1}^{y_2} cy\,dy$
δ_r	$C_{y_{\delta_r}} = \dfrac{S_v}{S}\tau C_{L\alpha_v}$	$C_{n_{\delta_r}} = -V_v\eta_v\tau C_{L\alpha_v}$	$C_{l_{\delta_r}} = \dfrac{S_v}{S}\left(\dfrac{z_v}{b}\right)\tau C_{L\alpha_w}$

AR	Aspect ratio
b	Wingspan
C_{L0}	Reference lift coefficient
$C_{L\alpha}$	Airplane lift curve slope
$C_{L\alpha_w}$	Wing lift curve slope
$C_{L\alpha_v}$	Tail lift curve slope
$\bar{c}$	Mean aerodynamic chord
K	empirical factor
l_v	Distance from center of gravity to vertical tail aerodynamic center
V_v	Vertical tail volume ratio
S	Wing area
S_v	Vertical tail area
z_v	Distance from center of pressure of vertical tail to fuselage centerline
Γ	Wing dihedral angle
Λ	Wing sweep angle
η_v	Efficiency factor of the vertical tail
λ	Taper ratio (tip chord/root chord)
$\dfrac{d\sigma}{d\beta}$	Change in sidewash angle with a change in sideslip angle

121

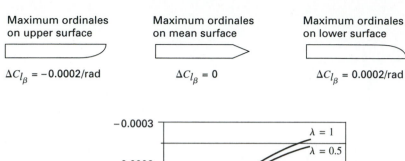

Maximum ordinales
on upper surface

$\Delta C_{l_\beta} = -0.0002/\text{rad}$

Maximum ordinales
on mean surface

$\Delta C_{l_\beta} = 0$

Maximum ordinales
on lower surface

$\Delta C_{l_\beta} = 0.0002/\text{rad}$

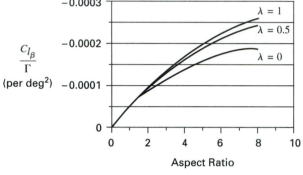

FIGURE 3.11
Tip shape and aspect ratio effect on C_{l_β}.

$$\eta = \frac{Y_1}{b_w/2} = \frac{\text{Spanwise distance from centerline to the inboard edge of the aileron control}}{\text{Semispan}}$$

FIGURE 3.12
Empirical factor for $C_{n_{\delta_a}}$ estimate.

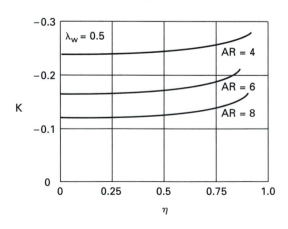

TABLE 3.5
Summary of longitudinal derivatives

$$X_u = \frac{-(C_{D_u} + 2C_{D_0})QS}{mu_0} \, (\text{s}^{-1}) \qquad X_w = \frac{-(C_{D_\alpha} - C_{L_0})QS}{mu_0} \, (\text{s}^{-1})$$

$$Z_u = \frac{-(C_{L_u} + 2C_{L_0})QS}{mu_0} \, (\text{s}^{-1})$$

$$Z_w = \frac{-(C_{L_\alpha} + C_{D_0})QS}{mu_0} \, (\text{s}^{-1}) \qquad Z_{\dot{w}} = -C_{z_{\dot\alpha}} \frac{c}{2u_0} QS/(u_0 m)$$

$$Z_\alpha = u_0 Z_{\dot w} \, (\text{ft/s}^2) \text{ or } (\text{m/s}^2) \qquad Z_{\dot\alpha} = u_0 Z_{\dot w} \, (\text{ft/s}) \text{ or } (\text{m/s})$$

$$Z_q = -C_{Z_q} \frac{c}{2u_0} QS/m \, (\text{ft/s}) \text{ or } (\text{m/s}) \qquad Z_{\delta_e} = -C_{Z_{\delta_e}} QS/m \, (\text{ft/s}^2)$$

$$M_u = C_{m_u} \frac{(QSc)}{u_0 I_y} \left(\frac{1}{\text{ft} \cdot \text{s}}\right) \text{ or } \left(\frac{1}{\text{m} \cdot \text{s}}\right)$$

$$M_w = C_{m_\alpha} \frac{(QS\bar c)}{u_0 I_y} \left(\frac{1}{\text{ft} \cdot \text{s}}\right) \text{ or } \left(\frac{1}{\text{m} \cdot \text{s}}\right) \qquad M_{\dot w} = C_{m_{\dot\alpha}} \frac{\bar c}{2u_0} \frac{QS\bar c}{u_0 I_y} \, (\text{ft}^{-1})$$

$$M_\alpha = u_0 M_w \, (\text{s}^{-2}) \qquad M_{\dot\alpha} = u_0 M_{\dot w} \, (\text{s}^{-1})$$

$$M_q = C_{m_q} \frac{\bar c}{2u_0} (QS\bar c)/I_y \, (\text{s}^{-1}) \qquad M_{\delta_e} = C_{m_{\delta_e}}(QS\bar c)/I_y \, (\text{s}^{-2})$$

TABLE 3.6
Summary of lateral directional derivatives

$$Y_\beta = \frac{QSC_{y\beta}}{m} \, (\text{ft/s}^2) \text{ or } (\text{m/s}^2) \qquad N_\beta = \frac{QSbC_{n\beta}}{I_z} \, (\text{s}^{-2}) \qquad L_\beta = \frac{QSbC_{l\beta}}{I_x} \, (\text{s}^{-2})$$

$$Y_p = \frac{QSbC_{yp}}{2mu_0} \, (\text{ft/s}) \, (\text{m/s}) \qquad N_p = \frac{QSb^2 C_{np}}{2I_x u_0} \, (\text{s}^{-1}) \qquad L_p = \frac{QSb^2 C_{lp}}{2I_x u_0} \, (\text{s}^{-1})$$

$$Y_r = \frac{QSbC_{yr}}{2mu_0} \, (\text{ft/s}) \text{ or } (\text{m/s}) \qquad N_r = \frac{QSb^2 C_{nr}}{2I_x u_0} \, (\text{s}^{-1}) \qquad L_r = \frac{QSb^2 C_{lr}}{2I_x u_0} \, (\text{s}^{-1})$$

$$Y_{\delta_a} = \frac{QSC_{y\delta_a}}{m} \, (\text{ft/s}^2) \text{ or } (\text{m/s}^2) \qquad Y_{\delta_r} = \frac{QSC_{y\delta_r}}{m} \, (\text{ft/s}^2) \text{ or } (\text{m/s}^2)$$

$$N_{\delta_a} = \frac{QSbC_{n\delta_a}}{I_z} \, (\text{s}^{-2}) \qquad N_{\delta_r} = \frac{QSbC_{n\delta_r}}{I_z} \, (\text{s}^{-2})$$

$$L_{\delta_a} = \frac{QSbC_{l\delta_a}}{I_x} \, (\text{s}^{-2}) \qquad L_{\delta_r} = \frac{QSbC_{l\delta_r}}{I_x} \, (\text{s}^{-2})$$

As noted earlier, there are many more derivatives for which we could develop prediction methods. The few simple examples presented here should give the reader an appreciation of how one would go about determining estimates of the aerodynamic stability coefficients. A summary of some of the theoretical prediction methods for some of the more important lateral and longitudinal stability coefficients is presented in Tables 3.3 and 3.4. Tables 3.5 and 3.6 summarize the longitidinal and lateral derivatives.

EXAMPLE PROBLEM 3.1. Estimate the longitudinal stability derivatives for the STOL transport described in Appendix B. A summary of the mass, geometric, and aerodynamic characteristics of the airplane were obtained from [3.6] and are given in Table 3.7.

Solution. The stability coefficients, $C_{x_u}, C_{x_\alpha}, C_{z_u}, C_{z_\alpha}, C_{z_{\dot\alpha}}, C_{z_q}, C_{z_{\delta_e}}, C_{m_u}, C_{m_\alpha}, C_{m_{\dot\alpha}}, C_{m_q}$, and $C_{m_{\delta_e}}$ can be calculated from the formulas given in Table 3.3. Because we are considering a low-speed flight condition, the terms related to the Mach number can be ignored; for example, $\partial C_m/\partial M$ and C_{D_u}, The stability coefficient for the STOL transport are calculated next.

The change in the X force coefficient, C_x, with respect to a change in the forward speed is given by

$$C_{x_u} = -(C_{D_u} + 2C_{D_0}) + C_{T_u}$$

C_{D_u} is set to 0 and C_{T_u} is assumed to be equal to $-C_{D_0}$ as explained in Section 3.6:

$$C_{x_u} = -3C_{D_0} = -3(0.057) = -0.171$$

TABLE 3.7
Geometric, aerodynamic, and mass data for the STOL transport

Wing area, S, ft²	945	Horizontal tail area, S_t	233
Wing span, b, ft	96	Horizontal tail span, b_t	32
Wing mean aerodynamic chord, $\bar{c}$, ft	10.1	Horizontal tail mean aerodynamic chord, $\bar{c}_t$	7.0
Wing aspect ratio, AR	9.75	Horizontal tail aspect ratio, AR_t	4.4
Location of wing 1/4 root chord on the fuselage, % of fuselage length, l_f	31.6	Horizontal tail moment arm, l_t, distance from center of gravity to tail aricraft characteristics	3.5
Wing lift curve slope, $C_{L_{\alpha_w}}$/rad	5.2	Horizontal tail lift curve slope, $C_{L_{\alpha_t}}$/rad	3.5
Aircraft lift coefficient, C_L	0.77	Elevator area, S_e, ft²	81.5
Span efficiency factor, e	0.75	C_{m_α} due to fuselage and power effects per rad	0.93
Fuselage length, l_f, ft	76	Fuselage width, w_f, ft	9.4
Aircraft weight, W, lbs	40,000	Aircraft altitude, ft	0
Center of gravity location, % $\bar{c}$, ft, measured from leading edge	40	Ambient air density, ρ, slug/ft³	0.00238
Aircraft mass moment of inertia, I_y, slug-ft², measured about center of gravity	21,500	Flight velocity u_0, ft/s	215

The change in the X-force coefficient, C_x, with respect to a change in angle of attack can be estimated from the following formula:

$$C_{x_\alpha} = C_{L_0}\left(1 - \frac{2\,C_{L_\alpha}}{\pi e AR}\right)$$

$$= (0.77)\left[1 - \frac{(2.0)(5.2/\text{rad})}{\pi(0.75)(9.75)}\right] = 0.42/\text{rad}$$

The Z-force coefficient, C_z, with respect to a change in forward speed is given by

$$C_{z_u} = -\left(\frac{\text{M}^2}{1 - \text{M}^2}\right)C_{L_0} - 2C_{L_0}$$

where the first term can be neglected due to the low flight speed:

$$C_{z_u} = -2(0.77) = -1.54$$

The Z-force coefficient, C_z, with respect to a change in angle of attack is given by the expression

$$C_{z_\alpha} = -(C_{L_\alpha} + C_{D_0})$$

$$= -[5.2 + 0.057] = -5.26/\text{rad}$$

The Z-force coefficient, C_z with respect to a change time rate of angle of attack $\dot{\alpha}$, is given by

$$C_{z_{\dot{\alpha}}} = -2C_{L_{\alpha_t}}\eta V_H \frac{d\varepsilon}{d\alpha}$$

The rate of change of the downwash angle with respect to the angle of attack can be estimated using the relationship presented in Section 2.3

$$\frac{d\varepsilon}{d\alpha} = \frac{2C_{L_{\alpha w}}}{\pi AR_w} = \frac{2(5.2/\text{rad})}{\pi(9.75)} = 0.34$$

and the horizontal tail volume ratio, V_H, is defined as

$$V_H = \frac{l_t S_t}{S\bar{c}} = \frac{(46\text{ ft})(233\text{ ft}^2)}{(965\text{ ft}^2)(10.1\text{ ft})} = 1.1$$

The tail efficiency factor, η, is assumed to be equal to unity. With this information we can now calculate $C_{z_{\dot{\alpha}}}$:

$$C_{z_{\dot{\alpha}}} = -2(3.5/\text{rad})(1.0)(1.1)(0.34)$$

or

$$C_{z_{\dot{\alpha}}} = -2.62/\text{rad}.$$

The change in the Z-force coefficient, C_Z, with respect to a nondimensional pitch rate $q\bar{c}/(2u_0)$ is given by

$$C_{z_q} = \frac{\partial C_z}{\partial\left(\dfrac{q\bar{c}}{2u_0}\right)} = -2C_{L_{\alpha_t}}\eta V_H$$

or

$$C_{z_q} = -(2.0)(3.5/\text{rad})(1.1) = -7.7/\text{rad}$$

The Z-force coefficient, C_z, with respect to a change in the elevator angle, δ_e, is given by

$$C_{z_{\delta_e}} = -C_{L_{\alpha_t}} \tau \eta \frac{S_t}{S}$$

The flap effectiveness parameter, τ, can be estimated from Figure 2.21. For the ratio of elevator area to tail plane area, $S_e/S_t = 81.5 \text{ ft}^2/233 \text{ ft}^2 = 0.35$ the flap effectiveness parameter is estimated to be $\tau = 0.55$.

$$C_{z_{\delta_e}} = -(3.5/\text{rad})(0.55)(1.0) \left(\frac{233 \text{ ft}^2}{965 \text{ ft}^2}\right) = -0.46/\text{rad}$$

The rate of change of the pitch moment coefficient, C_m, with respect to a change speed, u, is given by

$$C_{m_u} = \frac{\partial C_m}{\partial M} M_0$$

For low-speed flight $\partial C_m/\partial M$ can be assumed to be 0; therefore, $C_{m_u} = 0$.

The rate of change of the pitching moment coefficient, C_m, with respect to a change in angle of attack, α, is given by

$$C_{m_\alpha} = C_{L_{\alpha w}} \left(\frac{x_{cg}}{\bar{c}} - \frac{x_{ac}}{\bar{c}}\right) + C_{m_{\alpha_{fus}}} - \eta V_H C_{L_{\alpha_t}} \left(1 - \frac{d\varepsilon}{d\alpha}\right)$$

The fuselage contribution to C_{m_α} including power effects was given as $C_{m_{\alpha_{fus}}} = 0.93/\text{rad}$. The wing and tail contribution are added to the fuselage contribution:

$$C_{m_\alpha} = (5.2/\text{rad})(0.4 - 0.25) + 0.93 - (1.0)(1.1)(3.5/\text{rad})(1 - 0.34)$$

$$= -0.83/\text{rad}$$

The stability coefficients C_{m_α}, C_{m_q}, and $C_{m_{\delta_e}}$ are related to the corresponding Z-force coefficients times the ratio of the tail moment over the wing mean chord. For example,

$$C_{m_\alpha} = C_{z_\alpha} \frac{l_t}{\bar{c}} = (-2.62/\text{rad})(4.55) = -11.92/\text{rad}$$

$$C_{m_q} = C_{z_q} \frac{l_t}{\bar{c}} = (-7.7/\text{rad})(4.55) = -35/\text{rad}$$

$$C_{m_{\delta_e}} = C_{z_{\delta_e}} \frac{l_t}{\bar{c}} = (-0.46/\text{rad})(4.55) = -2.09/\text{rad}$$

The dimensional derivatives X_u, X_α, and the like can be estimated from the formulas in Tables 3.5 and 3.6. To complete this problem we need to multiply each stability coefficient by the appropriate parameter. The parameters included in the dimensional derivatives are QS/m, $QS/(mu_0)$, $(\bar{c}/2u_0) QS/m$, $QS\bar{c}/I_y$, or $(\bar{c}/2u_0) QS\bar{c}/I_y$. These

TABLE 3.8
Longitudinal dimensional derivatives for STOL transport

$$X_u = C_{x_u}\left(\frac{1}{u_0}\right)QS/m = -0.0.34/s \qquad M_u = C_{m_u}\left(\frac{1}{u_0}\right)QS\bar{c}/I_y = 0$$

$$X_\alpha = C_{x_\alpha}QS/m = 18.06 \text{ ft/s}^2 \qquad M_\alpha = C_{m_\alpha}QS\bar{c}/I_y = -2.1/s^2$$

$$Z_u = C_{z_u}\left(\frac{1}{u_0}\right)QS/m = -0.308/s \qquad M_{\dot\alpha} = C_{m_{\dot\alpha}}\left(\frac{\bar{c}}{2u_0}\right)QS\bar{c}/I_y = -0.7/s$$

$$Z_\alpha = C_{z_\alpha}QS/m = -226.2 \text{ ft/s}^2 \qquad M_q = C_{m_q}\left(\frac{\bar{c}}{2u_0}\right)QS\bar{c}/I_y = -2.03/s$$

$$Z_{\dot\alpha} = C_{z_{\dot\alpha}}\left(\frac{\bar{c}}{2\bar{u}_0}\right)QS/m = -2.6 \text{ ft/s} \qquad M_{\delta_e} = C_{m_{\delta_e}}QS\bar{c}/I_y = -5.27/s^2$$

$$Z_q = C_{z_q}\left(\frac{\bar{c}}{2\bar{u}_0}\right)QS/m = -7.6 \text{ ft/s}$$

$$Z_{\delta_e} = C_{z_{\delta_e}}QS/m = -19.8 \text{ ft/s}^2$$

quantities are calculated next:

$$m = W/g = 40,000 \text{ lb}/32.2 \text{ ft/s}^2 = 1242 \text{ slugs}$$

$$Q = \frac{1}{2}\rho u_0^2 = (0.5)(0.0238 \text{ slug/ft}^3)(215 \text{ ft/s})^2 = 55 \text{ lb/ft}^2$$

$$QS/m = (55 \text{ lb/ft}^2)(975 \text{ ft}^2)/(1242 \text{ slugs}) = 43 \text{ ft/s}^2$$

$$QS/(mu_0) = (43 \text{ ft/s})/(215 \text{ ft/s}) = 0.2/s$$

$$\bar{c}/(2u_0) = (10.1 \text{ ft})/[2(215 \text{ ft/s})] = 0.023 \text{ s}$$

$$QS\bar{c}/I_y = (55 \text{ lb/ft}^2)(975 \text{ ft}^2)(10.1 \text{ ft})/(215,000 \text{ slug-ft}^2)$$

$$QS\bar{c}/I_y = 2.52/s^2$$

$$\left(\frac{\bar{c}}{2u_0}\right)QS\bar{c}/I_y = (0.023 \text{ s})(2.52/s^2) = 0.058/s$$

A summary of the dimensional longitudinal derivatives are presented in Table 3.8.

3.7
SUMMARY

The nonlinear differential equations of motion of a rigid airplane were developed from Newton's second law of motion. Linearization of these equations was accomplished using the small-disturbance theory. In following chapters we shall solve the linearized equations of motion. These solutions will yield valuable information on the dynamic characteristics of airplane motion.

PROBLEMS

3.1. Starting with the Y force equation, use the small-disturbance theory to determine the linearized force equation. Assume a steady-level flight for the reference flight conditions.

3.2. Starting with the Z-force equation, use the small-disturbance theory to determine the linearized force equation. Assume a steady-level flight for the reference flight conditions.

3.3. Repeat Problem 3.2 assuming the airplane is experiencing a steady pull-up maneuver; that is, $q_0 = $ constant.

3.4. Discuss why the products of inertial I_{yz} and I_{xy} are usually 0 for an airplane configuration. Use simple sketches to support your arguments. The products of inertia I_{yz}, I_{xy}, and I_{xz} are defined as follows:

$$I_{yz} = \iiint yz\, dm \qquad I_{xy} = \iiint xy\, dm \qquad I_{xz} = \iiint xz\, dm$$

Why is I_{xz} usually not 0?

3.5. Using the geometric data given below and in Figure P3.5, estimate C_{m_α}, $C_{m_{\dot\alpha}}$, C_{m_q}, and $C_{m_{\delta_e}}$.

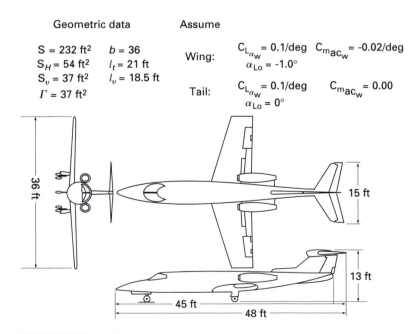

Geometric data		Assume	
$S = 232$ ft^2 $\quad b = 36$		Wing:	$C_{L_{\alpha_w}} = 0.1/$deg $\quad C_{m_{ac_w}} = -0.02/$deg
$S_H = 54$ ft^2 $\quad l_t = 21$ ft			$\alpha_{Lo} = -1.0°$
$S_v = 37$ ft^2 $\quad l_v = 18.5$ ft		Tail:	$C_{L_{\alpha_w}} = 0.1/$deg $\quad C_{m_{ac_w}} = 0.00$
$\Gamma = 37$ ft^2			$\alpha_{Lo} = 0°$

36 ft

15 ft

13 ft

45 ft

48 ft

FIGURE P3.5a
Three-view sketch of a business jet.

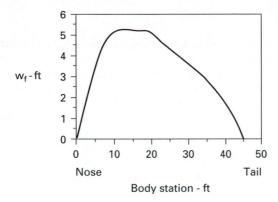

FIGURE P3.5b
Aircraft fuselage width as a function of body
station.

3.6. Estimate C_{l_p} and C_{n_r} for the airplane described in Problem 3.5.

3.7. Show that for a straight tapered wing the roll damping coefficient C_{l_p} can be expressed as

$$C_{l_p} = -\frac{C_{L_\alpha}}{12} \frac{1 + 3\lambda}{1 + \lambda}$$

3.8. Develop an expression for C_{m_q} due to a canard surface.

3.9. Estimate C_{y_β}, C_{n_β}, and C_{n_r} for the Boeing 747 at subsonic speeds. Compare your predictions with the data in Appendix B.

3.10. Estimate the lateral stability coefficients for the STOL transport. See Example 3.1 and Appendix B for the appropriate data.

3.11. Explain why deflecting the ailerons produces a yawing moment.

3.12. (a) The stability coefficient C_{l_r} is the change in roll moment due to the yawing rate. What causes this effect and how does the vertical tail contribute to the C_{l_r}? A simple discussion with appropriate sketches is required for this problem.
(b) The stability coefficient $C_{l_{\delta_r}}$ is the change in roll moment coefficient due to rudder deflection. Again, explain how this effect occurs.

3.13. In this chapter we developed an expression for C_{l_p} due to the wing. How would you estimate C_{l_p} due to the vertical and horizontal tail surfaces. Use simple sketches to support your discussion.

REFERENCES

3.1. McRuer, D.; I. Ashkemas; and D. Graham. *Aircraft Dynamics and Automatic Control.* Princeton, NJ: Princeton University Press, 1973.

3.2. Bryan, G. H.; and W. E. Williams. "The Longitudinal Stability of Aerial Gliders." *Proceedings of the Royal Society of London, Series A* 73 (1904), pp. 110–116.

3.3. Bryan, G. H. *Stability in Aviation.* London: Macmillan, 1911.

3.4. *USAF Stability and Control DATCOM*, Flight Control Division, Air Force Flight Dynamics Laboratory, Wright-Patterson Air Force Base, Fairborn, OH.

3.5. Smetana, F. O.; D. C. Summey; and W. D. Johnson. *Riding and Handling Qualities of Light Aircraft—A Review and Analysis.* NASA CR-1955, March 1972.

3.6. MacDonald, R. A.; M. Garelick; and J. O'Grady. "Linearized Mathematical Models for DeHavilland Canada 'Buffalo and Twin Otter' STOL Transports." U.S. Department of Transportation, Transportation Systems Center Report No. DOT-TSC-FAA-71-8, June 1971.

CHAPTER 4

Longitudinal Motion (Stick Fixed)

"The equilibrium and stability of a bird in flight, or an aerodome or flying machine, has in the past been the subject of considerable speculation, and no adequate explanation of the principles involved has hitherto been given."

Frederick W. Lanchester, *Aerodonetics* [4.1], published in 1908, in which he develops an elementary theory of longitudinal dynamic stability.

4.1
HISTORICAL PERSPECTIVE

The theoretical basis for the analysis of flight vehicle motion developed almost concurrently with the successful demonstration of a powered flight of a human-carrying airplane. As early as 1897, Frederick Lanchester was studying the motion of gliders. He conducted experiments with hand-launched gliders and found that his gliders would fly along a straight path if they were launched at what he called the glider's natural speed. Launching the glider at a higher or lower speed would result in an oscillatory motion. He also noticed that, if launched at its "natural speed" and then disturbed from its flight path, the glider would start oscillating along its flight trajectory. What Lanchester had discovered was that all flight vehicles possess certain natural frequencies or motions when disturbed from their equilibrium flight.

Lanchester called the oscillatory motion the phugoid motion. He wanted to use the Greek word meaning "to fly" to describe his newly discovered motion; actually, phugoid means "to flee." Today, we still use the term phugoid to describe the long-period slowly damped oscillation associated with the longitudinal motion of an airplane.

The mathematical treatment of flight vehicle motions was first developed by G. H. Bryan. He was aware of Lanchester's experimental observations and set out to develop the mathematical equations for dynamic stability analysis. His stability work was published in 1911. Bryan made significant contributions to the analysis of vehicle flight motion. He laid the mathematical foundation for airplane dynamic stability analysis, developed the concept of the aerodynamic stability derivative, and recognized that the equations of motion could be separated into a symmetric longitudinal motion and an unsymmetric lateral motion. Although the mathematical treatment of airplane dynamic stability was formulated shortly after the first successful human-controlled flight, the theory was not used by the inventors because of its mathematical complexity and the lack of information on the stability derivatives.

Experimental studies were initiated by L. Bairstow and B. M. Jones of the National Physical Laboratory (NPL) in England and Jerome Hunsaker of the Massachusetts Institute of Technology (MIT) to determine estimates of the aerodynamic stability derivatives used in Bryan's theory. In addition to determining stability derivatives from wind-tunnel tests of scale models, Bairstow and Jones nondimensionalized the equations of motion and showed that, with certain assumptions, there were two independent solutions; that is, one longitudinal and one lateral. During the same period, Hunsaker and his group at MIT conducted wind-tunnel studies of scale models of several flying airplanes. The results from these early studies were extremely valuable in establishing relationships between aerodynamics, geometric and mass characteristics of the airplanes, and its dynamic stability.*

Although these early investigators could predict the stability of the longitudinal and lateral motions, they were unsure how to interpret their findings. They were preplexed because when their analysis predicted an airplane would be unstable the airplane was flown successfully. They wondered how the stability analysis could be used to assess whether an airplane was of good or bad design. The missing factor in analyzing airplane stability in these early studies was the consideration of the pilot as an essential part of the airplane system.

In the late 1930s the National Advisory Committee of Aeronautics (NACA) conducted an extensive flight test program. Many airplanes were tested with the goal of quantitatively relating the measured dynamic characteristics of the airplane with the pilot's opinion of its handling characteristics. These experiments laid the foundation for modern flying qualities research. In 1943, R. Gilruth reported the results of the NACA research program in the form of flying qualities' specifications. For the first time, the designer had a list of specifications that could be used in designing the airplane. If the design complied with the specifications, one could be reasonably sure that the airplane would have good flying qualities [4.1–4.4].

In this chapter we shall examine the longitudinal motion of an airplane disturbed from its equilibrium state. Several different analytical techniques will be presented for solving the longitudinal differential equations. Our objectives are for the student to understand the various analytical techniques employed in airplane motion analysis and to appreciate the importance of aerodynamic or configuration changes on the airplane's dynamic stability characteristics. Later we shall discuss what constitutes good flying qualities in terms of the dynamic characteristics presented here. Before attempting to solve the longitudinal equations of motion, we will examine the solution of a simplified aircraft motion. By studying the simpler motions with a single degree of freedom, we shall gain some insight into the more complicated longitudinal motions we shall study later in this chapter.

---

* The first technical report by the National Advisory Committee of Aeronautics, NACA (forerunner of the National Aeronautics and Space Administration, NASA), summarizes the MIT research in dynamic stability.

4.2
SECOND-ORDER DIFFERENTIAL EQUATIONS

Many physical systems can be modeled by second-order differential equations. For example, control servomotors, special cases of aircraft dynamics, and many electrical and mechanical systems are governed by second-order differential equations. Because the second-order differential equation plays such an important role in aircraft dynamics we shall examine its characteristics before proceeding with our discussion of aircraft motions.

To illustrate the properties of a second-order differential equation, we examine the motion of a mechanical system composed of a mass, a spring, and a damping device. The forces acting on the system are shown in Figure 4.1. The spring provides a linear restoring force that is proportional to the extension of the spring, and the damping device provides a damping force that is proportional to the velocity of the mass. The differential equation for the system can be written as

$$m\,\frac{d^2x}{dt^2} + c\,\frac{dx}{dt} + kx = F(t) \qquad (4.1)$$

or
$$\frac{d^2x}{dt^2} + \frac{c}{m}\frac{dx}{dt} + \frac{k}{m}x = \frac{1}{m}F(t) \qquad (4.2)$$

This is a nonhomogeneous, second-order differential equation with constant coefficients. The coefficients in the equation are determined from the physical characteristics of the mechanical system being modeled, that is, its mass, damping coefficient, and spring constant. The function $F(t)$ is called the forcing function. If the forcing function is 0, the response of the system is referred to as the free response. When the system is driven by a forcing function $F(t)$ the response is referred to as the forced response. The general solution of the nonhomogeneous differential equation is the sum of the homogeneous and particular solutions. The homogeneous solution is the solution of the differential equation when the right-hand side of the equation is 0. This corresponds to the free response of the system. The particular solution is a solution that when substituted into the left-hand side of the

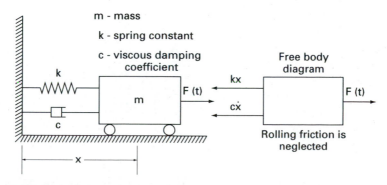

FIGURE 4.1
A spring mass damper system.

differential equation yields the nonhomogeneous or right-hand side of the differential equation. In the following section we will restrict our discussion to the solution of the free response or homogeneous equation.

The solution of the differential equation with constant coefficients is found by letting

$$x = Ae^{\lambda t} \tag{4.3}$$

and substituting into the differential equation yields

$$\lambda^2 Ae^{\lambda t} + \frac{c}{m}\lambda Ae^{\lambda t} + \frac{k}{m}Ae^{\lambda t}e = 0 \tag{4.4}$$

Clearing the equation of $Ae^{\lambda t}$ yields

$$\lambda^2 + \frac{c}{m}\lambda + \frac{k}{m} = 0 \tag{4.5}$$

which is called the characteristic equation. The roots of the characteristic equation are called the characteristic roots or eigenvalues of the system.

The roots of Equation (4.5) are

$$\lambda_{1,2} = -\frac{c}{2m} \pm \sqrt{\left(\frac{c}{2m}\right)^2 - \frac{k}{m}} \tag{4.6}$$

The solution of the differential equation can now be written as

$$x(t) = C_1 e^{\lambda_1 t} + C_2 e^{\lambda_2 t} \tag{4.7}$$

where C_1 and C_2 are arbitrary constants determined from the initial conditions of the problem. The type of motion that occurs if the system is displaced from its equilibrium position and released depends on the value of λ. But λ depends on the physical constants of the problem; namely, m, c, and k. We shall consider three possible cases for λ.

When $(c/2m) > \sqrt{k/m}$, the roots are negative and real, which means that the motion will die out exponentially with time. This type of motion is referred to as an overdamped motion. The equation of motion is given by

$$x(t) = C_1 \exp\left[-\frac{c}{2m} + \sqrt{\left(\frac{c}{2m}\right)^2 - \frac{k}{m}}\right]t$$
$$+ C_2 \exp\left[-\frac{c}{2m} - \sqrt{\left(\frac{c}{2m}\right)^2 - \frac{k}{m}}\right]t \tag{4.8}$$

For the case where $(c/2m) < \sqrt{k/m}$, the roots are complex:

$$\lambda = -\frac{c}{2m} \pm i\sqrt{\frac{k}{m} - \left(\frac{c}{2m}\right)^2} \tag{4.9}$$

The equation of motion is as follows:

$$x(t) = \exp\left(-\frac{c}{2m}t\right)\left[C_1 \exp\left[i\sqrt{\frac{k}{m} - \left(\frac{c}{2m}\right)^2}\, t\right]\right.$$

$$\left. + C_2 \exp\left[-i\sqrt{\frac{k}{m} - \left(\frac{c}{2m}\right)^2}\, t\right]\right] \tag{4.10}$$

which can be rewritten as

$$x(t) = \exp\left(-\frac{c}{2m}t\right)\left[A \cos\left[\sqrt{\frac{k}{m} - \left(\frac{c}{2m}\right)^2}\, t\right]\right.$$

$$\left. + B \sin\left[\sqrt{\frac{k}{m} - \left(\frac{c}{2m}\right)^2}\, t\right]\right] \tag{4.11}$$

The solution given by Equation (4.11) is a damped sinusoid having a natural frequency given by

$$\omega = \sqrt{\frac{k}{m} - \left(\frac{c}{2m}\right)^2} \tag{4.12}$$

The last case we consider is when $(c/2m) = \sqrt{k/m}$. This represents the boundary between the overdamped exponential motion and the damped sinusoidal motion. This particular motion is referred to as the critically damped motion. The roots of the characteristic equation are identical; that is,

$$\lambda_{1,2} = -\frac{c}{2m} \tag{4.13}$$

The general solution for repeated roots has the form

$$x(t) = (C_1 + C_2 t)\, e^{\lambda t} \tag{4.14}$$

If λ is a negative constant, then $e^{\lambda t}$ will go to 0 faster than $C_2 t$ goes to infinity as time increases. Figure 4.2 shows the motion for the three cases analyzed here.

The damping constant for the critically damped case, called the critical damping constant, is defined as

$$c_{cr} = 2\sqrt{km} \tag{4.15}$$

For oscillatory motion, the damping can be specified in terms of the critical damping:

$$c = \zeta c_{cr} \tag{4.16}$$

where ζ is called the damping ratio,

$$\zeta = \frac{c}{c_{cr}} \tag{4.17}$$

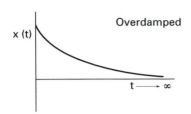

Overdamped

$x(t)$

$t \longrightarrow \infty$

FIGURE 4.2
Typical motions of a dynamic system.

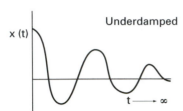

Underdamped

$x(t)$

$t \longrightarrow \infty$

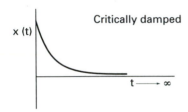

Critically damped

$x(t)$

$t \longrightarrow \infty$

For a system that has no damping, that is, $c = 0$, which implies that $\zeta = 0$, the motion is an undamped oscillation. The natural frequency, called the undamped natural frequency, can be obtained from Equation (4.12) by setting $c = 0$:

$$\omega_n = \sqrt{\frac{k}{m}} \qquad (4.18)$$

Since both the damping ratio and undamped natural frequency are specified as functions of the system physical constants, we can rewrite the differential equation in terms of the damping ratio and undamped natural frequency as follows:

$$\frac{d^2x}{dt^2} + 2\zeta\omega_n \frac{dx}{dt} + \omega_n^2 x = f(t) \qquad (4.19)$$

Equation (4.19) is the standard form of a second-order differential equation with constant coefficients. Although we developed the standard form of a second-order differential equation from a mechanical mass-spring-damper system, the equation could have been developed using any one of an almost limitless number of physical systems. For example, a torsional spring-mass-damper equation of motion is given by

$$\frac{d^2\theta}{dt^2} + \frac{c}{I}\frac{d\theta}{dt} + \frac{k}{I}\theta = f(t) \qquad (4.20)$$

where c, k, and I are the torsional damping coefficient, torsional spring constant, and moment of inertia, respectively.

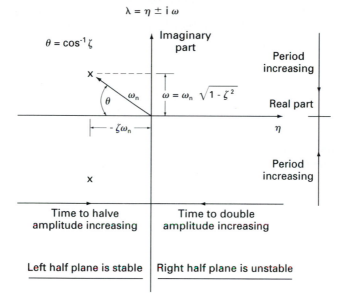

FIGURE 4.3
Relationship among η, ω, ζ, and ω_n.

The characteristic equation for the standard form of the second-order differential equation with constant coefficients can be shown to be

$$\lambda^2 + 2\zeta\omega_n\lambda + \omega_n^2 = 0 \tag{4.21}$$

The roots of the characteristic equation are

$$\lambda_{1,2} = -\zeta\omega_n \pm i\omega_n\sqrt{1 - \zeta^2} \tag{4.22}$$

or

$$\lambda_{1,2} = \eta \pm i\omega \tag{4.23}$$

where

$$\eta = -\zeta\omega_n \tag{4.24}$$

$$\omega = \omega_n\sqrt{1 - \zeta^2} \tag{4.25}$$

The real part of λ, that is, η, governs the damping of the response and the imaginary part, ω, is the damped natural frequency.

Figure 4.3 shows the relationship between the roots of the characteristic equation and η, ω, ζ, and ω_n. When the roots are complex the radial distance from the origin to the root is the undamped natural frequency. The system damping η is the real part of the complex root and the damped natural frequency is the imaginary part of the root. The damping ratio ζ is equal to the cosine of the angle between the negative real axis and the radial line from the origin to the root:

$$\cos(\pi - \theta) = -\cos \theta = \frac{-\zeta\omega_n}{\omega_n} \tag{4.26}$$

or $$\zeta = \cos \theta \tag{4.27}$$

The influence of the damping ratio on the roots of the characteristic equation can be examined by holding the undamped natural frequency constant and varying ζ from $-\infty$ to ∞ as shown in Figure 4.4. The response of the homogeneous equation to a displacement from its equilibrium condition can take on many forms depending on the magnitude of the damping ratio. The classification of the response is given in Table 4.1.

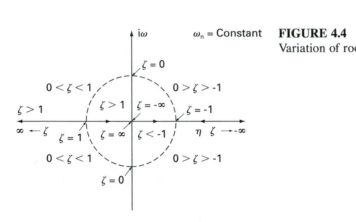

FIGURE 4.4
Variation of roots with damping ratio.

TABLE 4.1
Variation of response with damping ratio

Magnitude of damping ratio	Type of root	Time response
$\zeta < -1$	Two positive real distinct roots	Exponentially growing motion
$0 > \zeta > -1$	Complex roots with a positive real part	Exponentially growing sinusoidal motion
$\zeta = 0$	Complex roots with a real part 0	Undamped sinusoidal motion Pure harmonic motion
$0 < \zeta < 1$	Complex roots with a real part negative	Underdamped exponentially decaying sinusoidal motion
$\zeta = 1$	Two negative equal real roots	Critically damped exponentially decaying motion
$\zeta > 1$	Two negative distinct real roots	Overdamped exponentially decaying motion

4.3
PURE PITCHING MOTION

Consider the case in which the airplane's center of gravity is constrained to move in a straight line at a constant speed but the aircraft is free to pitch about its center of gravity. Figure 4.5 is the sketch of a wind-tunnel model constrained so that it can perform only in a pitching motion.

The equation of motion can be developed from the rigid body equations developed in Chapter 3 by making the appropriate assumptions. However, to aid our understanding of this simple motion, we shall rederive the governing equation from first principles. The equation governing this motion is obtained from Newton's second law:

$$\sum \text{Pitching moments} = \sum M_{cg} = I_y \ddot{\theta} \qquad (4.28)$$

The pitching moment M and pitch angle θ can be expressed in terms of an initial reference value indicated by a subscript, 0, and the perturbation by the Δ symbol:

$$M = M_0 + \Delta M \qquad (4.29)$$

$$\theta = \theta_0 + \Delta\theta \qquad (4.30)$$

If the reference moment M_0 is 0, then equation (4.28) reduces to

$$\Delta M = I_y \Delta\ddot{\theta} \qquad (4.31)$$

For the restricted motion that we are examining, the variables are the angle of attack, pitch angle, the time rate of change of these variables, and the elevator angle. The pitching moment is not a function of the pitch angle but of the other variables and can be expressed in functional form as follows:

$$\Delta M = \text{fn}(\Delta\alpha, \Delta\dot{\alpha}, \Delta q, \Delta\delta_e) \qquad (4.32)$$

Equation (4.32) can be expanded in terms of the perturbation variables by means

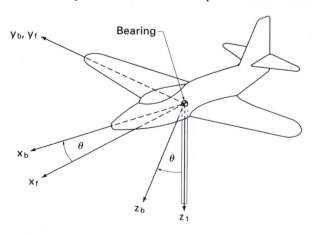

FIGURE 4.5
A model constrained to a pure pitching motion.

of a Taylor series:

$$\Delta M = \frac{\partial M}{\partial \alpha} \Delta\alpha + \frac{\partial M}{\partial \dot\alpha} \Delta\dot\alpha + \frac{\partial M}{\partial q} \Delta q + \frac{\partial M}{\partial \delta_e} \Delta\delta_e \tag{4.33}$$

If we align the body and fixed frames so they coincide at $t = 0$, the change in angle of attack and pitch angles are identical; that is,

$$\Delta\alpha = \Delta\theta \qquad \text{and} \qquad \Delta\dot\theta = \Delta q = \Delta\dot\alpha \tag{4.34}$$

This is true only for the special cases where the center of gravity is constrained. Substituting this information into Equation (4.31) yields

$$\Delta\ddot\alpha - (M_q + M_{\dot\alpha})\Delta\dot\alpha - M_\alpha\Delta\alpha = M_{\delta e}\Delta\delta_e \tag{4.35}$$

where

$$M_q = \frac{\partial M}{\partial q}\bigg/ I_y, \qquad M_{\dot\alpha} = \frac{\partial M}{\partial \dot\alpha}\bigg/ I_y, \qquad \text{and so forth}$$

Equation (4.35) is a nonhomogeneous second-order differential equation, having constant coefficients. This equation is similar to a torsional spring-mass-damper system with a forcing function, which was mentioned briefly in the previous section. The static stability of the airplane can be thought of as the equivalent of an aerodynamic spring, while the aerodynamic damping terms are similar to a torsional damping device. The characteristic equation for Equation (4.35) is

$$\lambda^2 - (M_q + M_{\dot\alpha})\lambda - M_\alpha = 0 \tag{4.36}$$

This equation can be compared with the standard equation of a second-order system:

$$\lambda^2 + 2\zeta\omega_n\lambda + \omega_n^2 = 0 \tag{4.37}$$

where ζ is the damping ratio and ω_n is the undamped natural frequency. By inspection we see that

$$\omega_n = \sqrt{-M_\alpha} \tag{4.38}$$

and

$$\zeta = \frac{-(M_q + M_{\dot\alpha})}{2\sqrt{-M_\alpha}} \tag{4.39}$$

Note that the frequency is related to the airplane's static stability and that the damping ratio is a function of the aerodynamic damping and static stability.

If we solve the characteristic Equation (4.37), we obtain the following roots:

$$\lambda_{1,2} = \frac{-2\zeta\omega_n \pm \sqrt{4\zeta^2\omega_n^2 - 4\omega_n^2}}{2} \tag{4.40}$$

or

$$\lambda_{1,2} = -\zeta\omega_n \pm i\omega_n\sqrt{1 - \zeta^2} \tag{4.41}$$

Expressing the characteristic root as

$$\lambda_{1,2} = \eta \pm i\omega \tag{4.42}$$

and comparing Equation (4.42) with (4.41), yields

$$\eta = -\zeta\omega_n \qquad (4.43)$$

and

$$\omega = \omega_n\sqrt{1 - \zeta^2} \qquad (4.44)$$

which are the real and imaginary parts of the characteristic roots. The angular frequency ω is called the damped natural frequency of the system.

The general solution to Equation (4.35) for a step change $\Delta\delta_e$ in the elevator angle can be expressed as

$$\Delta\alpha(t) = \Delta\alpha_{\mathrm{trim}}\left[\left(1 + \frac{e^{-\zeta\omega_n t}}{\sqrt{1 - \zeta^2}}\sin(\sqrt{1 - \zeta^2}\,\omega_n t + \phi)\right)\right] \qquad (4.45)$$

where $\Delta\alpha_{\mathrm{trim}}$ = change in trim angle of attack $= -(M_{\delta_e}\,\Delta\delta_e)/M_\alpha$

ζ = damping ratio $= -(M_q + M_{\dot\alpha})/(2\sqrt{-M_\alpha})$

ω_n = undamped natural frequency $= \sqrt{-M_\alpha}$

ϕ = phase angle $= \tan^{-1}(-\sqrt{1 - \zeta^2}/-\zeta)$

The solution is a damped sinusoidal motion with the frequency a function of C_{m_α} and the damping rate a function of $C_{m_q} + C_{m_{\dot\alpha}}$ and $C_{m_{\dot\alpha}}$. Figure 4.6 illustrates the angle of attack time history for various values of the damping ratio ζ. Note that as the system damping is increased the maximum overshoot of the response diminishes.

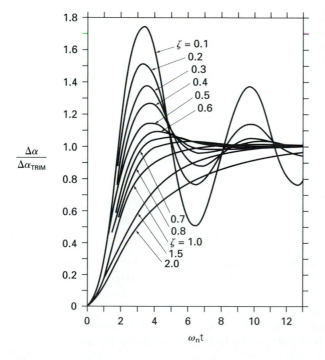

FIGURE 4.6
Angle of attack time history of a pitching model for various damping ratios.

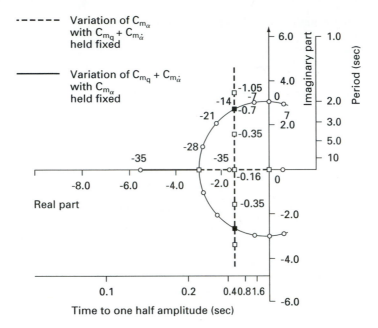

FIGURE 4.7
Variation of the characteristic roots of the pitching motion as a
function of the stability coefficients.

The influence of the stability coefficients on the roots of the characteristic
equation can be seen in Figure 4.7. The curves show the effect of variations in C_{m_α}
and $C_{m_q} + C_{m_{\dot{\alpha}}}$ on the roots. This type of curve is referred to as a root locus plot.
Notice that as the roots move into the right half plane the vehicle will become
unstable.

The roots of the characteristic equation tell us what type of response our
airplane will have. If the roots are real, the response will be either a pure divergence
or a pure subsidence, depending on whether the root is positive or negative. If the
roots are complex, the motion will be either a damped or undamped sinusoidal
oscillation. The period of the oscillation is related to the imaginary part of the root
as follows:

$$\text{Period} = \frac{2\pi}{\omega} \tag{4.46}$$

The rate of growth or decay of the oscillation is determined by the sign of the real
part of the complex root. A negative real part produces decaying oscillation,
whereas a positive real part causes the motion to grow. A measure of the rate of
growth or decay of the oscillation can be obtained from the time for halving or
doubling the initial amplitude of the disturbance. Figure 4.8 shows damped and
undamped oscillations and how the time for halving or doubling the amplitude can

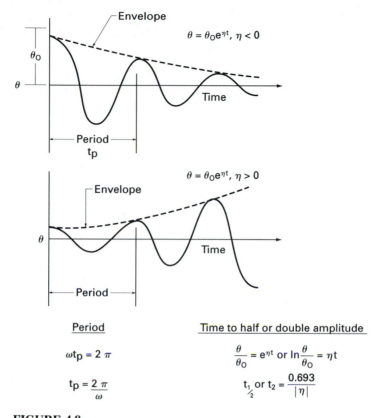

Period	Time to half or double amplitude
$\omega t_p = 2\pi$	$\dfrac{\theta}{\theta_0} = e^{\eta t}$ or $\ln\dfrac{\theta}{\theta_0} = \eta t$
$t_p = \dfrac{2\pi}{\omega}$	$t_{\frac{1}{2}}$ or $t_2 = \dfrac{0.693}{|\eta|}$

FIGURE 4.8
Relationships for time to halve or double amplitude and the period.

be calculated. The expression for the time for doubling or halving of the amplitude is

$$t_{\text{double}} \quad \text{or} \quad t_{\text{halve}} = \frac{0.693}{|\eta|} \tag{4.47}$$

and the number of cycles for doubling or halving the amplitude is

$$N(\text{cycles})_{\text{double or halve}} = 0.110 \frac{|\omega|}{|\eta|} \tag{4.48}$$

EXAMPLE PROBLEM 4.1. A flat plate lifting surface is mounted on a hollow slender rod as illustrated in Figure 4.9. The slender rod is supported in the wind tunnel by a transverse rod. A low friction bearing is used so that the slender rod-flat plate system can rotate freely in pitch. To have the center of gravity located at the pivot point ballast is placed inside the slender tube forward of the pivot. Estimate the damping ratio, ζ, the undamped natural frequency, ω_n, and the damped natural frequency of the tube-flat

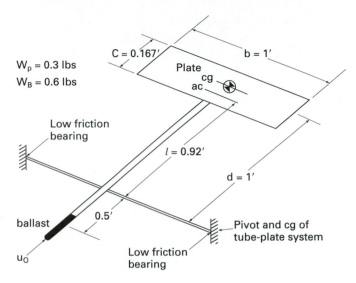

FIGURE 4.9
Rod-plate assembly constrained to a pure pitching motion.

plate assembly. The following assumptions are made in the analysis:

1. Neglect the mass of the slender rod.
2. Neglect the contribution of the pitching moment contribution due to the slender rod.
3. Neglect the mechanical friction of the bearings.

Solution. The equation of motion governing the pitching motion of the slender rod–flat plate model can be derived as follows:

$$\Sigma \text{ Pitching moments about the center of gravity} = I_y \ddot{\theta}$$

$$M = I_y \ddot{\theta}$$

The pitching moment for this model will be a function of only the angle of attack, α, and the pitch rate, q. The contribution due to $\dot{\alpha}$ is not included because this effect is due primarily to the interaction of the wing wake on an aft surface. Because there is no wing in this case the $\dot{\alpha}$ term can be ignored. The aerodynamic pitching moment can be expressed as follows:

$$M = \frac{\partial M}{\partial \alpha} \alpha + \frac{\partial M}{\partial q} q$$

Substituting the moment expression into the differential equation and rearranging yields

$$\ddot{\theta} - M_q q - M_{\dot{\alpha}} \alpha = 0$$

where

$$M_q = \frac{\partial M}{\partial q} \bigg/ I_y$$

$$M_\alpha = \frac{\partial M}{\partial \alpha} \bigg/ I_y$$

Because the center of gravity is constrained the angle of attack, α, and the pitch angle, θ, are the same. The pitch rate, q, is the same as $\dot{\theta}$; therefore, the equation of motion can be written in terms of either α or θ. In terms of θ the equation is as follows:

$$\ddot{\theta} - M_q\dot{\theta} - M_\alpha\theta = 0$$

This equation is similar to the differential equation developed for a pitching aircraft. The next step in the analysis is to develop expressions to estimate the stability derivatives M_q and M_α.

The moment contribution due to a change in angle of attack can be estimated from the geometric and aerodynamic characteristics of the flat plate lifting surface. The moment created by a change in angle of attack is due to the change in lift on the flat plate times the moment arm to the pivot (center of gravity location).

$$M(\alpha) = -l\,\Delta\,\text{Lift}$$

$$M(\alpha) = -l\,C_{L_\alpha}\alpha\,QS$$

where $Q = \frac{1}{2}\rho u_0^2$, l is the distance from the center of gravity to the aerodynamic center of the plate, S is the planform area of the plate, and C_{L_α} is the lift curve slope of the flat plate.

The derivative M_α can be estimated from the preceding formula:

$$M_\alpha = \frac{\partial M}{\partial \alpha}\bigg/ I_y = -l\,C_{L_\alpha}QS/I_y$$

In a similar manner the moment contribution due to the pitch rate, q, can be estimated. Recall that when an aft surface undergoes a pitching motion a change in the angle of attack is induced on the surface. The change in angle of attack can be approximated as

$$\tan \alpha = \frac{ql}{u_0}$$

or for small angles

$$\alpha \simeq \frac{ql}{u_0}$$

The pitching moment as a function of q is equal to the change in lift on the aft plate times the moment arm to the center of gravity:

$$M(q) = -l\,C_{L_\alpha}\left(\frac{ql}{u_0}\right)QS$$

The derivative M_q can be estimated from this equation:

$$M_q = \frac{\partial M}{\partial q}\bigg/ I_y = -l\,C_{L_\alpha}\left(\frac{l}{u_0}\right)QS/I_y$$

The next step in our analysis it to determine the appropriate values for C_{L_α}, Q, and I_y from the data given. The lift curve slope, C_{L_α}, can be estimated by using the theoretical value of an infinite flat plate, $C_{\ell_\alpha} = 2\pi$ /rad and correcting this value for the influence of aspect ratio:

$$C_{L_\alpha} = \frac{C_{\ell_\alpha}}{1 + C_{\ell_\alpha}/(\pi AR)}$$

The flat plate has an aspect ratio of 6, therefore, $C_{L_\alpha} = 4.7/\text{rad}$. The only term in the expression that is not known is the mass moment of inertia, I_y. The inertia of a thin flat plate about the y' axis through the plate's center of gravity is given in terms of ρ, b, t, and c, the mass density of the material and the dimensions of the plate, respectively.

$$I_{y'} = \frac{1}{12}\rho b t c^3 = \frac{1}{12}mc^2$$

$$= \frac{1}{12}(9.3 \cdot 10^{-3}\ \text{slugs})(0.167\ \text{ft})^2$$

$$= 2.16 \cdot 10^{-5}\ \text{slug} \cdot \text{ft}^2$$

The inertia of the plate about an axis through the pivot point can be determined using the parallel axis theorem:

$$I_y = I_{y'} + md^2$$

where d is the distance to the new axis:

$$I_y = 2.16 \times 10^{-5}\ \text{slug} \cdot \text{ft}^2 + (9.3 \times 10^{-3}\ \text{slugs})(1\ \text{ft})^2$$

$$= 9.32 \times 10^{-3}\text{slug} \cdot \text{ft}^2$$

The mass moment of inertia of the complete system, flat plate, and ballast is given by

$$I_y = I_{y\,\text{plate}} + I_{y\,\text{ballast}}$$

$$= 9.32 \times 10^{-3}\text{slug} \cdot \text{ft}^2 + (1.86 \times 10^{-2}\ \text{slugs})(0.5\ \text{ft})^2$$

$$= 1.4 \times 10^{-2}\text{slug} \cdot \text{ft}^2$$

With the expressions developed for M_α and M_q and the data in Figure 4.9 we now can develop estimates of the derivatives:

$$Q = \frac{1}{2}\rho u_0^2 = (0.5)(0.002378\ \text{slug-ft}^2)(25\ \text{ft/s})^2$$

$$= 0.7\ \text{lb/ft}^2$$

$$M_\alpha = -lC_{L_\alpha}QS/I_y$$

$$= -(0.92\ \text{ft})(4.7/\text{rad})(0.7\ \text{lb/ft}^2)(0.167\ \text{ft}^2)/(1.4 \times 10^{-2}\text{slugs} \cdot \text{ft}^2)$$

$$= -36.1/\text{s}^2$$

and $\quad M_q = -lC_{L_\alpha}\left(\frac{l}{u_0}\right)QS/I_y$

$$= -(0.92\ \text{ft})(4.7/\text{rad})[(0.96\ \text{ft})/(25\ \text{ft/s})](0.7\ \text{lb/ft}^2)(0.167\ \text{ft}^2)/$$
$$(1.4 \times 10^{-2}\text{slugs} \cdot \text{ft}^2)$$

$$= -1.38/\text{s}$$

Substituting these values into the differential equation yields

$$\ddot{\theta} + 1.38\,\dot{\theta} + 36.1\theta = 0$$

A second-order differential equation can be expressed in terms of the system damping ratio, ζ, and the system's undamped natural ω_n frequency as follows:

$$\ddot{\theta} + 2\zeta\,\omega_n\dot{\theta} + \omega_n^2\,\theta = 0$$

The system damping ratio and undamped natural frequency can be obtained by inspection:

$$\omega_n^2 = 36.1/s^2$$

or

$$\omega_n = 6.0 \text{ rad/s}$$

and

$$2\zeta\omega_n = 1.38$$

$$\zeta = 0.115$$

Finally the damped natural frequency, ω, is obtained from the following equation:

$$\omega = \omega_n\sqrt{1 - \zeta^2}$$

$$= 5.96 \text{ rad/s}$$

In this example problem we have developed the governing differential equation from Newton's second law. The aerodynamic moment was assumed to be linear and a function of α and q and was expressed in terms of stability derivatives. Expressions for estimating the stability derivatives were developed in terms of the aerodynamic, geometric, and inertia characteristics of the rod-plate system.

4.4
STICK FIXED LONGITUDINAL MOTION

The motion of an airplane in free flight can be extremely complicated. The airplane has three translation motions (vertical, horizontal, and transverse), three rotational motions (pitch, yaw, and roll), and numerous elastic degrees of freedom. To analyze the response of an elastic airplane is beyond the scope of this book.

The problem we shall address in this section is the solution of the rigid-body equations of motion. This may seem to be a formidable task; however, some simplifying assumptions will reduce the complexity of the problem. First, we shall assume that the aircraft's motion consists of small deviations from its equilibrium flight condition. Second, we shall assume that the motion of the airplane can be analyzed by separating the equations into two groups. The X-force, Z-force, and pitching moment equations embody the longitudinal equations, and the Y-force, rolling, and yawing moment equations form the lateral equations. To separate the equations in this manner, the longitudinal and lateral equations must not be coupled. These are all reasonable assumptions provided the airplane is not undergoing a large-amplitude or very rapid maneuver.

In aircraft motion studies, one must always be sure that the assumptions made in an analysis are appropriate for the problem at hand. Students are all too eager to use the first equation they can find to solve their homework problems. This type of approach can lead to many incorrect or ridiculous solutions. To avoid such

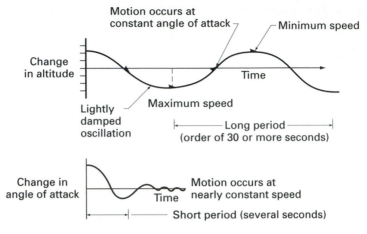

FIGURE 4.10
The phugoid and short-period motions.

embarrassment, one must always verify that the assumptions used in developing the equations one wishes to use are consistent with the problem one is attempting to solve. This is particularly important when solving problems related to aircraft dynamics.

In the following sections we shall examine the longitudinal motion of an airplane without control input. The longitudinal motion of an airplane (controls fixed) disturbed from its equilibrium flight condition is characterized by two oscillatory modes of motion. Figure 4.10 illustrates these basic modes. We see that one mode is lightly damped and has a long period. This motion is called the long-period or phugoid mode. The second basic motion is heavily damped and has a very short period; it is appropriately called the short-period mode.

4.4.1 State Variable Representation of the Equations of Motion

The linearized longitudinal equations developed in Chapter 3 are simple, ordinary linear differential equations with constant coefficients. The coefficients in the differential equations are made up of the aerodynamic stability derivatives, mass, and inertia characteristics of the airplane. These equations can be written as a set of first-order differential equations, called the state-space or state variable equations and represented mathematically as

$$\dot{\mathbf{x}} = \mathbf{A}\mathbf{x} + \mathbf{B}\boldsymbol{\eta} \tag{4.49}$$

where $\mathbf{x}$ is the state vector, $\boldsymbol{\eta}$ is the control vector, and the matrices $\mathbf{A}$ and $\mathbf{B}$ contain the aircraft's dimensional stability derivatives.

The linearized longitudinal set of equations developed earlier are repeated here:

$$\left(\frac{d}{dt} - X_u\right) \Delta u - X_w \, \Delta w + (g \cos \theta_0) \, \Delta\theta = X_\delta \, \Delta\delta + X_{\delta_T} \, \Delta\delta_T$$

$$-Z_u \, \Delta u + \left[(1 - Z_{\dot{w}})\frac{d}{dt} - Z_w\right] \Delta - \left[(u_0 + Z_q)\frac{d}{dt} - g \sin \theta_0\right] \Delta\theta \qquad (4.50)$$

$$= Z_\delta \, \Delta\delta + Z_{\delta_T} \, \Delta\delta_T$$

$$-M_u \, \Delta u - \left(M_{\dot{w}}\frac{d}{dt} + M_w\right) \Delta w + \left(\frac{d^2}{dt^2} - M_q\frac{d}{dt}\right) \Delta\theta = M_\delta \, \Delta\delta + M_{\delta_T} \, \Delta\delta_T$$

where $\Delta\delta$ and $\Delta\delta_T$ are the aerodynamic and propulsive controls, respectively.

In practice, the force derivatives Z_q and $Z_{\dot{w}}$ usually are neglected because they contribute very little to the aircraft response. Therefore, to simplify our presentation of the equations of motion in the state-space form we will neglect both Z_q and $Z_{\dot{w}}$. Rewriting the equations in the state-space form yields

$$\begin{bmatrix} \Delta\dot{u} \\ \Delta\dot{w} \\ \Delta\dot{q} \\ \Delta\dot{\theta} \end{bmatrix} = \begin{bmatrix} X_u & X_w & 0 & -g \\ Z_u & Z_w & u_0 & 0 \\ M_u + M_{\dot{w}}Z_u & M_w + M_{\dot{w}}Z_w & M_q + M_{\dot{w}}u_0 & 0 \\ 0 & 0 & 1 & 0 \end{bmatrix} \begin{bmatrix} \Delta u \\ \Delta w \\ \Delta q \\ \Delta\theta \end{bmatrix}$$

$$+ \begin{bmatrix} X_\delta & X_{\delta_T} \\ Z_\delta & Z_{\delta_T} \\ M_\delta + M_{\dot{w}}Z_\delta & M_{\delta_T} + M_{\dot{w}}Z_{\delta_T} \\ 0 & 0 \end{bmatrix} \begin{bmatrix} \Delta\delta \\ \Delta\delta_T \end{bmatrix} \qquad (4.51)$$

where the state vector $\mathbf{x}$ and control vector $\boldsymbol{\eta}$ are given by

$$\mathbf{x} = \begin{bmatrix} \Delta u \\ \Delta w \\ \Delta q \\ \Delta\theta \end{bmatrix}, \qquad \boldsymbol{\eta} = \begin{bmatrix} \Delta\delta \\ \Delta\delta_T \end{bmatrix} \qquad (4.52)$$

and the matrices $\mathbf{A}$ and $\mathbf{B}$ are given by

$$\mathbf{A} = \begin{bmatrix} X_u & X_w & 0 & -g \\ Z_u & Z_w & u_0 & 0 \\ M_u + M_{\dot{w}}Z_u & M_w + M_{\dot{w}}Z_w & M_q + M_{\dot{w}}u_0 & 0 \\ 0 & 0 & 1 & 0 \end{bmatrix} \qquad (4.53)$$

$$\mathbf{B} = \begin{bmatrix} X_\delta & X_{\delta_T} \\ Z_\delta & Z_{\delta_T} \\ M_\delta + M_{\dot{w}}Z_\delta & M_{\delta_T} + M_{\dot{w}}Z_{\delta_T} \\ 0 & 0 \end{bmatrix} \qquad (4.54)$$

TABLE 4.2
Summary of longitudinal derivatives

$$X_u = \frac{-(C_{D_u} + 2C_{D_0})QS}{mu_0} \qquad X_w = \frac{-(C_{D_\alpha} - C_{L_0})QS}{mu_0}$$

$$Z_u = \frac{-(C_{L_u} + 2C_{L_0})QS}{mu_0}$$

$$Z_w = \frac{-(C_{L_\alpha} + C_{D_0})QS}{mu_0} \qquad Z_{\dot{w}} = C_{z_{\dot{\alpha}}} \frac{\bar{c}}{2u_0} QS/(u_0 m)$$

$$Z_\alpha = u_0 Z_w \qquad\qquad Z_{\dot{\alpha}} = u_0 Z_{\dot{w}}$$

$$Z_q = C_{z_q} \frac{\bar{c}}{2u_0} QS/m \qquad Z_{\delta e} = C_{z_{\delta e}} QS/m$$

$$M_u = C_{m_u} \frac{(QS\bar{c})}{u_0 I_y}$$

$$M_w = C_{m_\alpha} \frac{(QS\bar{c})}{u_0 I_y} \qquad M_{\dot{w}} = C_{m_{\dot{\alpha}}} \frac{\bar{c}}{2u_0} \frac{QS\bar{c}}{u_0 I_y}$$

$$M_\alpha = u_0 M_w \qquad\qquad M_{\dot{\alpha}} = u_0 M_{\dot{w}}$$

$$M_q = C_{m_q} \frac{\bar{c}}{2u_0} (QS\bar{c})/I_y \qquad M_{\delta e} = C_{m_{\delta e}}(QS\bar{c})/I_y$$

The force and moment derivatives in the matrices have been divided by the mass of the airplane or the moment of inertia, respectively, as indicated:

$$X_u = \frac{\partial X/\partial u}{m}, \qquad M_u = \frac{\partial X/\partial u}{I_y}, \qquad \text{and so forth} \qquad (4.55)$$

Table 4.2 includes a list of the definitions of the longitudinal stability derivatives. Methods for estimating the stability coefficients were discussed in Chapter 3.

The homogeneous solution to Equation (4.49) can be obtained by assuming a solution of the form

$$\mathbf{x} = \mathbf{x}_r e^{\lambda_r t} \qquad (4.56)$$

Substituting Equation (4.56) into Equation (4.49) yields

$$[\lambda_r \mathbf{I} - \mathbf{A}]\mathbf{x}_r = 0 \qquad (4.57)$$

where $\mathbf{I}$ is the identity matrix

$$\mathbf{I} = \begin{bmatrix} 1 & 0 & 0 & 0 \\ 0 & 1 & 0 & 0 \\ 0 & 0 & 1 & 0 \\ 0 & 0 & 0 & 1 \end{bmatrix} \qquad (4.58)$$

For a nontrivial solution to exist, the determinant

$$|\lambda_r \mathbf{I} - \mathbf{A}| = 0 \qquad (4.59)$$

must be 0. The roots λ_r of Equation (4.59) are called the characteristic roots or eigenvalues. The solution of Equation (4.59) can be accomplished easily using a digital computer. Most computer facilities will have a subroutine package for determining the eigenvalues of a matrix. The software package MATLAB* was used by the author for solution of matrix problems.

The eigenvectors for the system can be determined once the eigenvalues are known from Equation (4.60).

$$[\lambda_j I - A]P_{ij} = 0 \tag{4.60}$$

where P_{ij} is the eigenvector corresponding to the jth eigenvalue. The set of equations making up Equation (4.60) is linearly dependent and homogeneous; therefore, the eigenvectors cannot be unique. A technique for finding these eigenvectors will be presented later in this chapter.

EXAMPLE PROBLEM 4.2. Given the differential equations that follow

$$\dot{x}_1 + 0.5x_1 - 10x_2 = -1\delta$$

$$\dot{x}_2 - x_2 + x_1 = 2\delta$$

where x_1 and x_2 are the state variables and δ is the forcing input to the system:

(a) Rewrite these equations in state space form; that is,

$$\dot{x} = Ax + B\eta$$

(b) Find the free response eigenvalues.
(c) What do these eigenvalues tell us about the response of this system?

Solution. Solving the differential equations for the highest order derivative yields

$$\dot{x}_1 = -0.5x_1 + 10x_2 - \delta$$

$$\dot{x}_2 = -x_1 + x_2 + 2\delta$$

or in matrix form

$$\begin{bmatrix} \dot{x}_1 \\ \dot{x}_2 \end{bmatrix} = \begin{bmatrix} -0.5 & 10 \\ -1.0 & 1.0 \end{bmatrix} \begin{bmatrix} x_1 \\ x_2 \end{bmatrix} + \begin{bmatrix} -1 \\ 2 \end{bmatrix} \delta$$

which is the state space formulation

$$\dot{x} = Ax + B\eta$$

where $A = \begin{bmatrix} -0.5 & 10 \\ -1.0 & 1.0 \end{bmatrix}$ and $B = \begin{bmatrix} -1 \\ 2 \end{bmatrix}$

The eigenvalues of the system can be determined by solving the equation

$$|\lambda I - A| = 0$$

---

* MATLAB is the trademark for the software package of scientific and engineering computrics produced by The Math Works, Inc.

where $\mathbf{I}$ is the identity matrix. Substituting the $\mathbf{A}$ matrix into the preceding equation yields

$$\left| \lambda \begin{bmatrix} 1 & 0 \\ 0 & 1 \end{bmatrix} - \begin{bmatrix} -0.5 & 10 \\ -1.0 & 1.0 \end{bmatrix} \right| = 0$$

$$\left| \begin{bmatrix} \lambda & 0 \\ 0 & \lambda \end{bmatrix} - \begin{bmatrix} -0.5 & 10 \\ -1.0 & 1.0 \end{bmatrix} \right| = 0$$

$$\begin{vmatrix} \lambda + 0.5 & -10 \\ 1.0 & \lambda - 1.0 \end{vmatrix} = 0$$

Expanding the determinant yields the characteristic equation

$$(\lambda + 0.5)(\lambda - 1.0) + 10 = 0$$

or

$$\lambda^2 - 0.5\lambda + 9.5 = 0$$

The characteristic equation can be solved for the eigenvalues for the system.

The eigenvalues for this particular characteristic equation are

$$\lambda_{1,2} = 0.25 \pm 3.07i$$

The eigenvalues are complex and the real part of the root is positive. This means that the system is dynamically unstable. If the system were given an initial disturbance, the motion would grow sinusoidally and the frequency of the oscillation would be governed by the imaginary part of the complex eigenvalue. The time to double amplitude can be calculated from Equation (4.47).

$$t_{\text{double}} = \frac{0.693}{|\eta|} = \frac{0.693}{0.25}$$

$$= 2.77 \text{ s}$$

The period of the sinusoidal motion can be calculated from Equation (4.46).

$$\text{Period} = \frac{2\pi}{\omega} = \frac{2\pi}{3.07} = 2.05 \text{ s}$$

4.5
LONGITUDINAL APPROXIMATIONS

We can think of the long-period or phugoid mode as a gradual interchange of potential and kinetic energy about the equilibrium altitude and airspeed. This is illustrated in Figure 4.10. Here we see that the long-period mode is characterized by changes in pitch attitude, altitude, and velocity at a nearly constant angle of attack. An approximation to the long-period mode can be obtained by neglecting the pitching moment equation and assuming that the change in angle of attack is 0; that is,

$$\Delta\alpha = \frac{\Delta w}{u_0} \qquad \Delta\alpha = 0 \rightarrow \Delta w = 0 \tag{4.61}$$

Making these assumptions, the homogeneous longitudinal state equations reduce to the following:

$$\begin{bmatrix} \Delta \dot{u} \\ \Delta \dot{\theta} \end{bmatrix} = \begin{bmatrix} X_u & -g \\ \dfrac{-Z_u}{u_0} & 0 \end{bmatrix} \begin{bmatrix} \Delta u \\ \Delta \theta \end{bmatrix} \tag{4.62}$$

The eigenvalues of the long-period approximation are obtained by solving the equation

$$|\lambda \mathbf{I} - \mathbf{A}| = 0 \tag{4.63}$$

or

$$\begin{vmatrix} \lambda - X_u & g \\ \dfrac{Z_u}{u_0} & \lambda \end{vmatrix} = 0 \tag{4.64}$$

Expanding this determinant yields

$$\lambda^2 - X_u \lambda - \frac{Z_u g}{u_0} = 0 \tag{4.65}$$

or

$$\lambda_p = \left[X_u \pm \sqrt{X_u^2 + 4\frac{Z_u g}{u_0}} \right] \bigg/ 2.0 \tag{4.66}$$

The frequency and damping ratio can be expressed as

$$\omega_{n_p} = \sqrt{\frac{-Z_u g}{u_0}} \tag{4.67}$$

$$\zeta_p = \frac{-X_u}{2\omega_{n_p}} \tag{4.68}$$

If we neglect compressibility effects, the frequency and damping ratios for the long-period motion can be approximated by the following equations:

$$\omega_{n_p} = \sqrt{2}\,\frac{g}{u_0} \tag{4.69}$$

$$\zeta_p = \frac{1}{\sqrt{2}}\frac{1}{L/D} \tag{4.70}$$

Notice that the frequency of oscillation and the damping ratio are inversely proportional to the forward speed and the lift-to-drag ratio, respectively. We see from this approximation that the phugoid damping is degraded as the aerodynamic efficiency (L/D) is increased. When pilots are flying an airplane under visual flight rules the phugoid damping and frequency can vary over a wide range and they will still find the airplane acceptable to fly. On the other hand, if they are flying the airplane under instrument flight rules low phugoid damping will become very objectable. To improve the damping of the phugoid motion, the designer would have to reduce the lift-to-drag ratio of the airplane. Because this would degrade the performance of the airplane, the designer would find such a choice unacceptable and would look for another alternative, such as an automatic stabilization system to provide the proper damping characteristics.

4.5.1 Short-Period Approximation

An approximation to the short-period mode of motion can be obtained by assuming $\Delta u = 0$ and dropping the X-force equation. The longitudinal state-space equations reduce to the following:

$$\begin{bmatrix} \Delta \dot{w} \\ \Delta \dot{q} \end{bmatrix} = \begin{bmatrix} Z_w & u_0 \\ M_w + M_{\dot{w}}Z_w & M_q + M_{\dot{w}}u_0 \end{bmatrix} \begin{bmatrix} \Delta w \\ \Delta q \end{bmatrix} \qquad (4.71)$$

This equation can be written in terms of the angle of attack by using the relationship

$$\Delta \alpha = \frac{\Delta w}{u_0} \qquad (4.72)$$

In addition, one can replace the derivatives due to w and $\dot{w}$ with derivatives due to α and $\dot{\alpha}$ by using the following equations. The definition of the derivative M_α is

$$M_\alpha = \frac{1}{I_y} \frac{\partial M}{\partial \alpha} = \frac{1}{I_y} \frac{\partial M}{\partial (\Delta w/u_0)} = \frac{u_0}{I_y} \frac{\partial M}{\partial w} = u_0 M_w \qquad (4.73)$$

In a similar way we can show that

$$Z_\alpha = u_0 Z_w \qquad \text{and} \qquad M_{\dot{\alpha}} = u_0 M_{\dot{w}} \qquad (4.74)$$

Using these expressions, the state equations for the short-period approximation can be rewritten as

$$\begin{bmatrix} \Delta \dot{\alpha} \\ \Delta \dot{q} \end{bmatrix} = \begin{bmatrix} \dfrac{Z_\alpha}{u_0} & 1 \\ M_\alpha + M_{\dot{\alpha}}\dfrac{Z_\alpha}{u_0} & M_q + M_{\dot{\alpha}} \end{bmatrix} \begin{bmatrix} \Delta \alpha \\ \Delta q \end{bmatrix} \qquad (4.75)$$

The eigenvalues of the state equation can again be determined by solving the equation

$$|\lambda \mathbf{I} - \mathbf{A}| = 0 \qquad (4.76)$$

which yields

$$\begin{vmatrix} \lambda - \dfrac{Z_\alpha}{u_0} & -1 \\ -M_\alpha - M_{\dot{\alpha}}\dfrac{Z_\alpha}{u_0} & \lambda - (M_q + M_{\dot{\alpha}}) \end{vmatrix} = 0 \qquad (4.77)$$

The characteristic equation for this determinant is

$$\lambda^2 - \left(M_q + M_{\dot{\alpha}} + \frac{Z_\alpha}{u_0} \right)\lambda + M_q \frac{Z_\alpha}{u_0} - M_\alpha = 0 \qquad (4.78)$$

TABLE 4.3
Summary of longitudinal approximations

	Long period (phugoid)	Short period
Frequency	$\omega_{n_p} = \sqrt{\dfrac{-Z_u g}{u_0}}$	$\omega_{n_{sp}} = \sqrt{\dfrac{Z_\alpha M_q}{u_0} - M_\alpha}$
Damping ratio	$\zeta_p = \dfrac{-X_u}{2\omega_{n_p}}$	$\zeta_{sp} = -\dfrac{M_q + M_{\dot{\alpha}} + \dfrac{Z_\alpha}{u_0}}{2\omega_{n\,sp}}$

The approximate short-period roots can be obtained easily from the characteristic equation,

$$\lambda_{sp} = \left(M_q + M_{\dot{\alpha}} + \frac{Z_\alpha}{u_0}\right)\bigg/ 2 \pm \left[\left(M_q + M_{\dot{\alpha}} + \frac{Z_\alpha}{u_0}\right)^2 \right.$$
$$\left. - 4\left(M_q \frac{Z_\alpha}{u_0} - M_\alpha\right)\right]^{1/2}\bigg/ 2 \tag{4.79}$$

or in terms of the damping and frequency

$$\omega_{n_{sp}} = \left[\left(M_q \frac{Z_\alpha}{u_0} - M_\alpha\right)\right]^{1/2} \tag{4.80}$$

$$\zeta_{sp} = -\left[M_q + M_{\dot{\alpha}} + \frac{Z_\alpha}{u_0}\right]\bigg/ (2\omega_{n_{sp}}) \tag{4.81}$$

Equations (4.80) and (4.81) should look familiar. They are very similar to the equations derived for the case of a constrained pitching motion. If we neglect the Z_α term (i.e., neglect the vertical motion), Equations (4.80) and (4.81) are identical to Equations (4.38) and (4.39). A summary of the approximate formulas is presented in Table 4.3.

To help clarify the preceding analysis, we shall determine the longitudinal characteristics of the general aviation airplane included in Appendix B.

EXAMPLE PROBLEM 4.3. Find the longitudinal eigenvalues and eigenvectors for the general aviation airplane included in Appendix B and Figure 4.11. Compare these results with the answers obtained by using the phugoid and short-period approximations. The exact solution was determined numerically using MATLAB.

Solution. First, we must determine the numerical values of the dimensional longitudinal stability derivatives. The dynamic pressure Q and the terms QS, $QS\bar{c}$, and $\bar{c}/2u_0$ are

$$Q = \tfrac{1}{2}\rho u_0^2 = (0.5)(0.002378 \text{ slug/ft}^3)(176 \text{ ft/s})^2$$
$$= 36.8 \text{ lb/ft}^2$$
$$QS = (36.8 \text{ lb/ft}^2)(184 \text{ ft}^2) = 6771 \text{ lb}$$
$$QS\bar{c} = (6771 \text{ lb})(5.7 \text{ ft}) = 38596 \text{ ft} \cdot \text{lb}$$
$$(\bar{c}/2u_0) = (5.7 \text{ ft})/(2 \times 176 \text{ ft/s}) = 0.016 \text{ s}$$

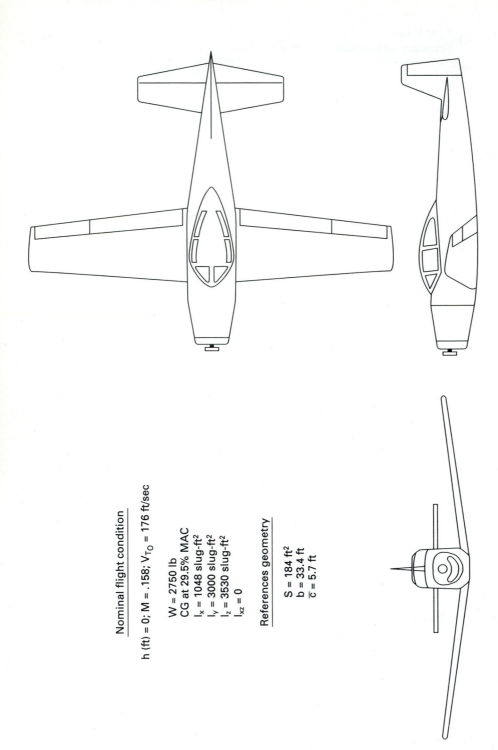

Nominal flight condition

h (ft) = 0; M = .158; V_{T_O} = 176 ft/sec

W = 2750 lb
CG at 29.5% MAC
I_x = 1048 slug-ft^2
I_y = 3000 slug-ft^2
I_z = 3530 slug-ft^2
I_{xz} = 0

References geometry

S = 184 ft^2
b = 33.4 ft
$\bar{c}$ = 5.7 ft

FIGURE 4.11
Geometric, mass, and aerodynamic properties of a general aviation airplane.

The longitudinal derivatives can be estimated from the formulas in Table 4.2.

u derivatives

$$\begin{aligned}
X_u &= -(C_{D_u} + 2C_{D_0})QS/(u_0 m) \\
&= -[0.0 + 2(0.05)](6771 \text{ lb})/[(176 \text{ ft/s})(85.4 \text{ slugs})] \\
&= -0.045 \ (\text{s}^{-1}) \\
Z_u &= -(C_{L_u} + 2C_{L_0})QS/(u_0 m) \\
&= -[0.0 + 2(0.41)](6771 \text{ lb})/[(176 \text{ ft/s})(85.4 \text{ slugs})] \\
&= -0.369 \ (\text{s}^{-1}) \\
M_u &= 0
\end{aligned}$$

w derivatives

$$\begin{aligned}
X_w &= -(C_{D_\alpha} - C_{L_0})QS/(u_0 m) \\
&= -(0.33 - 0.41)(6771 \text{ lb})/[(176 \text{ ft/s})(85.4 \text{ slugs})] \\
&= 0.036 \ (\text{s}^{-1}) \\
Z_w &= -(C_{L_\alpha} + C_{D_0})QS/(u_0 m) \\
&= -(4.44 + 0.05)(6771 \text{ lb})/[((176 \text{ ft/s})(85.4 \text{ slugs})) \\
&= -2.02 \ (\text{s}^{-1}) \\
M_w &= C_{m_\alpha}QS\bar{c}/(u_0 I_y) \\
&= (-0.683)(38\ 596 \text{ ft} \cdot \text{lb})/[(176 \text{ ft/s})(3000 \text{ slugs} \cdot \text{ft}^2)] \\
&= -0.05 \ [1/(\text{ft} \cdot \text{s})]
\end{aligned}$$

$\dot{w}$ derivatives

$$\begin{aligned}
X_{\dot{w}} &= 0 \\
Z_{\dot{w}} &= 0 \\
M_{\dot{w}} &= C_{m_{\dot{\alpha}}}\frac{\bar{c}}{2u_0} QS\bar{c}/(u_0 I_y) \\
&= (-4.36)(0.016 \text{ s})(38\ 596 \text{ ft} \cdot \text{lb})/[(176 \text{ ft/s})(3000 \text{ slugs} \cdot \text{ft}^2)] \\
&= -0.0051 \ (\text{ft}^{-1})
\end{aligned}$$

q derivatives

$$\begin{aligned}
X_q &= 0 \\
Z_q &= 0 \\
M_q &= C_{m_q}\frac{\bar{c}}{2u_0} QS\bar{c}/I_y \\
&= (-9.96)(0.016 \text{ s})(38\ 596 \text{ ft} \cdot \text{lb})/(3000 \text{ slugs} \cdot \text{ft}^2) \\
&= -2.05 \ (\text{s}^{-1})
\end{aligned}$$

Substituting the numerical values of the stability derivatives into Equation (4.51), we can obtain the stability matrix:

$$\dot{x} = Ax$$

or

$$
\begin{bmatrix} \Delta\dot{u} \\ \Delta\dot{w} \\ \Delta\dot{q} \\ \Delta\dot{\theta} \end{bmatrix} =
\begin{bmatrix}
-0.045 & 0.036 & 0.0000 & -32.2 \\
-0.369 & -2.02 & 176 & 0.0000 \\
0.0019 & -0.0396 & -2.948 & 0.000 \\
0.0000 & 0.0000 & 1.0000 & 0.0000
\end{bmatrix}
\begin{bmatrix} \Delta u \\ \Delta w \\ \Delta q \\ \Delta\theta \end{bmatrix}
$$

The eigenvalues can be determined by finding eigenvalues of the matrix A:

$$|\lambda I - A| = 0$$

The resulting characteristic equation is

$$\lambda^4 + 5.05\lambda^3 + 13.2\lambda^2 + 0.67\lambda + 0.59 = 0$$

The solution of the characteristic equation yields the eigenvalues:

$$\lambda_{1,2} = -0.0171 \pm i(0.213) \quad \text{(phugoid)}$$

$$\lambda_{3,4} = -2.5 \pm i\,(2.59) \quad \text{(short period)}$$

The period, time, and number of cycles of half amplitude are readily obtained once the eigenvalues are known.

Phugoid (long period)	Short period
$t_{1/2} = 0.69/|\eta| = \dfrac{0.69}{-0.0171}$	$t_{1/2} = 0.69/|\eta| = \dfrac{0.69}{-2.5}$
$t_{1/2} = 40.3$ s	$t_{1/2} = 0.28$ s
Period $= 2\pi/\omega = 2\pi/0.213$	Period $= 2\pi/\omega = 2\pi/2.59$
Period $= 29.5$ s	Period $= 2.42$ s
Number of cycles to half amplitude	**Number of cycles to half amplitude**
$N_{1/2} = \dfrac{t_{1/2}}{P} = 0.110\dfrac{\omega}{|\eta|}$	$N_{1/2} = 0.110\dfrac{\omega}{|\eta|}$
$= \dfrac{(0.110)(0.213)}{|-0.0171|}$	$= \dfrac{(0.110)(2.59)}{|-2.5|}$
$N_{1/2} = 1.37$ cycles	$N_{1/2} = 0.11$ cycles

Now let us estimate these parameters by means of the long- and short-period approximations. The damping ratio and undamped natural frequency for the long-period motion was given by Equations (4.69), (4.70), (4.80), and (4.81).

Phugoid approximation

$$\omega_{n_p} = \sqrt{\frac{-Z_u g}{u_0}} = \left[\frac{-(0.369)(32.21)}{(176)}\right]^{1/2} = 0.26 \text{ rad/s}$$

$$\zeta_p = \frac{-X_u}{2\omega_{n_p}} = \frac{-(-0.045)}{2(0.26)} = 0.087$$

$$\begin{aligned}
\lambda_{1,2} &= -\zeta_p\omega_{n_p} \pm i\omega_{n_p}\sqrt{1 - \zeta_p^2} \\
&= -(0.087)(0.26) \pm i(0.26)\sqrt{1 - (0.087)^2} \\
&= -0.023 \pm i0.26
\end{aligned}$$

$$\text{Period} = \frac{2\pi}{\omega} = \frac{2\pi}{0.26} = 24.2 \text{ s}$$

$$t_{1/2} = \frac{0.69}{\eta} = \frac{0.69}{|-0.023|} = 30 \text{ s}$$

$$N_{1/2} = 0.110\frac{\omega}{|\eta|} = 0.110\frac{[0.26]}{0.023} = 1.24 \text{ cycles}$$

Short-period approximation

$$\omega_{n_{sp}} = \sqrt{\frac{Z_\alpha M_q}{u_0} - M_\alpha}$$

Recall that $Z_\alpha = u_0 Z_w$, $M_\alpha = u_0 M_w$, and $M_{\dot{\alpha}} = u_0 M_{\dot{w}}$

$$\omega_{n_{sp}} = [(-2.02)(-2.05) - (-0.05)(176)]^{1/2} = 3.6 \text{ rad/s}$$

$$\begin{aligned}
\zeta_{sp} &= \left(M_q + M_{\dot{\alpha}} + \frac{Z_\alpha}{u_0}\right)\bigg/[2\omega_{n\,sp}] \\
&= [(-2.05) + (-0.88) + (-2.02)]/[(2)(3.6)] \\
&= 0.69
\end{aligned}$$

$$\begin{aligned}
\lambda_{1,2,sp} &= -\zeta_{sp}\omega_{n\,sp} \pm i\omega_{n\,sp}\sqrt{1 - \zeta_{sp}^2} \\
&= -(0.69)(3.6) \pm i(3.6)\sqrt{1 - (0.69)^2} \\
&= -2.48 \pm i2.61
\end{aligned}$$

$$\text{Period} = \frac{2\pi}{\omega} = \frac{2\pi}{2.61} = 2.4 \text{ s}$$

$$t_{1/2} = \frac{0.69}{|\eta|} = \frac{0.69}{|-2.48|} = 0.278 \text{ s}$$

$$N_{1/2} = 0.110\frac{\omega}{|\eta|} = 0.110\frac{3.6}{|-2.48|} = 0.16 \text{ cycles}$$

A summary of the results from the exact and approximate analyses is included in Table 4.4. In this analysis, the short-period approximation was found to be in closer agreement with the exact solution than the phugoid approximation. In general, the short-period approximation is the more accurate one.

The eigenvectors for this problem can be determined by a variety of techniques; however, we will discuss only one relatively straightforward method. For additional

TABLE 4.4
Comparison of exact and aproximate methods

	Exact method	Approximate method	Difference
Phugoid	$t_{1/2} = 40.3$ s	$t_{1/2} = 30$ s	25%
	$P = 29.5$ s	$P = 24.2$ s	18%
Short period	$t_{1/2} = 0.280$ s	$t_{1/2} = 0.278$ s	0%
	$P = 2.42$ s	$P = 2.4$ s	0%

information on other techniques, readers should go to their methematics library or computer center. Most computer facilities maintain digital computer programs suitable for extracting eigenvalues and eigenvectors of large-order systems.

To obtain the longitudinal eigenvectors for this example problem, we will start with Equation (4.60), which is expanded as follows:

$$(\lambda_j - A_{11}) \, \Delta u_j - A_{12} \, \Delta w_j - A_{13} \, \Delta q_j - A_{14} \, \Delta\theta_j = 0$$

$$-A_{21} \, \Delta u_j + (\lambda_j - A_{22})\Delta w_j - A_{23}q_j - A_{24} \, \Delta\theta_j = 0$$

$$-A_{31} \, \Delta u_j - A_{32} \, \Delta w_j + (\lambda_j - A_{33})\Delta q_j - A_{34} \, \Delta\theta_j = 0$$

$$- A_{41} \, \Delta u_j - A_{42} \, \Delta w_j - A_{43} \, \Delta q_j + (\lambda_j - A_{44})\Delta\theta_j = 0$$

In this set of equations, the only unknowns are the components of the eigenvector; the eigenvalues λ_j and the elements of the **A** matrix were determined previously. Dividing the preceding equations by any one of the unknowns (for this example we will use $\Delta\theta_j$), we obtain four equations for the three unknown ratios. Any three of the four equations can be used to find the eigenvectors. If we drop the fourth equation, we will have a set of three equations with the three unknown ratios, as follows:

$$(\lambda_j - A_{11})\left(\frac{\Delta u}{\Delta\theta}\right)_j - A_{12}\left(\frac{\Delta w}{\Delta\theta}\right)_j - A_{13}\left(\frac{\Delta q}{\Delta\theta}\right)_j = A_{14}$$

$$-A_{21}\left(\frac{\Delta u}{\Delta\theta}\right)_j + (\lambda_j - A_{22})\left(\frac{\Delta w}{\Delta\theta}\right)_j - A_{23}\left(\frac{\Delta q}{\Delta\theta}\right)_j = A_{24}$$

$$-A_{31}\left(\frac{\Delta u}{\Delta\theta}\right)_j - A_{32}\left(\frac{\Delta w}{\Delta\theta}\right)_j + (\lambda_j - A_{33})\left(\frac{\Delta q}{\Delta\theta}\right)_j = A_{34}$$

This set of equations can easily be solved by conventional techniques to yield the eigenvector $[\Delta u/\Delta\theta, \, \Delta w/\Delta\theta, \, \Delta q/\Delta\theta, \, 1]$.

The nondimensional eigenvectors for the example problem have been computed and are listed in Table 4.5. The longitudinal modes now can be examined by means of a vector or Argand diagram. The magnitude of the eigenvectors are arbitrary so only the relative length of the vectors is important.

Figure 4.12 is an Argand diagram illustrating the long-period and short-period modes. In this diagram the lengths of the vectors are decreasing exponentially with time, while the vectors are rotating with the angular rate ω. The motion of the airplane can be imagined as the projection of the eigenvectors along the real axis.

On close examination of Figure 4.12, several observations can be made. For the long-period mode, we see that the changes in angle of attack and pitch rate are

TABLE 4.5
Longitudinal eigenvectors for general aviation

Eigenvector	Long period	Short period
	$\lambda = -0.0171 \pm 0.213i$	$\lambda = -2.5 \pm 2.59i$
$\dfrac{\Delta u/u_0}{\Delta\theta}$	$-0.114 \pm 0.837i$	$0.034 \pm 0.025i$
$\dfrac{\Delta w/u_0}{\Delta\theta} = \dfrac{\Delta\alpha}{\Delta\theta}$	$0.008 \pm 0.05i$	$1.0895 \pm 0.733i$
$\dfrac{\Delta[qc/(2u_0)]}{\Delta\theta}$	$-0.000027 \pm 0.00347i$	$-0.039 \pm 0.041i$

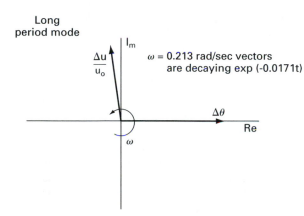

Long
period mode

$\omega = 0.213$ rad/sec vectors
are decaying exp (-0.0171t)

FIGURE 4.12
Eigenvectors for the general
aviation airplane in
Problem 4.3.

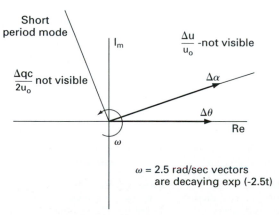

Short
period mode

$\dfrac{\Delta u}{u_o}$ -not visible

$\dfrac{\Delta qc}{2u_o}$ not visible

$\omega = 2.5$ rad/sec vectors
are decaying exp (-2.5t)

negligible. The motion is characterized by changes in speed and pitch attitude. Notice
that the velocity vector leads the pitch attitude by nearly 90° in phase. In contrast, the
short-period mode is characterized by changes in angle of attack and pitch attitude with
negligible speed variations. As we can see from the vector diagrams, the assumptions
we made earlier in developing the long- and short-period approximations indeed are
consistent with the exact solution.

4.6
THE INFLUENCE OF STABILITY DERIVATIVES
ON THE LONGITUDINAL MODES OF MOTION

The type of response we obtain from solving the differential equations of motion depends on the magnitude of the stability coefficients. This easily can be seen by examining the expressions for the damping ratio and frequency of the long- and short-period approximations. Table 4.6 summarizes the effect of each derivative on the longitudinal motion

Of the two characteristic modes, the short-period mode is the more important. If this mode has a high frequency and is heavily damped, then the airplane will respond rapidly to an elevator input without any undesirable overshoot. When the short-period mode is lightly damped or has a relatively low frequency, the airplane will be difficult to control and in some cases may even be dangerous to fly.

The phugoid or long-period mode occurs so slowly that the pilot can easily negate the disturbance by small control movements. Even though the pilot can correct easily for the phugoid mode it would become extremely fatiguing if the damping were too low.

Figures 4.13 and 4.14 show the effects of varying the center of gravity position and the horizontal tail area size on the long- and short-period responses. As the center of gravity is moved rearward the longitudinal modes become aperiodic and, eventually, unstable.

From a performance standpoint, it would be desirable to move the center of gravity further aft so that trim drags during the cruise portion of the flight could be reduced. Unfortunately, this leads to a less stable airplane. By using an active control stability augmentation system, the requirement of static stability can be relaxed without degrading the airplane's flying qualities.

Recent studies by the commercial aircraft industry have shown that fuel saving of 3 or 4 percent is possible if relaxed stability requirements and active control stability augmentation are incorporated into the design. With the ever-rising costs of jet fuel, this small percentage could mean the savings of many millions of dollars for the commercial airlines.

TABLE 4.6
Influence of stability derivatives on the long- and short-period motions

Stability derivative	Mode affected	How affected
$M_q + M_{\dot{\alpha}}$	Damping of short-period mode of motion	Increasing $M_q + M_{\dot{\alpha}}$ increases damping
M_α	Frequency of short-period mode of motion	Increasing M_α or static stability increases the frequency
X_u	Damping of the phugoid or long-period mode of motion	Increasing X_u increases damping
Z_u	Frequency of phugoid mode of motion	Increasing Z_u increases the frequency

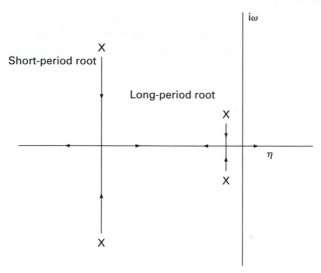

Arrow indicates direction of decreasing
static margin. Center of gravity is moving aft.

FIGURE 4.13
Influence of center of gravity position on longitudinal
response.

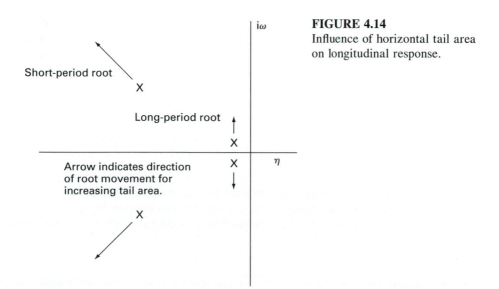

FIGURE 4.14
Influence of horizontal tail area
on longitudinal response.

4.7
FLYING QUALITIES

In the previous sections we examined the stick fixed longitudinal characteristics of an airplane. The damping and frequency of both the short- and long-period motions were determined in terms of the aerodynamic stability derivatives. Because the stability derivatives are a function of the geometric and aerodynamic characteristics of the airplane, designers have some control over the longitudinal dynamics by their selection of the vehicle's geometric and aerodynamic characteristics. For example, increasing the tail size would increase both the static stability of the airplane and the damping of the short-period motion.* However, the increased tail area also would increase the weight and drag of the airplane and thereby reduce the airplane's performance, The designer is faced with the challenge of providing an airplane with optimum performance that is both safe and easy to fly. To achieve such a goal, the designer needs to know what degree of stability and control is required for the pilot to consider the airplane safe and flyable.

The flying qualities of an airplane are related to the stability and control characteristics and can be defined as those stability and control characteristics important in forming the pilot's impression of the airplane. The pilot forms a subjective opinion about the ease or difficulty of controlling the airplane in steady and maneuvering flight. In addition to the longitudinal dynamics, the pilot's impression of the airplane is influenced by the feel of the airplane, which is provided by the stick force and stick force gradients. The Department of Defense and Federal Aviation Administration has a list of specifications dealing with airplane flying qualities. These requirements are used by the procuring and regulatory agencies to determine whether an airplane is acceptable for certification. The purpose of these requirements is to ensure that the airplane has flying qualities that place no limitation in the vehicle's flight safety nor restrict the ability of the airplane to perform its intended mission. The specification of the requirements for airplane flying qualities can be found in [4.5].

As one might guess, the flying qualities expected by the pilot depend on the type of aircraft and the flight phase. Aircraft are classified according to size and maneuverability as shown in Table 4.7. The flight phase is divided into three categories as shown in Table 4.8. Category A deals exclusively with military aircraft. Most of the flight phases listed in categories B and C are applicable to either commercial or military aircraft. The flying qualities are specified in terms of three levels:

Level 1   Flying qualities clearly adequate for the mission flight phase.
Level 2   Flying qualities adequate to accomplish the mission flight phase but with some increase in pilot workload and/or degradation in mission effectiveness or both.

---

*Because the aerodynamic derivatives also are a function of the Mach number, the designer can optimize the dynamic characteristics for only one flight regime. To provide suitable dynamic characteristics over the entire flight envelope, the designer must provide artificial damping by using stability augmentation.

TABLE 4.7
Classification of airplanes

Class I	Small, light airplanes, such as light utility, primary trainer, and light observation craft
Class II	Medium-weight, low-to-medium maneuverability airplanes, such as heavy utility/search and rescue, light or medium transport/cargo/tanker, reconnaissance, tactical bomber, heavy attack and trainer for Class II
Class III	Large, heavy, low-to-medium maneuverability airplanes, such as heavy transport/cargo/tanker, heavy bomber and trainer for Class III
Class IV	High-maneuverability airplanes, such as fighter/interceptor, attack, tactical reconnaissance, observation and trainer for Class IV

TABLE 4.8
Flight phase categories

Nonterminal flight phase

Category A	Nonterminal flight phase that require rapid maneuvering, precision tracking, or precise flight-path control. Included in the category are air-to-air combat ground attack, weapon delivery/launch, aerial recovery, reconnaissance, in-flight refueling (receiver), terrain-following, antisubmarine search, and close-formation flying
Category B	Nonterminal flight phases that are normally accomplished using gradual maneuvers and without precision tracking, although accurate flight-path control may be required. Included in the category are climb, cruise, loiter, in-flight refueling (tanker), descent, emergency descent, emergency deceleration, and aerial delivery.

Terminal flight phases

Category C	Terminal flight phases are normally accomplished using gradual maneuvers and usually require accurate flight-path control. Included in this category are takeoff, catapult takeoff, approach, wave-off/go-around and landing.

Level 3   Flying qualities such that the airplane can be controlled safely but pilot workload is excessive and/or mission effectiveness is inadequate or both. Category A flight phases can be terminated safely and Category B and C flight phases can be completed.

The levels are determined on the basis of the pilot's opinion of the flying characteristics of the airplane.

4.7.1 Pilot Opinion

Handling or flying qualities of an airplane are related to the dynamic and control characteristics of the airplane. For example, the short- and long-period damping ratios and undamped natural frequencies influence the pilot's opinion of how easy or difficult the airplane is to fly. Although we can calculate these qualities, the question that needs to be answered is what values should ζ and ω_n take so that the pilot finds the airplane easy to fly. Researchers have studied this problem using ground-based simulators and flight test aircraft. To establish relationships between

TABLE 4.9
Cooper-Harper scale

Pilot rating	Aircraft characteristic	Demand of pilot	Overall assessment
1	Excellent, highly desirable	Pilot compensation not a factor for desired performance	
2	Good, negligible deficiencies	Pilot compensation not a factor for desired performance	Good flying qualities
3	Fair, some mildly unpleasant deficiencies	Minimal pilot compensation required for desired performance	
4	Minor but annoying deficiencies	Desired performance requires moderate pilot compensation	
5	Moderately objectionable deficiencies	Adequate performance requires considerable pilot compensation	Flying qualities warrant improvement
6	Very objectionable but tolerable deficiencies	Adequate performance requires extensive pilot compensation	
7	Major deficiencies	Adequate performance not attainable with maximum tolerable pilot compensation; controllability not in question	
8	Major deficiencies	Considerable pilot compensation is required for control	Flying quality deficiencies require improvement
9	Major deficiencies	Intense pilot compensation is required to retain control	
10	Major deficiencies	Control will be lost during some portion of required operation	Improvement mandatory

the stability and control parameters of the airplane and the pilot's opinion of the airplane a pilot rating system was developed. A variety of rating scales have been used over the years; however, the rating system proposed by Cooper and Harper [4.6] has found widespread acceptance. The Cooper-Harper scale is presented in Table 4.9. The rating scale goes from 1 to 10 with low numbers corresponding to good flying or handling qualities. The scale is an indication of the difficulty in achieving the desired performance that the pilot expects.

Flying qualities research provides the designer information to assess the flying qualities of a new design early in the design process. If the flying qualities are found to be inadequate then the designer can improve the handing qualities by making design changes that influence the dynamic characteristics of the airplane. A designer that follows the flying qualities guidelines can be confident that when the airplane finally is built it will have flying qualities acceptable to its pilots.

Extensive research programs have been conducted by the government and the aviation industry to quantify the stability and control characteristics of the airplane with the pilot's opinion of the airplane's flying qualities. Figure 4.15 is an example of the type of data generated from flying qualities research. The figure shows the relationship between the level of flying qualities and the damping ratio and undamped natural frequency of the short-period mode. This kind of figure is sometimes referred to as a thumbprint plot. Table 4.10 is a summary of the longitudinal

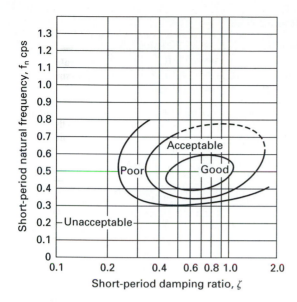

FIGURE 4.15
Short-period flying qualities.

TABLE 4.10
Longitudinal flying qualities

Phugoid mode	
Level 1	$\zeta > 0.04$
Level 2	$\zeta > 0$
Level 3	$T_2 > 55$ s

Short-period mode

	Categories A and C		Category B	
	ζ_{sp}	ζ_{sp}	ζ_{sp}	ζ_{sp}
Level	min	max	min	max
1	0.35	1.30	0.3	2.0
2	0.25	2.00	0.2	2.0
3	0.15	—	0.15	—

specifications for the phugoid and short-period motions that is valid for all classes of aircraft.

The information provided by Table 4.10 provides the designer with valuable design data. As we showed earlier, the longitudinal response characteristics of an airplane are related to its stability derivatives. Because the stability derivatives are related to the airplane's geometric and aerodynamic characteristics it is possible for the designer to consider flying qualities in the preliminary design phase.

EXAMPLE PROBLEM 4.4. A fighter aircraft has the aerodynamic, mass, and geometric characteristics that follow. Determine the short-period flying qualities at sea level, at 25,000 ft, and at 50,000 ft for a true airspeed of 800 ft/s. How can the designer improve the flying qualities of this airplane?

$$W = 17\ 580\ \text{lb} \qquad\qquad I_y = 25\ 900\ \text{slug} \cdot \text{ft}^2$$
$$S = 260\ \text{ft}^2 \qquad\qquad \bar{c} = 10.8\ \text{ft}$$
$$C_{L_\alpha} = 4.0\ \text{rad}^{-1} \qquad\qquad C_{m_q} = -4.3\ \text{rad}^{-1}$$
$$C_{m_\alpha} = -0.4\ \text{rad}^{-1} \qquad\qquad C_{m_{\dot\alpha}} = -1.7\ \text{rad}^{-1}$$

Solution. The approximate formulas for the short-period damping ratio and frequency are given by Equations (4.80) and (4.81):

$$\omega_{n_{sp}} = \sqrt{\frac{Z_\alpha M_q}{u_0} - M_\alpha}$$

$$\zeta_{sp} = -\frac{(M_q + M_{\dot\alpha} + Z_\alpha/u_0)}{2\omega_{n_{sp}}}$$

where $Z_\alpha = -C_{L_\alpha} QS/m$

$$M_q = C_{m_q}\left(\frac{\bar{c}}{2u_0}\right)\frac{QS\bar{c}}{I_y}$$

$$M_\alpha = C_{m_\alpha}\frac{QS\bar{c}}{I_y}$$

$$M_{\dot\alpha} = C_{m_{\dot\alpha}}\left(\frac{\bar{c}}{2u_0}\right)\frac{QS\bar{c}}{I_y}$$

If we neglect the effect of Mach number changes in the stability coefficients, the damping ratio and frequency can easily be calculated from the preceding equations. Figure 4.16 is a plot of ζ_{sp} and $\omega_{n_{sp}}$ as functions of the altitude. Comparing the estimated short-period damping ratio and frequency with the pilot opinion contours in Figure 4.15, we see that this airplane has poor handling qualities at sea level that deteriorate to unacceptable characteristics at altitude.

To improve the flying qualities of this airplane, the designer needs to provide more short-period damping. This could be accomplished by increasing the tail area or the tail moment arm. Such geometric changes would increase the stability coefficients C_{m_α}, C_{m_q}, and $C_{m_{\dot\alpha}}$. Unfortunately, this cannot be accomplished without a penalty in flight performance. The larger tail area results in increased structural weight and empennage drag. For low-speed aircraft geometric design changes usually can be used to provide suitable flying qualities; for aircraft that have an extensive flight envelope such as fighters it is not possible to provide good flying qualities over the entire flight regime

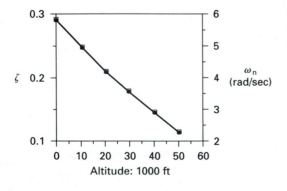

FIGURE 4.16
Variation of ζ_{sp} and $\omega_{n_{sp}}$ as a function of altitude.

from geometric considerations alone. This can be accomplished, however, by using a stability augmentation system.

4.8
FLIGHT SIMULATION

To determine the flying quality specifications described in a previous section requires some very elaborate test facilities. Both ground-based and in-flight simulators are used to evaluate pilot opinion on aircraft response characteristics, stick force requirements, and human factor data such as instrument design, size, and location.

The ground-based flight simulator provides the pilot with the "feel" of flight by using a combination of simulator motions and visual images. The more sophisticated flight simulators provide six degrees of freedom to the simulator cockpit. Hydraulic servo actuators are attached to the bottom of the simulator cabin and driven by computers to produce the desired motion. The visual images produced on the windshield of the simulator are created by projecting images from a camera mounted over a detailed terrain board or by computer-generated images. Figure 4.17 is a sketch of a five degree of freedom ground-based simulator used by the

FIGURE 4.17
Sketch of United States Air Force Large Amplitude Multimode Aerospace Research Simulator (LAMARS). Courtesy of the Flight Control Division, Flight Dynamics Directorate, Wright Laboratory.

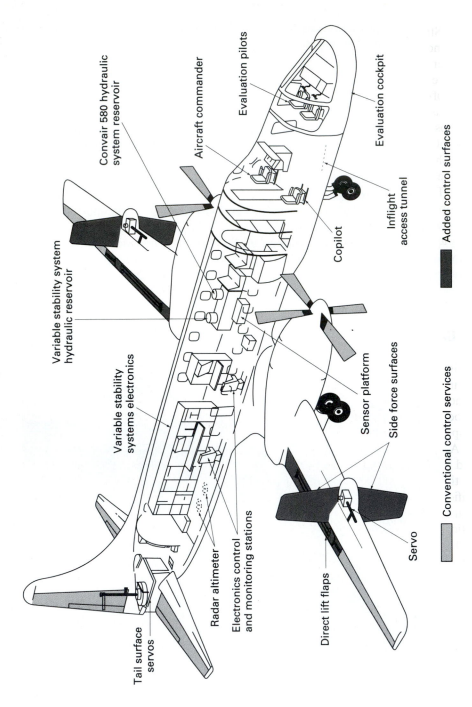

FIGURE 4.18
Airborne flight simulator.

Labels in figure:
- Convair 580 hydraulic system reservoir
- Aircraft commander
- Evaluation pilots
- Evaluation cockpit
- Inflight access tunnel
- Copilot
- Variable stability system hydraulic reservoir
- Variable stability systems electronics
- Sensor platform
- Side force surfaces
- Radar altimeter
- Electronics control and monitoring stations
- Tail surface servos
- Direct lift flaps
- Servo
- Added control surfaces
- Conventional control services

United States Air Force for handling qualities research. The crew station is located at the end of a 30 ft arm that can be controlled to provide the crew with vertical and lateral accelerations.

An example of an in-flight simulator is shown in Figure 4.18. This figure is a sketch of the U.S. Air Force's total in-flight simulator (TIFS), which is a modified C131 transport. By using special force-producing control surfaces such as direct lift flaps and side force generators, this airplane can be used to simulate a wide range of larger aircraft. The TIFS has been used to simulate the B-1, C-5, and space shuttle among other craft.

The stability characteristics of the simulator can be changed through the computer. This capability permits researchers to establish the relationship between pilot opinion and aircraft stability characteristics. For example, the short-period characteristics of the simulator could be varied and the simulator pilot would be asked to evaluate the ease or difficulty of flying the simulator. In this manner, the researcher can establish the pilot's preference for particular airplane response characteristics.

4.9
SUMMARY

In this chapter we examined the stick fixed longitudinal motion of an airplane using the linearized equations of motion developed in Chapter 3. The longitudinal dynamic motion was shown to consist of two distinct and separate modes: a long-period oscillation that is lightly damped, and a very short-period but heavily damped oscillation.

Approximate relationships for the long- and short-period modes were developed by assuming that the long-period mode occurred at constant angle of attack and the short-period mode occurred at a constant speed. These assumptions were verified by an examination of the exact solution. The approximate formulas permitted us to examine the relationship of the stability derivatives on the longitudinal motion.

Before concluding, it seems appropriate to discuss several areas of research that will affect how we analyze aircraft motions. As mentioned, active control technology in commercial aircraft can be used to improve aerodynamic efficiency. With active controls, the aircraft can be flown safely with more aft center of gravity position than would be possible with a standard control system. By shifting the center of gravity further aft, the trim drag can be reduced substantially. This allows for improved fuel economy during the cruise portion of the flight.

Active control technology also can be used to improve ride comfort and reduce wing bending during flight in turbulent air. With active controls located on the wing, a constant load factor can be maintained. This alleviates most of the unwanted response associated with encounters with a vertical gust field. In addition to improving the ride for passengers, the gust alleviation system reduces the wing bending moments, which means the wing can be lighter. Again, this will result in potential fuel savings.

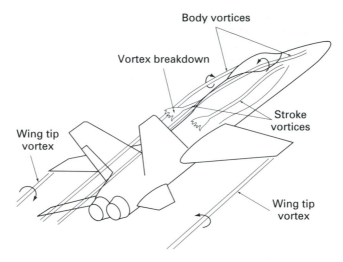

FIGURE 4.19
Sketch of a fighter aircraft illustrating separated vortical
flows.

The analysis presented in this chapter assumes that the aerodynamic characteristics are linear and can be represented by stability derivatives. This assumption is
quite good if the angle of attack of the airplane is small. However, modern fighter
aircraft are capable of performing transient maneuvers that involve high angular
rates and large angles of attack [4.7, 4.8]. The flow field around a slender fighter
aircraft at large angles of attack is dominated by vortices created by flow separation
around the forebody (nose of the fuselage), strake, wing and control surfaces.
Figure 4.19 is a sketch of the leeward wake over a slender fighter aircraft. The
interaction of these vortices with various components of the aircraft can create
significant nonlinear aerodynamic forces and moments. To further illustrate the
complexity of the wake flow around a fighter aircraft, we will examine the separated
flow over the forebody that is the nose region of the fuselage in the next section.

As the angle of attack of the airplane increases, the flow around the fuselage
separates. The separated flow field can cause nonlinear static and dynamic aerodynamic characteristics. An example of the complexity of the leeward wake flows
around a slender aircraft and a missile is sketched in Figure 4.20. Notice that as the
angle of attack becomes large the separated body vortex flow can become asymmetric. The occurence of this assymetry in the flow can give rise to large side
forces, yawing, and rolling moments on the airplane or missile even though the
vehicle is performing a symmetric maneuver (i.e., sideslip angle equals 0). The
asymmetric shedding of the nose vortices is believed to be a major contribution to
the stall spin departure characteristics of many high-performance airplanes.

Figure 4.21 a and b are multiple exposure photographs of the vortex pattern
above a cone finned model. A laser light sheet is used to illuminate smoke entrained
into the body vortices. The light sheet was positioned so that it intersected the flow
normal to the longitudinal axis of the model. The cross section of the body vortices
are observed at several axial locations along the model. The model was painted

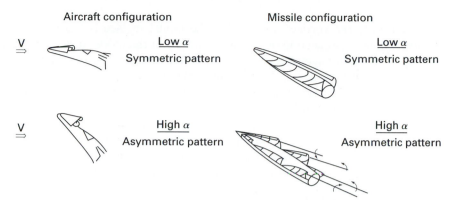

Aircraft configuration   Missile configuration

V ⇒   **Low α**
Symmetric pattern   **Low α**
Symmetric pattern

V ⇒   **High α**
Asymmetric pattern   **High α**
Asymmetric pattern

FIGURE 4.20
Vortex flows around an aircraft at large angles of attack.

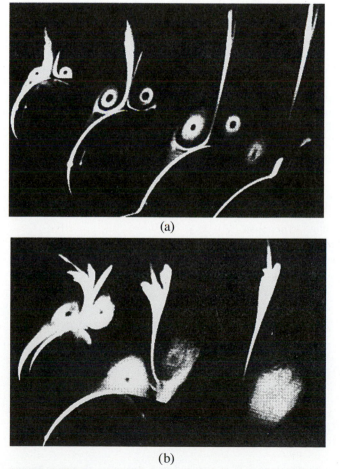

(a)

(b)

FIGURE 4.21
Flow visualization of body vortices. (a) Symmetric body
vortex pattern. (b) Asymmetric body vortex pattern.

black so that only the vortices are visible. The model surface is indicated by a curved line which is a reflection of the laser sheet from the model surface. In part a the body vortices are symmetric; however, as the angle of attack is increased further the wake vortices become asymmetric. The vortex on the right side of the model is farther away from the model surface than the left side vortex. When the wake vortices become asymmetric the body experiences both a side force and yawing moment even though the model is at zero sideslip angle.

The asymmetric vortex wake can lead to aerodynamic cross-coupling between the longitudinal and lateral equations of motion. Analyzing these motions requires a much more sophisticated analysis than that presented in this chapter.

PROBLEMS

Problems that require the use of a computer have the capital letter C after the problem number

4.1. Starting with Newton's second law of motion, develop the equation of motion for the simple torsional pendulum shown in Figure P4.1. The concept of the torsional pendulum can be used to determine the mass moment of inertia of aerospace vehicles or components. Discuss how one could use the torsional pendulum concept to determine experimentally the mass moment of inertia of a test vehicle.

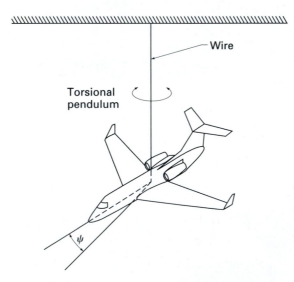

FIGURE P4.1
Aircraft model swinging as a torsional pendulum.

4.2. A mass weighing 5 lb is attached to a spring as shown in Figure P4.2 (a). The spring is observed to extend 1 in. when the mass is attached to the spring. Suppose the mass is given an instantaneous velocity of 10 ft/s in the downward direction from the equilibrium position. Determine the displacement of the mass as a function of time. Repeat your analysis for the spring mass damper system in Figure P4.2 (b), assume $F = -c\dot{y}$, where $c = 0.6$ (lb · s/ft.).

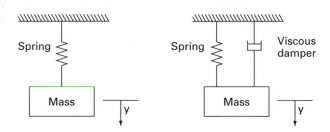

(a) Mass-spring system   (b) Mass-spring-damper-system

FIGURE P4.2
Spring-mass and spring-mass-damper systems.

4.3. The differential equation for the constrained center of gravity pitching motion of an airplane is computed to be

$$\ddot{\alpha} + 4\dot{\alpha} + 36\alpha = 0$$

Find the following:
(a) ω_n, natural frequency, rad/s
(b) ζ, damping ratio
(c) ω_d, damped natural frequency, rad/s

4.4. Given the second-order differential equation

$$\ddot{\theta} + 2\dot{\theta} + 5\theta = -\delta$$

(a) Rewrite this equation in the state space form:

$$\dot{x} = Ax + B\eta$$

(c) Determine the eigenvalues of the **A** matrix.

4.5(C). Determine the eigenvalues and eigenvectors for the following matrix:

$$A = \begin{bmatrix} 2 & -3 & 1 \\ 3 & 1 & 2 \\ -5 & 2 & -4 \end{bmatrix}$$

4.6. The characteristic roots of a second-order system are shown in Figure P4.6. If this system is disturbed from equilibrium, find the time to half-amplitude, the number of cycles to half amplitude, and the period of motion.

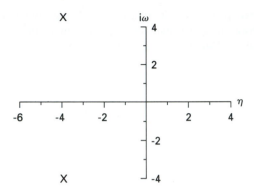

FIGURE P4.6
Second-order system roots.

4.7(C). The missile shown in Figure P4.7 is considered so that only a pitching motion is possible. Assume that the aerodynamic damping and static stability come completely from the tail surface (i.e., neglect the body contribution). If the model is displaced $10°$ from its trim angle of attack ($\alpha_t = 0$) and then released determine the angle of attack time history. Plot your results. What effect would moving the center of gravity have on the motion of the model?

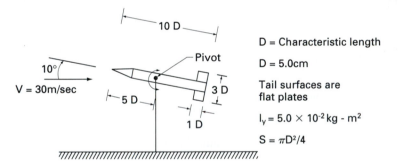

FIGURE P4.7
Pitching wind-tunnel model.

4.8. Develop the equation of motion for an airplane that has freedom only along the flight path; that is, variations in the forward speed. Assume that $X = \text{fn} (u, \delta_T)$, where u is the forward speed and δ_T is the propulsive control. If the airplane is perturbed from its equilibrium state, what type of motion would you expect?

4.9. Given the following differential equation

$$\dddot{x} + \ddot{x} - 4\dot{x} + 6x = r$$

(a) Rewrite the equation in state-space form; that is, $\dot{\mathbf{x}} = \mathbf{Ax} + \mathbf{B\eta}$. Hint: let $x_1 = x$, $x_2 = \dot{x}$, $x_3 = \ddot{x}$.

(b) If the characteristic equation is given by

$$(\lambda + 3)(\lambda^2 - 2\lambda + 2) = 0$$

describe the free response modes of motion.

4.10. Given the differential equation

$$\frac{d^2x}{dt^2} + 3\frac{dx}{dt} + 2x = 4$$

(a) Rewrite the equation in state-space form.
(b) Determine the characteristic equation of the system
(c) Find the eigenvalues of the system and describe the motion one might expect for these eigenvalues.

4.11(C). For the set of differential equations that follow

$$\dot{\alpha} + 2\alpha - q = 0$$

$$\ddot{\theta} + 10\alpha + 150 = -5\delta$$

(a) Rewrite the equations in state-space form.
(b) Use MATLAB or similar software to determine the eigenvalues of the **A** matrix.
(c) Determine the response of the system to a unit step input. Assume the initial states all are 0.

4.12. Use the short- and long-period approximations to find the damping ratio for the executive jet airplane described in Appendix B.

4.13. Show that if one neglects compressibility effects the frequency and damping ratio for the phugoid mode can be expressed as

$$\omega_{np} = \sqrt{2}\,\frac{g}{u_0} \qquad \text{and} \qquad \zeta_p = \frac{1}{\sqrt{2}}\frac{1}{L/D}$$

4.14. From data in Figure P4.14 estimate the time to half-amplitude and the number of cycles for both the short- and long-period modes.

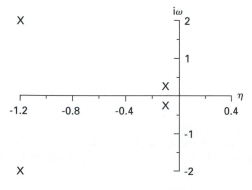

Longitudinal roots   **FIGURE P4.14**

4.15. The short-period equations for a particular airplane can be expressed as follows:

$$\begin{bmatrix} \Delta\dot{\alpha} \\ \Delta\dot{q} \end{bmatrix} = \begin{bmatrix} \dfrac{Z_\alpha}{u} & 1 \\ M_\alpha & M_q \end{bmatrix}\begin{bmatrix} \Delta\alpha \\ \Delta q \end{bmatrix}$$

Suppose $Z_\alpha/u_0 = -1$. Determine M_q and M_α so that the damping ration $\zeta = 0$, and the undamped natural frequency is 2 rad/s.

4.16. What effect will increasing altitude have on the short- and long-period modes? Use the approximate formulas in your analysis.

4.17. Develop the equation of motion for an airplane that has freedom only along the flight path; that is, variations in forward speed. If the airplane is perturbed from its equilibrium state what type of motion would you expect? Clearly state all of your assumptions.

4.18(C). Develop a computer program to compute the eigenvalues for the longitudinal equations of motion. Use your program to determine the characteristic roots for the executive jet airplane described in Appendix B. Compare your results with those obtained in Problem 4.12.

4.19(C). An airplane has the following stability and inertia characteristics:

$W = 564\ 000$ lb	$C_L = 1.11$
$I_x = 13.7 \times 10^6$ slug $\cdot$ ft^2	$C_D = 0.102$
$I_y = 30.5 \times 10^6$ slug $\cdot$ ft^2	$C_{L_\alpha} = 5.7$ rad^{-1}
$I_z = 43.1 \times 10^6$ slug $\cdot$ ft^2	$C_{D_\alpha} = 0.66$ rad^{-1}
h = sea level	$C_{m_\alpha} = -1.26$ rad^{-1}
$S = 5500$ ft^2	$C_{m_{\dot\alpha}} = -3.2$ rad^{-1}
$b = 195.68$ ft	$C_{m_q} = -20.8$ rad^{-1}
$\bar{c} = 27.3$ ft	
$V = 280$ ft/s	

(a) Find the frequency and damping ratios of the short- and long-period modes.
(b) Find the time to half-amplitude for each mode.
(c) Discuss the influence of the coefficients C_{m_q} and $C_{m_{\dot\alpha}}$ on the longitudinal motion.

4.20(C). Determine the longitudinal equations

$$\dot{x} = Ax + B\eta$$

for that STOL transport in Appendix B.
(a) Determine the eigenvalues of the **A** matrix.
(b) Determine the response of the airplane to a step input of the elevator, $\Delta\delta_e = -0.1$ rad.

4.21(C). Using the plant matrix **A** determined in Problem 4.18(C), examine the influence of the stability derivatives, C_{m_α}, C_{m_q}, C_{z_α}, and C_{x_u} on the longitudinal eigenvalues. Vary one stability coefficient at a time and plot the movement of the eigenvalues.

4.22. A wind-tunnel model is constrained so that only a pitching motion can occur. The model is in equilibrium when the angle of attack is 0. When the model is displaced from its equilibrium state and released, the motion shown in Figure P4.22 is

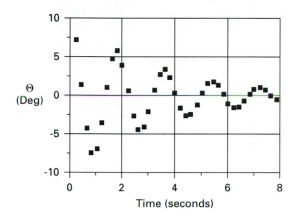

FIGURE P4.22

recorded. Using the following data determine C_{m_α} and $C_{m_q} + C_{m_{\dot\alpha}}$:

$$u_0 = 100 \text{ ft/s} \qquad c = 0.2 \text{ ft}$$
$$Q = 11.9 \text{ lb/ft}^2 \qquad I_y = 0.01 \text{ slug} \cdot \text{ft}^2$$
$$S = 0.5 \text{ ft}^2$$

Assume that equation of motion is

$$\theta(t) = \theta_0 \, e^{nt} \cos \omega t$$

where

$$\eta = (M_q + M_{\dot\alpha})/2.0$$

and

$$\omega = \sqrt{-M_\alpha}$$

REFERENCES

4.1. Lanchester, F. W. *Aerodonetics*. London: Archibald Constable, 1908.

4.2. Perkins, C. D. "Development of Airplane Stability and Control Technology." *AIAA Journal of Aircraft* 7, no. 4 (1970), pp. 290–301.

4.3. Bairstow, L. *Applied Aerodynamics,* 2nd ed. New York: Longmans, Green, 1939.

4.4. Garber, P. E. "The Wright Brothers' Contribution to Airplane Design" In *Proceedings of the AIAA Diamond Jubilee of Powered Flight—The Evolution of Aircraft Design.* New York: AIAA, 1978.

4.5. *MIL-F-8785B Military Specifications—Flying Qualities of Piloted Airplanes* (August 1969).

4.6. Cooper, G. E. and R. P. Harper. "The Use of Pilot Rating in the Evaluation of Aircraft Handling Qualities." NASA TN D-5153, 1969.
4.7. Kawamura, R. and Aihara, Y. (Editors), *Fluid Dynamics of High Angle of Attack,* Springer-Verlag, New York, NY, 1993.
4.8. Nelson, R. C. "The Role of Flow Visualization in the Study of High-Angle-of-Attack Aerodynamics." *Tactual Missle Aerodyanics,* Volume 104 of the Progress in Astronautics and Aeronautics Series, American Institute of Aeronautics and Astronautics, New York, NY, 1986.

CHAPTER 5

Lateral Motion (Stick Fixed)

"Dutch Roll is a complex oscillating motion of an aircraft involving rolling, yawing and sideslipping. So named for the resemblance to the characteristic rhythm of an ice skater."

F. D. Adams, *Aeronautical Dictionary* [5.1]

5.1
INTRODUCTION

The stick fixed lateral motion of an airplane disturbed from its equilibrium state is a complicated combination of rolling, yawing, and sideslipping motions. As was shown in Chapter 2, an airplane produces both yawing and rolling moments due to the sideslip angle. This interaction between the roll and the yaw produces the coupled motion. Three potential lateral dynamic instabilities are of interest to the airplane designer: directional divergence, spiral divergence, and the so-called Dutch roll oscillation.

Directional divergence can occur when the airplane lacks directional or weathercock stability. If disturbed from its equilibrium state such an airplane will tend to rotate to ever-increasing angles of sideslip. Owing to the side force acting on the airplane, it will fly a curved path at large sideslip angles. For an airplane that has lateral static stability (i.e., dihedral effect) the motion can occur with no significant change in bank angle. Obviously, such a motion cannot be tolerated and readily can be avoided by proper design of the vertical tail surface to ensure directional stability.

Spiral divergence is a nonoscillatory divergent motion that can occur when directional stability is large and lateral stability is small. When disturbed from equilibrium, the airplane enters a gradual spiraling motion. The spiral becomes tighter and steeper as time proceeds and can result in a high-speed spiral dive if corrective action is not taken. This motion normally occurs so gradually that the pilot unconsciously corrects for it.

The Dutch roll oscillation is a coupled lateral-directional oscillation that can be quite objectionable to pilots and passengers. The motion is characterized by a combination of rolling and yawing oscillations that have the same frequency but are out of phase with each other. The period can be on the order of 3 to 15 seconds, so that if the amplitude is appreciable the motion can be very annoying.

Before analyzing the complete set of lateral equations we shall examine several motions with a single degree of freedom. The purpose of examining the single degree of freedom equations is to gain an appreciation of the more complicated motion comprising the stick fixed lateral motion of an airplane.

5.2
PURE ROLLING MOTION

A wind-tunnel model free to roll about its x axis is shown in Figure 5.1. The equation of motion for this example of a pure rolling motion is

$$\sum \text{Rolling moments} = I_x \ddot{\phi} \tag{5.1}$$

or

$$\frac{\partial L}{\partial \delta_a} \Delta \delta_a + \frac{\partial L}{\partial p} \Delta p = I_x \Delta \ddot{\phi} \tag{5.2}$$

where $(\partial L / \partial \delta_a) \Delta \delta_a$ is the roll moment due to the deflection of the ailerons and $(\partial L / \partial p) \Delta p$ is the roll-damping moment. Methods for estimating these derivatives were presented in Chapters 2 and 3. The roll angle ϕ is the angle between z_b of the body axes and z_f of the fixed axis system. The roll rate Δp is equal to $\Delta \dot{\phi}$, which will allow us to rewrite Equation (5.2) as follows:

$$\tau \Delta \dot{p} + \Delta p = -\frac{L_{\delta a} \Delta \delta_a}{L_p} \tag{5.3}$$

Here τ, L_p, and $L_{\delta a}$ are defined as follows:

$$\tau = -\frac{1}{L_p} \quad \text{and} \quad L_p = \frac{\partial L / \partial p}{I_x} \quad L_{\delta a} = \frac{\partial L / \partial \delta_a}{I_x} \tag{5.4}$$

The parameter τ is referred to as the time constant of the system. The time constant tells us how fast our system approaches a new steady-state condition after being disturbed. If the time constant is small, the system will respond very rapidly; if the time constant is large, the system will respond very slowly.

The solution to Equation (5.3) for a step change in the aileron angle is

$$\Delta p(t) = -\frac{L_{\delta a}}{L_p}(1 - e^{-t/\tau}) \Delta \delta_a \tag{5.5}$$

Recall that C_{l_p} is negative; therefore, the time constant will be positive. The roll rate time history for this example will be similar to that shown in Figure 5.2. The steady-state roll rate can be obtained from Equation (5.5), by assuming that time t is large enough that $e^{-t/\tau}$ is essentially 0:

$$p_{ss} = \frac{-L_{\delta a}}{L_p} \Delta \delta_a \tag{5.6}$$

$$p_{ss} = \frac{-C_{l_{\delta a}} QSb/I_x}{C_{l_p}(b/2u_0)QSb/I_x} \Delta \delta_a \tag{5.7}$$

$$\frac{p_{ss}b}{2u_0} = -\frac{C_{l_{\delta a}}}{C_{l_p}} \Delta \delta_a$$

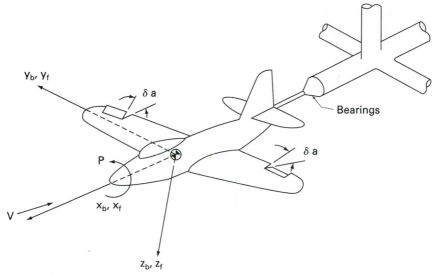

FIGURE 5.1
Wind-tunnel model constrained to a pure rolling motion.

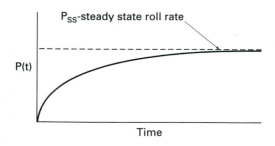

FIGURE 5.2
Typical roll response due to aileron deflection.

The term $(p_{ss}b/2u_0)$ for full aileron deflection can be used for sizing the aileron. The minimum requirement for this ratio is a function of the class of airplane under consideration:

Cargo or transport airplanes: $pb/2u_0 = 0.07$
                Fighter airplanes: $pb/2u_0 = 0.09$

EXAMPLE PROBLEM 5.1. Calculate the roll response of the F104A to a 5° step change in aileron deflection. Assume the airplane is flying at sea level with a velocity of 87 m/s. The F104A has the following aerodynamic and geometric characteristics:

$$C_{l_p} = -0.285 \text{ rad}^{-1} \qquad S = 18 \text{ m}^2$$

$$C_{l_{\delta_a}} = 0.039 \text{ rad}^{-1} \qquad b = 6.7 \text{ m}$$

$$I_x = 4676 \text{ kg} \cdot \text{m}^2$$

$$\frac{b}{2u_0} = \frac{6.7 \text{ m}}{2(87 \text{ m/s})} = 0.039 \text{ s}$$

$$Q = \frac{1}{2}\rho u_0^2 = (0.5)(1.225 \text{ kg/m}^3)(87 \text{ m/s})^2 = 4636 \text{ N/m}^2$$

$$L_p = C_{l_p}\frac{b}{2u_0}QSb/I_x$$

$$= (-0.285 \text{ rad}^{-1})(0.039 \text{ s}^{-1})(4636 \text{ N/m}^2)(18 \text{ m}^2)(6.7 \text{ m})(4676 \text{ kg} \cdot \text{m}^2)$$

$$L_p = -1.3(\text{s}^{-1})$$

$$\tau = \frac{1}{L_p} = -\frac{1}{(-1.3 \text{ s}^{-1})} = 0.77 \text{ s}$$

Steady-state roll rate

$$p_{ss} = -\frac{L_{\delta_a}}{L_p}\Delta\delta_a$$

$$L_{\delta_a} = C_{l_{\delta_a}}QSb/I_x$$

$$L_{\delta_a} = (0.039 \text{ rad}^{-1})(4636 \text{ N/m}^2)(18 \text{ m}^2)(6.7 \text{ m})/(4676 \text{ kg} \cdot \text{m}^2) = 4.66 \text{ (s}^{-2})$$

$$p_{ss} = -(4.661 \text{ s}^{-2})(5 \text{ deg})/[(-1.3 \text{ s}^{-1})(57.3 \text{ deg/rad})] = 0.31 \text{ rad/s}$$

Figure 5.3 is a plot of the roll rate time history for a step change in aileron deflection.

Let us reconsider this problem. Suppose that Figure 5.3 is a measured roll rate instead of a calculated response. The roll rate of the airplane could be measured by means of a rate gyro appropriately located on the airplane. If we know the mass and geometric properties of the airplane we can extract the aerodynamic stability coefficients from the measured motion data.

If we fit the solution to the differential equation of motion to the response we can obtain values for $C_{l_{\delta_a}}$ and C_{l_p}. It can be shown that after one time constant the response of a first-order system to a step input is 63% of its final value. With this

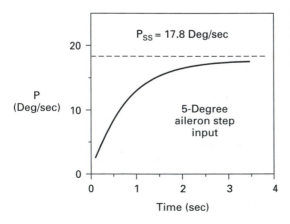

FIGURE 5.3
Roll time history of an F104A to a 5° step change in aileron deflection.

in mind we can obtain the time constant from Figure 5.3. The steady-state roll rate can also be measured directly from this figure. Knowing τ and p_{ss}, we can compute L_{δ_a} and L_p and, in turn, $C_{l_{\delta_a}}$ and C_{l_p}. The technique of extracting aerodynamic data from the measured response is often called the inverse problem or parameter identification.

5.2.1 Wing Rock

One of the most common dynamic phenomena experienced by slender-wing air-craft flying at high angles of attack is known as wing rock. Wing rock is a complicated motion that typically affects several degrees of freedom simultaneously; however, as the name implies the primary motion is an oscillation in roll. The rolling motion is self-induced and characterized by a limit cycle behavior. Obviously such a dynamic motion is unwanted and should be avoided.

A highly swept wing will undergo a wing rock motion at large angles of attack. Figure 5.4 shows the rolling motion for a delta wing having a leading edge sweep of 80° (from [5.2] and [5.3]). The wing was mounted on an air bearing system that permitted only a free to roll motion. The model was released with initial conditions $\phi = 0$ and $\dot{\phi} = 0$. The model is unstable in a roll: The motion begins to build up until it reaches some maximum amplitude at which time it continues to repeat the motion. This type of motion is called a limit cycle oscillation. The limit cycle motion clearly is indicated when the response data is plotted in a phase plane diagram. In the phase plane diagram, the amplitude, ϕ, is plotted versus the roll velocity, $\dot{\phi}$. The data in Figure 5.4 when plotted in the phase plane is as shown on

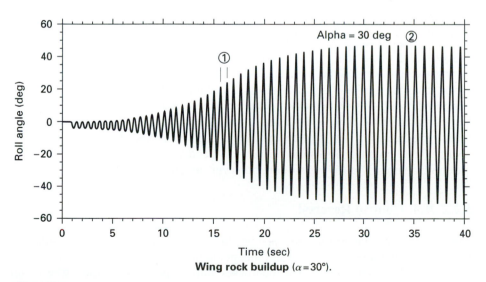

Wing rock buildup ($\alpha = 30°$).

FIGURE 5.4
Wing rock motion of a flat plate delta wing.
Leading edge sweep angle of 80° and $\alpha = 30°$

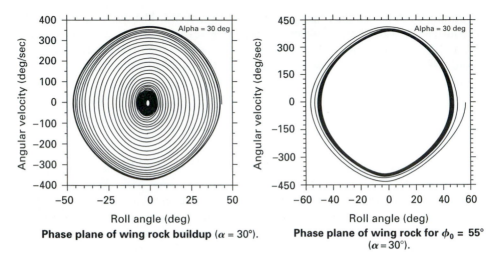

Phase plane of wing rock buildup ($\alpha = 30°$).

Phase plane of wing rock for $\phi_0 = 55°$ ($\alpha = 30°$).

FIGURE 5.5
Phase plane plots of the wing rock motion of a delta wing.

the left side of Figure 5.5. The motion is observed to spiral out to the limit cycle. If the initial conditions on release were any combination on ϕ and $\dot{\phi}$ within the limit cycle boundary the motion would still spiral out the limit cycle boundary. On the other hand if the initial conditions were outside the limit cycle boundary the motion would spiral into the limit cycle as illustrated on the right side of Figure 5.5. The limit cycle motion is due to the nonlinear aerodynamic characteristics of a slender delta wing at large angles of attack. Because the aerodynamics are nonlinear, the equation of motion also will be nonlinear. This type of motion can not be predicted using the linear differential equations presented in this chapter.

Airplanes most susceptible to this oscillatory phenomenon typically have highly swept planforms or long, slender forebodies that produce vortical flows during excursions into the high angle-of-attack regime. The wing rock motion arises from the unsteady behavior of the vortical flow fields associated with these planforms, coupled with the rolling degree of freedom of the aircraft. The unsteady loads created by the flow field produce a rolling oscillation that exhibits the classic limit cycle behavior. The motion can be quite complex and in many cases is the result of the coupling of several degrees of freedom. There are cases where the motion is primarily a rolling motion, however, as presented here.

5.2.2 Roll Control Reversal

The aileron control power per degree, $(pb/2u_0)/\delta_a$ is shown in Figure 5.6. Note that $(pb/2u_0)/\delta_a$ essentially is a constant, independent of speeds below 140 m/s. However, at high speeds $(pb/2u_0)/\delta_a$ decreases until a point is reached where roll control is lost. The point at which $(pb/2u_0)/\delta_a = 0$ is called the aileron reversal speed. The loss and ultimate reversal of aileron control is due to the elasticity of the wing.

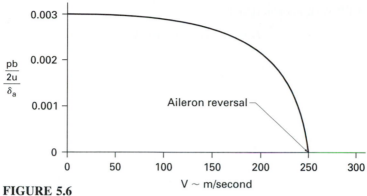

FIGURE 5.6
Aileron control power per degree versus flight velocity.

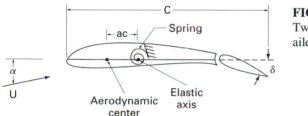

FIGURE 5.7
Two-dimensional wing and aileron.

Some understanding of this aeroelastic phenomenon can be obtained from the following simplified analysis. Figure 5.7 shows a two-dimensional wing with an aileron. As the aileron is deflected downward it increases the lift acting on the wing. The increased lift produces a rolling moment. Deflecting the aileron also produces a nose-down aerodynamic pitching moment that tends to twist the wing downward. Such a rotation will reduce the lift and rolling moment. The aerodynamic forces vary with the square of the airplane's velocity whereas the elastic stiffness of the wing is independent of the flight speed. Thus, the wing may twist enough that the ailerons become ineffective. The speed at which the ailerons become ineffective is called the critical aileron reversal speed.

To determine the aileron reversal speed, we shall use the information in Figure 5.7. The torsional stiffness of the wing will be modeled by the simple torsional spring located at the elastic axis of the wing. The lift and moment coefficients for the two-dimensional airfoil can be expressed as functions of the stability coefficients:

$$C_\ell = C_{\ell_\alpha}\alpha + C_{\ell_\delta}\delta \tag{5.8}$$

$$C_m = C_{m_{ac}} + C_{m_\delta}\delta \tag{5.9}$$

where δ is the flap angle; that is, aileron. Aileron reversal occurs when the rate of change of lift with aileron deflection is 0:

$$L = (C_{\ell_\alpha}\alpha + C_{\ell_\delta}\delta)\,Qc \tag{5.10}$$

$$\frac{dL}{d\delta} = \left(C_{\ell_\alpha}\frac{d\alpha}{d\delta} + C_{\ell_\delta}\right)Qc = 0 \tag{5.11}$$

or

$$\frac{d\alpha}{d\delta} = -\frac{C_{\ell_\delta}}{C_{\ell_\alpha}} \tag{5.12}$$

Note that the angle of attack is a function of the flap angle because the wing can twist. The aerodynamic moment acting about the elastic axis is

$$M = [C_{m_{ac}} + C_{m_\delta}\delta + (C_{\ell_\alpha}\alpha + C_{\ell_\delta}\delta)\,a]\,Qc^2 \tag{5.13}$$

This moment is balanced by the torsional moment to the wing:

$$k\alpha = [C_{m_{ac}} + C_{m_\delta}\delta + (C_{\ell_\alpha}\alpha + C_{\ell_\delta}\delta)\,a]\,Qc^2 \tag{5.14}$$

where k is the torsional stiffness of the wing.

Differentiating Equation (5.14) with respect to δ yields

$$k\frac{d\alpha}{d\delta} = \left[C_{m_\delta} + \left(C_{\ell_\alpha}\frac{d\alpha}{d\delta} + C_{\ell_\delta}\right)a\right]Qc^2 \tag{5.15}$$

Substituting Equation (5.12) into (5.15) and solving for Q yields the critical dynamic pressure when control reversal will occur:

$$Q_{rev} = -\frac{kC_{\ell_\delta}}{c^2 C_{\ell_\alpha} C_{m_\delta}} \tag{5.16}$$

The reversal speed is given by

$$U_{rev} = \sqrt{-\frac{2kC_{\ell_\delta}}{\rho c^2 C_{\ell_\alpha} C_{m_\delta}}} \tag{5.17}$$

Note that the reversal speed increases with increasing torsional stiffness and increasing altitude.

5.3
PURE YAWING MOTION

As our last example of a motion with a single degree of freedom, we shall examine the motion of an airplane constrained so that it can perform only a simple yawing motion. Figure 5.8 illustrates a wind-tunnel model that can only perform yawing motions. The equation of motion can be written as follows:

$$\sum \text{Yawing moments} = I_z\ddot{\psi} \tag{5.18}$$

The yawing moment N and the yaw angle ψ can be expressed as

$$N = N_0 + \Delta N \qquad \psi = \psi_0 + \Delta\psi \tag{5.19}$$

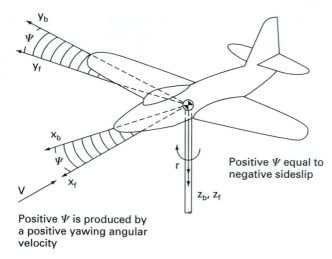

FIGURE 5.8
Wind-tunnel model
constrained to a pure
yawing motion.

Positive Ψ equal to
negative sideslip

Positive Ψ is produced by
a positive yawing angular
velocity

The yawing moment equation reduces to

$$\Delta N = I_z \, \Delta\ddot{\psi} \tag{5.20}$$

where $$\Delta N = \frac{\partial N}{\partial \beta} \, \Delta\beta + \frac{\delta N}{\delta \dot{\beta}} \, \Delta\dot{\beta} + \frac{\partial N}{\partial r} \, \Delta r + \frac{\partial N}{\partial \delta_r} \, \Delta\delta_r \tag{5.21}$$

Because the center of gravity is constrained, the yaw angle ψ and the sideslip angle β are related by the expression

$$\Delta\psi = -\Delta\beta \qquad \Delta\dot{\psi} = -\Delta\dot{\beta} \qquad \Delta\dot{\psi} = \Delta r \tag{5.22}$$

Substituting these relationships into Equation (5.20) and rearranging yields

$$\Delta\ddot{\psi} - (N_r - N_{\dot{\beta}}) \, \Delta\dot{\psi} + N_\beta \, \Delta\psi = N_{\delta_r} \, \Delta\delta_r \tag{5.23}$$

where $$N_r = \frac{\partial N/\partial r}{I_z} \qquad \text{and so forth.}$$

For airplanes, the term $N_{\dot{\beta}}$ usually is negligible and will be eliminated in future expressions.

The characteristic equation for Equation (5.23) is

$$\lambda^2 - N_r\lambda + N_\beta = 0 \tag{5.24}$$

The damping ratio ζ and the undamped natural frequency ω_n can be determined directly from Equation (5.24):

$$\omega_n = \sqrt{N_\beta} \tag{5.25}$$

$$\zeta = -\frac{N_r}{2\sqrt{N_\beta}} \tag{5.26}$$

The solution to Equation (5.23) for a step change in the rudder control will result in a damped sinusoidal motion, provided the airplane has sufficient aerodynamic damping. As in the case of the pure pitching we see that the frequency of

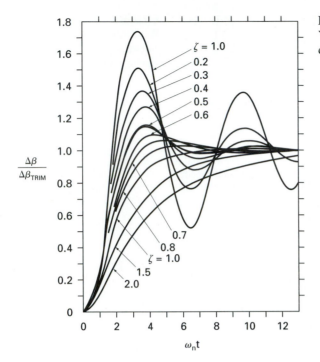

FIGURE 5.9
Yawing motion due to rudder deflection.

oscillation is a function of the airplane's static stability (weathercock or directional stability) and the damping ratio is a function of the aerodynamic damping derivative. Figure 5.9 illustrates the yawing motion due to a step change in rudder deflections for different levels of aerodynamic damping.

EXAMPLE PROBLEM 5.2. Suppose an airplane is constrained to a pure yawing motion as described in Section 5.3. Using the data for the general aviation airplane in Appendix B, determine the following:

(a) The yawing moment equation rewritten in state-space form.
(b) The characteristic equation and eigenvalues for the system.
(c) The damping ratio, ζ, and undamped natural frequency, ω_n.
(d) The response of the airplane to a 5° rudder input. Assume the initial conditions are $\Delta\beta(0) = 0$, $\Delta r(0) = 0$.

Solution. The lateral derivatives can be estimated from the data in Appendix B. For the sea-level flight condition, the weathercock static stability coefficient, C_{n_β}, the yawing damping coefficient, C_{n_r}, and the rudder control power, $C_{n_{\delta_r}}$, have the following numerical values:

$$C_{n_\beta} = 0.071/\text{rad} \qquad C_{n_r} = -0.125/\text{rad}$$

$$C_{n_{\delta_r}} = -0.072/\text{rad}$$

The derivative $C_{n_{\dot\beta}}$ is not included in the table of Appendix B and will be assumed to be 0 for this problem.

For a flight velocity of 176 ft/s, the dimensional derivatives N_β, N_r, and N_{δ_r} can be estimated from the mass, geometric, and aerodynamic stability coefficient data of

Appendix B. The dynamic pressure, Q, is calculated next:

$$Q = \frac{1}{2}\rho u_0^2 = (0.5)\,(0.002378\ \text{slug/ft}^3)\,(176\ \text{ft/s})^2$$

$$= 36.8\ \text{lb/ft}^2$$

The dimensional derivative, N_β, which is the yaw moment due to the airplane's weathercock stability, is obtained from the expression

$$N_\beta = \frac{C_{n_\beta} QSb}{I_z}$$

or

$$N_\beta = \frac{(0.071/\text{rad})\,(36.8\ \text{lb/ft}^2)\,(184\ \text{ft}^2)\,(33.4\ \text{ft})}{3530\ \text{slug}\cdot\text{ft}^2}$$

$$= 4.55/\text{s}^2$$

The dimensional derivative, N_r, which is the yaw damping of the airplane, is obtained from the expression

$$N_r = \frac{C_{n_r}\left(\dfrac{b}{2u_0}\right)QSb}{I_z}$$

$$= \frac{(-0.125/\text{rad})\,[33.4\ \text{ft}/(2(176\ \text{ft/s}))]\,(36.8\ \text{lb/ft}^2)\,(184\ \text{ft}^2)\,(33.4\ \text{ft})}{3530\ \text{slug}\cdot\text{ft}^2}$$

$$= -0.76/\text{s}$$

The dimensional derivative, N_{δ_r}, the rudder control derivative, is obtained from the expression

$$N_{\delta_r} = \frac{C_{n_{\delta_r}} QSb}{I_z}$$

$$= \frac{(-0.072/\text{rad})\,(36.8\ \text{lb/ft}^2)\,(184\ \text{ft}^2)\,(33.4\ \text{ft})}{3530\ \text{slug}\cdot\text{ft}^2}$$

$$= -4.6/\text{s}^2$$

Substituting the dimensional derivatives into the constrained yawing moment equation (Equation (5.23)) yields

$$\Delta\ddot{\psi} - (N_r - N_{\dot{\beta}})\,\Delta\dot{\psi} + N_\beta\,\Delta\psi = N_{\delta_r}\,\Delta\delta_r$$

where $N_{\dot{\beta}}$ is assumed to be 0:

$$\Delta\ddot{\psi} + 0.76\,\Delta\dot{\psi} + 4.55\,\Delta\psi = -4.6\,\Delta\delta_r$$

This is a second-order differential equation in terms of the dependent variable $\Delta\psi$. The preceding second-order differential equation can be written as a system of two first-order differential equations by defining the system states as $\Delta\psi$ and Δr. Recall that the time rate of change of the yaw angle is the same as the yaw rate; that is, $\Delta\dot{\psi} = \Delta r$. Solving the yaw moment equation for the highest order derivative $\Delta\ddot{\psi}$,

$$\Delta\ddot{\psi} = -0.76\,\Delta\dot{\psi} - 4.55\,\Delta\psi - 4.6\,\Delta\delta_r$$

or

$$\Delta\dot{r} = -0.76\,\Delta r - 4.55\,\Delta\psi - 4.6\,\Delta\delta_r$$

The two state equations are

$$\Delta\dot\psi = \Delta r$$

$$\Delta\dot r = -0.76\,\Delta r - 4.55\,\Delta\psi - 4.6\,\Delta\delta_r$$

which can be readily arranged in matrix form as

$$\begin{bmatrix} \Delta\dot\psi \\ \Delta\dot r \end{bmatrix} = \begin{bmatrix} 0 & 1 \\ -4.55 & -0.76 \end{bmatrix}\begin{bmatrix} \Delta\psi \\ \Delta r \end{bmatrix} + \begin{bmatrix} 0 \\ -4.6 \end{bmatrix}\Delta\delta_r$$

or

$$\dot x = Ax + B\eta$$

where the state vector, $x = \begin{bmatrix} \Delta\psi \\ \Delta r \end{bmatrix}$, the control vector is $\Delta\delta_r$, and the A and B matrices are

$$A = \begin{bmatrix} 0 & 1 \\ -4.55 & -0.76 \end{bmatrix}$$

$$B = \begin{bmatrix} 0 \\ -4.6 \end{bmatrix}$$

The characteristic equation for the system is found from the equation

$$|\lambda I - A| = 0$$

where on substituting in the A matrix yields

$$\left| \lambda\begin{bmatrix} 1 & 0 \\ 0 & 1 \end{bmatrix} - \begin{bmatrix} 0 & 1 \\ -4.55 & -0.76 \end{bmatrix} \right| = 0$$

$$\begin{vmatrix} \lambda & -1 \\ 4.55 & \lambda + 0.76 \end{vmatrix} = \lambda(\lambda + 0.76) + 4.55 = 0$$

or

$$\lambda^2 + 0.76\lambda + 4.55 = 0$$

The characteristic equation for a second-order system could have been obtained directly from the second-order differential equation.

The eigenvalues of the system are found by obtaining the roots of the characteristic equation. For this example the root or eigenvalues can be shown to be

$$\lambda_{1,2} = -0.38 \pm 2.1i$$

The eigenvalues are complex; therefore the free response motion will be a damped sinusoidal oscillation. The motion is damped because the real part of the eigenvalue is negative.

The damping ratio, ζ, and the undamped natural frequency can be estimated from Equations (5.25) and (5.26):

$$\omega_n = \sqrt{N_\beta} = \sqrt{4.55/s^2} = 2.13 \text{ rad/s}$$

and

$$\zeta = -\frac{N_r}{2\sqrt{N_\beta}} = -\frac{(0.76/s)}{2(2.13 \text{ rad/s})} = 0.178$$

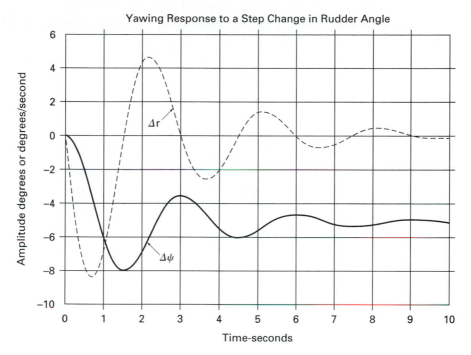

FIGURE 5.10
Yawing motion response to a 5° step input in the rudder angle.

Finally the response of the airplane to a 5° step input in the rudder is shown in Figure 5.10. The change in both heading angle $\Delta\psi$ and the yaw rate Δr are presented as a function of time. The response was determined using MATLAB.

5.4
LATERAL-DIRECTIONAL EQUATIONS OF MOTION

The lateral-directional equations of motion consist of the side force, rolling moment, and yawing moment equations of motion. The lateral equations of motion can be rearranged into the state-space form in the following manner. We start with a lateral set of Equations (5.27):

$$\left(\frac{d}{dt} - Y_v\right) \Delta v - Y_p \, \Delta p + (u_0 - Y_r) \, \Delta r - g \cos \theta_0 \, \Delta\phi = Y_{\delta_r} \, \Delta\delta_r$$

$$- L_v \, \Delta v + \left(\frac{d}{dt} - L_p\right) \Delta p - \left(\frac{I_{xz}}{I_x}\frac{d}{dt} + L_r\right) \Delta r = L_{\delta_a} \, \Delta\delta_a + L_{\delta_r} \, \Delta\delta_r \quad (5.27)$$

$$- N_v \, \Delta v - \left(\frac{I_{xz}}{I_z}\frac{d}{dt} + N_p\right) \Delta p + \left(\frac{d}{dt} - N_r\right) \Delta r = N_{\delta_a} \, \Delta\delta_a + N_{\delta_r} \, \Delta\delta_r$$

Rearranging and collecting terms, this equation can be written in the state variable form:

$$\dot{x} = Ax + B\eta \tag{5.28}$$

The matrices A and B are defined as follows:

$$A = \begin{bmatrix} Y_v & Y_p & -(u_0 - Y_r) & g\cos\theta_0 \\ L_v^* + \dfrac{I_{xz}}{I_x}N_v^* & L_p^* + \dfrac{I_{xz}}{I_x}N_p^* & L_r^* + \dfrac{I_{xz}}{I_x}N_r^* & 0 \\ N_v^* + \dfrac{I_{xz}}{I_z}L_v^* & N_p^* + \dfrac{I_{xz}}{I_z}L_p^* & N_r^* + \dfrac{I_{xz}}{I_z}L_r^* & 0 \\ 0 & 1 & 0 & 0 \end{bmatrix} \tag{5.29}$$

$$B = \begin{bmatrix} 0 & Y_{\delta_r} \\ L_{\delta_a}^* + \dfrac{I_{xz}}{I_x}N_{\delta_a}^* & L_{\delta_r}^* + \dfrac{I_{xz}}{I_x}N_{\delta_r}^* \\ N_{\delta_a}^* + \dfrac{I_{xz}}{I_z}L_{\delta_a}^* & N_{\delta_r}^* + \dfrac{I_{xz}}{I_z}L_{\delta_r}^* \\ 0 & 0 \end{bmatrix} \tag{5.30}$$

$$x = \begin{bmatrix} \Delta v \\ \Delta p \\ \Delta r \\ \Delta\phi \end{bmatrix} \quad \text{and} \quad \eta = \begin{bmatrix} \Delta\delta_a \\ \Delta\delta_r \end{bmatrix} \tag{5.31}$$

The starred derivatives are defined as follows:

$$L_v^* = \frac{L_v}{[1 - (I_{xz}^2/(I_x I_z))]} \qquad N_v^* = \frac{N_v}{[1 - (I_{xz}^2/(I_x I_z))]} \qquad \text{and the like.} \tag{5.32}$$

If the product of intertia $I_{xz} = 0$, the equations of motion reduce to the following form:

$$\begin{bmatrix} \Delta\dot{v} \\ \Delta\dot{p} \\ \Delta\dot{r} \\ \Delta\dot{\phi} \end{bmatrix} = \begin{bmatrix} Y_v & Y_p & -(u_0 - Y_r) & g\cos\theta_0 \\ L_v & L_p & L_r & 0 \\ N_v & N_p & N_r & 0 \\ 0 & 1 & 0 & 0 \end{bmatrix} \begin{bmatrix} \Delta v \\ \Delta p \\ \Delta r \\ \Delta\phi \end{bmatrix} + \begin{bmatrix} 0 & Y_{\delta_r} \\ L_{\delta_a} & L_{\delta_r} \\ N_{\delta_a} & N_{\delta_r} \\ 0 & 0 \end{bmatrix} \begin{bmatrix} \Delta\delta_a \\ \Delta\delta_r \end{bmatrix} \tag{5.33}$$

It sometimes is convenient to use the sideslip angle $\Delta\beta$ instead of the side velocity Δv. These two quantities are related to each other in the following way:

$$\Delta\beta \approx \tan^{-1}\frac{\Delta v}{u_0} = \frac{\Delta v}{u_0} \tag{5.34}$$

Using this relationship, Equation (5.33) can be expressed in terms of $\Delta\beta$:

$$
\begin{bmatrix} \Delta\dot{\beta} \\ \Delta\dot{p} \\ \Delta\dot{r} \\ \Delta\dot{\phi} \end{bmatrix} = \begin{bmatrix} \dfrac{Y_\beta}{u_0} & \dfrac{Y_p}{u_0} & -\left(1 - \dfrac{Y_r}{u_0}\right) & \dfrac{g\cos\theta_0}{u_0} \\ L_\beta & L_p & L_r & 0 \\ N_\beta & N_p & N_r & 0 \\ 0 & 1 & 0 & 0 \end{bmatrix} \begin{bmatrix} \Delta\beta \\ \Delta p \\ \Delta r \\ \Delta\phi \end{bmatrix} + \begin{bmatrix} 0 & \dfrac{Y_{\delta_r}}{u_0} \\ L_{\delta_a} & L_{\delta_r} \\ N_{\delta_a} & N_{\delta_r} \\ 0 & 0 \end{bmatrix} \begin{bmatrix} \Delta\delta_a \\ \Delta\delta_r \end{bmatrix} \quad (5.35)
$$

The solution of Equation (5.35) is obtained in the same manner as we solved the state equations in Chapter 4. The characteristic equation is obtained by expanding the following determinant:

$$ |\lambda_r \mathbf{I} - \mathbf{A}| = 0 \quad (5.36) $$

where $\mathbf{I}$ and $\mathbf{A}$ are the identity and lateral stability matrices, respectively. The characteristic equation determined from the stability matrix $\mathbf{A}$ yields a quartic equation:

$$ A\lambda^4 + B\lambda^3 + C\lambda^2 + D\lambda + E = 0 \quad (5.37) $$

where A, B, C, D, and E are functions of the stability derivatives, mass, and inertia characteristics of the airplane.

In general, we will find the roots to the lateral-directional characteristic equation to be composed of two real roots and a pair of complex roots. The roots will be such that the airplane response can be characterized by the following motions:

1. A slowly convergent or divergent motion, called the spiral mode.
2. A highly convergent motion, called the rolling mode.
3. A lightly damped oscillatory motion having a low frequency, called the Dutch roll mode.

Figures 5.11, 5.12, and 5.13 illustrate the spiral, roll, and Dutch roll motions. An unstable spiral mode results in a turning flight trajectory. The airplane's bank angle increases slowly and it flies in an ever-tightening spiral dive. The rolling motion usually is highly damped and will reach a steady state in a very short time. The combination of the yawing and rolling oscillations is called the Dutch roll motion because it reminded someone of the weaving motion of a Dutch ice skater.

5.4.1 Spiral Approximation

As indicated in Figure 5.11 the spiral mode is characterized by changes in the bank angle ϕ and the heading angle ψ. The sideslip angle usually is quite small but cannot be neglected because the aerodynamic moments do not depend on the roll angle ϕ or the heading angle ψ but on the sideslip angle β, roll rate p, and yawing rate r.

The aerodynamic contributions due to β and r usually are on the same order of magnitude. Therefore, to obtain an approximation of the spiral mode we shall

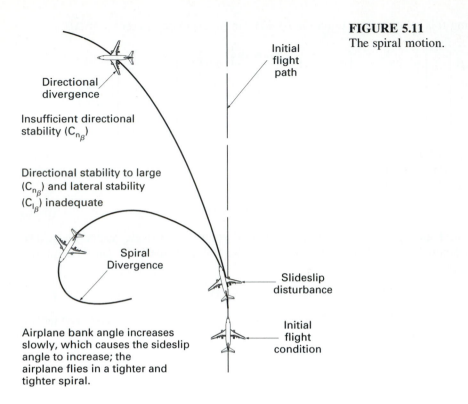

FIGURE 5.11
The spiral motion.

Initial
flight
path

Directional
divergence

Insufficient directional
stability (C_{n_β})

Directional stability to large
(C_{n_β}) and lateral stability
(C_{l_β}) inadequate

Spiral
Divergence

Slideslip
disturbance

Airplane bank angle increases
slowly, which causes the sideslip
angle to increase; the
airplane flies in a tighter and
tighter spiral.

Initial
flight
condition

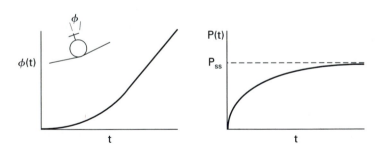

FIGURE 5.12
The roll motion.

neglect the side force equation and $\Delta\phi$. With these assumptions, the equations of motion for the approximation can be obtained from Equation (5.35):

$$L_\beta\,\Delta\beta + L_r\,\Delta r = 0 \tag{5.38}$$

$$\Delta\dot{r} = N_\beta\,\Delta\beta + N_r\,\Delta r \tag{5.39}$$

or

$$\Delta\dot{r} + \frac{L_r N_\beta - L_\beta N_r}{L_\beta}\,\Delta r = 0 \tag{5.40}$$

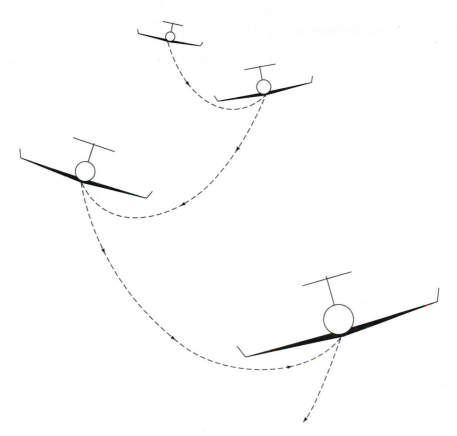

FIGURE 5.13
The Dutch roll motion.

The characteristic root for this equation is

$$\lambda_{\text{spiral}} = \frac{L_\beta N_r - L_r N_\beta}{L_\beta} \qquad (5.41)$$

The stability derivatives L_β (dihedral effect) and N_r (yaw rate damping) usually are negative quantities. On the other hand, N_β (directional stability) and L_r (roll moment due to yaw rate) generally are positive quantities. If the derivatives have the usual sign, then the condition for a stable spiral model is

$$L_\beta N_r - N_\beta L_r > 0 \qquad (5.42)$$

or
$$L_\beta N_r > N_\beta L_r \qquad (5.43)$$

Increasing the dihedral effect L_β or the yaw damping or both can make the spiral mode stable.

5.4.2 Roll Approximation

This motion can be approximated by the single degree of freedom rolling motion, which was analyzed earlier in the chapter:

$$\tau \, \Delta \dot{p} + \Delta p = 0$$

where τ is the roll time constant. Therefore,

$$\lambda_{\text{roll}} = -\frac{1}{\tau} = L_p \tag{5.44}$$

The magnitude of the roll damping L_p is dependent on the size of the wing and tail surfaces.

5.4.3 Dutch Roll Approximation

If we consider the Dutch roll mode to consist primarily of sideslipping and yawing motions, then we can neglect the rolling moment equation. With these assumptions, Equation (5.35) reduces to

$$\begin{bmatrix} \Delta \dot{\beta} \\ \Delta \dot{r} \end{bmatrix} = \begin{bmatrix} \dfrac{Y_\beta}{u_0} & -\left(1 - \dfrac{Y_r}{u_0}\right) \\ N_\beta & N_r \end{bmatrix} \begin{bmatrix} \Delta \beta \\ \Delta r \end{bmatrix} \tag{5.45}$$

Solving for the characteristic equation yields

$$\lambda^2 - \left(\frac{Y_\beta + u_0 N_r}{u_0}\right)\lambda + \frac{Y_\beta N_r - N_\beta Y_r + u_0 N_\beta}{u_0} = 0 \tag{5.46}$$

From this expression we can determine the undamped natural frequency and the damping ratio as follows:

$$\omega_{n_{\text{DR}}} = \sqrt{\frac{Y_\beta N_r - N_\beta Y_r + u_0 N_\beta}{u_0}} \tag{5.47}$$

$$\zeta_{\text{DR}} = -\frac{1}{2\omega_{n_{\text{DR}}}}\left(\frac{Y_\beta + u_0 N_r}{u_0}\right) \tag{5.48}$$

The approximations developed in this section give, at best, only a rough estimate of the spiral and Dutch roll modes. The approximate formulas should, therefore, be used with caution. The reason for the poor agreement between the approximate and exact solutions is that the Dutch roll motion is truly a three-degree-of-freedom motion with strong coupling between the equations.

EXAMPLE PROBLEM 5.3. Find the lateral eigenvalues of the general aviation airplane described in Chapter 4 and compare these results with the answers obtained using the lateral approximations. A summary of the aerodynamic and geometric data

TABLE 5.1
Summary of lateral directional derivatives

$$Y_\beta = \frac{QSC_{y\beta}}{m} \ \text{(ft/s}^2 \text{ or m/s}^2) \quad N_\beta = \frac{QSbC_{n\beta}}{I_z} \ \text{(s}^{-2}) \quad L_\beta = \frac{QSbC_{l\beta}}{I_x} \ \text{(s}^{-2})$$

$$Y_p = \frac{QSbC_{yp}}{2mu_0} \ \text{(ft/s) or (m/s)} \quad N_p = \frac{QSb^2C_{np}}{2I_zu_0} \ \text{(s}^{-1})$$

$$L_p = \frac{QSb^2C_{lp}}{2I_xu_0} \ \text{(s}^{-1})$$

$$Y_r = \frac{QSbC_{yr}}{2mu_0} \ \text{(ft/s) or (m/s)} \quad N_r = \frac{QSb^2C_{nr}}{2I_zu_0} \ \text{(s}^{-1})$$

$$L_r = \frac{QSb^2C_{lr}}{2I_xu_0} \ \text{(s}^{-1})$$

$$Y_{\delta a} = \frac{QSC_{y\delta a}}{m} \ \text{(ft/s}^2) \text{ or (m/s}^2) \quad Y_{\delta_r} = \frac{QSC_{y\delta_r}}{m} \ \text{(ft/s}^2) \text{ or (m/s}^2)$$

$$N_{\delta a} = \frac{QSbC_{n\delta a}}{I_z} \ \text{(s}^{-2}) \quad N_{\delta r} = \frac{QSbC_{n\delta_r}}{I_z} \ \text{(s}^{-2})$$

$$L_{\delta a} = \frac{QSbC_{l\delta a}}{I_x} \ \text{(s}^{-2}) \quad L_{\delta r} = \frac{QSbC_{l\delta_r}}{I_x} \ \text{(s}^{-2})$$

needed for this analysis is included in Appendix B. The stick fixed lateral equations follow:

$$\begin{bmatrix} \Delta\dot{\beta} \\ \Delta\dot{p} \\ \Delta\dot{r} \\ \Delta\dot{\phi} \end{bmatrix} = \begin{bmatrix} \dfrac{Y_\beta}{u_0} & \dfrac{Y_p}{u_0} & -\left(1 - \dfrac{Y_r}{u_0}\right) & \dfrac{g}{u_0}\cos\theta_0 \\ L_\beta & L_p & L_r & 0 \\ N_\beta & N_p & N_r & 0 \\ 0 & 1 & 0 & 0 \end{bmatrix} \begin{bmatrix} \Delta\beta \\ \Delta p \\ \Delta r \\ \Delta\phi \end{bmatrix}$$

Before we can determine the eigenvalues of the stability matrix **A**, we first must calculate the lateral stability derivatives. Table 5.1 is a summary of the lateral stability derivative definitions and Table 5.2 gives a summary of the values of these derivatives for the general aviation airplane.

Substituting the lateral stability derivatives into the stick fixed lateral equations yields

$$\dot{x} = Ax$$

or

$$\begin{bmatrix} \Delta\dot{\beta} \\ \Delta\dot{p} \\ \Delta\dot{r} \\ \Delta\dot{\phi} \end{bmatrix} = \begin{bmatrix} -0.254 & 0 & -1.0 & 0.182 \\ -16.02 & -8.40 & 2.19 & 0 \\ 4.488 & -0.350 & -0.760 & 0 \\ 0 & 1 & 0 & 0 \end{bmatrix} \begin{bmatrix} \Delta\beta \\ \Delta p \\ \Delta r \\ \Delta\phi \end{bmatrix}$$

The eigenvalues can be determined by finding the eigenvalues of the matrix **A**:

$$|\lambda I - A| = 0$$

TABLE 5.2
Lateral derivatives for the general aviation airplane

$Y_v = -0.254$ (s^{-1})	$L_v = -0.091$ (ft · s)$^{-1}$
$Y_\beta = -45.72$ (ft/s^2)	$L_\beta = -16.02$ (s^{-2})
$Y_p = 0$	$L_p = -8.4$ (s^{-1})
$Y_r = 0$	$L_r = 2.19$ (s^{-1})
$N_v = 0.025$ (ft · s)$^{-1}$	
$N_\beta = 4.49$ (s^{-2})	
$N_p = -0.35$ (s^{-1})	
$N_r = -0.76$ (s^{-1})	

The resulting characteristic equation is

$$\lambda^4 + 9.417\lambda^3 + 13.982\lambda^2 + 48.102\lambda + 0.4205 = 0$$

Solution of the characteristic equation yields the lateral eigenvalues:

$$\lambda = -0.00877 \qquad \text{(Spiral mode)}$$

$$\lambda = -8.435 \qquad \text{(Roll mode)}$$

$$\lambda = -0.487 \pm i(2.335) \qquad \text{(Dutch roll mode)}$$

The estimates for the lateral eigenvalues using the approximate expressions is obtained as follows:

$$\lambda_{\text{spiral}} = \frac{L_\beta N_r - L_r N_\beta}{L_\beta}$$

Susbtituting in the numerical values for the derivatives yields

$$\lambda_{\text{spiral}} = [(-16.02 \text{ s}^{-2})(-0.76 \text{ s}^{-1}) - (2.19 \text{ s}^{-1})(4.49 \text{ s}^{-2})]/(-16.02 \text{ s}^{-2})$$

$$= -0.144 \text{ s}^{-1}$$

$$\lambda_{\text{roll}} = L_p = -8.4 \text{ s}^{-1}$$

The Dutch roll roots are determined from the characteristic equation given by Equation (5.44):

$$\lambda^2 - \frac{(Y_\beta + u_0 N_r)}{u_0}\lambda + \frac{Y_\beta N_r - N_\beta Y_r + u_0 N_\beta}{u_0} = 0$$

or

$$\lambda^2 + 1.102\lambda + 4.71 = 0$$

which yields the following roots

$$\lambda_{\text{DR}} = -0.51 \pm 2.109i$$

and

$$\omega_{n_{\text{DR}}} = 2.17 \text{ rad/s}$$

$$\zeta_{\text{DR}} = 0.254$$

TABLE 5.3
Comparison of exact and approximate roots

	Exact			Approximate		
	$T_{1/2}$, s	T_2, s	P, s	$T_{1/2}$, s	T_2, s	P, s
Spiral	78.7	—	—	4.79	—	—
Roll	0.082	—	—	0.082	—	—
Dutch roll	1.42	—	2.69	1.35	—	2.98

Table 5.3 compares the results of the exact and approximate analysis. For this example, the roll and Dutch roll roots are in good agreement. On the other hand, the spiral root approximation is very poor.

The relationship between good spiral and Dutch roll characteristics presents a challenge to the airplane designer. In Chapter 2 it was stated that an airplane should possess static stability in both the directional and roll modes. This implies the $C_{n_\beta} > 0$ and $C_{l_\beta} < 0$. However, if we examine the influence of these stability coefficients on the lateral roots by means of a root locus plot, we observe the following. As the dihedral effect is increased, that is, C_{l_β} becomes more negative, the Dutch roll root moves toward the right half-plane, which means the Dutch roll root is becoming less stable and the spiral root is moving in the direction of increased stability. These observations are clearly shown in Figures 5.14 and 5.15.

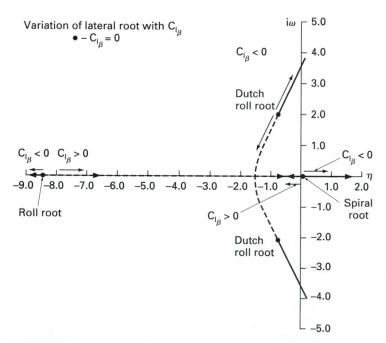

FIGURE 5.14
Variation of lateral roots with C_{l_β}.

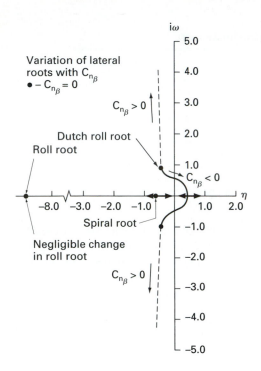

FIGURE 5.15
Variation of lateral roots with C_{n_β}.

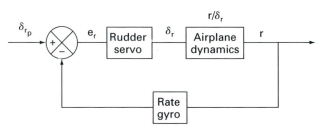

FIGURE 5.16
Block diagram of a yaw damper system.

Increasing directional stability of the airplane, that is, C_{n_β} becomes more positive, causes the spiral root to become less stable and the frequency of the Dutch roll root is increased. Increasing the yaw damping, that is, C_{n_r} becomes more negative, will result in better Dutch roll damping. Unfortunately, this is not easy to achieve simply by geometric design changes. Increasing the vertical tail size will cause an increase in both C_{n_β} and C_{n_r}. Many airplanes are provided with a rate damper to artificially provide adequate damping in Dutch roll. Figure 5.16 is a sketch of a simple control system to provide increased yaw damping for the airplane.

5.5
LATERAL FLYING QUALITIES

In this chapter we examined the lateral direction characteristics of an airplane. The relationship between the aerodynamic stability and control derivatives and the lateral response was discussed. We have developed the necessary equations and analysis procedures to calculate the lateral dynamics. Although these techniques allow us to determine whether an airplane design is stable or unstable, by itself the analysis does not tell us whether the pilot will judge the airplane to have acceptable flying characteristics. To determine this the designer needs to know what dynamic characteristics are considered favorable by the pilots who will fly the airplane. This information is available through the lateral-directional flying quality specifications.

The lateral-directional flying quality requirements are listed in Tables 5.4, 5.5, and 5.6. The definition of class and category were presented in Chapter 4. In Example Problem 5.2 the aircraft would be considered a Class 1 vehicle and the flight phase as Category B. Using the information from Table 5.4, we find that the aircraft studied here has Level 1 flying qualities.

EXAMPLE PROBLEM 5.4. As shown earlier, the Dutch roll motion can be improved by increasing the magnitude of the yaw damping term N_r. One means of increasing N_r is by increasing the vertical tail area. Unfortunately, increasing the vertical tail area will add additional drag to the airplane as well as increase the directional stability. The increase in directional stability will degrade the spiral characteristics of the airplane. For most transport and fighter aircraft, increased damping is provided artificially by means of a yaw damper.

In this example we examine the basic idea behind a yaw damper. More detailed information on stability augmentation systems and autopilots will be provided in

TABLE 5.4
Spiral mode (minimum time to double amplitude) flying qualities

Class	Category	Level 1	Level 2	Level 3
I and IV	A	12 s	12 s	4 s
	B and C	20 s	12 s	4 s
II and III	All	20 s	12 s	4 s

TABLE 5.5
Roll mode (maximum roll time constant) flying qualities (in seconds)

Class	Category	Level 1	Level 2	Level 3
I, IV	A	1.0	1.4	10
II, III		1.4	3.0	
All	B	1.4	3.0	10
I, IV	C	1.0	1.4	10
II, III		1.4	3.0	

TABLE 5.6
Dutch roll flying qualities

Level	Category	Class	Min ζ*	Min $\zeta\omega_n$,* rad/s	Min ω_n, rad/s
1	A	I, IV	0.19	0.35	1.0
		II, III	0.19	0.35	0.4
	B	All	0.08	0.15	0.4
	C	I, II-C	0.08	0.15	1.0
		IV			
		II-L, III	0.08	0.15	0.4
2	All	All	0.02	0.05	0.4
3	All	All	0.02	—	0.4

Where C and L denote carrier- or land-based aircraft.
*The governing damping requirement is that yielding the larger value of ζ.

Chapters 7–10. To examine how a yaw damper can be used to provide damping for an airplane, consider the yawing moment equation developed earlier:

$$\Delta\ddot{\psi} - N_r \, \Delta\dot{\psi} + N_\beta \, \Delta\psi = N_{\delta_r} \, \Delta\delta_r$$

Suppose that for a particular airplane the static directional stability, yaw damping, and control derivatives were as follows:

$$N_\beta = 1.77 \text{ s}^{-2} \qquad N_r = -0.10 \text{ s}^{-1} \qquad N_{\delta_r} = -0.84 \text{ s}^{-1}$$

For this airplane the damping ratio and undamped natural frequency would be

$$\zeta = -\frac{N_r}{2\sqrt{N_\beta}} = 0.037 \qquad \omega_n = \sqrt{N_\beta} = 1.33 \text{ rad/s}$$

The low damping ratio would result in a free response that would have a large overshoot and poor damping. Such an airplane would be very difficult for the pilot to fly. However, we could design a feedback control system such that the rudder deflection is proportional to the yaw rate; that is,

$$\Delta\delta_r = -k \, \Delta\dot{\psi}$$

Substituting the control deflection expression into the equation of motion and rearranging yields

$$\Delta\ddot{\psi} - (N_r - kN_{\delta_r}) \, \Delta\dot{\psi} + N_\beta \, \Delta\psi = 0$$

By proper selection of k we can provide the airplane whatever damping characteristics we desire. For the purpose of this example, consider the simple yawing motion to be an approximation of the Dutch roll motion. The flying quality specifications included in Table 5.6 state that a Level 1 flying quality rating would be achieved for the landing flight phase if

$$\zeta > 0.08 \qquad \zeta\omega_n > 0.15 \text{ rad/s} \qquad \omega_n > 0.4 \text{ rad/s}$$

A damping ratio of 0.2 and a frequency of 1.33 would be considered acceptable by pilots. The problem now is to select the unknown gain k so that the airplane has the desired damping characteristics. If we compare the yaw moment equation of motion to the standard form for a second-order system, we can establish a relationship for k as follows:

$$2\zeta\omega_n = -(N_r - kN_{\delta_r}) \qquad 0.532 = -[-0.1 - k(-0.84)] \qquad k = -0.514$$

Figure 5.16 is a sketch of a simple yaw damper stability augmentation system.

Although we designed a feedback system to provide improved damping, it is possible to control both the damping and the frequency. This can be accomplished by making the rudder deflection proportional to both the yaw rate and yaw angle; that is,

$$\Delta\delta_r = -k_1 \, \Delta\dot{\psi} - k_2 \, \Delta\psi$$

Substituting this expression back into the differential equation yields

$$\Delta\ddot{\psi} - (N_r - k_1 N_{\delta_r}) \, \Delta\dot{\psi} + (N_\beta + k_2) \, \Delta\psi = 0$$

The gains k_1 and k_2 then are selected so that the characteristic equation has the desired damping ratio and frequency. The use of feedback control to augment the stability characteristics of an airplane plays an important role in the design of modern aircraft. By using stability augmentation systems, the designer can ensure good flying qualities over the entire flight regime. Furthermore, with the addition of a stability augmentation system, the designer can reduce the inherent aerodynamic static stability of the airplane by reducing the vertical tail size. Thus, the designer can achieve an improvement in performance without compromising the level of flying qualities.

5.6
INERTIAL COUPLING

In the analysis presented in this and the previous chapter, we treated the longitudinal and lateral equations separately. In so doing we assumed that there is no coupling between the equations. However, slender high-performance fighter aircraft can experience significant roll coupling that can result in divergence from the desired flight path, causing loss of control or structural failure.

The mechanisms that cause this undesirable behavior can be due to inertial or aerodynamic coupling of the equations of motion. To explain how inertial coupling occurs, we examine the nonlinearized moment equations developed in Chapter 3. The moment equations are reproduced in Equation (5.49):

$$\sum \text{Roll moments} = I_x\dot{p} + qr(I_z - I_y) - (\dot{r} + qp)I_{xz}$$

$$\sum \text{Pitching moments} = I_y\dot{q} + pr(I_x - I_z) + (p^2 - r^2)I_{xz} \qquad (5.49)$$

$$\sum \text{Yawing moments} = I_z\dot{r} + pq(I_y - I_x) + (qr - \dot{p})I_{xz}$$

The first cases of inertial coupling started to appear when fighter aircraft designs were developed for supersonic flight. These aircraft were designed with low aspect ratio wings and long, slender fuselages. In these designs, more of the aircraft's weight was concentrated in the fuselage than in the earlier subsonic fighters. With the weight concentrated in the fuselage, the moments of inertia around the pitch angle yaw axis increased and the inertia around the roll axis decreased in comparison with subsonic fighter aircraft.

On examining Equation (5.49) we see that the second term in the pitch equation could be significant if the difference in the moments of inertia becomes large. For the case of a slender high-performance fighter executing a rapid rolling maneuver the term $pr(I_x - I_z)$ can become large enough to produce an uncontrollable pitching motion.

A similar argument can be made for the product of inertia terms in the equations of motion. The product of inertia I_{xz} is a measure of the uniformity of the distribution of mass about the x axis. For modern fighter aircraft I_{xz} typically is not 0. Again we see that if the airplane is executing a rapid roll maneuver the term $(p^2 - r^2)I_{xz}$ may be as significant as the other terms in the equation.

Finally, aerodynamic coupling also must be considered when aircraft are maneuvering at high angular rates or at high angles of attack. As was discussed in Chapter 4 high angle of attack flow asymmetries can cause out-of-plane forces and moments even for symmetric flight conditions. Such forces and moments couple the longitudinal and lateral equations of motion.

5.7
SUMMARY

In this chapter we examined the lateral modes of motion. The Dutch roll and spiral motions were shown to be influenced by static directional stability and dihedral effect in an opposing manner. The designer is faced with the dilemma of trying to satisfy the flying quality specifications for both the spiral and Dutch roll modes. This becomes particularly difficult for airplanes that have extended flight envelopes. One way designers have solved this problem is by incorporating a yaw damper in the design. The yaw damper is an automatic system that artificially improves the system damping. The increased damping provided by the yaw damper improves both the spiral and Dutch roll characteristics.

PROBLEMS

Problems that require the use of a computer have a capital C after the problem number.

5.1. Determine the response of the A-4D to a 5° step change in aileron deflection. Plot the roll rate versus time. Assume sea-level standard conditions and that the airplane is flying at $M = 0.4$. What is the steady-state roll rate and time constant for this motion?

5.2. For the roll response shown in Figure P5.2, estimate the aileron control power L_{δ_a} and the roll damping derivative L_p. Information on the characteristics of the airplane is in the figure.

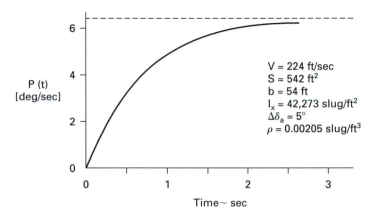

V = 224 ft/sec
S = 542 ft²
b = 54 ft
I_x = 42,273 slug/ft²
$\Delta\delta_a$ = 5°
ρ = 0.00205 slug/ft³

FIGURE P5.2
Roll rate time history.

5.3. A wind-tunnel model free to rotate about its x axis is spun up to 10.5 rad/s by means of a motor drive system. When the motor drive is disengaged, the model spin will decay as shown in Figure P5.3. From the spin time history determine the roll damping derivative L_p.

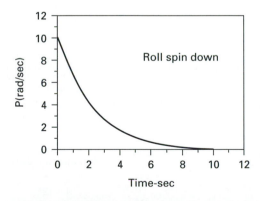

FIGURE P5.3
Roll rate time history.

5.4. A wind-tunnel model is constructed of two small lifting surfaces mounted to an axisymmetric body as illustrated in Figure P5.4. The body houses a set of ball bearings that permit the model to roll freely about the longitudinal or x axis. The right lifting surface (positive y axis) is mounted to the body at a $-3°$ and the left lifting surface is set at a $+3°$.
 (*a*) Estimate the rolling moment of inertia, I_x, of the model. Approximate the lifting surfaces as thin flat plates. Neglect the body contribution.
 (*b*) Estimate the roll torque due to the differential mounting incidence. Express your answer as a roll moment coefficient per unit deflection, C_{l_δ}.
 (*c*) Estimate the roll damping coefficient, C_{l_p}.

(d) Calculate the response of the model if it is released from the rest. Neglect the friction of the bearings.

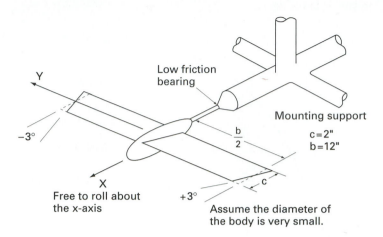

FIGURE P5.4

5.5. Suppose the wing segments for the model described in Problem 5.4 are set so that there is no differential incidence between the two sections. If the wings are mounted in this manner, the roll torque due to the differential incidences will be 0. Now consider what would happen if a half-span wing were mounted upstream of the free-to-roll model as illustrated in Figure P5.5. Assume that the free-to-roll wing is centered in the tip vortex. Estimate the maximum roll rate of the

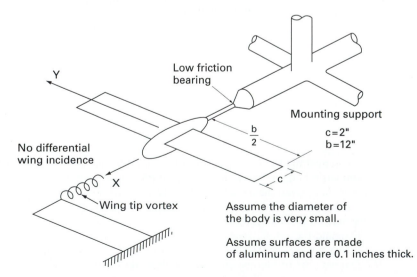

FIGURE P5.5

free-to-roll wing. The strength of the vortex can be shown to be as follows.

$$\Gamma = \frac{8C_L VS}{\pi b}$$

where C_L = wing lift coefficient
$\quad V$ = velocity of the tunnel
$\quad S$ = wing area of generating wing
$\quad b$ = span of generating wing.

Assume the vortex core is 5% of the generating wing span.

5.6. Assuming the cruciform finned model in Figure P5.6 is mounted in a wind tunnel so that it is constrained to a pure yawing motion. The model is displaced from its trim position by 10° and then released. Neglect the fuselage and $\dot{\beta}$ contribution and assume $S = \pi D^2/4$.
(a) Find the time for the motion to damp to half its initial amplitude.
(b) What is the period of the motion?

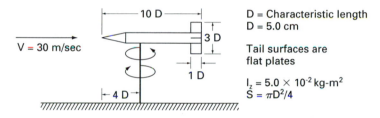

FIGURE P5.6
Yawing wind-tunnel model.

5.7. Figure P5.7. shows the stick fixed lateral roots of a jet transport airplane. Identify the roots and determine the time for the amplitude and period to halve or double where applicable.

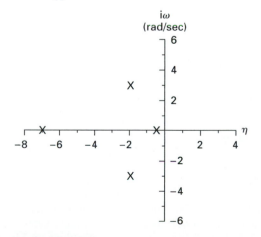

FIGURE P5.7
Lateral roots for a jet transport.

5.8(C). The Dutch roll motion can be approximated using the following equations:

$$\begin{bmatrix} \Delta\dot\beta \\ \Delta\dot r \end{bmatrix} = \begin{bmatrix} \dfrac{Y_\beta}{u_0} & -\left(1 - \dfrac{Y_r}{u_0}\right) \\ N_\beta & N_r \end{bmatrix} \begin{bmatrix} \Delta\beta \\ \Delta_r \end{bmatrix} + \begin{bmatrix} \dfrac{Y_{\delta_r}}{u_0} \\ N_{\delta_r} \end{bmatrix} \Delta\delta_r$$

Assume the coefficients in the plant matrix have the following numerical values:

$$Y_\beta = -7.8 \text{ ft/s}^2 \qquad N_r = -0.34 \text{ 1/s} \qquad Y_{\delta_r} = -5.236 \text{ ft/s}^2$$
$$Y_r = 2.47 \text{ ft/s} \qquad u_0 = 154 \text{ ft/s} \qquad N_{\delta_r} = 0.616 \text{ 1/s}^2$$
$$N_\beta = 0.64 \text{ 1/s}^2$$

(a) Determine the Dutch roll eigenvalues.
(b) What is the damping ratio and undamped natural frequency?
(c) What is the period and time to half amplitude of the motion?
(d) Determine the response of the system if the initial conditions are as follows:

$$\begin{bmatrix} \Delta\beta \\ \Delta r \end{bmatrix} = \begin{bmatrix} 0.1 \\ 0.0 \end{bmatrix}$$

From the time history plot, estimate the period and time to half amplitude.
(e) Determine the response of the system to a step input. For this part assume that the initial conditions are both 0.

The last two parts of this problem should be solved by computer.

5.9(C). Develop a computer code to obtain the stick fixed lateral eigenvalues from the lateral stability matrix. Use your computer program to analyze the lateral motion of the 747 jet transport. Estimated aerodynamic, mass, and geometric characteristics of the 747 are included in Appendix B. The MATLAB Software is suggested for this problem.

5.10(C). Using the program developed in problem 5.9, examine the influence of C_{l_β} and C_{n_r} on the lateral roots. Use the 747 data, but vary C_{l_β} and C_{n_r} separately.

5.11. Using the Dutch roll approximation, determine the state feedback gains so that the damping ratio and frequency of the Dutch roll are 0.3 and 1.0 rad/s, respectively. Assume the airplane has the following characteristics:

$$Y_\beta = -19.5 \text{ ft/s}^2 \qquad Y_r = 1.3 \text{ ft/s}$$
$$N_\beta = 1.5 \text{ s}^{-2} \qquad N_r = -0.21 \text{ s}^{-1}$$
$$Y_{\delta_r} = 4.7 \text{ ft/s}^2 \qquad N_{\delta_r} = -0.082 \text{ s}^{-2}$$
$$u_0 = 400 \text{ ft/s}$$

REFERENCES

5.1. Adams, F. D. *Aeronautical Dictionary*. Washington, DC: National Aeronautics and Space Administration, United States Government Printing Office, 1959.
5.2. Arena, A. S., Jr.; and R. C. Nelson. "Experimental Investigations on Limit Cycle Wing Rock of Slender Wings." AIAA Journal of Aircraft 31, no. 5 (September–October 1994) pp. 1148–1155.

5.3. Arena, A. S., Jr.; R. C. Nelson; and L. B. Schiff. "An Experimental Study of the Nonlinear Dynamic Phenomenon Known as Wing Rock." AIAA Paper No. 60–2813, August 1990.

5.4. Seckel, E. *Stability and Control of Airplanes and Helicopters*. New York: Academic Press, 1964.

5.5. Etkin, B. *Dynamics of Flight*. New York: Wiley, 1972.

5.6. Hage, R. E.; and C. D. Perkins. *Airplane Performance, Stability and Control*. New York: Wiley, 1949.

5.7. Roskam, J. *Flight Dynamics of Rigid and Elastic Airplanes*. Lawrence: University of Kansas Press, 1972.

5.8. Fung, Y. C. *The Theory of Aeroelasticity*. New York: Wiley, 1955.

5.9. Bisplinghoff, R. L.; H. Ashley; and R. L. Halfman. *Aeroelasticity*. Reading, MA: Addison Wesley, 1955.

5.10. Scanlan, R. H.; and R. Rosenbaum. *Introduction to the Study of Aircraft Vibration and Flutter*. New York: Macmillan, 1951.

5.11. Abramson, H. *The Dynamics of Airplanes*. New York: Ronald Press, 1958.

CHAPTER 6

Aircraft Response to Control or Atmospheric Inputs

6.1
INTRODUCTION

In the previous chapters we examined the free response of an airplane as well as several simple examples of single degree of freedom motions with step changes in control input. Another useful input function is the sinusoidal signal. The step and sinusoidal input functions are important for two reasons. First, the input to many physical systems takes the form of either a step change or sinusoidal signal. Second, an arbitrary function can be represented by a series of step changes or a periodic function can be decomposed by means of Fourier analysis into a series of sinusoidal waves. If we know the response of a linear system to either a step or sinusoidal input, then we can construct the system's response to an arbitrary input by the principle of superposition.

Of particular importance to the study of aircraft response to control or atmospheric inputs is the steady-state response to a sinusoidal input. If the input to a linear stable system is sinusoidal, then after the transients have died out the response of the system also will be a sinusoid of the same frequency. The response of the system is completely described by the ratio of the output to input amplitude and the phase difference over the frequency range from zero to infinity. The magnitude and phase relationship between the input and output signals is called the frequency response. The frequency response can be obtained readily from the system transfer function by replacing the Laplace variable s by $i\omega$. The frequency response information is usually presented in graphical form using either rectangular, polar, log-log or semi-log plots of the magnitude and phase angle versus the frequency. At first it might appear that the construction of the magnitude and phase plots would be extremely difficult for all but the simplest transfer functions. Fortunately, this is not the case. Consider the factored form of a transfer function, given by

$$G(s) = \frac{k(1 + T_a s)(1 + T_b s) \cdots}{s^m (1 + T_1 s)(1 + T_2 s) \cdots \left(1 + \frac{2\zeta}{\omega_n} s + \frac{s^2}{\omega_n^2}\right)} \tag{6.1}$$

The transfer function has been factored into first- and second-order terms. Replacing the Laplace variable s by $i\omega$ and rewriting the transfer function in polar form yields

$$M(\omega) = |G(i\omega)| = \frac{|k| \times |1 + T_a i\omega| \times |1 + T_b i\omega| \cdots}{|(i\omega)^m| \times |1 + T_1 i\omega| \cdots \times \left|1 - \left(\dfrac{\omega}{\omega_n}\right)^2 + 2\zeta\dfrac{\omega}{\omega_n}i\right| \cdots} \\ \times \exp[i\,(\phi_a + \phi_b \cdots - \phi_1 - \phi_2 \cdots)] \tag{6.2}$$

Now, if we take the logarithm of this equation, we obtain

$$\log M(\omega) = \log k + \log |1 + T_a i\omega| + \log |1 + T_b i\omega| \cdots - m \log |i\omega| \\ - \log |1 + T_1 i\omega| - \log |1 + T_2 i\omega| \\ - \log \left|1 - \left(\dfrac{\omega}{\omega_n}\right)^2 + 2\zeta\dfrac{\omega}{\omega_n}i\right| - \cdots \tag{6.3}$$

and
$$\angle G\,(i\omega) = \tan^{-1} \omega T_a + \tan^{-1} \omega T_b + \cdots - m(90°) \\ - \tan^{-1} \omega T_1 + \cdots - \tan^{-1}\left(\dfrac{2\zeta\omega_n \omega}{\omega_n^2 - \omega^2}\right) \tag{6.4}$$

By expressing the magnitude in terms of logarithms, the magnitude of the transfer function is readily obtained by the addition of the individual factors. The contribution of each of the basic factors, that is, gain, pole at the origin, simple poles and zeros, and complex poles and zeros, is presented in appendix D at the end of this book. In practice, the log magnitude is often expressed in decibels (dB). The magnitude in decibels is found by multiplying each term in Equation (6.3) by 20:

$$\text{Magnitude in dB} = 20 \log |G(i\omega)| \tag{6.5}$$

The frequency response information of a transfer function is represented by two graphs, one of the magnitude and the other of the phase angle, both versus the frequency on a logarithmic scale. When the frequency response data are presented in this manner, the plots are referred to as Bode diagrams after H. W. Bode who made significant contributions to frequency response analysis.

We shall now look at the application of the frequency response techniques to the longitudinal control transfer functions. As the first example, let us consider the longitudinal pitch angle to elevator transfer function that can be shown as indicated below, where the coefficients A_θ, B_θ, and so forth are functions of the aircraft stability derivatives. The longitudinal pitch angle to elevator transfer function is as follows:

$$\frac{\theta(s)}{\delta_e(s)} = \frac{A_\theta s^2 + B_\theta s + C_\theta}{As^4 + Bs^3 + Cs^2 + Ds + E} \tag{6.6}$$

which can be written in the factored form:

$$\frac{\theta(s)}{\delta_e(s)} = \frac{k_{\theta\delta}(T_{\theta 1} s + 1)(T_{\theta 2} s + 1)}{\left(\dfrac{s^2}{\omega_{nsp}^2} + \dfrac{2\zeta_{sp}}{\omega_{nsp}} s + 1\right)\left(\dfrac{s^2}{\omega_{np}^2} + \dfrac{2\zeta_p}{\omega_{np}} s + 1\right)} \tag{6.7}$$

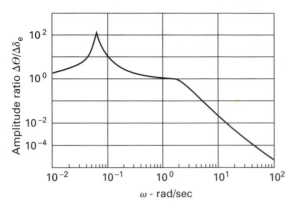

FIGURE 6.1

Magnitude plot of $\Delta\theta/\Delta\delta e$ versus frequency.

The magnitude and phase angle for the control transfer function is obtained by replacing s by $i\omega$ as follows:

$$\left|\frac{\theta(i\omega)}{\delta_e(i\omega)}\right| = \frac{|k_{\theta\delta}| |T_{\theta 1}i\omega + 1|}{\left|\dfrac{(i\omega)^2}{\omega_{nsp}^2} + \dfrac{2\zeta_{sp}}{\omega_{nsp}}i\omega + 1\right|} \frac{|T_{\theta 2}i\omega + 1|}{\left|\dfrac{(i\omega)^2}{\omega_{np}^2} + \dfrac{2\zeta_p}{\omega_{np}}i\omega + 1\right|} \tag{6.8}$$

$$\angle\theta(i\omega)/\delta_e(i\omega) = \tan^{-1}\omega T_{\theta 1} + \tan^{-1}\omega T_{\theta 2} - \tan^{-1}[2\zeta_{sp}\omega_{nsp}\omega/(\omega_{nsp}^2 - \omega^2)]$$
$$- \tan^{-1}[2\zeta_p\omega_{np}\omega/(\omega_{np}^2 - \omega^2)]$$

The frequency response for the pitch attitude to control deflection for the corporate business jet described in Appendix B is shown in Figure 6.1. The amplitude ratio at both the phugoid and short-period frequencies are of comparable magnitude. At very large frequencies the amplitude ratio is very small, which indicates that the elevator has a negligible effect on the pitch attitude in this frequency range.

The frequency response for the change in forward speed and angle of attack to control input is shown in Figure 6.2 and 6.3 for the same aircraft. For the speed elevator transfer function the amplitude ratio is large at the phugoid frequency and very small at the short-period frequency. Recall that in Chapter 4 we assumed that the short-period motion occurred at essentially constant speed. The frequency response plot confirms the validity of this assumption. Figure 6.3 shows the amplitude ratio of the angle of attack to elevator deflection; here we see that angle of attack is constant at the low frequencies. This again is in keeping with the assumption we made regarding the phugoid approximation. Recall that in the phugoid approximation the angle of attack was assumed to be constant. The phase plot shows that there is a large phase lag in the response of the speed change to elevator inputs. The phase lag for α/δ is much smaller, which means that the angle of attack will respond faster than the change in forward speed to an elevator input.

A similar type of analysis can be conducted for the lateral response to aileron or rudder control input. Several problems dealing with the lateral frequency response are presented at the end of this chapter.

Frequency response techniques also are useful in studying the motion of an aircraft encountering atmosphere turbulence. In Chapter 3 the equations of motion

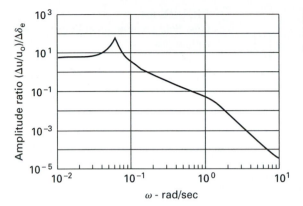

FIGURE 6.2
Magnitude plot of $(\Delta u/u_0)/\Delta \delta e$ versus frequency.

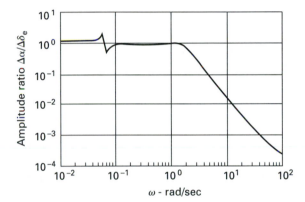

FIGURE 6.3
Magnitude plot of $\Delta \alpha/\Delta \delta e$ frequency.

were developed for flight in a stationary atmosphere. In the following sections we discuss the influence of wind gusts, that is, turbulence, on aircraft response.

6.2
EQUATIONS OF MOTION IN A NONUNIFORM ATMOSPHERE

The atmosphere rarely is calm but usually is characterized by winds, gusts, and turbulence. To study the influence of atmospheric disturbances on aircraft motions, the equations must be modified. The aerodynamic forces and moments acting on the airplane depend on the relative motion of the airplane to the atmosphere and not on the inertial velocities. Therefore, to account for atmospheric disturbances such as winds, gusts, or turbulence the forces and moments must be related to the relative motion with respect to the atmosphere. This is accomplished by expressing the velocities used in calculating the aerodynamics in terms of the inertial and gust velocities as follows:

$$\Delta u_a = \Delta u - u_g \qquad \Delta v_a = \Delta v - v_g \qquad \Delta w_a = \Delta w - w_g$$

$$\Delta p_a = \Delta p - p_g \qquad \Delta q_a = \Delta q - q_g \qquad \Delta r_a = \Delta r - r_g$$

$$(6.9)$$

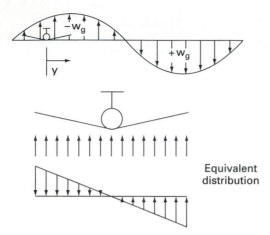

FIGURE 6.4
Gust field creating an effective rolling gust.

Equivalent distribution

where the Δ quantities are the perturbations in the inertial variables and the subscripted variables are the gust velocities. The aerodynamic forces and moments now can be expressed as follows:

$$\Delta X = \frac{\partial X}{\partial u}(\Delta u - u_g) + \frac{\partial X}{\partial w}(\Delta w - w_g) + \frac{\partial X}{\partial \dot{w}}(\Delta \dot{w} - \dot{w}_g)$$

$$+ \frac{\partial X}{\partial q}(\Delta q - q_g) + \frac{\partial X}{\partial \delta_e}\Delta \delta_e$$

$$\Delta Z = \frac{\partial Z}{\partial u}(\Delta u - u_g) + \frac{\partial Z}{\partial w}(\Delta w - w_g) + \frac{\partial Z}{\partial \dot{w}}(\Delta \dot{w} - \dot{w}_g) + \cdots \quad (6.10)$$

$$\vdots$$

$$\Delta N = \frac{\partial N}{\partial v}(\Delta v - v_g) + \frac{\partial N}{\partial r}(\Delta r - r_g) + \frac{\partial N}{\partial p}(\Delta p - p_g)$$

The disturbances in the atmosphere can be described by the spatial and temporal variations in the gust components. The rotational gusts q_g, p_g, and so forth included in Equations (6.10) arise from the variation of u_g, v_g, and w_g with position and time.

The rotary gusts p_g, q_g, and r_g occur due to the spatial variations of the gust components. For example, if the gust field wavelength is large in comparison with the airplane, as shown in Figure 6.4, the vertical gust produces a spanwise variation of velocity along the span of the wing. The linear variation of velocity across the span is the same as that produced on a rolling wing. The velocity normal to the wing at some point along the span is given by

$$w = py \quad (6.11)$$

or

$$\frac{\partial w}{\partial y} = p \quad (6.12)$$

Using this analogy, we can express the rotary gust velocity in terms of the gradient

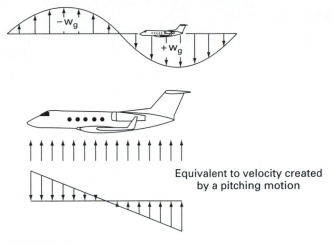

FIGURE 6.5
Gust field creating an effective pitching gust.

in the vertical gust field:

$$p_g = \frac{\partial w_g}{\partial y} \tag{6.13}$$

In a similar manner, the q_g can be developed. The variation of the vertical gust velocity along the X axis of the airplane is similar to the velocity distribution created on a pitching airplane. Figure 6.5 helps to show the origin of rotary gust q_g.

$$q_g = \frac{\partial w_g}{\partial x} \tag{6.14}$$

or

$$q_g = \frac{\partial w_g / \partial t}{\partial x / \partial t} = -\dot{w}_g / u_0 \tag{6.15}$$

The equations of motion, modified to account for atmospheric disturbances, can be written in the state-space form as follows:

$$\dot{\mathbf{x}} = \mathbf{A}\mathbf{x} + \mathbf{B}\boldsymbol{\eta} + \mathbf{C}\boldsymbol{\xi} \tag{6.16}$$

where $\mathbf{x}$, $\boldsymbol{\eta}$, and $\boldsymbol{\xi}$ are the state, control, and gust disturbance vectors. The longitudinal equations are

$$
\begin{bmatrix} \Delta\dot{u} \\ \Delta\dot{w} \\ \Delta\dot{q} \\ \Delta\dot{\theta} \end{bmatrix} =
\begin{bmatrix} X_u & X_w & 0 & -g \\ Z_u & Z_w & u_0 & 0 \\ M_u & M_w & M_q & 0 \\ 0 & 0 & 1 & 0 \end{bmatrix}
\begin{bmatrix} \Delta u \\ \Delta w \\ \Delta q \\ \Delta\theta \end{bmatrix} +
\begin{bmatrix} X_\delta & X_{\delta_T} \\ Z_\delta & Z_{\delta_T} \\ M_\delta & M_{\delta_T} \\ 0 & 0 \end{bmatrix}
\begin{bmatrix} \Delta\delta_e \\ \Delta\delta_T \end{bmatrix}
$$

$$
+ \begin{bmatrix} -X_u & -X_w & 0 \\ -Z_u & -Z_w & 0 \\ -M_u & -M_w & -M_q \\ 0 & 0 & 0 \end{bmatrix}
\begin{bmatrix} u_g \\ w_g \\ q_g \end{bmatrix} \tag{6.17}
$$

and the lateral equations are

$$
\begin{bmatrix} \Delta \dot{v} \\ \Delta \dot{p} \\ \Delta \dot{r} \\ \Delta \dot{\phi} \end{bmatrix} = \begin{bmatrix} Y_v & 0 & (Y_r - u_0) & g \\ L_v & L_p & L_r & 0 \\ N_v & N_p & N_r & 0 \\ 0 & 1 & 0 & 0 \end{bmatrix} \begin{bmatrix} \Delta v \\ \Delta p \\ \Delta r \\ \Delta \phi \end{bmatrix} + \begin{bmatrix} 0 & Y_{\delta_r} \\ L_{\delta_a} & L_{\delta_r} \\ N_{\delta_a} & N_{\delta_r} \\ 0 & 0 \end{bmatrix} \begin{bmatrix} \Delta \delta_a \\ \Delta \delta_r \end{bmatrix}
$$
$$
+ \begin{bmatrix} -Y_v & 0 & 0 \\ -L_v & -L_p & -L_r \\ -N_v & -N_p & -N_r \\ 0 & 0 & 0 \end{bmatrix} \begin{bmatrix} v_g \\ p_g \\ r_g \end{bmatrix} \tag{6.18}
$$

The longitudinal and lateral gust transfer functions can be determined by taking the Laplace transform of Equations (6.17) and (6.18) and then dividing by the gust function. A linear set of algebraic equations in terms of $\Delta u / u_g$ are obtained. These equations then can be solved for the transfer functions.

To provide some insight into the influence of atmospheric disturbances on aircraft response, we shall examine the vertical motion of an airplane that encounters a vertical gust field.

6.3
PURE VERTICAL OR PLUNGING MOTION

Consider an airplane constrained so that movement is possible only in the vertical direction. This type of motion could be simulated in the wind tunnel using a model constrained by a vertical rod as illustrated in Figure 6.6. The model is free to move up or down along the rod but no other motion is possible.

Now let us examine the response of this constrained airplane subjected to an external disturbance such as a wind gust. The equation of motion for this example is obtained by applying Newton's second law; that is

$$
\sum \text{Forces in the vertical direction} = m \frac{dw}{dt} \tag{6.19}
$$

$$
Z + W = m \frac{dw}{dt} \tag{6.20}
$$

where Z is the aerodynamic force in the z direction and W is the weight of the airplane model. If we assume the motion of the airplane will be confined to small perturbations from an initial unaccelerated flight condition, then the aerodynamic force and vertical velocity can be expressed as the sum of the reference flight condition plus the perturbation:

$$
Z = Z_0 + \Delta Z \qquad w = w_0 + \Delta w \tag{6.21}
$$

Substituting Equation (6.21) into (6.20) yields

$$
Z_0 + \Delta Z + W = m \frac{d}{dt} (w_0 + \Delta w) \tag{6.22}
$$

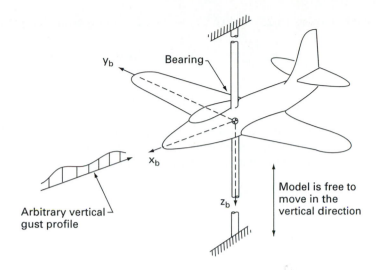

FIGURE 6.6
Wind tunnel model constrained to motion in the vertical
direction.

This equation can be simplified by recognizing that in unaccelerated flight the
condition for equilibrium is

$$Z_0 + W = 0 \tag{6.23}$$

Therefore, Equation (6.22) reduces to

$$\Delta Z/m = \frac{d}{dt} \Delta w \tag{6.24}$$

The aerodynamic force acting on the airplane is a function of the angle of attack
and time rate of change of the attack and it can be expressed in terms of the stability
derivatives as follows:

$$\Delta Z/m = Z_\alpha \, \Delta \alpha + Z_{\dot{\alpha}} \, \Delta \dot{\alpha} \tag{6.25}$$

or $$\Delta Z/m = C_{z_\alpha} \, \Delta \alpha \, QS/m + C_{z_{\dot{\alpha}}} \frac{\Delta \dot{\alpha} c}{2u_0} QS/m \tag{6.26}$$

where $$C_{z_\alpha} = -C_{L_\alpha} \qquad C_{z_{\dot{\alpha}}} = -C_{L_{\dot{\alpha}}}$$

To simplify our analysis we will assume that the lag in lift term, $Z_{\dot{\alpha}} \, \Delta \dot{\alpha}$, is negligible
in comparison to the $Z_\alpha \, \Delta \alpha$ term.

The change in angle of attack experienced by the airplane is due to its motion
in the vertical direction and also to the vertical wind gust. The angle of attack can
be written as

$$\Delta \alpha = \frac{\Delta w}{u_0} - \frac{w_g(t)}{u_0} \tag{6.27}$$

Substituting Equations (6.25) and (6.27) into (6.24) and rearranging yields

$$u_0 \frac{d\Delta w}{dt} - Z_\alpha \Delta w = -Z_\alpha w_g(t) \tag{6.28}$$

or

$$-\frac{u_0}{Z_\alpha} \frac{d\Delta w}{dt} + \Delta w = w_g(t) \tag{6.29}$$

Equation (6.29) is a first-order differential equation with constant coefficients. Systems characterized by first-order differential equations are referred to as first-order systems. We rewrite Equation (6.29) to have the form:

$$\tau \frac{d\Delta w}{dt} + \Delta w = \left(\tau \frac{d}{dt} + 1\right) \Delta w = w_g(t) \tag{6.30}$$

where

$$\tau = -\frac{u_0}{Z_\alpha} \tag{6.31}$$

and $w_g(t)$ is the gust velocity as a function of time.

The solution to Equation (6.30) for a sharp-edged or sinusoidal gust will now be examined. Figure 6.7 shows an airplane encountering a sharp-edged or step gust and a sinusoidal gust profile. The reason for selecting these two types of gust inputs is that they occur quite often in nature. Furthermore, as was mentioned earlier both the steps function and sinusoidal inputs can be used to construct an arbitrary gust profile. For example, Figure 6.8 shows the construction of an arbitrary gust profile as a series of step changes. Also in the case of an arbitrary-periodic gust function the profile can be decomposed into a series of sine waves by Fourier analysis.

The transient response of an airplane to an encounter with a sharp-edged gust can be modeled by expressing the gust profile as a step function:

$$w_g(t) = \begin{cases} 0 & t = 0^- \\ A_g u(t) & t = 0^+ \end{cases} \tag{6.32}$$

where $u(t)$ is a unit step change and A_g is the magnitude of the gust. The solution to Equation (6.30) for a step input can be obtained by taking the Laplace transformation of the differential equation

$$\tau s \, \Delta w(s) + \Delta w(s) = w_g(s) \tag{6.33}$$

or solving for the ratio of the output to input yields

$$\frac{\Delta w(s)}{w_g(s)} = \frac{1}{\tau s + 1} \tag{6.34}$$

Equation (6.34) is the transfer function of the change in vertical velocity to the vertical gust input. When the forcing function or input is a step change in the gust velocity,

$$w_g(s) = \frac{A_g}{s} \tag{6.35}$$

or

$$\Delta w(s) = \frac{A_g}{s(\tau s + 1)} \tag{6.36}$$

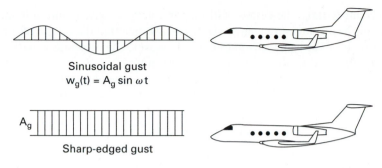

Sinusoidal gust
$w_g(t) = A_g \sin \omega t$

A_g

Sharp-edged gust

FIGURE 6.7
Idealized gust profiles.

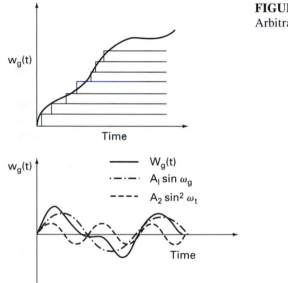

$w_g(t)$

Time

FIGURE 6.8
Arbitrary gust profiles.

$w_g(t)$

——— $W_g(t)$

—·—· $A_1 \sin \omega_g$

---- $A_2 \sin^2 \omega_t$

Time

Expanding Equation (6.36) by the method of partial factions and taking the inverse Laplace transformation yields

$$\Delta w(t) = A_g(1 - e^{-t/\tau}) \tag{6.37}$$

The vertical velocity of the airplane grows exponentially from 0 to a final value of A_g. The initial slope of the curve at $t = 0$ is given by the derivative

$$\frac{dw}{dt} = \frac{A_g}{\tau} e^{-t/\tau} \quad \text{or} \quad \left.\frac{dw}{dt}\right|_{t \to 0} = \frac{A_g}{\tau} \tag{6.38}$$

The parameter τ is referred to as the time constant of the system. The time constant tells us how fast our system approaches a new steady-state condition after being disturbed. If the time constant is small the system will respond very rapidly; if the time constant is large the system will respond very slowly. Figure 6.9 shows the response of the airplane to a sharp-edged gust. Notice that the output of the system approaches the final value asymptotically; however, the response is within 2 percent of the final value after only four time constants.

Additional insight into the vehicle's response can be obtained by looking at the maximum acceleration of the airplane. The maximum acceleration occurs at $t = 0$:

$$\Delta \dot{w} = \frac{C_{L_\alpha} QS}{mu_0} A_g = \frac{A_g}{\tau} \tag{6.39}$$

Dividing Equation (6.39) by the gravitational constant g we obtain an equation for the change in load factor due to a sharp-edged gust:

$$\frac{\Delta \dot{w}}{g} = \frac{C_{L_\alpha} QS}{mu_0 g} A_g = \frac{\Delta L}{W} = \Delta n \tag{6.40}$$

or

$$\Delta n = C_{L_\alpha} \frac{\rho u_0}{2} \frac{A_g}{W/S} \tag{6.41}$$

Equation (6.41) indicates that airplanes having low wing loading W/S will be much more responsive to the influence of vertical wing gust than airplanes with high wing loadings.

The takeoff and landing performance of an airplane can be shown to be a function of wing loading W/S, weight per unit of wing area. Airplanes having a low wing loading in general will have short takeoff and landing field requirements. Airplanes designed for minimum runway requirements, such as short-takeoff-and-landing (STOL) aircraft, will have low wing loadings compared with conventional transport and fighter airplanes and therefore should be more responsive to atmospheric disturbances.

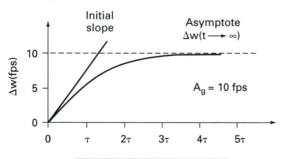

FIGURE 6.9
Response to a sharp edged gust.

t	$\Delta w/w_g = 1 - e^{-t/\tau}$
0	0
τ	0.632
2τ	0.865
3τ	0.950
4τ	0.982
5τ	0.993
6τ	0.998

If the gust profile encountered by the airplane is sinusoidal the response will consist of a transient phase followed by a steady-state sinusoidal oscillation. The steady-state response to a sinusoidal gust can be written as

$$\Delta w(t) = A_g \frac{1}{\sqrt{1 + \tau^2 \omega^2}} \sin(\omega t - \phi) \qquad (6.42)$$

where

$$\phi = -\tan^{-1}(\tau\omega)$$

The steady-state response of the airplane will have the following characteristics:

1. The response will have the same frequency as the gust wave.
2. The amplitude of the response will be

$$\text{Amplitude} = \frac{A_g}{\sqrt{1 + \tau^2 \omega^2}}$$

   where the amplitude of the gust is A_g.
3. The phase angle of the response is $\phi = -\tan^{-1}(\tau\omega)$; the phase angle of the input gust is 0. The response of the airplane lags the gust wave by the angle ϕ.

Figure 6.10 shows the vertical response of an airplane to a sinusoidal gust encountered for values of $\omega\tau$. Remember that ω is the frequency of the gust and τ is the time constant of the airplane. Notice for small values of $\omega\tau$, that is, low-frequency gusts or small airplane time constants, the phase angle ϕ is very small and the ratio of the response to gust input amplitudes is near unity. In this situation, the response is in phase with the gust wave and the amplitude of response of the airplane is nearly equal to the amplitude of the gust profile.

For very large values of $\omega\tau$ the response amplitude tends to 0; that is, the airplane is unaffected by the gust profile. These trends easily are observed in the frequency response curve shown in Figure 6.11. This analysis shows us that the rigid body motion of the airplane is excited by the low-frequency or long wavelength gusts and that the high-frequency or short wavelength gusts have little effect on the airplane's motion. Although the high-frequency gusts do not influence the rigid body motion they will excite the structural modes of the airplane.

Although this example gives us some insight into how atmospheric gusts will affect an airplane the turbulence in the atmosphere is not deterministic. That is to

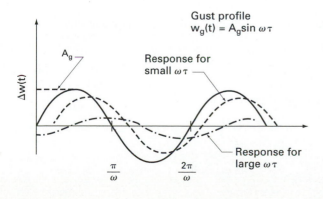

Gust profile
$w_g(t) = A_g \sin \omega\tau$

Response for small $\omega\tau$

Response for large $\omega\tau$

FIGURE 6.10
Response of a first order system to a sinusoidal input.

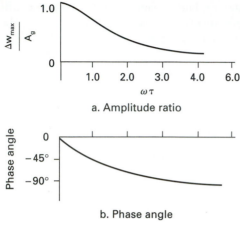

FIGURE 6.11
Frequency response information.

a. Amplitude ratio

b. Phase angle

Curves a and b are called
frequency response curves

say, no analytical expressions completely describe atmospheric turbulence. Rather, turbulence is a stochastic process or random process and can be described only in a statistical manner.

EXAMPLE PROBLEM 6.1. Determine the response of two different airplanes to an encounter with a sharp edge gust of 15 ft/s. Assume the airplanes are in final approach for landing. Data on the airplanes follows:

Aircraft	Weight, lbs.	Approach speed ft/s	Wing area ft²	Lift curve rad⁻¹
General aviation	2,750	125	184	4.44
Jet transport	126,000	225	2,000	4.52

Solution. The vertical response to a sharp edge gust can be computed using Equation (6.37).

$$\Delta w(t) = A_g(1 - e^{-t/\tau})$$

where A_g is the magnitude of the vertical gust and τ is the airplane time constant defined as

$$\tau = -\frac{u_0}{Z_\alpha}$$

The derivative Z_α can be computed from the formula

$$Z_\alpha = C_{Z_\alpha} QS/m$$

but

$$C_{Z_\alpha} = -C_{L_\alpha}$$

therefore

$$Z_\alpha = -C_{L_\alpha} QS/m$$

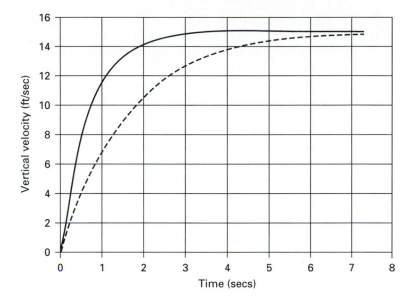

FIGURE 6.12
Response of light general aviation and jet transport to a vertical gust encounter.

Substituting the expression for Z_α into the equation for the time constant and rearranging yields

$$\tau = \frac{2(W/S)}{C_{L_\alpha}\rho u_0 g}$$

For the general aviation airplane,

$$\tau = 2(14.9 \text{ lb/ft}^2)/[(4.44)(0.002378 \text{ slug/ft}^3)(125 \text{ ft/s})(32.2 \text{ ft/s}^2)]$$

$$= 0.7 \text{ s}$$

For the jet transport τ is found to be 1.61 s. Figure 6.12 shows the response of the two airplanes to the vertical gust encounter. The general aviation airplane is much more responsive to the vertical gust than the jet transport. This is due primarily to the difference in wing loading for the two aircraft.

6.4
ATMOSPHERIC TURBULENCE

The atmosphere is in a continuous state of motion. The winds and wind gusts created by the movement of atmospheric air masses can degrade the performance and flying qualities of an airplane. In addition, the atmospheric gusts impose structural loads that must be accounted for in the structural design of an airplane.

The movement of atmospheric air masses is driven by solar heating, the Earth's rotation, and various chemical, thermodynamic, and electromagnetic processes.

The velocity field within the atmosphere varies in both space and time in a random manner. This random velocity field is called atmospheric turbulence. The velocity variations in a turbulent flow can be decomposed into a mean part and a fluctuating part. Figure 6.13 shows a typical atmospheric turbulence profile. The size or scale of the fluctuations vary from small wavelengths on the order of centimeters to wavelengths on the order of kilometers. Because atmospheric turbulence is a random phenomenon it can be described only in a statistical way.

To predict the effect of atmospheric disturbances on aircraft response, flying qualities, autopilot performance, and structural loads requires a mathematical model. In the following sections the discussion will include a description of statistical functions used in describing atmospheric turbulence, a mathematical model of turbulence, and finally an indication of how the turbulence model can be used to determine the response of an airplane to atmospheric disturbances.

Before presenting the mathematical model of turbulence, it is necessary to review some of the basic concepts used to describe turbulence. The discussion at best will be only a cursory review of an extremely complicated subject. The reader is referred to [6.2] and [6.3] for a more informative treatment of the subject.

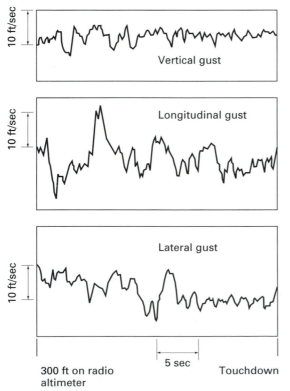

FIGURE 6.13
Atmospheric gust profiles.

6.5
HARMONIC ANALYSIS

An arbitrary periodic signal having a period T can be represented as an infinite series of cosine and sine functions as follows:

$$f(t) = a_0 + \sum_{n=1}^{\infty} a_n \cos(n\omega t) + \sum_{m=1}^{\infty} b_n \sin(m\omega t) \qquad (6.43)$$

where the angular frequency $\omega = 2\pi/T$ and the Fourier coefficients are found from the relationship

$$a_0 = \frac{\omega}{2\pi} \int_{t_0}^{t_0+2\pi/\omega} f(t)\ dt \qquad (6.44)$$

$$a_n = \frac{\omega}{\pi} \int_{t_0}^{t_0+2\pi/\omega} f(t) \cos(\omega t)\ dt \qquad (6.45)$$

$$b_n = \frac{\omega}{\pi} \int_{t_0}^{t_0+2\pi/\omega} f(t) \sin(n\omega t)\ dt \qquad (6.46)$$

When the function is not periodic the technique still can be used by allowing the period T to go to infinity; then the Fourier series becomes a Fourier integral:

$$f(t) = \frac{1}{\pi} \int_{-\infty}^{\infty} e^{i\omega t}\ d\omega \int_{-\infty}^{\infty} f(\tau)\ e^{-i\omega\tau}\ d\tau \qquad (6.47)$$

If we define the second integral to be

$$G(\omega) = \int_{-\infty}^{\infty} f(\tau)\ e^{-i\omega\tau}\ d\omega \qquad (6.48)$$

then

$$f(t) = \frac{1}{2\pi} \int_{-\infty}^{\infty} G(\omega)\ e^{i\omega t}\ d\omega \qquad (6.49)$$

where $G(\omega)$ and $f(t)$ are a Fourier transform pair. The integrand $G(\omega)\ d\omega$ gives the contribution of the harmonic components of $f(t)$ between the frequencies ω and $\omega + d\omega$. Unfortunately, this harmonic analysis does not hold for turbulence. For the Fourier integral to be applicable the integrals must be convergent. The nonperiodic turbulence disturbances persist for long periods of time without dying out in time. The persistence of turbulence yields integrals that do not converge.

To obtain a frequency representation for a continuing disturbance requires the use of the theory of random processes. A random process is one which is random by its nature, so that a deterministic description is not practical. For example, we are all familiar with board games. In most of these games we must roll dice to move around the board. The rolling of the dice constitutes a random experiment. If we denote the sum of the points on the two dice as X, then X is a random variable that can assume integer values between 2 and 12. If we roll the dice a sufficient number of times, we can determine the probabilities of the random variable X assuming any value in the range of X. A function $f(X)$ that yields the probabilities is called the probability or frequency function of a random variable.

Atmospheric turbulence also is a random process and the magnitude of the gust fields can be described only by statistical parameters. That is, we can conduct experiments to determine the magnitude of a gust component and its probability of occurrence. The properties of atmospheric turbulence include that it is homogeneous and stationary. The property of homogeneity means that the statistical properties of turbulence are the same throughout the region of interest; stationarity implies that the statistical properties are independent of time.

For the case when $f(t)$ is a stationary random process, the mean square $\overline{f^2(t)}$ is defined as

$$\overline{f^2(t)} = \lim_{T \to \infty} \frac{1}{T} \int_0^T [f(t)]^2 \, dt \tag{6.50}$$

where $\overline{f^2(t)}$ represents a measure of the disturbance intensity. The disturbance function $f(t)$ can be thought of as an infinite number of sinusoidal components having frequencies ranging from zero to infinity. That portion of $\overline{f^2(t)}$ that occurs from ω to $d\omega$ is called the power spectral density and denoted by the symbol $\Phi(\omega)$. The intensity of the random process can be related to the power spectral density.

The response of a physical system such as an airplane to a random disturbance such as atmospheric turbulence can be obtained from the power spectral density of the input function and the system transfer function. If $G(i\omega)$ represents the system frequency response function and $\Phi_i(\omega)$ is the power spectral density of the disturbance input function, then the output $\Phi_0(\omega)$ is given by

$$\Phi_0(\omega) = \Phi_i(\omega) |G(i\omega)|^2 \tag{6.51}$$

With Equation (6.51) we can determine the response of an airplane at atmospheric disturbances. The transfer function G is the system gust transfer function described earlier. All that remains now is to describe $\Phi_i(\omega)$ for the gust input.

6.5.1 Turbulence Models

Two spectral forms of random continuous turbulence are used to model atmospheric turbulence for aircraft response studies: the mathematical models named after von Karman and Dryden, the scientists who first proposed them. Because the von Karman model is more widely used in practice it will be the only one described here. The power spectral density for the turbulence velocities is given by

$$\Phi_{ug}(\Omega) = \sigma_u^2 \frac{2L_u}{\pi} \frac{1}{[1 + (1.339 L_u \Omega)^2]^{5/6}} \tag{6.52}$$

$$\Phi_{vg}(\Omega) = \sigma_v^2 \frac{2L_v}{\pi} \frac{1 + \frac{8}{3}(1.339 L_v \Omega)^2}{[1 + (1.339 L_v \Omega)^2]^{11/6}} \tag{6.53}$$

$$\Phi_{wg}(\Omega) = \sigma_w^2 \frac{2L_w}{\pi} \frac{1 + \frac{8}{3}(1.339 L_w \Omega)^2}{[1 + (1.339 L_w \Omega)^2]^{11/6}} \tag{6.54}$$

where σ is the root mean square intensity of the gust component, Ω is the spatial frequency, defined by $2\pi/\lambda$, where λ is the wavelength of a sinusoidal component,

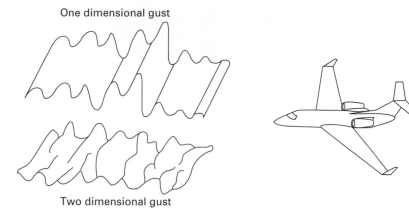

One dimensional gust

Two dimensional gust

FIGURE 6.14
One and two dimensional gust fields.

and L is the scale of the turbulence. The subscripts u, v, and w refer to the gust components. The scales and intensities of atmospheric turbulence depend on the altitude and the type of turbulence; that is, clear air (high or low altitude) and thunderstorm turbulences.

For an airplane passing through a gust field, it is assumed that the turbulence encountered is independent of time (i.e., the turbulence is stationary). This assumption can be visualized by considering the gust field to be frozen in both time and space, as illustrated in Figure 6.14. Assuming the frozen-field concept the turbulence-induced motion is due only to the motion of the airplane relative to the gust field.

The three power spectral densities presented earlier were a function of a spatial frequency; however, as the airplane passes through the frozen turbulent field it senses a temporal frequency. The relationship between the spatial and temporal frequency is given by

$$\Omega = \omega/u_0 \tag{6.55}$$

where ω is in rad/s and u_0 is the velocity of the airplane relative to the air mass it is passing through.

6.6
WIND SHEAR

Wind shear is defined as a local variation of the wind vector. The variations in wind speed and direction are measured in the vertical and horizontal directions. In a vertical wind shear the wind speed and direction vary with changing altitude; in a horizontal wind shear, wind variations are along some horizontal distance.

Wind shears are created by the movement of air masses relative to one another or to the Earth's surface. Thunderstorms, frontal systems, and the Earth's

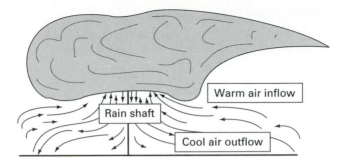

FIGURE 6.15
Wind shear created by a down burst.

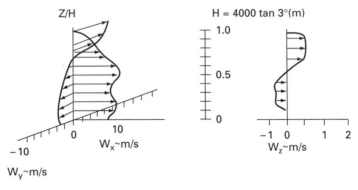

FIGURE 6.16
Measured wind shear velocity profiles.

boundary layer all produce wind shear profiles that at times can be hazardous to aircraft flying at low altitudes. The strong gust fronts associated with thunderstorms are created by downdrafts within the storm system. As the downdrafts approach the ground, they turn and move outward along the Earth's surface. The wind shear produced by the gust front can be quite severe.

The wind shear created by a frontal system occurs at the transition zone between two different air masses. The wind shear is created by the interaction of the winds in the two air masses. If the transition zone is gradual, the wind shear will be small. However, if the transition zone is small, the conflicting wind speeds and directions of the air masses can produce a very strong wind shear. Figure 6.15 shows some of the mechanisms that create a wind shear and Figure 6.16 shows an experimentally measured shear profile near the ground.

No simple mathematical formulations characterize the wind shears produced by the passage of frontal systems or thunderstorms. Generally, these shears are represented in simulation studies by tables of wind speed components with altitude.

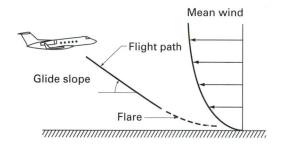

FIGURE 6.17
An aircraft descending into a
horizontal wind shear.

The surface boundary layer also produces wind shear. The shape of the profile is determined, primarily, by local terrain and atmospheric conditions. Additional problems arise when there is an abrupt change in surface roughness (which can be expected near airports), resulting in additional internal boundary layers, and when the direction of the wind varies with altitude.

To analyze the influence of wind shear on aircraft motion, the characteristics of wind shear must be known. The magnitude of the shear can be expressed in terms of the change in wind speed with respect to altitude, du/dh, where a positive wind shear increases with increasing altitude. The qualitative criteria for judging the severity of wind shear were proposed to the International Civil Aviation Organization (ICAO). It was suggested that shear be considered light if du/dh ranges from 0 to 0.08 s^{-1}, moderate for 0.08–0.15 s^{-1}, strong for 0.15–0.20 s^{-1}, and severe if greater than 0.2 s^{-1}. These criteria are useful in giving an idea of the magnitude of wind shear but the ICAO did not accept them. A shear that is moderate for an airplane with a high stall speed may be strong for one with a low stall speed, so universal criteria are impossible owing to differences among aircraft types.

EXAMPLE PROBLEM 6.2. Consider an airplane on a final approach encountering a vertical wind shear; that is, the variation of horizontal wind velocity with altitude. Figure 6.17 shows an airplane flying into a wind shear. To analyze this problem we can use Equation (6.17). The change in wind velocity is represented by

$$u_g = \frac{du}{dh} \, dh$$

where du/dh is the velocity gradient and dh is the change in altitude. If we assume that the controls are fixed, Equation (6.17) reduces to

$$
\begin{bmatrix} \Delta \dot{u} \\ \Delta \dot{w} \\ \Delta \dot{q} \\ \Delta \dot{\theta} \end{bmatrix}
=
\begin{bmatrix} X_u & X_w & 0 & -g \\ Z_u & Z_w & u_0 & 0 \\ M_u & M_w & M_q & 0 \\ 0 & 0 & 1 & 0 \end{bmatrix}
\begin{bmatrix} \Delta u \\ \Delta w \\ \Delta q \\ \Delta \theta \end{bmatrix}
+
\begin{bmatrix} -X_u \\ -Z_u \\ -M_u \\ 0 \end{bmatrix}
[u_g]
$$

But u_g is a function of altitude and therefore we must add other equations to the system. The vertical velocity of the airplane can be expressed as the time rate of change of altitude as follows:

$$\Delta \dot{h} = u_0 (\Delta \alpha - \Delta \theta)$$

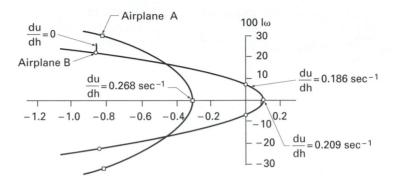

FIGURE 6.18
Influence of wind shear on longitudinal roots.

Adding this equation to the state equations and substituting for u_g yields

$$
\begin{bmatrix} \Delta \dot{u} \\[1em] \Delta \dot{\alpha} \\[1em] \Delta \dot{q} \\[1em] \Delta \dot{\theta} \\[1em] \Delta \dot{h} \end{bmatrix} = \begin{bmatrix} X_u & X_\alpha & 0 & -g & -X_u \dfrac{du}{dh} \\[1.2em] \dfrac{Z_u}{u_0} & \dfrac{Z_\alpha}{u_0} & 1 & 0 & \dfrac{-Z_u}{u_0}\dfrac{du}{dh} \\[1.2em] M_u & M_\alpha & M_q & 0 & -M_u\dfrac{du}{dh} \\[1.2em] 0 & 0 & 1 & 0 & 0 \\[1.2em] 0 & u_0 & 0 & -u_0 & 0 \end{bmatrix} \begin{bmatrix} \Delta u \\[1em] \Delta \alpha \\[1em] \Delta q \\[1em] \Delta \theta \\[1em] \Delta h \end{bmatrix}
$$

The solution to this system of equations yields five eigenvalues: two complex pairs representing the phugoid and short-period modes and a fifth, real, root indicating a nonoscillatory motion. These equations were solved in [6.6] for STOL aircraft for various magnitudes of the velocity gradient. The results showed that wind shear had very little affect on the short-period motion; however, the phugoid motion was found to be quite sensitive to du/dh. Figure 6.18 shows a root locus plot of the phugoid roots for variations in du/dh. For very large gradients the phugoid mode can become unstable. An unstable phugoid mode would make the landing approach very difficult for the pilot to control. Therefore, strong wind shears must be avoided for flight safety.

6.7
SUMMARY

In this chapter we examined some of the analytical techniques available to flight control engineers to study the dynamic response of an airplane to control deflection or atmospheric disturbances. Apart from the uncomfortable ride they create for the pilot and passengers, the loads imposed on the airframe structure by the gust fields must be calculated so that the structure can be properly designed.

Wind shear recently has been shown to be a greater hazard to commercial aviation than had been appreciated. Wind shears created by thunderstorm systems have been identified as the major contributor to several airline crashes. The techniques outlined in this chapter can be used by stability and control engineers to study the effects of atmospheric disturbances on aircraft flight characteristics. Such studies can be used to improve flight safety.

PROBLEMS

6.1. For the business jet aircraft whose details are included in Appendix B determine the lateral response curves for an aileron input. Present your results in the form of frequency response curves.

6.2. The vertical motion of an airplane subjected to a sharp-edged gust is described by the equation

$$\Delta w(t) = A_g(1 - e^{-t/\tau})$$

where Δw is in the vertical velocity, A_g is the magnitude of the gust, and τ is the time constant of the airplane. Using the information in Figure P6.2 determine the maximum vertical acceleration and the time constant of the airplane.

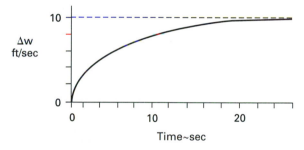

FIGURE P6.2
Vertical velocity response.

6.3. For the general aviation airplane whose details are included in Appendix B determine the vertical response to a sinusoidal gust field. Assume the problem can be modeled by a single degree of freedom vertical equation of motion. Present your results in the form of frequency response curves.

6.4. Discuss how changes in the aerodynamic stability characteristics would effect the response curves obtained in Problem 6.3.

6.5. Assume that an airplane is on final approach and encounters a wind shear that can be represented as

$$u_g = \frac{du}{dh} dh$$

where du/dh is the wind gradient. Assume that the pitch attitude of the airplane is maintained by an automatic control system. Develop the equations of motion governing the vertical and horizontal velocity of the airplane. How does the wind gradient effect the two-dimensional response?

REFERENCES

6.1. McRuer, D.; I. Ashkenas; and D. Graham. *Aircraft Dynamics and Automatic Control.* Princeton, NJ: Princeton University Press, 1973.

6.2. Batchelor, G. K. *The Theory of Homogeneous Turbulence.* London: Cambridge University Press, 1956.

6.3. Lumley, J. L.; and H. A. Panofsky. *The Structure of Atmospheric Turbulence.* New York: Wiley Interscience, 1964.

6.4. Houbolt, J. C.; R. Steiner; and K. G. Pratt. *Dynamic Response of Airplanes to Atmospheric Turbulence Including Flight Data on Input and Response.* NASA TR-R-199, June 1964.

6.5. Press, H.; M. T. Meadows; and I. Hadlock. *A Reevaluation of Data on Atmospheric Turbulence and Airplane Gust Loads for Application to Spectral Calculating.* NACA Report 1272, 1956.

6.6. Nelson, R. C.; M. M. Curtin; and F. M. Payne. *A Combined Experimental and Analytical Investigation of the Influence of Low Level Shear on the Handling Characteristics of Aircraft.* DOT Report-DOT/RSPA/ADMA-50/83/29, October 1979.

CHAPTER 7

Automatic Control Theory—
The Classical Approach

"The transport aircraft of the future may well be on automatic control from the moment of take-off to the automatic landing at its destination."

William Bollay, 14th Wright Brothers Lecture, 1950

7.1
INTRODUCTION

Control theory deals with the analysis and synthesis of logic for the control of a system. In the broadest sense, a system can be thought of as a collection of components or parts that work together to perform a particular function. The airplane is an example of a complex system designed to transport people and cargo.

What today we call control theory developed along two different analytical approaches. The first approach was based on frequency response methods, the root locus technique, transfer functions, and Laplace transforms. It had its beginning in the late 1930s. This approach to control theory is sometimes called classical or conventional control theory. A major feature of these analysis methods was their adaptability to simple graphical procedures, which was particularly important during this time period because computers were not available. Analysis techniques had to be suitable for calculations made without computers. The analysis tools, based upon the work of Bode, Nyquist, and Evans, form the foundation of "classical" control theory. To apply classical control theory to the design of a control system one needs to understand Laplace transforms and the concept of a transfer function.

With the advent of high-speed digital computers, control system analysis methods were developed based on the state-space formulation of the system. These analysis techniques, developed since the 1960s, are commonly called modern control theory. To understand modern control methods one must understand matrix algebra and the state-space concept of representing a system of governing equations. The selection of the names classical and modern is somewhat unfortunate in that it seems to relegate the classical approach to a lesser status when this is not the case. A control system designer needs to know both the classical and modern control approaches. In this and the next three chapters we divide control theory into

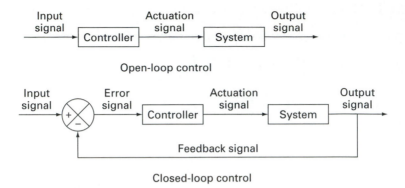

FIGURE 7.1
Examples of open-loop and closed-loop control systems.

the two categories, classical and modern, for convenience. Both approaches have their strengths and weaknesses and find wide acceptance and use by control system designers.

It is not possible to cover all aspects of control theory approach in just four chapters. Therefore, it has been assumed that the reader has had an undergraduate course in control theory. Chapters 7 and 9 provide a brief review of some of the theoretical aspects of the classical and the modern control; Chapters 8 and 10 apply the techniques to the design of simple airplane autopilots.

In each chapter we provide simple examples of the control analysis techniques that one can do readily with a simple pocket calculator. Once the theoretical basis of these techniques is understood more complicated problems can be attempted. A number of software packages are available for control system analysis and design. We have found the software package MATLAB* to be quite useful and used it in developing problems and examples for these chapters. Readers are encouraged to use whatever control software is available at their university or company to help them with the problems at the end of the chapters.

Before discussing control system design, a review of some of the basic concepts of control theory will be presented. Control systems can be classified as either open-loop or closed-loop systems, as illustrated in Figure 7.1. An open-loop control system is the simplest and least complex of all control devices. In the open-loop system the control action is independent of the output. In closed-loop system the control action depends on the output of the system. Closed-loop control systems are called feedback control systems. The advantage of the closed-loop system is its accuracy.

To obtain a more accurate control system, some form of feedback between the output and input must be established. This can be accomplished by comparing the controlled signal (output) with the commanded or reference input. In a feedback system one or more feedback loops are used to compare the controlled signal with the command signal to generate an error signal. The error signal then is used to

---

*MATLAB is a registered trademark of The Math Works, Inc.

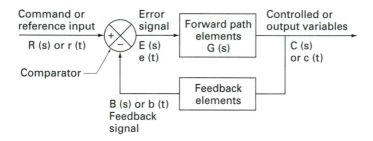

FIGURE 7.2
A feedback control system.

drive the output signal into agreement with the desired input signal. The typical closed-loop feedback system shown in Figure 7.2 is composed of a forward path, a feedback path, and an error-detection device called a comparator. Each component of the control system is defined in terms of its transfer function. The transfer function, T.F., is defined as the ratio of the Laplace transform of the output to the Laplace transform of the input where the initial conditions are assumed to be 0:

$$\text{T.F.} = \frac{\text{Laplace transform of the output}}{\text{Laplace transform of the input}} \tag{7.1}$$

The transfer function of each element of the control system can be determined from the equations that govern the dynamic characteristics of the element. The aircraft transfer functions are developed in Chapter 8 from the equations of motion.

The closed-loop transfer function for the feedback control system shown in Figure 7.2 can be developed from the block diagram. The symbols used in the block diagram are defined as follows:

$R(s)$ reference input
$C(s)$ output signal (variable to be controlled)
$B(s)$ feedback signal
$E(s)$ error or actuating signal
$G(s)$ $C(s)/E(s)$ forward path or open-loop transfer function
$M(s)$ $C(s)/R(s)$ the closed-loop transfer function
$H(s)$ feedback transfer function
$G(s)H(s)$ loop transfer function

The closed-loop transter function, $C(s)/R(s)$, can be obtained by simple algebraic manipulation of the block diagram. The actuating or error signal is the difference between the input and feedback signals:

$$E(s) = R(s) - B(s) \tag{7.2}$$

The feedback signal $B(s)$ can be expressed in terms of the feedback transfer function and the output signal:

$$B(s) = H(s)C(s) \tag{7.3}$$

and the output signal $C(s)$ is related to the error signal and forward path transfer function in the following manner:

$$C(s) = G(s)E(s) \tag{7.4}$$

Substituting Equations (7.2) and (7.3) into 7.4 yields

$$C(s) = G(s)R(s) - G(s)H(s)C(s) \tag{7.5}$$

Equation (7.5) can be solved for the closed-loop transfer function $C(s)/R(s)$:

$$\frac{C(s)}{R(s)} = \frac{G(s)}{1 + G(s)H(s)} \tag{7.6}$$

which is the ratio of the system output to the input. Most control systems are much more complex than the one shown in Figure 7.2. However, theoretically the more complex control systems consisting of many feedback elements can be reduced to the simple form just described.

The feedback systems described here can be designed to control accurately the output to some desired tolerance. However, feedback in itself does not ensure that the system will be stable. Therefore, to design a feedback control system one needs analysis tools that allow the designer to select system parameters so that the system will be stable. In addition to determining the absolute stability, the relative stability of the control system also must be determined. A system that is stable in the absolute sense may not be a satisfactory control system. For example, if the system damping is too low the output will be characterized by large amplitude oscillations about the desired output. The large overshooting of the response may make the system unacceptable.

Autopilots can be designed using either frequency- or time-domain methods developed from servomechanism theory or by time-domain analysis using state feedback design. In this chapter the techniques from servomechanism theory will be discussed and several simple applications of the design techniques will be demonstrated by applying the techniques to the design of autopilots.

The servomechanism design techniques include the Routh criterion, root locus, Bode, and Nyquist methods. A brief description of these techniques is presented either in the following sections or in the appendices at the end of this book. For a more rigorous treatment of this material, the reader is referred to [7.2–7.5].

7.2
ROUTH'S CRITERION

As noted earlier, the roots of the characteristic equation tell us whether or not the system is dynamically stable. If all the roots of the characteristic equation have negative real parts the system will be dynamically stable. On the other hand, if any root of the characteristic equation has a positive real part the system will be unstable. The system is considered to be marginally stable if one or more of the roots is a pure imaginary number. The marginally stable system represents the boundary between a dynamically stable or unstable system. For a closed-loop control system the denominator of Equation (7.6) is the characteristic equation.

A simple means of determining the absolute stability of a system can be obtained by the Routh stability criterion. The method allows us to determine whether any of the roots of the characteristic equation have positive real parts, without actually solving for the roots. Consider the characteristic equation

$$a_n \lambda^n + a_{n-1} \lambda^{n-1} + a_{n-2} \lambda^{n-2} \cdots a_1 \lambda + a_0 = 0 \qquad (7.7)$$

So that no roots of Equation (7.7) have positive real parts the necessary but not sufficient conditions are that

1. All the coefficients of the characteristic equation must have the same sign.
2. All the coefficients must exist.

To apply the Routh criterion, we must first define the Routh array as in Table 7.1. The Routh array is continued horizontally and vertically until only zeros are obtained. The last step is to investigate the signs of the numbers in the first column of the Routh table. The Routh stability criterion states

1. If all the numbers of the first column have the same sign then the roots of the characteristic polynominal have negative real parts. The system therefore is stable.
2. If the numbers in the first column change sign then the number of sign changes indicates the number of roots of the characteristic equation having positive real parts. Therefore, if there is a sign change in the first column the system will be unstable.

When developing the Routh array, several difficulties may occur. For example, the first number in one of the rows may be 0, but the other numbers in the row may not be. Obviously, if 0 appears in the first position of a row, the elements in the following row will be infinite. In this case, the Routh test breaks down. Another

TABLE 7.1
Definition of Routh array: Routh table

λ^n	a_n	a_{n-2}	a_{n-4}	$\cdots$
λ^{n-1}	a_{n-1}	a_{n-3}	a_{n-5}	$\cdots$
λ^{n-2}	b_1	b_2	b_3	$\cdots$
$\vdots$	c_1	c_2	c_3	$\cdots$

where $a_n, a_{n-1}, \ldots, a_0$ are the coefficients of the characteristic equation and the coefficients b_1, b_2, b_3, c_1, c_2, and so on are given by

$$b_1 \equiv \frac{a_{n-1}a_{n-2} - a_n a_{n-3}}{a_{n-1}} \qquad b_2 \equiv \frac{a_{n-1}a_{n-4} - a_n a_{n-5}}{a_{n-1}} \qquad \text{and so forth}$$

$$c_1 \equiv \frac{b_1 a_{n-3} - a_{n-1}b_2}{b_1} \qquad c_2 \equiv \frac{b_1 a_{n-5} - a_{n-1}b_3}{b_1} \qquad \text{and so forth}$$

$$d_1 \equiv \frac{c_1 b_2 - c_2 b_1}{c_1} \qquad \text{and so forth}$$

possibility is that all the numbers in a row are 0. Methods for handling these special cases can be found in most textbooks on automatic control theory.

Several examples of applying the Routh stability criterion are shown in Example Problem 7.1.

EXAMPLE PROBLEM 7.1. Determine whether the characteristic equations given below have stable or unstable roots.

(a) $\lambda^3 + 6\lambda^2 + 12\lambda + 8 = 0$

(b) $2\lambda^3 + 4\lambda^2 + 4\lambda + 12 = 0$

(c) $A\lambda^4 + B\lambda^3 + C\lambda^2 + D\lambda + E = 0$

Solution. The first two rows of the array are written down by inspection and the succeeding rows are obtained by using the relationship for each row element as presented previously:

$$
\begin{array}{ccc}
1 & 12 & 0 \\
6 & 8 & 0 \\
\dfrac{64}{6} & 0 & \\
8 & &
\end{array}
$$

There are no sign changes in column 1; therefore, the system is stable. The Routh array for the second characteristic equation is as follows:

$$
\begin{array}{ccc}
2 & 4 & 0 \\
4 & 12 & 0 \\
-2 & 0 & \\
12 & &
\end{array}
$$

Note that there are two sign changes in column 1; therefore, the characteristic equation has two roots with positive real parts. The system in unstable.

The Routh stability criterion can be applied to the quartic characteristic equation that describes either the longitudinal or lateral motion of an airplane. The quartic characteristic equation for either the longitudinal or lateral equation of motion is given in part c of this problem where A, B, C, D, and E are functions of the longitudinal or lateral stability derivatives. Forming the Routh array from the characteristic equation yields

$$
\begin{array}{ccc}
A & C & E \\
B & D & 0 \\
\dfrac{BC - AD}{B} & E & 0 \\
\dfrac{[D(BC - AC)/B] - BE}{(BC - AD)/B} & 0 & \\
E & &
\end{array}
$$

For the airplane to be stable requires that

$$A, B, C, D, E \qquad\qquad > 0$$

$$BC - AC \qquad\qquad > 0$$

$$D(BC - AD) - B^2E > 0$$

The last two inequalities were obtained by inspection of the first column of the Routh array.

If the first number in a row is 0 and the remaining elements of that row are nonzero, the Routh method breaks down. To overcome this problem the lead element that is 0 is replaced by a small positive number, ε. With the substitution of ε as the first element, the Routh array can be completed. After completing the Routh array we can examine the first column to determine whether there are any sign changes in the first column as ε approaches 0.

The other potential difficulty occurs when a complete row of the Routh array is 0. Again the Routh method breaks down. When this condition occurs it means that there are symmetrically located roots in the s plane. The roots may be real with opposite sign or complex conjugate roots. The polynomial formed by the coefficient of the first row just above the row of zeroes is called the auxiliary polynomial. The roots of the auxiliary polynomial are symmetrical roots of the characteristic equation. The situation can be overcome by replacing the row of zeroes by the coefficients of the polynomial obtained by taking the derivative of the auxiliary polynomial. These exceptions to the Routh method are illustrated by way of example problems.

EXAMPLE PROBLEM 7.2. In this example we will examine the two potential cases where the Routh method breaks down. The two characteristic equations are as follows:

(a) $\lambda^5 + \lambda^4 + 3\lambda^3 + 3\lambda^2 + 4\lambda + 6 = 0$

(b) $\lambda^6 + 3\lambda^5 + 6\lambda^4 + 12\lambda^3 + 11\lambda^2 + 9\lambda + 6 = 0$

For equation a, the lead element of the third row of the Routh table is 0 which prevents us from completing the table. This difficulty is avoided by replacing the lead element 0 in the third row by a small positive values ε. With the 0 removed and replaced by ε the Routh table can be completed as follows:

1	3	4
1	3	6
ε	-2	
$\dfrac{3\varepsilon + 2}{\varepsilon}$	6	
$\dfrac{-6\varepsilon^2 - 6\varepsilon - 4}{3\varepsilon + 2}$	0	
6		

Now as ε goes to 0 the sign of the first elements in rows 3 and 4 are positive. However, in row 5 the lead element goes to -2 as ε goes to 0. We note two sign changes in the first column of the Routh tables; therefore, the system has two roots with positive real parts, which means it is unstable.

The second difficulty that can cause a problem with the Routh method is a complete row of the Routh table being zeroes. This difficulty is illustrated by the Routh table for equation b.

The Routh table can be constructed as follows:

$$
\begin{array}{cccc}
1 & 6 & 11 & 6 \\
3 & 12 & 9 & \\
2 & 8 & 6 & \\
0 & 0 & &
\end{array}
$$

Note that the fourth row of the Routh table is all zeroes. The auxiliary equation is formed from the coefficients in the row just above the row of zeroes. For this example the auxiliary equation is

$$2\lambda^4 + 8\lambda^2 + 6 = 0$$

Taking the derivative of the auxiliary equation yields

$$8\lambda^3 + 16\lambda = 0$$

The row of zeroes in the fourth row is replaced by the coefficients 8 and 16. The Routh table now can be completed.

$$
\begin{array}{cccc}
1 & 6 & 11 & 6 \\
3 & 12 & 9 & \\
2 & 8 & 6 & \\
8 & 16 & & \\
4 & 6 & & \\
4 & 0 & & \\
6 & & &
\end{array}
$$

The auxiliary equation can also be solved to determine the symmetric roots,

$$\lambda^4 + 4\lambda^2 + 3 = 0$$

which can be factored as follows:

$$(\lambda^2 + 1)(\lambda^2 + 3) = 0$$

or $\qquad \lambda = \pm i \qquad$ and $\qquad \lambda = \pm\sqrt{3}\,i$

If we examine column 1 of the Routh table we conclude that there are no roots with positive real parts. However, solution of the auxiliary equations reveals that we have two pairs of complex roots lying on the imaginary axis. The purely imaginary roots lead to undamped oscillatory motions. In the absolute sense, the system is stable; that is, no part of the motion is growing with time. However, the purely oscillatory motions would be unacceptable for a control system.

Even though the method developed by Routh provides an easy way of assessing the absolute stability, it gives us no indication of the relative stability of the system. To assess the relative stability requires another analysis tool such as the root locus technique.

7.3
ROOT LOCUS TECHNIQUE

In designing a control system, it is desirable to be able to investigate the performance of the control system when one or more parameters of the system are varied. As has been shown repeatedly, the characteristic equation plays an important role in the dynamic behavior of aircraft motions. The same is true for linear control systems. In control system design, a powerful tool for analyzing the performance of a system is the root locus technique. Basically, the technique provides graphical information in the s plane on the trajectory of the roots of the characteristic equation for variations in one or more of the system parameters. Typically, most root locus plots consist of only one parametric variation. The control system designer can use the root locus method to obtain accurate time-domain response and frequency response information on a closed-loop control system.

The root locus technique was introduced by W. R. Evans in 1949. He developed a series of rules that allow the control systems engineer to quickly draw the root locus diagram. Although many software packages are available for accurately determining the root locus plots, the graphical rules remain important. They provide the control systems engineer a valuable tool to assessing system changes. With Evans's technique one can sketch a root locus plot in several minutes. The rules for constructing a root locus plot are presented later in this section.

The transfer function was described earlier as the ratio of the output to the input. On examining a transfer function we note that the denominator is the characteristic equation of the system. The roots of the denominator are the eigenvalues that describe the free response of the system, where the free response is the solution to the homogeneous equation. In controls terminology the characteristic roots are called the poles of the transfer function. The numerator of the transfer function governs the particular solution and the roots of the numerator are called zeros.

As was noted earlier in Chapters 4 and 5 the roots of the characteristic equation (or poles) must have negative real parts if the system is to be stable. In control system design the location of the poles of the closed-loop transfer function allows the designer to predict the time-domain performance of the system.

However, in designing a control system the designer typically will have a number of system parameters unspecified. The root locus technique permits the designer to view the movement of the poles of the closed-loop transfer function as one or more unknown system parameters are varied.

Before describing the root locus technique it would be helpful to examine the significance of the root placement in the complex plane and the type of response

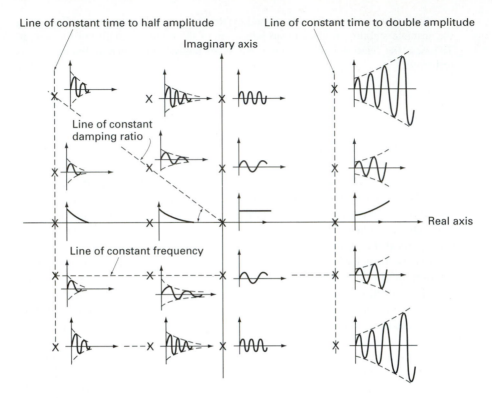

FIGURE 7.3
Impulse response as a function of the pole location in the complex s plane.

that can be expected to occur. Figure 7.3 illustrates some of the important features of pole location. First we note that any pole lying in the left half portion of the complex plane is stable; that is, the response decays with time. Any pole in the right half plane leads to a response that grows with time, which will result in an unstable system. The farther the root is to the left of the imaginary axis, the faster the response decays. All poles lying along a particular vertical line will have the same time to half amplitude. Poles lying along the same horizontal line have the same damped frequency, ω, and period. The farther the pole is from the real axis, the higher the frequency of the response will be. Poles lying along a radial line through the origin have the same damping ratio, ζ, and roots lying on the same circular arc around the origin will have the same undamped natural frequency. Finally, some comments must be made about the poles lying on the imaginary axis. Poles of the order 1 on the imaginary axis lead to undamped oscillations; however, multiple order poles result in responses that grow with time.

The closed-loop transfer function was shown earlier to be

$$M(s) = \frac{G(s)}{1 + G(s)H(s)} \tag{7.8}$$

The characteristic equation of the closed loop system is given by the denominator of equation (7.8):

$$1 + G(s)H(s) = 0 \qquad (7.9)$$

or
$$G(s)H(s) = -1 \qquad (7.10)$$

The transfer function $G(s)H(s)$ can be expressed in factored form as follows:

$$G(s)H(s) = \frac{k(s + z_1)(s + z_2) \cdots (s + z_m)}{(s + p_1)(s + p_2) \cdots (s + p_n)} \qquad (7.11)$$

where $n > m$ and k is an unknown system parameter. Substituting this equation into the characteristic equation yields.

$$\frac{k(s + z_1)(s + z_2) \cdots (s + z_m)}{(s + p_1)(s + p_2) \cdots (s + p_n)} = -1 \qquad (7.12)$$

The characteristic equation is complex and can be written in terms of a magnitude and angle as follows:

$$\frac{|k| |s + z_1| |s + z_2| \cdots |s + z_m|}{|s + p_1| |s + p_2| \cdots |s + p_n|} = 1 \qquad (7.13)$$

$$\sum_{i=1}^{m} \angle(s + z_i) - \sum_{i=1}^{n} \angle(s + p_i) = (2q + 1)\pi \qquad (7.14)$$

where $q = 0, 1, 2, \ldots, n - m - 1$. Solution of these equations yields the movement of the roots as a function of the unknown system parameter, k. These equations can be solved on the computer to determine the root locus contours. However, a simple graphical technique developed by W. R. Evans can be used to rapidly sketch a root locus plot. This graphical procedure is presented in the next section.

It can be shown easily that the root locus contours start at the poles of transfer function, $G(s)H(s)$ and end at the zeroes of the transfer function as k is varied from 0 to infinity. For example, if we rearrange the magnitude criteria in the following manner,

$$\frac{|s + z_1| |s + z_2| \cdots |s + z_m|}{|s + p_1| |s + p_2| \cdots |s + p_n|} = \frac{1}{|k|} \qquad (7.15)$$

then as k goes to 0 the function becomes infinite. This implies that the roots approach the poles as k goes to 0. On the other hand, as k goes to infinity the function goes to 0, which implies that the roots are at the transfer function zeros. Therefore, the root locus plot of the closed-loop system starts with a plot of the poles and zeros of the transfer function, $G(s)H(s)$. Evans developed a series of rules based on the magnitude and angle criteria for rapidly sketching the root locus branches on a pole zero map. A proof of these rules can be found in most control textbooks and will not be presented here. Table 7.2 is a summary of the rules for constructing a root locus contour.

TABLE 7.2
Rules for graphical construction of the root locus plot

1. The root locus contours are symmetrical about the real axis.
2. The number of separate branches of the root locus plot is equal to the number of poles of the transfer function $G(s)H(s)$. Branches of the root locus originate at the poles of $G(s)H(s)$ for $k = 0$ and terminate at either the open-loop zeroes or at infinity for $k = \infty$. The number of branches that terminate at infinity is equal to the difference between the number of poles and zeroes of the transfer function $G(s)H(s)$, where n = number of poles and m = number of zeros.
3. Segments of the real axis that are part of the root locus can be found in the following manner: Points on the real axis that have an odd number of poles and zeroes to their right are part of the real axis portion of the root locus.
4. The root locus branches that approach the open-loop zeroes at infinity do so along straight-line asymptotes that intersect the real axis at the center of gravity of the finite poles and zeroes. Mathematically this can be expressed as

$$\sigma = \left[\sum \text{Real parts of the poles} - \sum \text{Real parts of the zeroes} \right] \Big/ (n - m)$$

where n is the number of poles and m is the number of finite zeroes.
5. The angle that the asymptotes make with the real axis is given by

$$\phi_a = \frac{180° [2q + 1]}{n - m}$$

for $q = 0, 1, 2, \ldots , (n - m - 1)$
6. The angle of departure of the root locus from a pole of $G(s)H(s)$ can be found by the following expression:

$$\phi_p = \pm 180° (2q + 1) + \phi \qquad q = 0, 1, 2, \ldots$$

where ϕ is the net angle contribution at the pole of interest due to all other poles and zeroes of $G(s)H(s)$. The arrival angle at a zero is given by a similar expression:

$$\phi_z = \pm 180° (2q + 1) + \phi \qquad q = 0, 1, 2, \ldots$$

The angle ϕ is determined by drawing straight lines from all the poles and zeroes to the pole or zero of interest and then summing the angles made by these lines.
7. If a portion of the real axis is part of the root locus and a branch is between two poles, the branch must break away from the real axis so that the locus ends on a zero as k approaches infinity. The breakaway points on the real axis are determined by solving

$$1 + GH = 0$$

for k and then finding the roots of the equation $dk/ds = 0$. Only roots that lie on a branch of the locus are of interest.

The root locus technique discussed in this chapter provides the analyst or designer a convenient method for assessing the absolute and relative stability of a control system. In terms of the root locus diagram, if any of the roots of the characteristic equation of the closed-loop system lie in the right half plane the system is unstable. On the other hand, if all the roots lie in the left half plane the system is stable. Complex roots lying on the imaginary axis yield constant amplitude oscillations. Repeated roots on the imaginary axis result in unstable behavior.

For roots lying in the left side of the root locus plot the question becomes one of determining the relative stability of the system. A system that is stable in the absolute sense may not be a very useful control system. We need to know more about the relative stability of the system. Relative stability deals with how fast the system responds to control input and how fast disturbances are suppressed. The relative stability of the control system is measured by various performance indices such as time to half amplitude, percent over shoot, rise time, or settling time. These concepts will be discussed in the next section.

EXAMPLE PROBLEM 7.3. Sketch the root locus plot for the transfer function

$$G(s)H(s) = \frac{k(s + 3)}{s(s + 10)(s^2 + 8s + 20)}$$

Solution. This transfer function has one finite zero ($m = 1$) and four poles ($n = 4$):

zero: $s = -3$
poles: $s = 0, s = -10, s = -4 \pm 2i$

The poles and zeroes of the transfer function can be plotted on the root locus diagram. The poles and zeroes of $G(s)H(s)$ are denoted by a small x or 0, respectively, on the root locus plot. Using rule 3 from Table 7.2 we observe that the portion of the real axis that is part of the locus lies between $s = 0$ and -3 and from -10 to $-\infty$.

The number of branches of the root locus that terminate at a zero at infinity is equal to the difference between the number of poles (n) and the number of zeroes (m) of the transfer function (rule 2). In this case we have four poles and one zero; therefore, we have three branches of the locus going to zeroes at infinity.

The branches of the locus that go to a zero at infinity do so along straight-line asymptotes. The intersection of the asymptotes with the real axis and the angle of the asymptotes follows (see rules 4 and 5 of Table 7.2):

$$\sigma = \frac{\Sigma \text{ real parts of the poles} - \Sigma \text{ real parts of the zero}}{[n - m]}$$

$$\sigma = \frac{(-0 - 10 - 4 - 4) - (-3)}{4 - 1} = \frac{-15}{3} = -5$$

and $\phi_A = \dfrac{180°[2q + 1]}{n - m}$

or $\phi_A = \dfrac{180°[2q + 1]}{3}$ and $q = 0, 1, \ldots, n - m - 1,$

where $n - m - 1 = 4 - 1 - 1 = 2$

$\phi_A = 60°, \quad 180°, \quad 300°$

The pole at the origin approaches zero at $s = -3$, the pole at $s = -10$ goes to $-\infty$ on the real axis, and the complex poles go to zeroes along asymptotes making an angle of $60°$ and $300°$ with the real axis as k goes from 0 to ∞. Figure 7.4 is a sketch of the root locus plot.

7.3.1 Addition of Poles and Zeroes

The root locus method gives a graphic picture of the movement of the poles of the closed-loop system with the variation of one of the system parameters that needs to be selected by the designer. Later in this chapter we discuss how the relative

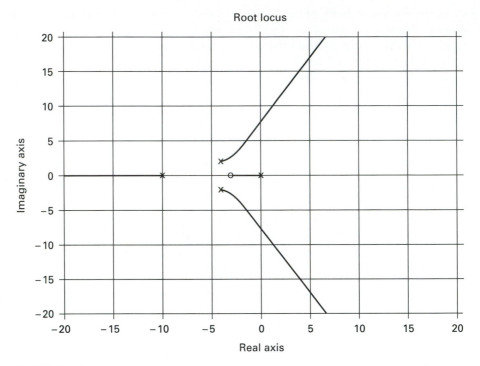

FIGURE 7.4
Root locus plot for Example Problem 7.3.

stability of the system and its performance can be obtained from the root locus diagram.

In many cases it is not possible to satisfy all the performance specifications using a single parameter such as the system gain. This requires the designer to add some form of compensation to the basic control system. The compensators may be electrical circuits, mechanical devices, or electromechanical devices that are added to the system to improve its performance. The compensators may be added to either the forward or feedback path. The compensator has a transfer function composed of poles and zeroes. Before discussing various methods of providing compensation to a control system it would be useful to examine the influence of the addition of poles and zeroes to the loop transfer function $G(s)H(s)$. We will do this by way of a simple example.

EXAMPLE PROBLEM 7.4. Construct a root locus plot from the transfer function $G(s)H(s)$ given by

$$G(s)H(s) = \frac{k}{s(s + p_1)}$$

then examine how the locus is affected by the addition of one of the following to the original transfer function.

i. simple pole   ii. multiple pole   iii. simple zero.

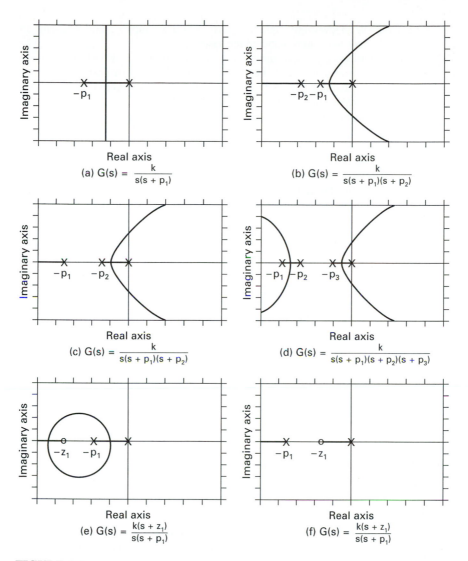

FIGURE 7.5
Sketch of root locus plot for Example Problem 7.4.

Solution. The root locus plot can be easily constructed by the rules outlined in this chapter. A sketch of the root locus is shown in Figure 7.5. For this particular transfer function the system is stable for $0 < k < \infty$. Now if we add a simple pole, $s + p_2$, to $G(s)H(s)$ the root locus will bend into the right half plane, which limits the range of k for which the system is stable. Notice that the plots for $p_1 > p_2$ or $p_2 > p_1$ have the same shape (see Figure 7.5(b) and (c)). The addition of yet another pole adds another branch of the locus that goes to zero at infinity, and the system can still become unstable if the system gain exceeds a certain value as shown in Figure 7.5(d). From this simple analysis we can conclude that the addition of a pole to a given transfer function causes the root locus plot to bend toward the right half portion of the complex plane. Thus, the additon of a simple pole tends to destabilize the system.

The addition of a simple zero, $s + z_1$, to the original transfer function, $G(s)H(s)$, will cause the root locus plot to bend further into the left half portion of the complex plane as illustrated in Figure 7.5(e) and (f). By adding a zero to $G(s)H(s)$, the system will be more stable than the original system.

The importance of this example is to show that the root locus plot of a control system can be altered by the addition of poles or zeroes. In practice a designer can use this idea to reshape the root locus contour so that the desired performance can be achieved. The compensator basically is a device that provides a transfer function consisting of poles or zeroes or both that can be chosen to move the root locus contour of the compensated system to the desired closed-loop pole configuration. Note that the addition of a compensator in general increases the order of the system.

7.4
FREQUENCY DOMAIN TECHNIQUES

The frequency response of a dynamic system was discussed in Chapter 6. The same techniques can be applied to the design of feedback control systems. The transfer function for a closed-loop feedback system can be written as

$$M(s) = \frac{C(s)}{R(s)} = \frac{G(s)}{1 + G(s)H(s)} \tag{7.16}$$

If we excite the system with a sinusoidal input such as

$$r(t) = A_I \sin(\omega t) \tag{7.17}$$

the steady-state output of the system will have the form

$$c(t) = A_O \sin(\omega t + \phi) \tag{7.18}$$

The magnitude and phase relationship between the input and output signals is called the frequency response of the system. The ratio of output to input for a sinusoidal steady state can be obtained by replacing the Laplace transform variable s with $i\omega$:

$$M(i\omega) = \frac{G(i\omega)}{1 + G(i\omega)H(i\omega)} \tag{7.19}$$

Expressing the previous equation in terms of its magnitude and phase angle yields

$$M(i\omega) = M(\omega)\underline{/\phi(\omega)} \tag{7.20}$$

where

$$M(\omega) = \left| \frac{G(i\omega)}{1 + G(i\omega)H(i\omega)} \right| \tag{7.21}$$

and

$$\phi(\omega) = \underline{/G(i\omega)} - \underline{/[1 + G(i\omega)H(i\omega)]} \tag{7.22}$$

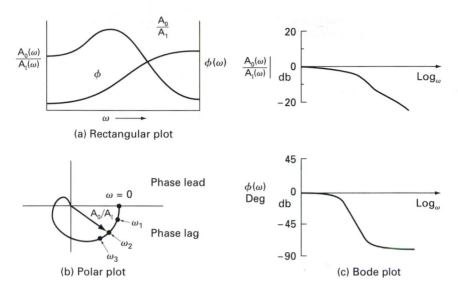

FIGURE 7.6
Various graphical ways of presenting frequency response data.

The frequency response information can be plotted in rectangular, polar, or logarithmic (Bode) plots. Figure 7.6 is a sketch of the various ways of presenting the frequency response data. The relationship between the frequency- and time-domain performance of a control system is discussed in the next section.

7.5
TIME-DOMAIN AND FREQUENCY-DOMAIN SPECIFICATIONS

The first step in the design of a feedback control system is to determine a set of specifications for the desired system performance. In the following section we shall present both time- and frequency-domain specifications and their relationship to one another for a second-order system. The transfer function of a second-order system can be expressed as

$$\frac{C(s)}{R(s)} = \frac{\omega_n^2}{s^2 + 2\zeta\omega_n s + \omega_n^2} \tag{7.23}$$

where ζ is the damping ratio and ω_n is the undamped natural frequency of the system. Figure 7.7 shows the response to a step input of an underdamped second-order system. The performance of the second-order system is characterized by the overshoot, delay time, rise time, and settling time of the transient response to a unit step. The time response of a second-order system to a step input for an

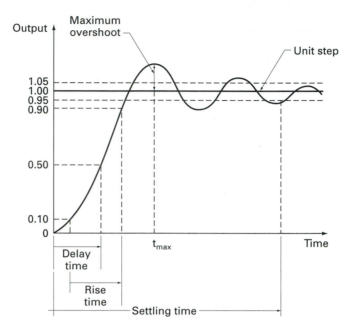

FIGURE 7.7
Time response of a second-order system.

underdamped system; that is, $\zeta < 1$, is given by Equations (7.24) and (7.25):

$$c(t) = 1 + \frac{e^{-\zeta\omega_n t}}{\sqrt{1 - \zeta^2}} \sin(\omega_n \sqrt{1 - \zeta^2}\, t - \phi) \tag{7.24}$$

$$\phi = \tan^{-1}\left(\frac{\sqrt{1 - \zeta^2}}{-\zeta}\right) \tag{7.25}$$

The delay and rise time give a measure of how fast the system responds to a step input. Delay time t_d is the time it takes for the response to reach for the first time 50 percent of the final value of the response. The rise time t_r is the time required for the response to rise from 10 to 90 percent of the final value. The other two parameters of interest are the settling time and peak overshoot. Settling time t_s is the time it takes for the response to stay within a specified tolerance band of 5 percent of the final value. The peak overshoot is a measure of the oscillations about the final output. From the standpoint of control system design, we would like to have a system that responds rapidly with minimum overshoot. Equations (7.24) and (7.25) can be used to determine the relationships between the time-domain specifications t_d, t_r, and the like and the damping ratio ζ and undamped natural frequency ω_n. Table 7.3 is a summary of these relationships.

Figure 7.8 is a sketch of the typical magnitude and phase characteristics of a feedback control system. As in the time-domain analysis it is desirable to have a set of specifications to describe the control system performance in the frequency

TABLE 7.3
Time domain specifications

Delay time t_d	Rise time, t_r
$$t_d \approx \frac{1 + 0.6\zeta + 0.15\zeta^2}{\omega_n}$$	$$t_r \approx \frac{1 + 1.1\zeta + 1.4\zeta^2}{\omega_n}$$
Time to peak amplitude, t_p	**Settling time, t_s**
$$t_p = \frac{\pi}{\omega_n\sqrt{1-\zeta^2}}$$	$$t_s = \frac{3.0}{\omega_n \zeta}$$

Peak overshoot, M_p

$$M_p = \frac{c(t_p) - c(\infty)}{c(\infty)} \times 100\%$$

For a unit step

$$\text{Percent maximum overshoot} = 100 \exp(-\pi\zeta/\sqrt{1-\zeta^2})$$

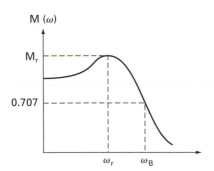

M (ω)

M_r

0.707

ω_r ω_B

FIGURE 7.8
Frequency response of a closed-loop control system.

domain. In the frequency domain the design specifications are given in terms of the response peak M_r, the resonant frequency ω_r, the system bandwidth ω_B, and the gain and phase margins. The maximum value of $M(\omega)$, called the resonance peak, is an indication of the relative stability of the control system. If M_r is large the system will have a large peak overshoot to a step input. The resonant frequency, ω_r, is the frequency at which the resonance peak occurs. It is related to the frequency of the oscillations and speed of the transient response. The bandwidth ω_B is the band of frequencies from 0 to the frequency at which the magnitude $M(\omega)$ drops to 70 percent of the zero-frequency magnitude. The bandwidth gives an indication of the transient response of the system. If the bandwidth is large, the system will respond rapidly, whereas a small bandwidth will result in a sluggish control system.

The gain and phase margins are measures of the relative stability of the system and are related to the closeness of the poles of the closed-loop system to the $i\omega$ axis.

For a second-order system the frequency domain characteristics M_r, ω_r, and ω_B can be related to the system damping ratio and the undamped natural frequency ω_n.

The relationships will be presented here without proof:

$$M_r = \frac{1}{2\zeta\sqrt{1 - \zeta^2}} \tag{7.26}$$

$$\omega_r = \omega_n\sqrt{1 - 2\zeta^2} \tag{7.27}$$

$$\omega_B = \omega_n\left[(1 - 2\zeta^2) + \sqrt{4\zeta^4 - 4\zeta^2 + 2}\right]^{1/2} \tag{7.28}$$

The peak response and the peak overshoot of the transient response in the time domain is given by the following approximation:

$$c(t)_{max} \leq 1.17M_r \tag{7.29}$$

The phase margin of a second-order system can be related to the system damping ratio as follows:

$$\phi = \tan^{-1}\left[2\zeta\left(\frac{1}{(4\zeta^4 + 1)^{1/2} - 2\zeta^2}\right)^{1/2}\right] \tag{7.30}$$

This very formidable equation can be approximated by the simple relationship

$$\zeta \approx 0.01\phi \qquad \text{for} \qquad \zeta \leq 0.7 \tag{7.31}$$

The phase margin ϕ is in degrees.

From the preceding relationships developed for the second-order system the following observations can be made:

1. The maximum overshoot for a unit step in the time domain is a function of only ζ.
2. The resonance peak of the closed-loop system is a function of only ζ.
3. The maximum peak overshoot and resonance peak are related through the damping ratio.
4. The rise time increases while the bandwidth decreases for increases in system damping for a fixed ω_n. The bandwidth and rise time are inversely proportional to one another.
5. The bandwidth is directly proportional to ω_n.
6. The higher the bandwidth, the larger is the resonance peak.

7.5.1. Gain and Phase Margin from Root Locus

The gain and phase margin used to determine the relative stability of a control system using frequency response techniques also can be determined from the root locus plot. The gain margin can be estimated by taking the ratio of the gain when the locus crosses the imaginary axis to the gain selected for the system:

Gain margin

$$= \frac{\text{Value of system gain } k \text{ when locus crosses the imaginary axis}}{\text{Selected value of system gain } k} \tag{7.32}$$

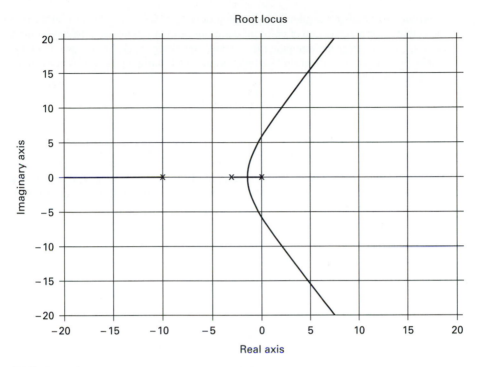

Root locus

FIGURE 7.9

Root locus plot for the transfer function $G(s)H(s) = \dfrac{k}{s(s + 3)(s + 10)}$.

The value of ω at the intersection on the root locus is the phase crossover frequency. If the root locus plot has no branches that cross over the imaginary axis the gain margin is infinite.

The phase margin can be determined for the selected gain by estimating the frequency on the imaginary axis that satisfies the relationship

$$|G(i\omega_g)H(i\omega_g)| = 1 \tag{7.33}$$

The frequency can be determined by trial and error. The frequency that satisfies this relationship is called the gain crossover frequency. The phase margin can be calculated from the equation

$$\phi_{PM} = 180° + \arg G(i\omega_g)H(i\omega_g). \tag{7.34}$$

EXAMPLE PROBLEM 7.5. The root locus plot for a system having the following transfer function is given in Figure 7.9:

$$G(s)H(s) = \frac{k}{s(s + 3)(s + 10)}$$

Determine the following information:

(a) Select the system gain so that the dominant roots have a damping ratio, $\zeta = 0.6$.
(b) Estimate the settling time.
(c) Find the gain and phase margin for the gain selected in part (a).

Solution. To estimate the gain for a damping ratio, $\zeta = 0.6$, the value of s on the root locus that intersects the line of constant damping ratio of 0.6 needs to be determined. As was shown earlier the damping ratio is constant along radial lines drawn from the origin of the root locus diagram. The magnitude of the damping ratio is related to the angle θ as follows:

$$\zeta = \cos \theta$$

Solving for theta yields

$$\theta = \cos^{-1}[\zeta] = \cos^{-1}[0.6] = 53°$$

The intersection of the line of constant damping ratio ($\theta = 53° \Rightarrow \zeta = 0.6$) with the root locus occurs at $s = -1.2 + 1.65i$. The magnitude of the system gain at this point can be determined using the magnitude criteria:

$$|G(s)H(s)| = 1$$

or

$$\frac{|k|}{|s||s + 3||s + 10|} = 1$$

Substituting in the value of $s = -1.2 + 1.65i$ yields

$$\frac{|k|}{\left(\sqrt{(1.2)^2 + (1.65)^2}\right)\left(\sqrt{(1.8)^2 + (1.65)^2}\right)\left(\sqrt{(8.8)^2 + (1.65)^2}\right)} = 1$$

or

$$|k| = (2.04)(2.44)(8.95) = 44.55$$

The settling time t_s can be estimated from the approximate formula given in Table 7.3:

$$t_s = \frac{3.0}{\zeta\omega_n}$$

where $\zeta\omega_n$ is the magnitude of the real part of the complex root,

$$\zeta\omega_n = 1.2$$

Therefore

$$t_s = \frac{3.0}{\zeta\omega_n} = \frac{3.0}{1.2} = 2.5 \text{ s}$$

To determine the gain margin from the root locus plot we can use Equation (7.33). We need to determine the gain for the system when the root locus crosses the imaginary axis. From the root locus plot we can determine that $s = +5.5i$ at the crossover point. The gain is determined from the magnitude criteria

$$\frac{|k|}{|s||s + 3||s + 10|} = 1$$

where $s = +5.5i$ and

$$\frac{k}{(5.5)(6.26)(11.41)} = 1$$

or $k = 393$.

The gain margin can be calculated from Equation (7.33):

$$\text{Gain margin} = \frac{\text{Value of system gain } k \text{ when locus crosses imaginary axis}}{\text{Selected value of system gain } k}$$

$$= \frac{393}{44.55} = 8.82$$

The phase margin can be determined by finding the frequency ω_g, the gain crossover frequency, so that $|G(i\omega_g)H(i\omega_g)| = 1.0$.

$$\frac{44.55}{\omega_g \sqrt{\omega_g^2 + 3^2} \sqrt{\omega_g^2 + 10^2}} = 1$$

Solving this equation by trial and error yields $\omega_g = 1.3$.

The phase margin now can be estimated from Equation (7.34) where the arg $G(i\omega_g) H(i\omega_g)$ is found in the following way:

$$\arg G(i\omega_g)H(i\omega_g) = -\angle i\omega_g - \angle(i\omega_g + 3) - \angle(i\omega_g + 10)$$

$$= -90° - 23.4 - 7.4° = 120.8$$

$$\phi_{PM} = 180° - \arg G(i\omega_g)H(i\omega_g)$$

$$= 180° - 120.8° = 59.2°$$

7.5.2 Higher-Order Systems

Most feedback control systems are usually of a higher order than the second-order system discussed in the previous sections. However, many higher-order control systems can be analyzed by approximating the system by a second-order system. Obviously, when this can be accomplished, the design and analysis of the equivalent system is greatly simplified.

For a higher-order system to be replaced by an equivalent second-order system, the transient response of the higher-order system must be dominated by a pair of complex conjugate poles. These poles, called the dominant poles or roots, are located closest to the origin in a pole-zero plot. The other poles must be located far to the left of the dominant poles or near a zero of the system. The transient response caused by the poles located to the far left of the dominant poles will diminish rapidly in comparison with the dominant root response. On the other hand, if the pole is not located to the far left of the dominant poles, then the poles must be near a zero of the system transfer function. The transient response of a pole located near a zero is characterized by a very small amplitude motion, which can readily be neglected.

The transfer function of a second-order system can be expressed in terms of the system damping ratio, ζ, and the undamped natural frequency, ω_n, as follows:

$$\frac{C(s)}{R(s)} = \frac{\omega_n^2}{s^2 + 2\zeta\omega_n s + \omega_n^2} \tag{7.35}$$

Consider the case where the system is underdamped; that is, $0 < \zeta < 1$. This implies that the second-order roots are complex. If the input is a unit step, that is, $R(s) = 1/s$, then the output is

$$\frac{\omega_n^2}{s(s^2 + 2\zeta\omega_n s + \omega_n^2)} \tag{7.36}$$

which can be inverted to the time domain as

$$C(t) = 1 + \frac{1}{\sqrt{1 - \zeta^2}} e^{-\zeta\omega_n t} \sin(\omega_n\sqrt{1 - \zeta^2}\, t - \phi) \tag{7.37}$$

where

$$\phi = \tan^{-1}(\sqrt{1 - \zeta^2}/-\zeta). \tag{7.38}$$

The response is a damped sinusoidal motion.

Now, if we add a simple pole in the form $1/(1 + Ts)$ to Equation (7.35), the response to a step input would be given by

$$C(t) = 1 - \frac{T^2\omega_n^2}{1 - 2T\zeta\omega_n + T^2\omega_n^2} e^{-t/T} + \frac{e^{-\zeta\omega_n t}\sin(\omega_n\sqrt{1 - \zeta^2}\, t - \phi)}{\sqrt{1 - \zeta^2}(1 - 2\zeta T\omega_n + T^2\omega_n^2)} \tag{7.39}$$

and

$$\phi = \tan^{-1}\frac{\sqrt{1 - \zeta^2}}{-\zeta} + \tan^{-1}\frac{T\omega_n\sqrt{1 - \zeta^2}}{1 - T\zeta\omega_n} \tag{7.40}$$

The pole is located at $s = -1/T$ and the smaller T is the farther the pole is from the imaginary axis. As the simple pole is moved farther to the left of the complex root the response of Equation (7.39) will approach that of Equation (7.37). This would occur when T is small and $1/T \gg \zeta\omega_n$. If we examine Equation (7.39) the second term vanishes much more quickly than the third term. The mathematical expression defining the third term approaches that of the second-order expression when T is small. A similar argument can be made for higher-order systems.

7.6
STEADY-STATE ERROR

The accuracy of a control system is measured by how well it tracks a given command input. Even if a system has good overall transient response it also must have good steady-state behavior. The accuracy of the control system is expressed in terms of the steady-state error to a given commanded input. The usual input signals used to evaluate the steady-state error are step, ramp, and parabolic input. Figure 7.10 shows a typical step, ramp, and parabolic input signal.

If we examine Figure 7.2 at the beginning of this chapter, an expression for the error signal can be developed. The error signal $E(s)$ can be shown to be

$$E(s) = \frac{R(s)}{1 + G(s)H(s)} \tag{7.41}$$

where $R(s)$ is the input signal and $G(s)H(s)$ is the loop transfer function. The steady-state error e_{ss} is the tracking error as time approaches a large value for a

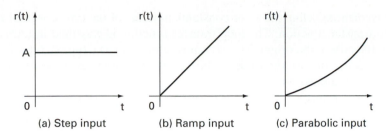

(a) Step input   (b) Ramp input   (c) Parabolic input

FIGURE 7.10
Typical input signals.

particular input command. Rather than inverting $E(s)$ back into the time domain and evaluating $e(t)$ as t goes to infinity we can use the final value theorem. This theorem states that if the Laplace transform of a function $f(t)$ is $F(s)$ and if the function $s\,F(s)$ is analytic on the imaginary axis and right half plane then

$$\text{Limit}_{t\to 0} f(t) = \text{Limit}_{s\to 0} sF(s) \tag{7.42}$$

The steady-state error can be found by applying the final value theorem:

$$e_{ss} = \text{Limit}_{t\to\infty} e(t) = \text{Limit}_{s\to 0} sE(s) \tag{7.43}$$

The steady-state error will depend on the input command $R(s)$ and the loop transfer function $G(s)H(s)$. The steady-state error for the three stipulated input signals is expressed in terms of error coefficients, which will be defined shortly. First we need to classify the open-loop transfer function. This is done by determining the order of the pole in $G(s)H(s)$ at the origin; that is $s = 0$. The loop transfer function $G(s)H(s)$ can be written in the pole-zero form as

$$G(s)H(s) = \frac{k}{s^l} \frac{(s + z_1)(s + z_2) \cdots (s + z_m)}{(s + p_1)(s + p_2) \cdots (s + p_n)} \tag{7.44}$$

An alternate form of this expression is

$$G(s)H(s) = \frac{K(1 + T_{z_1}s)(1 + T_{z_2}s) \cdots (1 + T_{z_m}s)}{s^l(1 + T_{p_1}s)(1 + T_{p_2}s) \cdots (1 + T_{p_n}s)} \tag{7.45}$$

which is referred to as the time-constant form of the transfer function. The time constants are simply

$$T_{z_i} = \frac{1}{z_i} \qquad i = 1 \text{ to } m \tag{7.46}$$

$$T_{p_j} = \frac{1}{p_j} \qquad j = 1 \text{ to } n \tag{7.47}$$

and

$$K = k \frac{\prod\limits_{i=1}^{m} z_i}{\prod\limits_{j=1}^{n} p_j} \tag{7.48}$$

It is convenient to define the error constants in terms of the time constant form of the loop transfer function. The loop transfer function is classified in terms of the order of the pole at the origin. The system is referred to as a type 0, type 1, type 2, and so on depending on the value of the exponent of the pole at the origin, l; that is, $l = 0, 1, 2$, and so on.

Now let us return to defining the error constants. We first examine the tracking error to a step input. The step input can be expressed as

$$r = Au(t)$$

where A is the amplitude of the step and $u(t)$ is a unit step. The Laplace transform of the step input is given by $R(s) = A/s$. The steady-state error can be found using Equations (7.41) and (7.45) and the final value theorem:

$$e_{ss} = \underset{t \to \infty}{\text{Limit}}\ e(t) = \underset{s \to 0}{\text{Limit}}\ sE(s)$$

$$e_{ss} = \underset{s \to 0}{\text{Limit}}\ \frac{s(A/s)}{1 + G(s)H(s)}$$

$$e_{ss} = \underset{s \to 0}{\text{Limit}}\ \frac{A}{1 + G(s)H(s)} = \frac{A}{1 + \underset{s \to 0}{\text{Limit}}\ G(s)H(s)}$$

or finally

$$e_{ss} = \frac{A}{1 + K_p}$$

where K_p, called the positional error constant, is defined as

$$K_p = \underset{s \to 0}{\text{Limit}}\ G(s)H(s)$$

When the input signal is a ramp $r(t) = At$. The Laplace transform of a ramp input is $R(s) = A/s^2$. The steady-state error can be found as previously:

$$e_{ss} = \underset{s \to 0}{\text{Limit}}\ sE(s) = \underset{s \to 0}{\text{Limit}}\ \frac{s(A/s^2)}{1 + G(s)H(s)}$$

$$e_{ss} = \underset{s \to 0}{\text{Limit}}\ \frac{A}{s + sG(s)H(s)}$$

or

$$e_{ss} = \frac{A}{K_v}$$

where K_v is called the velocity error constant, is defined as

$$K_v = \underset{s \to 0}{\text{Limit}}\ sG(s)H(s)$$

The final input signal is that of a parabolic input or acceleration. The input signal is given as

$$r(t) = At^2/2$$

or in the Laplace domain

$$R(s) = A/s^3$$

where A is acceleration amplitude. The steady-state error for an acceleration input

TABLE 7.4
Steady-state errors

System type	Step input $r(t) = Au(t)$	Ramp input $r(t) = At$	Parabolic input $r(t) = At^2/2$
0	$\dfrac{A}{1 + K_p}$	∞	∞
1	0	$\dfrac{A}{K_v}$	∞
2	0	0	$\dfrac{A}{K_a}$

is as follows:

$$e_{ss} = \underset{s \to 0}{\text{Limit }} sE(s) = \underset{s \to 0}{\text{Limit }} \frac{sA/s^3}{1 + G(s)H(s)}$$

$$e_{ss} = \underset{s \to 0}{\text{Limit }} \frac{A}{s^2 + s^2 G(s)H(s)} = \frac{A}{K_a}$$

where K_a is the acceleration error constant, defined as

$$K_a = \underset{s \to 0}{\text{Limit }} s^2 G(s)H(s)$$

The steady-state error depends on the system type and input function. A summary of the steady-state error is given in Table 7.4.

EXAMPLE PROBLEM 7.6. Given the following transfer function, determine the steady-state error of the system to unit step, ramp, and parabolic inputs:

$$G(s)H(s) = \frac{k(s + 2)}{s(s + 1)(s + 4)(s + 5)}$$

Solution. The transfer function $G(s)H(s)$ is in the pole-zero form. Rewriting the transfer function in the time constant from yields

$$G(s)H(s) = \frac{2k(1 + 0.5s)}{20s(1 + s)(1 + 0.25s)(1 + 0.2s)}$$

$$= \frac{k}{10} \frac{(1 + 0.5s)}{s(1 + s)(1 + 0.25s)(1 + 0.2s)}$$

$$= \frac{K(1 + 0.5s)}{s(1 + s)(1 + 0.25s)(1 + 0.2s)}$$

where $K = k/10$.

This transfer function is a type 1 system because of the first-order pole at the origin. From Table 7.4 we see that the steady error is 0 for a step input, $1/K_v$ for the ramp input, and ∞ for the parabolic input. The velocity error constant K_v can be found as follows:

$$K_v = \underset{s \to 0}{\text{Limit }} sG(s)H(s)$$

$$K_v = \underset{s \to 0}{\text{Limit }} \frac{K(1 - 0.5s)}{(1 + s)(1 + 0.25s)(1 + 0.2s)}$$

$$K_v = K = \frac{k}{10}$$

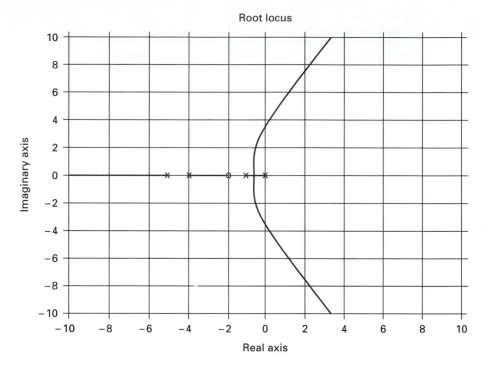

FIGURE 7.11

Root locus plot of $G(s) H(s) = \dfrac{k(s + 2)}{s(s + 1)(s + 4)(s + 5)}$.

The steady-state error for the ramp input is

$$e_{ss} = 10/k$$

As the system gain is increased, the steady-state error will decrease. However, for this particular example, the system gain is limited because too large a gain will cause the system to be unstable. Figure 7.11 shows the root locus plot for this system.

7.7
CONTROL SYSTEM DESIGN

In this section we will try to provide a simple overview of the design process in developing a new control system. Figure 7.12 is a simple flow chart indicating the basic elements in the design of a new product. Design often is divided into three phases: conceptual design, preliminary design, and detailed design. In conceptual design, the designer attempts to develop one or more concepts that can provide the overall system performance required by the customer. In the next phase, the preliminary design phase, additional analysis is performed to optimize the system. In

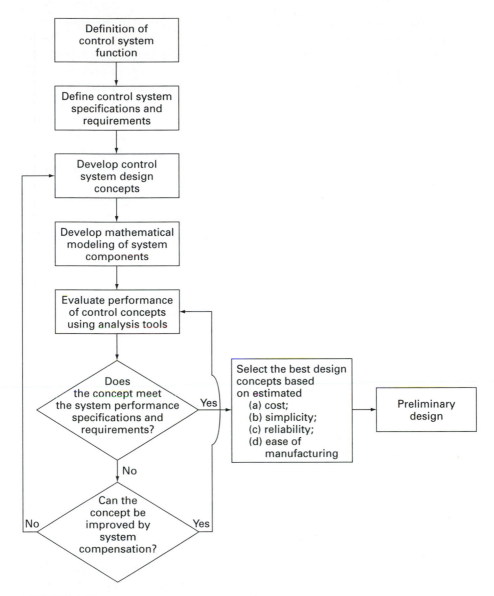

FIGURE 7.12
Flowchart of conceptual design process.

the final design phase the engineering team develops the detailed engineering drawings and stipulates the manufacturing details.

The design process begins with the recognition of a need for a new control system. This need may originate within the engineering department but is just as likely to come from the marketing or sales department through feedback from the company's customers. Regardless of how or where the idea originates, the recognition of the need for a new control system starts the engineering design process.

Once a product need is established this provides a definition of the purpose or function of the control system.

Having defined the purpose of the control system, the designer needs to identify its requirements and specifications. These consist of items such as control system performance, cost, reliability, maintainability, and other constraints. The performance of the system usually is given in terms of time or frequency domain characteristics or a combination of both. Time domain performance specifications include rise time, setting time, peak overshoot, steady-state error, and the like. On the other hand, the frequency domain specifications are given in terms of phase margin, gain margin, and so forth. Additional constraints may be weight and volume requirements, which might be critical in an aerospace application.

With the purpose and specifications defined the designer must develop one or more concepts to achieve the desired control function. The control system concepts in large part are based on the designer's creativity and experience. The concepts are simply ideas of how to implement the desired control function, which can be presented in the form of a simple block diagram. For example, if one were interested in designing a simple autopilot to maintain a wing's level attitude the control concept could be presented as shown in Figure 7.13.

The next phase of the design process is to evaluate the performance of each concept against the specifications. This requires the designer to develop the appropriate mathematical models for each of the design components, such as controller, actuators, plant, and sensor. The challenge at this point is to keep the mathematical model as simple as possible but accurate enough to retain the essential dynamic characteristics of each component.

Once the mathematical formulation is completed the control system can be analyzed using the techniques presented in this chapter or the state-space design methods presented in Chapter 9. These analysis methods allow the designer to evaluate the control system performance as a function of various control system design parameters. The performance of the control system concepts now can be compared with the desired performance. In practice, the designer often is faced with the problem that the concept does not meet all of the performance specifications. The designer basically has three options: One is to try to convince the potential customer that a particular performance specification is unrelated and not essential for the overall performance of the system if this indeed is the case. The second option is to select another control concept that can satisfy the specification. The third is to add some form of compensation to the concept to improve the system performance so that the specifications are satisfied.

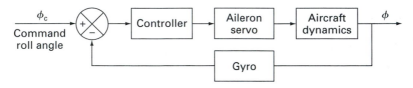

FIGURE 7.13
Wing-leveling autopilot.

7.7.1 Compensation

As stated in the previous section the ultimate test of a design concept is whether it meets the desired performance specifications. The control system performance is specified in terms of the transient behavior and the steady-state error. The transient performance in the time domain can be described in terms of the damping ratio, ζ, the peak overshoot, and the speed of the response as measured by the rise and settling time. The relative stability also can be specified in terms of frequency-domain performance indices such as the resonant peak, M_r, and gain and phase margins. The speed of response is measured by the resonant frequency, ω_r, and the system bandwidth, ω_B.

In general the designer on analyzing a control system concept finds that some but not all of the performance specifications are met by a particular control concept. Using the root locus analysis technique discussed earlier the designer can adjust the system gain to vary the control system performance; however, in most cases the designer cannot meet all the design performance objectives by gain adjustment alone. When the performance cannot be satisfied the designer can add an additional component to the control system, called a compensator. The purpose of the compensator is to improve the overall performance of the control system concept. Recall that when discussing the root locus techniques we examined the influence of the addition of either a simple pole, zero, or combination pole and zero to the root locus plot. We found that the addition of poles and zeroes allowed us to contour or change the shape of the root locus plot. The addition of some combination of poles and zeroes to a given control system transfer function represents a compensator. By selecting the parameter in the compensator the designer can change the shape of the root locus plot so that the overall performance specification can be met.

The compensators can be thought of as an additional transfer function $G_c(s)$ that can be added to either the forward or feedback path of the control system. As illustrated in Figure 7.14, when the compensator is added to the forward path it is called a cascade or series compensator and when it is placed in the feedback path it is called feedback or parallel compensator. In general, the compensators are electrical circuits or mechanical subsystems that provide the designer parameters that can be adjusted to improve the overall system performance.

7.7.2 Forward-Path Compensation

To examine how a compensator can be used to improve the performance of a control system we consider the simple control system shown in Figure 7.15. Suppose that the performance requirements are given in terms of the damping ratio and settling time as follows:

$$\zeta = 0.707$$

$$t_s < 3 \text{ s.}$$

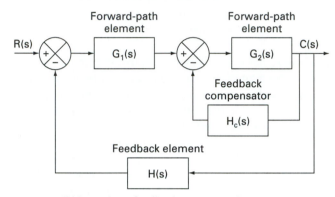

FIGURE 7.14
Series and parallel compensation.

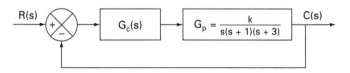

FIGURE 7.15
Control system with a forward-path compensator.

From the root locus plot shown in Figure 7.16 we can achieve the desired damping ratio by finding the gain for the point on the locus that interesects the radial line from the origin that makes an angle of 45° with respect to the negative real axis. The undamped natural frequency ω_n is the distance along the radial line of constant ζ from the origin to the root locus. For this case $\omega_n = 0.5$ rad/s.

The settling time which can be estimated by

$$t_s = \frac{3.0}{\zeta\omega_n} \tag{7.49}$$

for an $\omega_n = 0.5$ rad/s—the settling time is not less than 3 s. If the root locus plot could be made to intersect the $\zeta = 0.707$ line at a larger value of ω_n the settling time constraint could be met. As we noted earlier in this chapter a simple zero

Root locus

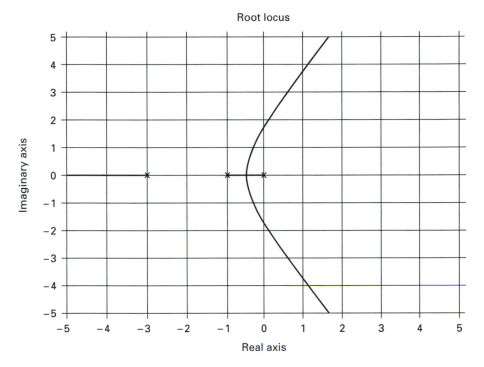

FIGURE 7.16

Root locus plot of $G(s)H(s) = \dfrac{k}{s(s+1)(s+3)}$.

added to an open-loop transfer function $G(s)H(s)$ causes the locus to bend more toward the left in the complex plane. Figure 7.17 is a root locus plot with the addition of a zero as $s = -1.1$. With the addition of the zero, the root locus plot bends toward the left. The value of ω_n for the damping ratio of 0.707 is now 1.98 rad/s, which yields a settling time less than 3 s.

Unfortunately a simple zero is not very practical. In practice we add a transfer function of the form

$$G_c(s) = \frac{s + z_c}{s + p_c} \tag{7.50}$$

where $z_c/p_c < 1$, or the compensator poles is located to the left of the compensator zero. Such a compensator is called a lead compensator. The designer can adjust the pole and zero location of the compensator to shape the root locus so that both the damping ratio and settling time specifications can be met. The movement of the compensator pole and zero is achieved by proper selection of the components in the electrical circuit. In summary the lead compensator can be used to improve the transient response characteristics of the control system.

It is possible to have a control system design with good transient characteristics but a large steady-state error. When the steady-state error is large a lag

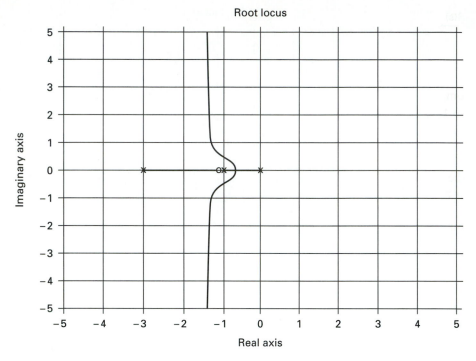

FIGURE 7.17

Root locus plot of $G(s)H(s) = \dfrac{k(s + 1.1)}{s(s + 1)(s + 3)}$.

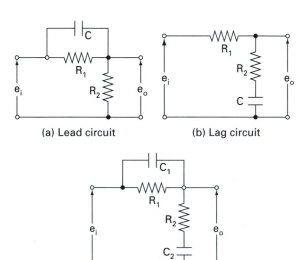

(a) Lead circuit

(b) Lag circuit

(c) Lag-lead circuit

FIGURE 7.18
Electrical circuits used as a compensator.

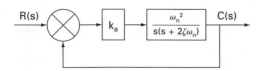

FIGURE 7.19
A second-order control system.

compensator can be used to improve the steady-state error. The lag compensator has the following form:

$$G_c(s) = \frac{(s + z_c)}{(s + p_c)} \qquad (7.51)$$

where the compensator pole near the origin is located to the right of the compensator zero ($z_c/p_c > 1$).

For the case where both the transient and steady response are unsatisfactory a combination of a lag and lead compensator can be used. An example of a lag-lead compensator follows:

$$G_c(s) = \frac{(s + z_1)\ (s + z_2)}{(s + p_1)\ (s + p_2)} \qquad (7.52)$$

Figure 7.18 shows electrical circuits that could be used to create a lead, lag, or lag-lead compensator.

7.7.3 Feedback-Path Compensation

Feedback compensation can be used to improve the damping of the system by incorporating an inner rate feedback loop. The stabilizing effect of the inner loop rate feedback can be demonstrated by a simple example. Suppose we have the second-order system shown in Figure 7.19. The amplifier gain can be adjusted to vary the system response as shown in the accompanying root locus plot presented in Figure 7.20. The closed-loop transfer function for this system is given by

$$M(s) = \frac{k_a \omega_n}{s^2 + 2\zeta\omega_n s + k_a \omega_n^2}$$

Now if we add an inner rate feedback loop as shown in Figure 7.21, the closed-loop transfer function can be obtained as follows. The inner loop transfer functions are

$$G_1(s) = \frac{\omega_n^2}{s(s + 2\zeta\omega_n)}$$

$$H_1(s) = k_r s$$

which can be combined as

$$M(s)_{\text{I.L.}} = \frac{G_1(s)}{1 + G_1(s)H_1(s)}$$

$$= \frac{\omega_n^2}{s^2 + (2\zeta\omega_n + k_r\omega_n^2)s}$$

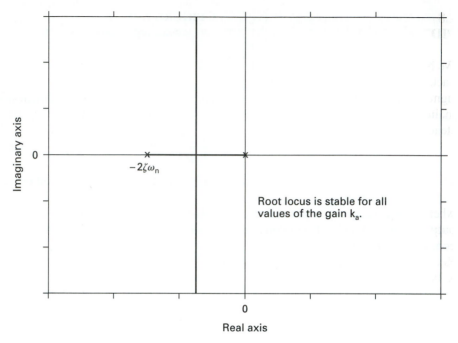

FIGURE 7.20
Root locus for second order system.

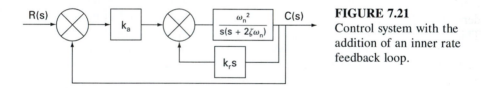

FIGURE 7.21
Control system with the addition of an inner rate feedback loop.

The closed-loop transfer function can be obtained by letting

$$G(s)_2 = \frac{k_a \omega_n^2}{s^2 + (2\zeta\omega_n + k_r\omega_n^2)s}$$

$$H_2(s) = 1$$

which can be combined as

$$M(s)_{\text{O.L.}} = \frac{G_2(s)}{1 + G_2(s)H_2(s)}$$

$$= \frac{k_a \omega_n^2}{s^2 + (2\zeta\omega_n + k_r\omega_n^2)s + k_a\omega_n^2}$$

If we compare the closed-loop transfer function for the cases with and without rate feedback we observe that in the closed-loop characteristic equation the damping term has been increased by $k_r\omega_n^2$. The gain k_r can be used to increase the system damping.

7.8
PID CONTROLLER

We have shown examples of various kinds of control concepts. The simplest feedback controller is one for which the controller output is proportional to the error signal. Such a controller is called a proportional control. Obviously the controller's main advantage is its simplicity. It has the disadvantage that there may be a steady-state error.

The steady-state error can be eliminated by using an integral controller

$$\eta(t) = k_i \int_0^t e(t) \, dt \qquad \text{or} \qquad \eta(s) = \frac{k_i}{s} e(s) \tag{7.53}$$

where k_i is the integral gain. The advantage of the integral controller is that the output is proportional to the accumulated error. The disadvantage of the integral controller is that we make the system less stable by adding the pole at the origin. Recall that the addition of a pole to the forward-path transfer function was shown to bend the root locus toward the right half plane.

It is also possible to use a derivative controller defined as follows:

$$\eta(t) = k_d \frac{de}{dt} \qquad \text{or} \qquad \eta(s) = k_d s e(s) \tag{7.54}$$

The advantage of the derivative controller is that the controller will provide large corrections before the error becomes large. The major disadvantage of the derivative controller is that it will not produce a control output if the error is constant. Another difficulty of the derivative controller is its susceptibility to noise. The derivative controller in its present form would have difficulty with noise problems. This can be avoided by using a derivative controller of the form

$$\eta(s) = k_d \frac{s}{\tau s + 1} e(s) \tag{7.55}$$

The term $1/(\tau s + 1)$ attentuates the high-frequency components in the error signal, that is, noise, thus avoiding the noise problems.

Each of the controllers—providing proportional, integral, and derivative control—has its advantages and disadvantages. The disadvanatages of each controller can be eliminated by combining all three controllers into a single PID controller, or proportional, integral, and derivative, controller.

The selection of the gains for the PID controller can be determined by a method developed by Ziegler and Nichols, who studied the performance of PID controllers by examining the integral of the absolute error (IAE):

$$\text{IAE} = \int_0^\infty |e(t)| \, dt \tag{7.56}$$

From their analysis they observed that when the error index was a minimum the control system responded to a step input as shown in Figure 7.22. Note that the second overshoot is one quarter of the magnitude of the maximum overshoot. They called this the quarter decay criterion. Based on their analysis they derived a set of rules for selecting the PID gains. The gains k_p, k_i, and k_d are determined in terms

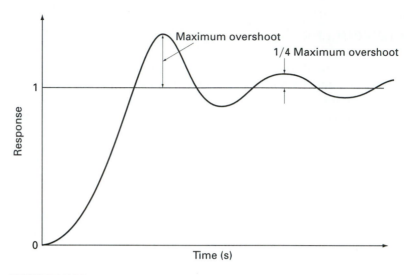

FIGURE 7.22
The quarter-decay response.

of two parameters, k_{p_u}, called the ultimate gain, and T_u, the period of the oscillation that occurs at the ultimate gain. Table 7.5 gives the values for the gains for proportional (P), proportional-integral (PI), and the proportional-integral-derivative (PID) controllers.

To apply this technique the root locus plot for the control system with the integral and derivative gains set to 0 must become marginally stable. That is, as the proportional gain is increased the locus must intersect the imaginary axis. The proportional gain, k_p, for which this occurs is called the ultimate gain, k_{p_u}. The purely imaginary roots, $\lambda = \pm i\omega$, determine the value of T_u:

$$T_u = \frac{2\pi}{\omega} \tag{7.57}$$

One additional restriction must be met: All other roots of the system must have negative real parts; that is, they must be in the left-hand portion of the complex s plane. If these restrictions are satisfied the P, PI, or PID gains easily can be determined.

EXAMPLE PROBLEM 7.7. Design a PID controller for the control system shown in Figure 7.23.

TABLE 7.5
Gains for P, PI, and PID controllers

Type of controller	k_p	k_i	k_d
P (proportional controller)	$k_p = 0.5k_{p_u}$		
PI (proportional-integral controller)	$k_p = 0.45k_{p_u}$	$k_i = 0.45k_{p_u}/(0.83T_u)$	
PID (proportional-integral-derivative controller)	$k_p = 0.6k_{p_u}$	$k_i = 0.6k_{p_u}/(0.5T_u)$	$k_d = 0.6k_{p_u}(0.125T_u)$

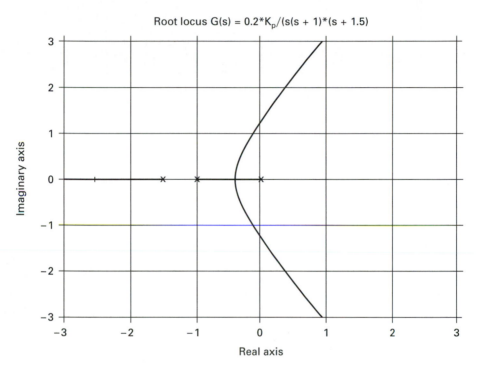

FIGURE 7.23
PID controller.

FIGURE 7.24
Root locus plot.

Solution. The gains of the PID controller can be estimated using the Ziegler-Nichols method provided the root locus for the plant becomes marginally stable for some value of the proportional gain k_p when the integral and derivative control gains have been set to 0. The root locus plot for

$$G(s) = \frac{0.2k_p}{s(s + 1)(s + 1.5)}$$

is shown in Figure 7.24. The root locus plot meets the requirements for the Ziegler-Nichols method. Two branches of the locus cross the imaginary axis and all other roots lie in the left half plane. The ultimate gain k_{p_u} is found by finding the gain when the root locus intersects the imaginary axis. The locus intersects the imaginary axis at $s = \pm 1.25i$. The gain at the crossover point can be estimated from the magnitude criteria:

$$\frac{|0.2| \, k_{p_u}}{|s| \, |s + 1| \, |s + 1.5|} = 1$$

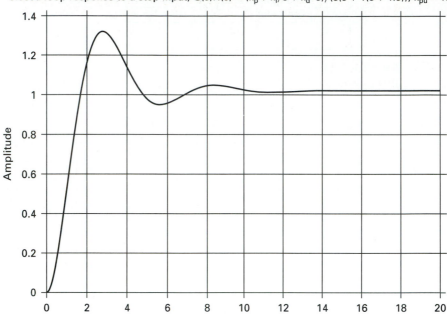

Closed loop response to a step input, $G(s)H(s) = (k_p + k_i/s + k_d*s)/(s(s + 1(s + 1.5))$, $k_{pu} = 19.8$

FIGURE 7.25
Transient response to a step input.

Substituting $s = 1.25i$ into the magnitude criteria yields

$$k_{p_u} = 19.8$$

The period of the undamped oscillation T_u is obtained as follows:

$$T_u = \frac{2\pi}{\omega} = \frac{2\pi}{1.25} = 5.03$$

Knowing k_{p_u} and T_u the proportional, integral, and derivative gains k_p, k_i, and k_d can be evaluated:

$$k_p = 0.6\, k_{p_u} = (0.6)(19.8) = 11.88$$
$$k_1 = 0.6\, k_{p_u}/(0.5T_u) = (0.6)(11.88)/[(0.5)(19.8)] = 0.72$$
$$k_d = 0.6\, k_{p_u}\, (0.125T_u) = (0.6)(19.8)(0.125)(5.03) = 7.47$$

The response of control system to a step input is given in Figure 7.25.

7.9
SUMMARY

In this chapter we examined some of the analytical tools available to the control system designer. The root locus technique allows the designer to examine the movement of the closed-loop poles of the control system as a function of one or more of the design variables. We also examined the relationship between the root location in the root locus diagram and the time and frequency domain performance of the system.

The conceptual design of a control system was presented. Once the control function has been identified, the designer must develop one or more concepts to meet the performance objectives of the control system. This phase of the design relies heavily on the designer's creativity and experience. Having developed some control system concepts the designer must evaluate the system performance. This requires mathematically modeling the various elements in the control system and selecting system parameters and analyzing the system performance using, for example, the root locus technique. In general, the designer usually will find that one or more of the concepts comes close to meeting the design objectives but that some of the requirements are not satisfied. In this case the designer must consider adding some form of compensating elements to the control system. We examined a number of compensators commonly used to improve control system performance. The type of compensation that needs to be added to a control system depends on what system performance specification needs to be improved.

PROBLEMS

Problems that require the use of a computer have a capital letter C after the problem number.

7.1. Given the characteristic equation

$$\lambda^3 + 3\lambda^2 + 3\lambda + 1 + k = 0$$

find the range of values of k for which the system is stable.

7.2. Given the fourth-order characteristic equation

$$\lambda^4 + 6\lambda^3 + 11\lambda^2 + 6\lambda + k = 0$$

for what values of k will the system be stable?

7.3. Given the following characteristic equation determine the stability of the system using the Routh criterion. If the system is unstable determine the number of roots lying in the left portion of the complex plane.

$$\lambda^6 + 3\lambda^5 + 5\lambda^4 + 9\lambda^3 + 8\lambda^2 + 6\lambda + 4 = 0$$

7.4. The characteristic equations for several feedback control systems follow. Determine the range of values of k for which the following systems are stable:
(a) $s^3 + 3ks^2 + (k + 2)s + 4 = 0$
(b) $s^4 + 4s^3 + 13s^2 + 36s + k = 0$

7.5.(C). The loop transfer function $G(s)H(s)$ is

(a) $\dfrac{k}{s(s^2 + 6s + 18)}$ (b) $\dfrac{k}{s(s + 2)(s + 5)}$ (c) $\dfrac{k(s + 4)}{s(s + 3)(s + 5)}$

(d) $\dfrac{k(s + 3)}{s^2 + 4s + 20}$ (e) $\dfrac{k(s + 4)}{(s^2 + 2s + 6)(s^2 + 4s + 8)}$

Sketch the root locus plot for variations of k, $0 \le k \le \infty$, for each transfer function. Check your results by using an appropriate root locus program.

7.6. Given the loop transfer function

$$G(s)H(s) = \frac{k}{s(s + 3)(s + 10)}$$

(a) Sketch the root locus plot for $G(s)H(s)$.
(b) Add a simple pole, $(s + 2)$, to $G(s)H(s)$ and examine the resulting root locus.
(c) Add a simple zero, $(s + 2)$, to $G(s)H(s)$ and examine the resulting root locus.

7.7. The root locus plot for the transfer function

$$G(s)H(s) = \frac{k}{s(s + 2)(s + 8)}$$

is shown in Figure P7.7.
(a) Estimate the system gain, k, when the system is critically damped.
(b) What is the value of the system gain, k, for which the system neutrally stable?

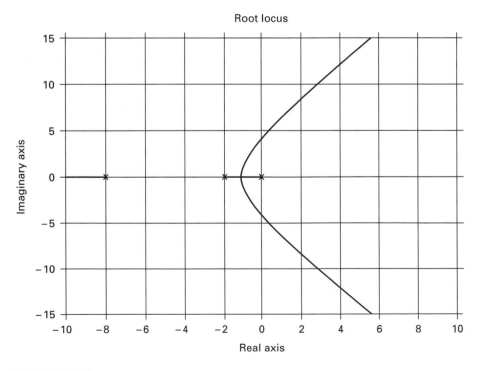

Root locus

FIGURE P7.7

7.8. The single degree of freedom pitching motion of an airplane was shown to be represented by a second-order differential equation. If the equation is given as

$$\ddot{\theta} + 0.5\dot{\theta} + 2\theta = \delta_e$$

where the θ and δ_e are in radians, estimate the rise time, peak overshoot, and settling time for step input of the elevator angle of 0.10 rad.

7.9. Determine the frequency domain characteristic for Problem 7.8. In particular estimate the resonance peak, M_r, resonant frequency, ω_r, bandwidth, ω_B, and the phase margin.

7.10(C). The root locus plot for the loop transfer function

$$G(s)H(s) = \frac{k}{(s + 8)(s^2 + 6s + 13)}$$

is shown in Figure P7.10.
(a) Find the system gain when the damping ratio is $\zeta = 0.707$.
(b) Estimate the time-domain characteristic for the dominant roots for the gain determined in part (a).
(c) Estimate the frequency response characteristics, that is, gain and phase margin, from the root locus plot for the gain selected in part (a).

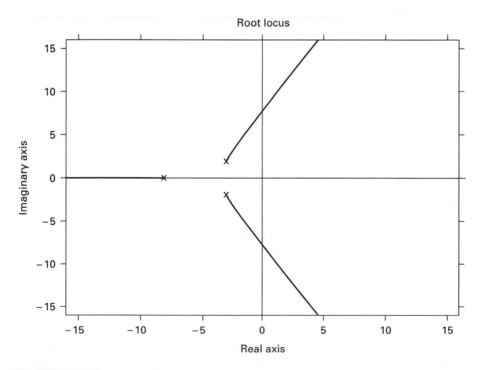

FIGURE P7.10

7.11. Calculate the position, velocity, and acceleration error constants K_p, K_v, and K_a for the loop transfer function $G(s)H(s)$ that follows:

(a) $\dfrac{10}{s(s + 1)(s + 10)}$

(b) $\dfrac{k}{s(1 + 0.1s)(1 + s)}$

(c) $\dfrac{k}{s(s^2 + 4s + 100)}$

(d) $\dfrac{s + 2}{s(s^2 + 4s + 6)}$

(e) $\dfrac{15\,(s + 2)}{s^2(s + 5)(s + 3)}$

7.12. The lead compensator can be constructed from a simple electrical circuit shown in Figure P7.12. Show that the transfer function for this circuit can be written as

$$G(s) = \frac{e_o}{e_i} = a\,\frac{(T_1 s + 1)}{(aT_1 s + 1)}$$

where $a = R_2/R_1 + R_2$ and $T_1 = R_1 C$.

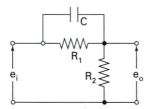

FIGURE P7.12
Lead circuit.

7.13. The lag compensator also can be constructed from a simple electrical circuit as shown in Figure P7.13. Show that the transfer function for this circuit can be written as

$$G(s) = \frac{e_o}{e_i} = \frac{T_2 s + 1}{(T_2/b)s + 1}$$

where $b = R_2/(R_1 + R_2)$

$T_2 = R_2 C$

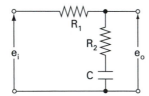

FIGURE P7.13
Lag circuit.

7.14(C). The control system shown in Figure P7.14 must meet the following performance specifications:

Damping ratio, $\zeta = 0.6$
Settling time, $t_s \leq 2.0$ s
Positional error constant, $K_p \geq 10$

(a) Assume that no compensation is used and estimate the system performance.
(b) Design a lead compensator to achieve this system performance.

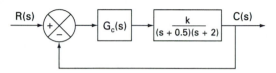

FIGURE P7.14

7.15. In the control system shown in Figure P7.15 rate feedback is to be used to increase the system damping. Estimate the gains k_a and k_r so that the system meets the following performance specifications:

Damping ratio, $\zeta = 0.7$
Settling time, ≤ 3.0 s

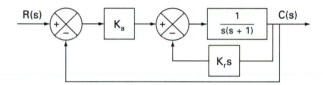

FIGURE P7.15

7.16(C). Given the control system shown in Figure P7.16 where the plant transfer function $G(s)$ is given by

$$G(s) = \frac{2.0}{s(s + 1)(s + 3)}$$

design a PID controller for this system.

R(s) ⊗ → $k_p + \dfrac{k_i}{s} + k_d s$ → $\dfrac{2.0}{s(s+1)(s+3)}$ → C(s)

PID controller   Plant

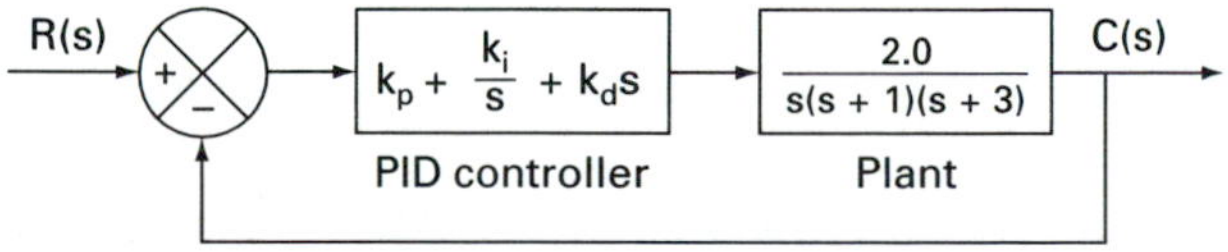

FIGURE P7.16

7.17(C). If the plant transfer function for Problem 7.16 is changed to

$$G(s) = \frac{7.0}{(s + 5)(s^2 + 2s + 5)}$$

design a PID controller for this system.

REFERENCES

7.1. Bollay W. "Aerodynamic Stability and Automatic Control." *Journal of the Aeronautical Sciences* 18, no. 9 (1951), pp. 569–617.
7.2. Raven, F. H. *Automatic Control Engineering.* New York: McGraw-Hill, 1995.
7.3. Kuo, B. C. *Automatic Control Systems.* Englewood Cliffs, NJ: Prentice-Hall, 1975.
7.4. Shinners, S. M. *Modern Control System Theory and Application.* Reading, MA: Addison Wesley, 1978.
7.5. D'Souza, A. F. *Design of Control Systems.* Englewood Cliffs, NJ: Prentice-Hall, 1988.
7.6. Hale, F. J. *Introduction to Control System Analysis and Design.* Englewood Cliffs, NJ: Prentice-Hall, 1988.
7.7. Nagrath, I. J.; and M. Gopal. *Control Systems Engineering.* New York: John Wiley and Sons, 1975.

CHAPTER 8

<hr>

Application of Classical Control Theory to Aircraft Autopilot Design

"The application of automatic control systems to aircraft promises to bring about the most important new advances in aeronautics in the future."

William Bollay, 14th Wright Brothers Lecture, 1950

8.1
INTRODUCTION

The rapid advancement of aircraft design from the very limited capabilities of the Wright brothers' first successful airplane to today's high performance military, commercial, and general aviation aircraft required the development of many technologies: aerodynamics, structures, materials, propulsion, and flight controls. Today's aircraft designs rely heavily on automatic control systems to monitor and control many of the aircraft's subsystems.

The development of automatic control systems has played an important role in the growth of civil and military aviation. Modern aircraft include a variety of automatic control systems that aid the flight crew in navigation, flight management, and augmenting the stability characteristics of the airplane. In this chapter we use control theory to design simple autopilots that can be used by the flight crew to lessen their workload during cruising and help them land their aircraft during adverse weather conditions. In addition, we also discuss how automatic control systems can be used to provide artificial stability to improve the flying qualities of an airplane.

Table 8.1 lists some of the functions that automatic control systems provide for flight control. In addition to the automatic flight control system, modern aircraft use control systems to aid in the navigation of the aircraft.

The development of autopilots closely followed the successful development of a powered, human-carrying airplane by the Wright brothers. In 1914 the Sperry brothers demonstrated the first successful autopilot. The autopilot was capable of maintaining pitch, roll, and heading angles. To demonstrate the effectiveness of their design, Lawrence Sperry trimmed his airplane for straight and level flight and then engaged the autopilot. He then proceeded to stand in the cockpit with his hands raised above his head while his mechanic walked out along the wings in an

TABLE 8.1
Automatic flight control system

Flight control system to reduce pilot workload
  Attitude control systems to maintain pitch, roll, or heading

  Altitude hold control system to maintain a desired altitude

  Speed control system to maintain a constant speed or Mach number

Stability augmentation systems
  If an airplane is marginally stable or unstable, automatic control systems can provide
  proper flight vehicle stability

  Automatic control can be used to ensure an airplane has the appropriate handling qualities;
  additional damping is incorporated by using a roll, pitch, or yaw damper

Landing aids
  A glide slope control system to guide the airplane down an electronic beam to the runway

  A localizer to align the aircraft in the lateral direction with the runway centerline as the
  airplane descends down the glide slope

  A flare control system that helps the aircraft make the transition from the glide slope
  to the runway

FIGURE 8.1
Sperry's flight demonstration of a three-axis automatic control system (from [8.1]).

attempt to upset the airplane's equilibrium. Figure 8.1 shows a photograph of the remarkable flight. The autopilot provided aileron, rudder, and elevator commands so that the airplane remained in a wings-level attitude.

8.2
AIRCRAFT TRANSFER FUNCTIONS

The longitudinal and lateral equations of motion were described by a set of linear differential equations in Chapter 3. A very useful concept in the analysis and design of control systems is the transfer function. The transfer function gives the relationship between the output of and input to a system. In the case of aircraft dynamics it specifies the relationship between the motion variables and the control input. The transfer function is defined as the ratio of the Laplace transform of the output to the Laplace transform of the input with all the initial conditions set to 0. (i.e., the system is assumed to be initially in equilibrium). For the reader who is not familiar with theory of Laplace transformations, a brief review of the basic concepts of Laplace transformation theory is included in Appendix C at the end of this book. In the following sections we develop the transfer function based on the longitudinal and lateral approximations developed in Chapters 4 and 5. We develop these simpler mathematical models so that we can examine the idea behind various autopilots without undue mathematical complexity.

8.2.1 Short-Period Dynamics

In Chapter 4 the equations for the short-period motions were developed for the case where the control was held fixed. The equation with control input from the elevator in state space form can be written as

$$\begin{bmatrix} \Delta\dot{\alpha} \\ \Delta\dot{q} \end{bmatrix} = \begin{bmatrix} Z_\alpha/u_0 & 1 \\ M_\alpha + M_{\dot{\alpha}}Z_\alpha/u_0 & M_q + M_{\dot{\alpha}} \end{bmatrix} \begin{bmatrix} \Delta\alpha \\ \Delta q \end{bmatrix} + \begin{bmatrix} Z_{\delta_e}/u_0 \\ M_{\delta_e} + M_{\dot{\alpha}}Z_{\delta_e}/u_0 \end{bmatrix} [\Delta\delta_e] \quad (8.1)$$

The control due to the propulsion system is neglected here for simplicity. Taking the Laplace transform of this equation yields

$$(s - Z_\alpha/u_0)\,\Delta\alpha(s) - \Delta q(s) = Z_{\delta_e}/u_0\,\Delta\delta_e(s) \quad (8.2)$$

$$-(M_\alpha + M_{\dot{\alpha}}Z_\alpha/u_0)\,\Delta\alpha(s) + [s - (M_q + M_{\dot{\alpha}})]\,\Delta q(s) \\ = (M_{\delta_e} + M_{\dot{\alpha}}Z_{\delta_e}/u_0)\,\Delta\delta_e \quad (8.3)$$

If we divide these equations by $\Delta\delta_e(s)$ we obtain a set of algebraic equations in terms of the transfer functions $\Delta\alpha(s)/\Delta\delta_e(s)$ and $\Delta q(s)/\Delta\delta_e(s)$:

$$(s - Z_\alpha/u_0)\,\frac{\Delta\alpha(s)}{\Delta\delta_e(s)} - \frac{\Delta q(s)}{\Delta\delta_e(s)} = Z_{\delta_e}/u_0 \quad (8.4)$$

$$-(M_\alpha + M_{\dot\alpha} Z_\alpha/u_0) \frac{\Delta\alpha(s)}{\Delta\delta_e(s)} + [s - (M_q + M_{\dot\alpha})] \frac{\Delta q(s)}{\Delta\delta_e(s)} = M_{\delta_e} + M_{\dot\alpha} \frac{Z_{\delta_e}}{u_0} \quad (8.5)$$

Solving for $\Delta\alpha(s)/\Delta\delta_e(s)$ and $\Delta q(s)/\Delta\delta_e(s)$ by Cramer's rule yields

$$\frac{\Delta\alpha(s)}{\Delta\delta_e(s)} = \frac{N^\alpha_{\delta_e}(s)}{\Delta_{sp}(s)} = \frac{\begin{vmatrix} Z_{\delta_e}/u_0 & -1 \\ M_{\delta_e} + M_{\dot\alpha}\dfrac{Z_{\delta_e}}{u_0} & s - (M_q + M_{\dot\alpha}) \end{vmatrix}}{\begin{vmatrix} s - Z_\alpha/u_0 & -1 \\ -(M_\alpha + M_{\dot\alpha} Z_\alpha/u_0) & s - (M_q + M_{\dot\alpha}) \end{vmatrix}} \quad (8.6)$$

When expanded, the numerator and denominator are polynomials in the Laplace variable s. The coefficients of the polynomials are a function of the stability derivatives. McRuer, Ashkenas, and Graham [8.2] use a shorthand notation to express the transfer function polynomials. We will use this convenient notation to present the transfer function developed here. An example of the notation follows:

$$\frac{\Delta\alpha(s)}{\Delta\delta_e(s)} = \frac{N^\alpha_{\delta_e}(s)}{\Delta_{sp}(s)} = \frac{A_\alpha s + B_\alpha}{As^2 + Bs + C} \quad (8.7)$$

where the coefficients in the numerator and denominator are given in Table 8.2. The transfer function for the change in pitch rate to the change in elevator angle can be shown to be

$$\frac{\Delta q(s)}{\Delta\delta_e(s)} = \frac{N^q_{\delta_e}(s)}{\Delta_{sp}(s)} = \frac{\begin{vmatrix} s - Z_\alpha/u_0 & Z_{\delta_e}/u_0 \\ -(M_\alpha + M_{\dot\alpha} Z_\alpha/u_0) & M_{\delta_e} + M_{\dot\alpha}\dfrac{Z_{\delta_e}}{u_0} \end{vmatrix}}{\begin{vmatrix} s - Z_\alpha/u_0 & -1 \\ -(M_\alpha + M_{\dot\alpha} Z_\alpha/u_0) & s - (M_q + M_{\dot\alpha}) \end{vmatrix}} \quad (8.8)$$

or

$$\frac{\Delta q(s)}{\Delta\delta_e(s)} = \frac{N^q_{\delta_e}(s)}{\Delta_{sp}(s)} = \frac{A_q s + B_q}{As^2 + Bs + C} \quad (8.9)$$

Again the coefficients of the polynomials are defined in Table 8.2.

TABLE 8.2
Short-period transfer function approximations

	A, A_α, or A_q	B, B_α, or B_q	C
$\Delta_{sp}(s)$	1	$-(M_q + M_{\dot\alpha} + Z_\alpha/u_0)$	$Z_\alpha M_q/u_0 - M_\alpha$
$N^\alpha_{\delta_e}(s)$	Z_{δ_e}/u_0	$M_{\delta_e} - M_q Z_{\delta_e}/u_0$	
$N^q_{\delta_e}(s)$	$M_{\delta_e} + M_{\dot\alpha} Z_{\delta_e}/u_0$	$M_\alpha Z_{\delta_e}/u_0 - M_{\delta_e} Z_\alpha/u_0$	

8.2.2 Long-Period or Phugoid Dynamics

The state-space equation for the long period or phugoid approximation are as follows:

$$\begin{bmatrix} \Delta \dot{u} \\ \Delta \dot{\theta} \end{bmatrix} = \begin{bmatrix} X_u & -g \\ -\dfrac{Z_u}{u_0} & 0 \end{bmatrix} \begin{bmatrix} \Delta u \\ \Delta \theta \end{bmatrix} + \begin{bmatrix} X_{\delta_e} & X_{\delta_T} \\ -\dfrac{Z_{\delta_e}}{u_0} & -\dfrac{Z_{\delta_T}}{u_0} \end{bmatrix} \begin{bmatrix} \Delta \delta_e \\ \Delta \delta_T \end{bmatrix} \tag{8.10}$$

The Laplace transformation of the approximate equations for the long period are

$$(s - X_u)\,\Delta u(s) + g\,\Delta \theta(s) = X_{\delta_e}\,\Delta \delta_e(s) + X_{\delta_T}\,\Delta \delta_T(s) \tag{8.11}$$

$$\frac{Z_u}{u_0}\,\Delta u(s) + s\,\Delta \theta(s) = -\frac{Z_{\delta_e}}{u_0}\,\Delta \delta_e(s) - \frac{Z_{\delta_T}}{u_0}\,\Delta \delta_T(s) \tag{8.12}$$

The transfer function $\Delta u(s)/\Delta \delta_e(s)$ and $\Delta \theta(s)/\Delta \delta_e(s)$ can be found by setting $\Delta \delta_T(s)$ to 0 and solving for the appropriate transfer function as follows:

$$(s - X_u)\frac{\Delta u(s)}{\Delta \delta_e(s)} + g\,\frac{\Delta \theta(s)}{\Delta \theta_e(s)} = X_{\delta_e} \tag{8.13}$$

$$\frac{Z_u}{u_0}\frac{\Delta u(s)}{\Delta \delta_e(s)} + s\,\frac{\Delta \theta(s)}{\Delta \delta_e(s)} = -\frac{Z_{\delta_e}}{u_0} \tag{8.14}$$

The equations of motion have been reduced to a set of algebraic equations in terms of the desired transfer function. These equations can be solved to yield the transfer functions

$$\frac{\Delta u(s)}{\Delta \delta_e(s)} = \frac{\begin{vmatrix} X_{\delta_e} & g \\ -\dfrac{Z_{\delta_e}}{u_0} & s \end{vmatrix}}{\begin{vmatrix} s - X_u & g \\ \dfrac{Z_u}{u_0} & s \end{vmatrix}} \tag{8.15}$$

$$\frac{\Delta u(s)}{\Delta \delta_e(s)} = \frac{X_{\delta_e}s + gZ_{\delta_e}/u_0}{s^2 + X_u s - \dfrac{Z_u g}{u_0}} \tag{8.16}$$

In a similar manner $\Delta \theta(s)/\Delta \delta(s)$ can be shown to be

$$\frac{\Delta \theta(s)}{\Delta \delta_e(s)} = \frac{-\dfrac{Z_{\delta e}}{u_0}s + \left(\dfrac{X_u Z_{\delta e}}{u_0} - \dfrac{Z_u X_{\delta e}}{u_0}\right)}{s^2 - X_u s - \dfrac{Z_u g}{u_0}} \tag{8.17}$$

TABLE 8.3
Long-period transfer function approximations

	A, A_u, or A_θ	B, B_u, or B_θ	C
$\Delta_p(s)$	1	$-X_u$	$-Z_u g/u_0$
$N^u_{\delta_e}(s)$	X_{δ_e}	gZ_{δ_e}/u_0	
$N^\theta_{\delta_e}(s)$	$-Z_{\delta_e}/u_0$	$X_u Z_{\delta_e}/u_0 - Z_u X_{\delta_e}/u_0$	

The transfer functions can be written in a symbolic form in the following manner:

$$\frac{\Delta u(s)}{\Delta \delta_e(s)} = \frac{N^u_{\delta_e}(s)}{\Delta_p(s)} = \frac{A_u s + B_u}{As^2 + Bs + C} \tag{8.18}$$

$$\frac{\Delta \theta(s)}{\Delta \delta_e(s)} = \frac{N^\theta_{\delta_e}}{\Delta_p(s)} = \frac{A_\theta s + B_\theta}{As^2 + Bs + C} \tag{8.19}$$

where A_u, B_u, and so forth are defined in Table 8.3. The transfer functions for the propulsive control, that is, $\Delta u(s)/\Delta \delta_T(s)$ and $\Delta \theta(s)/\Delta \delta_T(s)$, have the same form except that the derivatives with respect to δ_e are replaced by derivatives with respect to δ_T. Therefore, Table 8.3 can be used for both aerodynamic and propulsive control transfer functions provided that the appropriate control derivatives are used.

8.2.3 Roll Dynamics

The equation of motion for a pure rolling motion, developed in Chapter 5, is

$$\Delta \dot{p} - L_p \, \Delta p = L_{\delta_a} \, \Delta \delta_a \tag{8.20}$$

The transfer function $\Delta p(s)/\delta_a(s)$ and $\Delta \phi(s)/\Delta \delta_a(s)$ can be obtained by taking the Laplace transform of the roll equation:

$$(s - L_p) \, \Delta p(s) = L_{\delta_a} \, \Delta \delta_a(s) \tag{8.21}$$

or

$$\frac{\Delta p(s)}{\Delta \delta_a(s)} = \frac{L_{\delta a}}{s - L_p} \tag{8.22}$$

But the roll rate Δp is defined as $\Delta \dot{\phi}$; therefore,

$$\Delta p(s) = s \Delta \phi(s) \tag{8.23}$$

or

$$\frac{\Delta \phi(s)}{\Delta \delta_a(s)} = \frac{L_{\delta_a}}{s(s - L_p)} \tag{8.24}$$

8.2.4 Dutch Roll Approximation

The final simplified transfer function we will develop is for the Dutch roll motion. The approximate equations can be shown to be

$$\begin{bmatrix} \Delta\dot\beta \\ \Delta\dot r \end{bmatrix} = \begin{bmatrix} Y_\beta/u_0 & -(1 - Y_r/u_0) \\ N_\beta & N_r \end{bmatrix}\begin{bmatrix} \Delta\beta \\ \Delta r \end{bmatrix} + \begin{bmatrix} Y_{\delta_r}/u_0 & 0 \\ N_{\delta_r} & N_{\delta_a} \end{bmatrix}\begin{bmatrix} \Delta\delta_r \\ \Delta\delta_a \end{bmatrix} \qquad (8.25)$$

Taking the Laplace transform and rearranging yields

$$(s - Y_\beta/u_0)\,\Delta\beta(s) + (1 - Y_r/u_0)\,\Delta r(s) = Y_{\delta_r}/u_0\,\Delta\delta_r(s) \qquad (8.26)$$

$$-N_\beta\,\Delta\beta(s) + (s - N_r)\,\Delta r(s) = N_{\delta_a}\,\Delta\delta_a(s) + N_{\delta_r}\,\Delta\delta_r(s) \qquad (8.27)$$

The transfer functions $\Delta\beta(s)/\Delta\delta_r(s)$, $\Delta r(s)/\Delta\delta_r(s)$, $\Delta\beta(s)/\Delta\delta_a(s)$, and $\Delta r(s)/\Delta\delta_a(s)$ can be obtained by setting $\Delta\delta_a(s)$ to 0 and solving for $\Delta\beta(s)/\Delta\delta_r(s)$ and $\Delta r(s)/\Delta\delta_r(s)$. Next set $\Delta\delta_r(s)$ equal to 0 and solve for $\Delta\beta(s)/\Delta\delta_a(s)$ and $\Delta r(s)/\Delta\delta_a(s)$. The transfer functions $\Delta\beta(s)/\Delta\delta_r(s)$ and $\Delta r(s)/\Delta\delta_r(s)$ are obtained as follows:

$$(s - Y_\beta/u_0)\frac{\Delta\beta(s)}{\Delta\delta_r(s)} + (1 - Y_r/u_0)\frac{\Delta r(s)}{\Delta\delta_r(s)} = Y_{\delta_r}/u_0 \qquad (8.28)$$

$$-N_\beta\frac{\Delta\beta(s)}{\Delta\delta_r(s)} + (s - N_r)\frac{\Delta r(s)}{\Delta\delta_r(s)} = N_{\delta_r} \qquad (8.29)$$

Solving for the transfer function yields

$$\frac{\Delta\beta(s)}{\Delta\delta_r(s)} = \frac{\begin{vmatrix} Y_{\delta_r}/u_0 & 1 - Y_r/u_0 \\ N_{\delta_r} & s - N_r \end{vmatrix}}{\begin{vmatrix} s - Y_\beta/u_0 & 1 - Y_r/u_0 \\ -N_\beta & s - N_r \end{vmatrix}} \qquad (8.30)$$

$$\frac{\Delta r(s)}{\Delta\delta_r(s)} = \frac{\begin{vmatrix} s - Y_\beta/u_0 & Y_{\delta_r}/u_0 \\ -N_\beta & N_{\delta_r} \end{vmatrix}}{\begin{vmatrix} s - Y_\beta/u_0 & 1 - Y_r/u_0 \\ -N_\beta & s - N_r \end{vmatrix}} \qquad (8.31)$$

or

$$\frac{\Delta\beta(s)}{\Delta\delta_r(s)} = \frac{N^\beta_{\delta_r}(s)}{\Delta_{DR}(s)} = \frac{A_\beta s + B_\beta}{As^2 + Bs + C} \qquad (8.32)$$

$$\frac{\Delta r(s)}{\Delta\delta_r(s)} = \frac{N^\beta_{\delta_r}(s)}{\Delta_{DR}(s)} = \frac{A_r s + B_r}{As^2 + Bs + C} \qquad (8.33)$$

In a similar manner the aileron transfer function can be shown to be

$$\frac{\Delta\beta(s)}{\Delta\delta_a(s)} = \frac{N^\beta_{\delta_a}(s)}{\Delta_{DR}(s)} = \frac{A_\beta s + B_\beta}{As^2 + Bs + C} \qquad (8.34)$$

$$\frac{\Delta r(s)}{\Delta\delta_a(s)} = \frac{N^r_{\delta_a}(s)}{\Delta_{DR}(s)} = \frac{A_r s + B_r}{As^2 + Bs + C} \qquad (8.35)$$

TABLE 8.4
Dutch roll transfer function approximations

	A, B_β, or A_r	B, B_β, or B_r	C
$\Delta_{DR}(s)$	1	$-(Y_\beta + u_0 N_r)/u_0$	$(Y_\beta N_r - N_\beta Y_r + N_\beta u_0)/u_0$
$N^\beta_{\delta_r}(s)$	Y_r/u_0	$(Y_r N_{\delta_r} - Y_{\delta_r} N_r - N_{\delta_r} u_0)/u_0$	
$N^r_{\delta_r}(s)$	N_{δ_r}	$(N_\beta Y_{\delta_r} - Y_\beta N_{\delta_r})/u_0$	
$N^\beta_{\delta_a}(s)$	0	$(Y_r N_{\delta_a} - u_0 N_{\delta_a})/u_0$	
$N^r_{\delta_a}(s)$	N_{δ_a}	$-Y_\beta N_{\delta_a}/u_0$	

The coefficients of the polynomials in the Dutch roll transfer functions are included in Table 8.4. The denominator coefficients are in the first row and the numerator coefficients are defined for each transfer function in the subsequent rows.

In the previous section, transfer functions were derived for both longitudinal and lateral dynamics based on the approximations to these motions. For a preliminary autopilot design these approximations are appropriate. However, as the autopilot concept is refined and developed it is necessary to examine the autopilot performance using transfer functions based on the complete set of either the longitudinal or lateral equations. This is particularly important for the lateral equations. As we showed in Chapter 5 the lateral approximations do not generally give a very accurate representation of the Dutch roll motion.

The longitudinal and lateral transfer functions for the complete set of equations are determined in the same manner as the approximate transfer functions derived here. The transfer functions for the complete set of rigid body equations are given in Tables 8.5 and 8.6.

8.3
CONTROL SURFACE ACTUATOR

In addition to the various transfer functions that represent the aircraft dynamics, we need to develop the transfer functions for the other elements that make up the control system. This would include the servo actuators to deflect the aerodynamic control surfaces as well as the transfer function for any sensors in the control loop; for example, an attitude gyro, rate gyro, altimeter, or velocity sensor. The transfer functions for most sensors can be approximated by a gain, k. In this section we develop an expression for the transfer function of a simple position control servo that is used to accurately deflect the aerodynamic control surfaces in an automatic system.

Control surface servo actuators can be either electrical, hydraulic, pneumatic, or some combination of the three. The transfer function is similar for each type. We will develop the control surface servo actuator transfer function for a servo based on an electric motor.

TABLE 8.5
Longitudinal control transfer functions

	A	B	C	D	E
Δ_{long}	1	$-M_q - u_0 M_{\dot{w}} - Z_w - X_u$	$Z_w M_q - u_0 M_w - X_w Z_u + X_u(M_q + u_0 M_{\dot{w}} + Z_w)$	$-X_u(Z_w M_q - u_0 M_w) + Z_u(X_w M_q + g M_{\dot{w}}) - M_u(u_0 X_w - g)$	$g(Z_u M_w - M_u Z_w)$
N^θ_δ	$M_\delta + Z_\delta M_{\dot{w}}$	$X_\delta(Z_u M_{\dot{w}} + M_u) + Z_\delta(M_w - X_u M_{\dot{w}}) - M_\delta(X_u + Z_w)$	$X_\delta(Z_u M_w - Z_w M_u) + Z_\delta(M_u X_w - M_w X_u) + M_\delta(Z_w X_u - X_w Z_u)$		
N^w_δ	Z_δ	$X_\delta Z_u - Z_\delta(X_u + M_q) + M_\delta u_0$	$X_\delta(u_0 M_u - Z_u M_q) + Z_\delta X_u M_q - u_0 M_\delta X_u$	$g(Z_\delta M_u - M_\delta Z_u)$	
N^u_δ	X_δ	$-X_\delta(Z_w + M_q + u_0 M_{\dot{w}}) + Z_\delta X_w$	$X_\delta(Z_w M_q - u_0 M_w) - Z_\delta(X_w M_q + g M_{\dot{w}}) + M_\delta(u_0 X_w - g)$	$g(M_\delta Z_w - Z_\delta M_w)$	

TABLE 8.6
Lateral control transfer functions

	A	B	C	D	E
Δ_{lat}	$1 - \dfrac{I_{xz}^2}{I_x I_z}$	$-Y_v\left(1 - \dfrac{I_{xz}^2}{I_x I_z}\right) - L_p - N_r$ $- \dfrac{I_{xz}}{I_x}N_p - \dfrac{I_{xz}}{I_x}L_r$	$u_0 N_v + L_p(Y_v + N_r) + N_p\left(\dfrac{I_{xz}}{I_x}Y_v - L_r\right)$ $+ Y_v\left(\dfrac{I_{xz}}{I_x}L_r + N_r\right) + u_0\dfrac{I_{xz}}{I_z}L_v$	$-u_0 N_v L_p - Y_v(N_p L_r - L_p N_r)$ $+ u_0 N_p L_v - g\left(L_v + \dfrac{I_{xz}}{I_x}N_v\right)$	$g(L_v N_r - N_v L_r)$
N_δ^v	$Y_\delta\left(1 - \dfrac{I_{xz}^2}{I_x I_z}\right)$	$-Y_\delta\left(L_p + N_r + \dfrac{I_{xz}}{I_x}N_p + \dfrac{I_{xz}}{I_z}L_r\right)$ $- u_0\left(\dfrac{I_{xz}}{I_z}L_\delta + N_\delta\right)$	$Y_\delta(L_p N_r - N_p L_r) + u_0(N_\delta L_p - L_\delta N_p)$ $+ g\left(L_\delta + \dfrac{I_{xz}}{I_x}N_\delta\right)$	$g(N_\delta L_r - L_\delta N_r)$	
N_δ^ϕ	$L_\delta + \dfrac{I_{xz}}{I_x}N_\delta$	$Y_\delta\left(L_v + \dfrac{I_{xz}}{I_x}N_v\right) - L_\delta(N_r + Y_v)$ $+ N_\delta\left(L_r - \dfrac{I_{xz}}{I_x}Y_v\right)$	$Y_\delta(L_r N_v - L_v N_r) + L_\delta(Y_v N_r + u_0 N_v)$ $- N_\delta(u_0 L_v + Y_v L_r)$		
N_δ^r	$N_\delta + \dfrac{I_{xz}}{I_z}L_\delta$	$Y_\delta\left(N_v + \dfrac{I_{xz}}{I_x}L_v\right)$ $+ L_\delta\left(N_p - \dfrac{I_{xz}}{I_z}Y_v\right)$ $- N_\delta(Y_v + L_p)$	$Y_\delta(L_v N_p - N_v L_p) - L_\delta Y_v N_p + N_\delta Y_v L_p$	$g(L_\delta N_v - N_\delta L_v)$	

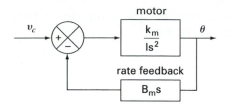

FIGURE 8.2
Motor with rate feedback.

The torque produced by an electric motor is proportional to the control voltage as follows:

$$T_m = k_m v_c \qquad (8.36)$$

where k_m is a constant. The angular position of the motor shaft can be determined from the equation

$$I\ddot{\theta} = T_m \qquad (8.37)$$

The relationship between the angular position of the motion shaft (output) and the motor control voltage (input) is given by the transfer function

$$\frac{\theta}{v_c} = \frac{k_m}{Is^2} \qquad (8.38)$$

In general, the motor will incorporate a rate feedback loop as illustrated in Figure 8.2. The transfer function for the system with rate feedback can be shown to be

$$\frac{\theta}{v_c} = \frac{k}{s(\tau_m s + 1)} \qquad (8.39)$$

where
$$\tau_m = \frac{I}{k_m B_m} \quad \text{and} \quad k = \frac{1}{B_m} \qquad (8.40)$$

The motor time constant τ_m is a measure of how fast the motor responds to a change in control voltage. If τ_m is small, the motor responds rapidly and the transfer function of the motor with rate feedback can be approximated as

$$\frac{\theta}{v_c} = \frac{k}{s} \qquad (8.41)$$

A simple position control servo system can be developed from the control diagram shown in Figure 8.3. The motor shaft angle, θ, can be replaced by the flap angle,

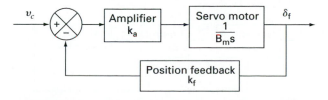

FIGURE 8.3
Simple position control servo for control surface deflection.

δ_f, of the control surface. For the positional feedback system the closed loop transfer function can be shown to have the following form:

$$\frac{\delta_f}{v_c} = \frac{k}{\tau s + 1} \tag{8.42}$$

where k and τ are defined in terms of characteristics of the servo,

$$k = 1/k_f \qquad \text{and} \qquad \tau = \frac{B_m}{k_f k_a} \tag{8.43}$$

The time constant of the control surface servo is typical of the order of 0.1 s. In the problems that follow we assume this value as representative of typical control surface servo time constants.

8.4
DISPLACEMENT AUTOPILOT

One of the earliest autopilots to be used for aircraft control is the so-called displacement autopilot. A displacement type autopilot can be used to control the angular orientation of the airplane. Conceptually, the displacement autopilot works in the following manner. In a pitch attitude displacement autopilot, the pitch angle is sensed by a vertical gyro and compared with the desired pitch angle to create an error angle. The difference or error in pitch attitude is used to produce proportional displacements of the elevator so that the error signal is reduced. Figure 8.4 is a block diagram of either a pitch or roll angle displacement autopilot.

The heading angle of the airplane also can be controlled using a similar scheme. The heading angle is sensed by a directional gyro and the error signal is used to displace the rudder to reduce the error signal. A displacement heading autopilot also is shown in Figure 8.5.

In practice, the displacement autopilot is engaged once the airplane has been trimmed in straight and level flight. To maneuver the airplane while the autopilot

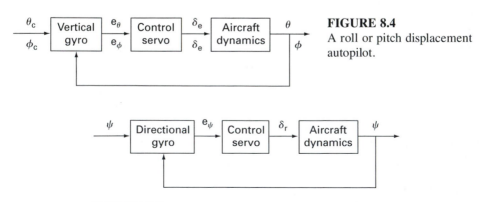

FIGURE 8.4
A roll or pitch displacement autopilot.

FIGURE 8.5
A heading displacement autopilot.

is engaged, the pilot must adjust the commanded signals. For example, the airplane can be made to climb or descend by changing the pitch command. Turns can be achieved by introducing the desired bank angle while simultaneously changing the heading command. In the following sections we examine several displacement autopilot concepts.

8.4.1 Pitch Displacement Autopilot

The basic components of a pitch attitude control system are shown in Figure 8.4. For this design the reference pitch angle is compared with the actual angle measured by a gyro to produce an error signal to activate the control servo. In general the error signal is amplified and sent to the control surface actuator to deflect the control surface. Movement of the control surface causes the aircraft to achieve a new pitch orientation, which is fed back to close the loop.

To illustrate how such an autopilot would be designed, we will examine this particular pitch displacement autopilot concept for a business jet aircraft. Once we have decided on a control concept, our next step must be to evaluate the performance of the control system. To accomplish this we must define the transfer functions for each of the elements in the block diagram describing the system. For this discussion we assume that the transfer functions of both the gyro and amplifier can be represented by simple gains. The elevator servo transfer function can be represented as a first-order system:

$$\frac{\delta_e}{v} = \frac{k_a}{\tau s + 1}$$

where δ_e, v, k_a, and τ are the elevator deflection angle, input voltage, elevator servo gain, and servomotor time constant. Time constants for typical servomotors fall in a range $0.05-0.25$ s. For our discussion we assume a time constant of 0.1 s. Finally, we need to specify the transfer function for the airplane. The transfer function relating the pitch attitude to elevator deflection was developed earlier. To keep the description of this design as simple as possible, we represent the aircraft dynamics by using the short-period approximation. The short-period transfer function for the business jet in Appendix B can be shown to be

$$\frac{\Delta\theta}{\Delta\delta_e} = \frac{-2.0(s + 0.3)}{s(s^2 + 0.65s + 2.15)}$$

Figure 8.6 is the block diagram representation of the autopilot. The problem now is one of determining the gain k_a so that the control system will have the desired performance. Selection of the gain k_a can be determined using a root locus plot of the loop transfer function. Figure 8.7 is the root locus plot for the business jet pitch autopilot. As the gain is increased from 0, the system damping decreases rapidly and the system becomes unstable. Even for low values of k_a, the system damping would be too low for satisfactory dynamic performance. The reason for the poor performance of this design is that the airplane has very little natural damping. To

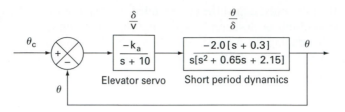

FIGURE 8.6
A pitch displacement autopilot for a business jet.

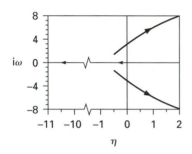

FIGURE 8.7
Root locus pilot of the system gain for a pitch displacement autopilot.

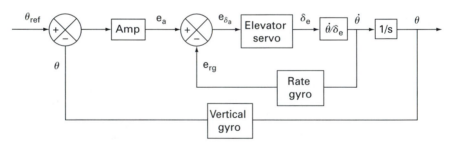

FIGURE 8.8
A pitch attitude control system employing pitch rate feedback.

improve the design we could increase the damping of the short-period mode by adding an inner feedback loop. Figure 8.8 is a block diagram of a displacement autopilot with pitch rate feedback for improved damping. In the inner loop the pitch rate is measured by a rate gyro and fed back to be added with the error signal generated by the difference in pitch attitude. Figure 8.9 is a block diagram for the business jet when pitch rate is incorporated into the design. For this problem we now have two parameters to select; namely, the gains k_a and k_{rg}. The root locus method can be used to pick both parameters. The procedure essentially is by trial and error. First, the root locus diagram is determined for the inner loop, a gyro gain is selected, and then the outer root locus plot is constructed. Several iterations may be required until the desired overall system performance is achieved.

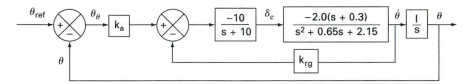

FIGURE 8.9
A business jet pitch attitude control system with pitch rate feedback.

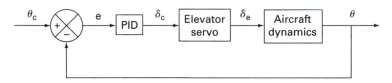

FIGURE 8.10
Pitch attitude autopilot with a PID controller.

EXAMPLE PROBLEM 8.1. Use the PID controller for a pitch attitude autopilot as illustrated in Figure 8.10. The transfer functions for each component are given in Table 8.7.

Solution. Using the Ziegler and Nichols method discussed in Section 7.8, the PID gains can be estimated from the ultimate gain k_{p_u}, which is the gain for which the system is marginally stable when only the proportional control is being used. Figure 8.11 is the root locus sketch of the transfer function:

$$G(s)H(s) = \frac{3.0k_p}{(s + 10)(s^2 + 2s + 5)}$$

The root locus crosses the imaginary axis at $s = \pm 5.13i$. The gain of the system can be found from the magnitude criteria to be $k_{p_u} = 88.7$. The period, $T_u = 2\pi/\omega = 1.22$. Table 8.8 gives the gains for the proportional, proportional-integral and proportional-integral-derivative controllers. Figure 8.12 shows the response of the pitch attitude

TABLE 8.7
Data for Example Problem 8.1

Control element	Parameters	Transfer function
PID	$k_p = ?$ $k_i = ?$ $k_d = ?$	$\dfrac{\delta_c}{e} = k_p + \dfrac{k_i}{s} + k_d s$
Elevator servo	$A = -0.1$ $\tau = 0.1$	$\dfrac{\delta_e}{\delta_c} = \dfrac{A}{\tau s + 1}$
Aircraft dynamics	$M_{\delta e} = -3 \text{ s}^{-2}$ $M_q = -2 \text{ s}^{-1}$ $M_\alpha = -5 \text{ s}^{-2}$	$\dfrac{\theta}{\delta_e} = \dfrac{M_{\delta e}}{s^2 - M_q s - M_\alpha}$

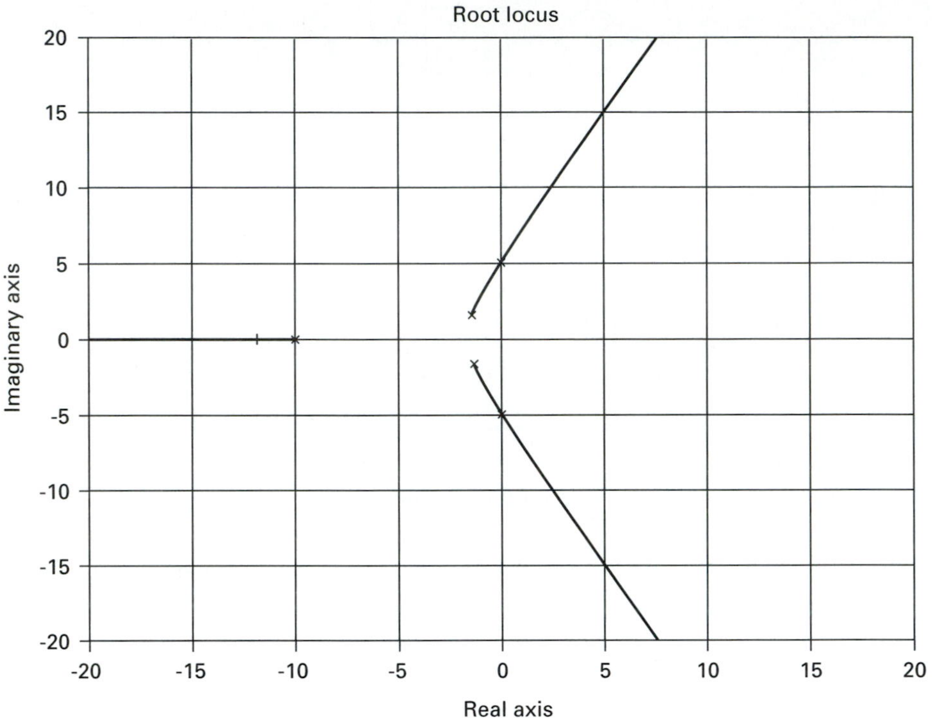

FIGURE 8.11
Root locus plot of $G(s)H(s)$.

TABLE 8.8
Gains for P, PI, and PID controllers

P control	$k_p = 0.5k_{pu} = 44.35$
PI control	$k_p = 0.45k_{pu} = 39.92$
	$k_i = 0.45k_{pu}/(0.83T_u) = 39.42$
PID control	$k_p = 0.6k_{pu} = 53.22$
	$k_i = 0.6k_{pu}/(0.5T_u) = 87.24$
	$k_d = 0.6k_{pu}(0.125T_u) = 8.12$

autopilot for the three different controllers to a step input. Notice that the proportional controller has a steady-state error; that is, it does not go to 1 but converges to a value of approximately 0.7. The magnitude of the steady-state error can be predicted using the steady-state error constants in Chapter 7:

$$e_{ss} = \frac{1}{1 + K_p}$$

where

$$K_p = \underset{s \to 0}{\text{Limit}} \ G(s)H(s) = \underset{s \to 0}{\text{Limit}} \ \frac{3.0k_p}{s^3 + 12s^2 + 25s + 50}$$

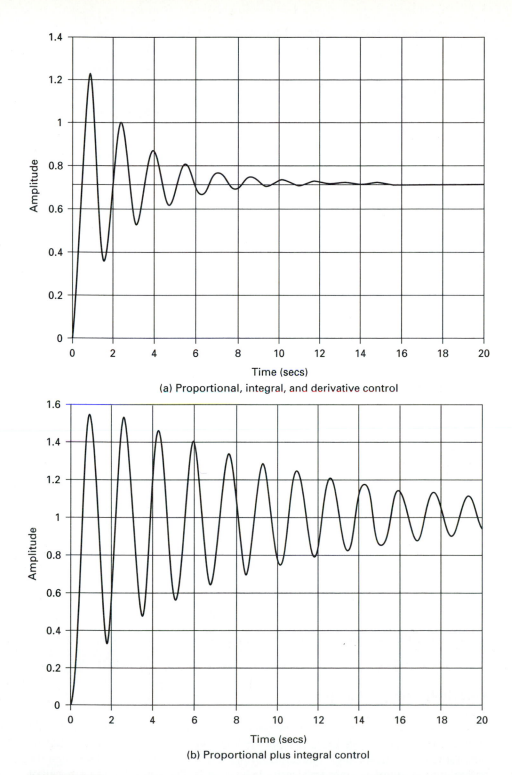

FIGURE 8.12

Response to a step input of a pitch autopilot with either a P, PI, or PID controller.

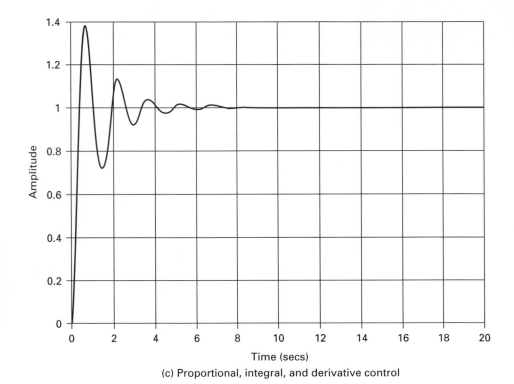

FIGURE 8.12
Concluded.

for a proportional gain $k_p = 44.35$

$$K_p = 2.66$$

The steady-state error e_{ss} can then be calculated:

$$e_{ss} = \frac{1}{1 + K_p} = \frac{1}{3.66} = 0.27$$

Therefore the response will go to 0.73 instead of 1 due to the steady-state error.

8.4.2 Roll Attitude Autopilot

The roll attitude of an airplane can be controlled by a simple bank angle autopilot as illustrated in Figure 8.13. Conceptually the roll angle of the airplane can be maintained at whatever angle one desires. In practice we would typically design the autopilot to maintain a wings level attitude or $\phi = 0$. The autopilot is composed of a comparator, aileron actuator, aircraft equation of motion (i.e., transfer function), and an attitude gyro to measure the airplane's roll angle.

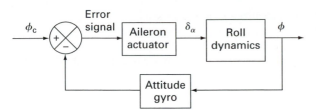

FIGURE 8.13
Simple roll attitude control system.

EXAMPLE PROBLEM 8.2. Design a roll attitude control system to maintain a wings level attitude for a vehicle having the following characteristics:

$$L_{\delta_a} = 2.0/s^2 \qquad L_p = -0.5/s$$

The system performance is to have a damping ratio, $\zeta = 0.707$, and an undamped natural frequency, $\omega_n = 10$ rad/s. A potential concept of a roll attitude control system is shown in the block diagram in Figure 8.14.

Solution. Once we have decided on one or more concepts our next step is to evaluate the performance of the proposed control system. To accomplish this we need to develop the appropriate mathematical model for each system component. For this example we assume that the servo actuator and sensor can be represented by gains k_a and k_s, for the actuator and sensor, respectively. The equation of motion for an airplane constrained to a pure rolling motion was developed in Chapter 5 and transfer function $\Delta\phi(s)/\Delta\delta_a(s)$ was developed earlier in this chapter. The roll angle to aileron input transfer function for an airplane can be shown to be

$$\frac{\Delta\phi(s)}{\Delta\delta_a(s)} = \frac{L_{\delta_a}}{s(s - L_p)}$$

For this example we consider the sensor to be a perfect device; the feedback path then can be represented as a unity feedback (see Figure 8.15). The forward path transfer function is obtained by combining the elements in the forward path:

$$G(s) = \frac{\Delta\delta_a(s)}{e(s)} \frac{\Delta\phi(s)}{\Delta\delta_a(s)}$$

$$= k_a \frac{L_{\delta_a}}{s(s - L_p)}$$

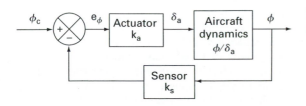

FIGURE 8.14
Roll attitude control concept.

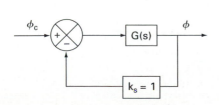

FIGURE 8.15
Simplified roll control system.

The feedback transfer function is idealized as a perfect sensor:

$$H(s) = 1$$

Finally the loop transfer function, $G(s)H(s)$, can be determined by combining the forward and feedback path transfer functions:

$$G(s)H(s) = \frac{k}{s(s - L_p)}$$

where

$$k = k_a L_{\delta_a}$$

$$G(s)H(s) = \frac{k}{s(s + 0.5)}$$

The desired damping ratio of $\zeta = 0.707$ can be achieved with the present control system. The gain for the system is determined by drawing a line from the origin at 45° as indicated in the root locus plot. Recall that the damping ratio was shown to be equal to the following expression:

$$\zeta = \cos \theta$$

where θ is measured from the positive real axis in the counterclockwise direction. Any root intersecting this line has a damping ratio of 0.707. The gain at this point can be determined from the magnitude criteria as follows:

$$\frac{|k|}{|s|\,|s + 0.5|} = 1$$

where $s = -0.25 + 0.25i$.

Substituting s into the magnitude equation and determining the magnitude of each component yields a value for k:

$$k = 0.0139$$

For this example we see that it is possible to select a gain so that the damping ratio requirement is satisfied; however, the undamped natural frequency is much lower than specified:

$$\omega_n = 0.35 \text{ rad/s}$$

Recall that the undamped natural frequency is equal to the radial distance from the origin to the point on the locus as illustrated in the root locus sketch. The problem with this system is the low roll damping. If the roll root, L_p, were greater in the negative sense, the vertical asymptotes of the root locus would shift to the left. This is noted in the root locus sketch (Figure 8.16) by the dotted root locus contour.

L_p, the roll damping root, was shown to be a function of the wing span; therefore, we could make L_p more negative by increasing the wing span of the vehicle. This may be impractical and so we need to look at providing increased damping by means of a stability augmentation system. This can be accomplished by incorporating a rate feedback loop as illustrated in Figure 8.17.

The inner loop transfer function can be expressed as follows:

$$\frac{\Delta p(s)}{\Delta \delta_a(s)} = \frac{L_{\delta_a}}{(s - L_p)}$$

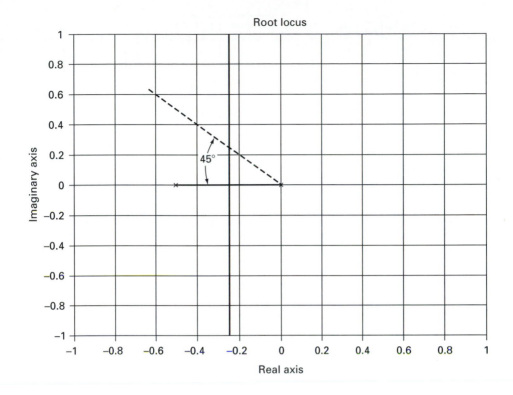

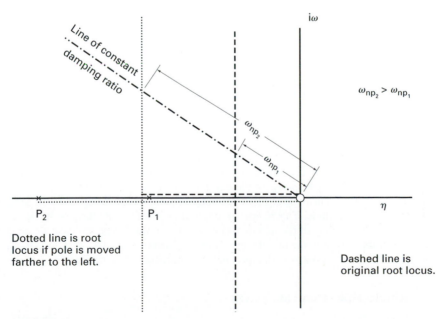

FIGURE 8.16
Root locus plot of $G(s)H(s) = k/s(s + 0.5)$.

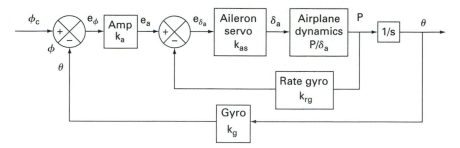

FIGURE 8.17
Rate feedback block diagram.

for the aircraft dynamics, k_{as} for the aileron servo, and $k_{rg} = 1$ for the rate gyro. The inner loop transfer functions are

$$G(s)_{\mathrm{IL}} = \frac{k_{\mathrm{IL}}}{s + 0.5}$$

where

$$k_{\mathrm{IL}} = k_{as}L_{\delta_a}$$

$$H(s)_{\mathrm{IL}} = 1$$

The inner loop can be replaced by the transfer function

$$M(s)_{\mathrm{IL}} = \frac{G(s)_{\mathrm{IL}}}{1 + G(s)_{\mathrm{IL}}H(s)_{\mathrm{IL}}}$$

$$= \frac{k_{\mathrm{IL}}}{s + 0.5 + k_{\mathrm{IL}}}$$

The inner loop gain can be selected to move the augmented roll root farther out along the negative real axis. If the inner loop root is located at $s = -14.14$ the root locus will be shifted to the left so that both the desired damping and undamped natural frequency, ω_n, can be achieved. This means that the inner loop gain k_{IL} must equal 13.64. The loop transfer function $G(s)H(s)_{\mathrm{OL}}$ for the outer loop can be expressed as

$$G(s)H(s) = \frac{k_a(13.64)}{s(s + 14.14)}$$

with the augmentation, provided by the inner loop damping the specifications for ω_n and ζ are both satisfied. The amplifier gain k_a can be shown to equal 7.33. Figure 8.18 shows the time history response of the control system with rate feedback to an initial disturbance in the bank angle of 15°. The control system rapidly brings the vehicle back to a wings level attitude. This simple example illustrates the challenges the designer must face in satisfying all the design specifications. In this particular case we needed to add a compensator to the initial concept in the form of a rate feedback loop to meet both the damping ratio and undamped natural frequency specifications.

8.4.3 Altitude Hold Control System

The altitude of an airplane can be maintained by an altitude hold autopilot. A simplified altitude hold autopilot is shown in Figure 8.19. Basically the autopilot is

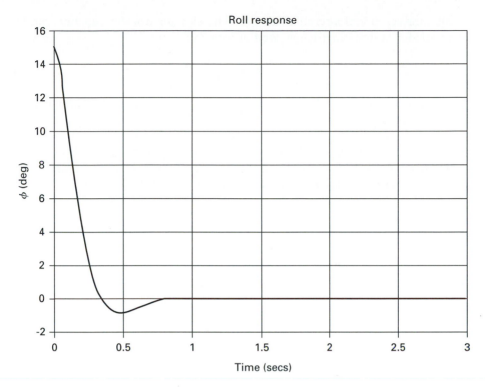

FIGURE 8.18
Time response of roll attitude control system to an initial disturbance in the roll angle.

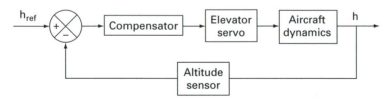

FIGURE 8.19
Altitude hold control system.

constructed to minimize the deviation between the actual altitude and the desired altitude.

To analyze how such an autopilot would function we examine an idealized case. We make the following assumptions: First, the airplane's speed will be controlled by a separate control system; second, we neglect any lateral dynamic effects. With these restrictions we are assuming that the only motion possible is in the vertical plane. The transfer functions necessary for performing this analysis are the elevator servo and aircraft dynamics. The elevator transfer function can be represented as a first-order lag as used previously:

$$\frac{\delta_e}{e} = \frac{k_a}{s + 10}$$

The aircraft dynamics will be represented by the short period approximation developed in Section 8.3.

To examine the altitude hold control system we need to find the transfer function $\Delta h / \Delta \delta_e$. This can be obtained by examining Figure 8.20, which shows the kinematic relationship between the airplane's rate of climb, pitch angle, and angle of attack. From Figure 8.20 we can write the following relationship:

$$\Delta \dot{h} = u_0 \sin(\Delta \theta - \Delta \alpha)$$

For small angles this can be reduced to

$$\Delta \dot{h} = u_0 (\Delta \theta - \Delta \alpha)$$

Now we can find $\Delta h / \Delta \delta_e$ as follows:

$$s \Delta h(s) = u_0 [\Delta \theta(s) - \Delta \alpha(s)]$$

or

$$\Delta h(s) = \frac{u_0}{s} [\Delta \theta(s) - \Delta \alpha(s)]$$

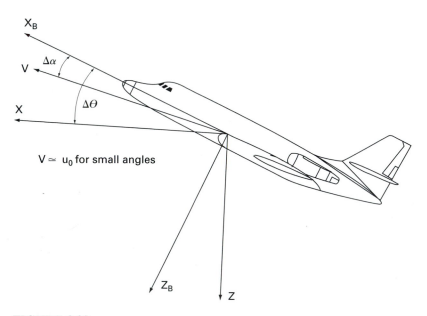

FIGURE 8.20
Kinematic relationship for determining vertical rate of climb.

and on dividing by $\Delta\delta_e$ we obtain the desired transfer function relationship:

$$\frac{\Delta h(s)}{\Delta\delta_e(s)} = \frac{u_0}{s}\left[\frac{\Delta\theta(s)}{\Delta\delta_e(s)} - \frac{\Delta\alpha(s)}{\Delta\delta_e(s)}\right]$$

The transfer function $\Delta\theta(s)/\Delta\delta_e(s)$ can be obtained from $\Delta q(s)/\Delta\delta_e(s)$ in the following way:

$$\Delta q = \Delta\dot{\theta}$$

therefore,

$$\Delta q(s) = s\,\Delta\theta(s)$$

or

$$\frac{\Delta\theta(s)}{\Delta\delta_e(s)} = \frac{1}{s}\frac{\Delta q(s)}{\Delta\delta_e(s)}$$

$$= \frac{A_q s + B_q}{s(As^2 + Bs + C)}$$

The transfer function $\Delta\alpha(s)/\Delta\delta_e(s)$ was developed earlier as

$$\frac{\Delta\alpha(s)}{\Delta\delta_e(s)} = \frac{A_\alpha s + B_\alpha}{As^2 + Bs + C}$$

where the coefficients in both the transfer function $\Delta\theta(s)/\Delta\delta_e(s)$ and $\Delta\alpha(s)/\Delta\delta_e(s)$ are given the Table 8.3.

EXAMPLE PROBLEM 8.3. A STOL transport has been modified to include direct-lift control surfaces. Unlike conventional high-lift flaps, the direct-lift flaps can be rotated up and down to increase or decrease the lift force on the wing. In this example, we are going to design an altitude hold control system that uses the direct-lift control surfaces. To simplify our analysis we assume that the airplane's velocity and pitch attitude are controlled by separate autopilots. The aerodynamic characteristics of the STOL airplane and the desired performance expected of the altitude autopilot follow:

Z_α ft/s²	Z_{δ_f} ft/s²	u_0 ft/s
-560	-50	400

Autopilot performance specifications are a settling time, $t_s < 2.5$ s, and a damping ratio, $\zeta = 0.6$.

Solution. One potential concept for controlling the altitude of the airplane is given in Figure 8.21. The transfer functions for each element of the control system is described next. The amplifier transfer function is a gain, k_a, the direct-lift servo is modeled as a first-order lag, and the altitude sensor is assumed to be a perfect sensor, which gives us a unity feedback system:

$$\frac{e_h}{e_s} = k_a$$

$$\frac{\delta_f}{e_s} = \frac{-10}{s + 10}$$

The transfer function for the aircraft dynamics can be obtained from the equation of motion in the vertical direction. Recall that we have assumed that the speed and pitch

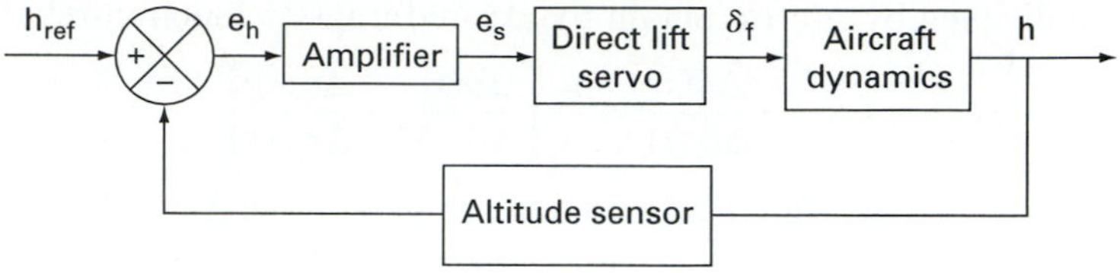

FIGURE 8.21
Altitude control concept.

attitude of the airplane are held at some desired values by separate autopilots. The equation of motion in the vertical direction is given by

$$\sum \text{Forces in vertical direction} = m \frac{dw}{dt}$$

or
$$W + Z = m \frac{dw}{dt}$$

Expressing the variables in terms of a reference value and a perturbation yields

$$W + Z_0 + \Delta Z = m \frac{d}{dt} (w_0 + \Delta w)$$

but $W + Z_0 = 0$ and $w_0 = 0$; for level equilibrium flight therefore,

$$\Delta Z = m \, \Delta \dot{w}$$

The change in the aerodynamic force ΔZ is assumed to be only a function of Δw and $\Delta \delta_f$, that is,

$$\Delta Z = \frac{\partial Z}{\partial w} \Delta w + \frac{\partial Z}{\partial \delta_f} \Delta \delta_f$$

Substituting into the differential equation yields

$$\Delta \dot{w} = Z_w \, \Delta w + Z_{\delta_f} \, \Delta \delta_f$$

where
$$Z_w = \frac{\partial Z/\partial w}{m}, \qquad Z_{\delta_f} = \frac{\partial Z/\partial \delta_f}{m}$$

Recall that Z_w and Z_α are related in the following manner:

$$Z_w = \frac{\partial Z/\partial w}{m} = \frac{1}{u_0} \frac{\partial Z/\partial (w/u_0)}{m} = \frac{1}{u_0} Z_\alpha$$

The transfer function $\Delta h / \Delta \delta_f$ now can be obtained:

$$\frac{\Delta w(s)}{\Delta \delta_f(s)} = \frac{Z_{\delta_f}}{s - Z_w}$$

but $\dot{h} = -\Delta w$; therefore,

$$\frac{\Delta h(s)}{\Delta \delta_f(s)} = -\frac{1}{s} \frac{Z_{\delta_f}}{(s - Z_w)}$$

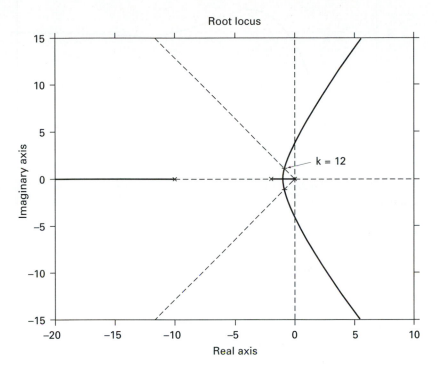

FIGURE 8.22
Root locus plot of $G(s)H(s)$, altitude hold control system.

Substituting the aerodynamic data for the STOL transport yields

$$\frac{\Delta h(s)}{\Delta \delta_f(s)} = -\frac{50}{s(s + 1.4)}$$

The forward path transfer function is

$$G(s) = \frac{k}{s(s + 1.4)(s + 10)}$$

where $k = k_a(-10)(-50) = 500 \, k_a$.

  The root locus plot of $G(s)H(s)$ is shown in Figure 8.22. Although the desired damping ratio $\zeta = 0.6$ can be achieved, the settling time is greater than 2.5 s. The closed-loop system response to a unit step change in altitude is shown in Figure 8.23. To improve the system performance we need to include some form of compensation. A lead circuit in the forward path can be used to improve the system performance. Figure 8.24 shows the root locus plot of $G(s)H(s)$ with the addition of a lead circuit

$$\text{T.F.} = \frac{s + a}{s + b} \qquad a < b$$

The zero of the lead circuit was positioned just to the left of the pole at $s = -1.4$. With the addition of the lead circuit the root locus plot is shifted to the left compared to the uncompensated system. For the compensated system we can meet both the damping ratio and settling time specification (Figure 8.25).

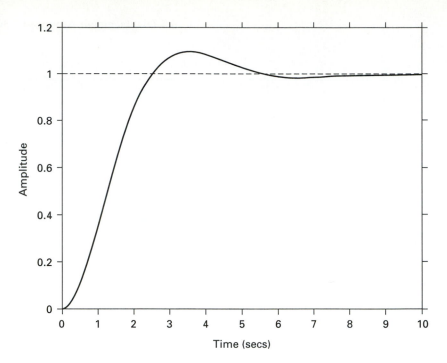

FIGURE 8.23
Closed-loop response to a step input altitude hold control system.

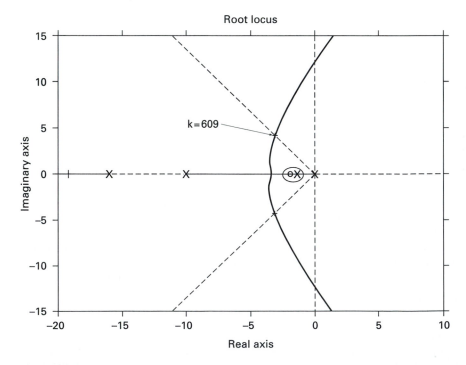

FIGURE 8.24
Root locus plot of compensated altitude hold control system.

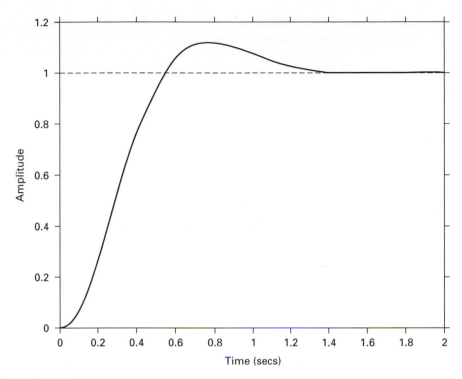

FIGURE 8.25
Closed-loop response to a step input for an altitude hold control system with a compensator.

8.4.4 Velocity Hold Control System

The forward speed of an airplane can be controlled by changing the thrust produced by the propulsion system. The function of the speed control system is to maintain some desired flight speed. This is accomplished by changing the engine throttle setting to increase or decrease the engine thrust. Figure 8.26 is a simplified concept for a speed control system described in [8.3]. The components that make up the system include a compensator, engine throttle, aircraft dynamics, and a feedback path consisting of the velocity and acceleration feedback.

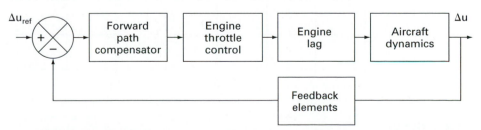

FIGURE 8.26
A block diagram for a speed control system.

EXAMPLE PROBLEM 8.4. Examine the performance characteristics of a speed control autopilot similar to the one shown in Figure 8.26 for the STOL transport included in Appendix B. The transfer functions for the throttle servo, engine lag, forward path compensation, and feedback elements follow:

$$G_{\text{throttle}}(s) = \frac{10}{s + 10}$$

$$G(s)_{\text{engine lag}} = \frac{1}{s + 0.1}$$

$$G_c(s) = 1 + 0.1/s = \frac{k_a(s + 0.1)}{s}$$

$$H(s) = 10s + 1$$

Solution. The aircraft dynamics can be approximated by using the long-period or phugoid approximation developed earlier in this chapter:

$$X_{\delta_T} = 0.038 \, \frac{\text{ft/s}^2}{\text{deg}} \qquad Z_{\delta_T} = 0$$

Substituting these values into the aircraft transfer function yields

$$\frac{\Delta u}{\Delta \delta_T} = \frac{0.038s}{s^2 + 0.039s + 0.039s + 0.053}$$

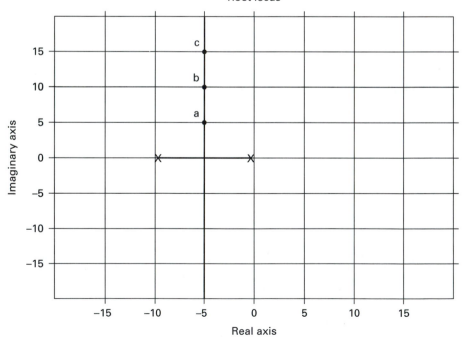

Root locus

FIGURE 8.27

Root locus plot $G(s)H(s) = \dfrac{3.8k_a(s + 0.1)}{(s + 10)(s^2 + 0.039s + 0.053)}$.

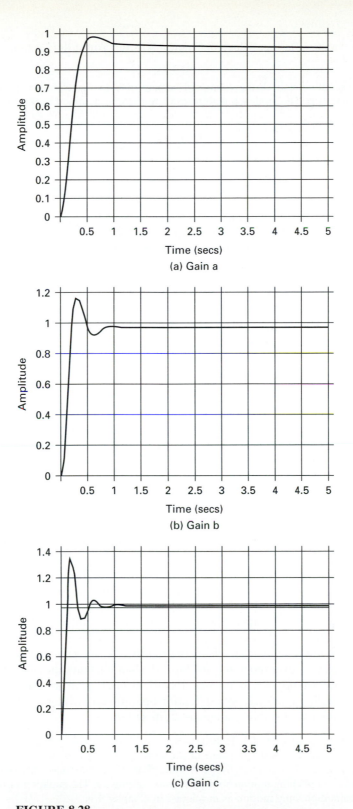

FIGURE 8.28
Response of speed control system to a unit step command for
different gains.

For this autopilot both the change in velocity and the acceleration are used in the feedback path. The feedback path transfer function is assumed to be of the form that follows:

$$H(s) = 10s + 1$$

The loop transfer function, $G(s)H(s)$, follows:

$$G(s)H(s) = \frac{3.8k_a(s + 0.1)}{(s + 10)(s^2 + 0.039s + 0.053)}$$

The root locus plot of the loop transfer function is shown in Figure 8.27.

Figure 8.28 shows the response of the speed control system to a unit step for several different values of the amplifier gain, k_a. The three gains are indicated on Figure 8.27. Note that for a gain corresponding to a damping ratio of 0.707 the response is very fast but there is a steady-state error. On the other hand, the steady-state error can be reduced by increasing the gain. However, larger gains mean a lower damping ratio and the response has a larger overshoot. To improve the performance of this system an additional compensator should be considered.

8.5
STABILITY AUGMENTATION

Another application of automatic devices is to provide artificial stability for an airplane that has undesirable flying characteristics. Such control systems are commonly called stability augmentation systems (SAS).

As we showed earlier, the inherent stability of an airplane depends on the aerodynamic stability derivatives. The magnitude of the derivatives affects both the damping and frequency of the longitudinal and lateral motions of an airplane. Furthermore, it was shown that the stability derivatives were a function of the airplane's aerodynamic and geometric characteristics. For a particular flight regime it would be possible to design an airplane to possess desirable flying qualities. For example, we know that the longitudinal stability coefficients are a function of the horizontal tail volume ratio. Therefore we could select a tail size and or location so that C_{m_α} and C_{m_q} provide the proper damping and frequency for the short-period mode. However, for an airplane that will fly throughout an extended flight envelope, one can expect the stability to vary significantly, owing primarily to changes in the vehicle's configuration (lowering of flaps and landing gear) or Mach and Reynolds number effects on the stability coefficients. Because the stability derivatives vary over the flight envelope, the handling qualities also will change. Obviously, we would like to provide the flight crew with an airplane that has desirable handling qualities over its entire operational envelope. This is accomplished by employing stability augmentation systems.

EXAMPLE PROBLEM 8.5. To help understand how a stability augmentation system works, we shall consider the case of an airplane having poor short-period dynamic characteristics. In our analysis we assume that the aircraft has only one degree of freedom—a pitching motion about the center of gravity. The equation of motion for a constrained pitching motion as developed in Chapter 4 is

$$\ddot{\theta} - (M_q + M_{\dot{\alpha}})\dot{\theta} + M_\alpha\theta = M_\delta\delta$$

The damping ratio and undamped natural frequency are given by

$$\zeta_{sp} = -(C_{m_q} + C_{m_{\dot{\alpha}}})\frac{\rho u_0 S \bar{c}^2}{4 I_y}/(2\omega_{nsp})$$

$$\omega_{nsp}^2 = -C_{m_\alpha}\frac{\rho u_0^2 S \bar{c}}{2 I_y}$$

If the aerodynamic and inertial characteristics of a business jet during cruise are such that the preceding equations have the numerical values

$$\ddot{\theta} + 0.071\dot{\theta} + 5.49\theta = -6.71\delta_e$$

then the damping ratio and frequency are given by

$$\zeta_{sp} = 0.015 \qquad \omega_{nsp} = 2.34 \text{ rad/s}$$

For these short-period characteristics the airplane has poor flying qualities. On examining the flying quality specification, we see that to provide level 1 flying qualities the short-period damping must be increased so that $\zeta_{sp} > 0.3$.

One means of improving the damping of the system is to provide rate feedback, as illustrated in Figure 8.29. This type of system is called a pitch rate damper. The stability augmentation system provides artificial damping without interfering with the pilot's control input. This is accomplished by producing an elevator deflection in proportion to the pitch rate and adding it to the pilot's control input:

$$\delta_e = \delta_{e_p} + k\dot{\theta}$$

where δ_{e_p} is that part of the elevator deflection created by the pilot. A rate gyro is used to measure the pitch rate and creates an electrical signal that is used to provide elevator deflections. If we substitute the expression for the elevator angle back into the equation of motion, we obtain

$$\ddot{\theta} + (0.071 + 6.71k)\dot{\theta} + 5.49\theta = -6.71\delta_{e_p}$$

Comparing this equation with the standard form of a second-order system yields

$$2\zeta\omega_n = (0.071 + 6.71k) \qquad \text{and} \qquad \omega_n^2 = 5.49$$

The short-period damping ratio is now a function of the gyro gain k and can be selected so that the damping ratio will provide level 1 handling qualities. For example, if k is chosen to be 0.2, then the damping ratio $\zeta = 0$.

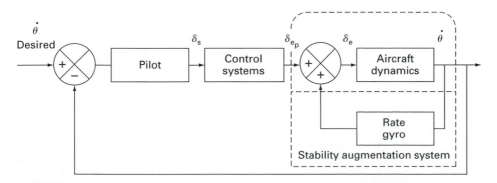

FIGURE 8.29
Stability augmentation system using pitch rate feedback.

8.6
INSTRUMENT LANDING

With the advent of the instrument landing system (ILS), aircraft became able to operate safely in weather conditions with restricted visibility. The instrument landing system is composed of ground-based signal transmitters and onboard receiving equipment. The ground-based equipment includes radio transmitters for the localizer, glide path, and marker beacons. The equipment on the airplane consists of receivers for detecting the signals and indicators to display the information.

The basic function of the ILS is to provide pilots with information that will permit them to guide the airplane down through the clouds to a point where the pilot re-establishes visual sighting of the runway. In a completely automatic landing, the autopilot guides the airplane all the way down to touchdown and roll out.

Before addressing the autoland system, we briefly review the basic ideas behind the ILS equipment. To guide the airplane down toward the runway, the guidance must be lateral and vertical. The localizer beam is used to position the aircraft on a trajectory so that it will intercept the centerline of the runway. The transmitter radiates at a frequency in a band of 108–112 MHz. The purpose of this beam is to locate the airplane relative to a centerline of the runway. This is accomplished by creating azimuth guidance signals that are detected by the onboard localizer receiver. The azimuth guidance signal is created by superimposing a 90-Hz signal directed toward the left and a 150-Hz signal directed to the right on the carrier signal. Figure 8.30 shows an instrument landing localizer signal. When the aircraft is flying directly along the projected extension of the runway centerline, both superimposed signals are detected with equal strength. However, when the aircraft deviates say to the right of centerline, the 150-Hz signal is stronger. The receiver in the cockpit detects the difference and directs the pilot to fly the aircraft to the left by way of a vertical bar on the ILS indicator that shows the airplane to the right of the runway. If the airplane deviates to the left, the indicator will deflect the bar to the left of the runway marker.

The glide path or glide slope beam is located near the runway threshold and radiates at a frequency in the range 329.3–335.0 MHz. Its purpose is to guide the aircraft down a predetermined descent path. The glide slope is typically an angle

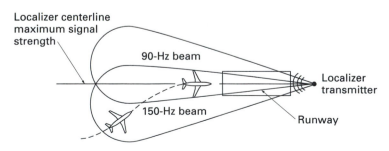

FIGURE 8.30
A localizer beam system.

of 2.5–3° to the horizontal. Figure 8.31 shows a schematic of the glide path beam. Note that the glide path angle has been exaggerated in this sketch. As in the case of the localizer, two signals are superimposed on the carrier frequency to create an error signal if the aircraft is either high or low with respect to the glide path. This usually is indicated by a horizontal bar on the ILS indicator that moves up or down with respect to the glide path indicator. The marker beacons are used to locate the aircraft relative to the runway. Two markers are used. One, located 4 nautical miles from the runway, is called the outer marker. The second, or inner, marker is located 3500 ft from the runway threshold. The beams are directed vertically into the descent path at a frequency of 75 MHz. The signals are coded, and when the airplane flies overhead the signals are detected by an onboard receiver. The pilot is alerted to the passage over a marker beacon by both an audio signal and visual signal. The audio signal is heard over the aircraft's communication system and the visual signal is presented by way of a colored indicator light on the instrument panel.

In flying the airplane in poor visibility, the pilot uses the ILS equipment in the following manner. The pilot descends from cruise altitude under direction of ground control to an altitude of approximately 1200 ft above the ground. The pilot then is vectored so that the aircraft intercepts the localizer at a distance of at least 6 nautical miles from the runway. The pilot positions the airplane using the localizer display so that it is on a heading toward the runway centerline. When the aircraft approaches the outer marker, the glide path signal is intercepted. The aircraft is placed in its final approach configuration and the pilot flies down the glide path slope. The pilot follows the beams by maneuvering the airplane so that the vertical and horizontal bars on the ILS indicator show no deviation from the desired flight path. The ILS system does not guide the aircraft all the way to touchdown. At some point during the approach the pilot must look away from the instruments and outside the window to establish a visual reference for the final portion of the

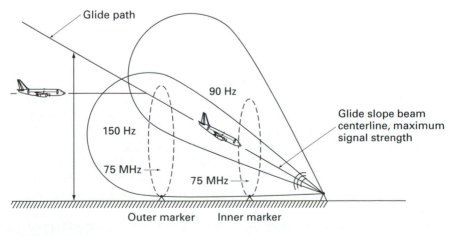

FIGURE 8.31
A glide slope beam system.

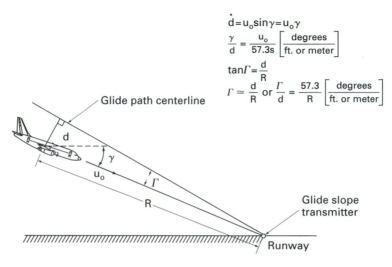

FIGURE 8.32
An airplane displaced from the glide path.

landing. The pilot may take 5 or 6 seconds to establish an outside visual reference. Obviously the pilot must do this at sufficient altitude and distance from the runway so that if the runway is not visible the pilot can abort the landing. This gives rise to a "decision height," which is a predetermined height above the runway that the pilot cannot go beyond without visually sighting the runway.

The ILS as outlined in the previous paragraphs is an integral part of a fully automatic landing system. To be able to land an airplane with no visual reference to the runway requires an automatic landing system that can intercept the localizer and glide path signals, then guide the airplane down the glide path to some pre-selected altitude at which the aircraft's descent rate is reduced and the airplane executes a flare maneuver so that it touches down with an acceptable sink rate. The autoland system comprises a number of automatic control systems, which include a localizer and glide path coupler, attitude and airspeed control, and an automatic flare control system.

Figure 8.32 shows an airplane descending toward the runway. The airplane shown is below the intended glide path. The deviation d of the airplane from the glide path is the normal distance of the airplane above or below the desired glide path. The angle Γ is the difference between the actual and desired glide path angle and R is the radial distance of the airplane from the glide slope transmitter. To maintain the airplane along the glide path, one must make Γ equal 0. Figure 8.33 is a conceptual design of an autopilot that will keep the airplane on the glide path. The transfer functions for d and Γ are obtained from the geometry and are noted in Figure 8.32.

As the airplane descends along the glide path, its pitch attitude and speed must be controlled. This again is accomplished by means of a pitch displacement and speed control autopilot. The pitch displacement autopilot would be conceptually

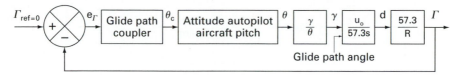

FIGURE 8.33
An automatic glide path control system.

the same as the one discussed earlier in this chapter. Figure 8.34 shows an automatic control system that could be used to maintain a constant speed along the flight path. The difference in flight speed is used to produce a proportional displacement of the engine throttle so that the speed difference is reduced. The component of the system labeled compensation is a device incorporated into the design so that the closed-loop system can meet the desired performance specifications. Finally, as the airplane gets very close to the runway threshold, the glide path control system is disengaged and a flare maneuver is executed. Figure 8.35 illustrates the flare maneuver just prior to touchdown. The flare maneuver is needed

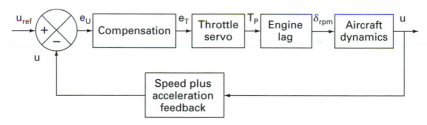

FIGURE 8.34
An automatic speed control system.

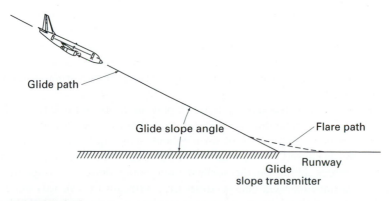

FIGURE 8.35
A flare maneuver.

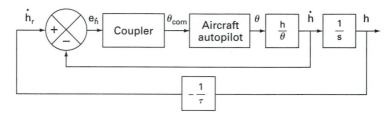

FIGURE 8.36
An automatic flare control system.

to decrease the vertical descent rate to a level consistent with the ability of the landing gear to dissipate the energy of the impact at landing. An automatic flare control system is shown in Figure 8.36. A detailed discussion of the autoland system is provided by Blakelock [8.3].

8.7
SUMMARY

In this chapter we examined briefly the use of an automatic control system that can be used to reduce the pilot's workload, guide the airplane to a safe landing in poor visibility, and provide stability augmentation to improve the flying qualities of airplanes with poor stability characteristics. Additional applications of automatic control technology include load alleviation and flutter suppression.

Load alleviation can be achieved by using active wing controls to reduce the wing-bending moments. By reducing the wing design loads through active controls, the designer can increase the wing span or reduce the structural weight of the wing. Increasing the span for a given wing area improves the aerodynamic efficiency of the wing; that is, it increases the lift-to-drag ratio. The improvement in aerodynamic efficiency and the potential for lower wing weight result in better cruise fuel efficiency.

Stability augmentation systems also can be used to improve airplane performance without degrading the vehicle's flying qualities. If the horizontal and vertical tail control surfaces are used in an active control system, the tail area can be reduced. Reducing the static stability results in smaller trim drag forces. The combination of smaller tail areas and reduced static stability yields a lower drag contribution from the tail surfaces, which will improve the performance characteristics of the airplane.

Another area in which active control can play an important role is in suppressing flutter. Flutter is an unstable structural motion that can lead to structural failure of any of the major components of an airplane: wing, tail, fuselage, or control surfaces. Flutter is caused by the interaction between structural vibration and the aerodynamic forces acting on the surface undergoing flutter. During flutter the aerodynamic surface extracts energy from the airstream to feed this undesirable motion. An automatic control system incorporating active controls can be designed to prevent flutter from occurring by controlling the structural vibration.

PROBLEMS

Problems that require the use of a computer have the capital letter C after the problem number.

8.1(C). A roll control system is shown in Figure P8.1. Sketch the root locus diagram for this system.
  (a) Determine the value of the gain, k, so that control system has a damping ratio of $\zeta = 0.707$.
  (b) What is the steady-state error for a step and ramp input?
  (c) Sketch the response of the control system to a 5° step change in bank angle command.
  (d) Repeat this problem using control synthesis software such as MATLAB.

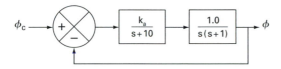

FIGURE P8.1

8.2(C). Use a rate feedback inner loop to improve the transient response of the control system in Problem 8.1. The system damping ratio is to remain at $\zeta = 0.707$.

8.3(C). For the pitch rate feedback control system shown in Figure P8.3, determine the gain necessary to improve the system characteristics so that the control system has the following performance: $\zeta = 0.3$, $\omega_n = 2.0$ rad/s. Assume that the aircraft characteristics are the same as given in Figure 8.9 in Section 8.4.

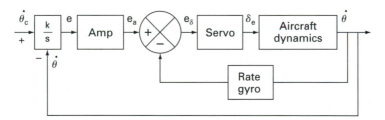

FIGURE P8.3

8.4(C). A simplified pitch control system is shown in Figure P8.4. Design a PID controller for this system and plot the response of the system to a 5° step change in the commanded pitch attitude.

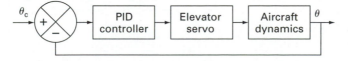

FIGURE P8.4

PID	$k_p + \dfrac{k_i}{s} + k_d s$
Elevator servo	$-\dfrac{10}{s + 10}$
Aircraft dynamic	$\dfrac{-3}{s^2 + 3s + 4.0}$

8.5(C). The Wright Flyer was statically and dynamically unstable. However, because the Wright brothers incorporated sufficient control authority into their design they were able to fly their airplane successfully. Although the airplane was difficult to fly, the combination of the pilot and airplane could be a stable system. In [8.5] the closed-loop pilot is represented as a pure gain, k_p, and the pitch attitude to canard deflection is given as follows:

$$\frac{\theta}{\delta_c} = \frac{11.0(s + 0.5)(s + 3.0)}{(s^2 + 0.72s + 1.44)(s^2 + 5.9s - 11.9)}$$

Determine the root locus plot of the closed-loop system shown in Figure P8.5. For what range of pilot gain is the system stable?

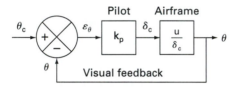

FIGURE P8.5

8.6(C). The block diagram for a pitch attitude control system for a spacecraft is shown in Figure P8.6a. Control of the spacecraft is achieved through thrusters located on the side of the spacecraft as illustrated in Figure P8.6b.
  (a) Determine the root locus plot for the control system if the rate loop is disconnected. Comment on the potential performance of this system for controlling the pitch attitude.
  (b) Determine the rate gain k_{rg} and the outer loop gyro gain k_g so that the system has a damping ratio $\zeta = 0.707$ and a settling time, $t_s = 1.5$ s.

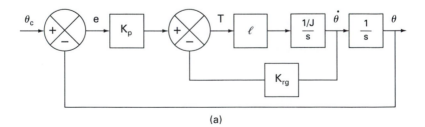

(a)

FIGURE P8.6

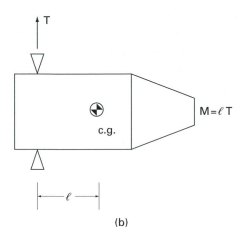

T

M = ℓ T

c.g.

|← ℓ →|

(b)

FIGURE P8.6 (continued)

8.7(C). A wind-tunnel model is constrained so that it can rotate only about the z axis; that is, pure yawing motion. The equation of motion for a constrained yawing motion was shown in Chapter 5 to be as follows:

$$\Delta\ddot{\psi} - N_r\,\Delta\dot{\psi} + N_\beta\,\Delta\psi = N_\delta\,\Delta\delta_r$$

where $N_\beta = 2.0 \text{ s}^{-2}$, $N_r = -0.5 \text{ s}^{-1}$ and $N_{\delta_r} = -10 \text{ s}^{-2}$. Design a heading control system so that the model has the following closed-loop performance characteristics:

$$\zeta = 0.6$$

$$t_s \leq 2.5$$

Assume that the rudder servo transfer function can be represented as

$$\frac{\Delta\delta_r}{e} = \frac{k}{s + 10}$$

8.8(C). Every pilot or airline passenger has encountered a rough flight due to atmospheric turbulence. The bumpy ride is due to the airplane encountering a vertical gust field. When an airplane encounters a vertical gust the effective angle of attack of the wing is changed, causing the airplane to accelerate in the vertical direction. This unwanted motion can be eliminated by means of a gust alleviation system. If the wing lift can be controlled, the acceleration due to the gust can be attenuated. One means of controlling the wing lift is by using direct lift controls. Basically, direct lift control surfaces are wing flaps that can be rotated up or down to either decrease or increase the wing lift. Consider a wind-tunnel model constrained to motion in only the vertical direction; that is, pure plunging motion. Also assume that the model is equipped with direct lift flaps. See Example Problem 8.3. Design a control system for the wind-tunnel model so that the vertical velocity is held near 0. Assume the direct lift actuator can be represented by the transfer function

$$\frac{\delta_f}{e} = \frac{k}{s + 10}$$

8.9(C). Design a control system for the wind tunnel model of Problem 8.8 to maintain a constant vertical position in the wind tunnel.

REFERENCES

8.1. Bollay, W. "Aerodynamic Stability and Automatic Control." *Journal of the Aeronautical Sciences,* 18, no. 9 (1951), pp. 569–617.

8.2. McRuer, D.; I. Ashkenas; and D. Graham. *Aircraft Dynamics and Automatic Control,* Princeton, N.J.: Princeton University Press, 1973.

8.3. Blakelock, J. H. *Automatic Control of Aircraft and Missiles.* New York: Wiley, 1991.

8.4. Pallett, E. H. J. *Automatic Flight Control,* London: Granada Publishing, 1979.

8.5. Culick, F. E. C. "Building a 1903 Wright Flyer—by Committee," *AIAA Paper* 88-0094, 1988.

CHAPTER 9

Modern Control Theory

9.1
INTRODUCTION

In Chapters 7 and 8, the design of feedback control systems was accomplished using the root locus technique and Bode methods developed by Evans and Bode, respectively. These techniques are very useful in designing many practical control systems. However, the design of a control system using either of the techniques essentially is by trial and error. The major advantage of these design procedures is their simplicity and ease of use. This advantage disappears quickly as the complexity of the system increases.

With the rapid development of high-speed computers during the recent decades, a new approach to control system design has evolved. This new approach, commonly called modern control theory, permits a more systematic approach to control system design. In modern control theory, the control system is specified as a system of first-order differential equations. By formulating the problem in this manner, the control system designer can fully exploit the digital computer for solving complex control problems. Another advantage of modern control theory is that optimization techniques can be applied to design optimal control systems. To comprehend this theory fully one needs to have a good understanding of matrix algebra; a brief discussion of matrix algebra is included in Appendix C.

It is not possible in a single chapter to present a thorough discussion of modern control theory. Our purpose is to expose the reader to some of the concepts of modern control theory and then apply the procedures to the design of aircraft autopilots. It is hoped that this brief discussion will provide the reader with an appreciation of modern control theory and its application to the design of aircraft flight control systems. Additional background material on modern control theory can be found in the references included at the end of this chapter [9.1–9.5].

9.2
STATE-SPACE MODELING

The state-space approach to control system analysis and design is a time-domain method. As was shown in Chapters 4 and 5, the equations of motion can be written easily in the state-space form. The application of state variable techniques to control problems is called modern control theory. The state equations are simply first-order differential equations that govern the dynamics of the system being analyzed. It should be noted that any higher-order differential equation can be decomposed into a set of first-order differential equations. This will be shown later by an illustration.

In the mathematical sense, the state variables and state equation completely describe the system. The definition of state variables is as follows. The state variables of a system are a minimum set of variables $x_1(t) \cdots x_n(t)$ that, when known at time t_0 and along with the input, are sufficient to determine the state of the system at any other time $t > t_0$. State variables should not be confused with the output of the system. An output variable is one that can be measured, but state variables do not always satisfy this condition. The output, as we will see shortly, is defined as a function of the state variables.

Once a physical system has been reduced to a set of differential equations, the equation can be rewritten in a convenient matrix form:

$$\dot{\mathbf{x}} = \mathbf{Ax} + \mathbf{B\eta} \tag{9.1}$$

The output of the system is expressed in terms of the state and control inputs as follows:

$$\mathbf{y} = \mathbf{Cx} + \mathbf{D\eta} \tag{9.2}$$

The state, control, and output vectors are defined as follows:

$$\mathbf{x} = \begin{bmatrix} x_1(t) \\ x_2(t) \\ \vdots \\ x_n(t) \end{bmatrix} \quad \text{State vector } (n \times 1) \tag{9.3}$$

$$\mathbf{\eta} = \begin{bmatrix} \delta_1(t) \\ \delta_2(t) \\ \vdots \\ \delta_p(t) \end{bmatrix} \quad \text{Control or input vector } (p \times 1) \tag{9.4}$$

$$\mathbf{y} = \begin{bmatrix} y_1(t) \\ y_2(t) \\ \vdots \\ y_q(t) \end{bmatrix} \quad \text{Output vector } (q \times 1) \tag{9.5}$$

The matrices **A**, **B**, **C**, and **D** are defined in the following manner:

$$\mathbf{A} = \begin{bmatrix} a_{11} & a_{12} & \cdots & a_{1n} \\ a_{21} & & & \vdots \\ \vdots & & & \vdots \\ a_{n1} & a_{n2} & \cdots & a_{nn} \end{bmatrix} \qquad \text{Plant matrix } (n \times n) \qquad (9.6)$$

$$\mathbf{B} = \begin{bmatrix} b_{11} & b_{12} & \cdots & b_{1p} \\ b_{21} & & & \vdots \\ \vdots & & & \\ b_{n1} & b_{n2} & \cdots & b_{np} \end{bmatrix} \qquad \text{Control or input matrix } (n \times p) \qquad (9.7)$$

$$\mathbf{C} = \begin{bmatrix} c_{11} & c_{12} & \cdots & c_{1n} \\ c_{21} & & & \vdots \\ \vdots & & & \\ c_{q1} & & & c_{qn} \end{bmatrix} \qquad (q \times n) \qquad (9.8)$$

$$\mathbf{D} = \begin{bmatrix} d_{11} & d_{12} & \cdots & d_{1p} \\ d_{21} & & & \vdots \\ \vdots & & & \\ d_{q1} & & & a_{qp} \end{bmatrix} \qquad (q \times p) \qquad (9.9)$$

Figure 9.1 is a block diagram representation of the state equation given by Equations (9.1) and (9.2).

The state equations are a set of first-order differential equations. The matrices **A** and **B** may be either constant or functions of time. For the application we are considering, namely, aircraft equations of motion, the matrices are composed of an array of constants. The constants making up either the **A** or **B** matrix are the stability and control derivatives of the airplane. It should be noted that if the governing differential equations are of higher order they can be reduced to a system of first-order differential equations.

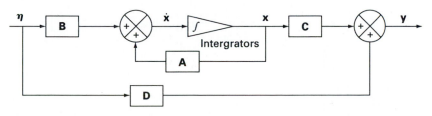

FIGURE 9.1
The linear state equations.

For example, suppose that the physical system being modeled can be described by an nth-order differential equation:

$$\frac{d^n c(t)}{dt^n} + a_1 \frac{d^{n-1} c(t)}{dt^{n-1}} + a_2 \frac{d^{n-2} c(t)}{dt^{n-2}} + \cdots + a_{n-1} \frac{dc(t)}{dt} + a_n c(t) = r(t) \quad (9.10)$$

The variables $c(t)$ and $r(t)$ are the output and input variables, respectively. This differential equation can be reduced to a set of first-order differential equations by defining the state variables as follows:

$$
\begin{aligned}
x_1(t) &= c(t) \\
x_2(t) &= \frac{dc(t)}{dt} \\
&\vdots \\
x_n(t) &= \frac{d^{n-1} c(t)}{dt^{n-1}}
\end{aligned}
\quad (9.11)
$$

The state equations can now be written as

$$
\begin{aligned}
\dot{x}_1(t) &= x_2(t) \\
\dot{x}_2(t) &= x_3(t) \\
&\vdots \\
\dot{x}_n(t) &= a_n x_1(t) - a_{n-1} x_2(t) - \cdots - a_1 x_n(t) + r(t)
\end{aligned}
\quad (9.12)
$$

The last equation is obtained by solving for the highest-order derivative in the original differential equation. Rewriting the equation in the state vector form yields

$$\dot{\mathbf{x}} = \mathbf{A}\mathbf{x} + \mathbf{B}\boldsymbol{\eta} \quad (9.13)$$

where

$$\mathbf{A} = \begin{bmatrix}
0 & 1 & 0 & 0 & 0 & \cdots & 0 \\
0 & 0 & 1 & 0 & 0 & & 0 \\
0 & 0 & 0 & 1 & 0 & & 0 \\
\vdots & \vdots & \vdots & \vdots & \vdots & & \vdots \\
0 & 0 & 0 & 0 & 0 & & 1 \\
-a_n & -a_{n-1} & -a_{n-2} & -a_{n-3} & -a_{n-4} & \cdots & -a_1
\end{bmatrix} \quad (9.14)$$

$$\mathbf{B} = \begin{bmatrix} 0 \\ 0 \\ 0 \\ 0 \\ \vdots \\ 1 \end{bmatrix} \quad (9.15)$$

and the output equation is

$$y = \mathbf{Cx} \tag{9.16}$$

where

$$\mathbf{C} = [1 \quad 0 \quad 0 \quad \cdots \quad 0] \tag{9.17}$$

For this particular differential equation the output vector is not a function of the control vector, therefore, the $\mathbf{D}$ matrix is a null matrix; that is, a matrix consisting of only zeroes. For the problems we consider in this chapter the $\mathbf{D}$ matrix will be a null matrix.

In most cases the physical system being analyzed is described by a number of differential equations. The state-space formulation can be applied to a set of equations and will be illustrated by an example.

EXAMPLE PROBLEM 9.1. Rewrite the following differential equations in state-space form:

$$\frac{d^2 c_1}{dt^2} + 5 \frac{d c_1}{dt} + 4 c_2 = r_1$$

$$\frac{d c_2}{dt} + \frac{d c_1}{dt} + c_1 + 3 c_2 = r_2$$

Solution. Let the states be

$$x_1 = c_1$$

$$x_2 = \frac{d c_1}{dt}$$

$$x_3 = c_2$$

Taking the derivative of the states yields

$$\dot{x}_1 = \frac{d c_1}{dt} = x_2$$

$$\dot{x}_2 = \frac{d^2 c_1}{dt^2} = -5 \frac{d c_1}{dt} - 4 c_2 + r_1$$

$$\dot{x}_2 = -5 x_2 - 4 x_3 + r_1$$

$$\dot{x}_3 = \frac{d c_2}{dt} = -\frac{d c_1}{dt} - c_1 - 3 c_2 + r_2$$

$$\dot{x}_3 = -x_2 - x_1 - 3 x_3 + r_2$$

These equations can now be put into the state-space form, $\dot{\mathbf{x}} = \mathbf{Ax} + \mathbf{B\eta}$:

$$\begin{bmatrix} \dot{x}_1 \\ \dot{x}_2 \\ \dot{x}_3 \end{bmatrix} = \begin{bmatrix} 0 & 1 & 0 \\ 0 & -5 & -4 \\ -1 & -1 & -3 \end{bmatrix} \begin{bmatrix} x_1 \\ x_2 \\ x_3 \end{bmatrix} + \begin{bmatrix} 0 & 0 \\ 1 & 0 \\ 0 & 1 \end{bmatrix} \begin{bmatrix} r_1 \\ r_2 \end{bmatrix}$$

where the plant and control matrices are

$$\mathbf{A} = \begin{bmatrix} 0 & 1 & 0 \\ 0 & -5 & -4 \\ -1 & -1 & -3 \end{bmatrix} \quad \text{and} \quad \mathbf{B} = \begin{bmatrix} 0 & 0 \\ 1 & 0 \\ 0 & 1 \end{bmatrix}$$

and the state and control vectors are

$$\mathbf{x} = \begin{bmatrix} x_1 \\ x_2 \\ x_3 \end{bmatrix}, \quad \mathbf{\eta} = \begin{bmatrix} r_1 \\ r_2 \end{bmatrix}$$

The output equation

$$\mathbf{y} = \mathbf{Cx} + \mathbf{D\eta}$$

can be expressed as follows:

$$\begin{bmatrix} y_1 \\ y_2 \end{bmatrix} = \begin{bmatrix} 1 & 0 & 0 \\ 0 & 0 & 1 \end{bmatrix} \begin{bmatrix} x_1 \\ x_2 \\ x_3 \end{bmatrix}$$

where $\mathbf{D}$ is a null matrix. It also should be noted that a transfer function can be rewritten in the state variable form.

The solution of the state equations will be discussed in the next several sections. Both analytical and numerical solutions of the state equations will be presented.

9.2.1 State Transition Matrix

The state transition matrix is defined as a matrix that satisfies the linear homogeneous state equation; that is,

$$\dot{\mathbf{x}} = \mathbf{Ax} \qquad \text{Homogeneous state equation} \qquad (9.18)$$

$$\mathbf{x}(0) = \begin{bmatrix} x_1(0) \\ \vdots \\ x_n(0) \end{bmatrix} \qquad \text{Initial state at time } t = 0 \qquad (9.19)$$

$$\mathbf{x}(t) = \mathbf{\Phi}(\mathbf{t})\, \mathbf{x}(0) \qquad (9.20)$$

where $\mathbf{\Phi}(t)$ is the state transition matrix.

State transition matrix by the Laplace transformation technique

We begin with

$$\dot{\mathbf{x}} = \mathbf{Ax} \quad \text{and} \quad \mathbf{x}(0) = \begin{bmatrix} x_1(0) \\ \vdots \\ x_n(0) \end{bmatrix} \qquad (9.21)$$

Taking the Laplace transformation of this equation yields

$$sx(s) - x(0) = Ax(s) \tag{9.22}$$

or

$$x(s) = [sI - A]^{-1}x(0) \tag{9.23}$$

The term $[sI - A]^{-1}$, called the resolvent, is the Laplace transform of the state transition matrix:

$$\boldsymbol{\Phi}(s) = [sI - A]^{-1} \tag{9.24}$$

The state transition matrix is obtained by taking the inverse Laplace transform of $\boldsymbol{\Phi}(s)$:

$$\boldsymbol{\Phi}(t) = \mathcal{L}^{!}[\boldsymbol{\Phi}(s)] = \mathcal{L}^{-1}[(sI - A)^{-1}] \tag{9.25}$$

Once the state transition matrix, $\boldsymbol{\Phi}(t)$, is known the homogenous solution can be found using Equation (9.20).

State Transition Matrix by the Matrix Exponential Method

An alternate definition of the state transition matrix can be determined by expressing the solution of the homogeneous equation in terms of an infinite series with undetermined coefficients. The solution of

$$\dot{\mathbf{x}}(\mathbf{t}) = \mathbf{A}\mathbf{x}(\mathbf{t}) \tag{9.26}$$

is given as

$$\mathbf{x}(t) = \boldsymbol{\Phi}(t)\mathbf{x}(0) \tag{9.27}$$

where

$$\boldsymbol{\Phi}(t) = \mathbf{I} + \mathbf{a}_1 t + \mathbf{a}_2 t^2 + \cdots + \mathbf{a}_n t^n + \cdots \tag{9.28}$$

and $\mathbf{x}(0)$ is the initial value of the state vector at time $t = 0$. Substituting the solution into the homogeneous equation yields

$$\frac{d}{dt}[\boldsymbol{\Phi}(t)\mathbf{x}(0)] = (\mathbf{a}_1 + 2\mathbf{a}_2 t + 3\mathbf{a}_3 t^2 + \cdots + n\mathbf{a}_n t^{n-1} + \cdots)\mathbf{x}(0)$$

$$= (\mathbf{A} + \mathbf{A}\mathbf{a}_1 t + \mathbf{A}\mathbf{a}_2 t^2 + \mathbf{A}\mathbf{a}_3 t^3 + \cdots \\ + \mathbf{A}\mathbf{a}_n t^{n-1} + \cdots)\mathbf{x}(0) \tag{9.29}$$

Equating the coefficients of like powers of t yields

$$\mathbf{a}_1 = \mathbf{A}$$

$$\mathbf{a}_2 = \frac{1}{2}\mathbf{A}\mathbf{a}_1 = \frac{1}{2}\mathbf{A}^2$$

$$\mathbf{a}_3 = \frac{1}{3}\mathbf{A}\mathbf{a}_2 = \frac{1}{3!}\mathbf{A}^3 \tag{9.30}$$

$$\vdots$$

$$\mathbf{a}_n = \frac{1}{n!}\mathbf{A}^n$$

or

$$\boldsymbol{\Phi}(t) = \mathbf{I} + \mathbf{A}t + \frac{1}{2!}\mathbf{A}^2 t^2 + \frac{1}{3!}\mathbf{A}^3 t^3 + \cdots + \frac{1}{n!}\mathbf{A}^n t^n + \cdots \tag{9.31}$$

The matrix series is similar to the scalar series representation of an exponential and is called a matrix exponential:

$$e^{At} = I + At + \frac{1}{2!}A^2t^2 + \frac{1}{3!}A^3t^3 + \cdots + \frac{1}{n!}A^nt^n + \cdots \qquad (9.32)$$

or
$$\Phi(t) = e^{At} \qquad (9.33)$$

The matrix exponential is defined in terms of the plant matrix A.

Properties of the state transition matrix

Some of the properties of the state transition matrix follow:

1. $\Phi(0) = e^{A0} = I$. $\qquad\qquad$ (9.34)
2. $[\Phi(t)]^{-1} = [\Phi(-t)]$. $\qquad\qquad$ (9.35)
3. $\Phi(t_1 + t_2) = e^{A(t_1+t_2)} = e^{At_1}e^{At_2} = \Phi(t_1)\Phi(t_2) = \Phi(t_2)\Phi(t_1)$. $\qquad$ (9.36)
4. $[\Phi(t)]^k = \Phi(kt)$, where k is an integer. $\qquad\qquad$ (9.37)

Once the state transition matrix has been found, the solution to the nonhomogeneous equation can be determined as follows:

$$\dot{x} = Ax + B\eta \qquad (9.38)$$

Taking the Laplace transform of the above equation yields

$$sx(s) - x(0) = Ax(s) + B\eta(s) \qquad (9.39)$$

solving for $x(s)$ yields

$$x(s) = [sI - A]^{-1}x(0) + [sI - A]^{-1}B\eta(s) \qquad (9.40)$$

$$x(t) = \mathcal{L}^{-1}[sI - A]^{-1}x(0) + \mathcal{L}^{-1}[(sI - A)^{-1}B\eta(s)] \qquad (9.41)$$

or
$$x(t) = \Phi(t)x(0) + \int_0^1 \Phi(t - \tau)B\eta(\tau)\, d\tau \qquad (9.42)$$

EXAMPLE PROBLEM 9.2. Given the following state equations,

$$\begin{bmatrix} \dot{x}_1 \\ \dot{x}_2 \end{bmatrix} = \begin{bmatrix} 0 & 1 \\ -1 & -3 \end{bmatrix}\begin{bmatrix} x_1 \\ x_2 \end{bmatrix} + \begin{bmatrix} 0 \\ 2 \end{bmatrix}u$$

$$y = [3 \quad 1]\begin{bmatrix} x_1 \\ x_2 \end{bmatrix}$$

The initial conditions for the system are

$$\begin{bmatrix} x_1(0) \\ x_2(0) \end{bmatrix} = \begin{bmatrix} 0 \\ 1 \end{bmatrix}$$

Determine the response of the system if u is a unit step function.

Solution. First we will need to determine the state transition matrix $\Phi(t)$. The Laplace transform of the state transition matrix yields

$$\Phi(s) = (s\mathbf{I} - \mathbf{A})^{-1}$$

$$\Phi(s) = \left(\begin{bmatrix} s & 0 \\ 0 & s \end{bmatrix} - \begin{bmatrix} 0 & 1 \\ -2 & -3 \end{bmatrix} \right)^{-1}$$

$$\Phi(s) = \begin{bmatrix} s & -1 \\ 2 & s+3 \end{bmatrix}^{-1}$$

or

$$\Phi(s) = \begin{bmatrix} \dfrac{s+3}{s^2 + 3s + 2} & \dfrac{1}{s^2 + 3s + 2} \\[2ex] \dfrac{-2}{s^2 + 3s + 2} & \dfrac{s}{s^2 + 3s + 2} \end{bmatrix}$$

Using partial fraction expansion, the elements of the transition matrix can be written as

$$\Phi(s) = \begin{bmatrix} \dfrac{2}{s+1} - \dfrac{1}{s+2} & \dfrac{1}{s+1} - \dfrac{1}{s+2} \\[2ex] \dfrac{-2}{s+1} + \dfrac{2}{s+2} & \dfrac{-1}{s+1} + \dfrac{2}{s+2} \end{bmatrix}$$

The state transition matrix now can be obtained by taking the inverse Laplace transform of $\Phi(s)$:

$$\Phi(t) = \begin{bmatrix} 2e^{-t} - e^{-2t} & e^{-t} - e^{-2t} \\ -2[e^{-t} - e^{-2t}] & -e^{-t} + 2e^{-2t} \end{bmatrix}$$

Knowing the state transition matrix we now can determine the response from the equation

$$\mathbf{x}(t) = \Phi(t)\mathbf{x}(0) + \int_0^t \Phi(t - \tau)\, \mathbf{B}\mathbf{u}\, d\tau$$

$$\mathbf{x}(t) = \begin{bmatrix} e^{-t} - e^{-2t} \\ -e^{-t} + 2e^{-2t} \end{bmatrix} + \begin{bmatrix} 2\int_0^t (e^{-(t-\tau)} - e^{-2(t-\tau)})\, d\tau \\ 2\int_0^t (2e^{-2(t-\tau)} - e^{-(t-\tau)})\, d\tau \end{bmatrix}$$

The integrals in the second term can be solved as follows. Consider the integral

$$2\int_0^t [e^{-(t-\tau)} - e^{-2(t-\tau)}]\, d\tau = 2e^{-t} \int_0^t e^{\tau}\, d\tau - 2e^{-2t} \int_0^t e^{2\tau}\, d\tau$$

$$= 2e^{-t}e^{\tau}\Big|_0^t - (2e^{-2t})\dfrac{e^{2\tau}}{2}\Big|_0^t$$

$$= 2e^{-t}[e^t - 1] - 2e^{-2t}\left[\dfrac{e^{2t}}{2} - \dfrac{1}{2}\right]$$

$$= 1 - 2e^{-t} + e^{-2t}$$

The other integral can be shown to have the following solution:

$$2\int_0^t (2e^{-2(t-\tau)} - e^{-(t-\tau)})\, d\tau = 2e^{-t} - 2e^{-2t}$$

Substituting the integral solution back into $\mathbf{x}(t)$ and combining terms yields

$$\mathbf{x}(t) = \begin{bmatrix} 1 - e^{-t} \\ e^{-t} \end{bmatrix}$$

The output of the system is given by

$$y = \mathbf{C}\mathbf{x}$$

or

$$y = [3 \quad 1]\begin{bmatrix} 1 - e^{-t} \\ e^{-t} \end{bmatrix} = 3 - 2e^{-t}$$

9.2.2 Numerical Solution of State Equations

The complete solution of the state equations was shown to be

$$\mathbf{x}(t) = \boldsymbol{\Phi}(t)\mathbf{x}(0) + \int_0^t \boldsymbol{\Phi}(t - \tau)\, \mathbf{B}\boldsymbol{\eta}(\tau)\, d\tau \tag{9.43}$$

The solution of Equation (9.43) can be obtained numerically by replacing the continuous system by a discrete time system. Takahashi, Rabins, and Auslander [9.4] present a numerical algorithm based on a technique developed by Paynter [9.6]. For this example a sampling interval Δt is specified so that

$$k\,\Delta t < t \le (k + 1)\,\Delta t$$

The Equation (9.43) can be rewritten as

$$\mathbf{x}_{k+1} = e^{\mathbf{A}\Delta t}\,\mathbf{x}_k + e^{\mathbf{A}\Delta t}\int_0^{\Delta t} e^{-\mathbf{A}\tau}\mathbf{B}\boldsymbol{\eta}(\tau)\, d\tau \tag{9.44}$$

If we assume the control input $\boldsymbol{\eta}(\tau)$ is constant over the time interval Δt then the integral can be evaluated.

$$\int_0^{\Delta t} e^{-\mathbf{A}\tau}\mathbf{B}\boldsymbol{\eta}(\tau)\, d\tau = (\mathbf{I} - e^{-\mathbf{A}\Delta t})\mathbf{A}^{-1}\mathbf{B}\boldsymbol{\eta}_k \tag{9.45}$$

Substituting the solution of the integral back into Equation (9.44) yields

$$\mathbf{x}_{k+1} = e^{\mathbf{A}\Delta t}\mathbf{x}_k + [e^{\mathbf{A}\Delta t} - \mathbf{I}]\mathbf{A}^{-1}\mathbf{B}\boldsymbol{\eta}_k \tag{9.46}$$

This equation can be simplified further by letting

$$\mathbf{M} = e^{\mathbf{A}\Delta t} \tag{9.47}$$

$$\mathbf{N} = (e^{\mathbf{A}\Delta t} - \mathbf{I})\mathbf{A}^{-1}\mathbf{B} \tag{9.48}$$

The solution vector can now be expressed as

$$\mathbf{x}_{k+1} = \mathbf{M}\mathbf{x}_k + \mathbf{N}\boldsymbol{\eta}_k \tag{9.49}$$

Equation (9.49) can be used to determine the time domain solution; for example,

$$\mathbf{x}_1 = \mathbf{Mx}_0 + \mathbf{N\eta}_0$$
$$\mathbf{x}_2 = \mathbf{Mx}_1 + \mathbf{N\eta}_1$$
$$\mathbf{x}_3 = \mathbf{Mx}_2 + \mathbf{N\eta}_2 \tag{9.50}$$
$$\vdots$$
$$\mathbf{x}_{k+1} = \mathbf{Mx}_k + \mathbf{N\eta}_k$$

On combining these equations one obtains

$$\mathbf{x}_k = \mathbf{M}^k \mathbf{x}_0 + \sum_{i=0}^{k-1} \mathbf{M}^{k-1-i} \mathbf{N\eta}_i \tag{9.51}$$

Once a satisfactory time interval is selected the matrices $\mathbf{M}$ and $\mathbf{N}$ need be calculated only one time. These matrices can be evaluated by the matrix expansion

$$\mathbf{M} = e^{\mathbf{A}\Delta t} = \mathbf{I} + \mathbf{A}\,\Delta t + \frac{1}{2!}\mathbf{A}^2\,\Delta t^2 \cdots \tag{9.52}$$

$$\mathbf{N} = \Delta t \left(\mathbf{I} + \frac{1}{2!}\mathbf{A}\,\Delta t + \frac{1}{3!}\mathbf{A}^2\,\Delta t^2 + \cdots \right)\mathbf{B} \tag{9.53}$$

The number of terms required in the series expansion depends on the time interval Δt. An algorithm developed by Paynter [9.6] can be used to determine the number of terms in the series expansion. This algorithm is presented in Table 9.1.

EXAMPLE PROBLEM 9.3. Use the numerical algorithm described in this section to determine the solution to the state equation given in Example Problem 9.2. The equations follow:

$$\begin{bmatrix} \dot{x}_1 \\ \dot{x}_2 \end{bmatrix} = \begin{bmatrix} 0 & 1 \\ -2 & -3 \end{bmatrix} \begin{bmatrix} x_1 \\ x_2 \end{bmatrix} + \begin{bmatrix} 0 \\ 2 \end{bmatrix} u$$

$$y = [3 \quad 1] \begin{bmatrix} x_1 \\ x_2 \end{bmatrix}$$

$$\begin{bmatrix} x_1(0) \\ x_2(0) \end{bmatrix} = \begin{bmatrix} 0 \\ 1 \end{bmatrix}$$

Solution. Assume that u is a unit step input.

In this example we assume that $\Delta t = 0.05$ s. Having specified the time increment we must determine the number of terms needed in the $\mathbf{M}$ and $\mathbf{N}$ matrices. The parameter q is found using the equation

$$q = \max |A_{ij}\,\Delta t| = 0.15$$

starting with $p = 2$ we see if the inequality

$$\frac{1}{p!}(nq)^p\, e^{nq} \leq 0.001$$

TABLE 9.1

Algorithm for the computation of M and N matrices by Paynter

1. Select a time interval, Δt.
2. Estimate the parameter, q, from the equation

$$q = \max |A_{ij}\, \Delta t|$$

where A_{ij} are the elements of the plant matrix **A**.

3. Determine the integer value of p, the number of terms in the **M** and **N** matrix expansion, from the equation

$$\frac{1}{p!}\,(nq)^P e^{nq} \le 0.001$$

where n is the order of the system. This equation is solved by trial and error. Starting with a value of $p = 2$, keep selecting a higher value of p until this equation is satisfied.

4. Once p is known, calculate **M** and **N** from Equation (9.52) and (9.53).

is satisfied. For example, for $p = 2$

$$\frac{1}{p!}\,(nq)^P e^{nq} = 0.06$$

which does not satisfy the inequality. A new value of p is selected and the process is continued until a value of p is found that meets the inequality relationship. For this example $p = 4$ was found to meet the requirement. Next we evaluate the matrices **M** and **N** by retaining only the first four terms in each series:

$$\mathbf{M} = \mathbf{I} + \mathbf{A}\,\Delta t + \frac{1}{2!}\mathbf{A}^2\,\Delta t^2 + \frac{1}{3!}\mathbf{A}^3\,\Delta t^3$$

$$\mathbf{N} = \Delta t\left[\mathbf{I} + \frac{1}{2!}\mathbf{A}\,\Delta t + \frac{1}{3!}\mathbf{A}^2\,\Delta t^2 + \frac{1}{4!}\mathbf{A}^3\,\Delta t^3\right][\mathbf{B}]$$

Evaluating the **M** and **N** matrices for the selected Δt yields

$$\mathbf{M} = \begin{bmatrix} 0.996 & 0.0464 \\ -0.0928 & 0.8584 \end{bmatrix}$$

$$\mathbf{N} = \begin{bmatrix} 0.0024 \\ 0.0928 \end{bmatrix}$$

The matrices **M** and **N** are fixed and the solution can be calculated by using the equations

$$\mathbf{x}[(k + 1)\,\Delta t] = \mathbf{M}\mathbf{x}(k\,\Delta t) + \mathbf{N}u(k\,\Delta t)$$

in a recursive manner for $k = 0$ to nk where $nk\,\Delta t$ is the final time selected for the solution. Figure 9.2 is a plot of the output vector for the exact and numerical solution:

$$y(k\,\Delta t) = \begin{bmatrix} 3 & 1 \end{bmatrix}\begin{bmatrix} x_1(k\,\Delta t) \\ x_2(k\,\Delta t) \end{bmatrix}$$

and the exact solution is given by

$$y = 3 - 2e^{-t}$$

The exact and numerical solutions are indistinguishable from one another.

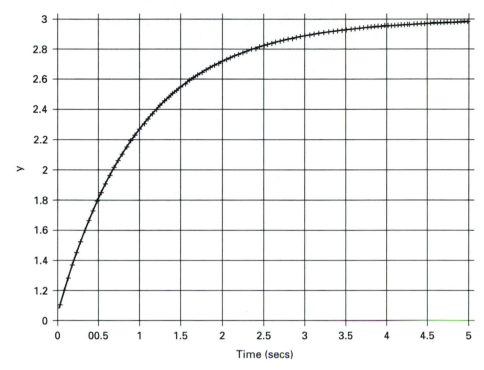

FIGURE 9.2
Numerical solution of state-space equation.

9.3
CANONICAL TRANSFORMATIONS

In formulating a physical system into the state-space representation we must select a set of state variables to describe the system. The set of state variables we select may not be the most convenient from the standpoint of the mathematical operations we need to perform to determine the solution of the state equations. It is possible to define a transformation matrix, **P**, that will transform the original state equations into a more convenient form.

To examine the characteristics of a given state equation it is useful to have the state equations in a canonical form where the plant matrix is a diagonal matrix. Consider a system that can be modeled by this state equation:

$$\dot{\mathbf{x}} = \mathbf{A}\mathbf{x} + \mathbf{B}\boldsymbol{\eta} \tag{9.54}$$

$$\mathbf{y} = \mathbf{C}\mathbf{x} \tag{9.55}$$

where the plant matrix **A** is not a diagonal matrix. Defining a new state vector **z** so that **x** and **z** are related by way of a transformation matrix **P**,

$$\mathbf{x} = \mathbf{P}\mathbf{z} \tag{9.56}$$

Rewriting the state equation in terms of the new state vector $\mathbf{z}$ yields

$$\dot{\mathbf{z}} = \mathbf{P}^{-1}\mathbf{A}\mathbf{P}\mathbf{z} + \mathbf{P}^{-1}\mathbf{B}\boldsymbol{\eta} \tag{9.57}$$

which can be written as

$$\dot{\mathbf{z}} = \boldsymbol{\Lambda}\mathbf{z} + \overline{\mathbf{B}}\boldsymbol{\eta} \tag{9.58}$$

$$\mathbf{y} = \overline{\mathbf{C}}\mathbf{z} \tag{9.59}$$

where $\boldsymbol{\Lambda}$ is a diagonal or nearly diagonal matrix. The matrices $\boldsymbol{\Lambda}$, $\overline{\mathbf{B}}$, and $\overline{\mathbf{C}}$ are defined as

$$\boldsymbol{\Lambda} = \mathbf{P}^{-1}\mathbf{A}\mathbf{P} \tag{9.60}$$

$$\overline{\mathbf{B}} = \mathbf{P}^{-1}\mathbf{B} \tag{9.61}$$

$$\overline{\mathbf{C}} = \mathbf{C}\mathbf{P} \tag{9.62}$$

The transformed state equation has the same form as the original equation. If the transformation matrix $\mathbf{P}$ is chosen so that $\boldsymbol{\Lambda}$ is a diagonalized matrix then the equations are in the canonical form.

The transformation matrix $\mathbf{P}$ is determined from the eigenvectors of the plant matrix $\mathbf{A}$. As has been shown earlier the eigenvalues of $\mathbf{A}$ are determined by solving the following equation:

$$|\lambda\mathbf{I} - \mathbf{A}| = 0 \tag{9.63}$$

which yields the characteristic equation

$$\lambda^n + a_n\lambda^{n-1} + a_{n-1}\lambda^{n-2} + \cdots + a_2\lambda + a_1 = 0 \tag{9.64}$$

The roots of the characteristic equation are the eigenvalues of the system. The eigenvectors can be determined by solving the equations

$$(\lambda_i\mathbf{I} - \mathbf{A})\mathbf{P}_i = 0 \quad \text{where} \quad i = 1, 2, 3, \ldots, n \tag{9.65}$$

The transformation matrix $\mathbf{P}$ is formed from the eigenvectors of the plant matrix. The eigenvectors form the columns of the transformation matrix as

$$\mathbf{P} = [\mathbf{P}_1\ \mathbf{P}_2\ \mathbf{P}_3 \cdots \mathbf{P}_n] \tag{9.66}$$

9.3.1 Real Distinct Eigenvalues

For these nonrepeated real eigenvalues, the transformation matrix $\mathbf{P}$ depends on the eigenvalues of the plant matrix $\mathbf{A}$. If the eigenvalues of $\mathbf{A}$ are real and distinct, the transformation matrix $\mathbf{P}$ is made up of the eigenvectors of $\mathbf{A}$ as follows:

$$\mathbf{P} = [\mathbf{P}_1\ \mathbf{P}_2\ \mathbf{P}_3 \cdots \mathbf{P}_n] \tag{9.67}$$

We illustrate how the transformation is determined by the following example problem.

EXAMPLE PROBLEM 9.4. Given the following state equations, determine the transformation matrix **P** so that the new state equations are in the state canonical form:

$$\begin{bmatrix} \dot{x}_1 \\ \dot{x}_2 \end{bmatrix} = \begin{bmatrix} 0 & 1 \\ -2 & -3 \end{bmatrix} \begin{bmatrix} x_1 \\ x_2 \end{bmatrix} + \begin{bmatrix} 0 \\ 2 \end{bmatrix} [u]$$

$$y = [3 \quad 1] \begin{bmatrix} x_1 \\ x_2 \end{bmatrix}$$

$$\begin{bmatrix} x_1(0) \\ x_2(0) \end{bmatrix} = \begin{bmatrix} 0 \\ 1 \end{bmatrix}$$

Solution. First find the eigenvalues of **A**:

$$|\lambda \mathbf{I} - \mathbf{A}| = 0$$

$$\left| \begin{bmatrix} \lambda & 0 \\ 0 & \lambda \end{bmatrix} - \begin{bmatrix} 0 & 1 \\ -2 & -3 \end{bmatrix} \right| = 0$$

$$\begin{vmatrix} \lambda & -1 \\ 2 & \lambda + 3 \end{vmatrix} = 0$$

or $\quad \lambda^2 + 3\lambda + 2 = 0 \Rightarrow \lambda = -2 \quad \text{and} \quad \lambda = -1$

The eigenvector for $\lambda = -1$ is found using Equation (9.65):

$$(\lambda_i \mathbf{I} - \mathbf{A})\mathbf{P}_i = 0$$

$$\left(\begin{bmatrix} -1 & 0 \\ 0 & -1 \end{bmatrix} - \begin{bmatrix} 0 & 1 \\ -2 & -3 \end{bmatrix} \right) \begin{bmatrix} P_{11} \\ P_{21} \end{bmatrix} = 0$$

$$-P_{11} - P_{21} = 0$$

$$2P_{11} + 2P_{21} = 0$$

Both equations yield the same relationship between P_{11} and P_{21}. We will arbitrarily select

$$P_{11} = 1$$

then $\qquad\qquad\qquad\qquad\qquad P_{21} = -1$

The eigenvector for $\lambda = -1$ is

$$\mathbf{P}_1 = \begin{bmatrix} 1 \\ -1 \end{bmatrix}$$

In a similar manner we can obtain the eigenvector for $\lambda = -2$. Solving Equation (9.65) yields the following equations:

$$\left(\begin{bmatrix} -2 & 0 \\ 0 & -2 \end{bmatrix} - \begin{bmatrix} 0 & 1 \\ -2 & -3 \end{bmatrix} \right) \begin{bmatrix} P_{12} \\ P_{22} \end{bmatrix} = 0$$

or $\qquad\qquad\qquad\qquad -2P_{12} - P_{22} = 0$

$$2P_{12} + 1P_{22} = 0$$

Again we will specify $P_{12} = 1$ and then solve for P_{22}. The eigenvector $\mathbf{P}_2$ becomes

$$\mathbf{P}_2 = \begin{bmatrix} 1 \\ -2 \end{bmatrix}$$

The transformation matrix $\mathbf{P}$ now can be constructed by stacking the eigenvectors as follows:

$$\mathbf{P} = [\mathbf{P}_1 \, \mathbf{P}_2]$$

or

$$\mathbf{P} = \begin{bmatrix} 1 & 1 \\ -1 & -2 \end{bmatrix}$$

To determine the new state equation we need the inverse of $\mathbf{P}$:

$$\mathbf{P}^{-1} = \begin{bmatrix} 2 & 1 \\ -1 & -1 \end{bmatrix}$$

The diagonal matrix $\mathbf{\Lambda}$ is defined in terms of $\mathbf{P}$ and $\mathbf{A}$:

$$\mathbf{\Lambda} = \mathbf{P}^{-1}\mathbf{A}\mathbf{P}$$

$$\mathbf{\Lambda} = \begin{bmatrix} 2 & 1 \\ -1 & -1 \end{bmatrix} \begin{bmatrix} 0 & 1 \\ -2 & -3 \end{bmatrix} \begin{bmatrix} 1 & 1 \\ -1 & -2 \end{bmatrix}$$

or

$$\mathbf{\Lambda} = \begin{bmatrix} -1 & 0 \\ 0 & -2 \end{bmatrix}$$

where the eigenvalues are on the diagonal.

In a similar manner $\overline{\mathbf{B}}$ and $\overline{\mathbf{C}}$ can be computed

$$\overline{\mathbf{B}} = \mathbf{P}^{-1}\mathbf{B}$$

$$\overline{\mathbf{B}} = \begin{bmatrix} 2 & 1 \\ -1 & -1 \end{bmatrix} \begin{bmatrix} 0 \\ 2 \end{bmatrix}$$

$$\overline{\mathbf{B}} = \begin{bmatrix} 2 \\ -2 \end{bmatrix}$$

$$\overline{\mathbf{C}} = \mathbf{C}\mathbf{P}$$

$$\overline{\mathbf{C}} = \begin{bmatrix} 3 & 1 \end{bmatrix} \begin{bmatrix} 1 & 1 \\ -1 & -2 \end{bmatrix}$$

$$\overline{\mathbf{C}} = \begin{bmatrix} 2 & 1 \end{bmatrix}$$

The new state equations are

$$\begin{bmatrix} \dot{z}_1 \\ \dot{z}_2 \end{bmatrix} = \begin{bmatrix} -1 & 0 \\ 0 & -2 \end{bmatrix} \begin{bmatrix} z_1 \\ z_2 \end{bmatrix} + \begin{bmatrix} 2 \\ -2 \end{bmatrix} [u]$$

$$y = \begin{bmatrix} 2 & 1 \end{bmatrix} \begin{bmatrix} z_1 \\ z_2 \end{bmatrix}$$

$$\begin{bmatrix} z_1(0) \\ z_2(0) \end{bmatrix} = \mathbf{P}^{-1}\mathbf{x}(0)$$

$$\begin{bmatrix} z_1(0) \\ z_2(0) \end{bmatrix} = \begin{bmatrix} 1 \\ -1 \end{bmatrix}$$

This example demonstrates an important property of eigenvalues; namely, that the eigenvalues and the corresponding characteristic equations are invariant under a nonsingular transformation. The eigenvalues of the $\mathbf{A}$ matrix and $\boldsymbol{\Lambda}$ are the same.

In this example the transformed plant matrix is a purely diagonal matrix having the eigenvalues of the original $\mathbf{A}$ matrix along the diagonal. For this particular case, the state transition matrix can be shown to be the following:

$$\boldsymbol{\Phi}(t) = e^{\Lambda t} = \begin{bmatrix} e^{\lambda_1 t} & 0 \\ 0 & e^{\lambda_2 t} \end{bmatrix}$$

or

$$\boldsymbol{\Phi}(t) = \begin{bmatrix} e^{-t} & 0 \\ 0 & e^{-2t} \end{bmatrix}$$

The solution of the transformed state equations would be similar to Equation (9.42):

$$\mathbf{z}(t) = \boldsymbol{\Phi}(t)\mathbf{z}(0) + \int_0^t \boldsymbol{\Phi}(t - \tau)\, \bar{\mathbf{B}}\boldsymbol{\eta}(\tau)\, d\tau$$

$$\begin{bmatrix} z_1(t) \\ z_2(t) \end{bmatrix} = \begin{bmatrix} e^{-t} & 0 \\ 0 & e^{-2t} \end{bmatrix} \begin{bmatrix} 1 \\ -1 \end{bmatrix} + \begin{bmatrix} \int_0^t 2e^{-(t-\tau)}\, d\tau \\ -\int_0^t 2e^{-2(t-\tau)}\, d\tau \end{bmatrix}$$

$$= \begin{bmatrix} 2 - e^{-t} \\ -1 \end{bmatrix}$$

The output of the system is given by

$$y = \bar{\mathbf{C}}\mathbf{z}$$

or

$$y = \begin{bmatrix} 2 & 1 \end{bmatrix} \begin{bmatrix} 2 - e^{-t} \\ -1 \end{bmatrix}$$

$$y = 3 - 2e^{-t}$$

9.3.2 Repeated Eigenvalues

Where the eigenvalues are repeated, the procedure outlined for the distinct eigenvalues produces a singular transformation matrix. The eigenvectors for the repeated roots are the same; therefore, two or more columns of the transformation matrix are identical, which results in a nonsingular matrix. For repeated eigenvalues an almost diagonal matrix, called a Jordan matrix, can be obtained. The Jordan matrix is

$$\boldsymbol{\Lambda} = \begin{bmatrix} \lambda_1 & 1 & 0 & 0 & 0 \\ 0 & \lambda_1 & 1 & 0 & 0 \\ 0 & 0 & \lambda_1 & 0 & 0 \\ 0 & 0 & 0 & \lambda_2 & 0 \\ 0 & 0 & 0 & 0 & \lambda_3 \end{bmatrix} \tag{9.68}$$

Notice that the diagonal immediately above the repeated eigenvalues is composed of ones. The eigenvectors associated with the distinct eigenvalues are determined as before. For the repeated eigenvalues the eigenvectors are determined using the following relationships:

$$(\lambda_i \mathbf{I} - \mathbf{A})\mathbf{P}_1 = 0$$

$$(\lambda_i \mathbf{I} - \mathbf{A})\mathbf{P}_2 = -\mathbf{P}_1 \tag{9.69}$$

$$(\lambda_i \mathbf{I} - \mathbf{A})\mathbf{P}_m = -\mathbf{P}_{m-1}$$

EXAMPLE PROBLEM 9.5. Given the state-space equations

$$\dot{\mathbf{x}} = \mathbf{A}\mathbf{x} + \mathbf{B}\eta$$

where

$$\mathbf{A} = \begin{bmatrix} 0 & -1 & -3 \\ -6 & 0 & -2 \\ 5 & -2 & -4 \end{bmatrix}$$

$$\mathbf{B} = \begin{bmatrix} 0 \\ 1 \\ 1 \end{bmatrix}$$

determine the transformation matrix $\mathbf{P}$ so that the new state equations are in the Jordan canonical form.

Solution. The transformation matrix $\mathbf{P}$ is determined from the eigenvectors of the $\mathbf{A}$ matrix:

$$|\lambda \mathbf{I} - \mathbf{A}| = 0$$

$$\begin{vmatrix} \lambda & 1 & 3 \\ 6 & \lambda & 2 \\ -5 & 2 & \lambda + 4 \end{vmatrix} = \lambda^3 + 4\lambda^2 + 5\lambda + 2$$

The roots of the characteristic equation are $\lambda = -2$, $\lambda = -1$, and $\lambda = -1$. We have a repeated eigenvalue $\lambda = -1$. The eigenvectors for the repeated roots are determined using equation (9.69):

$$(\lambda_i \mathbf{I} - \mathbf{A})\mathbf{P}_1 = 0$$

$$(\lambda_i \mathbf{I} - \mathbf{A})\mathbf{P}_2 = -\mathbf{P}_1$$

The eigenvector $\mathbf{P}_1$ is determined from the following equations:

$$\begin{bmatrix} -1 & 1 & 3 \\ 6 & -1 & 2 \\ -5 & 2 & 3 \end{bmatrix} \begin{bmatrix} P_{11} \\ P_{21} \\ P_{31} \end{bmatrix} = 0$$

$$-P_{11} + P_{21} + 3P_{31} = 0$$

$$6P_{11} - P_{21} + 2P_{31} = 0$$

$$-5P_{11} + 2P_{21} + 3P_{31} = 0$$

From the first two equations we can eliminate P_{21}:

$$5P_{11} + 5P_{31} = 0$$

Let $P_{11} = 1$ then $P_{31} = -1$.

From the first equation

$$-P_{11} + P_{21} + 3P_{31} = 0$$

or
$$P_{21} = P_{11} - 3P_{31} = 4$$

The eigenvector $\mathbf{P}_1$ is as follows:

$$\mathbf{P}_1 = \begin{bmatrix} 1 \\ 4 \\ -1 \end{bmatrix}$$

The second eigenvector for $\lambda = -1$ is determined from the equation $(\lambda_i \mathbf{I} - \mathbf{A})\mathbf{P}_2 = -\mathbf{P}_1$:

$$-P_{12} + P_{22} + 3P_{32} = -1$$

$$6P_{12} - P_{22} + 2P_{32} = -4$$

$$-5P_{12} + 2P_{22} + 3P_{32} = 1$$

Eliminating P_{22} from the first two equations yields

$$5P_{12} + 5P_{32} = -5$$

Let $P_{12} = 1$, therefore $P_{32} = -2$. Substituting P_{12} and P_{32} into the first equation yields P_{22}:

$$P_{22} = -1 + P_{12} - 3P_{32} = 6$$

The second eigenvector is

$$\mathbf{P}_2 = \begin{bmatrix} 1 \\ 6 \\ -2 \end{bmatrix}$$

The eigenvector for the distinct eigenvalue $\lambda = -2$ is found in the usual way:

$$\mathbf{P}_3 = \begin{bmatrix} 1 \\ 2.75 \\ -0.25 \end{bmatrix}$$

The transformation matrix $\mathbf{P}$ is formed by stacking the eigenvectors:

$$\mathbf{P} = [\mathbf{P}_1 \, \mathbf{P}_2 \, \mathbf{P}_3]$$

or
$$\mathbf{P} = \begin{bmatrix} 1 & 1 & 1 \\ 4 & 6 & 2.75 \\ -1 & -2 & -0.25 \end{bmatrix}$$

9.3.3 Complex Eigenvalues

In many engineering problems the eigenvalues may be complex. If the complex eigenvalues are not of multiple order then the procedure outlined earlier for distinct eigenvalues can be used to determine the transformation matrix, $\mathbf{P}$. This however, will result in a complex matrix. An alternate way of treating the complex eigen-values is to define the diagonal matrix as follows:

$$
\Lambda =
\begin{bmatrix}
\lambda_1 & 0 & \cdots & 0 & 0 & 0 & \cdots & 0 \\
0 & \lambda_2 & & 0 & 0 & & & \\
 & \vdots & & & \vdots & \vdots & & \\
0 & \cdots & & \lambda_m & 0 & \cdots & & 0 \\
0 & \cdots & & 0 & \Lambda_1 & \cdots & & 0 \\
 & \vdots & & & 0 & \Lambda_2 & & \vdots \\
 & \vdots & & & & \vdots & & \\
0 & 0 & \cdots & 0 & 0 & \cdots & & \Lambda_n
\end{bmatrix}
\tag{9.70}
$$

where λ_1, λ_2, and λ_3 are real distinct eigenvalues and Λ_1, Λ_2, and Λ_3 are the complex eigenvalues. The matrices $\Lambda_1 = \begin{bmatrix} \sigma_1 & \omega_1 \\ -\omega_1 & \sigma_1 \end{bmatrix}$ has the real part of the eigenvalue on the diagonal and the imaginary part on the off-diagonal. The matrix for two distinct eigenvalues and two pairs of distinct complex eigenvalues follows:

$$
\Lambda =
\begin{bmatrix}
\lambda_1 & 0 & 0 & 0 & 0 & 0 \\
0 & \lambda_2 & 0 & 0 & 0 & 0 \\
0 & 0 & \sigma_1 & \omega_1 & 0 & 0 \\
0 & 0 & -\omega_1 & \sigma_1 & 0 & 0 \\
0 & 0 & 0 & 0 & \sigma_2 & \omega_2 \\
0 & 0 & 0 & 0 & -\omega_2 & \sigma_2
\end{bmatrix}
\tag{9.71}
$$

EXAMPLE PROBLEM 9.6. Given the state equation

$$\dot{\mathbf{x}}(t) = \mathbf{A}\mathbf{x}(t) + \mathbf{B}\boldsymbol{\eta}(t)$$

where

$$\mathbf{A} = \begin{bmatrix} 0 & 1 & 0 \\ 0 & 0 & 1 \\ -5 & -7 & -3 \end{bmatrix}$$

$$\mathbf{B} = \begin{bmatrix} 0 \\ 0 \\ 1 \end{bmatrix}$$

find the transformation $\mathbf{x} = \mathbf{Pz}$ that transforms $\mathbf{A}$ into a canonical form.

Solution. The eigenvalues of $\mathbf{A}$ are complex:

$$|\lambda\mathbf{I} - \mathbf{A}| = 0$$

$$
\begin{vmatrix}
\lambda & -1 & 0 \\
0 & \lambda & -1 \\
5 & 7 & \lambda + 3
\end{vmatrix} = 0
$$

$$\lambda^3 + 3\lambda^2 + 7\lambda + 5 = 0$$

The roots of the characteristic equation are

$$\lambda = -1, \qquad \lambda = -1 \pm 2i$$

The eigenvectors can be found by solving the equation

$$(\lambda_i \mathbf{I} - \mathbf{A})\mathbf{P}_i = 0$$

For $\lambda = -1$

$$-P_{11} - P_{21} = 0$$

$$-P_{21} - P_{31} = 0$$

$$5P_{11} + 7P_{21} + 2P_{31} = 0$$

If in the first equation we let $P_{11} = 1$, we find that $P_{21} = -1$. From the second equation we can determine $P_{31} = -P_{21} = 1$. Therefore the first eigenvector is

$$\mathbf{P}_1 = \begin{bmatrix} 1 \\ -1 \\ 1 \end{bmatrix}$$

The third equation can be used to check if an error has been made.

The eigenvector for the complex root $\lambda = -1 + 2i$ can be found in a similar manner. The equations are

$$(-1 + 2i)P_{12} - P_{22} = 0$$

$$(-1 + 2i)P_{22} - P_{32} = 0$$

$$5P_{12} + 7P_{22} + (2 + 2i)P_{32} = 0$$

Again we let the first element of the eigenvector be 1, $P_{12} = 1$, then $P_{22} = -1 + 2i$. From the second equation

$$P_{32} = (-1 + 2i)P_{22}$$

$$P_{32} = -3 - 4i$$

Therefore, the eigenvector for $\lambda = -1 + 2i$ is

$$\mathbf{P}_2 = \begin{bmatrix} 1 \\ -1 + 2i \\ -3 - 4i \end{bmatrix}$$

The eigenvector for the complex conjugate eigenvalue $\lambda = -1 - 2i$ will be the complex conjugate of $\mathbf{P}_2$:

$$\mathbf{P}_3 = \begin{bmatrix} 1 \\ -1 - 2i \\ -3 + 4i \end{bmatrix}$$

Now the new plant matrix can be determined

$$\Lambda = \mathbf{P}^{-1}\mathbf{A}\mathbf{P}$$

$$\Lambda = \begin{bmatrix} -1.0 & 0 & 0 \\ 0 & -1 + 2i & 0 \\ 0 & 0 & -1 - 2i \end{bmatrix}$$

When the eigenvalues are complex an alternate way to express the Λ matrix is as follows:

$$\Lambda = \begin{bmatrix} \lambda_1 & 0 & 0 \\ 0 & \sigma_1 & \omega_1 \\ 0 & -\omega_1 & \sigma_1 \end{bmatrix}$$

where σ_1 is the real part and ω_1 is the imaginary part of the complex root. The elements of transformation matrix $\mathbf{P}$ for the complex eigenvalues can be expressed as

$$\mathbf{P}_1 = \alpha + i\beta \tag{9.72}$$

$$\mathbf{P}_2 = \alpha - i\beta$$

The complex eigenvector can be expressed in terms of the real and imaginary parts as follows:

$$\mathbf{P} = [\alpha \quad \beta] \tag{9.73}$$

For this example we have one real eigenvector and one complex eigenvector and its conjugate. The transformation matrix can be expressed for this example as

$$\mathbf{P} = [\mathbf{P}_1 \quad \alpha \quad \beta] \tag{9.74}$$

where $\mathbf{P}_1$ is the eigenvector for the real root and α and β are determined from the complex eigenvector as follows:

$$\mathbf{P}_2 = \begin{bmatrix} 1 \\ -1 \\ -3 \end{bmatrix} + i \begin{bmatrix} 0 \\ 2 \\ -4 \end{bmatrix}$$

Therefore

$$\mathbf{P} = \begin{bmatrix} 1 & 1 & 0 \\ -1 & -1 & 2 \\ 1 & -3 & -4 \end{bmatrix}$$

The diagonalized matrix Λ is

$$\Lambda = \mathbf{P}^{-1}\mathbf{A}\mathbf{P} = \begin{bmatrix} -1 & 0 & 0 \\ 0 & -1 & 2 \\ 0 & -2 & -1 \end{bmatrix}$$

9.4
CONTROLLABILITY AND OBSERVABILITY

In the following sections we examine the application of state feedback design and optimal control theory to aircraft control problems. Two concepts that play an important role in modern control theory are controllability and observability. Controllability is concerned with whether the states of the dynamic system are affected by the control input. A system is said to be completely controllable if some control transfers any initial state $\mathbf{x}_i(t)$ to any final state $\mathbf{x}_f(t)$ in some finite time. If one or more of the states are unaffected by the control, the system is not completely controllable.

A mathematical definition of controllability for a linear dynamical system can be expressed as follows. If the dynamic system can be described by the state equation

$$\dot{\mathbf{x}} = \mathbf{A}\mathbf{x} + \mathbf{B}\boldsymbol{\eta} \tag{9.75}$$

where $\mathbf{x}$ and $\boldsymbol{\eta}$ are the state and control vectors of order n and m, respectively, then the necessary and sufficient condition for the system to be completely controllable is that the rank of the controllability matrix $\mathbf{V}$ is equal to the number of states. The matrix $\mathbf{V}$ is constructed from the $\mathbf{A}$ and $\mathbf{B}$ matrices in the following way:

$$\mathbf{V} = [\mathbf{B}, \mathbf{A}\mathbf{B}, \mathbf{A}^2\mathbf{B}, \ldots, \mathbf{A}^{n-1}\mathbf{B}] \tag{9.76}$$

The rank of a matrix is defined as the largest nonzero determinant. Although this definition is abstract, the test for controllability easily can be applied.

Observability deals with whether the states of the system can be identified from the output of the system. A system is said to be completely observable if every state $\mathbf{x}$ can be determined by the measurement of the output $\mathbf{y}(t)$ over a finite time interval. If one or more states cannot be identified from the output of the system, the system is not observable. A mathematical test for observability of an nth-order dynamic system governed by the equations

$$\dot{\mathbf{x}} = \mathbf{A}\mathbf{x} + \mathbf{B}\boldsymbol{\eta} \tag{9.77}$$

$$\mathbf{y} = \mathbf{C}\mathbf{x} + \mathbf{D}\boldsymbol{\eta} \tag{9.78}$$

is given as follows. The necessary and sufficient condition for a system to be completely observable is that the observability matrix $\mathbf{U}$, defined as

$$\mathbf{U} = [\mathbf{C}^T, \mathbf{A}^T\mathbf{C}^T, \ldots, (\mathbf{A}^T)^{n-1}\mathbf{C}^T] \tag{9.79}$$

is of the rank n.

The mathematical definitions of controllability and observability easily are calculated but are somewhat abstract. An alternate way of looking at either controllability or observability is to transform the state equations to a canonical form. If the state equations are transformed so that the new plant matrix is a diagonal matrix the equations governing the system have been decoupled. The control matrix for the modified state system can be examined to determine if the system is completely state controllable. Because the equations have been decoupled, if any row of the control matrix, $\overline{\mathbf{B}}$, is all zeroes then that particular state is uncontrollable. In a similar manner one can determine whether the system is observable by examining the new output matrix, $\overline{\mathbf{C}}$. If any column of the output matrix is all zeroes then the corresponding state is not observable in the output vector.

EXAMPLE PROBLEM 9.7. Determine whether the system that follows is state controllable and observable. The $\mathbf{A}$, $\mathbf{B}$, and $\mathbf{C}$ matrices of the state and output equation are

$$\mathbf{A} = \begin{bmatrix} 0 & 1 \\ -6 & -5 \end{bmatrix}$$

$$\mathbf{B} = \begin{bmatrix} 0 \\ 1 \end{bmatrix}$$

$$\mathbf{C} = \begin{bmatrix} 1 & 0 \end{bmatrix}$$

Solution. The controllability matrix, **V**, is defined for this problem as

$$\mathbf{V} = [\mathbf{B} \quad \mathbf{AB}]$$

$$\mathbf{AB} = \begin{bmatrix} 0 & 1 \\ -6 & -5 \end{bmatrix} \begin{bmatrix} 0 \\ 1 \end{bmatrix} = \begin{bmatrix} 1 \\ -5 \end{bmatrix}$$

$$\mathbf{V} = \begin{bmatrix} 0 & 1 \\ 1 & -5 \end{bmatrix}$$

The rank of **V** is of the same as the order of the system. Therefore the system is state controllable.

The observability matrix, **U**, for this example is

$$\mathbf{U} = [\mathbf{C}^T \quad \mathbf{A}^T\mathbf{C}^T]$$

$$\mathbf{A}^T\mathbf{C}^T = \begin{bmatrix} 0 & -6 \\ 1 & -5 \end{bmatrix} \begin{bmatrix} 1 \\ 0 \end{bmatrix} = \begin{bmatrix} 0 \\ 1 \end{bmatrix}$$

$$\mathbf{U} = \begin{bmatrix} 1 & 0 \\ 0 & 1 \end{bmatrix}$$

The rank of the observability matrix also is of the same as the order of the system. Therefore the system is state observable.

An alternate way of examining the concept of controllability and observability is to transform the equation to a new state as shown in Example Problem 9.4. The new state equations are decoupled, and if a row of the new control matrix is 0 then that particular state is not controllable. For this example the new state equations were found to be

$$\begin{bmatrix} \dot{z}_1 \\ \dot{z}_2 \end{bmatrix} = \begin{bmatrix} -2 & 0 \\ 0 & -3 \end{bmatrix} \begin{bmatrix} z_1 \\ z_2 \end{bmatrix} + \begin{bmatrix} 1 \\ -1 \end{bmatrix} [u]$$

$$\dot{\mathbf{z}} = \mathbf{\Lambda z} + \mathbf{\bar{B}\eta}$$

$$y = \begin{bmatrix} 1 & 1 \end{bmatrix} \begin{bmatrix} z_1 \\ z_2 \end{bmatrix}$$

$$y = \mathbf{\bar{C}z}$$

The control matrix **B̄** of the decoupled state system has no zero rows, therefore each state is completely controllable. On the other hand, if the output matrix has a column of zeroes then that particular state is not observable in the output vector. Again for this example both z_1 and z_2 are observed in the output, therefore the system is completely state observable.

EXAMPLE PROBLEM 9.8. Consider the system represented by the following equations:

$$\begin{bmatrix} \dot{x}_1 \\ \dot{x}_2 \end{bmatrix} = \begin{bmatrix} 0 & 2 \\ -1 & -3 \end{bmatrix} \begin{bmatrix} x_1 \\ x_2 \end{bmatrix} + \begin{bmatrix} 1 \\ -1 \end{bmatrix} [u]$$

Determine whether the system is state controllable.

Solution. For a second-order system the controllability matrix is defined as

$$\mathbf{V} = [\mathbf{B} \quad \mathbf{AB}]$$

The matrix product **AB** follows:

$$\mathbf{AB} = \begin{bmatrix} 0 & 2 \\ -1 & -3 \end{bmatrix} \begin{bmatrix} 1 \\ -1 \end{bmatrix} = \begin{bmatrix} -2 \\ 2 \end{bmatrix}$$

The controllability matrix now can be expressed as

$$\mathbf{V} = \begin{bmatrix} 1 & -2 \\ -1 & 2 \end{bmatrix}$$

The determinant of **V** is 0, which means the rank of the matrix is less than the order of the system. Therefore the system is not state controllable.

If we select a new state variable so that the plant matrix is diagonalized we can determine if the system is controllable by inspection. Using the methods discussed earlier the state equation can be transformed to the following:

$$\begin{bmatrix} \dot{z}_1 \\ \dot{z}_2 \end{bmatrix} = \begin{bmatrix} -1 & 0 \\ 0 & -2 \end{bmatrix} \begin{bmatrix} z_1 \\ z_2 \end{bmatrix} + \begin{bmatrix} 0 \\ 1 \end{bmatrix} [u]$$

The new state equations are decoupled. Notice that state z_1 can not be controlled, therefore the system is not state controllable.

9.5
STATE FEEDBACK DESIGN

State feedback can be used to design a control system with a specific eigenvalue structure. Consider the system represented by the state equations

$$\dot{\mathbf{x}} = \mathbf{Ax} + \mathbf{B\eta} \tag{9.80}$$

$$\mathbf{y} = \mathbf{Cx} \tag{9.81}$$

It can be shown that if the system is state controllable, then it is possible to define a linear control law to achieve any closed loop eigenvalue structure. For the case of a single input system the control law is given by

$$\eta = \mathbf{k}^T\mathbf{x} + \eta' \tag{9.82}$$

where η' is the control input without state feedback and **k** is a column matrix or vector of the feedback gains. Figure 9.3 shows a block diagram representation of the system.

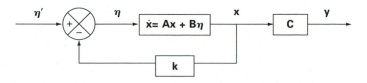

FIGURE 9.3
A linear system with state feedback.

If we combine Equations (9.80) and (9.82) the closed-loop system is given by

$$\dot{\mathbf{x}} = (\mathbf{A} - \mathbf{Bk}^T)\mathbf{x} + \mathbf{B}\eta' \tag{9.83}$$

or

$$\dot{\mathbf{x}} = \mathbf{A}^*\mathbf{x} + \mathbf{B}\eta' \tag{9.84}$$

where $\mathbf{A}^*$ is the augmented matrix. For the case in which the $\mathbf{A}$ matrix may have had undesirable eigenvalues the augmented matrix $\mathbf{A}^*$ can be made to have specific eigenvalues by properly selecting the feedback gains. Application of this technique to multiple input systems is discussed later in this section.

The application of state feedback as presented here requires that the states be state controllable. As stated earlier, a system is said to be completely controllable if the control can be used to move the system from its initial state at $t = t_0$ to the desired state at $t = t_1$. Another way of stating this concept is to say that every state is affected by the control input signal.

EXAMPLE PROBLEM 9.9. The state equations for a system follow:

$$\dot{\mathbf{x}} = \mathbf{Ax} + \mathbf{B}\eta$$

$$\mathbf{y} = \mathbf{Cx}$$

where

$$\mathbf{A} = \begin{bmatrix} -3 & 8 \\ 0 & 0 \end{bmatrix}$$

$$\mathbf{B} = \begin{bmatrix} 0 \\ 4 \end{bmatrix}$$

$$\mathbf{C} = \begin{bmatrix} 1 & 0 \end{bmatrix}$$

Use state feedback so that the closed-loop system has the following characteristics:

$$\omega_n = 25 \text{ rad/s}$$

$$\zeta = 0.707$$

Solution. First we must test to see if the system is state controllable. This is accomplished by examining the controllability matrix, $\mathbf{V}$. If the controllability matrix, $\mathbf{V}$, has a rank that is on the same order as the system then the system is state controllable. The controllability matrix, $\mathbf{V}$, for this problem follows:

$$\mathbf{V} = \begin{bmatrix} \mathbf{B} & \mathbf{AB} \end{bmatrix}$$

$$\mathbf{AB} = \begin{bmatrix} -3 & 8 \\ 0 & 0 \end{bmatrix}\begin{bmatrix} 0 \\ 4 \end{bmatrix} = \begin{bmatrix} 32 \\ 0 \end{bmatrix}$$

$$\mathbf{V} = \begin{bmatrix} 0 & 32 \\ 4 & 0 \end{bmatrix}$$

$$\det [\mathbf{V}] = -128$$

The rank of $\mathbf{V}$ is 2, which is on the same order as the system, therefore, the system is state controllable.

The desired characteristic equation for the closed-loop system can be written as

$$\lambda^2 + 2\zeta\omega_n\lambda + \omega_n^2 = 0$$

which yields upon substitution of the numerical values of ζ and ω_n for this problem the following equation:

$$\lambda^2 + 35.35\lambda + 625 = 0$$

The augmented matrix with state feedback $\mathbf{A}^*$ follows:

$$\mathbf{A}^* = \mathbf{A} - \mathbf{B}\mathbf{k}^T$$

Substituting the matrices $\mathbf{A}$ and $\mathbf{B}$ and the gain vector $\mathbf{k}$ into the preceding equation and expanding yields

$$\mathbf{A}^* = \begin{bmatrix} -3 & 8 \\ 0 & 0 \end{bmatrix} - \begin{bmatrix} 0 \\ 4 \end{bmatrix}[k_1 \quad k_2]$$

$$= \begin{bmatrix} -3 & 8 \\ -4k_1 & -4k_2 \end{bmatrix}$$

The eigenvalues of the augment matrix can be determined in the usual manner:

$$|\lambda\mathbf{I} - \mathbf{A}^*| = 0$$

$$\left| \begin{bmatrix} \lambda & 0 \\ 0 & \lambda \end{bmatrix} - \begin{bmatrix} -3 & 8 \\ -4k_1 & -4k_2 \end{bmatrix} \right| = 0$$

$$\begin{vmatrix} \lambda+3 & -8 \\ 4k_1 & \lambda+4k_2 \end{vmatrix} = 0$$

or

$$\lambda^2 + (3 + 4k_2)\lambda + 12k_2 + 32k_1 = 0$$

The augmented system can be made to have the desired performance by adjusting the gains k_1 and k_2 so that the augmented characteristic equation is as desired. The two characteristic equations are the same if the coefficient of like powers of λ are the same. Equating coefficients of the polynomial yields

$$3 + 4k_2 = 35.35$$
$$12k_2 + 32k_1 = 625$$

Solving these equations yields the state feedback gains for the closed loop system.

$$k_1 = 16.5$$
$$k_2 = 8.09$$

Figure 9.4 shows the response of the closed loop system to an initial displacement from the equilibrium state. With state feedback the system quickly returns to the equilibrium state.

9.5.1 Numerical Method for Determining Feedback Gains

As shown in the previous section, it is possible to use state feedback to locate the eigenvalues so that the system has the desired performance. In this section we

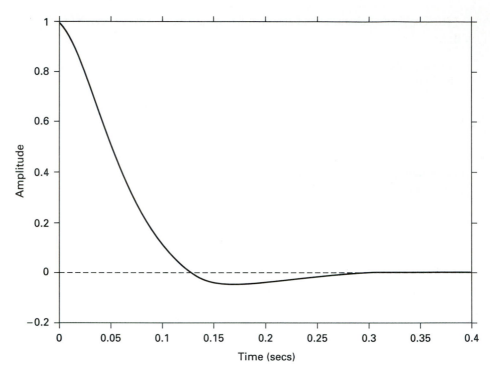

FIGURE 9.4
Response of augmented system to initial condition disturbance.

examine an analytical technique for determining the gains for a given eigenvalue structure. Friedland [9.5] presents a numerical algorithm developed by Bass and Gura [9.7] to find the state feedback gains. This method will be discussed here. The method will be demonstrated for placement of the eigenvalues for a single input-output system. For this particular case the state equations take the form

$$\dot{\mathbf{x}} = \mathbf{A}\mathbf{x} + \mathbf{B}\eta \tag{9.85}$$

where **B** is a column matrix

$$\mathbf{B} = \begin{bmatrix} b_1 \\ \vdots \\ b_k \end{bmatrix} \tag{9.86}$$

and the control law is expressed as follows

$$\eta = -\mathbf{k}^T\mathbf{x} \tag{9.87}$$

where **k** is a vector of the unknown gains for a single input-output system.

If the original system is in what is called the companion form the plant matrix will look like this:

$$
\mathbf{A} =
\begin{bmatrix}
-a_1 & -a_2 & -a_3 & \cdots & & -a_n \\
1 & 0 & 0 & & & 0 \\
0 & 1 & 0 & & & 0 \\
& & & \cdots & & \\
& & & \cdots & & \\
0 & & & \cdots & 1 & 0
\end{bmatrix}
\tag{9.88}
$$

where the terms a_i are the coefficients in the differential equation. The control matrix in the companion form reduces to the simplified form that follows. Note that several arrangements are called the companion form:

$$
\mathbf{B} =
\begin{bmatrix}
1 \\
0 \\
\cdot \\
\cdot \\
\cdot \\
0
\end{bmatrix}
\tag{9.89}
$$

If we substitute the control law into the state equations we obtain the following:

$$
\dot{\mathbf{x}} = (\mathbf{A} - \mathbf{B}\mathbf{k}^T)\mathbf{x}
\tag{9.90}
$$

or

$$
\mathbf{A}^* = \mathbf{A} - \mathbf{B}\mathbf{k}^T
\tag{9.91}
$$

where $\mathbf{A}^*$ is the matrix of the system with the desired eigenvalues.

The eigenvalues of the derived system can be expressed as follows:

$$
\lambda^n + \overline{a}_1 \lambda^{n-1} + \cdots + \overline{a}_n
\tag{9.92}
$$

where $\overline{a}_1$ and the like are the coefficients of the desired characteristic equation. The augmented matrix $\mathbf{A}^*$ can be found by performing the following matrix operations.

The coefficients of the augmented matrix can be adjusted by way of the gains to give the desired plant matrix.

$$
\mathbf{A}^* =
\begin{bmatrix}
-a_1 - k_1 & -a_2 - k_2 & \cdots & & -a_n - k_n \\
1 & 0 & \cdots & & 0 \\
0 & 1 & \cdots & & 0 \\
\vdots & & & & \vdots \\
\vdots & & & & \\
0 & 0 & \cdots & 1 & 0
\end{bmatrix}
\tag{9.93}
$$

$$
-a_i - k_i = -\overline{a}_i \text{ or } \quad i = 1, \ldots, n
\tag{9.94}
$$

$$
\mathbf{k} = (\overline{\mathbf{a}} - \mathbf{a})
\tag{9.95}
$$

and

$$
\mathbf{a} = \begin{pmatrix} a_1 \\ \vdots \\ a_n \end{pmatrix} \quad \text{and} \quad \overline{\mathbf{a}} = \begin{pmatrix} \overline{a}_1 \\ \vdots \\ \overline{a}_n \end{pmatrix}
\tag{9.96}
$$

where **a** and **ā** are the coefficients of the companion form of the plant matrix and desired characteristic equation, respectively. The Bass-Gura method easily can be used to determine the gains for a particular eigenvalue structure. The plant matrix in general may not be in the companion form. In the next section we will examine how the Bass-Gura method can be extended to plant matrices not in the companion form.

If the system is not in the companion form we can find a transformation to accomplish this:

$$\mathbf{k} = [(\mathbf{VW})^T]^{-1}[\bar{\mathbf{a}} - \mathbf{a}] \tag{9.97}$$

where **V** = controllability test matrix
W = a triangular matrix

$$\mathbf{W} = \begin{bmatrix} 1 & a_1 & \cdots & a_{n-1} \\ 0 & 1 & \cdots & a_{n-2} \\ \vdots & & \cdots & \vdots \\ 0 & 0 & \cdots & 1 \end{bmatrix} \tag{9.98}$$

ā = coefficients of desired closed-loop characteristic equation
a = coefficients of open-loop plant matrix characteristic equation.

EXAMPLE PROBLEM 9.10. Given the open-loop system having the following plant and control matrix

$$\mathbf{A} = \begin{bmatrix} -1 & 1 & 0 \\ 0 & -4 & 5 \\ 0 & -1 & -6 \end{bmatrix}$$

$$\mathbf{B} = \begin{bmatrix} 0 \\ 0 \\ 10 \end{bmatrix}$$

$$\mathbf{C} = \begin{bmatrix} 1 & 0 & 0 \end{bmatrix}$$

use state feedback to locate the closed loop eigenvalues at $\lambda = -3, -2 \pm 2i$ using the Bass-Gura method.

Solution. The characteristic equation for the plant matrix

$$|\lambda \mathbf{I} - \mathbf{A}| = 0 \Rightarrow \lambda^3 + 11\lambda^2 + 39\lambda + 29 = 0$$

or

$$\lambda^3 + a_1\lambda^2 + a_2\lambda + a_3 = 0$$

where the coefficients $a_1 = 11, a_2 = 39$, and $a_3 = 29$. The characteristic equation for the desired closed-loop system is given by

$$\lambda^3 + 7\lambda^2 + 20\lambda + 24 = 0$$

$$\lambda^3 + \bar{a}_1\lambda^2 + \bar{a}_2\lambda + \bar{a}_3 = 0$$

where $\bar{a}_1 = 7, \bar{a}_2 = 20$, and $\bar{a}_3 = 24$. The feedback gains can be calculated from the equation

$$\mathbf{k} = [(\mathbf{VW})^T]^{-1}[\bar{\mathbf{a}} - \mathbf{a}]$$

The controllability matrix, $\mathbf{V}$, is determined from

$$\mathbf{V} = [\mathbf{B} \quad \mathbf{AB} \quad \mathbf{A}^2\mathbf{B}]$$

$$\mathbf{V} = \begin{bmatrix} 0 & 0 & 50 \\ 0 & 50 & -500 \\ 10 & -60 & 310 \end{bmatrix}$$

$$\mathbf{W} = \begin{bmatrix} 1 & a_1 & a_2 \\ 0 & 1 & a_1 \\ 0 & 0 & 1 \end{bmatrix} = \begin{bmatrix} 1 & 11 & 39 \\ 0 & 1 & 11 \\ 0 & 0 & 1 \end{bmatrix}$$

$$[(\mathbf{VW}^T)]^{-1} = \begin{bmatrix} 0.02 & -0.02 & 0.02 \\ -0.10 & 0.02 & 0.00 \\ 0.10 & 0.00 & 0.00 \end{bmatrix}$$

$$\mathbf{k} = [(\mathbf{VW})^T]^{-1}[\bar{\mathbf{a}} - \mathbf{a}]$$

$$\mathbf{k} = \begin{bmatrix} 0.02 & -0.02 & 0.02 \\ -0.10 & 0.02 & 0.00 \\ 0.10 & 0.00 & 0.00 \end{bmatrix} \begin{bmatrix} \begin{bmatrix} 7 \\ 20 \\ 24 \end{bmatrix} - \begin{bmatrix} 11 \\ 39 \\ 29 \end{bmatrix} \end{bmatrix}$$

$$\mathbf{k} = \begin{bmatrix} 0.20 \\ 0.02 \\ -0.40 \end{bmatrix}$$

The response of the closed loop system to an initial displacement is shown in Figure 9.5. The system returns to the equilibrium state rapidly.

9.5.2 Multiple Input-Output System

In the previous section we examined the use of state feedback control for placement of the closed-loop eigenvalues. For a single-input system a unique set of gains can be found by solving the state feedback problem. A single-input system is a specialized case of the more general multi-input system (see Figure 9.6). For a multi-input system having p controls the state feedback control law is given by the following expression:

$$\boldsymbol{\eta} = -\mathbf{Kx} \tag{9.99}$$

where the gain matrix $\mathbf{K}$ is $n \times p$. We now have a situation where there are $n \times p$ gains, but we still only have n eigenvalues to be specified. Therefore we have p times as many gains as necessary for eigenvalue placement. At first this may seem to be a problem but actually the additional gains can be used to provide the designer with greater flexibility in configuring the control system.

The number of gains can be reduced to n, that is, the number of closed-loop eigenvalues, by defining the gain matrix as follows:

$$\mathbf{K} = \mathbf{gk}^T \tag{9.100}$$

where $\mathbf{g}$ is a $p \times 1$ vector of constants chosen by the designer and $\mathbf{k}$ is an $n \times 1$ vector of gains that can be determined by the desired eigenvalue placement.

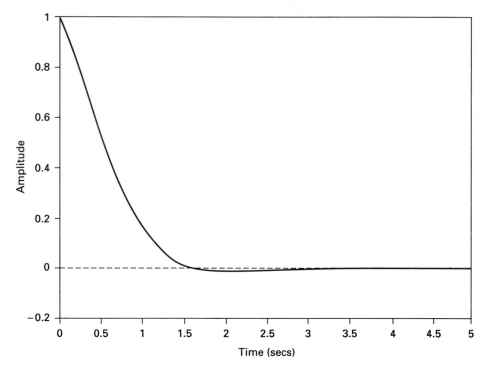

FIGURE 9.5
Response of closed-loop system to an initial condition disturbance.

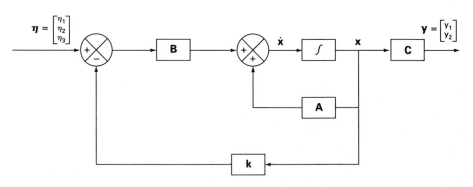

FIGURE 9.6
Sketch of a multiple input-output system.

9.5.3 Eigenvalue Placement

In this chapter we discussed the use of state feedback to locate the eigenvalues or poles of the closed-loop system. The methods presented here allow us to position the closed-loop eigenvalues at any location we desire. The question that must now be asked is this: Is there a preferred location? Several factors should guide us on locating the closed-loop eigenvalues. The factors include actuator saturation, actuator size, unmodeled structural dynamics, and noise.

The control law for a single input system is proportional to the gains times the states

$$\eta = -\mathbf{k}^T\mathbf{x} \qquad (9.101)$$

The larger the gains the bigger the control action becomes for a given state vector. The gains increase the further we move the closed-loop poles from the open-loop poles. This clearly is demonstrated by examining the Bass-Gura formula:

$$\mathbf{k} = [(\mathbf{VW})^T]^{-1}[\overline{\mathbf{a}} - \mathbf{a}] \qquad (9.102)$$

For a given state vector the control input can become very large if the gains are too high. This may mean that the control input might exceed a servo actuator's capability to respond due to physical limitations. In such a case the actuator is said to be saturated. If saturation occurs through most of the control process the system will not perform as expected. This could be fixed by replacing the servo actuator with a more powerful one.

Recall that when setting up the state equations that model a physical system we often times ignore the structural dynamics equations. For example, in the aircraft equations of motion we treat the airplane as a rigid body, thus neglecting the structural modes. Therefore we want to avoid increasing the closed-loop frequency response so that we will not excite an unmodeled structural mode.

9.6
STATE VARIABLE RECONSTRUCTION:
THE STATE OBSERVER

The state feedback design discussed in the previous section requires the measurement of each state variable. In some systems this is not possible, owing either to the complexity of the system or to the expense required to measure certain states. If the states cannot be measured for these reasons the control law cannot be implemented. An alternate approach for designing the controller when all the states are not available is to use an approximation to the state vector. The approximation to the unavailable states is obtained by a subsystem called an observer. The design of a state feedback control system when some of the states are inaccessible can be divided into two phases. In the first phase, the control system is designed as though all the states were known; for example, the method discussed in the previous section. The second part of the design deals with determining the design of the system that estimates the unavailable states. Figure 9.7 shows a linear system with state feedback and a state observer.

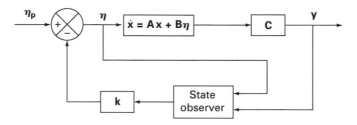

FIGURE 9.7
A linear system with state feedback and a state observer.

The designer can select the eigenvalues of the state observer. In choosing the eigenvalues, it should be obvious that one would want the observer to respond faster than the observed system. This means that the eigenvalues of the observer should be more negative than those of the observed system. In practice, the observer eigenvalues are chosen so that they are only slightly more negative than the observed system eigenvalues. If the observer eigenvalues were chosen to be extremely large negative values the observer would have extremely rapid response. Such an observer would be highly sensitive to noise. Hence, it has been found that good closed-loop response with an observer is best achieved by selecting eigenvalues of the observer that make the observer only slightly more responsive than the observed system.

A state observer can be designed in a number of ways. The basic idea is to make the estimated state x_e to be very close to the actual state x. Because x is unknown there is no direct way of comparing the estimated state to the actual state of the system. However, we do know the output of the system and we can compare it with the estimated output of the observer. In the following analysis we will examine how one can design a state observer for a single input and output system. The output vector y in this case is a scalar. The estimated output can be expressed in terms of the estimated states as follows:

$$y_e = Cx_e \qquad (9.103)$$

where C is a $1 \times n$ row matrix.

The observer can be constructed as a state feedback problem as illustrated in Figure 9.8. The problem now is one of determining the observer feedback gains k_e

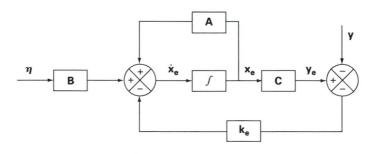

FIGURE 9.8
Design for a state observer multi-input and -output system.

so that $\mathbf{y}_e$ approaches $\mathbf{y}$ as rapidly as possible. The dynamic characteristics of the observer can be expressed as

$$\dot{\mathbf{x}}_e = (\mathbf{A} - \mathbf{k}_e\mathbf{C})\mathbf{x}_e + \mathbf{B}\eta + \mathbf{k}_e y \tag{9.104}$$

but

$$y = \mathbf{C}\mathbf{x} \tag{9.105}$$

or

$$\dot{\mathbf{x}}_e = (\mathbf{A} - \mathbf{k}_e\mathbf{C})\mathbf{x}_e + \mathbf{B}\eta + \mathbf{k}_e\mathbf{C}\mathbf{x} \tag{9.106}$$

If we subtract Equation (9.106) from the state equation for the actual system, we obtain

$$\dot{\mathbf{x}} - \dot{\mathbf{x}}_e = (\mathbf{A} - \mathbf{k}_e\mathbf{C})(\mathbf{x} - \mathbf{x}_e) \tag{9.107}$$

The characteristic equation for the observer can be determined by solving

$$|\lambda\mathbf{I} - (\mathbf{A} - \mathbf{k}_e\mathbf{C})| = 0 \tag{9.108}$$

The gain matrix of the observer is selected so that Equation (9.108) decays rapidly to 0.

The approach outlined here can be extended to a multi-input and -output system in a manner similar to that outlined in section 9.5.2.

EXAMPLE PROBLEM 9.11. For Example Problem 9.9 assume that all the states are not available for feedback control. Because some of the states are not available we need to design a state observer to generate estimates of the system states. This problem is solved by first determining the state feedback gains to meet the desired closed-loop performance as if all the states were available for feedback. Once this has been accomplished a state observer is designed to generate estimates of the system states. The estimated states then will be used in the state feedback control system.

Solution. Having determined the state feedback gains in Example Problem 9.9 we next turn our attention to design the state observer. Before attempting to design an observer we will first determine whether the system is observable. This is accomplished by examining the observability matrix, $\mathbf{U}$. If the system is observable then the rank of the observability matrix $\mathbf{U}$ is the same as the order of the system. The observability matrix for this example problem is as follows:

$$\mathbf{U} = [\mathbf{C}^T \quad \mathbf{A}^T\mathbf{C}^T]$$

$$\mathbf{A}^T\mathbf{C}^T = \begin{bmatrix} -3 & 0 \\ 8 & 0 \end{bmatrix}\begin{bmatrix} 1 \\ 0 \end{bmatrix} = \begin{bmatrix} -3 \\ 8 \end{bmatrix}$$

$$\mathbf{U} = \begin{bmatrix} 1 & -3 \\ 0 & 8 \end{bmatrix}$$

$$\det \mathbf{U} = \begin{vmatrix} 1 & -3 \\ 0 & 8 \end{vmatrix} = 8$$

The rank of $\mathbf{U}$ is 2, which is the same as the order of the system, therefore the system is state observable.

The observer is determined by solving Equation (9.108):

$$|\lambda\mathbf{I} - (\mathbf{A} - \mathbf{k}_e\mathbf{C})| = 0$$

Substituting in the appropriate matrices and performing the indicated matrix operations yields

$$\begin{vmatrix} \lambda + 3 + k_{e_1} & -8 \\ k_{e_2} & \lambda \end{vmatrix} = 0$$

or

$$\lambda^2 + (3 + k_{e_1})\lambda + 8k_{e_2} = 0$$

The dynamics of the observer must be faster than the system being controlled. For this example we assume that the observer roots are four times as large as the desired closed loop performance.

The roots for the closed loop system were

$$\lambda_{1,2} = -17.68 \pm 17.68i$$

therefore the observer roots are selected as

$$\lambda_{1,2_{OB}} = -70.72 \pm 70.72i$$

The characteristic equation desired for the observer is given as

$$(\lambda - \lambda_{1_{OB}})(\lambda - \lambda_{2_{OB}}) = 0$$

or

$$\lambda^2 + 141.44\lambda + 10{,}003 = 0$$

This allows us to select the observer gains by equating the desired observer characteristic equation to the observation characteristic equation in terms of observer gains:

$$3 + k_{e_1} = 141.44 \Rightarrow k_{e_1} = 138.4$$

$$8k_{e_2} = 10{,}003 \Rightarrow k_{e_2} = 1250$$

Figure 9.9 is a sketch of closed loop system incorporating state feedback and a state observer.

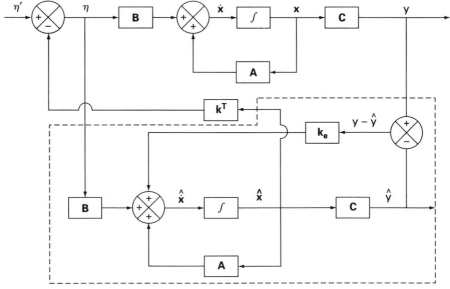

State observer within dashed lines.

FIGURE 9.9
Sketch of closed-loop system with state observer (shown within the dashed lines).

9.7
OPTIMAL STATE-SPACE CONTROL SYSTEM DESIGN

The control system can be written in the state-space form:

$$\dot{\mathbf{x}} = \mathbf{A}\mathbf{x} + \mathbf{B}\boldsymbol{\eta} \qquad (9.109)$$

For the optimal control problem, given an initial state $\mathbf{x}(t_0)$ we want to find a control vector $\boldsymbol{\eta}$ that drives the state $\mathbf{x}(t_0)$ to the desired final state $\mathbf{x}_d(t_f)$ in such a way that a selected performance index of the form

$$J = \int_{t_0}^{t_f} g(\mathbf{x}, \boldsymbol{\eta}, t)\, dt \qquad (9.110)$$

is minimized. The functional form of the performance index can be expressed in a variety of forms. The most useful form is a quadratic index:

$$J = \int_0^{t_f} \mathbf{x}^T \mathbf{Q} \mathbf{x}\, dt \qquad (9.111)$$

where $\mathbf{Q}$ is a weighting matrix. For many practical control problems it is desirable to include a penalty for physical constraints such as expenditure of control energy. The performance index can be rewritten as

$$J = \int_0^{t_f} (\mathbf{x}^T \mathbf{Q} \mathbf{x} + \boldsymbol{\eta}^T \mathbf{R} \boldsymbol{\eta})\, dt \qquad (9.112)$$

Using the quadratic performance index just defined it can be shown that for a linear feedback control the optimal control law for a single input system is

$$\boldsymbol{\eta} = -\mathbf{k}^T \mathbf{x} \qquad (9.113)$$

where $\mathbf{k}$ is a matrix of unknown gains. This problem is often referred to as the linear regulator problem.

If we apply the principles of the calculus of variations to the minimization of the performance index, we obtain the Riccati equation. A complete development of the Riccati equation can be found in [9.4] and [9.8]. The Riccati equation is a set of nonlinear differential equations that must be solved for the Riccati gains $\mathbf{S}(t)$:

$$\frac{d\mathbf{S}(t)}{dt} = \mathbf{S}(t)\mathbf{B}\mathbf{R}^{-1}\mathbf{B}^T\mathbf{S}(t) - \mathbf{S}(t)\mathbf{A} - \mathbf{A}^T\mathbf{S}(t) - \mathbf{Q} \qquad (9.114)$$

The Riccati matrix, $\mathbf{S}$, is a symmetric positive definite matrix. The time-varying gains are related to the Riccati gains in the following manner:

$$\mathbf{k}(t) = \mathbf{R}^{-1}\mathbf{B}^T\mathbf{S}(t) \qquad (9.115)$$

For the case in which the final time t_f approaches infinity the Riccati gain matrix becomes a constant matrix and Equation 9.114 reduces to

$$\mathbf{S}\mathbf{B}\mathbf{R}^{-1}\mathbf{B}^T\mathbf{S} - \mathbf{S}\mathbf{A} - \mathbf{A}^T\mathbf{S} - \mathbf{Q} = 0 \qquad (9.116)$$

In this form the Riccati equation is a set of nonlinear algebraic equations in terms of the Riccati gains. Except for the simplest of examples the solution to Equation (9.116) requires sophisticated computer codes.

EXAMPLE PROBLEM 9.12. Find the control law that minimizes the performance index

$$J = \int_0^\infty (x_1^2 + x_2^2 + u^2)\, dt$$

for the system

$$\begin{bmatrix} \dot{x}_1 \\ \dot{x}_2 \end{bmatrix} = \begin{bmatrix} 0 & 1 \\ 0 & 0 \end{bmatrix} \begin{bmatrix} x_1 \\ x_2 \end{bmatrix} + \begin{bmatrix} 0 \\ 1 \end{bmatrix} [u]$$

Solution. First we need to determine the weighting matrices **Q** and **R**. The performance index is expressed as

$$J = \int_0^\infty (\mathbf{x}^T \mathbf{Q} \mathbf{x} + \boldsymbol{\eta}^T \mathbf{R} \boldsymbol{\eta})\, dt$$

The first part of the integrand can be expanded in the following manner.

$$\mathbf{x}^T \mathbf{Q} \mathbf{x} = \begin{bmatrix} x_1 & x_2 \end{bmatrix} \begin{bmatrix} Q_{11} & Q_{12} \\ Q_{21} & Q_{22} \end{bmatrix} \begin{bmatrix} x_1 \\ x_2 \end{bmatrix}$$

$$= x_1^2 Q_{11} + x_2 x_1 Q_{21} + x_2 x_1 Q_{12} + x_2^2 Q_{22}$$

But that part of the integrand related to the state variables is given as $x_1^2 + x_2^2$, therefore $Q_{11} = Q_{22} = 1$ and $Q_{12} = Q_{21} = 0$. In a similar manner one can show that $\mathbf{R} = [1]$. The weighting matrices **Q** and **R** follow:

$$\mathbf{Q} = \begin{bmatrix} 1 & 0 \\ 0 & 1 \end{bmatrix}$$

$$\mathbf{R} = [1]$$

The reduced Riccati equations can be rearranged as follows:

$$\mathbf{A}^T \mathbf{S} + \mathbf{S} \mathbf{A} - \mathbf{S} \mathbf{B} \mathbf{R}^{-1} \mathbf{B}^T \mathbf{S} + \mathbf{Q} = 0$$

We will perform the indicated matrix operations for first two terms in the Riccati equation:

$$\mathbf{A}^T \mathbf{S} = \begin{bmatrix} 0 & 0 \\ 1 & 0 \end{bmatrix} \begin{bmatrix} S_{11} & S_{12} \\ S_{21} & S_{22} \end{bmatrix} = \begin{bmatrix} 0 & 0 \\ S_{11} & S_{12} \end{bmatrix}$$

$$\mathbf{S} \mathbf{A} = \begin{bmatrix} S_{11} & S_{12} \\ S_{21} & S_{22} \end{bmatrix} \begin{bmatrix} 0 & 1 \\ 0 & 0 \end{bmatrix} = \begin{bmatrix} 0 & S_{11} \\ 0 & S_{21} \end{bmatrix}$$

The third term $\mathbf{S} \mathbf{B} \mathbf{R}^{-1} \mathbf{B}^T \mathbf{S}$ will be calculated in steps:

$$\mathbf{S} \mathbf{B} \mathbf{R}^{-1} \mathbf{B}^T \mathbf{S} = \begin{bmatrix} S_{11} & S_{12} \\ S_{21} & S_{22} \end{bmatrix} \begin{bmatrix} 0 \\ 1 \end{bmatrix} \mathbf{R}^{-1} \mathbf{B}^T \mathbf{S}$$

$$= \begin{bmatrix} S_{12} \\ S_{22} \end{bmatrix} \mathbf{R}^{-1} \mathbf{B}^T \mathbf{S}$$

$$= \begin{bmatrix} S_{12} \\ S_{22} \end{bmatrix} \begin{bmatrix} 0 & 1 \end{bmatrix} \mathbf{S}$$

$$= \begin{bmatrix} 0 & S_{12} \\ 0 & S_{22} \end{bmatrix} \mathbf{S}$$

$$= \begin{bmatrix} 0 & S_{12} \\ 0 & S_{22} \end{bmatrix} \begin{bmatrix} S_{11} & S_{12} \\ S_{21} & S_{22} \end{bmatrix}$$

$$= \begin{bmatrix} S_{12}S_{21} & S_{12}S_{22} \\ S_{22}S_{21} & S_{22}^2 \end{bmatrix}$$

Note that in this problem $\mathbf{R}^{-1} = 1$. Substituting matrices into the Riccati equation yields

$$\begin{bmatrix} 0 & 0 \\ S_{11} & S_{12} \end{bmatrix} + \begin{bmatrix} 0 & S_{11} \\ 0 & S_{21} \end{bmatrix} - \begin{bmatrix} S_{12}S_{21} & S_{12}S_{22} \\ S_{22}S_{21} & S_{22}^2 \end{bmatrix} + \begin{bmatrix} 1 & 0 \\ 0 & 1 \end{bmatrix} = \begin{bmatrix} 0 & 0 \\ 0 & 0 \end{bmatrix}$$

Combining the matrices yields

$$\begin{bmatrix} -S_{12}S_{21} + 1 & S_{11} - S_{12}S_{22} \\ S_{11} - S_{22}S_{21} & S_{12} + S_{21} - S_{22}^2 + 1 \end{bmatrix} = \begin{bmatrix} 0 & 0 \\ 0 & 0 \end{bmatrix}$$

We now must solve the nonlinear algebraic equations for the unknown Riccati gains:

$$-S_{12}S_{21} + 1 = 0$$

$$S_{11} - S_{12}S_{22} = 0$$

$$S_{12} + S_{21} - S_{22}^2 + 1 = 0$$

From symmetry
$$S_{12} = S_{21}$$

$$-S_{12}^2 + 1 = 0 \Rightarrow S_{12} = \pm\sqrt{1} = \pm 1$$

$$2S_{12} - S_{22}^2 + 1 = 0$$

For $S_{12} = 1$,

$$-S_{22}^2 + 3 = 0 \Rightarrow S_{22} = \pm\sqrt{3}$$

$$S_{11} - S_{12}S_{22} = 0 \Rightarrow S_{11} = \pm\sqrt{3}$$

The Riccati matrix $\mathbf{S}$ follows:

$$\mathbf{S} = \begin{bmatrix} \sqrt{3} & 1 \\ 1 & \sqrt{3} \end{bmatrix}$$

The control law $\eta = -\mathbf{k}^T\mathbf{x}$, where

$$\mathbf{k} = \mathbf{R}^{-1}\mathbf{B}^T\mathbf{S}$$

$$\mathbf{k} = [1][0 \quad 1] \begin{bmatrix} \sqrt{3} & 1 \\ 1 & \sqrt{3} \end{bmatrix} = [1 \quad \sqrt{3}]$$

The control law can now be written

$$\eta = -\mathbf{k}^T\mathbf{x} = -[1 \quad \sqrt{3}] \begin{bmatrix} x_1 \\ x_2 \end{bmatrix}$$

$$= -x_1 - \sqrt{3}x_2$$

For a higher-order system numerical techniques are required. The MATLAB control system toolbox has numerical algorithms for solving optimal control problems.

9.8
SUMMARY

In this chapter we examined another approach to control system analysis and design called modern control theory. This theory is based on the state-space formulation of the differential equations that govern the system. We showed that higher-order differential equations can be reduced to a system of first-order differential equations; that is, the state-space approach. These equations can be solved easily using a computer.

Once the system has been formulated in the state-space format we can use state feedback to locate the closed-loop eigenvalues so that the system meets whatever performance requirements are desired. When some of the states are not available for feedback we can design a state observer to estimate or predict the states. The estimated states then can be used in place of the actual states in the feedback system.

Finally, a short presentation of optimal control was presented. Optimal control allows the designer to specify constraints on maximum allowable excursion of the states and control input. This is accomplished by specifying weighting matrices for the states and control in an integral performance index. The optimal control gains are determined by solving the steady-state Riccati equation.

Modern control theory provides the control system designer with a set of very powerful tools for designing control systems.

PROBLEMS

Problems that require the use of a computer have the capital letter C after the problem number.

9.1. For the differential equations that follow, rewrite the equations in the state-space formulation. Each part—(a), (b), and (c)—is to be treated as a separate problem. Also identify the output equation.

(a) $\dfrac{d^2c}{dt^2} + 2\zeta\omega_n \dfrac{dc}{dt} + \omega_n^2 c = r$

(b) $\dfrac{d^3c}{dt^3} + \dfrac{d^2c}{dt^2} + 2\dfrac{dc}{dt} + c = 2\dfrac{dr}{dt} + 3r$

(c) $\dfrac{d^2\theta}{dt^2} + 3\dfrac{d\theta}{dt} + 2\dfrac{d\alpha}{dt} + 5\alpha = -6\delta_e$

$\dfrac{d\alpha}{dt} + 4\alpha - 15\dfrac{d\theta}{dt} = -3\delta_e$

Hint: For problem (b), assume that one of the states includes the derivative dr/dt.

9.2. The transfer functions for a feedback control system follow. Determine the state-space equations for the closed-loop system.

(a) $G(s) = \dfrac{k}{s(s + 2)(s + 3)}$ $H(s) = 1$

(b) $G(s) = \dfrac{k}{s(s^2 + 8s + 10)}$ $H(s) = 1$

9.3. Given the second-order differential equation

$$\frac{d^2c(t)}{dt^2} + 3\frac{dc(t)}{dt} + 2c(t) = r(t)$$

having the initial conditions $c(0) = 1$ and $dc/dt(0) = 0$, write the equation in state vector form.
(a) Find the state transition matrix.
(b) Determine the solution if $r(t)$ is a unit step function.

9.4. Given the linear time-invariant dynamical system that is governed by the equations

$$\begin{bmatrix} \dot{x}_1 \\ \dot{x}_2 \end{bmatrix} = \begin{bmatrix} 1 & 0 \\ 1 & 1 \end{bmatrix}\begin{bmatrix} x_1 \\ x_2 \end{bmatrix} + \begin{bmatrix} 1 \\ 1 \end{bmatrix}[\eta]$$

where

$$\begin{bmatrix} x_1(0) \\ x_2(0) \end{bmatrix} = \begin{bmatrix} 0 \\ 1 \end{bmatrix}$$

determine the state transition matrix and the response of the system if the input signal is a unit step function.

9.5(C). Use the numerical algorithm discussed in Section 9.2 to solve Problem 9.3.

9.6(C). Use the numerical algorithm discussed in Section 9.2 to solve Problem 9.4.

9.7. Given the following matrix

$$A = \begin{bmatrix} -2 & 1 \\ -5 & 0 \end{bmatrix}$$

(a) Determine the eigenvalues of **A**.
(b) Determine the transformation matrix **P** that can be used to diagonalize the **A** matrix

$$\Lambda = P^{-1}AP$$

9.8. Given the following matrix

$$A = \begin{bmatrix} -4 & 1 \\ 0 & -2 \end{bmatrix}$$

(a) Determine the eigenvalues of **A**.
(b) Determine the transformation matrix **P** that can be used to diagonalize the **A** matrix

$$\Lambda = P^{-1}AP$$

9.9(C). The state-space equations are given as follows:

$$\begin{bmatrix} \dot{x}_1 \\ \dot{x}_2 \\ \dot{x}_3 \end{bmatrix} = \begin{bmatrix} 1 & 2 & -1 \\ 0 & 1 & 0 \\ 1 & -4 & 2 \end{bmatrix}\begin{bmatrix} x_1 \\ x_2 \\ x_3 \end{bmatrix} + \begin{bmatrix} 1 \\ 0 \\ 0 \end{bmatrix}u$$

Determine the transformation, **P**, that transforms the state equations so that the new plant matrix is a diagonal matrix.

9.10(C). Given the following matrix determine the transformation **P** that transforms the **A** matrix into a diagonalized matrix **Λ**.

$$\mathbf{A} = \begin{bmatrix} 0 & 1 & 0 \\ 0 & 0 & 1 \\ -6 & -11 & -6 \end{bmatrix}$$

$$\mathbf{\Lambda} = \begin{bmatrix} -1 & 0 & 0 \\ 0 & -2 & 0 \\ 0 & 0 & -3 \end{bmatrix}$$

9.11. Given the following matrix determine the transformation matrix **P**, that transforms the **A** matrix into a diagonal matrix **Λ**.

$$\mathbf{A} = \begin{bmatrix} -3 & -1 \\ 5 & -1 \end{bmatrix}$$

$$\mathbf{\Lambda} = \begin{bmatrix} -2 + 2i & 0 \\ 0 & -2 - 2i \end{bmatrix}$$

What form would **P** take to obtain **Λ** in the following forms?

$$\mathbf{\Lambda} = \begin{bmatrix} -\sigma_1 & \omega_1 \\ -\omega_1 & \sigma_1 \end{bmatrix}$$

or

$$\mathbf{\Lambda} = \begin{bmatrix} -2 & 2 \\ -2 & -2 \end{bmatrix}$$

9.12. When a new state vector is selected so that the transformed equation has a diagonalized plant matrix

$$\mathbf{\Lambda} = \begin{bmatrix} \lambda_1 & 0 & 0 \\ 0 & \lambda_2 & 0 \\ 0 & 0 & \lambda_3 \end{bmatrix}$$

show that the state transition matrix **Φ**(t) can be expressed as

$$\mathbf{\Phi}(t) = e^{\mathbf{\Lambda}t} = \begin{bmatrix} e^{\lambda_1 t} & 0 & 0 \\ 0 & e^{\lambda_2 t} & 0 \\ 0 & 0 & e^{\lambda_3 t} \end{bmatrix}$$

The series expansion for e^{at} is given as $e^{at} = 1 + at + \dfrac{a^2 t^2}{2!} + \dfrac{a^3 t^3}{3!} + \dfrac{a^4 t^4}{4!} + \cdots$

9.13. When the eigenvalues are repeated, the **Λ** matrix takes on the following

$$\mathbf{\Lambda} = \begin{bmatrix} \lambda_1 & 0 & 0 \\ 0 & \lambda_2 & 0 \\ 0 & 0 & \lambda_2 \end{bmatrix}$$

Show that the state transition matrix for this case is

$$\Phi(t) = e^{\Lambda t} = \begin{bmatrix} e^{\lambda_1 t} & 0 & 0 \\ 0 & e^{\lambda_2 t} & te^{\lambda_2 t} \\ 0 & 0 & e^{\lambda_2 t} \end{bmatrix}$$

9.14(C). Given the state equations

$$\begin{bmatrix} \dot{x}_1 \\ \dot{x}_2 \\ \dot{x}_3 \end{bmatrix} = \begin{bmatrix} 0 & 1 & 0 \\ 0 & 0 & 1 \\ -3 & -6 & -4 \end{bmatrix} \begin{bmatrix} x_1 \\ x_2 \\ x_3 \end{bmatrix} + \begin{bmatrix} 0 \\ 0 \\ 1 \end{bmatrix} [\eta]$$

determine whether the system is completely controllable.

9.15. If the output matrix for Problem 9.9 is

$$y = \begin{bmatrix} 1 & -1 & 1 \end{bmatrix} \begin{bmatrix} x_1 \\ x_2 \\ x_3 \end{bmatrix}$$

determine the following:
(a) Is the system controllable?
(b) Is the system observable?

9.16. Given the system governed by the following state equations

$$\begin{bmatrix} \dot{x}_1(t) \\ \dot{x}_2(t) \end{bmatrix} = \begin{bmatrix} 0 & 1 \\ -3 & -4 \end{bmatrix} \begin{bmatrix} x_1(t) \\ x_2(t) \end{bmatrix} + \begin{bmatrix} 0 \\ 1 \end{bmatrix} [\eta] \quad \text{and} \quad \begin{bmatrix} x_1(0) \\ x_2(0) \end{bmatrix} = \begin{bmatrix} 1 \\ 1 \end{bmatrix}$$

that can be decoupled by defining a new state variable $z(t)$ so that

$$x(t) = P z(t)$$

or

$$\dot{z}(t) = \Lambda z + \bar{B}\eta$$

where $\Lambda = P^{-1}AP$ and $\bar{B} = P^{-1}B$, the Λ matrix is a diagonal matrix and P is a transformation matrix.
(a) Show that the transformation matrix P is as follows:

$$P = \begin{bmatrix} 1 & 1 \\ -1 & -3 \end{bmatrix}$$

(b) Determine the state transition matrix $\Phi(t)*$ for the new state equations

$$\dot{z}(t) = \Lambda z + \bar{B}\eta$$

(c) Determine the state transition matrix $\Phi(t)$ for the original state equations

$$\dot{x}(t) = Ax + B\eta$$

from $\Phi(t)*$.
(d) The free response $x(t) = $?

9.17. A single-axis, attitude control system for a satellite can be modeled as follows:

$$\begin{bmatrix} \dot{\theta} \\ \dot{q} \end{bmatrix} = \begin{bmatrix} 0 & 1 \\ 0 & 0 \end{bmatrix} \begin{bmatrix} \theta \\ q \end{bmatrix} + \begin{bmatrix} 0 \\ \dfrac{\ell}{I} \end{bmatrix} T$$

where θ, q, T, ℓ, and I are defined as follows:
θ = the pitch angle of the satellite
q = the pitch rate of the satellite
T = the thrust of the control thrusters
ℓ = the distance of the thrusters from the satellite's center of gravity
I = the mass moment of inertia about the axis of rotation.

If $\ell/I = 50$ determine the state feedback gains so that the closed-loop system has the following performance:

$$\omega_n = 20 \text{ rad/s}$$

$$\zeta = 0.707$$

9.18(C). An open-loop control system has the following state-space model:

$$\mathbf{A} = \begin{bmatrix} 0 & 1 & 0 \\ -1 & 0 & 2 \\ -4 & -2 & -2 \end{bmatrix}$$

$$\mathbf{B} = \begin{bmatrix} 0 \\ 2 \\ 1 \end{bmatrix}$$

(a) Determine the characteristic equations and eigenvalues for the open-loop system.
(b) Use the Bass-Gura method to locate the closed-loop eigenvalues at $\lambda_1 = -5$, $\lambda_{2,3} = -2 \pm 3i$.

REFERENCES

9.1. Kuo, B. C. *Automatic Control Systems.* Englewood Cliffs, NJ: Prentice-Hall, 1975.
9.2. D'Souza, A. F. *Design of Control Systems.* Englewood Cliffs, NJ: Prentice-Hall, 1988.
9.3. Hale, F. J. *Introduction to Control System Analysis and Design.* Englewood Cliffs, NJ: Prentice-Hall, 1988.
9.4. Takahashi, Y.; M. J. Rabins; and D. M. Auslander. *Control and Dynamic Systems.* Reading, MA: Addison-Wesley, 1970.
9.5. Friedland, B. *Control System Design: An Introduction to State-Space Methods.* New York: McGraw-Hill, 1986.
9.6. Paynter, H. M. *Analysis and Design of Engineering Systems.* Cambridge, MA: MIT Press, 1961.
9.7. Bass, R. W.; and I. Gura. "High-Order System Design via State-Space Considerations." In *Proceeding of the Joint Automatic Control Conference,* June 1965.
9.8. Bryson, A. E.; and Y. C. Ho. *Applied Optimal Control.* Washington, D.C.: Hemisphere, 1975.

CHAPTER 10

Application of Modern Control Theory to Aircraft Autopilot Design

"While the Wright brothers are justly famed for their priority in many fields of aviation, their most notable contribution was the implicit appreciation that the secret to the control of flight was feedback."

Duane McRuer and Dunstan Graham [10.1]

10.1
INTRODUCTION

In this final chapter we apply modern control theory to the design of aircraft autopilots. This is accomplished through a series of example problems to illustrate the control techniques presented in Chapter 9. State feedback is used to provide a stability augmentation system (SAS) to improve an aircraft's longitudinal and lateral flying qualities. In addition, an altitude hold autopilot is designed using state feedback.

Next we discuss the design of a state observer. Recall that a state observer or estimator is required to implement a state feedback control law if some of the states are unavailable. Obviously a state that is not measured cannot be used in the state feedback controller. The observer provides estimates of the states so the controller can be implemented. Finally we examine several examples where we apply optimal control theory.

10.2
STABILITY AUGMENTATION

State feedback control can be used to improve the stability characteristics of airplanes that lack good flying qualities. As shown in Chapter 9 the eigenvalues of a system can be changed by using state feedback. The longitudinal eigenvalues are the short- and long-period roots. If the longitudinal eigenvalues do not meet the handling quality specifications discussed in Chapter 4 the airplane would be considered difficult to fly and deemed unacceptable by the pilots.

10.2.1 Longitudinal Stability Augmentation

Starting with the longitudinal state equations given in Chapter 4, we develop a set of linear algebraic equations in terms of the unknown feedback gains. The state equations for the longitudinal motion have been simplified by neglecting the affect of the control on the X-force equation and the stability derivative $M_{\dot{w}}$. The state equations are given below:

$$\begin{bmatrix} \Delta \dot{u} \\ \Delta \dot{w} \\ \Delta \dot{q} \\ \Delta \dot{\theta} \end{bmatrix} = \begin{bmatrix} X_u & X_w & 0 & -g \\ Z_u & Z_w & u_0 & 0 \\ M_u & M_w & M_q & 0 \\ 0 & 0 & 1 & 0 \end{bmatrix} \begin{bmatrix} \Delta u \\ \Delta w \\ \Delta q \\ \Delta \theta \end{bmatrix} + \begin{bmatrix} 0 \\ Z_\delta \\ M_\delta \\ 0 \end{bmatrix} [\Delta \delta_e] \tag{10.1}$$

or
$$\dot{\mathbf{x}} = \mathbf{A}\mathbf{x} + \mathbf{B}\eta \tag{10.2}$$

where $\mathbf{A}$ and $\mathbf{B}$ are the stability and control matrices just shown and $\mathbf{x}$ and η are the state and control vectors.

The eigenvalues of the $\mathbf{A}$ matrix are the short- and long-period roots. If these roots are unacceptable to the pilot, a stability augmentation system will be required. State feedback design can be used to provide the stability augmentation system. In state feedback design we assume a linear control law that is proportional to the states; that is,

$$\eta = -\mathbf{k}^T\mathbf{x} + \eta_p \tag{10.3}$$

where $\mathbf{k}^T$ is the transpose of the feedback gain vector and η_p is the pilot input. Substituting the control law into the state equation yields

$$\dot{\mathbf{x}} = (\mathbf{A} - \mathbf{B}\mathbf{k}^T)\mathbf{x} + \mathbf{B}\eta_p \tag{10.4}$$

or
$$\dot{\mathbf{x}} = \mathbf{A}^*\mathbf{x} + \mathbf{B}\eta_p \tag{10.5}$$

where $\mathbf{A}^*$ is the augmented matrix, expressed as

$$\mathbf{A}^* = \mathbf{A} - \mathbf{B}\mathbf{k}^T \tag{10.6}$$

The augmented matrix for the longitudinal system of equations is

$$\mathbf{A}^* = \begin{bmatrix} X_u & X_w & 0 & -g \\ Z_u - Z_\delta k_1 & Z_w - Z_\delta k_2 & u_0 - Z_\delta k_3 & -Z_\delta k_4 \\ M_u - M_\delta k_1 & M_w - M_\delta k_2 & M_q - M_\delta k_3 & -M_\delta k_4 \\ 0 & 0 & 1 & 0 \end{bmatrix} \tag{10.7}$$

The characteristic equation for the augmented matrix is obtained by solving the equation

$$|\lambda \mathbf{I} - \mathbf{A}^*| = 0 \tag{10.8}$$

which yields a quartic characteristic equation,

$$A\lambda^4 + B\lambda^3 + C\lambda^2 + D\lambda + E = 0 \tag{10.9}$$

where the coefficients are defined as follows:

$$A = 1.0$$

$$\left.\begin{aligned}
B &= Z_\delta k_2 + M_\delta k_3 - (X_u + Z_w + M_q) \\
C &= Z_\delta X_w k_1 + (u_0 M_\delta - X_u Z_\delta - Z_\delta M_q)k_2 \\
&\quad + (Z_\delta M_w - X_u M_\delta - Z_w M_\delta)k_3 + M_\delta k_4 \\
&\quad + X_u M_q + X_u Z_w + Z_w M_q - u_0 M_w - X_w Z_u \\
D &= (u_0 X_w M_\delta - gM_\delta - X_w Z_\delta M_q)k_1 + (X_u Z_\delta M_q - u_0 X_u M_\delta)k_2 \\
&\quad + (X_u Z_w M_\delta - X_u Z_\delta M_w - X_w Z_u M_\delta + X_w Z_\delta M_u)k_3 \\
&\quad + (Z_\delta M_w - X_u M_\delta - Z_w M_\delta)k_4 + gM_u - X_u Z_w M_q \\
&\quad + u_0 X_u M_w + X_w Z_u M_q - u_0 X_w M_u \\
E &= (gZ_w M_\delta - gZ_\delta M_w)k_1 + (gZ_\delta M_u - gZ_u M_\delta)k_2 \\
&\quad + (X_u Z_w M_\delta - X_u Z_\delta M_w - X_w Z_u M_\delta + X_w Z_\delta M_u)k_4 \\
&\quad + gZ_u M_w - gZ_w M_u
\end{aligned}\right\} \quad (10.10)$$

The characteristic equation of the augmented system is a function of the known stability derivatives and the unknown feedback gains. The feedback gains can be determined once the desired longitudinal characteristics are specified. For example, if the desired characteristic roots are

$$\lambda_{1,2} = -\zeta_{sp}\omega_{n_{sp}} \pm i\omega_{n_{sp}}\sqrt{1 - \zeta_{sp}^2} \qquad (10.11)$$

and

$$\lambda_{3,4} = -\zeta_p\omega_{n_p} \pm i\omega_{n_p}\sqrt{1 - \zeta_p^2} \qquad (10.12)$$

then the desired characteristic equation is

$$\lambda^4 - [(\lambda_1 + \lambda_2 + \lambda_3 + \lambda_4)]\lambda^3 + [\lambda_1\lambda_2 + \lambda_3\lambda_4 + (\lambda_1 + \lambda_2)(\lambda_3 + \lambda_4)]\lambda^2$$
$$- [\lambda_1\lambda_2(\lambda_3 + \lambda_4) + \lambda_3\lambda_4(\lambda_1 + \lambda_2)]\lambda + \lambda_1\lambda_2\lambda_3\lambda_4 = 0 \qquad (10.13)$$

By equating the coefficients of like powers of λ for the augmented and desired characteristic equations one obtains a set of four linear algebraic equations in terms of the unknown gains. These equations can be solved for the feedback gains.

EXAMPLE PROBLEM 10.1. An airplane is found to have poor short-period flying qualities in a particular flight regime. To improve the flying qualities, a stability augmentation system using state feedback is to be employed. Determine the feedback gains so that the airplane's short-period characteristics are $\lambda_{sp} = -2.1 \pm 2.14i$. Assume that the original short-period dynamics are given by

$$\begin{bmatrix} \Delta\dot{\alpha} \\ \Delta\dot{q} \end{bmatrix} = \begin{bmatrix} -0.334 & 1.0 \\ -2.52 & -0.387 \end{bmatrix}\begin{bmatrix} \Delta\alpha \\ \Delta q \end{bmatrix} + \begin{bmatrix} -0.027 \\ -2.6 \end{bmatrix}[\Delta\delta_e]$$

Solution. The augmented matrix $\mathbf{A}^*$ can be obtained from Equation (10.6):

$$\mathbf{A}^* = \mathbf{A} - \mathbf{B}\mathbf{k}^T$$

$$\mathbf{A}^* = \begin{bmatrix} -0.334 + 0.027k_1 & 1.0 + 0.027k_2 \\ -2.52 + 2.6k_1 & -0.387 + 2.6k_2 \end{bmatrix}$$

The eigenvalues of the augmented matrix $\mathbf{A}^*$ are determined from the characteristic equation, which is obtained from

$$|\lambda\mathbf{I} - \mathbf{A}^*| = 0$$

or

$$\begin{vmatrix} \lambda + 0.334 - 0.027k_1 & -1.0 - 0.027k_2 \\ 2.52 - 2.6k_1 & \lambda + 0.387 - 2.6k_2 \end{vmatrix} = 0$$

Expanding the determinant yields the characteristic equation of the augmented system in terms of the unknown feedback gains, k_1 and k_2:

$$\lambda^2 + (0.721 - 0.027k_1 - 2.6k_2)\lambda + 2.65 - 2.61k_1 - 0.8k_2 = 0$$

The desired characteristic equation is given as

$$\lambda^2 + 4.2\lambda + 9 = 0$$

Comparing like powers of λ we obtain a set of algebraic equations for the unknown feedback gains:

$$0.721 - 0.027k_1 - 2.6k_2 = 4.2 \qquad 2.65 - 2.61k_1 - 0.8k_2 = 9$$

Solving for the gains yields

$$k_1 = -2.03 \qquad k_2 = -1.318$$

and the state feedback control is given as

$$\Delta\delta_e = 2.03\ \Delta\alpha + 1.318\ \Delta q$$

Figure 10.1 shows the response of the airplane with and without the stability augmentation system. An initial angle of attack disturbance of 5° is used to excite the airplane. Without the stability augmentation, the airplane responds in its natural short-period motion. However, when the state feedback stability augmentation system is active the disturbance is quickly damped out.

In Example Problem 10.1 the state feedback gains for the second-order system are relatively easy to determine. Through some simple algebraic manipulations and calculations we can estimate the state feedback gains. On the other hand, when the order of

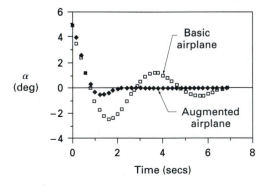

FIGURE 10.1
Longitudinal response of an airplane with and without state feedback.

the system is greater than 2 the algebraic manipulations and calculations can become quite tedious. For higher-order systems, numerical techniques usually are used to find the state feedback gains.

As mentioned, numerous computer software codes are available to solve control problems and in particular to determine the state feedback gains. In the following example problem we rely on the Bass-Gura method to determine state feedback gains for improving the longitudinal dynamics using the complete or fourth-order model of longitudinal equations. To solve this problem using the Bass-Gura method we use matrix software that is readily available for most personal computers.

EXAMPLE PROBLEM 10.2. The longitudinal equations for an airplane having poor handling qualities follow. Use state feedback to provide stability augmentation so that the augmented aircraft has the following short- and long-period (phugoid) characteristics:

$$\begin{bmatrix} \Delta \dot{u} \\ \Delta \dot{w} \\ \Delta \dot{q} \\ \Delta \dot{\theta} \end{bmatrix} = \begin{bmatrix} -0.01 & 0.1 & 0 & -32.2 \\ -0.40 & -0.8 & 180 & 0 \\ 0 & -0.003 & -0.5 & 0 \\ 0 & 0 & 1 & 0 \end{bmatrix} \begin{bmatrix} \Delta u \\ \Delta w \\ \Delta q \\ \Delta \theta \end{bmatrix} + \begin{bmatrix} 0 \\ -10 \\ -2.8 \\ 0 \end{bmatrix} [\Delta \delta_e]$$

$$\zeta_{sp} = 0.6 \qquad \omega_{n_{sp}} = 3.0 \text{ rad/s}$$

$$\zeta_p = 0.05 \qquad \omega_{n_p} = 0.1 \text{ rad/s}$$

Solution. As the order of the system increases beyond 3, simple hand calculations similar to Example Problem 10.1 become quite difficult. As stated earlier, software packages are available for solving state feedback design problems. Later in this chapter we use such programs to solve selected problems; however, for this example problem we use the Bass-Gura method, which lends itself to simple matrix manipulations. The state feedback gains can be estimated using the Bass-Gura technique described in Chapter 9. The feedback gains are found by solving the following equations:

$$\mathbf{k} = [(\mathbf{VW})^T]^{-1}[\bar{\mathbf{a}} - \mathbf{a}]$$

where $\mathbf{V}$ is the controllability matrix, $\mathbf{W}$ is a transformation matrix, and $\bar{\mathbf{a}}$ and $\mathbf{a}$ are vectors made up of the coefficients of the characteristic equation of the augmented or closed-loop system $(\mathbf{A} - \mathbf{Bk}^T)$ and the characteristic equation of the open-loop plant matrix $\mathbf{A}$.

The characteristic equation for the augmented or closed-loop system is determined by deciding on what closed-loop performance is desired. For this particular problem the desired eigenvalues are specified in terms of the short- and long-period damping ratio and undamped natural frequency. The desired characteristic equation can be written in terms of the damping and frequency as follows:

$$(\lambda^2 + 2\zeta_{sp}\omega_{n_{sp}}\lambda + \omega_{n_{sp}}^2)(\lambda^2 + 2\zeta_p\omega_{n_p}\lambda + \omega_{n_p}^2) = 0$$

Substituting the numerical values of ζ_{sp}, $\omega_{n_{sp}}$, ζ_p, and ω_{n_p} into the preceding equation and expanding yields

$$(\lambda^2 + 3.6\lambda + 9)(\lambda^2 + 0.01\lambda + 0.01) = 0$$

or
$$\lambda^4 + 3.61\lambda^3 + 9.05\lambda^2 + 0.126\lambda + 0.09 = 0$$

The vector $\bar{\mathbf{a}}$ is created from the coefficients of the desired characteristic equation:

$$\lambda^4 + \bar{a}_1\lambda^3 + \bar{a}_2\lambda^2 + \bar{a}_3\lambda + \bar{a}_4 = 0$$

or
$$\bar{\mathbf{a}} = \begin{bmatrix} \bar{a}_1 \\ \bar{a}_2 \\ \bar{a}_3 \\ \bar{a}_4 \end{bmatrix} = \begin{bmatrix} 3.61 \\ 9.05 \\ 0.126 \\ 0.09 \end{bmatrix}$$

The characteristic equation of the open-loop system is obtained by solving the equation

$$|\lambda\mathbf{I} - \mathbf{A}| = 0$$

which yields

$$\lambda^4 + 1.31\lambda^3 + 0.993\lambda^2 + 0.0294\lambda + 0.0386 = 0$$

The vector $\mathbf{a}$ is created from the coefficients of the open-loop characteristic equation:

$$\lambda^4 + a_1\lambda^3 + a_2\lambda^2 + a_3\lambda + a_4 = 0$$

or
$$\mathbf{a} = \begin{bmatrix} a_1 \\ a_2 \\ a_3 \\ a_4 \end{bmatrix} = \begin{bmatrix} 1.31 \\ 0.993 \\ 0.0294 \\ 0.0386 \end{bmatrix}$$

Continuing with the solution, we need to determine the controllability matrix, $\mathbf{V}$. In Chapter 9 we showed that the controllability matrix is defined in terms of the plant and control matrices. For the fourth-order system under consideration here, the controllability matrix is

$$\mathbf{V} = [\mathbf{B} \quad \mathbf{AB} \quad \mathbf{A}^2\mathbf{B} \quad \mathbf{A}^3\mathbf{B}]$$

The elements of the $\mathbf{V}$ matrix can be readily calculated by performing the appropriate matrix multiplications:

$$\mathbf{AB} = \begin{bmatrix} -0.01 & 0.1 & 0 & -32.2 \\ -0.40 & -0.8 & 180 & 0 \\ 0 & -0.003 & -0.5 & 0 \\ 0 & 0 & 1.0 & 0 \end{bmatrix} \begin{bmatrix} 0 \\ -10 \\ -2.8 \\ 0 \end{bmatrix} = \begin{bmatrix} -1.0 \\ -496 \\ 1.43 \\ -2.8 \end{bmatrix}$$

$$\mathbf{A}^2\mathbf{B} = \mathbf{A}[\mathbf{AB}] = \begin{bmatrix} -0.01 & 0.1 & 0 & -32.2 \\ -0.40 & -0.8 & 180 & 0 \\ 0 & -0.003 & -0.5 & 0 \\ 0 & 0 & 1.0 & 0 \end{bmatrix} \begin{bmatrix} -1.0 \\ -496 \\ 1.43 \\ -2.8 \end{bmatrix}$$

$$\mathbf{A}^2\mathbf{B} = \begin{bmatrix} 40.57 \\ 654.6 \\ 0.773 \\ 1.43 \end{bmatrix}$$

$$\mathbf{A^3B} = \mathbf{A[A^2B]} = \begin{bmatrix} -0.01 & 0.1 & 0 & -32.2 \\ -0.40 & -0.8 & 180 & 0 \\ 0 & -0.003 & -0.5 & 0 \\ 0 & 0 & 1.0 & 0 \end{bmatrix} \begin{bmatrix} 40.57 \\ 654.6 \\ 0.773 \\ 1.43 \end{bmatrix}$$

$$\mathbf{A^3B} = \begin{bmatrix} 19.008 \\ -400.77 \\ -2.35 \\ 0.773 \end{bmatrix}$$

Substituting the column matrices into the definition of $\mathbf{V}$ yields

$$\mathbf{V} = \begin{bmatrix} 0 & -1.0 & 40.57 & 19.008 \\ -10 & 496 & 654.6 & -400.77 \\ -2.8 & 1.43 & 0.773 & -2.35 \\ 0 & -2.8 & 1.43 & 0.773 \end{bmatrix}$$

The transformation matrix $\mathbf{W}$ is required if the plant matrix $\mathbf{A}$ is not in the companion form. For this particular problem the $\mathbf{A}$ matrix is not in companion form; therefore, the transformation matrix must be developed. As was shown in Chapter 9 the transformation matrix is defined in terms of the coefficients of the characteristic equation of the plant matrix. For this particular example of a fourth-order system the $\mathbf{W}$ matrix is defined as

$$\mathbf{W} = \begin{bmatrix} 1 & a_1 & a_2 & a_3 \\ 0 & 1 & a_1 & a_2 \\ 0 & 0 & 1 & a_1 \\ 0 & 0 & 0 & 1 \end{bmatrix} = \begin{bmatrix} 1 & 1.31 & 0.993 & 0.0294 \\ 0 & 1 & 1.31 & 0.993 \\ 0 & 0 & 1 & 1.31 \\ 0 & 0 & 0 & 1 \end{bmatrix}$$

Now we are in a position to calculate $[(\mathbf{VW})^T]^{-1}$. This will be accomplished in the following steps:

$$\mathbf{VW} = \begin{bmatrix} 0 & -1 & 40.57 & 19.008 \\ -10.0 & -496 & 654.6 & -400.781 \\ -2.8 & 1.43 & 0.773 & -2.35 \\ 0 & -2.8 & 1.43 & 0.773 \end{bmatrix} \begin{bmatrix} 1 & 1.31 & 0.993 & 0.0294 \\ 0 & 1.0 & 1.31 & 0.993 \\ 0 & 0 & 1.0 & 1.31 \\ 0 & 0 & 0 & 1.0 \end{bmatrix}$$

$$\mathbf{VW} = \begin{bmatrix} 0 & -1.0 & 39.23 & 71.2 \\ -10.0 & -509.1 & -5.01 & -36.1 \\ -2.8 & -2.24 & -0.134 & 0 \\ 0 & -2.8 & -2.24 & -0.13 \end{bmatrix}$$

The transpose of the matrix $\mathbf{VW}$ is obtained by interchanging the rows and columns:

$$(\mathbf{VW})^T = \begin{bmatrix} 0 & -10.0 & -2.8 & 0 \\ -1.0 & -509 & -2.234 & -2.8 \\ 39.3 & -5.1 & -0.13 & -2.24 \\ 71.2 & -36.1 & 0.0 & -0.13 \end{bmatrix}$$

The inverse of the matrix $[(\mathbf{VW})]^T)^{-1}$ follows:

$$([\mathbf{VW}]^T)^{-1} = \begin{bmatrix} 0.0008 & -0.0010 & 0.0004 & 0.0138 \\ 0.0014 & -0.0019 & 0.0025 & -0.0014 \\ -0.3622 & 0.0068 & -0.0089 & 0.0050 \\ 0.0321 & -0.0135 & -0.4446 & 0.2451 \end{bmatrix}$$

The state feedback gains can now be calculated from the equation

$$\mathbf{k} = ([\mathbf{VW}]^T)^{-1} (\bar{\mathbf{a}} - \mathbf{a})$$

$$= \begin{bmatrix} 0.0008 & -0.0010 & 0.0004 & 0.0138 \\ 0.0014 & -0.0019 & 0.0025 & -0.0014 \\ -0.3622 & 0.0068 & -0.0089 & 0.0050 \\ 0.0321 & -0.0135 & -0.4446 & 0.2451 \end{bmatrix} \left(\begin{bmatrix} 3.61 \\ 9.05 \\ 0.126 \\ 0.09 \end{bmatrix} - \begin{bmatrix} 1.31 \\ 0.993 \\ 0.0294 \\ 0.0386 \end{bmatrix} \right)$$

$$= \begin{bmatrix} -0.0055 \\ -0.0120 \\ -0.7785 \\ -0.0656 \end{bmatrix}$$

Having determined the feedback gains we can now define the control law. The stability augmentation control law is

$$\Delta \delta_e = -\mathbf{k}^T \mathbf{x} = -[-0.0055 \;\; -0.0120 \;\; -0.7785 \;\; -0.0656] \begin{bmatrix} \Delta u \\ \Delta w \\ \Delta q \\ \Delta \theta \end{bmatrix}$$

$$= 0.0055 \,\Delta u + 0.0120 \,\Delta w + 0.7785 \,\Delta q + 0.0656 \,\Delta \theta$$

10.2.2 Lateral Stability Augmentation

The lateral eigenvalues of an airplane also can be modified using state feedback. The lateral state equations are expressed in state-space form as follows

$$\begin{bmatrix} \Delta \dot{v} \\ \Delta \dot{p} \\ \Delta \dot{r} \\ \Delta \dot{\phi} \end{bmatrix} = \begin{bmatrix} Y_v & 0 & -u_0 & g \\ L_v & L_p & L_r & 0 \\ N_v & N_p & N_r & 0 \\ 0 & 1 & 0 & 0 \end{bmatrix} \begin{bmatrix} \Delta v \\ \Delta p \\ \Delta r \\ \Delta \phi \end{bmatrix} + \begin{bmatrix} Y_{\delta_a} & Y_{\delta_r} \\ L_{\delta_a} & L_{\delta_r} \\ N_{\delta_a} & N_{\delta_r} \\ 0 & 0 \end{bmatrix} \begin{bmatrix} \Delta \delta_a \\ \Delta \delta_r \end{bmatrix} \qquad (10.14)$$

or in shorthand mathematical form

$$\dot{\mathbf{x}} = \mathbf{A}\mathbf{x} + \mathbf{B}\boldsymbol{\eta} \qquad (10.15)$$

Note that the control vector is made up of two control inputs; namely, the aileron and rudder deflector angle. The control matrix $\mathbf{B}$ no longer is just a column matrix but a 4×2 rectangular matrix.

When we have a multiple input system the state feedback gain vector becomes a gain matrix of order $n \times m$ where n is the order of the system and m is the number of control input signals. Placing the eigenvalues at some desired location allows the designer to identify n of the gains; however, we still have $n \times (m - 1)$ gains that must be selected. There are techniques that can be used to handle the multiple input system but these techniques are beyond the scope of this book.

One technique for handling the multiple input system was discussed in Chapter 9. Basically this technique reduces the gain matrix to a gain vector. Oehman and Suddath [10.2] use this approach to apply state feedback control for lateral stability augmentation. The control law can be expressed in terms of a constant row matrix, $\mathbf{g}$, the gain vector, $\mathbf{k}$, and the pilot's control input, η_p:

$$\eta = -\mathbf{g}\mathbf{k}^T\mathbf{x} + \eta_p \qquad (10.16)$$

The procedure is identical to that for the longitudinal equations. The constant vector $\mathbf{g}$ establishes the relationship between the aileron and rudder for augmentation. Either g_1 or g_2 is equal to 1, and the ratio $g_1/g_2 = \Delta\delta_a/\Delta\delta_r$ is specified by control deflection limits.

Substituting the control vector into the state equation yields

$$\dot{\mathbf{x}} = (\mathbf{A} - \mathbf{B}\mathbf{g}\mathbf{k}^T)\mathbf{x} + \mathbf{B}\eta_p \qquad (10.17)$$

or

$$\dot{\mathbf{x}} = \mathbf{A}^*\mathbf{x} + \mathbf{B}\eta_p \qquad (10.18)$$

where $\mathbf{A}^*$ is the augmented matrix, expressed as

$$\mathbf{A}^* = \mathbf{A} - \mathbf{B}\mathbf{g}\mathbf{k}^T \qquad (10.19)$$

EXAMPLE PROBLEM 10.3. Use state feedback to improve the Dutch roll characteristics of an airplane. For this example we use a 2-degrees-of-freedom model to approximate the Dutch roll motion. The equations used to approximate the Dutch roll motion follow:

$$\begin{bmatrix} \Delta\dot{\beta} \\ \Delta\dot{r} \end{bmatrix} = \begin{bmatrix} Y_\beta/u_0 & -(1 - Y_r/u_0) \\ N_\beta & N_r \end{bmatrix}\begin{bmatrix} \Delta\beta \\ \Delta r \end{bmatrix} + \begin{bmatrix} 0 & Y_{\delta_r}/u_0 \\ N_{\delta_a} & N_{\delta_r} \end{bmatrix}\begin{bmatrix} \Delta\delta_a \\ \Delta\delta_r \end{bmatrix}$$

Assume that the stability derivatives have the following numerical values.

$$Y_\beta = -19.5 \text{ ft/s}^2 \qquad Y_{\delta_r} = 4.8 \text{ ft/s}$$

$$Y_r = 1.3 \text{ ft/s} \qquad N_{\delta_r} = -0.082 \text{ 1/s}^2$$

$$N_\beta = 1.5 \text{ 1/s}^2 \qquad N_{\delta_a} = -0.008 \text{ 1/s}^2$$

$$N_r = -.21 \text{ 1/s} \qquad u_0 = 400 \text{ ft/s}$$

The desired damping ratio for the Dutch roll motion is $\zeta_{DR} = 0.3$ and the undamped natural frequency is $\omega_n = 1.0$ rad/s.

Substituting the numerical values of the stability derivatives into the Dutch roll equations yields

$$\begin{bmatrix} \Delta\dot{\beta} \\ \Delta\dot{r} \end{bmatrix} = \begin{bmatrix} -0.049 & -0.997 \\ 1.5 & -0.21 \end{bmatrix}\begin{bmatrix} \Delta\beta \\ \Delta r \end{bmatrix} + \begin{bmatrix} 0 & 0.012 \\ -0.008 & -0.082 \end{bmatrix}\begin{bmatrix} \Delta\delta_a \\ \Delta\delta_r \end{bmatrix}$$

Solution. For a multiple-input system the control law is modified as follows:

$$\eta = -\mathbf{g}\mathbf{k}^T\mathbf{x}$$

where

$$\eta = \begin{bmatrix} \Delta\delta_a \\ \Delta\delta_r \end{bmatrix}$$

$$\mathbf{g} = \begin{bmatrix} g_1 \\ g_2 \end{bmatrix}$$

$$\mathbf{k} = \begin{bmatrix} k_1 \\ k_2 \end{bmatrix}$$

$$\mathbf{x} = \begin{bmatrix} \Delta\beta \\ \Delta r \end{bmatrix}$$

The elements of the constant vector $\mathbf{g}$ represent a weighting of the relative authority of the ailerons and rudder for augmentation. For this problem we assume that $g_1 = 1$ and $g_2 = \Delta\delta_r/\delta_a$ is taken as the ratio of the maximum control deflection angles. With this assumption the maximum authority of the rudder and aileron would be achieved simultaneously. We assume that $g_2 = \Delta\delta_a/\Delta\delta_r = 0.25$ for this problem. Substituting the control law into the state equation yields

$$\dot{\mathbf{x}} = (\mathbf{A} - \mathbf{Bgk}^T)\mathbf{x}$$

The augmented matrix $\mathbf{A}^*$ is given as

$$\mathbf{A}^* = \mathbf{A} - \mathbf{Bgk}^T$$

The characteristic equation of the augmented system can now be determined:

$$|\lambda\mathbf{I} - \mathbf{A}^*| = 0$$

or

$$\left| \begin{bmatrix} \lambda & 0 \\ 0 & \lambda \end{bmatrix} - \begin{bmatrix} -0.049 & -0.997 \\ 1.5 & -0.21 \end{bmatrix} + \begin{bmatrix} 0 & 0.012 \\ -0.008 & -0.082 \end{bmatrix} \begin{bmatrix} 1 \\ 0.25 \end{bmatrix} [k_1 \quad k_2] \right| = 0$$

$$\left| \begin{matrix} \lambda + 0.049 + 0.003k_1 & 0.997 + 0.003k_2 \\ -1.5 - 0.0285k_1 & \lambda + 0.21 - 0.285k_2 \end{matrix} \right| = 0$$

Expanding this determinant yields the characteristic equation of the augmented matrix in terms of the unknown gains k_1 and k_2:

$$\lambda^2 + (0.259 + 0.003k_1 - 0.0285k_2)\lambda + 1.51 + 0.029k_1 + 0.0031k_2 = 0$$

The desired characteristic equation can be expressed in terms of the Dutch roll damping ratio and frequency:

$$\lambda^2 + 2\zeta_{DR}\omega_{n_{DR}}\lambda + \omega_{n_{DR}}^2 = 0$$

Substituting in the values for ζ_{DR} and $\omega_{n_{DR}}$ yields

$$\lambda^2 + 0.6\lambda + 1.0 = 0$$

Equating the coefficients of the two polynomials yields a set of linear algebraic equations in terms of the unknown gains:

$$\begin{bmatrix} 0.003 & -0.0285 \\ 0.029 & 0.0031 \end{bmatrix} \begin{bmatrix} k_1 \\ k_2 \end{bmatrix} = \begin{bmatrix} 0.341 \\ -0.51 \end{bmatrix}$$

Solving for the gains yields

$$\mathbf{k} = \begin{bmatrix} -16.1 \\ -13.7 \end{bmatrix}$$

Substituting the gain vector back into the control law yields

$$\eta = -\mathbf{gk}^T\mathbf{x}$$

or

$$\begin{bmatrix} \Delta\delta_a \\ \Delta\delta_r \end{bmatrix} = -\begin{bmatrix} g_1 \\ g_2 \end{bmatrix}[k_1 \quad k_2]\begin{bmatrix} \Delta\beta \\ \Delta r \end{bmatrix}$$

$$\Delta\delta_a = -g_1 k_1 \Delta\beta - g_1 k_2 \Delta r$$

$$\Delta\delta_r = -g_2 k_1 \Delta\beta - g_2 k_2 \Delta r$$

For the selected values of **g** and the feedback gains determined here, we have the following control law:

$$\Delta\delta_a = 16.1 \ \Delta\beta + 13.7 \ \Delta r$$

$$\Delta\delta_r = 4.0 \ \Delta\beta + 3.42 \ \Delta r$$

This problem could have been solved using the Bass-Gura method once the **g** matrix was selected. The augmented system for a single- and multiple-input system follow:

$$\mathbf{A}^* = \mathbf{A} - \mathbf{Bk}^T \qquad \text{Single-input system}$$

$$\mathbf{A}^* = \mathbf{A} - \mathbf{Bgk}^T \qquad \text{Multiple-input system}$$

For a multiple-input system the control matrix **B** is $n \times m$ where n is the order of the system and m is the number of control input signals. The constant matrix **g** is $n \times 1$, therefore the matrix product **Bg** is $n \times 1$. The Bass-Gura method can be used if we replace the control matrix by $\overline{\mathbf{B}}$ where

$$\overline{\mathbf{B}} = \mathbf{Bg}$$

The constant vector reduces the problem to determining n gains instead of $n \times m$ gains.

Now let us apply the Bass-Gura method to this problem. First we determine the modified control matrix $\overline{\mathbf{B}}$:

$$\overline{\mathbf{B}} = \mathbf{Bg} = \begin{bmatrix} 0 & 0.012 \\ -0.008 & -0.082 \end{bmatrix}\begin{bmatrix} 1 \\ 0.25 \end{bmatrix}$$

$$\overline{\mathbf{B}} = \begin{bmatrix} 0.003 \\ -0.0285 \end{bmatrix}$$

The vector $\overline{\mathbf{a}}$ is determined from the desired characteristic equation

$$\lambda^2 + 0.6\lambda + 1.0 = 0$$

or

$$\lambda^2 + \overline{a}_1\lambda + \overline{a}_2 = 0$$

therefore

$$\overline{\mathbf{a}} = \begin{bmatrix} 0.6 \\ 1.0 \end{bmatrix}$$

The vector **a** is determined from the characteristic equation of the plant matrix **A**. The characteristic equation for the **A** matrix can be calculated easily:

$$\lambda^2 + 0.259\lambda + 1.5058 = 0$$

or

$$\lambda^2 + a_1\lambda + a_2 = 0$$

therefore

$$\mathbf{a} = \begin{bmatrix} 0.259 \\ 1.506 \end{bmatrix}$$

The controllability matrix is defined in terms of $\overline{\mathbf{B}}$ and $\mathbf{A}$:

$$\mathbf{V} = [\overline{\mathbf{B}} \quad \mathbf{A}\overline{\mathbf{B}}]$$

$$= \begin{bmatrix} 0.003 & 0.028 \\ -0.0285 & 0.011 \end{bmatrix}$$

Because the plant matrix is not in companion form we need to determine the transformation matrix $\mathbf{W}$:

$$\mathbf{W} = \begin{bmatrix} 1 & a_1 \\ 0 & 1 \end{bmatrix} = \begin{bmatrix} 1 & 0.259 \\ 0 & 1 \end{bmatrix}$$

Finally the feedback gains can be calculated by

$$\mathbf{k} = [(\mathbf{V}\mathbf{W})^T]^{-1}[\overline{\mathbf{a}} - \mathbf{a}]$$

where

$$[(\mathbf{V}\mathbf{W})^T]^{-1} = \begin{bmatrix} 3.71 & 34.05 \\ -34.70 & 3.58 \end{bmatrix}$$

and

$$\mathbf{k} = \begin{bmatrix} -16.0 \\ -13.7 \end{bmatrix}$$

Figure 10.2 is a plot of the Dutch roll motion for an initial displacement in β for an airplane with and without a stability augmentation system working.

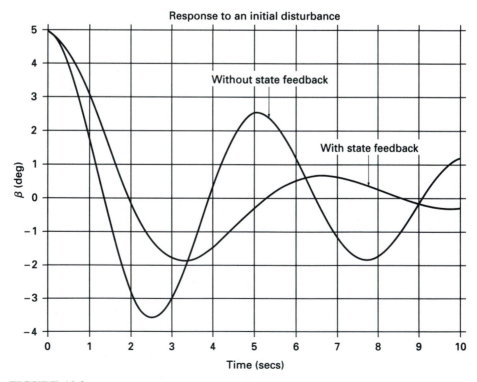

Response to an initial disturbance

Without state feedback

With state feedback

FIGURE 10.2
Dutch roll response with and without state feedback.

10.3
AUTOPILOT DESIGN

The stability augmentation system discussed in the previous section is an autopilot. The function of an SAS autopilot is to provide good handling qualities for the airplane so that the pilots do not find the airplane difficult to fly. Other types of autopilots discussed in Chapter 8 were used to lessen the flight crew's workload during cruise and help them land the airplane during adverse weather conditions. We examined autopilots to maintain the airplane's orientation, speed, and altitude.

The state feedback design approach can be used to design autopilots to perform the same functions. In the following example problem we demonstrate how the state feedback design approach can be used to design an altitude hold autopilot.

EXAMPLE PROBLEM 10.4. Use state feedback to design an autopilot to maintain a constant altitude. To simplify this problem we will assume that the forward speed of the airplane, u_0, is held fixed by a separate velocity control system and furthermore we neglect the control surface actuator dynamics. If the actuator dynamics were included the order of the system would be increased by 1. This assumption was made solely for the purposes of keeping the system as simple as possible. The airplane selected for this example is the STOL transport used in Example Problem 8.3.

The state equation for the airplane can be represented by the short-period approximation. The kinematic equation representing the change in vertical height in terms of the angles $\Delta\alpha$ and $\Delta\theta$, developed in Chapter 8 is:

$$\Delta\dot{h} = u_0(\Delta\theta - \Delta\alpha)$$

If we add the vertical velocity equation to the short-period equations we obtain the following fourth-order system:

$$\begin{bmatrix} \Delta\dot{\alpha} \\ \Delta\dot{q} \\ \Delta\dot{\theta} \\ \Delta\dot{h} \end{bmatrix} = \begin{bmatrix} Z_\alpha/u_0 & 1 & 0 & 0 \\ M_\alpha + M_{\dot{\alpha}}Z_\alpha/u_0 & M_q + M_{\dot{\alpha}} & 0 & 0 \\ 0 & 1 & 0 & 0 \\ -u_0 & 0 & u_0 & 0 \end{bmatrix} \begin{bmatrix} \Delta\alpha \\ \Delta q \\ \Delta\theta \\ \Delta h \end{bmatrix} + \begin{bmatrix} Z_{\delta_e}/u_0 \\ M_{\delta_e} \\ 0 \\ 0 \end{bmatrix} [\Delta\delta_e]$$

Substituting the numerical values of the stability derivatives for the STOL transport yields

$$\begin{bmatrix} \Delta\dot{\alpha} \\ \Delta\dot{q} \\ \Delta\dot{\theta} \\ \Delta\dot{h} \end{bmatrix} = \begin{bmatrix} -1.397 & 1 & 0 & 0 \\ -5.47 & -3.27 & 0 & 0 \\ 0 & 1 & 0 & 0 \\ -400 & 0 & 400 & 0 \end{bmatrix} \begin{bmatrix} \Delta\alpha \\ \Delta q \\ \Delta\theta \\ \Delta h \end{bmatrix} + \begin{bmatrix} -0.124 \\ -13.2 \\ 0 \\ 0 \end{bmatrix} [\Delta\delta_e]$$

In state feedback design the designer can specify the desired location of the eigenvalues. For this example we choose to locate the eigenvalues at

$$\lambda_{1,2} = -1.0 \pm 3.5i$$

$$\lambda_{3,4} = -2.0 \pm 1.0i$$

Solution. The state feedback gains can be again determined using the Bass-Gura method. The gains are determined by the matrix equation

$$\mathbf{k} = [\mathbf{V}\,\mathbf{W}^T]^{-1}[\overline{\mathbf{a}} - \mathbf{a}]$$

where $\mathbf{V}$ is the controllability matrix, $\mathbf{W}$ is a transformation matrix, and $\bar{\mathbf{a}}$ and $\mathbf{a}$ are vectors made up of the coefficients of the characteristic equations for the closed-loop system $\mathbf{A}^* = (\mathbf{A} - \mathbf{B}\mathbf{k}^T)$ and the characteristic equation for open-loop plant matrix $\mathbf{A}$, respectively. The eigenvalues for the desired closed-loop system can be multiplied together to give the closed-loop characteristic equation

$$(\lambda - \lambda_1)(\lambda - \lambda_2)(\lambda - \lambda_3)(\lambda - \lambda_4) = 0$$

Substituting the desired eigenvalues into the above equation and performing the indicated multiplication yields the following characteristic equation:

$$\lambda^4 + 6.0\lambda^3 + 26.25\lambda^2 + 63\lambda + 66.25 = 0$$

The vector $\bar{\mathbf{a}}$ is composed of the coefficients of the desired characteristic equation:

$$\lambda^4 + \bar{a}_1\lambda^3 + \bar{a}_2\lambda^2 + \bar{a}_3\lambda + \bar{a}_4 = 0$$

where

$$\bar{\mathbf{a}} = \begin{bmatrix} \bar{a}_1 \\ \bar{a}_2 \\ \bar{a}_3 \\ \bar{a}_4 \end{bmatrix} = \begin{bmatrix} 6.0 \\ 26.25 \\ 63.0 \\ 66.25 \end{bmatrix}$$

The characteristic equation for the $\mathbf{A}$ matrix is found by solving for the eigenvalues of the $\mathbf{A}$ matrix:

$$|\lambda\mathbf{I} - \mathbf{A}| = 0$$

which was solved on the computer

$$\lambda^4 + 4.667\lambda3 + 10.04\lambda^2 + 0\lambda + 0 = 0$$

or

$$\lambda^4 + a_1\lambda^3 + a_2\lambda^2 + a_3\lambda + a_4 = 0$$

therefore

$$\mathbf{a} = \begin{bmatrix} a_1 \\ a_2 \\ a_3 \\ a_4 \end{bmatrix} = \begin{bmatrix} 4.667 \\ 10.04 \\ 0.0 \\ 0.0 \end{bmatrix}$$

The next step is to determine the controllability matrix $\mathbf{V}$. The controllability matrix is defined in terms of the plant matrix $\mathbf{A}$ and control matrix $\mathbf{B}$. For this example it is

$$\mathbf{V} = [\mathbf{B} \quad \mathbf{A}\mathbf{B} \quad \mathbf{A}^2\mathbf{B} \quad \mathbf{A}^3\mathbf{B}]$$

The elements of the $\mathbf{V}$ matrix can be calculated readily by simple matrix multiplication:

$$\mathbf{A}\mathbf{B} = \begin{bmatrix} -1.397 & 1.00 & 0 & 0 \\ -5.47 & -3.27 & 0 & 0 \\ 0 & 1.00 & 0 & \\ -400 & 0 & 400 & 0 \end{bmatrix} \begin{bmatrix} -0.124 \\ -13.20 \\ 0 \\ 0 \end{bmatrix} = \begin{bmatrix} -13.03 \\ 43.84 \\ -13.20 \\ 49.6 \end{bmatrix}$$

$$\mathbf{A}^2\mathbf{B} = \mathbf{A}[\mathbf{A}\mathbf{B}] = \begin{bmatrix} -1.397 & 1.00 & 0 & 0 \\ -5.47 & -3.27 & 0 & 0 \\ 0 & 1.0 & 0 & 0 \\ -4.00 & 0 & 400 & 0 \end{bmatrix} \begin{bmatrix} -13.03 \\ 43.84 \\ -13.20 \\ 49.6 \end{bmatrix}$$

$$\mathbf{A^2B} = \begin{bmatrix} 62.04 \\ -72.11 \\ 43.84 \\ -69.29 \end{bmatrix}$$

$$\mathbf{A^3B} = \mathbf{A[A^2B]} = \begin{bmatrix} -1.397 & 1.0 & 0 & 0 \\ -5.47 & -3.27 & 0 & 0 \\ 0 & 1.0 & 0 & 0 \\ -400 & 0 & 400 & 0 \end{bmatrix} \begin{bmatrix} 62.04 \\ -72.11 \\ 43.84 \\ -69.29 \end{bmatrix}$$

$$\mathbf{A^3B} = \begin{bmatrix} -158.8 \\ -103.6 \\ -72.1 \\ -7279.4 \end{bmatrix}$$

$$\mathbf{V} = \begin{bmatrix} -0.12 & -13.03 & 62.04 & -158.8 \\ -13.20 & 43.84 & -72.11 & -103.6 \\ 0 & -13.20 & 43.84 & -72.1 \\ 0 & 49.60 & -69.29 & -7279.4 \end{bmatrix}$$

The rank of the $\mathbf{V}$ matrix is 4; therefore the system is completely state controllable. Our next step is to determine the transformation matrix $\mathbf{W}$, which for this particular problem is

$$\mathbf{W} = \begin{bmatrix} 1 & a_1 & a_2 & a_3 \\ 0 & 1 & a_1 & a_2 \\ 0 & 0 & 1 & a_1 \\ 0 & 0 & 0 & 1 \end{bmatrix} = \begin{bmatrix} 1 & 4.66 & 10.04 & 0.0 \\ 0 & 1 & 4.66 & 10.04 \\ 0 & 0 & 1 & 4.66 \\ 0 & 0 & 0 & 1 \end{bmatrix}$$

We can now calculate the state feedback gains

$$\mathbf{k} = [(\mathbf{VW})^T]^{-1}[\mathbf{\bar{a}} - \mathbf{a}]$$

where

$$\mathbf{VW} = \begin{bmatrix} -0.12 & 13.03 & 62.04 & -158.8 \\ -13.20 & 43.84 & -72.11 & -103.6 \\ 0 & -13.20 & 43.84 & -72.1 \\ 0 & 49.60 & -69.29 & 72.79 \end{bmatrix} \begin{bmatrix} 1 & 4.66 & 10.04 & 0 \\ 0 & 1 & 4.66 & 10.04 \\ 0 & 0 & 1 & 4.66 \\ 0 & 0 & 0 & 1 \end{bmatrix}$$

$$= \begin{bmatrix} -0.12 & -13.6 & 0.1 & -0.5 \\ -13.2 & -17.7 & -0.3 & 0.6 \\ 0 & -13.2 & -17.7 & -0.3 \\ 0 & 49.6 & 161.8 & -7{,}104 \end{bmatrix}$$

The transpose of the matrix $\mathbf{VW}$ is obtained by interchanging the rows and columns of $\mathbf{VW}$:

$$(\mathbf{VW})^T = \begin{bmatrix} -0.12 & -13.2 & 0 & 0 \\ -13.6 & -17.7 & -13.2 & 49.6 \\ 0.1 & -0.3 & -17.7 & 161.8 \\ -0.5 & 0.6 & -0.3 & -7{,}104 \end{bmatrix}$$

The inverse of the matrix $(\mathbf{VW})^T$ follows:

$$[(\mathbf{VW})^T]^{-1} = \begin{bmatrix} 0.0978 & -0.0741 & 0.0553 & 0.0007 \\ -0.0767 & 0.0007 & -0.0005 & 0.000 \\ 0.0018 & -0.0003 & -0.0563 & -0.0013 \\ 0.000 & 0.000 & 0.000 & -0.0001 \end{bmatrix}$$

The state feedback gains are

$$\mathbf{k} = [(\mathbf{VW})^T]^{-1}[\overline{\mathbf{a}} - \mathbf{a}]$$

$$= \begin{bmatrix} 0.0978 & -0.0741 & 0.0553 & 0.0007 \\ -0.0767 & 0.0007 & -0.0005 & 0.000 \\ 0.0018 & -0.0003 & -0.0563 & -0.0013 \\ 0.000 & 0.000 & 0.000 & -0.0001 \end{bmatrix} \left(\begin{bmatrix} 6.0 \\ 20.5 \\ 63.0 \\ 66.25 \end{bmatrix} - \begin{bmatrix} 4.67 \\ 10.04 \\ 0.00 \\ 0.00 \end{bmatrix} \right)$$

$$= \begin{bmatrix} 2.445 \\ -0.124 \\ -3.636 \\ -0.009 \end{bmatrix}$$

The control law developed to maintain a constant altitude was evaluated using a numerical simulation. The autopilot was given an initial altitude excursion of 100 ft

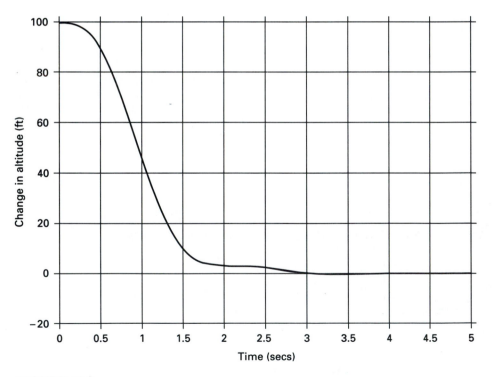

FIGURE 10.3
Response of the STOL transport to a 100-ft initial displacement from the designated altitude.

from the desired attitude. Figure 10.3 shows the response to the change in altitude. The autopilot quickly brings the airplane back to the designated altitude.

10.4
STATE OBSERVER

In Example Problems 10.1 and 10.2 we determined the state feedback gains to relocate the longitudinal eigenvalues so that the airplane would have better handling qualities. The state feedback design approach assumes that all the states are available for feedback. By available we mean that the states must be able to be measured by sensors onboard the aircraft. This may not always be the case. One could imagine that one or more states may not be easily measured and therefore would not be available for feedback. If all the states cannot be measured the control law developed in these examples could not be implemented. Obviously if state feedback were used to locate the eigenvalues at some desired location so the system would have certain time domain performance, then all the states would have to be used to accomplishing this task. A state observer could be used to provide estimates of the states that cannot be measured.

Recall in Chapter 9 that the state observed can be constructed if the output is observable. In the following example problems we design a state observer to predict the states of the system. The predicted states then could be used to implement the state feedback control law [10.3–10.6].

EXAMPLE PROBLEM 10.5. In Example Problem 10.1 we designed a state feedback control law, $\eta = -\mathbf{k}^T\mathbf{x}$, to improve the handling qualities of the airplane. Through state feedback we were able to relocate the eigenvalues (short-period roots) of the airplane. To implement the stability augmentation system all the states must be available. In this problem we assume that the states are not measured by onboard sensors and therefore are unavailable for feedback. To overcome this difficulty we design a state observer to provide predictions of the necessary states. The predicted states then can be used in conjunction with the state feedback control law determined in Example Problem 10.1.

Solution. The characteristic equation of the observer can be determined by expanding the following equation:

$$|\lambda\mathbf{I} - (\mathbf{A} - \mathbf{k}_e\mathbf{C})| = 0$$

where $\mathbf{A}$ and $\mathbf{C}$ are the plant and output matrices and $\mathbf{k}_e$ is the observer gain vector. For this problem the output matrix is given by

$$\mathbf{C} = [1 \quad 0]$$

Substituting the appropriate matrices into the preceding equation and expanding yields

$$\left| \begin{bmatrix} \lambda & 0 \\ 0 & \lambda \end{bmatrix} - \begin{bmatrix} -0.334 & 1.0 \\ -2.52 & -0.387 \end{bmatrix} + \begin{bmatrix} k_{e_1} \\ k_{e_2} \end{bmatrix} [1 \quad 0] \right| = 0$$

$$\begin{vmatrix} \lambda + 0.334 + k_{e_1} & -1.0 \\ 2.52 + k_{e_2} & \lambda + 0.387 \end{vmatrix} = 0$$

$$\lambda^2 + (0.721 + k_{e_1})\lambda + 2.65 + 0.387 k_{e_1} + k_{e_2} = 0$$

As stated in Chapter 9 the observer roots should be more responsive than the roots of the state feedback system. We assume for this example problem that the observer roots are four times as responsive as the state feedback roots. From a mathematical standpoint the observer roots can be located anywhere in the left-hand portion of the complex plane, provided they are to the left of the desired closed-loop system roots. However, practical constraints similar to those discussed in Chapter 9 for the state feedback root location also apply to the placement of the observer roots. In Example Problem 10.1 the roots for the state feedback system were located at $\lambda_{SF} = -2.1 \pm 2.14i$. The desired observer characteristic equation is obtained by

$$(\lambda - \lambda_{OB_1})(\lambda - \lambda_{OB_2}) = 0$$
$$(\lambda + 8.4 + 8.56i)(\lambda + 8.4 - 8.56i) = 0$$
$$\lambda^2 + 16.8\lambda + 143.8 = 0$$

By equating the desired observer characteristic equation with the one as a function of the observer gains we obtain a set of equations for the unknown observer gains.

$$0.721 + k_{e_1} = 16.8$$
$$2.65 + 0.387 k_{e_1} + k_{e_2} = 143.8$$

Solving for each k_e yields

$$k_{e_1} = 16.08$$
$$k_{e_2} = 134.9$$

In Example Problem 10.5, the observer gains were easily obtained for the second-order system through simple algebraic manipulations. However, as the order of the system increases the analysis becomes quite tedious. Numerical techniques such as the Bass-Gura method can be used to solve for the observer gains for higher-order systems.

Friedland [10.7] shows that the state observer gains can be determined by the Bass-Gura method. The observer gains are obtained from the equation

$$\mathbf{k}_e = [(\mathbf{UW})^T]^{-1}(\hat{\mathbf{a}} - \mathbf{a}) \tag{10.20}$$

where $\mathbf{U}$ is the observability matrix, $\mathbf{W}$ is a transformation matrix defined earlier, and $\hat{\mathbf{a}}$ and $\mathbf{a}$ are vectors of the coefficients of the desired observer characteristic equation and the plant matrix, respectively.

EXAMPLE PROBLEM 10.6. Solve Example Problem 10.5 using the Bass-Gura method.

Solution. In Example Problem 10.5 the desired observer characteristic equation was shown to be

$$\lambda^2 + 16.8\lambda + 143.8 = 0$$

therefore
$$\hat{\mathbf{a}} = \begin{bmatrix} \hat{a}_1 \\ \hat{a}_2 \end{bmatrix} = \begin{bmatrix} 16.8 \\ 143.8 \end{bmatrix}$$

The characteristic equation of the plant matrix $\mathbf{A}$ can be shown to be

$$\lambda^2 + 0.721\lambda + 2.65 = 0$$

or
$$\mathbf{a} = \begin{bmatrix} a_1 \\ a_2 \end{bmatrix} = \begin{bmatrix} 0.721 \\ 2.65 \end{bmatrix}$$

The observability matrix for a second-order system is given by

$$U = [C^T \quad A^T C^T]$$

$$C^T = \begin{bmatrix} 1 \\ 0 \end{bmatrix}$$

$$A^T C^T = \begin{bmatrix} -0.334 & -2.52 \\ 1.0 & -0.387 \end{bmatrix} \begin{bmatrix} 1 \\ 0 \end{bmatrix} = \begin{bmatrix} -0.334 \\ 1 \end{bmatrix}$$

$$U = \begin{bmatrix} 1 & -0.334 \\ 0 & 1 \end{bmatrix}$$

The transformation matrix W is defined in terms of the coefficient of the plant matrix:

$$W = \begin{bmatrix} 1 & a_1 \\ 0 & 1 \end{bmatrix} = \begin{bmatrix} 1 & 0.721 \\ 0 & 1 \end{bmatrix}$$

The observer gains can now be estimated from Equation (10.20):

$$k_e = [(UW)^T]^{-1}(\hat{a} - a)$$

where

$$UW = \begin{bmatrix} 1 & -0.334 \\ 0 & 1 \end{bmatrix} \begin{bmatrix} 1 & 0.721 \\ 0 & 1 \end{bmatrix}$$

$$= \begin{bmatrix} 1 & 0.387 \\ 0 & 1 \end{bmatrix}$$

$$(UW)^T = \begin{bmatrix} 1 & 0 \\ 0.387 & 1 \end{bmatrix}$$

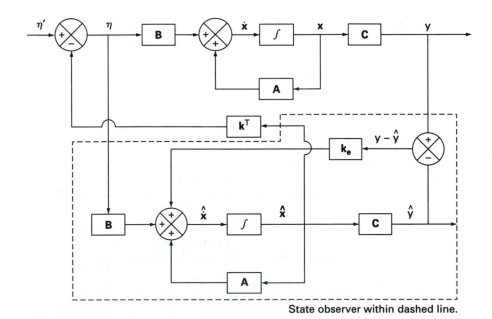

State observer within dashed line.

FIGURE 10.4
State feedback controller with an observer (within the dashed line).

The inverse of $(\mathbf{UW})^T$ is

$$[(\mathbf{UW})^T]^{-1} = \begin{bmatrix} 1 & 0 \\ -0.387 & 1 \end{bmatrix}$$

Therefore the observer gains are

$$\mathbf{k}_e = \begin{bmatrix} 1 & 0 \\ -0.387 & 1 \end{bmatrix} \left[\begin{bmatrix} 16.8 \\ 143.8 \end{bmatrix} - \begin{bmatrix} 0.721 \\ 2.65 \end{bmatrix} \right]$$

$$= \begin{bmatrix} 1 & 0 \\ -0.387 & 1 \end{bmatrix} \begin{bmatrix} 16.079 \\ 141.13 \end{bmatrix}$$

$$= \begin{bmatrix} 16.08 \\ 134.9 \end{bmatrix}$$

Figure 10.4 is a block diagram of a system using state feedback and an observer.

10.5
OPTIMAL CONTROL

In the previous sections we examined the use of state feedback control for the placement of the closed-loop eigenvalues. By placing the eigenvalues in the left half portion of the complex plane we can be sure that the system is stable. However, as we move the eigenvalues farther to the left in the complex plane the gains may become large, resulting in excessive control deflection. For some systems the designer may not have a good idea or feel for the best location of the closed-loop eigenvalues.

Optimal control theory can be used to overcome these difficulties. In the following example we apply optimal control theory to provide an optimal controller for maintaining a desired roll angle while placing constraints on the maximum permissible roll angle and aileron deflection, respectively [10.8–10.10]. This problem is simple enough that we can solve the steady-state Riccati equations by hand. However, for higher-order systems computer methods are required. A second example of a higher-order system is examined using the software package MATLAB.

EXAMPLE PROBLEM 10.7. Most guided missiles require that the roll attitude of the missile be kept at a fixed orientation throughout its flight so that the guidance system can function properly. A roll autopilot is needed to maintain the desired roll orientation. Figure 10.5 is a sketch of a wing-controlled missile.

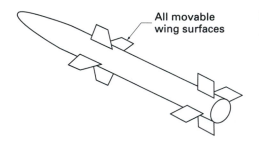

All movable
wing surfaces

FIGURE 10.5
A wing-controlled missile.

Solution. In this example we design a feedback control system that will keep the roll orientation near $0°$ while not exceeding a given limit on the aileron deflection angle. The following equations of motion for the rolling motion of the missile were developed in Chapter 5:

$$I_x \dot{p} = \frac{\partial L}{\partial P} p + \frac{\partial L}{\partial \delta_a} \delta_a \qquad \dot{\phi} = p$$

Rewriting these equations as

$$\dot{p} = L_p p + L_{\delta_a} \delta_a \qquad \dot{\phi} = p$$

where

$$L_p = \frac{\partial L/\partial p}{I_x} \qquad \text{and} \qquad L_{\delta_a} = \frac{\partial L/\partial \delta_a}{I_x}$$

the equations can easily be written in the state variable form as follows:

$$\begin{bmatrix} \dot{\phi} \\ \dot{p} \end{bmatrix} = \begin{bmatrix} 0 & 1 \\ 0 & L_p \end{bmatrix} \begin{bmatrix} \phi \\ p \end{bmatrix} + \begin{bmatrix} 0 \\ L_{\delta_a} \end{bmatrix} \{\delta_a\}$$

or

$$\dot{x} = Ax + B\eta$$

where

$$A = \begin{bmatrix} 0 & 1 \\ 0 & L_p \end{bmatrix}$$

$$B = \begin{bmatrix} 0 \\ L_{\delta_a} \end{bmatrix}$$

The quadratic performance index that is to be minimized is

$$J = \int_0^\infty \left[\left(\frac{\phi}{\phi_{max}} \right)^2 + \left(\frac{p}{p_{max}} \right)^2 + \left(\frac{\delta_a}{\delta_{max}} \right)^2 \right] dt$$

where ϕ_{max} = the maximum desired roll angle
p_{max} = the maximum desired roll rate
δ_{max} = maximum aileron deflection.

Comparing the performance index given here with the general form allows us to specify the matrices Q and R:

$$Q = \begin{bmatrix} \dfrac{1}{\phi^2_{max}} & 0 \\ 0 & \dfrac{1}{p^2_{max}} \end{bmatrix}$$

$$R = \frac{1}{\delta^2_{max}}$$

The optimum control law is determined by solving the steady-state Riccati matrix equation:

$$A^T S + SA - SBR^{-1}B^T S + Q = 0$$

for the values of the S matrix. The optimal control law is given by

$$\eta = -k^T x$$

where

$$k^T = R^{-1}B^T S$$

Substituting the matrices **A**, **B**, **Q**, and **R** into the Ricatti equation yields a set of nonlinear algebraic equations for the unknown elements of the **S** matrix:*

$$\frac{1}{\phi_{max}^2} - S_{12}^2 L_{\delta_a}^2 \delta_{max}^2 = 0$$

$$S_{11} + S_{12} L_p - S_{12} S_{22} L_{\delta_a}^2 \delta_{max}^2 = 0$$

$$2S_{12} + 2S_{22} L_p + \frac{1}{p_{max}^2} - S_{22}^2 L_{\delta_a}^2 \delta_{max}^2 = 0$$

For the case in which the missile has the aerodynamic characteristics

$$L_p = -2 \text{ rad/s}$$

$$L_{\delta_a} = 9000 \text{ s}^{-2}$$

$$\phi_{max} = 10° = 0.174 \text{ rad}$$

$$p_{max} = 300°/s = 5.23 \text{ rad/s}$$

$$\delta_{max} = \pm 30° = \pm 0.524 \text{ rad}$$

the nonlinear Ricatti equations can be solved for the elements of the Ricatti matrix **S**:

$$\mathbf{S} = \begin{bmatrix} 1.135 & 0.0012 \\ 0.0012 & 0.00005 \end{bmatrix}$$

The control law gains can now be calculated from the equation

$$\mathbf{k}^T = \mathbf{R}^{-1} \mathbf{B}^T \mathbf{S}$$

and the control law is found to be $\delta_a = -3.0\phi - 0.103p$.

In Example Problem 10.6 it was possible to solve the Ricatti equation through simple algebraic calculations. For more complex problems the Ricatti equation must be solved by numerical algorithms incorporated into computer software.

A computer software package to solve for the optimal gains can be found in MATLAB. A program called *lqr* solves the Ricatti equations for the continuous linear-quadratic regulator problem. The *lqr* program is one of a collection of control system analysis and design algorithms found in the MATLAB control system toolbox.

To use this program the user must supply the plant matrix **A**, the control matrix **B**, and the weighting matrices **Q** and **R** that are in the performance index, *J*:

$$J = \int_0^\infty (\mathbf{x}^T \mathbf{Q} \mathbf{x} + \eta^T \mathbf{R} \eta) \, dt$$

As a final example problem, we will determine the optimal control law to maintain a fixed altitude.

EXAMPLE PROBLEM 10.8. Determine the optimal control law for Example Problem 10.4 if we place constraints on the angle of attack, altitude excursion, and control

---

* Remember that the **S** matrix is symmetric, so it is necessary to solve only the equation generated for the elements along and above the diagonal of the matrix.

deflection. The weighting matrices are assumed to have the following form:

$$Q = \begin{bmatrix} \left(\dfrac{1}{\alpha_{max}}\right)^2 & 0 & 0 & 0 \\ 0 & 0 & 0 & 0 \\ 0 & 0 & 0 & 0 \\ 0 & 0 & 0 & \left(\dfrac{1}{h_{max}}\right)^2 \end{bmatrix}$$

$$R = \left[\left(\dfrac{1}{\delta_{e_{max}}}\right)^2\right]$$

where $\Delta\alpha_{max} = 5° = 0.087$ rad
$\Delta h_{max} = 100$ ft
$\Delta\delta_{e_{max}} = 10° = 0.175$ rad

Solution. The equations for the STOL transport follow:

$$\begin{bmatrix} \Delta\dot{\alpha} \\ \Delta\dot{q} \\ \Delta\dot{\theta} \\ \Delta\dot{h} \end{bmatrix} = \begin{bmatrix} -1.397 & 1 & 0 & 0 \\ -5.47 & -3.27 & 0 & 0 \\ 0 & 1 & 0 & 0 \\ -400 & 0 & 400 & 0 \end{bmatrix} \begin{bmatrix} \Delta\alpha \\ \Delta q \\ \Delta\theta \\ \Delta h \end{bmatrix} + \begin{bmatrix} -0.124 \\ -13.2 \\ 0 \\ 0 \end{bmatrix} [\Delta\delta e]$$

The MATLAB program *lqr* was used to determine the Riccati matrix. Figure 10.6 is a listing of the MATLAB instructions used to solve this problem. The Ricatti matrix was found to be

$$S = \begin{bmatrix} 75.6886 & -0.9547 & -74.8768 & -0.0865 \\ -0.9547 & 0.7648 & 4.9711 & 0.0052 \\ -74.8768 & 4.9711 & 106.1849 & 0.1208 \\ -0.0865 & 0.0052 & 0.1208 & 0.0002 \end{bmatrix}$$

```
A = [-1.397 1 0 0; -5.47 -3.27 0 0; 0 1 0 0; -400 0 400 0]
B = [-0.124; -13.2; 0; 0]
Q = [132.12 0 0 0; 0 0 0 0; 0 0 0 0; 0 0 0 0.0001]
R = [32.84]
[K,S,E] = lqr(A,B,Q,R)
```

FIGURE 10.6
Listing of MATLAB instruction.

Once the Ricatti matrix has been determined the optimal control gains can be determined by the equation

$$\mathbf{k}^T = \mathbf{R}^{-1}\mathbf{B}^T\mathbf{S}$$

where

$$\mathbf{R}^{-1} = [\delta^2_{e_{max}}] = 0.0306$$

$$\mathbf{k}^T = [0.0306][-0.124 \quad -13.2 \quad 0 \quad 0] \begin{bmatrix} 75.6886 & -0.9547 & -74.8768 & -0.0865 \\ -0.9547 & 0.7648 & 4.9711 & 0.0052 \\ -74.8768 & 4.9711 & 106.1849 & 0.1208 \\ -0.0865 & 0.0052 & 0.1208 & 0.0002 \end{bmatrix}$$

$$= [0.098 \quad -0.0304 \quad -1.715 \quad -0.0017]$$

The optimal control law can now be written

$$\eta = -\mathbf{k}^T\mathbf{x}$$

or $\quad\quad \Delta\delta_e = -0.098\Delta\alpha + 0.0304\Delta q + 1.715\Delta\theta + 0.0017\Delta h$

Figure 10.7 shows the response of the airplane to an initial displacement of 100 ft from the desired altitude. The control system is observed to rapidly bring the aircraft

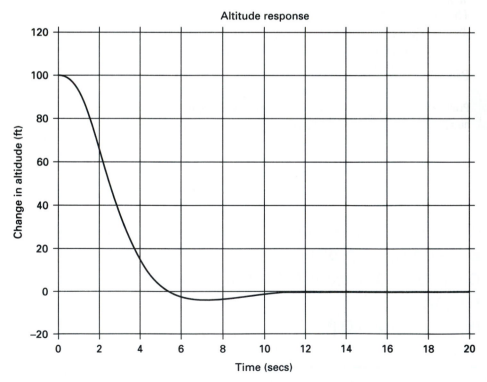

Altitude response

FIGURE 10.7
Response of the STOL aircraft to a 100-ft deviation from the desired altitude.

back to the desired altitude while keeping the angle of attack and control deflection under $\Delta\alpha_{max}$ and $\Delta\delta_{e max}$, respectively.

10.6
SUMMARY

Modern control theory provides the control systems engineer with a valuable design tool. Unlike the classical control methods presented in Chapter 7, modern control theory is ideally suited for synthesis of a control system with multiple inputs and for determining optimal control strategies.

In state feedback design the designer can place the closed-loop system poles at any location in the complex plane. In principle this technique permits the designer to completely specify the dynamic performance of the system. From a mathematical standpoint the poles can be placed anywhere. However, practical considerations such as signal noise and control actuator saturation place limitations on pole placement.

To use a state feedback design the system had to be state controllable and all the states must be accessible to measurement. If any state is unavailable for feedback the design cannot be implemented. This limitation can be overcome by the use of a state observer. The state observer provides estimates of the system states. Therefore the state observer can provide information on the unavailable states so that the state feedback design can be implemented.

PROBLEMS

Problems that require the use of a computer have the capital letter C after the problem number.

10.1. A wind-tunnel model is mounted on a bearing system so that the model is free to pitch about its center of gravity. No other motion is possible. Design a control system to maintain the model at some reference pitch attitude. The equation of motion for the model is

$$\begin{bmatrix} \Delta\dot{\theta} \\ \Delta\dot{q} \end{bmatrix} = \begin{bmatrix} 0 & 1 \\ M_\alpha & M_q \end{bmatrix} \begin{bmatrix} \Delta\theta \\ \Delta q \end{bmatrix} + \begin{bmatrix} 0 \\ M_\delta \end{bmatrix} [\Delta\delta_e]$$

where $M_\alpha = -1 \text{ s}^{-2}$
$\quad\quad M_q = -3 \text{ s}^{-1}$
$\quad\quad M_\delta = -4 \text{ s}^{-2}$

Use state feedback to locate the closed-loop eigenvalues at $\lambda_{1,2} = -1 \pm 2i$.

10.2. The longitudinal motion of an airplane is approximated by the differential equations

$$\dot{w} = -2.0w + 179\dot{\theta} - 27\delta$$
$$\ddot{\theta} = -0.25w - 15\dot{\theta} - 45\delta$$

(a) Rewrite the equations in state-space form

$$\dot{x} = Ax + B\eta$$

(b) Find the eigenvalues of **A**.
(c) Determine a state feedback control law

$$\eta = -k^T x$$

so that the augmented system has a damping ratio $\zeta = 0.5$ and the undamped natural frequency $\omega_n = 20$ rad/s.

10.3.(C). An airplane is found to have poor lateral handling qualities. Use state feedback to provide stability augmentation. The lateral equations of motion and the desired lateral eigenvalues follow. The lateral state equations are

$$
\begin{bmatrix} \Delta\dot{\beta} \\ \Delta\dot{p} \\ \Delta\dot{r} \\ \Delta\dot{\phi} \end{bmatrix}
=
\begin{bmatrix}
-0.05 & -0.003 & -0.98 & .2 \\
-1.0 & -0.75 & 1.0 & 0 \\
0.3 & -0.3 & -0.15 & 0 \\
0 & 1 & 0 & 0
\end{bmatrix}
\begin{bmatrix} \Delta\beta \\ \Delta p \\ \Delta r \\ \Delta\phi \end{bmatrix}
+
\begin{bmatrix}
0 & 0 \\
1.7 & -0.2 \\
0.3 & -0.6 \\
0 & 0
\end{bmatrix}
\begin{bmatrix} \Delta\delta_a \\ \Delta\delta_r \end{bmatrix}
$$

The desired lateral eigenvalues are

$$\lambda_{roll} = -1.5$$

$$\lambda_{spiral} = 0.05$$

$$\lambda_{DR} = -0.35 \pm 1.5i$$

Assume the relative authority of the ailerons and rudder are $g_1 = 1.0$ and $g_2 = \delta_r / \delta_a = 0.33$.

10.4. Assume that states in Problem 10.1 are unavailable for state feedback. Design a state observer to estimate the states. Assume the state observer eigenvalues are three times as fast as the desired closed-loop eigenvalues; that is, $\lambda_{OB} = 3\lambda_{SF}$.

10.5.(C). Design a state observer to estimate the states for the airplane described in Problem 10.2. Assume that observer roots are twice as fast as the closed-loop eigenvalues of the augmented system; that is, $\lambda_{OB} = 2\lambda$ where $\lambda_{1,2} = -10 \pm 17.3i$.

10.6.(C). Use state feedback to design an altitude hold control system. Assume the forward speed is held constant and the longitudinal equation can be modeled using the short-period approximation. The short-period equations are

$$
\begin{bmatrix} \Delta\dot{\alpha} \\ \Delta\dot{q} \\ \Delta\dot{\theta} \end{bmatrix}
=
\begin{bmatrix}
-1.5 & 1 & 0 \\
-4.0 & -1.0 & 0 \\
0 & 1 & 0
\end{bmatrix}
\begin{bmatrix} \Delta\alpha \\ \Delta q \\ \Delta\theta \end{bmatrix}
+
\begin{bmatrix} -0.2 \\ -8.0 \\ 0 \end{bmatrix}
\Delta\delta_e
$$

Assume the $\Delta\dot{h} = u_0(\Delta\theta - \Delta\alpha)$ where $u_0 = 200$ ft/s. Determine the state-feedback gain if the closed-loop eigenvalues are located at

$$\lambda = -1.5 \pm 2.5i$$

$$\lambda = -0.75 \pm 1.0i$$

10.7. Use state feedback to design a control system to maintain a wings level attitude. Assume the aircraft can be modeled by the following state equations:

$$\begin{bmatrix} \dot{p} \\ \dot{\phi} \end{bmatrix} = \begin{bmatrix} L_p & 0 \\ 1 & 0 \end{bmatrix} \begin{bmatrix} p \\ \phi \end{bmatrix} + \begin{bmatrix} L_{\delta_a} \\ 0 \end{bmatrix} \delta_a$$

where $L_{\delta_a} = 2.0/s^2$ and $L_p = -0.5/s$.

The closed loop system should have the following performace

$$\zeta = 0.707$$

$$\omega_n = 10 \text{ rad/s}$$

10.8. Design an optimal control law for Problem 10.1. Assume these constraints on the pitch angle and elevator angle:

$$\Delta\theta_{max} = \pm 10° = 0.175 \text{ rad}$$

$$\Delta\delta_{e\,max} = \pm 15° = 0.26 \text{ rad}$$

The weighting function for the performance index J are

$$Q = \begin{bmatrix} \dfrac{1}{\Delta\theta_{max}^2} & 0 \\ 0 & 0 \end{bmatrix}$$

$$R = \begin{bmatrix} \dfrac{1}{\delta_{e\,max}^2} \end{bmatrix}$$

10.9(C). Design an automatic control system to maintain zero vertical acceleration. The equations of motion governing the aircraft's motion are

$$\Delta\dot{\alpha} = \frac{Z_\alpha}{u_0} \Delta\alpha - \Delta q$$

$$\Delta\dot{q} = M_\alpha \Delta\alpha + M_q \Delta q + M_\delta \Delta\delta_e$$

Find the nonlinear algebraic equations that must be solved to determine the gains for the control law $\eta = -k^T x$, that satisfies the performance index

$$J = \int_0^\infty \left[\left(\frac{\alpha}{\alpha_{max}}\right) + \left(\frac{\delta}{\delta_{max}}\right) + \left(\frac{q}{q_{max}}\right)^2 \right] dt$$

where δ_{max} = maximum control deflection
α_{max} = maximum angle to attack
q_{max} = maximum pitch rate.

10.10(C). The rolling motion of an aerospace vehicle is given by these state equations:

$$\begin{bmatrix} \dot{\delta}_a \\ \dot{p} \\ \dot{\phi} \end{bmatrix} = \begin{bmatrix} -1/\tau & 0 & 0 \\ L_{\delta_a} & L_p & 0 \\ 0 & 1 & 0 \end{bmatrix} \begin{bmatrix} \delta_a \\ p \\ \phi \end{bmatrix} + \begin{bmatrix} 1/\tau \\ 0 \\ 0 \end{bmatrix} [\delta_v]$$

where δ_a, p, ϕ, and δ_v are the aileron deflection angle, roll rate, roll angle, and voltage input to the aileron actuator motor. Note that in this problem the aileron angle is considered a state and the control voltage, δ_v, is the input. Determine the optimal control law that minimizes the performance index, J, as follows:

$$J = \int_0^\infty (\mathbf{x}^T \mathbf{Q} \mathbf{x} + \boldsymbol{\eta}^T \mathbf{R} \boldsymbol{\eta}) dt$$

where

$$\mathbf{Q} = \begin{bmatrix} \dfrac{1}{\delta_{a\,max}^2} & 0 & 0 \\ 0 & 0 & 0 \\ 0 & 0 & \dfrac{1}{\phi_{max}^2} \end{bmatrix}$$

$$\mathbf{R} = \begin{bmatrix} \dfrac{1}{\delta_{v\,max}^2} \end{bmatrix}$$

For this problem assume the following:

$$\tau = 0.1 \text{ s}$$

$$L_{\delta_a} = 30/\text{s}^2$$

$$L_p = -1.0 \text{ rad/s}$$

$$\delta_{a\,max} = \pm 25° = 0.436 \text{ rad}$$

$$\phi_{max} = \pm 45° = 0.787 \text{ rad}$$

$$\delta_{v\,max} = 10 \text{ volts}$$

REFERENCES

10.1. McRuer, D.; and D. Graham. "Eighty Years of Flight Control: Triumphs and Pitfalls of the Systems Approach." *AIAA Journal of Guidance and Control* 4, no. 4 (1981), pp. 353–362.

10.2. Oehman, W. E.; and J. H. Suddath. "State-Vector Control Applied to Lateral Stability of High Performance Aircraft." NASA TN D-29084, July 1965.

10.3. Kuo, B. C. *Automatic Control Systems.* Englewood Cliffs, NJ: Prentice-Hall, 1975.

10.4. D'Souza, A. F. *Design of Control Systems.* Englewood Cliffs, NJ: Prentice-Hall, 1988.

10.5. Hale, F. J. *Introduction to Control System Analysis and Design.* Englewood Cliffs, NJ: Prentice-Hall, 1988.

10.6. Takahashi, Y.; M. J. Rabins; and D. M. Auslander. *Control and Dynamic Systems.* Reading, MA: Addison-Wesley, 1970.

10.7. Friedland, B. *Control System Design: An Introduction to State-Space Methods.* New York: McGraw-Hill, 1986.

10.8. Bryson, A. E.; and Y. C. Ho. *Applied Optimal Control.* Washington, DC: Hemisphere, 1975.

10.9. Nesline, F. W.; and P. Zarchan. "A Classical Look at Modern Control for Missile Autopilot Design." AIAA Paper 82-1512, August 1982.

10.10. Bryson, A. E. *Control of Spacecraft and Aircraft.* Princeton, NJ: Princeton University Press, 1994.

APPENDIX A

Atmospheric Tables (ICAO Standard Atmosphere)

TABLE A.1
Geometric altitude (metric units)

H_G, m	H, m	T,° K	P, N/m²	P/P_0		ρ, kg/m⁻³		ρ/ρ_0		a, m/s	ν, m²/s	
0	0	288.150	1.01325 +5	1.00000	+0	1.2250	+0	1.0000	+1	340.294	1.4607	−5
1,000	1,000	281.651	8.9876 +4	8.87009	−1	1.1117	+0	9.0748	−1	336.435	1.5813	−5
2,000	1,999	275.154	7.9501 +4	7.84618	−1	1.0066	+0	8.2168	−1	332.532	1.7147	−5
3,000	2,999	268.659	7.0121 +4	6.92042	−1	9.0925	−1	7.4225	−1	328.583	1.8628	−5
4,000	3,997	262.166	6.1660 +4	6.08541	−1	8.1935	−1	6.6885	−1	324.589	2.0275	−5
5,000	4,996	255.676	5.4048 +4	5.33415	−1	7.3643	−1	6.0117	−1	320.545	2.2110	−5
6,000	5,994	249.187	4.7217 +4	4.66001	−1	6.6011	−1	5.3887	−1	316.452	2.4162	−5
7,000	6,992	242.700	4.1105 +4	4.05677	−1	5.9002	−1	4.8165	−1	312.306	2.6461	−5
8,000	7,990	236.215	3.5651 +4	3.51854	−1	5.2579	−1	4.2921	−1	308.105	2.9044	−5
9,000	8,987	229.733	3.0800 +4	3.03979	−1	4.6706	−1	3.8128	−1	303.848	3.1957	−5
10,000	9,984	223.252	2.6500 +4	2.61533	−1	4.1351	−1	3.3756	−1	299.532	3.5251	−5
11,000	10,981	216.774	2.2700 +4	2.24031	−1	3.6480	−1	2.9780	−1	295.154	3.8988	−5
12,000	11,977	216.650	1.9399 +4	1.91457	−1	3.1194	−1	2.5464	−1	295.069	4.5574	−5
13,000	12,973	216.650	1.4170 +4	1.63628	−1	2.6660	−1	2.1763	−1	295.069	5.3325	−5
14,000	13,969	216.650	1.4170 +4	1.39851	−1	2.2786	−1	1.8600	−1	295.069	6.2391	−5
15,000	14,965	216.650	1.2112 +4	1.19534	−1	1.9475	−1	1.5898	−1	295.069	7.2995	−5
16,000	15,960	216.650	1.0353 +4	1.02174	−1	1.6647	−1	1.3589	−1	295.069	8.5397	−5
17,000	16,955	216.650	8.8496 +3	8.73399	−2	1.4230	−1	1.1616	−1	295.069	9.9902	−5
18,000	17,949	216.650	7.5652 +3	7.46629	−2	1.2165	−1	9.9304	−2	295.069	1.1686	−4
19,000	18,943	216.650	6.4674 +3	6.38291	−2	1.0400	−1	8.4894	−2	295.069	1.3670	−4
20,000	19,937	216.650	5.5293 +3	5.45700	−2	8.8910	−2	7.2579	−2	295.069	1.5989	−4
21,000	20,931	217.581	4.7274 +3	4.66709	−2	7.5715	−2	6.1808	−2	295.703	1.8843	−4
22,000	21,924	218.574	4.0420 +3	3.99456	−2	6.4510	−2	5.2661	−2	296.377	2.2201	−4
23,000	22,917	219.567	3.4562 +3	3.42153	−2	5.5006	−2	4.4903	−2	297.049	2.6135	−4
24,000	23,910	220.560	2.9554 +3	2.93288	−2	4.6938	−2	3.8317	−2	297.720	3.0743	−4
25,000	24,902	221.552	2.6077 +3	2.51588	−2	4.0084	−2	3.2722	−2	298.389	3.6135	−4
26,000	25,894	222.544	2.1632 +3	2.15976	−2	3.4257	−2	2.7965	−2	299.056	4.2439	−4
27,000	26,886	223.536	1.8555 +3	1.85539	−2	2.9298	−2	2.3917	−2	299.722	4.9805	−4
28,000	27,877	224.527	1.5949 +3	1.59506	−2	2.5076	−2	2.0470	−2	300.386	5.8405	−4
29,000	28,868	225.518	1.3737 +3	1.37224	−2	2.1478	−2	1.7533	−2	301.048	6.8438	−4
30,000	29,859	226.509	1.1855 +3	1.18138	−2	1.8410	−2	1.5029	−2	301.709	8.0134	−4

TABLE A.2
Geometric altitude (English units)

H_G, ft	H, ft	T, °R	P, lb/ft²	P/P_0	ρ, slug/ft⁻³	ρ/ρ_0	a, ft/s	ν, ft²/s
0	0	518.670	2.1162 +3	1.00000 +0	2.3769 −3	1.0000 +0	1116.45	1.5723 −4
2,500	2,500	509.756	1.9319 +3	9.12910 −1	2.2079 −3	9.2887 −1	1106.81	1.6700 −4
5,000	4,999	500.843	1.7609 +3	8.32085 −1	2.0482 −3	8.6170 −1	1097.10	1.7755 −4
7,500	7,497	491.933	1.6023 +3	7.57172 −1	1.8975 −3	7.9832 −1	1087.29	1.8896 −4
10,000	9,995	483.025	1.4556 +3	6.87832 −1	1.7556 −3	7.3859 −1	1077.40	2.0132 −4
12,500	12,493	474.120	1.3200 +3	6.23741 −1	1.6219 −3	6.8235 −1	1067.43	2.1472 −4
15,000	14,989	465.216	1.1948 +3	5.64587 −1	1.4962 −3	6.2946 −1	1057.36	2.2927 −4
17,500	17,485	456.315	1.0794 +3	5.10072 −1	1.3781 −3	5.7977 −1	1047.19	2.4509 −4
20,000	19,981	447.415	9.7327 +2	4.59912 −1	1.2673 −3	5.3316 −1	1036.93	2.6233 −4
22,500	22,476	438.518	8.7576 +2	4.13834 −1	1.1634 −3	4.8947 −1	1026.57	2.8113 −4
25,000	24,970	429.623	7.8633 +2	3.71577 −1	1.0663 −3	4.4859 −1	1016.10	3.0167 −4
27,500	27,464	420.730	7.0447 +2	3.32892 −1	9.7544 −4	4.1039 −1	1005.53	3.2416 −4
30,000	29,957	411.839	6.2962 +2	2.97544 −1	8.9068 −4	3.7473 −1	994.85	3.4882 −4
32,500	32,449	402.950	5.6144 +2	2.65305 −1	8.1169 −4	3.415 −1	984.05	3.7591 −4
35,000	34,941	394.064	4.9934 +2	2.35962 −1	7.3820 −4	3.1058 −1	973.14	4.0573 −4
37,500	37,432.5	389.970	4.4312 +2	2.09396 −1	6.6196 −4	2.7850 −1	968.08	4.48535 −4
40,000	39,923	389.970	3.9312 +2	1.85769 −1	5.8727 −4	2.4708 −1	968.08	5.0560 −4
42,500	42,413.5	389.970	3.4878 +2	1.64816 −1	5.2103 −4	2.1921 −1	968.08	5.69855 −4
45,000	44,903	389.970	3.0945 +2	1.46227 −1	4.6227 −4	1.9449 −1	968.08	6.4228 −4
47,500	47,392.5	389.970	2.7456 +2	1.29742 −1	4.1015 −4	1.7256 −1	968.08	7.2391 −4
50,000	49,880	389.970	2.4361 +2	1.15116 −1	3.6391 −4	1.5311 −1	968.08	8.1587 −4

H_G, ft	H, ft	T, °R	P, lb/ft²	P/P_0	ρ, slug/ft⁻³	ρ/ρ_0	a, ft/s	ν, ft²/s
52,500	52,368.5	389.970	2.1615 +2	1.02143 −1	3.2290 −4	1.3585 −1	968.08	9.19505 −4
55,000	54,855	389.970	1.9180 +2	9.06336 −2	2.8652 −4	1.2055 −1	968.08	1.0363 −3
57,500	57,341.5	389.970	1.7019 +2	8.04248 −2	2.5424 −4	1.0697 −1	968.08	1.1678 −3
60,000	59,828	389.970	1.5103 +2	7.13664 −2	2.2561 −4	9.4919 −2	968.08	1.3160 −3
62,500	62,313.5	389.970	1.3402 +2	6.33315 −2	2.0021 −4	8.4232 −2	968.08	1.483 −3
65,000	64,798	389.970	1.1893 +2	5.62015 −2	1.7767 −4	7.4749 −2	968.08	1.6711 −3
67,500	67,282.5	390.8835	1.0555 +2	4.98815 −2	1.5767 −4	6.6188 −2	969.21	1.891 −3
70,000	69,766	392.246	9.3672 +1	4.42898 −2	1.3993 −4	5.8565 −2	970.90	2.1434 −3
72,500	72,249	393.6085	8.3134 +1	3.93432 −2	1.2419 −4	5.1843 −2	972.58	2.4283 −3
75,000	74,731	394.971	7.3784 +1	3.49635 −2	1.1022 −4	4.5914 −2	974.26	2.7498 −3
77,500	77,213	396.3325	6.5487 +1	3.10856 −2	9.7829 −5	4.0168 −2	975.94	3.1125 −3
80,000	79,694	397.693	5.8125 +1	2.76491 −2	8.6831 −5	3.6060 −2	977.62	3.5213 −3
82,500	82,174	399.0545	5.1592 +1	2.46035 −2	7.7022 −5	3.1978 −2	979.285	3.98215 −3
85,000	84,655	400.415	4.5827 +1	2.19023 −2	6.7706 −5	2.8371 −2	980.95	4.5012 −3
87,500	87,134.5	401.7755	4.0757 +1	1.95063 −2	5.9598 −5	2.5181 −2	982.62	5.0857 −3
90,000	89,613	403.135	3.6292 +1	1.73793 −2	5.2531 −5	2.2360 −2	984.28	5.7434 −3
92,500	92,091.5	404.495	3.2354 +1	1.54919 −2	4.6362 −5	1.9864 −2	985.94	6.48345 −3
95,000	94,569	405.854	2.8878 +1	1.38133 −2	4.0970 −5	1.7653 −2	987.59	7.3155 −3
97,500	97,046	407.2135	2.5805 +1	1.23226 −2	3.6251 −5	1.5695 −2	989.245	8.25085 −3
100,000	99,523	408.572	2.3085 +1	1.09971 −2	3.2114 −5	1.3960 −2	990.90	9.3017 −3

APPENDIX B

Geometric, Mass, and Aerodynamic Characteristics of Selected Airplanes

Data on the geometric, mass, and aerodynamic stability and control characteristics are presented for seven airplanes. The airplanes include a general aviation airplane, two jet fighters, an executive business jet, two jet transports, and a STOL transport. The stability coefficients are presented in tabular form for each airplane. Coefficients that were unavailable have been presented with a numerical value of 0 in the following tables. The stability coefficients for the A-4D are presented in graphical form as a function of the Mach number and altitude. These plots show the large variations in the coefficients due to compressibility effects. The definitions of the stability coefficients and geometric data presented in the figures are given in the following nomenclature list. The information presented in this appendix was taken from [B.1], [B.2] and [B.3] given after the nomenclature list.

NOMENCLATURE

b Wing span

$$C_{L_\alpha} = \frac{\partial C_L}{\partial \alpha} \ (\text{rad}^{-1})$$

$\bar{c}$ Mean chord

$$C_{L_{\dot\alpha}} = \frac{\partial C_L}{\partial \left(\frac{\dot\alpha \bar{c}}{2u_0} \right)} \ (\text{rad}^{-1})$$

$$C_L = \frac{L}{QS}$$

$$C_{L_M} = \frac{\partial C_L}{\partial M}$$

$$C_{l_{\delta_a}} = \frac{\partial C_l}{\partial \delta_r} \ (\text{rad}^{-1})$$

$$C_{L_{\delta_e}} = \frac{\partial C_L}{\partial \delta_e} \ (\text{rad}^{-1})$$

$$C_{l_{\delta_r}} = \frac{\partial C_l}{\partial \delta_r} \ (\text{rad}^{-1})$$

$$C_D = \frac{D}{QS}$$

$$C_n = \frac{N}{QSb}$$

$$C_{D_\alpha} = \frac{\partial C_D}{\partial \alpha} \ (\text{rad}^{-1})$$

$$C_{n_\beta} = \frac{\partial C_n}{\partial \beta} \ (\text{rad}^{-1})$$

398

$$C_{D_M} = \frac{\partial C_D}{\partial M}$$

$$C_{n_p} = \frac{\partial C_n}{\partial(pb/2u_0)} \ (\text{rad}^{-1})$$

$$C_{D_{\delta_e}} = \frac{\partial C_D}{\partial \delta_e} \ (\text{rad}^{-1})$$

$$C_{n_r} = \frac{\partial C_n}{\partial(rb/2u_0)} \ (\text{rad}^{-1})$$

$$C_m = \frac{M}{QS\bar{c}}$$

$$C_{m_{\dot{\alpha}}} = \frac{\partial C_m}{\partial(\dot{\alpha}\bar{c}/2u_0)} \ (\text{rad}^{-1})$$

$$C_{m_\alpha} = \frac{\partial C_m}{\partial \alpha} \ (\text{rad}^{-1})$$

$$C_{m_M} = \frac{\partial C_m}{\partial M}$$

$$C_y = \frac{Y}{QS}$$

$$C_{m_q} = \frac{\partial C_m}{\partial(q\bar{c}/2u_0)} \ (\text{rad}^{-1})$$

$$C_{y_\beta} = \frac{\partial C_y}{\partial \beta} \ (\text{rad}^{-1})$$

$$C_{n_{\delta_a}} = \frac{\partial C_n}{\partial \delta_a} \ (\text{rad}^{-1})$$

$$C_{y_{\delta_r}} = \frac{\partial C_y}{\partial \delta_r} \ (\text{rad}^{-1})$$

$$C_{n_{\delta_r}} = \frac{\partial C_n}{\partial \delta_r} \ (\text{rad}^{-1})$$

$$C_l = \frac{L}{QSb}$$

I_x Rolling moment of inertia
I_y Pitching moment of intertia
I_z Yawing moment of inertia

$$C_{l_\beta} = \frac{\partial C_l}{\partial \beta} \ (\text{rad}^{-1})$$

I_{xz} Product of inertia about xz axis
M   Mach number

$$C_{l_p} = \frac{\partial C_l}{\partial(pb/2u_0)} \ (\text{rad}^{-1})$$

Q   Dynamic pressure
S   Wing planform area

$$C_{l_r} = \frac{\partial C_l}{\partial(rb/2u_0)} \ (\text{rad}^{-1})$$

u_0 Reference flight speed

REFERENCES

B.1. Teper, G. L. *Aircraft Stability and Control Data*. Hawthorne, CA: System Technology, Technical Report 176-1, April 1969.

B.2. Heffley, R. K.; and W. F. Jewell. *Aircraft Handling Qualities Data*. NASA CR-2144, December 1972.

B.3. Mac Donald, R.A.; M. Garelick; and J.O'Grady. "Linearized Mathematical Models for De Havilland Canada 'Buffalo and Twin Otter' STOL Transports." U.S. Department of Transportation – Transportation System Center Report No. DOT-TSC-FAA-71-8, June 1971.

TABLE B.1
General aviation airplane: NAVION

Longitudinal M = 0.158	C_L	C_D	$C_{L\alpha}$	$C_{D\alpha}$	$C_{m\alpha}$	$C_{L\dot\alpha}$	$C_{m\dot\alpha}$	C_{L_q}	C_{m_q}	C_{L_M}	C_{D_M}	C_{m_M}	$C_{L\delta_e}$	$C_{m\delta_e}$
Sea level	0.41	0.05	4.44	0.33	−0.683	0.0	−4.36	3.8	−9.96	0.0	0.0	0.0	0.355	−0.923

Lateral M = 0.158	$C_{y\beta}$	$C_{l\beta}$	$C_{n\beta}$	C_{l_p}	C_{n_p}	C_{l_r}	C_{n_r}	$C_{l\delta_a}$	$C_{n\delta_a}$	$C_{y\delta_r}$	$C_{l\delta_r}$	$C_{n\delta_r}$
Sea level	−0.564	−0.074	0.071	−0.410	−0.0575	0.107	−0.125	−0.134	−0.0035	0.157	0.107	−0.072

Note: All derivatives are per radian.

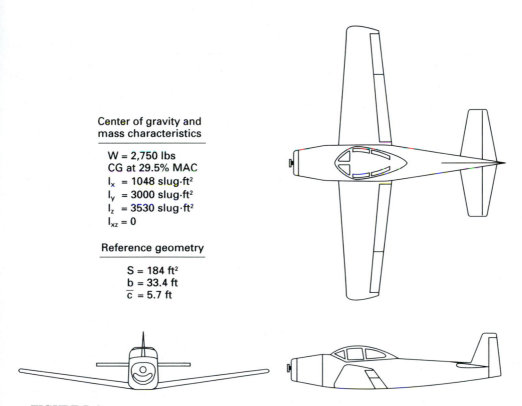

Center of gravity and
mass characteristics

W = 2,750 lbs
CG at 29.5% MAC
I_x = 1048 slug·ft²
I_y = 3000 slug·ft²
I_z = 3530 slug·ft²
I_{xz} = 0

Reference geometry

S = 184 ft²
b = 33.4 ft
$\overline{c}$ = 5.7 ft

FIGURE B.1
Three-view sketch and stability data for a general aviation airplane.

TABLE B.2
Fighter aircraft: F104-A

Longitudinal	C_L	C_D	C_{L_α}	C_{D_α}	C_{m_α}	$C_{L_{\dot\alpha}}$	$C_{m_{\dot\alpha}}$	C_{L_q}	C_{m_q}	C_{L_M}	C_{D_M}	C_{m_M}	$C_{L_{\delta e}}$	$C_{m_{\delta e}}$
M = 0.257 Sea level	0.735	0.263	3.44	0.45	−0.64	0.0	−1.6	0.0	−5.8	0.0	0.0	0.0	0.68	−1.46
M = 1.8 55,000 ft	0.2	0.055	2.0	0.38	−1.30	0.0	−2.0	0.0	−4.8	−0.2	0.0	−0.01	0.52	−0.10

Lateral	C_{y_β}	C_{l_β}	C_{n_β}	C_{l_p}	C_{n_p}	C_{l_r}	C_{n_r}	$C_{l_{\delta a}}$	$C_{n_{\delta a}}$	$C_{y_{\delta r}}$	$C_{l_{\delta r}}$	$C_{n_{\delta r}}$
M = 0.257 Sea level	−1.17	−0.175	0.50	−0.285	−0.14	0.265	−0.75	0.039	0.0042	0.208	0.045	−0.16
M = 1.8 55,000 ft	−1.0	−0.09	0.24	−0.27	−0.09	0.15	−0.65	0.017	0.0025	0.05	0.008	−0.04

Note: All derivatives are per radian.

Center of gravity and
mass characteristics

W = 16,300 lb
CG at 7% MAC
I_x = 3549 slug·ft²
I_y = 58,611 slug·ft²
I_z = 59,669 slug·ft²
I_{xz} = 0

Reference geometry

S = 196.1 ft²
b = 21.94 ft
$\bar{c}$ = 9.55 ft

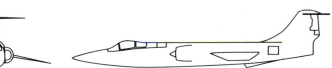

FIGURE B.2
Three-view sketch and stability data for the F-104-A fighter.

TABLE B.3
Fighter aircraft: A-4D

Longitudinal	C_L	C_D	$C_{L\alpha}$	$C_{D\alpha}$	$C_{m\alpha}$	$C_{L\dot\alpha}$	C_{Lq}	C_{mq}	C_{LM}	C_{DM}	C_{mM}	$C_{L\delta_e}$	$C_{m\delta_e}$
M = 0.4 Sea level	0.28	0.03	3.45	0.30	−0.38	0.72	0.0	−3.6	0.0	0.0	0.0	0.36	−0.50
M = 0.8 35,000 ft	0.30	0.038	4.0	0.56	−0.41	1.12	0.0	−4.3	0.15	0.03	−0.05	0.4	−0.60

Lateral	$C_{y\beta}$	$C_{l\beta}$	$C_{n\beta}$	C_{lp}	C_{np}	C_{lr}	C_{nr}	$C_{l\delta_a}$	$C_{n\delta_a}$	$C_{y\delta_r}$	$C_{l\delta_r}$	$C_{n\delta_r}$
M = 0.4 Sea level	−0.98	−0.12	0.25	−0.26	0.022	0.14	−0.35	0.08	0.06	0.17	−0.105	0.032
M = 0.8 35,000 ft	−1.04	−0.14	0.27	−0.24	0.029	0.17	−0.39	0.072	0.04	0.17	−0.105	0.032

Note: All derivatives are per radian.

Center of gravity and
mass characteristics

W = 17,578 lb
CG at 25% MAC
I_x = 8090 Slug·ft²
I_y = 25,900 Slug·ft²
I_z = 29,200 Slug·ft²
I_{xz} = 1300 Slug·ft²

Reference geometry

S = 260 ft²
b = 27.5 ft
$\overline{c}$ = 10.8 ft

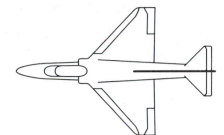

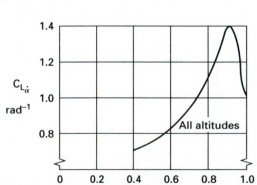

FIGURE B.3
Three-view sketch and stability data for the A-4D fighter.

FIGURE B.4
C_{L_α} versus the Mach number.

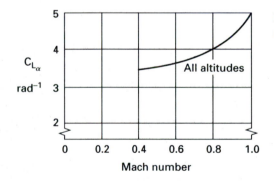

FIGURE B.5
$C_{L_{\dot{\alpha}}}$ versus the Mach number.

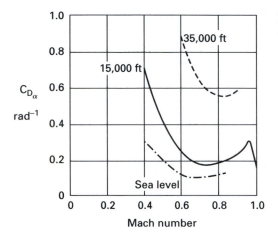

FIGURE B.6
C_{D_α} versus the Mach number.

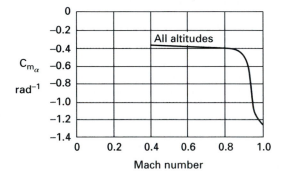

FIGURE B.7
C_{m_α} versus the Mach number.

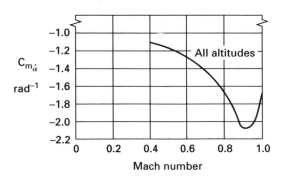

FIGURE B.8
$C_{m_{\dot\alpha}}$ versus the Mach number.

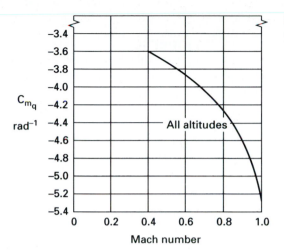

FIGURE B.9
C_{m_q} versus the Mach number.

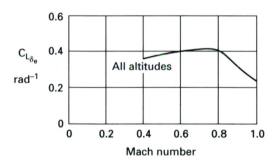

FIGURE B.10
$C_{L_{\delta_e}}$ versus the Mach number.

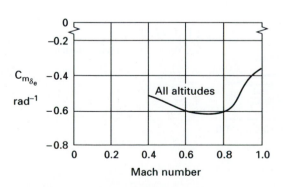

FIGURE B.11
$C_{m_{\delta_e}}$ versus the Mach number.

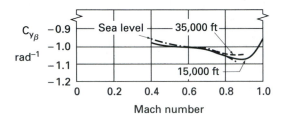

FIGURE B.12
C_{y_β} versus the Mach number.

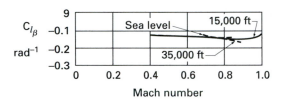

FIGURE B.13
C_{l_β} versus the Mach number.

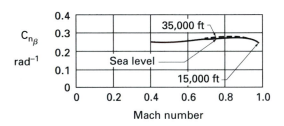

FIGURE B.14
C_{n_β} versus the Mach number.

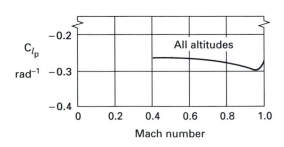

FIGURE B.15
C_{l_p} versus the Mach number.

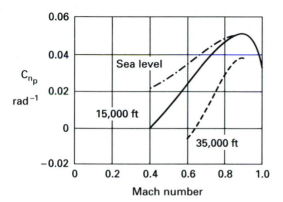

FIGURE B.16
C_{n_p} versus the Mach number.

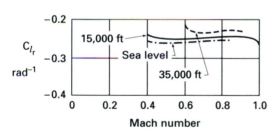

FIGURE B.17
C_{l_r} versus the Mach number.

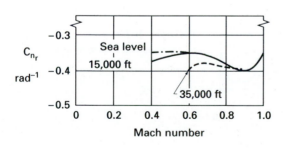

FIGURE B.18
C_{n_r} versus the Mach number.

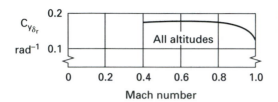

FIGURE B.19
$C_{y_{\delta_r}}$ versus the Mach number.

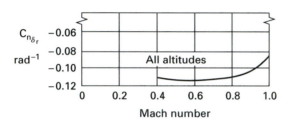

FIGURE B.20
$C_{n_{\delta_r}}$ versus the Mach number.

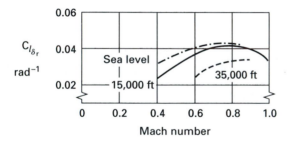

FIGURE B.21
$C_{l_{\delta_r}}$ versus the Mach number.

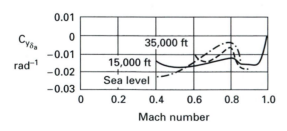

FIGURE B.22
$C_{y_{\delta_a}}$ versus the Mach number.

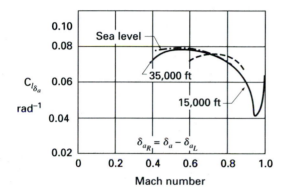

FIGURE B.23
$C_{l_{\delta a}}$ versus the Mach number.

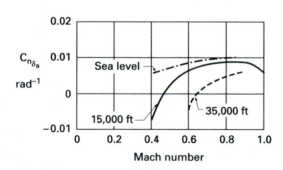

FIGURE B.24
$C_{n_{\delta a}}$ versus the Mach number.

TABLE B.25
Business Jet: Jetstar

Longitudinal	C_L	C_D	$C_{L\alpha}$	$C_{D\alpha}$	$C_{m\alpha}$	$C_{L\dot{\alpha}}$	$C_{m\dot{\alpha}}$	C_{L_q}	C_{m_q}	C_{L_M}	C_{D_M}	C_{m_M}	$C_{L_{\delta e}}$	$C_{m_{\delta e}}$
M = 0.20 Sea level	0.737	0.095	5.0	0.75	−0.80	0.0	−3.0	0.0	−8.0	0.0	0.0	−0.05	0.4	−0.81
M = 0.80 40,000 ft	0.4	0.04	6.5	0.60	−0.72	0.0	−0.4	0.0	−0.92	0.0	−0.6	−0.60	0.44	−0.88

Lateral	$C_{y\beta}$	$C_{l\beta}$	$C_{n\beta}$	C_{l_p}	C_{n_p}	C_{l_r}	C_{n_r}	$C_{l_{\delta a}}$	$C_{n_{\delta a}}$	$C_{y_{\delta r}}$	$C_{l_{\delta r}}$	$C_{n_{\delta r}}$
M = 0.20 Sea level	−0.72	−0.103	0.137	−0.37	−0.14	0.11	−0.16	0.054	0.0075	0.175	0.029	−0.063
M = 0.80 40,000 ft	−0.75	−0.06	0.13	−0.42	−0.756	0.04	−0.16	0.060	−0.06	0.16	0.029	−0.057

Note: All derivatives are per radian.

Center of gravity and
mass characteristics

W = 38,200 lb
CG at 25% MAC
I_x = 118,773 Slug·ft²
I_y = 135,869 Slug·ft²
I_z = 243,504 Slug·ft²
I_{xz} = 5061 Slug·ft²

Reference geometry

S = 542.5 ft²
b = 53.75 ft
$\bar{c}$ = 10.93 ft

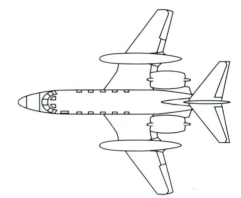

FIGURE B.25
Three-view sketch and stability data for a Jetstar executive business jet.

TABLE B.26
Transport aircraft: Convair 880

Longitudinal

	C_L	C_D	C_{L_u}	C_{D_α}	C_{m_α}	C_{L_α}	$C_{m_{\dot\alpha}}$	C_{L_q}	C_{m_q}	C_{L_M}	C_{D_M}	C_{m_M}	$C_{L_{\delta_e}}$	$C_{m_{\delta_e}}$
M = 0.25 Sea level	0.68	0.08	4.52	0.27	−0.903	2.7	−4.13	7.72	−12.1	0.0	0.0	0.0	0.213	−0.637
M = 0.8 35,000 ft	0.347	0.024	4.8	0.15	−0.65	2.7	−4.5	7.5	−4.5	0.0	0.0	0.0	0.190	−0.57

Lateral

	C_{y_β}	C_{l_β}	C_{n_β}	C_{l_p}	C_{n_p}	C_{l_r}	C_{n_r}	$C_{l_{\delta_a}}$	$C_{n_{\delta_a}}$	$C_{y_{\delta_r}}$	$C_{l_{\delta_r}}$	$C_{n_{\delta_r}}$
M = 0.25 Sea level	−0.877	−0.196	0.139	−0.381	−0.049	0.198	−0.185	−0.038	0.017	0.216	0.0226	−0.096
M = 0.8 35,000 ft	−0.812	−0.177	0.129	−0.312	−0.011	0.153	−0.165	−0.050	0.008	0.184	0.019	−0.076

Note: All derivatives are per radian

414

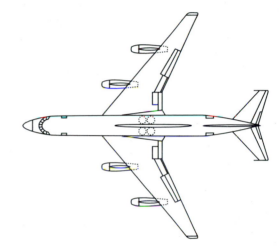

Center of gravity and mass characteristics

W = 126,000 lb
CG at 25% MAC
I_x = 115,000 Slug·ft²
I_y = 2450,000 Slug·ft²
I_z = 4070,000 Slug·ft²
I_{xz} = 0

Reference geometry

S = 2,000 ft²
b = 120 ft
$\overline{c}$ = 18.94 ft

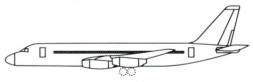

FIGURE B.26
Three-view sketch and stability data for a Convair 880 jet transport.

TABLE B.27
Transport aircraft: Boeing 747

Longitudinal	C_L	C_D	C_{L_α}	C_{D_α}	C_{m_α}	$C_{L_{\dot\alpha}}$	$C_{m_{\dot\alpha}}$	C_{L_q}	C_{m_q}	C_{L_M}	C_{D_M}	C_{m_M}	$C_{L_{\delta_e}}$	$C_{m_{\delta_e}}$
M = 0.25 Sea level	1.11	0.102	5.70	0.66	−1.26	6.7	−3.2	5.4	−20.8	−0.81	0.0	0.27	0.338	−1.34
M = 0.90 40,000 ft	0.5	0.042	5.5	0.47	−1.6	0.006	−9.0	6.58	−25.0	0.2	0.25	−0.10	0.3	−1.2

Lateral	C_{y_β}	C_{l_β}	C_{n_β}	C_{l_p}	C_{n_p}	C_{l_r}	C_{n_r}	$C_{l_{\delta_a}}$	$C_{n_{\delta_a}}$	$C_{y_{\delta_r}}$	$C_{l_{\delta_r}}$	$C_{n_{\delta_r}}$
M = 0.25 Sea level	−0.96	−0.221	0.150	−0.45	−0.121	0.101	−0.30	0.0461	0.0064	0.175	0.007	−0.109
M = 0.90 40,000 ft	−0.85	−0.10	0.20	−0.30	0.20	0.20	−0.325	0.014	0.003	0.075	0.005	−0.09

Note: All derivatives are per radian.

Center of gravity and
mass characteristics

W = 636,600 lb
CG at 25% MAC
I_x = 18.2 × 10^6 Slug·ft^2
I_y = 33.1 × 10^6 Slug·ft^2
I_z = 49.7 × 10^6 Slug·ft^2
I_{xz} = 0.97 × 10^6 Slug·ft^2

Reference geometry

S = 5,500 ft^2
b = 195.68 ft
$\bar{c}$ = 27.31 ft

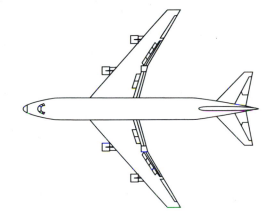

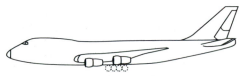

FIGURE B.27
Three-view sketch and stability data for a large Boeing 747 jet transport.

TABLE B.28
STOL Transport

Longitudinal	C_L	C_D	C_{L_α}	C_{D_α}	C_{m_α}	$C_{L_{\dot\alpha}}$	$C_{m_{\dot\alpha}}$	C_{L_q}	C_{m_q}	C_{L_M}	C_{D_M}	C_{M_M}	$C_{L_{\delta_e}}$	$C_{m_{\delta_e}}$
M = 0.14 Sea level	1.5	0.127	5.24	0.67	−0.78	1.33	−6.05	7.83	−35.6	0	0	0	0.465	−2.12
M = 0.37 10,000 ft	0.3	0.036	5.24	0.67	−0.78	1.33	−6.05	7.83	−35.6	0	0	0	0.465	−2.12

Lateral	C_{y_β}	C_{l_β}	C_{n_β}	C_{l_p}	C_{n_p}	C_{l_r}	C_{n_r}	$C_{l_{\delta_a}}$	$C_{n_{\delta_a}}$	$C_{y_{\delta_a}}$	$C_{l_{\delta_r}}$	$C_{n_{\delta_r}}$
M = 0.14 Sea level	−0.362	−0.125	0.101	−0.53	−0.283	0.410	−0.188	0.20	0	−0.233	−0.024	0.107
M = 0.37 10,000 ft	−0.362	−0.125	0.101	−0.53	−0.037	0.113	−0.171	0.20	0	−0.233	−0.024	0.107

Note: All derivatives are per radian.

418

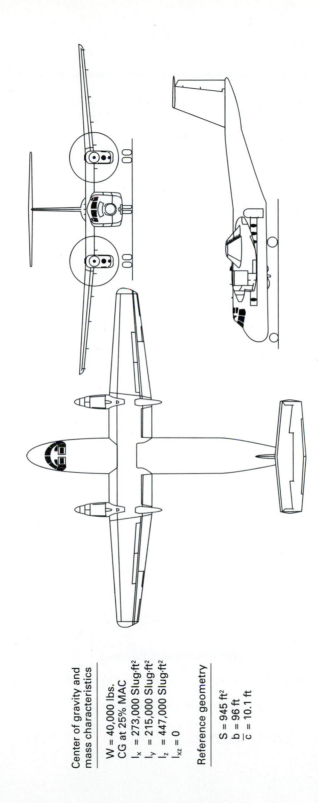

Center of gravity and
mass characteristics

W = 40,000 lbs.
CG at 25% MAC
I_x = 273,000 Slug·ft²
I_y = 215,000 Slug·ft²
I_z = 447,000 Slug·ft²
I_{xz} = 0

Reference geometry

S = 945 ft²
b = 96 ft
$\bar{c}$ = 10.1 ft

FIGURE B.28
Three-view sketch and stability data for a STOL transport.

APPENDIX C

Mathematical Review of Laplace Transforms and Matrix Algebra

REVIEW OF MATHEMATICAL CONCEPTS

Laplace Transformation

The Laplace transform is a mathematical technique that has been used extensively in control system synthesis. It is a very powerful mathematical tool for solving differential equations. When the Laplace transformation technique is applied to a differential equation it transforms the differential equation to an algebraic equation. The transformed algebraic equation can be solved for the quantity of interest and then inverted back into the time domain to provide the solution to the differential equation.

The Laplace transformation is a mathematical operation defined by

$$\mathscr{L}[f(t)] = \int_0^\infty f(t) \, e^{-st} \, dt = F(s) \tag{C.1}$$

where $f(t)$ is a function of time. The operator $\mathscr{L}$ and the complex variable s are the Laplace operator and variable, respectively, and $F(s)$ is the transform of $f(t)$. The Laplace transformation of various functions $f(t)$ can be obtained by evaluating Equation (C.1). The process of obtaining $f(t)$ from the Laplace transform $F(s)$, called the inverse Laplace transformation, is given by

$$f(t) = \mathscr{L}^{-1}[F(s)] \tag{C.2}$$

where the inverse Laplace transformation is given by the following integral relationship:

$$f(t) = \frac{1}{2\pi i} \int_{c-\infty}^{c+\infty} F(s) \, e^{st} \, ds \tag{C.3}$$

Several examples of Laplace transformations follow.

EXAMPLE PROBLEM C.1. Consider the function $f(t) = e^{-at}$.

Solution. The Laplace transform of this expression yields

$$\mathscr{L}[f(t)] = \mathscr{L}[e^{-at}] = \int_0^\infty e^{-at} \, e^{st} \, dt = \int_0^\infty e^{-(a+s)t} \, dt$$

and the evaluation of the integral gives the transform $F(s)$:

$$F(s) = -\frac{e^{-(a+s)t}}{a+s}\bigg|_0^\infty = \frac{1}{s+a}$$

As another example suppose that $f(t) = \sin \omega t$. Substituting into the definition of the Laplace transformation one obtains

$$F(s) = \mathcal{L}[\sin \omega t] = \int_0^\infty \sin \omega t \, e^{-st} \, dt = \frac{1}{2i} \int_0^\infty (e^{i\omega t} - e^{i\omega t}) e^{-st} \, dt$$

Evaluating this integral yields

$$F(s) = \frac{\omega}{s^2 + \omega^2}$$

EXAMPLE PROBLEM C.2. Consider the Laplace transformation of operations such as the derivative and definite integral. When $f(t)$ is a derivative, for example $f(t) = dy/dt$,

$$\mathcal{L}[f(t)] = \int_0^\infty \frac{dy}{dt} e^{-st} \, dt$$

Solution. Solution of this integral can be obtained by applying the method of integration by parts. Mathematically integration by parts is given by the following expression:

$$\int_a^b u \, dv = uv \bigg|_a^b - \int_a^b v \, du$$

Letting u and dv be as follows

$$u = e^{-st}$$

$$dv = \frac{dy}{dt} \, dt$$

then

$$du = -s \, e^{-st} \, dt$$

$$v = y(t)$$

Substituting and integrating by parts yields

$$\mathcal{L}[f(t)] = y(t) e^{-st} \bigg|_0^\infty + s \int_0^\infty y(t) e^{-st} \, dt$$

but the integral

$$\int_0^\infty y(t) e^{-st} \, dt = Y(s)$$

therefore

$$\mathcal{L}\left[\frac{dy}{dt}\right] = -y(0) + sY(s)$$

In a similar manner the Laplace transformation of higher-order derivatives can be shown to be

$$\mathcal{L}\left[\frac{d^n y}{dt^n}\right] = s^n Y(s) - s^{n-1} y(0) - s^{n-2} \frac{dy}{dt}\bigg|_{t=0} - \cdots - \frac{d^{n-1} y}{dt^{n-1}}\bigg|_{t=0}$$

When all initial conditions are 0 the transform simplifies to the following expression.

$$\mathcal{L}\left[\frac{d^n y}{dt^n}\right] = s^n Y(s)$$

Now consider the Laplace transform of a definite integral:

$$\mathcal{L}\left[\int_0^1 y(\tau) \, d\tau\right] = \int_0^\infty e^{-st} \, dt \int_0^t y(\tau) \, d\tau$$

This integral can also be evaluated by the method of integration by parts. Letting u and dv be as follows,

$$u = \int_0^1 y(\tau) \, d\tau$$

$$dv = e^{-st} \, dt$$

then

$$du = y(t)$$

$$v = \frac{1}{s} e^{-st}$$

Substituting and integrating by parts yields

$$\mathcal{L}\left[\int_0^t y(\tau) \, d\tau\right] = \frac{1}{s} e^{-st} \int_0^t y(\tau) \, d\tau \Big|_0^\infty - \frac{1}{s} \int_0^\infty e^{-st} y(t) \, dt$$

or

$$\mathcal{L}\left[\int_0^t y(\tau) \, d\tau\right] = \frac{Y(s)}{s}$$

By applying the Laplace transformation to various functions of $f(t)$ one can develop a table of transform pairs as shown in Table C.1. This table is a list of some of the most commonly used transform pairs that occur in control system analysis.

TABLE C.1
Table of Laplace transform pairs

$f(t)$	$F(s)$	$f(t)$	$F(s)$
$u(t)$	$1/s$	$\sin \omega t$	$\omega/(s^2 + \omega^2)$
t	$1/s^2$	$\cos \omega t$	$s/(s^2 + \omega^2)$
t^n	$n!/s^{n+1}$	$\sinh \omega t$	$\dfrac{\omega}{s^2 - \omega^2}$
$\delta(t)$ Unit impulse	1	$\cosh \omega t$	$\dfrac{s}{s^2 - \omega^2}$
$\int_{-\varepsilon}^{+\varepsilon} \delta(t) \, dt = 1$		$e^{-at} \sin \omega t$	$\dfrac{\omega}{(s - a)^2 + \omega^2}$
e^{-at}	$1/(s + a)$	$t \cos \omega t$	$\dfrac{s^2 - \omega^2}{(s^2 + \omega^2)}$
$t e^{-at}$	$\dfrac{1}{(s + a)^2}$	$t \sin \omega t$	$\dfrac{2\omega s}{(s^2 + \omega^2)^2}$
$t^n e^{-at}$	$n!/(s + a)^{n+1}$		

Solution of Ordinary Linear Differential Equations

In control system design, a linear differential equation of the form

$$a_n \frac{d^n y}{dt^n} + a_{n-1} \frac{d^{n-1} y}{dt^{n-1}} + \cdots + a_1 \frac{dy}{dt} + a_0 y = f(t) \qquad (C.4)$$

is common. This is a nonhomogeneous linear differential equation with constant coefficients. The Laplace transformations of a differential equation results in an algebraic equation in terms of the transform of the derivatives and the Laplace variables. The resulting algebraic equation can be manipulated to solve for the unknown function $Y(s)$. The expression for $Y(s)$ then can be inverted back into the time domain to determine the solution $y(t)$.

EXAMPLE PROBLEM C.3. Given a second-order differential equation

$$\frac{d^2 y}{dt^2} + 2\zeta\omega_n \frac{dy}{dt} + \omega_n^2 y = \omega_n^2 u(t)$$

where $u(t)$ is a unit step function. Find the solution $y(t)$ if the initial conditions are as follows

$$y(0) = 0$$

$$\frac{dy(0)}{dt} = 0$$

Solution. Taking the Laplace transformation of the differential equation yields

$$(s^2 + 2\zeta\omega_n s + \omega_n^2)Y(s) = \frac{\omega_n^2}{s}$$

Solving for $Y(s)$ yields

$$Y(s) = \frac{\omega_n^2}{s(s^2 + 2\zeta\omega_n s + \omega_n^2)}$$

Now $y(t)$ can be obtained by inverting $Y(s)$ back into the time domain:

$$y(t) = 1 + \frac{1}{\sqrt{1 - \zeta^2}} e^{-\zeta\omega_n t} \sin(\omega_n \sqrt{1 - \zeta^2} t - \phi)$$

where
$$\phi = \tan^{-1}(\sqrt{1 - \zeta^2} / - \zeta)$$

Partial Fractions Technique for Finding Inverse Transformations

When solving a differential equation using the Laplace transformation approach, the major difficulty is in inverting the transformation back into the time domain. The dependent variable is found as a rational function of the ratio of two polynomials in the Laplace variable, s. The inverse of this function can be obtained by the inverse Laplace transform defined by Equation (C.3). However, in practice it generally is not necessary to evaluate the inverse in this manner. If this function can be found in a table of Laplace transform pairs the solution in the time domain is easily obtained. On the other hand, if the transform cannot be found in the table then an alternate approach must be used. The method of partial fractions reduces the rational fraction to a sum of elementary terms which are available in the Laplace tables.

The Laplace transform of a differential equation typically takes the form of a ratio of polynomials in the Laplace variable, s:

$$F(s) = \frac{N(s)}{D(s)}$$

The denominator can be factored as follows:

$$D(s) = (s + p_1)(s + p_2) \cdots (s + p_n)$$

These roots can be either real or complex conjugate pairs and can be of multiple order. When the roots are real and of order 1 the Laplace transform can be expanded in the following manner:

$$F(s) = \frac{N(s)}{D(s)} = \frac{N(s)}{(s + p_1)(s + p_2) \cdots (s + p_n)}$$

$$= \frac{C_{p_1}}{s + p_1} + \frac{C_{p_2}}{s + p_2} + \cdots + \frac{C_{p_n}}{s + p_n}$$

where the constants C_{p_i} are defined as

$$C_{p_1} = \left[(s + p_1) \frac{N(s)}{D(s)} \right]_{s=-p_1}$$

$$C_{p_2} = \left[(s + p_2) \frac{N(s)}{D(s)} \right]_{s=-p_2}$$

$$C_{p_i} = \left[(s + p_i) \frac{N(s)}{D(s)} \right]_{s=-p_i}$$

When some of the roots are repeated the Laplace transform can be represented as

$$F(s) = \frac{N(s)}{D(s)} = \frac{N(s)}{(s + p_1)(s + p_2) \cdots (s + p_i)^r (s + p_n)}$$

and in expanded form as

$$F(s) = \frac{C_{p_1}}{s + p_1} + \frac{C_{p_2}}{s + p_2} + \cdots + \frac{k_1}{(s + p_i)} + \frac{k_2}{(s + p_i)^2} + \cdots + \frac{k_r}{(s + p_i)^r}$$

The coefficients for the nonrepeated roots are determined as shown previously, and the coefficients for the repeated roots can be obtained from the following expression:

$$k_j = \frac{1}{(r - j)!} \frac{d^{r-j}}{ds^{r-j}} \left[(s + p_i)^r \frac{N(s)}{D(s)} \right]_{s=-p_i}$$

With the partial fraction technique the Laplace transform of the differential equation can be expressed as a sum of elementary transforms that easily can be inverted to the time domain.

Matrix Algebra

In this section we review some of the properties of matrices. A matrix is a collection of numbers arranged in a square or rectangular array. Matrices are used in the solution of simultaneous equations and are of great utility as a shorthand notation for large systems of equations. A brief review of some of the basic algebraic properties of matrices are presented in the following section.

A rectangular matrix is a collection of elements that can be arranged in rows and columns as follows:

$$\mathbf{A} = a_{ij} = \begin{bmatrix} a_{11} & a_{12} & \cdots & a_{1j} \\ a_{21} & & & \\ a_{31} & & & \\ a_{41} & & & \\ \vdots & & & \\ a_{i1} & a_{i2} & \cdots & a_{ij} \end{bmatrix}$$

where the indexes i and j represent the row and column, respectively. The rectangular matrix reduces to a square matrix when $i = j$.

A unit matrix or identity matrix is a square matrix with the elements along the diagonal being unity and all other elements of the array zero. The identity matrix is denoted in the following manner:

$$\mathbf{I} = \begin{bmatrix} 1 & 0 & \cdots & 0 \\ 0 & 1 & \cdots & 0 \\ \vdots & \vdots & & \vdots \\ 0 & 0 & \cdots & 1 \end{bmatrix}$$

Addition and Subtraction of Matrices

Two matrices are equal if they are of the same order; that is, they have the same number of rows and columns and the corresponding elements of the matrices are identical. Mathematically this can be stated as

$$\mathbf{A} = \mathbf{B}$$

if

$$a_{ij} = b_{ij}$$

Matrices can be added provided they are of the same order. Matrix addition is accomplished by adding together corresponding elements.

$$\mathbf{C} = \mathbf{A} + \mathbf{B}$$

or

$$c_{ij} = a_{ij} + b_{ij}$$

Subtraction of matrices is defined in a similar manner:

$$\mathbf{C} = \mathbf{A} - \mathbf{B}$$

or

$$c_{ij} = a_{ij} - b_{ij}$$

Multiplication of Two Matrices

Two matrices $\mathbf{A}$ and $\mathbf{B}$ can be multiplied provided that the number of columns of $\mathbf{A}$ is equal to the number of rows of $\mathbf{B}$. For example, suppose the matrices $\mathbf{A}$ and $\mathbf{B}$ are defined as follows:

$$\mathbf{A} = [a_{ij}]_{n,p}$$

$$\mathbf{B} = [b_{ij}]_{q,m}$$

These matrices can be multiplied if the number of columns of $\mathbf{A}$ is equal to the number of rows of $\mathbf{B}$; that is, $p = q$:

$$\mathbf{C} = \mathbf{AB} = [a_{ij}]_{n,p}[b_{ij}]_{q,m} = [c_{ij}]_{n,m}$$

where
$$c_{ij} = \sum_{k=1}^{P} a_{ik}b_{kj} \qquad \begin{aligned} i &= 1, 2, \ldots, n \\ j &= 1, 2, \ldots, m \end{aligned}$$

EXAMPLE PROBLEM C.4. Given the matrices $\mathbf{A}$ and $\mathbf{B}$, determine the product $\mathbf{AB}$:

$$\mathbf{A} = \begin{bmatrix} a_{11} & a_{12} & a_{13} \\ a_{21} & a_{22} & a_{23} \\ a_{31} & a_{32} & a_{33} \end{bmatrix}$$

$$\mathbf{B} = \begin{bmatrix} b_{11} & b_{12} \\ b_{21} & b_{22} \\ b_{31} & b_{32} \end{bmatrix}$$

Solution. $\mathbf{A}$ and $\mathbf{B}$ can be multiplied together because the number of columns of $\mathbf{A}$ is equal to the number of rows of $\mathbf{B}$:

$$\mathbf{C} = \mathbf{AB}$$

$$\mathbf{C} = \begin{bmatrix} (a_{11}b_{11} + a_{12}b_{21} + a_{13}b_{31}) & (a_{11}b_{12} + a_{12}b_{22} + a_{13}b_{32}) \\ (a_{21}b_{11} + a_{22}b_{21} + a_{23}b_{31}) & (a_{21}b_{12} + a_{22}b_{22} + a_{23}b_{32}) \\ (a_{31}b_{11} + a_{32}b_{21} + a_{33}b_{31}) & (a_{31}b_{12} + a_{32}b_{22} + a_{33}b_{32}) \end{bmatrix}$$

Some additional properties of matrix multiplication are included in Table C.2. Notice that in general matrix multiplication is not commutative. Multiplication of a

TABLE C.2
Properties of matrix multiplication

$(AB)C = A(BC)$	Associative
$(A + B)C = AC + BC$	Distributive
$A(B + C) = AB + AC$	Distributive
$AB \neq BA$	Commutative

matrix A by a scalar constant k is equivalent to multiplying each element of the matrix by the scalar k:

$$k\mathbf{A} = \begin{bmatrix} ka_{11} & ka_{12} & ka_{13} \\ ka_{21} & ka_{22} & ka_{23} \\ ka_{31} & ka_{32} & ka_{33} \end{bmatrix}$$

Matrix Division (Inverse of a Matrix)

The solution of a system of algebraic equations requires matrix inversion. For example, if a set of algebraic equations can be written in matrix form as

$$\mathbf{Ax} = \mathbf{y}$$

then the solution is given as

$$\mathbf{x} = \mathbf{A}^{-1}\mathbf{y}$$

where $\mathbf{A}^{-1}$ is the inverse of the matrix $\mathbf{A}$. For the inverse of $\mathbf{A}$ to exist matrix $\mathbf{A}$ must be square and nonsingular. The condition that $\mathbf{A}$ be nonsingular means that the determinant of $\mathbf{A}$ must be a nonzero value. The inverse of a matrix is defined as follows:

$$\mathbf{A}^{-1} = \frac{\text{Adj}\mathbf{A}}{|\mathbf{A}|}$$

where Adj $\mathbf{A}$ is called the adjoint of $\mathbf{A}$. The adjoint of a matrix is obtained by taking the transpose of the cofactors of the $\mathbf{A}$ matrix, where the cofactors are determined as follows:

$$C_{ij} = (-1)^{i+j}D_{ij}$$

and D_{ij} is the determinant obtained by eliminating the ith row and jth column of $\mathbf{A}$. Some additional properties of the inverse matrix are given in Table C.3.

The transpose of a matrix is obtained by interchanging the rows and columns of the matrix. Given the matrix $\mathbf{A}$,

$$\mathbf{A} = \begin{bmatrix} a_{11} & a_{12} & a_{13} \\ a_{21} & a_{22} & a_{23} \\ a_{31} & a_{32} & a_{33} \end{bmatrix}$$

TABLE C.3
Properties of an inverse matrix

1. $\mathbf{AA}^{-1} = \mathbf{A}^{-1}\mathbf{A} = \mathbf{I}$
2. $[\mathbf{A}^{-1}]^{-1} = \mathbf{A}$
3. If $\mathbf{A}$ and $\mathbf{B}$ are nonsingular and square matrices
   then $(\mathbf{AB})^{-1} = \mathbf{B}^{-1}\mathbf{A}^{-1}$

then the transpose of $\mathbf{A}$ is

$$\mathbf{A}^T = \begin{bmatrix} a_{11} & a_{21} & a_{31} \\ a_{12} & a_{22} & a_{32} \\ a_{13} & a_{23} & a_{33} \end{bmatrix}$$

For additional properties of matrices the reader should consult his or her mathematics library.

APPENDIX D

Review of Control System Analysis Techniques

BODE DIAGRAMS

The frequency response of a linear system is determined experimentally by applying a sinusoidal input signal and then measuring the sinusoidal response of the system. The frequency response data includes the measurement of the amplitude and phase shift of the sinusoidal output compared to the amplitude and phase of the input signal as the input frequency is varied. The relationship between the output and input to the system can be used by the designer to determine the performance of the system. Furthermore, frequency response data can be used to deduce the performance of a system to an arbitrary input that may or may not be periodic.

The magnitude of the amplitude ratio and phase angle can be presented graphically in a number of ways. However, one of the most useful presentations of the data is in the so-called Bode diagram, named after H. W. Bode for his pioneering work in frequency response analysis. In a Bode diagram the logarithm of the magnitude of the system transfer function, $|G(i\omega)|$, and the phase angle, ϕ, are plotted separately versus the frequency.

The frequency response, output-input amplitude ratio, and phase with respect to the input can be determined analytically from the system transfer function written in factored time constant form:

$$G(s) = \frac{k(1 + T_a s)(1 + T_b s) \cdots}{s^r (1 + T_1 s)(1 + T_2 s) \cdots \left(1 + \dfrac{2\zeta}{\omega_n} s + \dfrac{s^2}{\omega_n^2}\right)} \tag{D.1}$$

This transfer function has simple zeros at $-1/T_a$, $-1/T_b$, . . ., a pole at the origin of order r, simple poles at $-1/T_1$, $-1/T_2$, . . ., and complex poles at $-\zeta\omega_n \pm i\omega_n\sqrt{1 - \zeta^2}$. The steady-state response can be shown to be determined by substituting $i\omega$ for the Laplace variable s in the system transfer function. Substituting $i\omega$ for s one can express the transfer function in terms of the magnitude of its amplitude ratio and phase angle as follows:

$$\begin{aligned}
20 \log |G(i\omega)| &= 20 \log k + 20 \log |1 + i\omega T_a| \\
&\quad + 20 \log |1 + i\omega T_b| + \cdots - 20\, r \log |i\omega| \\
&\quad - 20 \log |1 + i\omega T_1| - 20 \log |1 + i\omega T_2| \\
&\quad - 20 \log|1 + 2\zeta(\omega/\omega_n)i - (\omega/\omega_n)^2| \cdots
\end{aligned} \tag{D.2}$$

and the phase angle in degrees

$$\angle G(i\omega) = \tan^{-1} \omega T_a + \tan^{-1} \omega T_b + \cdots - r(90°) - \tan^{-1} \omega T_1$$

$$-\tan^{-1} \omega T_2 \cdots - \tan^{-1}\left(\frac{2\zeta\omega\omega_n}{\omega^2_n - \omega^2}\right) \tag{D.3}$$

The magnitude has been expressed in terms of decibels. A magnitude in decibels is defined as follows:

$$\text{Magnitude in dB} = 20 \log \frac{|\text{magnitude of output}|}{|\text{magnitude of input}|} \tag{D.4}$$

where the logarithm is to the base 10.

The Bode diagram now can be constructed using a semilog plot. The magnitude in decibels and phase angle are plotted separately on a linear ordinate versus the frequency on a logarithmic abscissa. Because the Bode diagram is obtained by adding the various factors of $G(i\omega)$ one can construct the Bode diagram quite rapidly.

In the general case the factors that will make up the transfer function are a constant term (system gain), poles at the origin, simple poles and zeros on the real axis, and complex conjugate poles and zeros. The graphical representation of each of these individual factors is described in the following section.

System Gain

The log magnitude of the system gain is as follows:

$$20 \log k = \text{constant dB} \tag{D.5}$$

and the phase angle by

$$\angle k = \begin{array}{cc} 0° & k > 0 \\ 180° & k < 0 \end{array} \tag{D.5}$$

Figure D.1 shows the Bode plot for a positive system gain.

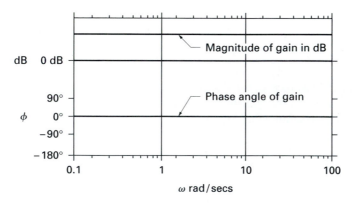

FIGURE D.1
Bode representation of the magnitude and phase of the system gain k.

Poles or Zeros at the Origin $(i\omega)^{\pm r}$

The log magnitude of a pole or zero at the origin of order r can be written as

$$20 \log |(i\omega)^{\pm r}| = \pm 20r \log \omega \text{ dB} \qquad \text{(D.6)}$$

and the phase angle is given by

$$\angle (i\omega)^{\pm r} = \pm 90°r \qquad \text{(D.7)}$$

The log-magnitude is 0 dB at $\omega = 1.0$ rad/s and has a slope of 20 dB/decade, where a decade is a factor of 10 change in frequency. Figure D.2 is a sketch of the log magnitude and phase angle for a multiple zero or pole.

Simple Poles or Zeros $(1 + i\omega T)^{\pm 1}$

The log magnitude of a simple pole or zero can be expressed as

$$\pm 20 \log |1 + i\omega T| = \pm 20 \log \sqrt{1 + (\omega T)^2} \qquad \text{(D.8)}$$

For very low values of ωT, that is, $\omega T \ll 1$, then

$$\pm 20 \log \sqrt{1 + (\omega T)^2} \cong 0 \qquad \text{(D.9)}$$

and for very large values of ωT, that is, $\omega T \gg 1$, then

$$\pm 20 \log \sqrt{1 + (\omega T)^2} \cong \pm 20 \log \omega T \qquad \text{(D.10)}$$

From this simple analysis one can approximate the log magnitude plot of a simple pole or zero by two straight line segments as shown in Figure D.3. One of the asymptotic lines is the 0 dB line and the second line segment has a slope of 20 dB/decade that intersects the 0 dB line at the frequency $\omega = 1/T$. The intersection

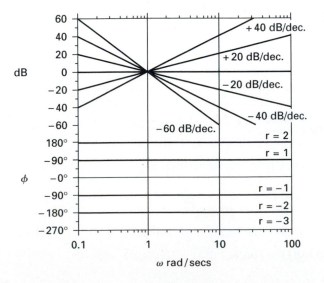

FIGURE D.2
Bode representation of the magnitude and phase of a pole or zero at the origin.

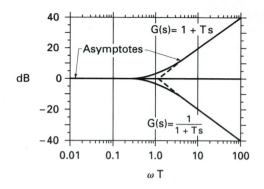

FIGURE D.3
Bode representation of the magnitude of a simple pole or zero.

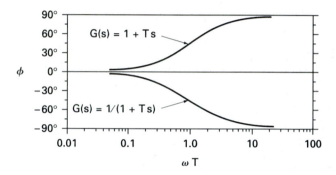

FIGURE D.4
Bode representation of the phase angle of a simple pole or zero.

frequency is called the corner frequency. The actual log magnitude differs from the asymptotic approximation in the vicinity of the corner frequency.

The phase angle for a simple pole or zero is given by

$$\angle(1 + i\omega T)^{\pm 1} = \pm\tan^{-1}\omega T \tag{D.11}$$

Figure D.4 is a sketch of the phase angle.

Complex Conjugate Pole or Zero
$$[1 + i2\zeta\omega/\omega_n - (\omega/\omega_n)^2]^{\pm 1}$$

The log magnitude of the complex pole can be written as

$$
20 \log \left| \frac{1}{1 + i2\zeta\omega/\omega_n + (\omega/\omega_n)^2} \right|
$$
$$
= -20 \log[(1 - (\omega/\omega_n)^2)^2 + (2\zeta\omega/\omega_n)^2]^{1/2} \tag{D.12}
$$
$$
= -10 \log[(1 - (\omega/\omega_n)^2)^2 + (2\zeta\omega/\omega_n)^2]
$$

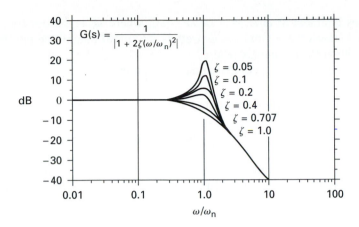

FIGURE D.5
Bode representation of the magnitude of a complex conjugate pole.

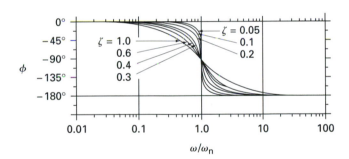

FIGURE D.6
Bode representation of the phase angle of a complex conjugate pole.

The log magnitude can be approximated by two straight line segments. For example, when $\omega/\omega_n \ll 1$

$$20 \log \left| \frac{1}{1 + i2\zeta\omega/\omega_n - (\omega/\omega_n)^2} \right| \cong 0 \qquad (D.13)$$

and when $\omega/\omega_n \gg 1$

$$20 \log \left| \frac{1}{1 + i2\zeta\omega/\omega_n - (\omega/\omega_n)^2} \right| \cong -40 \log \omega/\omega_n \qquad (D.14)$$

The two straight line asymptotes consist of a straight line along the 0 dB line for $\omega/\omega_n = 1 \ll 1$ and a line having a slope of -40 dB/decade for $\omega/\omega_n \gg 1$. The asymptotes intersect at $\omega/\omega_n = 1$ or $\omega = \omega_n$, where ω_n is the corner frequency. Figure D.5 shows the asymptotes as well as the actual magnitude plot for various damping ratios for a complex pole.

The phase angle for a complex pole is given by

$$\angle[1 + i2\zeta\omega/\omega_n - (\omega/\omega_n)^2]^{-1} = -\tan^{-1}\left[\frac{2\zeta\omega/\omega_n}{1 - (\omega/\omega_n)^2}\right] \qquad (D.16)$$

Figure D.6 shows the phase angle for a complex pole. Similar curves can be developed for a complex zero.

If the transfer function is expressed in time constant form, then the Bode diagram easily can be constructed from the simple expressions developed in this section.

Index